Personnel Management

Functions and Issues

Personnel Management

Functions and Issues

William H. Holley
Auburn University

Kenneth M. Jennings
University of North Florida

The Dryden Press
Chicago
New York
Philadelphia
San Francisco
Montreal
Toronto
London
Sydney
Tokyo
Mexico City
Rio de Janeiro
Madrid

This book is dedicated to our parents—Bill and Grace, Ken and Doris—who have given us many things, including positively rough acts to follow.

Acquisitions Editor: Anne Elizabeth Smith
Developmental Editor: Patricia Locke
Project Editor: Ruta S. Graff
Design Director: Alan Wendt
Production Manager: Mary Jarvis
Managing Editor: Jane Perkins
Text and cover design by James Buddenbaum
Copy editing by Beverly Peavler, Naples Editing Services
Indexing by Bernice Eisen
Permissions by Joyce Miller, Naples Editing Services
Compositor: York Graphic Services
Text type: 10 on 12 Serifa 55

Address orders to:

383 Madison Avenue
New York, New York 10017

Address editorial correspondence to:

One Salt Creek Lane
Hinsdale, Illinois 60521

Library of Congress Catalog Card Number:
ISBN 0-03-058903-7
Printed in the United States of America
345-016-98765432

CBS College Publishing
The Dryden Press
Holt, Rinehart and Winston
Saunders College Publishing

Preface

Many good personnel textbooks are presently available, a situation that should discourage prospective authors from writing a similar text. We reviewed these books with the following question in mind: How does one successfully differentiate a book from existing books of high quality? Our review found that competitive textbooks have tended to overlook one or more considerations.

First, many texts fail to stress the provocative, real-world aspects of personnel; instead, these books emphasize techniques that, if followed, will presumably result in a trouble-free work environment. However, this approach tends to ignore the fact that organizational participants are unique individuals offering varied prospects and problems to managers. Our book presents the acceptable techniques but also accounts for individual differences among employees. Further, it recognizes that employee problems can occur even in the best-managed organizations. Part 5 of our book, which embodies this acknowledgment, discusses such controversial areas as alcoholism, drug abuse, white-collar crime, and changing employee values, as well as potential solutions to these problems. Personnel's provocative and exciting aspects are discussed throughout the book; most chapters conclude with a controversial issue (Chapter 18, for example, ends with the issue "How Are Fair Employment Laws Interpreted? The Cases of Religious Discrimination and Sexual Harassment").

Second, changing laws and business conditions combine with the highly varied subject of employees to make personnel a complex study area. Some personnel books have reacted to this situation by ignoring complications, while others have attempted to fully explain every possibility and contradictory research finding. The first approach appears too simplistic; the second tends to overwhelm the student. The book takes a middle-ground approach to ensure its primary objective: *to present the subject matter to students in a realistic, interesting, and understandable fashion.*

This objective is also enhanced by other features of the text, such as an analytical framework for the personnel function in Chapter 1 to place the subsequent chapters in clearer perspective. Numerous quotations by practitioners and academics are inserted throughout the book to provide the inexperienced reader with insights and the experienced scholar with a means to compare various points of view. The notes at the end of each chapter should provide the reader with useful points for continued research.

Finally, personnel activities will likely relate to all readers of this book, but in different ways. Most textbooks assume that their readers will either seek a career in personnel or are presently employed in that field. Our experiences and those of many other professors do not support this assumption; many students enrolled in a personnel course are preparing for a management career in another field, such as marketing, accounting, or public administration. However, all readers, regardless of their chosen careers, will be concerned with personnel matters such as equal employment opportunity and communication. Also, all readers, regardless of career, will both implement and be affected by personnel decisions. In a real sense, every manager is a personnel manager. For example, sales managers must make performance appraisals and wage and salary decisions regarding their subordinates. Individuals are also directly affected by personnel decisions when their bosses determine what wage increases, performance appraisals, and promotional opportunities they will receive.

Personnel is therefore one of the most widely relevant subjects taught in a business curriculum. The problem is to present related material in a way that will apply to students with diverse academic backgrounds and career interests. This problem has been approached and, we hope, resolved in our text.

Those students or classes desiring a full treatment of personnel techniques and activities will be best served by reading all the chapters. However, while this book has been designed to cover the fundamentals of these personnel technques, it places much emphasis on managerial applications. Many of the chapters have a section that emphasizes the respective roles and responsibilities of personnel managers and other management officials in implementing personnel activities. Cases included at the end of each part reinforce understanding of personnel techniques and their implications for other organizational managers.

As mentioned, issues are also included at the ends of most chapters. In some cases, a professor may not want to stress certain subjects (say, employee benefits or recruiting). Instead of neglecting these subjects entirely, the professor can assign related issues ("How Can Benefits Help Accomplish Organizational Objectives?" and "How Can the College Student Improve His or Her Chances with the Campus Recruiter?") that summarize and extend the chapter's contents in a more general way.

Acknowledgments

Many individuals have enhanced the quality of this book. We are most grateful to the following professors, who have read either the entire book or parts of it and have made valuable suggestions: John Bruckman, California Polytechnical Institute—Pomona; Ben Burdetsky, George Washington University; David Caldwell, The University of Santa Clara; Michael Crino, Louisiana State University; Geraldine Ellenbrock, California Polytechnic State University; Gerald Ferris, University of Illinois; Durward Hofler, Northeastern Illinois State University; Des Martin, University of Cincinnati; Lena Prewitt, University of Alabama; and George Stevens, Arizona State University.

Special thanks is extended to those who helped along the way: Fred Adams, Ron Adams, Jo-Anne Alcorn, Ernie Brown, Kathy Cohen, Sally Coltrin, Anita Constant, Dawn Holinbonich, Charles Jones, Dave Moore, Steve Shapiro, Jay Smith, Bill Tomlinson, Earle Traynham, Achilles Armenakis, Art Bedeian, John Darr, Kerry Davis, Junior Feild, Bill Giles, Langston Hawley, Harold Janes, Don Mosley, Tom Noble, Kevin Mossholder, Dwight Norris, and Rudy White.

We also wish to thank those individuals who have either directly or indirectly aided in the preparation of the book: Kathy Atkins, Judson Brooks, Karen Burns, Anne Davis, Ouida Doughty, Rose Dunphy, June Holland, Marian Gay, Linda Pearson, Ellen Sides, Pat Watson, and Ron Touchton and Bess Yellen.

The Dryden staff and others deserve our appreciation for their fine work on this text. We are especially grateful to Anne Smith, Jane Perkins, Alan Wendt, Patricia Locke, Ruta Graff, Beverly Peavler and Bernice Eisen.

Finally, credit goes to our wives and children—Betty, Jackie, Ali, and Bret—whose patience, endurance, and humor made this book an almost entirely pleasant project.

Series List

Albanese and Van Fleet
Organizational Behavior: A Managerial Viewpoint

Bedeian
Organizations: Theory and Analysis

Bedeian and Glueck
Management, Third Edition

Boone and Kurtz
Contemporary Business, Third Edition

Chen and McGarrah
Productivity Management: Text and Cases

Gaither
Production and Operations Management: A Problem-Solving and Decision-Making Approach

Gellerman
The Management of Human Resources

Grad, Glans, Holstein, Meyers, and Schmidt
Management Systems: A Guide to the Study and Design of Information Systems, Second Edition

Higgins
Organizational Policy and Strategic Management: Text and Cases, Second Edition

Hodgetts
Management Fundamentals

Hodgetts
Management: Theory, Process and Practice, Third Edition

Hodgetts
Modern Human Relations

Holley and Jennings
Personnel Management: Functions and Issues

Holley and Jennings
The Labor Relations Process

Hollingsworth and Hand
A Guide to Small Business Management: Text and Cases

Huseman, Lahiff, and Hatfield
Business Communication: Strategies and Skills

Huseman, Lahiff and Hatfield
Readings in Business Communication

Jauch, Coltrin, Bedeian, and Glueck
The Managerial Experience: Cases, Exercises, and Readings, Third Edition

Karmel
Point and Counterpoint in Organizational Behavior

Lee
Introduction to Management Science

Lindauer
Communicating in Business, Second Edition

McFarlan, Nolan, and Norton
Information Systems Administration

Mayerson
Shoptalk: Foundations of Managerial Communication

Miner
Theories of Organizational Behavior

Miner
Theories of Organizational Structure and Process

Paine and Anderson
Strategic Management

Paine and Naumes
Organizational Strategy and Policy: Text and Cases, Third Edition

Penrose
Applications in Business Communication

Ray and Eison
Supervision

Robinson
International Business Management, Second Edition

Smith
Management System: Analysis and Applications

Stone
Understanding Personnel Management

Viola
Organizations in a Changing Society: Administration and Human Values

Bradley and South
Introductory Statistics for Business and Economics

Gulati
A Short Course in Calculus

Trueman
Quantitative Methods for Decision Making in Business

Howell, Henley, and Allison
Business Law: Text and Cases, Second Edition

Howell, Henley, and Allison
Business Law: Text and Cases, Second Alternate Edition

Contents

**Part Four
Preserving Effective
Employee-Management
Relationships**

Part One   Personnel in an Organizational Setting

Organizations exist through employees, who are in turn deeply affected by the organizations' personnel decisions. Personnel represents the most pervasive organizational concern. Chapter 1 provides an analytical framework that places this broad and significant topic into a proper perspective. The chapter describes personnel's general functional areas and related activities, objectives, and issues. Also discussed are the participants in personnel matters, as well as external and internal influences on them.

Chapter 2 traces the historical development of the personnel function and tells how it is typically implemented in today's organization. Concluding insights into the personnel function in an organizational setting are furnished in Chapter 3, which discusses the essential components of all organizations and describes various factors, including job characteristics, that motivate employees to perform in a manner consistent with organizational objectives.

Chapter 1

Introduction to the Personnel Function and Its Analytical Framework

The name of the game in business today is personnel. . . . You can't hope to show a good financial or operating report unless your personnel relations are in order, and I don't care what kind of a company you're running. A chief executive is nothing without his people.

Tom Beebe, Chief Executive of Delta Airlines, as cited in Herbert E. Meyer, "Personnel Directors Are the New Corporate Heroes," *Fortune,* February 1976, p. 88.

Figure 1.1   **Analytical Framework of the**
                                 Personnel Function

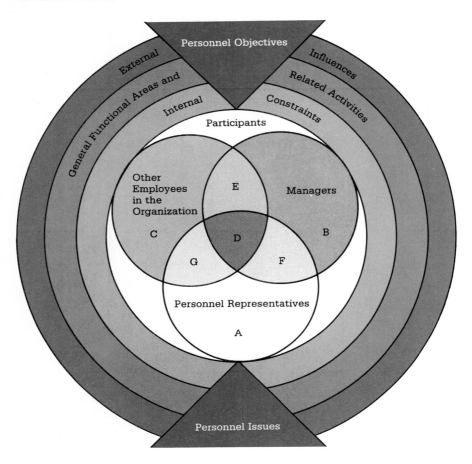

Most of us have participated in personnel activities. We have interviewed for part-time or full-time jobs and perhaps received training, performance appraisals, pay increases, even promotions. We may have seen other personnel activities, such as an employment discrimination suit or the decision to discharge a popular professor, publicized through newspapers or television. Yet questions probably remain as to the exact nature of these activities, the people responsible for their implementation, and the various factors that influence their content and direction.

This chapter attempts to partially answer these questions by using the analytical framework illustrated in Figure 1.1. This framework defines and operationalizes the personnel function and introduces the reader to topics discussed throughout the book. It should also help in sorting out complex (often contradictory) information about the academic and practical aspects of the personnel function.[1]

This chapter will briefly discuss functional personnel areas and related activities, giving additional attention to personnel objectives and issues. It will also discuss various participants in the personnel function and the external influences and internal constraints that can shape personnel concerns and activities.

Before discussing this framework, we should distinguish between *employees* and *personnel.* The latter term refers to beliefs, policies, functions, activities, and issues that pertain to employees or to the personnel department. It has been suggested that *human resource management* should be substituted for *personnel management* to signify the importance of employees as organizational investments which require careful planning, organization, development, and control.[2] *Human resource management* has also been used to stress the significance of the people (usually in the personnel department) charged with assuring that workers with the required mix of knowledge and skills will be available at the right time and price to perform the work the company has undertaken.[3] However, largely for the sake of brevity, this book mainly uses *personnel* instead of *human resources* with no difference intended between the terms.

General Functional Areas and Related Activities, Objectives, and Issues

Many activities may be included in the overall personnel function; in fact, a detailed list would probably include several hundred items. These activities can be grouped into general functional areas. Chapter 2 discusses some of the factors which determine the number and type of such functional areas for a particular organization. However, the following five areas and some related activities are given for illustrative purposes. These five areas serve as an introduction to most of the remaining chapters of this book.

1. *Determining and staffing for employment needs*—Carrying out job analysis to determine jobs' essential characteristics; forecasting the number of employees needed for various jobs; recruiting employees from inside and outside the organization by using techniques such as testing, interviewing, and career path planning and development.
2. *Measuring performance and developing employee potential*—Constructing valid performance appraisals; determining which types of performance appraisal are appropriate for certain employee classifications; analyzing organizational training needs, conducting related training programs, and assessing their effectiveness.
3. *Preserving effective employee-management relationships*—Evaluating the relative importance of jobs; determining appropriate compensation programs, including various incentive systems and financial benefits; negotiating collective bargaining agreements and resolving grievances in unionized firms.

4. *Uncovering and resolving employee problems*—Assessing the extent to which organizational conditions cause employee stress, which coupled with changing employee values can cause a variety of problems such as drug abuse, alcoholism, white-collar crime, and absenteeism; devising strategies to resolve these problems, such as communication, counseling, discipline, and quality of worklife programs.

5. *Anticipating and coping with organizational change*—Implementing the principles of fair employment legislation concerning black, female, older, and handicapped employees; conducting research to assess effectiveness of present personnel activities; anticipating future personnel trends and concerns.

Personnel activities are often shaped and guided by personnel policies. Consider, for example, recruiting entry-level accountants. Related policies might require that applicants have college degrees or even that they be recruited from certain schools. Another personnel policy might state that no employee may be discharged without complete documentation of poor work performance and previous attempts by the supervisor to correct the problem.

Personnel activities also have specific objectives. For example, recruiting has the objective of successfully matching the applicant's qualifications and interests to the available job opening. There are also general objectives, which cut across the more specific activities and apply to the entire personnel function and to the individuals (usually in the personnel department) who implement the personnel function on a full-time basis. General personnel objectives include:

Fostering the attitude that employees are the organization's most important resource and thus deserve organizational attention and recognition.

Working with and through employees to enhance organizational effectiveness.

Assisting other managers in carrying out their personnel-related responsibilities.

Personnel functions and their component activities often involve controversial issues that extend beyond the immediate situation. For example, union-management activities (Chapters 14 and 15) involve the following issue: "Can union-management cooperation become the rule rather than the exception?" Specific issues are discussed for each personnel function at the end of each chapter to reflect some of the implications of personnel management.

There are also some broader issues that can help predict whether an organization can achieve its personnel objectives. These issues, approached indirectly throughout the book, include the following:

To what extent can the organization adapt to employee's concerns, and vice versa?

What is the relationship between the personnel department and other organizational departments?

To what degree is the personnel department presently effective in its various activities?

Personnel functions do not occur in a vaccum. They are implemented by people within the organization and are subject to external influences and internal constraints.

Participants

The inner circles of Figure 1.1 show the three major groups involved, directly or indirectly, in personnel activities. *Personnel representatives* at various organizational levels devote full-time effort to the development and implementation of personnel functions, activities, and policies. Chapter 2 describes in more detail the varied organizational roles and relationships involving personnel representatives. Other participants include *managers of functions other than personnel,* such as accounting, sales, production, and so forth, and *other organizational employees.*

Two factors complicate describing the roles of these participants. First, each participant group pursues its own specialized interests in an organizational setting (areas A, B, and C in Figure 1.1). Personnel representatives are involved in their own activities, such as conducting wage and salary surveys and designing and implementing employment tests. Managers of functions other than personnel focus on establishing and implementing their departmental goals. Employees often balance job requirements with personal priorities (family, education, recreation, and so forth) and life styles.

Second, not all personnel activities and decisions involve all the participants. Possible combinations are discussed below:

Involvement of all participant groups (area D in Figure 1.1)—activities such as safety programs, training programs, performance appraisals, and alcoholism rehabilitation programs.

Involvement of managers and employees (area E in Figure 1.1)—activities such as scheduling overtime, determining content and direction of daily work assignments, and so forth.

Involvement of personnel representatives and managers (area F in Figure 1.1)—areas such as manpower forecasting, college recruiting, and wage and salary adjustments. This combination is important in many organizations. Also, many students in personnel courses will become managers in areas other than personnel. Therefore, it seems appropriate to discuss this combination as it applies to particular personnel concerns. Such

discussions appear in most of the chapters in sections, titled
"The Role of the Personnel Department and Other Managers."

Involvement of personnel representatives and employees (area G
in Figure 1.1)—activities such as counseling, determining benefit eligibility and payment, and conducting employee attitude
surveys.

In summary, personnel activities involve personnel representatives,
other managers, and employees in varying degrees and combinations.
Also, each group has exclusive concerns and priorities. In fact, as discussed further in Chapter 2, some managers and employees may consider that carrying out various personnel-related activities (completing
a performance appraisal, transferring an employee to another location,
and so forth) intrudes upon their priorities.

The seven areas of autonomy and interrelationship of the participants in the personnel function (areas A through G in Figure 1.1) illustrate a realistic representation of how the personnel function operates
within a typical organization. The following sections of this chapter
discuss the two remaining components of Figure 1.1.

External Influences and Internal Constraints

The outer circle in Figure 1.1 represents several interrelated external
influences that help determine and shape personnel functions and activities. These influences are introduced here and discussed in more
detail in later chapters.

External Influences

State of the Economy The economy is referred to here in a broad sense,
although it has many specific implications for the personnel function.
The president of a large corporation assessed the state of the economy
from 1969 to the present in the following terms:[4]

> In 1969 and 1970, the economy experienced the first recession in
> nine years, rebounded to very strong growth in 1972 and 1973 and
> then spiraled into recession. Basic inflationary trends were set off
> which have not yet been arrested.

> These wide swings in the economy in the face of inflationary pres-
> sures were very difficult for business to handle. Planning was par-
> ticularly perplexing. I think most of us believed that this uncertain
> period was temporary, that long term and favorable business condi-
> tions would resume and, therefore, planning for expansion contin-
> ued, despite the lower profit margins from inflation.

Inflation directly affects personnel activities such as wage and salary
increases. For example, the 1980 average wage increase was 10.1
percent and the 1981 wage increase was 9.3 percent.[5] Another effect
of inflation on wages is the almost standard reliance on cost of living
indexes as a factor in wage determination (see Chapter 10 for

more details); yet another effect is an increase in pension costs. In one company, 1970 pension costs equaled $2 million, while 1976 pension costs for a workforce of about the same size were $10 million and projected 1995 pension costs are $42 million (a figure equal to the company's 1974 before-tax profits).[6] Less direct impacts on personnel concerns include those on home purchasing and financing; high interest rates have prompted many employees to turn down job transfers to other locations. A survey of 600 major organizations found 9 percent fewer employees moved in 1979 than in 1978.[7] Some companies have overcome employee reluctance with mortgage rate subsidies and other home purchase benefits. One company, for example, provided an executive a $61,000 loan free for five years as a down payment on a Los Angeles home.[8]

Sharp upward swings in the business cycle are often accompanied by an increase in available jobs. This situation often increases turnover (employees' voluntarily quitting to take jobs with other companies), which, in turn, increases recruiting and training activities while complicating employment forecasting efforts. Downswings in the economy have an opposite effect: turnover declines as employees become concerned with job security, and hiring and training slacken.

Competition in Product and Labor Markets Within the product market are competitive pressures, concerns over market share, interest in expanding the size of the market, and so forth. A company facing reduced demand for its products often has to consider a variety of personnel activities related to cost cutting. Texas Instruments, for example, had to impose "ordered vacation days" on employees at the end of 1980[9] and reduced work schedules for a portion of its workforce at the start of 1981.[10] Permanent employee reductions may also take place. Even companies with reputations as "lifetime employers" have been known to discharge hundreds of managers and executives within a short period.[11]

Competition in the product market also forces most companies to seriously examine pricing practices, production costs, and productivity issues. Productivity problems can be caused by many factors, such as government regulation and lack of investment in plant and equipment; some of the barriers to productivity improvements are personnel related, such as lack of cooperation between management and union officials and changing employee attitudes toward work.[12]

Employees, particularly those with extensive experience and skills, are usually scarce. Many times, companies must compete for high-quality employees. This competition extends across industrial categories. Even governmental agencies, especially at the federal level, are no longer "second-class" bidders for employee services. Employees, particularly at lower organizational levels, may be attracted to governmental positions because of comparable (in some cases, higher) wages and challenging career opportunities.

Government Regulations, Legislation, and Public Policy Governmental agencies at the local, state, and federal levels have increasingly become part of a company's way of life. Many executives openly acknowledge their involvement in political activities to ensure that their organizations' interests are represented in legislative decisions.[13] Many companies have also established political action committees (PACs), which contribute funds for political candidates at local, state, and federal levels.[14]

Closely related to corporate political involvement are government regulations, which affect nearly all aspects of the business firm. Much of this regulation occurs through various pieces of legislation[15] and through some 116 government agencies and programs.[16] Because these regulations limit organizations' flexibility and restrict many of their activities, confrontation between government and business can occur. One former CEO, when asked about significant challenges to management, commented, "We will all have to learn how to be effective in keeping the government from doing damn fool things that could put us out of business."[17] Government regulation is extensive; for example:[18]

As of the end of [1979], we had 100,980 federal government business regulators—appointed, not elected. They added 7,496 regulations to those that already filled 60,000 pages—most of them aimed at business and many of them carrying jail sentences.

Annually, the federal government issues over 9,800 different forms to be filled out by business requiring 556 million responses—and, in most cases, response is mandatory.

Much governmental regulation pertains to the personnel issues discussed throughout this book. (For a summary of these varied laws, see the appendix at the end of this chapter.) The effects of laws on the growth and status of the personnel function is discussed in Chapter 2. Here we need only point out that some legislation and related governmental regulation can result in extensive personnel activities. For example, fair employment legislation (discussed throughout the book, particularly in Chapter 18) prohibits discrimination in employment on the basis of sex, age, religion, race, and national origin. Some effects of these laws on personnel activities are illustrated in Exhibit 1.1.

Compliance with government regulation involves time and money. For example, in 1974, General Motors' activities related to compliance with personnel legislation involved 25,300 full-time employees and costs exceeding $1.3 billion.[19]

Characteristics of the Labor Force Potential as well as existing employees can be examined along several dimensions, such as: (1) experience, skill, and educational levels; (2) socio-demographic characteristics

Exhibit 1.1	**Implications of Equal Employment Opportunity (EEO) Legislation on Selected Personnel Functions**

Personnel Functions

Recruitment, Selection and Employment

Labor Relations

Training Staff

Work Force Forecasting

Compensation and Benefits

EEO Implications

Responsible for assuring that company intake, promotion and transfer policies, programs and practices are neither deliberately discriminatory nor have disparate effects on minorities and females protected under the law. To meet affirmative action goals, staff is called upon to develop and provide to operating managers any special new skills in their fields needed to reach and tap minority and female labor markets.

Generally responsible for assuring that collective bargaining agreements do not contain clauses that illegally discriminate or are discriminatory in their effects. Further, labor relations is generally responsible for achieving agreement with labor unions to changes in staffing, development and promotion practices undertaken to achieve affirmative action goals.

In many of the companies, labor relations staff represents the company when EEO charges or complaints have been brought. A number of recent court rulings have made it extremely advantageous for companies to locate and resolve internally and as quickly as possible any grievances that have potential for developing into EEO cases. Grievance procedures have been redesigned—via telephone "hot-line" procedures, for example—to bring such problems to the almost immediate attention of corporate labor relations and EEO staffs.

May have to assess the need for and, where necessary, develop special training and development programs for minority and female employees. Without such special training, it may not be possible for them to perform adequately in their present jobs or to be ready for promotion. Programs may have to be developed to prepare managers, supervisors and personnel staff for their responsibilities under the law.

May assure that company business plans, and analyses of the company's labor markets take into account the design and implementation of affirmative action plans.

May assure that minorities and women receive equal pay for equal work. Compensation and benefit plans may be modified better to meet the needs of the new work force.

Exhibit 1.1   **Continued**

Personnel Functions	EEO Implications
Safety Training and Management	May assure that requirements for working procedures and maintenance, training for workers and supervisors, and measurement procedures are suitable for the new work force.
Medical Departments	May need to reshape the preemployment physical for employees to avoid disparate effects or to make it job related. Departments may also expand their expertise in the diseases that especially afflict female employees or disadvantaged minority groups. Requirements for staffing medical facilities may also change. Medical staff may get more involved in diagnosis and treatment of illnesses where minority group members have only limited access to community or private medical care.
Organization Planning and Development	May be called into play to redesign jobs or to establish special management-development programs for minorities and women.

Source: Allen R. Janger, *The Personnel Function: Changing Objectives and Organization* (New York: Conference Board, 1977), pp. 89, 93. Reprinted by permission.

(sex, race, age, and so forth); and (3) work-related attitudes pertaining to authority, achievement, and the importance of work in life.[20] These dimensions are subject to broad trends and changes over time, which can in turn have implications for the personnel function.

Some chief executive officers regard the growing shortage of skilled personnel as the single most important issue companies will face in the 1980s.[21] The effects of this situation on recruiting and compensation have been previously mentioned in relation to competition in the labor market. Retaining employees in a tight labor market has other implications as well. For example, some employees might receive unwarranted promotions to justify wage increases, which in turn could result in morale and efficiency problems.[22]

On the other hand, the increasing educational level of the work force can create additional personnel challenges. One estimate by the Bureau of Labor Statistics suggests that the number of college educated employees is currently greater than the number of jobs requiring a college education.[23] Employers, therefore, must focus attention on motivating a better-educated work force through job and organizational design efforts. Such attention is particularly significant because many high-potential executives in their forties leave industry to pursue alternative life styles.[24]

One of the more recent and significant socio-demographic shifts in the labor force involves the female population. During the years 1955–1980, the number of women in the labor force more than doubled; and females currently represent over 40 percent of the civilian labor force.[25] Statistical differences reflect only one aspect of this shift. Not too long ago, many females were encouraged to pursue nonbusiness careers such as teaching in elementary and secondary schools or being housewives. New interests of female members of the labor force correspond with changes in educational patterns. For example, a survey of one million students conducted in 1980 found that for the first time, more female than male high school seniors expressed an interest in studying business courses in college.[26]

Females as well as racial minorities have increased their expectations for employment and career opportunities. However, these groups are not evenly distributed among occupations in our society. White males, on average, continue to hold higher-paying positions and have a lower unemployment rate than black and female employees. This situation, coupled with employment legislation, has several implications for personnel policies (see, for example, Exhibit 1.1 and Chapter 18).

People in the labor force hold sharply defined attitudes toward work and other social aspects of life. Changing work values and their implications for the personnel function are discussed in Chapters 2 and 16.[27] Other social beliefs and trends may also affect the personnel function, even though they are not directly related to work. Such changes are varied in topic and significance (consider, for example, hair and dress styles, political beliefs,[28] and attitudes toward marriage). Changes in social values always carry the potential to cause organizational confrontation and change. For example, the continued increase (since 1963)[29] in the U.S. divorce rate runs counter to a recent survey of top executives, 89 percent of whom have never been divorced.[30] Confrontation might occur when a divorced employee is considered for a promotion.

Technology Technology is a broad term that refers to the pace of work, the tasks to be performed, the work environment, the equipment used, and the workflow. Technology affects many personnel activities, most notably recruiting, staffing, training, and compensation of skilled personnel (Chapters 4, 5, 6, 7, 9, 10, and 11); negotiation of work rules by management and labor union officials (Chapter 15); and work design (Chapter 17).

Extensive technological development has occurred in the communications and data processing industries. Cable TV companies are now connecting homes with central communications centers to form networks that soon may facilitate electronic education, shopping, banking, and entertainment. Substantial personnel changes (layoffs, retraining, and so forth) might occur in these and other affected industries. For example, computer transmittal of banking and billing activities might substantially reduce Post Office activities and personnel.[31]

Many technological innovations, particularly data processing, have been applied to the personnel function. One recent survey found that over 80 percent of personnel executives rely on electronic data processing for at least some, if not all, record keeping and report preparation. Some of the more common computerized reports pertain to the basic employee information (name, social security number, date of hire, and the like), hours and earnings, equal employment opportunity information, insurance claims, benefits, turnover, attendance, safety records, and performance appraisals.[32]

International Conditions World conditions can focus attention on the personnel function. For example, World War I aided in the growth of the personnel function because it created a desperate need to recruit, test, and place people in military and civilian positions in a short period of time. Today, competition with foreign countries has forced many companies to engage in multinational operations (Chapter 19) and attempts to improve productivity (Chapter 17). Both these actions directly affect the personnel function. For example, many corporations are hiring specialists (political scientists and former Foreign Service officers) to methodically assess the political and economic risks of investing abroad.[33]

The recent energy crisis, initiated by foreign oil producers, has had several implications for the personnel function. Domestic demand for fuel-efficient transportation has caused production and employee cutbacks in the manufacturing of larger automobiles. The energy crisis might also prompt the establishment of new organizational positions. Since 1978, the number of organizations with full time ''energy managers'' has significantly increased.[34] These positions, of course, often affect such personnel activities as establishing employees' van pool and car pool programs to conserve gasoline.[35]

Internal Constraints

Internal constraints, like external influences, can modify personnel activities, often in ways that hinder the attainment of personnel goals and objectives. Three internal constraints may have major impacts on personnel activities: *unions,* the *nature of many personnel activities,* and the *attitudes of other managers toward the personnel function.*

Unions The impact of labor organizations or unions on personnel activities is discussed in Chapter 2 and, in much more detail, in Chapters 14 and 15. It should be briefly noted here, however, that unions reduce managerial discretion and that managers in unionized firms have less flexibility in implementing many personnel policies and activities.

Nature of Personnel Activities The characteristics of many personnel activities can represent a second internal constraint. Some personnel activities have been labeled "trash can"[36] activities, because they are trivial or unpleasant. In some cases, personnel activities are of the "no win" variety. For example, suppose some nurses in a hospital believe pantsuits are more comfortable and conducive to performing hospital duties, while other nurses and hospital administrators favor the more traditional uniforms, labeling them more "professional." Either way the dress code is determined will cause negative reactions. Establishing dress code policies, which are relatively inconsequential in terms of major organizational objectives, consumes time and sometimes arouses emotional reactions. Some other no-win activities and policies pertain to making rules about romances between company employees,[37] hair styles, smoking, and employment rights of homosexual and transexual persons. Even one of the more conspicuous personnel issues, equal employment opportunity, can involve a no-win situation in two respects: (a) when a minority employee is promoted, an employee not in this classification may claim reverse discrimination; and, (b) much of the printed publicity on the subject emphasizes the negative aspects (such as lost legal suits) instead of the positive results of affirmative action activity.

Many personnel activities also involve requirements of confidentiality, which can result in two problems. The requirement of confidentiality can restrict input necessary for accurate personnel decisions. Various laws have restricted the amount of information a company can legally request from its job applicants. One company, for example, requires applicants to furnish virtually no personal information other than name, address, and whether he or she has been convicted of any crime within the last five years. If the applicant is a veteran, all the company asks is the date he or she left the service; it doesn't require the applicant to tell whether the discharge was honorable.[38] Making an accurate assessment of the applicant's employment potential based on such limited information is difficult.

Other personnel activities may also involve confidential information from employees. Consider, for example, an employee concerned about his or her immediate supervisor's drinking problem. This employee informs another management official of the situation, asking that the information be kept in confidence. A problem then arises for the manager who received the information. How can the manager attempt to deal with the supervisor's drinking problem without betraying the employee's confidence?

Many personnel activities lack precise effectiveness measures.[39] One reason for this situation is that the personnel function's focal point—people—cannot be manipulated as easily as machines and capital.[40] Also, the success or failure of many personnel activities (safety, college recruiting, training programs, and so forth) depends on many organizational participants. Estimating individual contributions to these activities becomes extremely difficult.

Attitudes of Other Managers The third internal constraint concerns managerial attitudes toward personnel activities, which can either impede or enhance the accomplishment of related objectives. This constraint is related to the measurement problem just discussed. Managers will view personnel activities negatively if they cannot gauge their contribution to the firm. Managerial attitudes also pertain to the individuals whose full-time efforts are concerned with personnel. Reactions toward personnel representatives or the personnel department can be quite varied, as illustrated by the two following quotations:

Good managers recognize the importance of good human relations. That's why they don't let the personnel departments handle the important questions . . . . In our organization if you took the personnel function away it would never be missed.[41]

Corporations are setting new criteria and priorities for the personnel officer. So important has this executive become that many companies now view him as a star in his own right, courting him and paying him accordingly.[42]

Historical as well as current reasons for these varied attitudes are discussed in the next chapter.

Summary

Personnel describes beliefs, policies, functions, activities, and issues that pertain to employees or to the personnel department. The numerous and divergent personnel activities can be grouped into the following general functional areas: determining and staffing for employment needs; measuring performance and developing employee potential; preserving effective employee-management relationships; uncovering and resolving employee problems; and anticipating and coping with organizational change. Personnel functions and activities are undertaken to achieve organizational objectives and often involve controversial issues.

Personnel activities can involve three general categories of participants. Personnel representatives are the individuals concerned with the personnel function on a full-time basis. However, most, if not all, organizational managers are also concerned with at least some personnel activities—for example, recommending wage increases for their subordinates. Other organizational employees are also involved in personnel activities, such as safety and training programs. These three participant categories are not jointly involved in every personnel activity; they act in various combinations and also have mutually exclusive organizational concerns.

The personnel function is subject to many external influences. For example, characteristics of the labor force, such as increased female participation in it, coupled with related government regulations and legislation will likely modify organizational recruiting and training activities. Wage increases can be affected by the state of the economy and by the extent to which employers face labor or product market competition. Technological innovations and international conditions can also modify working conditions and arrangements.

Three internal constraints can modify personnel activities, often in ways that hinder the attainment of personnel goals and objectives. Unions can reduce managerial discretion in such personnel activities as employee layoffs and work assignments. Characteristics of personnel activities, such as "no win" situations and confidentiality requirements, can also act as internal constraints. Finally, the attitudes of other managers toward the personnel function can either impede or enhance the accomplishment of objectives.

Discussion Questions

1. Define *personnel management* and *human resource management,* indicating the similarities and possible differences between these terms.

2. Cite one of the five general functional areas of the personnel function. Based on your own part-time or full-time work experiences, briefly discuss one specific personnel activity that could be included in this area but that has not been previously mentioned in this chapter. Formulate one specific objective for that activity.

3. Explain with some specific examples how even though managers are sometimes excluded from personnel activities, the personnel function is every manager's responsibility.

4. Explain how the state of the economy can have implications for the personnel function. Name another external influence that could affect the personnel function and tell how.

5. Formulate two original examples of "no-win" personnel activities. For one of these examples, discuss specific strategies you would use to minimize this internal constraint.

Notes

1. Walter L. Wallace, *The Logic of Science in Sociology* (New York: Aldine, 1979), pp. 103–106.
2. Frederick G. Lippert, "Whither HRM in the Seventies?" *Michigan Business Review* 24 (March 1972), p. 11. For a brief case study which illustrates this shift in emphases see N. R. Kleinfield, "A Human Resource at Allied Corp.," June 6, 1981, p. 4F.
3. Robert R. Guthrie, "Personnel's Emergency Role," *Personnel Journal* 53 (September 1974), p. 658.
4. J. A. Henderson, "What the Chief Executive Expects of the Personnel Function," *Personnel*
5. Arthur Sackley, "Wage Increases Moderate in 1981," *Monthly Labor Review* 105 (May 1982), p. 4.

6. Henderson, "What the Chief Executive Expects," p. 42.
7. "Labor Letter," *Wall Street Journal,* August 12, 1980, p. 1.
8. "Labor Letter," *Wall Street Journal,* March 22, 1981, p. 1.
9. "Many Texas Instruments Employees to Get 'Ordered Vacation' Days at End of Year," *Wall Street Journal,* December 3, 1980, p. 7.
10. "Texas Instruments to Trim Workweeks, Cites Soft Market for Computer Products," *Wall Street Journal,* December 19, 1980, p. 3.
11. See, for example, Priscilla S. Meyer, "No More Nice Guy: Traditionally Paternal, Equitable Life Rattles Staff by Mass Firings," *Wall Street Journal,* December 11, 1978, pp. 1, 30.
12. Bureau of National Affairs, *Daily Labor Report,* November 11, 1980, p. 213; Bureau of National Affairs, *Daily Labor Report,* November 4, 1980, p. 3.
13. David G. Moore, *Politics and the Corporate Chief Executive* (New York: Conference Board, 1980), p. 23.
14. Stephen J. Sansweet, "PAC Pressure? Political-Action Units at Firms Are Assailed by Some over Tactics," *Wall Street Journal,* July 24, 1980, pp. 1, 12.
15. For a provocative discussion of the implications of legislation on corporate activities, see Christopher D. Stone, *Where the Law Ends: The Social Control of Corporate Behavior* (New York: Harper & Row, 1975).
16. "VPs of Red Tape: More Firms Upgraded Government Relations Jobs because of Sharp Growth in Federal Regulations," *Wall Street Journal,* January 11, 1980, p. 42.
17. Fred R. Edney, "The Greening of the Profession," *Personnel Administrator* 25 (July 1980), p. 28.
18. Ibid. See also Robert A. Leone, "The Real Costs of Regulation," *Harvard Business Review* 55 (November/December 1977), pp. 57–66.
19. For more details concerning these statistical allocations, see Allen R. Janger, *The Personnel Function: Changing Objectives and Organization* (New York: Conference Board, 1977), p. 3.
20. V. V. Murray, Harish C. Jain, and Roy J. Adams, "A Framework for the Comparative Analysis of Personnel Administration," *Academy of Management Review* 6 (July 1976), p. 48. It should be emphasized that this article contains many more variables than are listed in this text. The article offers an excellent starting point for assessing the personnel function. See also Earl G. Gottschalk, Jr., "Firms Increasingly Help Spouses of Transferred Employees Find Jobs," *Wall Street Journal,* January 21, 1982, p. 29.
21. Ross A. Hennigar, "People Management in the 1980s: A CEO's View," *Personnel Journal* 59 (November 1980), pp. 898–899.
22. Richard V. Scacchetti and J. Robert Parket, "How to Recognize the Promotables," *S.A.M. Advanced Management Journal* 37 (April 1972), p. 38.
23. Fred K. Foulkes, "The Expanding Role of the Personnel Function," *Harvard Business Review* 53 (March/April 1975), p. 72.
24. *Ibid.*
25. Maryann H. Albrecht, "The New Labor Force: Implications for Better Personnel Practices," in E. L. Miller, E. H. Burack, and M. H. Albrecht, eds., *Management of Human Resources* (Englewood Cliffs, N.J.: Prentice-Hall, 1980), p. 42.
26. "Labor Letter," *Wall Street Journal,* October 21, 1980, p. 1. It should be noted that these figures have tripled since 1973.
27. See, for example, Dean Rotbart, "Doctor's Husband: Father Quit His Job for the Family's Sake; Now Hirers Shun Him," *Wall Street Journal,* April 13, 1981, pp. 1, 14.
28. Thomas J. Murray, "It's Hell in Personnel," *Dun's* 97 (March 1971), pp. 40–43.
29. "Nation's Divorce Rate Climbing Again," *Miami Herald,* August 17, 1980, p. 2–A.
30. "Labor Letter," *Wall Street Journal,* March 4, 1980, p. 1.
31. D. Quinn Mills, "Human Resources in the 1980s," *Harvard Business Review* 57 (July/August 1979), p. 155.
32. *Aspects of the Personnel Function: Structure, Use of Electronic Data Processing, and Professional Activities* (Washington, D.C.: Bureau of National Affairs, 1979), p. 7.
33. Ronald Alsop, "Foreign Ventures: More Firms Are Hiring Own Political Analysts to Limit Risks Abroad," *Wall Street Journal,* March 30, 1981, pp. 1, 17.
34. "Labor Letter," *Wall Street Journal,* October 21, 1980, p. 1.
35. See, for example, "Labor Letter," *Wall Street Journal,* April 15, 1980, p. 1.
36. See, for example, George Ritzer and Harrison M. Trice, *An Occupation in Conflict* (Ithaca, N.Y.: New York State School of Industrial and Labor Relations, Cornell University, 1969), pp. 42–44.
37. See, for example, "Labor Letter," *Wall Street Journal,* October 17, 1977, p. 1.
38. "Corporate Life: Butting Out," *Newsweek,* November 10, 1975, pp. 95–96.
39. T. F. Cawsey, "Why Line Managers Don't Listen to Their Personnel Departments," *Personnel* 57 (January/February, 1980), p. 14.
40. Karen Legge and Margaret Exley, "Authority, Ambiguity and Adaptation: The Personnel Specialist's Dilemma," *Industrial Relations Journal* 6 (Autumn 1975), p. 55.
41. Cawsey, "Why Line Managers," p. 11.
42. Isadore Barmash, "Personnel Chief Has New Role," *New York Times,* April 21, 1981, p. D–2.

Selected Federal Legislation That Affects Personnel Activities

Name of Law/ Executive Order	Major Reference Category	Federal Government Agency Charged with Enforcement	Representative Activities Covered by Provisions	Scope of Law and Exemptions
Davis-Bacon Act of 1931	Wages	Department of Labor	Determination of prevailing wage rates and fringe benefits; overtime compensation; standard eight-hour workday.	Private contractors engaged in public works construction involving more than $2,000. Public construction projects financed with $2,000 or more in federal funds.
Social Security Act of 1935 (Act has been amended approximately every two years.)	Employee Benefits	Social Security Administration	Retirement benefits; disability benefits; old age and survivors' insurance; "Medicare" for hospitalization of covered patients over sixty-five; partial funding by employers of unemployment compensation; financial assistance for laid-off employees; maximum benefits; automatic adjustments of benefits because of rises in CPI.	Currently insured employees must have worked in covered employment during one and one-half years out of last three years. Fully insured employees must have worked in covered employment for ten years. Employees must be fully insured to receive retirement benefits. Only partial benefits may be collected by employees under the age of seventy-two who elect to continue working.
Walsh-Healey Act of 1936	Wages and Safety	Department of Labor	Differing minimum wage rates for specific industries; safety and health regulations; overtime compensation for work in excess	Employers receiving annual federal government contracts involving $10,000 or more. Executive, administrative, and profes-

Name of Law/ Executive Order	Major Reference Category	Federal Government Agency Charged with Enforcement	Representative Activities Covered by Provisions	Scope of Law and Exemptions
			of eight-hour day or forty-hour week.	sional employees exempt under Fair Labor Standards Act are exempt from this act. Employees who perform only office or custodial work are also exempted.
Employee Retirement Income Security Act of 1974	Employee Benefit Plans	Pension Benefit Guaranty Corporation Department of Labor Department of the Treasury	Minimum participation standards; minimum vesting standards; minimum funding standards; benefit accrual requirements; disclosure of plan provisions to employees; pension benefit guaranty funds; Individual Retirement Accounts; standards of conduct for plan officials.	Private sector employers and employee organizations engaged in commerce. Exempted are: government plans, church plans, plans maintained outside U.S., plans maintained solely for purpose of complying with workman's compensation laws, unemployment compensation, or disability insurance.
Fair Labor Standards Act of 1938 (Amended in 1949, 1955, 1961, 1966, 1974, 1977)	Hours Wages	Wage and Hour Division, Department of Labor Secretary of Labor EEOC	Minimum wage; maximum hours; overtime compensation; restrictions on child labor; wages for apprentices, students, and handicapped workers; home work regulations; maintenance of employer records; acts prohibited employers.	Employers engaged in commerce; hospitals; educational institutions; federal, state, and local governments; postal service. There are extensive exemptions varying according to particular provisions of act.
Equal Pay Act of 1963 (Amendment to Fair Labor Standards Act)	Sex Discrimination in Wages	EEOC	Prohibition of wage differentials based on sex.	Employers subject to Fair Labor Standards Act. Employees not covered by Fair Labor Standards Act are exempted.
Civil Rights Act of 1964 (Amended in 1972, 1978)	Discrimination in Employment	EEOC Civil Service (for Federal Violations)	Prohibition of hiring, discharge, segregation, or discrimination be-	Employers with fifteen or more employees; employment agencies;

Name of Law/ Executive Order	Major Reference Category	Federal Government Agency Charged with Enforcement	Representative Activities Covered by Provisions	Scope of Law and Exemptions
			cause of race, color, religion, sex, or national origin; bona fide occupational qualifications; investigations of discriminatory actions; filing of reports by EEOC; unlawful employment practices; posting of notices.	labor organizations with fifteen or more members; training programs; federal, state, and local governments. Aliens and individuals performing activities of religious organizations are exempted.
Executive Order 11246 of 1965 Executive Order 11375 of 1967	Equal Employment Opportunity and Affirmative Action for Minorities	OFCCP Office of Personnel Management	Prohibition of employment discrimination; affirmative action programs to increase the percentage of minority employees regarding employment, promotions, demotions, transfers, recruitment advertising, layoffs, termination, compensation, and training; integrated facilities in the workplace.	Employers receiving government contracts in excess of $10,000; for employers with fifty or more employees and $50,000 in contracts, affirmative action plans are mandatory; U.S. Postal Service; federal government agencies.
Age Discrimination in Employment Act of 1967 (Amended in 1974, 1978)	Employees Aged Forty through Seventy	EEOC	Hiring of, discharge of, or discrimination against employees in protected age group; limiting, segregating, or classifying of employees because of age; advertisements for employment; bona fide occupational qualifications; bona fide seniority systems or benefit plans; good cause dismissal.	Employers with twenty or more employees; employment agencies; labor organizations with twenty-five or more members; federal, state, and local governments. Bona fide executives aged sixty-five or older who are entitled to annuities of $27,000 or more are exempted.
Rehabilitation Act of 1973 (Amended in 1974, 1976, 1978)	Handicapped Employees (Includes Rehabilitated Alcoholics and Drug Addicts)	Office of Federal Contract Compliance Programs Rehabilitation Services Administration	Mandatory affirmative action programs for hiring, placement, and advancement of qualified handicapped persons;	Private sector firms receiving $2,500 or more annually in federal contracts; federal, state, and local governments.

Name of Law/ Executive Order	Major Reference Category	Federal Government Agency Charged with Enforcement	Representative Activities Covered by Provisions	Scope of Law and Exemptions
			accommodations for physical and mental limitations of the handicapped; counseling and guidance services for handicapped persons; evaluation of affirmative action programs.	
Vietnam Era Veterans Readjustment Act of 1974	Employment of Veterans	OFCCP	Reemployment rights of veterans; restoration of seniority, status, and compensation; protection of reservists and National Guardsmen from discharge; affirmative action plans to employ and advance disabled veterans and veterans of Vietnam era; employment rights of widows and wives of veterans.	Employers receiving government contracts of $10,000 or more.
Federal Privacy Act of 1974	Privacy of Individuals	Office of Management and Budget	Accuracy and security of records concerning individuals; limitation of agency's rights to maintain records; rights of individuals regarding release of records without their consent.	All federal agencies.
Fair Credit Reporting Act of 1971	Consumer Credit Reports	Federal Trade Commission	Consumer's right to review and correct information on file; omission of obsolete credit information; prohibitions against release of credit information to unauthorized agencies; notification of consumer by users of information; notification of agency if employment is	Users of credit and investigative reports; consumer reporting agencies.

Name of Law/ Executive Order	Major Reference Category	Federal Government Agency Charged with Enforcement	Representative Activities Covered by Provisions	Scope of Law and Exemptions
			denied because of credit information.	
Occupational Safety and Health Act of 1970	Safety of Employees	Occupational Safety and Health Administration of (Department of Labor) Occupational Safety and Health Review Commission	Mandatory occupational safety and health standards; inspections and investigations of the workplace; maintenance of employer's records; warning employees of potential hazards; reporting of accidents; prohibition of discrimination against employees for exercising the rights of this law.	All private sector employers engaged in business affecting commerce. Executive Order 12196 (1980) extends OSHA coverage to federal agencies. Self-employed persons, family owned and operated farms are exempted.
Comprehensive Employment and Training Act of 1973 (Amended in 1977, 1978)	Disadvantaged, Unemployed, or Underemployed Persons	Department of Labor	Wages and allowances for individuals receiving training; occupational upgrading and re-training programs; job search and relocation assistance; development of job opportunities for veterans; evaluation of effectiveness of all programs; allocation of funds.	All private-sector businesses; states; units of local government that serve populations of more than 100,000; rural areas with high levels of unemployment.
Railway Labor Act of 1926 (Amended in 1934, 1936, 1966)	Union-Management Relationships	National Railroad Adjustment Board (NRAB) National Mediation Board (NMB)	Rights of employees to organize and bargain collectively without employer interference; good faith bargaining; rates of pay; working conditions; arbitration procedures; enactment of emergency procedures when interstate commerce is substantially threatened.	All railroads engaged in interstate commerce; all airlines engaged in interstate or foreign commerce.
National Labor Relations Act of 1935 (Amended in 1947 and 1959)	Union-Management Relationships	National Labor Relations Board (NLRB)	Rights of employees to organize and bargain collec-	Private-sector employers affecting interstate com-

Name of Law/ Executive Order	Major Reference Category	Federal Government Agency Charged with Enforcement	Representative Activities Covered by Provisions	Scope of Law and Exemptions
			tively; unfair labor practices of employer and union; rights of employees to strike; good faith bargaining; union security; regulation of internal union affairs; filing of reports; representation elections; determination of appropriate bargaining units.	merce, although NLRB may exempt firms not regarded as having a "substantial impact" on interstate commerce. Also exempted are wholly owned government corporations; Federal Reserve banks; states; agricultural laborers; domestic servants; independent contractors; those employed by parents or spouse; supervisors; and employees covered by Railway Labor Act.

Source: Prepared by Dawn Holibonich from material in *Federal Labor Laws,* 4th ed. (St. Paul, Minn.: West Publishing, 1979). Copyright © 1979 by West Publishing. All rights reserved. Used with permission of West Publishing and Dawn Holibonich.

Chapter 2

The Development of the Personnel Function and Its Contemporary Role

Although evolutionary developments have occurred in personnel work, many of the activities associated with the personnel function over the years continue. However, it is encouraging that the personnel function is being challenged by management at all levels to demonstrate its ability to contribute in new and different ways to organizational effectiveness and performance. The transition from minor to major league is not without its problems. However, the growing acknowledgment of personnel's importance is not to be confused with automatic attainment of full responsibility and privileges of corporate citizenship.

Edwin L. Miller and Elmer Burack, "The Emerging Personnel Function," *MSU Business Topics* 25 (Autumn 1977), p. 27. Reprinted by permission of the publisher, Division of Research, Graduate School of Business Administration, Michigan State University.

As discussed in Chapter 1, the personnel function includes a wide variety of activities performed by many people in the organization. Some of these people—the personnel representatives—typically work in a specialized personnel department while others (sales managers, for example) are involved with personnel duties in addition to other organizational responsibilities. Understanding the personnel function, therefore, involves considering its varied organizational participants.

Also necessary is some historical appreciation of the personnel function. Previous personnel practices, the development of the personnel department, and related beliefs concerning employees have influenced the contemporary personnel function. A historical perspective can furnish insights into current personnel problems and prospects and can provide a basis for predicting future direction.

This chapter's first section provides a brief historical overview of the personnel function. The second section describes some current organizational arrangements and relationships involving the personnel function. The issue at the end of the chapter discusses whether the personnel function is an important one to the organization.

A Historical Overview

Making historical generalizations concerning the personnel function is difficult. There are several million companies with a variety of personnel orientations.[1] These companies have retained from the past specific blends of beliefs about and approaches to the personnel function. Looking at the personnel function in terms of chronological time periods can offer only broad generalizations. Given these cautions, this section will discuss three general time periods: 1870–1910, 1910–1930, and 1930 to the present.

The Turn of the Century: 1870–1910

The turn of the century witnessed an unprecedented shift of employees into manufacturing industries.[2] Managers needed to formulate a philosophy and corresponding activities to deal with these employees. Personnel philosophies concern: (1) *the relative positions of management and other employees* and (2) *managerial obligations toward employees.* One important general philosophy of this period, *social Darwinism,* helped industrial owners (Andrew Carnegie, for example[3]) and managers formulate a philosophy about the relative positions of managers and other employees. Social Darwinism applied Darwin's laws to social situations. "Survival of the fittest" was believed to pertain to the social as well as the natural world; thus, the weak (the employees) were thought to have lost the struggle for dominance and so were expected to submit to the successful competitors (the managers).

Social Darwinism represented a "natural law" to its adherents; therefore, they believed any change in the relative positions of managers and employees should proceed slowly if at all. Religious overtones of social Darwinism reinforced this conservative approach, since the unsuccessful were viewed as having no virtue.[4] Consider, for example, the following remarks made by a manager and a minister during this period:

The rights and interests of the laboring man will be protected and cared for, not by the labor agitators, but by the Christian men to whom God in his infinite wisdom has given the control of the property interests of the country.[5]

Business is religion and religion is business. . . . If God gives us the possibilities and power to get wealth, to acquire influence, to be forces in the world, what is the true conception of life but divine ownership and human administration.[6]

Managers who accepted this philosophy contended that employees must wholly conform to the expectations of their social betters;[7] outside advice on how to handle employees was unnecessary. Around 1900, for example, one manager responded in the following manner to a suggestion that employers during prosperous times set aside a fund for wage payments in the time of adversity:

Who are the men engaged in promulgating these so-called reforms, ostensibly for the benefit of workingmen? Are they not for the most part theorists with unbalanced minds, who have adopted unsound principles and are pushing them to the extreme? Are they not men without the knowledge and experience necessary to deal successfully with men of affairs? Why should men of affairs permit them, undisputed, unanswered, unchallenged, to arrogate to themselves the right to teach the world how we shall conduct our business?[8]

This managerial belief was reinforced by governmental and judicial philosophies (laissez-faire and the doctrine of private property) that basically said private industry should operate in its own best interest.

There was, however, less managerial agreement over the personnel philosophy relating to employers' obligations to employees. In fact, there were two general approaches to this matter during the period: *treating labor as a commodity*[9] and *social welfare and paternalism.* Under the commodity approach, employees represented a factor of production to be procured as cheaply as possible and discarded when no longer useful. The human factor was at best irrelevant in employment decisions. Some employers, for example, viewed employees' desires for education as harmful, spoiling these people for the realities of hard work.[10]

The commodity approach provided little room for personnel activities. Employment levels were determined solely by the laws of supply and demand. Employees were usually in abundant supply; therefore, little centralized attention was given to training, recruiting, and discipline. These activities were assigned to a first-line supervisor or foreman, who usually preferred to concentrate on production, since employees were readily available. The one exception pertained to clerical work such as keeping records of time worked and pay received. Although some hiring offices existed, it is doubtful that any personnel department existed before 1900.[11]

Other managers believed their dominant position included the obligation: "to give careful examination to all plans which contemplate man's improvement and elevation."[12] Social welfare and paternalism represented a moralistic interpretation of social Darwinism; for example, work rules posted in 1872 by one owner included the following:

Men employees will be given an evening off each week for courting purposes, or two evenings a week if they go regularly to church.

Every employee should lay aside from each day a goodly sum of his earnings for his benefits during his declining years, so that he will not become a burden upon the charity of his betters.

Any employee who smokes Spanish cigars, uses liquor in any form, gets shaved at a barber shop, or frequents pool or public halls, will give me good reason to suspect his worth, intentions, integrity and honesty.[13]

Some companies pursued this approach by hiring "welfare secretaries," who were typically drawn from the ranks of philanthropic organizations such as the Y.M.C.A. Paternalism, or fatherly concern for employees, was evidenced by the company-owned services, schools, stores, and housing provided by some companies to employees.[14] While few would now argue that employers should disregard their employees' concerns, the motives of paternalism have been frequently challenged. Some say paternalistic policies were established so that employers could manipulate employees through kindness and (in the case of company stores and housing) indebtedness. Others have concluded that employers adopted paternalistic policies because they believed employees were unable to think for themselves, plan ahead, and arrange their own personal affairs.

In summary, three general conclusions regarding managers and employees during the period 1870–1910 are: (1) employers and managers often justified their dominant organizational positions in terms of scientific and even moral laws; (2) employees were expected to obey managerial directives to the letter and adapt entirely to the organization's needs; and (3) nonmanagerial employees were considered to be all alike, a rather passive group offering no unique or significant challenges to the organization. Personnel activities were few during this period and usually involved social welfare and paternalism.

Growth of the Personnel Function: 1910–1930

Neither an immediate nor a steady increase in personnel activities occurred between 1910 and 1930. Economic conditions in 1921, for example, set back the expansion of such activities.[15] Yet three interrelated influences on personnel activities did occur during this time period: (1) recognition of employees' uniqueness and importance, (2) World War I, and (3) increased trade union activity. The Hawthorne Studies also began during this period and will be discussed here even though their influence on personnel activities and approaches did not exert itself until much later.

Recognition of Employees' Uniqueness and Importance Two general movements during the period 1910–1930 encouraged employers to seriously consider employees as human beings with unique attributes. One of these movements could be labeled *psychological reform.* A leader of this movement was Whiting Williams, a former business executive who toured the country working as an hourly employee to learn about employees' views. Many managers read his book, *What's on the Worker's Mind,* and were impressed with his main point that "everyone wants to be a near normal human being in addition to being a worker."[16] Another writer emphasized that all employees in the organization had a wide range of human desires and impulses, such as "love of family," "the creative impulse," and "the desire for justice."[17] Related management books published between 1916 and 1920 suggested that successful managers must realize employees were becoming more complicated because of their increasing intelligence and more subject to mental strain from the workplace (boredom and "antagonism of spirit").[18]

Many managers, while believing these conclusions, still needed reasons to act on them. The *efficiency movement* provided this motivation. Two significant features of the efficiency movement were Frederick Taylor's "scientific management" and the personnel policy changes at Ford Motor. Taylor had begun discussing efficient managerial techniques in 1895;[19] however, his most publicized effort, *The Principles of Scientific Management,* was published in 1911.

Managers already knew production waste and inefficiency cost money. Taylor, however, informed them of previously "hidden wastes" that resulted from haphazard, "rules-of-thumb" management techniques. He believed that when an employee did not perform a job properly, the fault was management's.

One essential element of scientific management was the *task,* a written, detailed series of directions indicating what was to be done, how it was to be done, and the exact time allowed to do it. Management was to plan the task by observing job behaviors, determining efficient movements, and leaving no room for employee discretion. *Careful recruitment* according to the duties specified in the task was also needed. A potential employee's work and personal background was to be carefully checked, since "each workman has his own special abilities and limitations."[20]

Taylor urged employers and employees to set mutually beneficial goals: higher employer profits and higher employee wages. Employees needed *inducements* to work hard. Wage incentives for exceeding production standards were to be established and promptly paid after the task so the employee could readily see the relationship between effort and reward.

Henry Ford adopted some of Taylor's principles with dramatic effect in 1914 when he raised the employees' base salary from $2.34 to $5.00 a day. Ford also severely reduced the foreman's freedom to hire, train, pay, and discharge employees. Indeed, under the new system, foremen could not discharge any employee; they were also held accountable if an employee did not rise through job progressions and pay grades at a normal rate.[21] Ford's policies reflected the social welfare concerns and paternalism of the previous period as well as the principles of scientific management. A sociological department of some 100 employees was established in the company. Representatives from this department investigated employees' financial and moral stability—qualifications for receiving wage increases.

There were two general reasons for Ford's dramatic shift in personnel policies, both of them related to scientific management principles. Ford believed that hourly employees should share in the company's financial success (Ford Motor's net income, for example, rose from approximately $4 million in 1910 to over $13.5 million in 1913).[22] He stated that hourly employees were "indispensible partners" to the organization and their investments in energy and skill should be rewarded with high wages.[23] Ford was also one of the first large employers to recognize a personnel problem—employee turnover, caused largely by haphazard recruiting and training policies. Before implementation of the 1914 plan, the company hired about 53,000 employees a year to keep a constant workforce of 14,000.

In 1915 [a year after the personnel changes] we had to hire only 6,508 men and the majority of those new men were taken on because of the growth of the business. With the old turnover of labour and our present force we should have to hire at the rate of nearly 200,000 men a year which would be pretty nearly an impossible proposition.[24]

Ford's personnel policies were given extensive, generally favorable[25] publicity throughout the United States and abroad, making him "the best known manufacturer in the world" by mid-1914.[26] The subsequent successes of these policies (high profits[27] and dramatically reduced turnover[28]) were also highly publicized.

The publicity given to the psychological reform and efficiency movements encouraged research on personnel topics such as employee services,[29] recruiting and selection, training, and wages and salaries (job analysis and methods of payment). Two professional journals, *Personnel* and the *Journal of Personnel Research* (later called *Personnel Journal*) were founded by 1922, stimulating further investigations in these areas. Many of the early articles in these journals attempted to match employee traits to successful job performance. Some investigators examined physical aspects such as hair color,[30] height and weight,[31] skin texture and facial profiles,[32] and sex[33] as well as social aspects such as marital status and ethnic and religious backgrounds.[34] Other early articles analyzed testing,[35] training,[36] and compensation activities. Personnel departments, first established around 1912,[37] also encouraged research into personnel topics.

World War I World War I affected the development of the personnel function into an important organizational activity in several ways. Wartime demand for production coupled with the induction of many employees into the Armed Services resulted in employees' receiving more managerial attention and concern.[38] In fact, the government insisted that personnel departments be installed in any facility manufacturing war equipment to ensure efficient operations.[39]

The government also created a committee (the Committee on Classification of Personnel in the Army) charged with effectively matching soldiers' varied skills and characteristics to different military tasks. This committee's massive efforts pertained to employee qualifications, job analysis, testing, and evaluation systems. Their techniques were modified and extensively applied in industry after the war.

Wartime efforts further altered the managerial philosophies that had been prevalent during the 1870–1910 period. "Instead of the struggle for survival, they emphasized cooperation; instead of regarding success as self-explanatory, they began to consider the duties of managers."[40] This "cooperative spirit" extended beyond the war years. Warren G. Harding, then president of the United States, wrote in 1921:

In a period of readjustment such as this, it is all the more important that we should all work out our problems in harmony together. A closer contact, a better understanding between managers and men is one of the first essentials to a prompt return to industrial prosperity.[41]

Trade Union Activity A brief history of labor unions in the United States is presented in Chapter 14 and won't be repeated here. However, two interrelated points should be noted. First, many employers of this period, fearing their employees might join a labor union, paid more attention to employees' economic and social concerns.[42] Increased emphasis on the personnel function represented "preventive medicine" to keep unions out of the organization.[43] Employers developed new personnel techniques to remain nonunion. One popular type of program, *the employee representation plan,* established a procedure to resolve employee complaints in nonunion settings. This activity attempted to match union grievance procedures (discussed in Chapter 15), even though management typically had the final decision on the issue.[44]

Second, unions also increased the scope of personnel topics and issues. A prominent union leader of the period, Samuel Gompers, publicized union-management issues in a variety of ways, including thorough articles written in personnel journals.[45]

The Hawthorne Studies Any historical assessment of the personnel function has to acknowledge the studies conducted at Western Electric's Hawthorne facilities between 1924 and 1932. The details and controversies concerning these experiments have been recorded elsewhere;[46] space permits only a summary of some of the studies to be reported here.

Illumination studies (1924–1927) were conducted with female employees in three series to determine the effects of various lighting intensities on production output. These studies found that production varied independently of the illumination level.

Rest pause studies, three in all, were carried out, the most publicized being the relay test room efforts, which began in 1927, lasted twenty-six months, and focused on six female employees. These efforts attempted to examine whether employees' physical characteristics were associated with productivity. Productivity had a nearly unbroken increase throughout the experiments, and the study group became much closer and friendlier to each other on and off the job.

The bank wiring room project (beginning in November 1931) represented a six-and-a-half month investigation of male employees' behavior, standards, sentiments, ideas, and codes. Major conclusions were that relationships between group members influenced each member's behavior and that the small work group, not management, determined production levels.

In addition, some 10,000 employee attitude interviews were conducted at Western Electric.

**Experimental Test
Group at the
Hawthorne Works**

Photo courtesy of Western Electric.

The Hawthorne Studies used a variety of methods (interviews, personal observation, and experiments) in a manner that subsequently influenced personnel practices.[47] This influence was not immediate, however; a review of *Personnel* and *Personnel Journal* for the years 1930–1950 found only nine articles on the subject.[48] Contrary to popular belief, the Hawthorne studies did not completely refute Taylor's scientific management theories. For example, participants in the first rest pause study were carefully selected to match employees' characteristics to task requirements, and they received a more favorable wage incentive system; both factors may have contributed to higher productivity.[49] Also, Taylor was aware that social interactions between employees could restrict productivity long before the bank wiring room studies at Hawthorne.[50]

Hawthorne did, however, suggest that scientific management's "one best way" might be too simplistic. Personnel activities such as those involving job tasks and performance standards must also include interpersonal considerations. Perhaps Hawthorne's major accomplishment was suggesting that industry might benefit from the input of academicians trained in the social sciences.[51]

**1930 to the
Present**

Contemporary personnel philosophies and activities are discussed throughout the remainder of this book. However, the development of the personnel function during the past fifty years can be briefly illustrated by a comparison of the situation found in 1930 with that found today.

Some contend that the personnel function has not changed much over the years.[52] By 1930, most employers had realized that employees were unique and important to the organization; and their approaches to personnel matters represented a blend of scientific management, industrial psychology, and corporate morality.[53] This situation also exists today; although, as discussed in Chapter 3, various behavioral science theories have refined contemporary personnel management approaches. Firms in 1930 also included many of the personnel activities found in today's organization.[54]

One major difference that developed during this period involves the increased responsibility given to people and departments specializing in the personnel function. Personnel departments in 1930 displayed the limited approaches characteristic of earlier periods.[55] The implementation of personnel activities was often left to the discretion of other managers.[56] Today, personnel representatives have more direct organizational responsibilities, a situation explained partially by three interrelated historical shifts in *personnel legislation, employees' values,* and *personnel philosophy.*

Personnel Legislation Virtually no laws affecting working conditions existed in 1930. This situation changed dramatically in subsequent years, particularly under the Roosevelt and Johnson administrations. In fact, laws have been implemented throughout this period, with impacts on almost every personnel activity.

The effect of legislation on the role and status of the personnel department often involves three phases. First, legislation *forces managerial awareness of the particular issue.* Sometimes, this awareness is sudden; the introduction of wage guidelines in 1971 is one example.

Personnel managers came to work one Monday morning in August 1971 to find that the federal government had imposed wage controls. Administering salaries was a whole new ballgame. The rules were fuzzy, complex, and subject to interpretation and change. Nor was the game any easier when controls were lifted.[57]

The second phase, *managerial acceptance of the personnel issues,* often occurs after companies have compiled with new governmental regulations over a period of time. Management officials gradually recognize that additional activities might be necessary for compliance and that these activities are inescapable and in many cases even necessary. Consider for example, labor legislation. Two years after the National Labor Relations Act was passed (in 1935), one industrial official commented, "Let us face the fact that collective bargaining is here to stay and that the wise thing is to use this device as a means of developing collective cooperation and better industrial relations."[58] Managerial acceptance of the role of the personnel function is increased when employees use governmental agencies (Equal Employment Opportunity Commission, National Labor Relations Board, and so forth) and the courts to enforce personnel legislation and win substantial sums in legal suits.

The third phase, *centralization of compliance activities and responsibilities,* occurs when increased time and attention is given to personnel legislation. This phase requires that personnel representatives obtain more knowledge about related laws and more sophistication and creativity in applying these laws to the industrial setting.[59]

Legislation therefore offers opportunities and challenges to the personnel function. One author contends that personnel legislation has transformed personnel representatives into the "new corporate heroes,"[60] although another author cautions:

If legislation is used as a club to gain more status or control—if personnel sets itself up as the moral guardian of the company's posture under the law—line operating management may have to listen on certain specific issues, but will be even more unlikely to include personnel in true organizational and business planning discussions. Personnel will merely have graduated from "flunky" to "necessary evil."[61]

Personnel representatives must therefore implement legislation in a responsible fashion and must show that compliance not only satisfies legal mandates but benefits the organization as well. For example, equal employment opportunity legislation can be an impetus for tapping new sources of employees who will do well if they know their efforts will be appreciated and rewarded.[62]

Employee's Values Employees' values (discussed in more detail in Chapter 16) appear to have changed since 1930. One personnel representative has summarized this change as follows:

Surely, the push for more entitlements and more rights by individuals; higher expectation levels resulting from more education and communication; and more focus on self and more loyalty to self and the profession as opposed to the company and institutions are . . . readable trends.[63]

Personnel Philosophy Changing employee values have combined with personnel legislation to alter companies' personnel philosophies since 1930. While managers in the period 1910–1930 realized that employees were unique and important, they still believed that employees were clearly subordinates in the organization. Employees who did not follow directions or who rebelled against narrowly defined job tasks like those prescribed by Taylor's scientific management could seek jobs elsewhere. Today, organizations' beliefs about and approaches to personnel matters reflect, to some extent, an adaptation to employees' needs for greater self-development, job responsibility, and growth. Related examples, such as flexible working schedules and drug and alcohol rehabilitation programs, are discussed throughout this book. Organizations often attempt to accommodate employees' interests to the mutual benefit of the employee and the organization. For example, IBM Corporation initiated a program encouraging employees to defer taking their vacation days during "booming years" and to take the accumulated vacation days during "lean years."[64] This arrangement benefited both organization and employees.

Role of the Personnel Function in Today's Organization: Arrangements and Relationships

As suggested in the preceding section, personnel activities in a typical organization have become increasingly specialized. Contemporary organizations often have personnel departments involved in coordinating personnel activities to ensure that these activities contribute to organizational objectives in a consistent and efficient manner. An understanding of the personnel function therefore has to consider the personnel department—more specifically, its location and roles in the organization and its relationships with other organizational participants.

Location of the Personnel Function in the Organization

There is no one common organizational arrangement of the personnel function, since each organization must take into account its unique combination of size, location, product mix, and markets. For example, the proper organizational structure for an auto maker may be unsuitable for an insurance company.[65] Variations in the organization of the personnel function occur in two major areas: (1) the number of organizational levels primarily concerned with the personnel function and (2) the number of separate departments primarily concerned with the personnel function. Figures 2.1 and 2.2 illustrate these areas of variation.

Variation in Number of Organizational Levels It is easiest to pinpoint the personnel setup in a single firm or a local governmental agency with one facility for its operation. The personnel function in such situations is normally carried out at one organizational level. Often, however, an organization's operations are spread out over many locations or facilities and involve many products or services. Figure 2.1 illustrates this situation for an industrial organization that produces several products.

The personnel network in this instance can be located at three different organizational levels: *corporate, divisional,* and *plant.* However,

Figure 2.1   Partial Organizational Chart
Illustrating Possible Levels of
Personnel Function

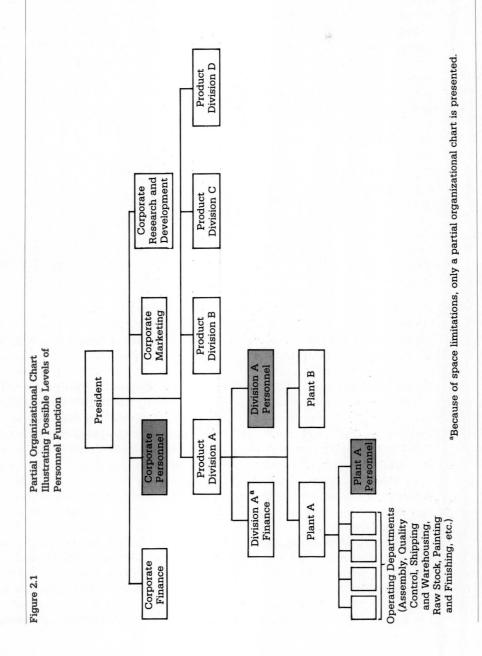

Operating Departments
(Assembly, Quality
Control, Shipping
and Warehousing,
Raw Stock, Painting
and Finishing, etc.)

[a]Because of space limitations, only a partial organizational chart is presented.

some organizations do not have distinct personnel departments at all three levels. The number of employees in the organization usually influences the number of levels at which personnel staffs are found. One survey of over 700 companies found that almost 75 percent of the companies with fewer than 1,000 employees had only corporate-level personnel staff units, while all the companies with more than 60,000 employees had personnel units at other levels as well.[66]

Multilevel personnel departments should help ensure that personnel policies and activities are consistently developed and applied throughout the organization. Yet, problems still can occur, particularly in coordinating the efforts of the various levels.[67] Consider, for example, college recruiting, which can be performed at the corporate, divisional, or plant level. Often, overlapping responsibilities can lead to confusion and duplication of effort among these levels. A plant personnel representative who must fill an immediate employment vacancy might recruit students at a nearby college, not knowing that subsequent recruiting trips to the same college are planned by divisional or corporate personnel representatives.

Plant personnel representatives often have too many bosses. Typically, these individuals report to the plant manager. However, they are also accountable to personnel representatives at divisional and corporate levels, particularly if their career objectives involve advancing up the corporate ladder by way of the personnel function. Problems can occur when the plant manager's priorities differ from those of divisional and corporate personnel representatives. Assume, for example, that the plant personnel representative is required to attend a corporate seminar on recent developments in equal employment opportunity legislation at the same time the plant manager needs thirty additional hourly employees.

Variation in Number of Personnel Departments Figure 2.2 shows the personnel departments in one organization. Determination of the number and type of such departments is primarily influenced by the number of employees in the organization. The personnel manager or department head in a small firm (one that employs fewer than 150 people) must be a generalist, familiar with most if not all personnel activities. Specializaton increases in larger firms (those that employ 5,000 to 6,000 people), where each department devotes its attention to one specific activity such as training, college recruiting, or wage and salary administration.[68]

The number of personnel departments is also influenced by the interests of company executives, as well as by the aggressiveness and skills of the personnel representatives. In some cases, events encourage the creation of a new personnel department. A firm whose employees have just become unionized, will probably establish a separate labor relations department. Similarly, passage of equal employment opportunity legislation prompted the establishment of related departments in many organizations. However, many personnel functions, such as employee or human resource forecasting, do not reach departmental status unless executives are convinced of their necessity.

The various personnel departments are seldom regarded as being of equal importance. The wage and salary department might be viewed as the most important in a nonunionized company, whereas the labor relations department might receive higher status in a unionized company. Two rather crude indicators of relative importance are the number of employees in the departments and the salaries of the department managers. One recent survey of 4,300 personnel practitioners found that managers of personnel research had the highest median income, followed closely by managers of labor relations. Other personnel management positions in the order of their median income were: training and organizational development, compensation and benefits, equal employment opportunity, and employment.[69] (Of course, wages reflect several factors—size of company, industry, geographical location, and so on—in addition to the particular job held.)

Specialization of personnel functions offer both career opportunities and career drawbacks. On the one hand, it enables personnel representatives to concentrate on developing techniques and knowledge in a rather narrow area. However, an individual who carries out one particular function, such as wage and salary administration, runs the risk of becoming "pigeonholed" if he or she continues long in that role.

Regardless of what organizational levels and how many departments it includes, the personnel function involves other organizational members in policy design and implementation. Two related topics are: the various roles the personnel function performs for the organization and the involvement of other members of the organization in the personnel function.

The Personnel Department's Organizational Roles

At least four organizational roles can apply to personnel representatives regardless of organizational level.

Firefighter One of the more common roles for the personnel representative is *firefighter*. The term implies that personnel representatives are largely reactive—that is, they wait until a problem (such as absenteeism, employee grievances, work slowdown, or turnover) becomes evident, then act to alleviate it. Personnel representatives do not like this role for two reasons. First, it tends to make them dependent on unpredictable organizational events, particularly those other managers do not want to handle. Second, it diverts them from long-range policy planning and professional development.[70]

Figure 2.2   **Organizational Chart of the Personnel Function in a Large Western Communication Company**

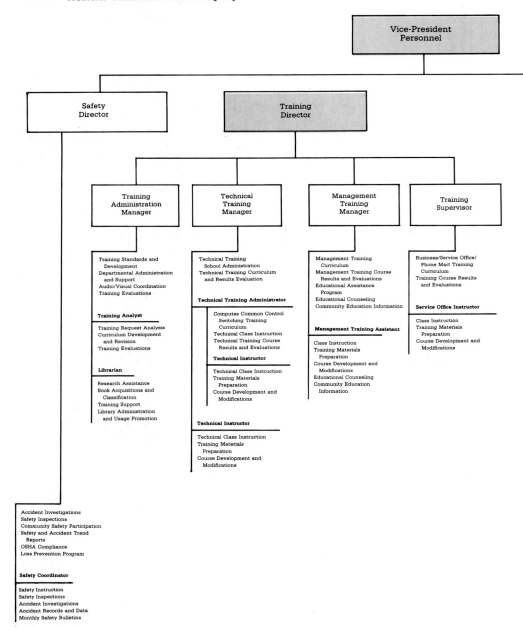

Source: Reprinted by permission from *Aspects of the Personnel Function*, p. 23, copyright 1979 by The Bureau of National Affairs, Inc., Washington, D.C.

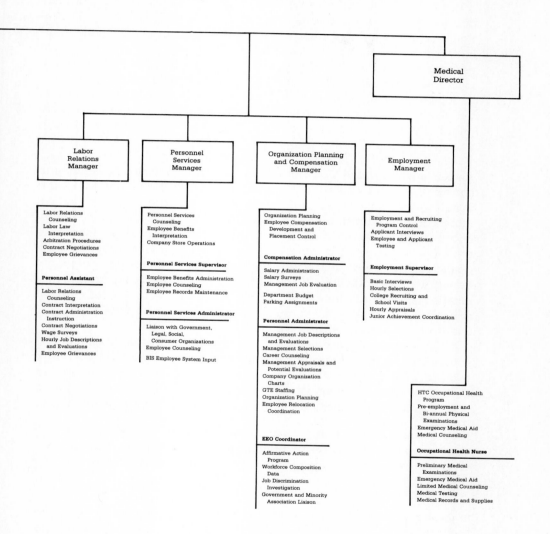

Medical Director

Labor Relations Manager

Labor Relations
  Counseling
Labor Law
  Interpretation
Arbitration Procedures
Contract Negotiations
Employee Grievances

Personnel Assistant

Labor Relations
  Counseling
Contract Interpretation
Contract Administration
  Instruction
Contract Negotiations
Wage Surveys
Hourly Job Descriptions
  and Evaluations
Employee Grievances

Personnel Services Manager

Personnel Services
  Counseling
Employee Benefits
  Interpretation
Company Store Operations

Personnel Services Supervisor

Employee Benefits Administration
Employee Counseling
Employee Records Maintenance

Personnel Services Administrator

Liaison with Government,
  Legal, Social,
  Consumer Organizations
Employee Counseling

BIS Employee System Input

Organization Planning and Compensation Manager

Organization Planning
Employee Compensation
  Development and
  Placement Control

Compensation Administrator

Salary Administration
Salary Surveys
Management Job Evaluation

Department Budget
Parking Assignments

Personnel Administrator

Management Job Descriptions
  and Evaluations
Management Selections
Career Counseling
Management Appraisals and
  Potential Evaluations
Company Organization
  Charts
GTE Staffing
Organization Planning
Employee Relocation
  Coordination

EEO Coordinator

Affirmative Action
  Program
Workforce Composition
  Data
Job Discrimination
  Investigation
Government and Minority
  Association Liaison

Employment Manager

Employment and Recruiting
  Program Control
Applicant Interviews
Employee and Applicant
  Testing

Employment Supervisor

Basic Interviews
Hourly Selections
College Recruiting and
  School Visits
Hourly Appraisals
Junior Achievement Coordination

HTC Occupational Health
  Program
Pre-employment and
  Bi-annual Physical
  Examinations
Emergency Medical Aid
Medical Counseling

Occupational Health Nurse

Preliminary Medical
  Examinations
Emergency Medical Aid
Limited Medical Counseling
Medical Testing
Medical Records and Supplies

Conciliator A second personnel role is a *conciliator* of opposing values and interest groups in the decision-making process.[71] Some might contend that personnel decisions should be made in an environment governed by efficiency considerations and professional knowledge. This rationale seems logical but is unrealistic.

Personnel representatives must at least acknowledge the existence of various interest groups and power structures within an organization. For example, they must be aware that managers may avoid limiting their employee forecasting and staffing levels for fear that such reductions might lower their status in the organization. Similarly, advice from organizational executives has to be considered regardless of its merits. In some cases, this advice is implemented even though its value to the organization is questionable. For example, a top executive might insist that his or her niece be interviewed for a marketing trainee position.

Auditor and Controller The third personnel role pertains to *audit and control*,[72] whereby personnel policies and activities are monitored and evaluated to ensure that they are effectively carried out. One of the more common audits involves a statistical analysis of employees by occupational level and minority category. This audit helps determine whether a company is meeting its equal employment opportunity goals. As will be discussed further in Chapter 12, various personnel benefits are periodically reviewed to determine their cost to the organization as well as the extent of their use. Such a review can reveal abuses of benefits—for example, by employees who year after year use up all their paid sick leave.

Audit and control are necessary components of organizational personnel efforts; however, some managers regard the related paperwork and justification to personnel representatives as time consuming and not worth the effort. This attitude can expand to a negative stereotype of personnel representatives' activities, as illustrated by the following:

Their common denominator is paper shuffling; their criterion is how many times and to how many different documents a person can sign his name. These are the members of the chairborne division of the paragraph troopers.[73]

Innovator and Agent of Change Finally, personnel representatives have the role of *innovator and agent of change*, a counterpart of the firefighter role. In this capacity, they analyze organizational problems and processes, usually those that pertain to the complex network of relationships among employees (the formal and informal groups discussed in more detail in Chapter 3). Personnel representatives must anticipate[74] a wide variety of societal events (potential employment legislation, changing workforce trends,[75] and so on) that could affect

Exhibit 2.1   **Personnel Changes Predicted
                                      for the Near Future**

Percentage of Respondents Who
Expect These Major Changes
To Take Place by Mid-1980s

0	10	20	30	40	50	60	70

Mandatory Retirement Illegal (at Any Age)

Mandatory Privacy Protection Programs

Mandatory Private Pension Plans—Fully
Portable and Integrated with Social Security

Women Achieve Parity Status with Men

Minorities Achieve Parity Status with Whites

Large Segment of Workforce on a Shorter
Work Week (35 or less hours)

Large Segment of Workforce Living Under
High Degree of Participative Management

Flexible Benefit Plan (with broad variety of
options) Available to Major Segment of
Workforce

Recruitment of Dual-Career Combinations
(husband/wife)

Note: N = 1,500 personnel representatives.

Source: Reprinted from ''Personnel Managers Look to the '80s,'' by Harold L. Schneider, p. 49 of the November 1979 issue of *Personnel Administrator,* copyright 1979, the American Society for Personnel Administration, 30 Park Drive, Berea, OH 44017, $26 per year.

the organization. Exhibit 2.1 summarizes various changes predicted for the near future in a recent survey of 1,500 personnel representatives.

The innovator role also includes long-range planning, which is typified by employment forecasting (discussed in Chapter 4). Planning involves the application of sound personnel knowledge and techniques to important and dynamic challenges faced by the organization.[76]

Naturally, the innovative role must be in tune with the times and the set of issues confronting a particular company. In periods of ris-

Exhibit 2.2   **Participants in Selected**
                                   Personnel Activities

	President		Senior Personnel Executive Staff		Operating Level Management	
	Number of Companies	Percent	Number of Companies	Percent	Number of Companies	Percent
Have Executives	644	100%	647	100%	155	100%
Participated significantly in *policy formulation* regarding:						
Equal Employment Opportunity	363	56	596	92	37	24
Manpower Training	125	19	497	77	29	19
Occupational Safety and Health	122	19	463	72	52	34
Benefits	360	56	582	90	32	21
Participated significantly in *program design* regarding:						
Equal Employment Opportunity	108	17	596	92	51	33
Manpower Training	52	8	485	75	43	28
Occupational Safety and Health	39	6	486	67	60	39
Benefits	180	28	484	90	35	23
Participated significantly in *monitoring* company performance regarding:						
Equal Employment Opportunity	145	23	603	93	52	34
Manpower Training	53	8	468	72	32	21
Occupational Safety and Health	60	9	437	68	67	43
Benefits	130	20	574	89	39	25

Source: Allen R. Janger, *The Personnel Function: Changing Objectives and Organization* (New York: Conference Board, 1977), pp. 20–21. Reprinted by permission.

ing inflation and escalating wage and salary demands, the emphasis
may be on compensation issues. In times of retrenchment and falling profits, creative work sharing and lay-off plans may be needed.[77]

This consideration assumes that personnel representatives will
sometimes need to be concerned not only with employee affairs but
also with other organizational matters such as sales, production, and
finance.[78] This concern is necessary to ensure that personnel policies
are not implemented to the detriment of the needs of other
organizational participants.[79]

**Relationships of
the Personnel
Department to
Other
Organizational
Participants**

We have indicated that many personnel functions involve members of
the organization other than the personnel representatives. This situation is illustrated in Exhibit 2.2, which shows that some personnel
activities involve company presidents, personnel executives, and operating managers in policy formulation, program design, and program
monitoring. The input of company presidents is often solicited by the
highest-ranking personnel executive. In some cases, the information
and direction they provide can benefit the personnel function. For ex-

Figure 2.3   **Line-Staff Relationships at**
Various Organizational Levels

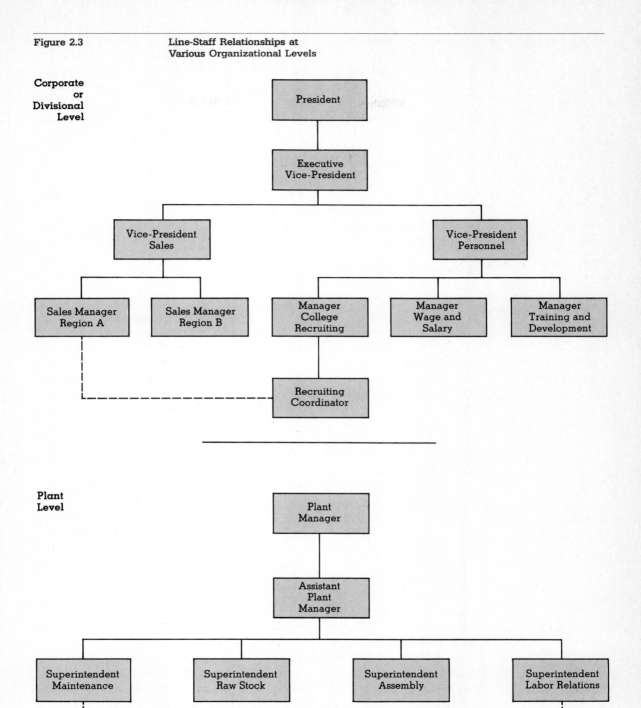

Corporate
or
Divisional
Level

President

Executive
Vice-President

Vice-President
Sales

Vice-President
Personnel

Sales Manager
Region A

Sales Manager
Region B

Manager
College
Recruiting

Manager
Wage and
Salary

Manager
Training and
Development

Recruiting
Coordinator

Plant
Level

Plant
Manager

Assistant
Plant
Manager

Superintendent
Maintenance

Superintendent
Raw Stock

Superintendent
Assembly

Superintendent
Labor Relations

Note: The dashed lines represent line-staff relationships. Because of space limitations, only partial organizational charts are presented as illustrations.

ample, the chief executive officer of Xerox recently played an active and positive role in restructuring certain employee benefit plans.[80]

Personnel executives often have access to top-level organizational officials. For example, one survey found that 83 percent of the chief personnel executives report to either the company's highest official or to a vice-president.[81] However, this situation does not always result in adequate direction and cooperation.[82] For example, one personnel executive reported the following overall objective given by his boss: "You are to make the company a more exciting and less certain place to work."[83]

As indicated by Figure 2.1, managers of other operations such as sales and production are also involved in the personnel function. The following discussion describes the effects of this situation on the personnel department.

Line-Staff Relationships The structure of an organization has many dimensions, which are further discussed in Chapter 3. However, one such dimension, line-staff relationships, is discussed here to put the personnel department into proper organizational perspective. The personnel function often involves line-staff relationships, which occur when *two or more organizational members from different lines of authority work together on a particular policy or activity. No participant is the direct organizational superior or subordinate of another in terms of the organization chart.* For example, the relationship illustrated by the dashed line in the top portion of Figure 2.3 might concern, among other things, selection of colleges to be included in the company's annual recruiting schedule. The plant level line-staff relationship illustrated in the bottom portion of Figure 2.3 might pertain to an employee's grievance over a particular work assignment.

Line-staff relationships can be initiated in a variety of ways. For example, the superintendent of maintenance might request the opinion of the superintendent of labor relations, or the assistant plant manager might "volunteer" the superintendent of maintenance to help the superintendent of labor relations determine appropriate questions for a safety survey. Thus, advice might come from either of the participants.

Line-staff relationships can offer many advantages. The participants typically have different perspectives and technical knowledge, which can ensure that a more complete approach to a particular activity is taken. Also, problem solving might be enhanced by compromise and persuasion, since none of the line-staff relationship's participants have organizational authority over the others. Line-staff relationships can, however, create tension and conflict. The following comments might well pertain to the previously mentioned example of line-staff relationships at the plant level:

Jefferson's [the superintendent of labor relations] idea was a good one. But his damned overbearing manner. . . . He came out here and

tried to ram the scheme down our throats. He made me so damn mad I could not see. The thing about him and the whole white-collar bunch that burns me up is the way they expect you to jump when they come around. I have been in this plant twenty-two years. I've worked in tool rooms too. I've forgot more than most of those college punks will ever know. I've worked with all kinds of schemes and all kinds of people. You see what I mean? I've been around and I don't need a punk like Jefferson telling me where to head in. I would not take that kind of stuff from my own kid and he's an engineer too. No, his scheme may have had some good points, but not good enough to have an ass like him lording it over you. He acted like we had to use his scheme. Damn that noise! Him and the whole white-collar bunch . . . can go to hell. We've got too many bosses already.[84]

Conflict in line-staff relationships can be caused by struggles for authority and by the varying backgrounds and orientations of the participants.

Struggles for Authority Defining *authority* is usually easier than pinpointing the details of its existence in a particular organization. Authority creates *an attitude of responsiveness and deference as well as an admission of subordination,* which is essential for social *order in an organization.*[85] Individuals can assume authority through personal characteristics (age, experience, and so on) or through formal organizational positions.[86]

As previously mentioned, authority in line-staff relationships seldom, if ever, stems from the participants' formal positions in the organization. Line-staff relationships do not involve superior-subordinate relationships in terms of the formal organization chart. However, personnel representatives retain at least some elements of authority in terms of their ability to limit organizational participants' choices.[87] For example, they can:

Specify safety equipment to be used in a particular area.

Prohibit managers from seeing test results or other information in an employee's file.

Establish a maximum allowable wage and salary increase.

Determine which job applicants will not be further considered in the hiring process.

The use of authority not expressly derived from the organization chart can become a complicated business. Returning to the example in Figure 2.3, assume the sales manager for Region A insists that his or her university be included on the company's recruiting schedule, and the recruiting coordinator disagrees. The argument could not be resolved on the basis of the participants' formal positions in the organization.

The two participants are relatively free to carve out their own strategies to resolve the problem in terms they consider favorable.[88]

One alternative is to pass the dispute up organizational channels to a point where an individual on the organization chart who can finally decide the issue is reached. Conceivably, the issue described earlier could involve the vice-presidents of sales and personnel, who, if unable to reach agreement, might ask the executive vice-president for a decision. In reality, however, such decisions are sought infrequently and most likely involve only concerns considered important, such as affirmative action programs and employee layoffs. More frequent than final decisions are *resolutions* agreed on by the personnel representatives and other organizational members involved. These resolutions offer solutions all the parties can live with. "And such a resolution is, as often as not, a matter of compromise, negotiation, appeals, pleadings, tears, and sometimes even lying."[89]

Conflicts can be successfully resolved if each participant has an appreciation of the others' situations and abilities. The background of personnel representatives and its effects on their relationships within the organization are discussed in the following section.

Background of Personnel Representatives   The formal education of personnel representatives represents an important starting point, particularly since relatively few organizations have formal instruction or training programs in the personnel function.[90] Two independent surveys of personnel representatives at various organizational levels have found that at least 90 percent of these individuals have had some college education, and nearly half have received some education at the graduate level.[91] Some evidence also suggests that personnel representatives tend to have, or place greater value on having, more formal education than their organizational peers.[92]

Additional training and educational direction for personnel representatives is provided by the American Society of Personnel Administration (ASPA), which was formed in 1948 and is currently the only national organization of personnel representatives in private industry. At present, personnel representatives can become formally accredited by taking tests or by possessing outstanding credentials in seven areas (training and development, safety, employee and labor relations, and so forth). Regardless of accreditation method, a practitioner's accreditation must be updated every three years. The ASPA conducts seminars and workshops for this updating. Accreditation can offer advantages; for example, it encourages personnel practitioners to keep up with developments in their fields. The accreditation process might also help universities design related courses and materials to better prepare students for a career in personnel.

As mentioned earlier, personnel representatives must be aware of other organizational operations and concerns so that they can effectively implement personnel activities throughout their organizations. Some of this knowledge can be gained through on-the-job experience, particularly in other departments such as sales, production, and accounting. Two surveys found that over 64 percent of the personnel representatives who responded had work experience in other organizational units.[93]

Thus, many personnel representatives appear to have an ideal background in terms of work and educational experience. They typically have the fairly high degree of specialized education necessary to perform specific personnel activities such as designing and assessing training programs and also have the experience in other departments needed to better understand the problems faced by the organization.[94]

However, education and experience, while necessary, do not ensure the success of line-staff relationships between the personnel representative and other organizational members. Some have suggested that personnel representatives, perhaps because of their formal educational attainment, tend to have a smug, even superior, attitude when dealing with others.[95]

In some cases, though, it is the other organizational participants who regard themselves as personnel "experts." Of course, successful implementation of personnel policies and activities depends on the interests and skills of other managers in the organization. All managers have performed at least some personnel duties, such as recruiting, interviewing, administering performance appraisals, and recommending salary increases for their subordinates. Therefore, the notion that "all managers are personnel managers" is at least partially correct. Problems can occur, however, when other managers believe their own personnel approaches to be the only correct ones. For example, *Up the Organization,* a best-selling book based on an executive's organizational experiences, suggested that the personnel department could be eliminated and replaced by a few clerks or secretaries. The author suggested that non-personnel managers know as much or more about personnel activities than personnel specialists. However, his insights regarding employee selection typify the problems inherent in such an approach:

The most important thing about hiring is the chemistry or the vibrations between boss and candidate: good, bad or not at all.[96]

While some may agree with this view, an employer would have some difficulty convincing a federal district judge in an employment discrimination suit of its validity.

Issue   ## Is Personnel an Important Organizational Function?

The first two chapters have emphasized that the personnel function is important because employees' actions can have significant consequences (either positive or negative) for the organization. This realization first gained attention around 1910, and today most corporate executives sincerely believe that employees represent an organization's most important asset. Two industrial executives have commented:

The old cliche, "The strength of an organization is in its people" will not be glibly mouthed in the years ahead.[97]

We feel that between 90 and 95 percent of our problems are people. . . . If we notice . . . that a division that has been going along very well begins to show a downward trend . . . every time we investigate it, we find that it was an attitude situation, a people situation, of some nature. It could be due to a shift. We could lose a key person. You can find out too late that something developed . . . that a man had a problem that was not taken care of.[98]

The importance of the personnel department in an organization must also be assessed if the issue of employee's importance to the organization is to be approached in a thorough manner. Executives may believe personnel management is a significant subject but may at the same time attach little significance to their organizations' personnel departments or to the individuals working in these departments. Such a situation probably will result in haphazard administration of the personnel function. Instead of turning to the personnel department for guidance and expertise, these executives will likely leave the implementation of personnel activities to the discretion of other organizational managers, who usually have to give most of their attention to other functions.

There are some indications that the personnel department and its members are increasing in importance. Since 1970, salaries of personnel executives appear to have increased more than those of their organizational counterparts.[99] A similar situation has occurred with respect to dollars assigned to the personnel function. Surveys conducted in 1969 and in 1977 reveal that the average operating budget for personnel as a percent of total payroll doubled in that period.[100]

However, other indicators are not as positive. Two such indicators are the number of chief executive officers who have had substantial experience in the personnel function and the belief of organizational members that personnel executives have a good chance of eventually becoming chief executive officers.

These indicators are, at best, only loosely associated with the merits of the personnel function. Some evidence suggests that most personnel representatives prefer to continue to work in the personnel field[101] (a tend-

Exhibit 2.3	**Functional Areas Considered Fastest Routes to the Top**		

		Current Fastest Route	Future Fastest Route
	Functional Area	(Figures Expressed in Percentages)	
	Finance/Accounting	33.3	30.4
	Marketing/Sales	30.6	20.3
	Personnel	0.2	0.9
	Professional/Technical	6.9	10.1
	Production/Manufacturing	4.2	3.6
	International	1.6	3.9
	General Management	18.2	22.9
	Other Area	0.6	0.7
	No Response	4.4	7.0
	Total	100.0	100.0

Note: Survey results from 3,640 senior level executives, of which 117 were in the personnel function. (Less than 1% of the 117 personnel executives saw the personnel function representing the current fastest route to the top, while 10.3% of those respondents saw personnel as the future fastest route.)

Source: Reprinted from "Profile of the Successful Personnel Executive" by John Sussman, p. 80 of the February 1980 issue of *Personnel Administrator,* copyright 1980, the American Society for Personnel Administration, 30 Park Drive, Berea, OH 44017, $26 per year.

ency that assures continued competent performance of personnel activities). Additional findings suggest that personnel representatives tend to be pleased with their career progress, present status in the organization, and prospects for further progress.[102]

However, the functional expertise of the chief executive officer can symbolize to organizational participants those skills which are rewarded by the organization. The comments of one company president illustrate this logic:

I would think that if management is getting things done through other people, the human resources officer should have more skill in this area than the heads of other functions and that this alone should suggest that more and more human resource officers will become CEOs in the future.[103]

As Exhibit 2.3 indicates, not many personnel representatives or other managers believe that the personnel function is now or will soon be the fastest route to the top.

The importance of the personnel function may vary across organizations,[104] depending upon the existence of four general factors:

1. Extent to which top management believes employees are unique resources capable of significant contributions to the organization's goals and objectives.

2. Access of personnel representatives to top management as well as to significant issues and decisions confronting the organization.
3. Ability of personnel representatives to formulate key personnel policies that directly relate to achieving organizational objectives in a more efficient manner.
4. Willingness of personnel representatives to implement personnel activities in an accountable manner, one that will convince organizational participants of the necessity for their continued existence.

As previously suggested, the first two factors are often found in organizations. Top executives appear to have a sincere interest in their employees, although they might be inconsistent in expressing and channeling this interest. Personnel representatives at higher organizational levels also typically report either to the company's highest official or to a vice-president.

The third factor could pertain to the variety of personnel activities and concerns discussed in the remaining chapters of this book. The personnel representative must be willing to carry out such activities even if some risk is involved. Personnel representatives must take initiative, because top management seldom furnishes specific direction.

One author suggests that the personnel function will face both challenges and opportunities in the near future:

The 1980's will be the decade in which "personnel" as it has traditionally been known may cease to exist, . . . at least in its present form, or it could rise to heights of accomplishment.[105]

Summary

The development of the personnel function and related philosophies and approaches in the United States can be placed into three general time periods: 1870–1910; 1910–1930; and 1930 to the present. The first period saw an unprecedented shift of employees into manufacturing industries, and managers were faced with developing a personnel philosophy. Many managers accepted the ideas of social Darwinism, which said that the weak (employees) must submit to the successful competitors (managers). The two approaches to employees taken during this period—treating them as a commodity and treating them according to the precepts of social welfare and paternalism—both emphasized that all employees were alike and should obey managerial directives.

The growth of the personnel function accelerated during the period 1910–1930. Two parallel movements, psychological reform and scientific management, convinced many managers that employees were unique and that careful attention to their differences could benefit the organization. World War I, trade union activity, and the Hawthorne studies also stimulated the growth of the personnel function during this period.

Some contend that the personnel function has not changed much since 1930, since many personnel activities found in firms today were used at that time. However, increased personnel legislation and changing employee values have given personnel representatives more organizational responsibility today than in 1930. A shift in personnel philosophy has also occurred. Managers now realize that employees will not blindly submit to managerial directives; in some cases the organization has to adapt to employee interests.

While the personnel function is often implemented by diverse members of the organization, particular attention must be given to the personnel department, which coordinates personnel activities to ensure that they contribute to organizational objectives in a consistent and efficient manner. The personnel department can be located at corporate, divisional, or plant levels. In some cases, organizations have several personnel departments, each charged with a particular function, such as wage and salary administration. The number of such departments is influenced by the number of employees in the organization, the interests of company executives, and outside events such as equal employment opportunity legislation.

People who work in personnel departments have four organizational roles: firefighter, conciliator, auditor and controller, and innovator and agent of change. These roles typically involve line-staff relationships, in which two or more organizational members from different lines of authority work together on a particular policy or activity.

There are no bosses in line-staff relationships, since the participants report to different individuals on the organizational chart. Line-staff relationships can ensure that a more thorough approach to an activity or problem is taken, but they can also involve tensions and conflict. Struggles for authority produce conflict that can be resolved either by passing the dispute up organizational channels or through resolutions. In some cases, the formal education and industrial experience of the line-staff participants can increase tensions. Personnel representatives often have had more education than some other organization members, which can result in their taking a superior attitude when dealing with others. This attitude can also be seen in other organizational managers who regard themselves as personnel experts.

The personnel function appears to be important in the organization, although this importance does not automatically carry over to the personnel department. While personnel executives have fairly high salaries and operating budgets, few executives believe the personnel function is the fastest route to the top. The future of the personnel department depends on several factors, such as organizational personnel philosophies, access to top executives, and willingness of personnel representatives to assert themselves and demonstrate the effectiveness of their contributions to organizational objectives.

Discussion Questions

1. Define *social Darwinism,* discussing its several dimensions. Also discuss how this concept could influence two seemingly different approaches to employees (the commodity approach and social welfare and paternalism).

2. Cite and briefly discuss two dimensions of a personnel philosophy. Indicate specifically how scientific management and the changes at Ford Motor in 1914 modified the personnel philosophy prevalent in the period 1870–1910.

3. Fully assess the argument that "the personnel function was legislated into existence." In addition to legislation, briefly discuss another difference between today's personnel function and that common in 1930, finishing with a specific example of this difference.

4. Explain the various factors that determine organizational location and variation in the personnel departments.

5. Discuss the following statement: "Line-staff relationships are exciting but unpredictable in terms of organizational effectiveness."

6. Explain how the future of the personnel department depends on both individual and organizational considerations.

Notes

1. One estimate indicates there were 14,559,000 proprietorships, partnerships, and corporations in 1976. Bureau of the Census, *Statistical Abstract of the United States,* 100th ed. (Washington, D.C.: Government Printing Office, 1979), p. 553.
2. Reinhard Bendix, *Work and Authority in Industry* (Berkeley; University of California Press, 1956), p. 254.
3. Richard Hofstadter, *Social Darwinism in American Thought,* rev. ed. (Boston: Beacon Press, 1955), p. 45.
4. *Ibid,* p. 57.
5. Leon Litwack, *The American Labor Movement* (Englewood Cliffs: Prentice-Hall, 1962), pp. 66–67.
6. Bendix, *Work and Authority,* p. 257.
7. Ida M. Tarbell, *The Nationalizing of Business 1878–1898* (New York: Macmillan, 1927; reprint ed., 1969), p. 114.
8. C. R. Henderson, "Business Men and Social Theorists," *American Journal of Sociology* 1 (January 1896), p. 388. This article also represents an early attempt to explain the role of academicians in industry. The author stated "It is the duty of the scholar to place and keep before the public the supreme criterion of social conduct, the common welfare. In a boiler factory, where the din and noise drown all sounds, the cry of a child cannot be heard. So men of affairs are apt to be deafened, by the uproar of those very affairs, to the neglected and forgotten members of our common humanity. A table of statistics, interpreted and illustrated by literary skill, may induce business men to enlarge the scope of their life plans. The scholar's duty is to aid in forming a judicial public opinion, as distinguished from the public opinion of a class and its special pleaders" (pp. 389–390).
9. Cyril Curtis Ling, *The Management of Personnel Relations: History and Origins* (Homewood, Ill.: Richard D. Irwin, 1965), p. 46.
10. Litwack, *American Labor Movement,* pp. 63–64.
11. Henry Eilbert, "The Development of Personnel Management in the United States," *Business History Review* 33 (Autumn 1959), p. 346.
12. Henderson, "Business Men," p. 392.
13. Fred J. Carvell, *Human Relations in Business* (New York: Macmillan, 1970), p. 21.
14. For an example of paternalism, see "Welfare Work in Company Towns," *Monthly Labor Review* 25 (August 1927), pp. 314–321.

15. The annual meeting of the Industrial Relations Association of America was postponed in 1921, a year which also began the six-year discontinuation of the professional journal *Personnel*. Allan N. Nash and John B. Miner, eds., *Personnel and Labor Relations, an Evolutionary Approach* (New York: Macmillan, 1973), p. 117.

16. Whiting Williams, *What's on the Worker's Mind* (New York: Charles Scribner's Sons, 1921), p. 130.

17. Ordway Tead and Henry Metcalf, *Personnel Administration,* 2d ed. (New York: McGraw-Hill, 1926; reprint ed., New York: Arno Press, 1979), pp. 17–27.

18. See, for example, Dexter S. Kimball, *Principles of Industrial Organization,* 2d ed. (New York: McGraw-Hill, 1919), p. 53; Charles Gerstenberg, *Principles of Business* (Englewood Cliffs, N.J.: Prentice-Hall, 1918), p. 18; John R. Commons, *Industrial Goodwill* (New York: McGraw-Hill, 1919); and Daniel Bloomfield, *Labor Maintenance* (New York: Ronald Press, 1920), p. 71. For one of the more widely quoted related articles of this period, see Mark M. Jones, "What I Would Do if I Were a Foreman," *Personnel* 1 (September 1919), p. 3.

19. Stanley M. Herman, *The People Specialists* (New York: Alfred A. Knopf, 1968), p. 40.

20. Frederick Winslow Taylor, *The Principles of Scientific Management* (reprint ed., New York: Norton), 1967, p. 43. See also, Edwin A. Locke, "The Ideas of Frederick W. Taylor: An *Evaluation,*" 7, (January 1982), pp. 14–24.

21. Allen Nevins, *Ford: The Times, the Man, the Company,* vol. 1 (New York: Charles Scribner's Sons, 1954), p. 530.

22. *Ibid.,* p. 527.

23. Henry Ford, *My Life and Work* (Garden City, N.Y.: Doubleday, Page and Company, 1922; reprint ed., New York: Arno Press, 1973), p. 119.

24. *Ibid.,* p. 129.

25. Some expressed concern that Ford was instituting these policies to make it difficult for competitors to attract an adequate workforce. Keith Sward, *The Legend of Henry Ford* (New York: Rinehart and Company, 1948), p. 59.

26. David L. Lewis, *The Public Image of Henry Ford* (Detroit: Wayne State University Press, 1976), p. 75. Additional details on related publicity are discussed on pp. 69–77.

27. "For the period 1914–1916, the company's net income after taxes read for three successive years, $30,000,000; $24,000,000; $60,000,000." Sward, *The Legend,* p. 55.

28. For example, in the six months ending April 1916, only one man was discharged. Nevins, *Ford,* p. 530.

29. *Personnel* 2 (1920), p. 3. For other classifications of employer welfare work, see Ling, *Management of Personnel,* pp. 76–77; and *Personnel* 2 (October 1920), p. 10.

30. Donald G. Paterson and Katherine E. Ludgate, "Blond and Brunette Traits: A Quantitative Study." *Journal of Personnel Research* 1 (July 1922), pp. 122–127.

31. Harry D. Kitson, "Height and Weight as Factors in Salesmanship," *Journal of Personnel Research* 1 (October/November 1922), p. 289.

32. For a thorough discussion of physical characteristics, see Katherine M. H. Blackford and Arthur Newcomb, *The Job, the Man, the Boss* (Garden City, N.Y.: Doubleday, Page and Company, 1914).

33. Morris S. Viteles and Helen M. Gardner, "Women Taxicab Drivers: Sex Differences in Proneness to Motor Vehicle Accidents," *Personnel Journal* 7 (February 1929), pp. 341–348. See also Marion Bills, "Relative Permanency of Men and Women Office Workers," *Personnel* 5 (August 1928), p. 214.

34. Henry E. Garrett, "Jews and Others," *Personnel Journal* 7 (February 1929), pp. 341–348.

35. There were many articles on testing, particularly after World War I. For example, in the first volume of the *Journal of Personnel Research* (May 1922–April 1923), seven of the sixteen articles on personnel activities concerned testing.

36. Many of the training articles published during this period concerned foremen or first-line supervisors and salesmen. The latter group received almost the complete attention of one issue of *Personnel* (August 1929).

37. Eilbert, "Development of Personnel," p. 353.

38. Loren Baritz, *The Servants of Power* (New York: John Wiley and Sons, 1965), p. 43.

39. Ling, *Management of Personnel,* p. 323.

40. Bendix, *Work and Authority,* p. 285.

41. Letter written by Warren G. Harding, *Personnel* 3 (May/June 1921), p. 1.

42. Sam Lewishon, "Employers' Responsibility for Industrial Peace," *Personnel* 3 (August 1928), p. 191.

43. Edward J. Giblin, "The Evolution of Personnel," *Human Resource Management* 17 (Fall 1978), p. 25.

44. For additional insights into employee representation plans, see E. K. Hall, "What is Employee Representation?" *Personnel* 4 (February 1928), pp. 71–83; Julian J. Aresty and Gordon S. Miller, "The Technique of Arousing and Maintaining the Interest of Foremen

and Workers in Plans of Employee Representation," *Personnel* 6 (February 1930), p. 115; and several articles in *Personnel* 4 (February 1928).

45. See, for example, Samuel Gompers, "Cooperation of Workers in Study of Industrial Personnel Matters," *Journal of Personnel Research* 1 (June 1922), pp. 53–55.

46. F. J. Roethlisberger and W. J. Dixon, *Management and the Worker* (Cambridge, Mass.: Harvard University Press, 1939); Henry A. Landsberger, *Hawthorne Revisited* (Ithaca, N.Y.: Cornell University, 1958); Richard Herbert Franke, "The Hawthorne Experiments: Re-View," *American Sociological Review* 44 (October 1979), pp. 861–866; and Berkley Rice, "The Hawthorne Defect: Persistence of a Flawed Theory," *Psychology Today* 16 (February 1982), pp. 71–74.

47. "Hawthorne Revisited: The Legend and the Legacy," *Organizational Dynamics* 3 (Winter 1975), p. 79.

48. Three of the articles devoted solely to Hawthorne appeared in the February 1930 issue of *Personnel Journal.* Other significant articles on this subject were written by G. A. Pennock and M. L. Putman, "Growth of an Employee Relations Research Study," *Personnel Journal* 9 (June 1930), pp. 82–85; Elton Mayo, "Research in Human Relations," *Personnel* 17 (May 1941), pp. 264–269; and T. N. Whitehead, "Human Relations within Industrial Groups," *Harvard Business Review* 14 (Autumn 1935), p. 1.

49. The influence of wage incentives on production prompted the second and third rest pause experiments. Studies pertaining to the second relay assembly group focused on converting wage incentives to smaller group standards similar to those found in phase 3 of the first relay assembly room study. Production increases were higher (13 percent), although not as high as the 30-percent increase in the first study. Landsberger, *Hawthorne Revisited,* pp. 12–13.

50. Charles D. Wrege and A. G. Perroni, "Taylor's Pig Tale: A Historical Analysis of Frederick W. Taylor's Pig-Iron Experiments," *Academy of Management Journal* 17 (March 1974), pp. 6–27.

51. For a summary of trends in human relations research, see George Strauss, "Human Relations—1968 Style," *Industrial Relations* 7 (May 1968), pp. 262–276.

52. See, for example, Peter F. Drucker, *The Practice of Management* (New York: Harper and Row, 1954), pp. 273–274.

53. "Sixty Years of Hiring Practices," *Personnel Journal* 59 (June 1980), p. 462.

54. Stanley B. Mathewson, "A Survey of Personnel Management in 195 Concerns," *Personnel Journal* 10 (December 1931), pp. 225–231. Some wage determination factors reported here differ from those used today. The 195 firms in the study used the following selected wage determination factors: nationality of the worker, 9 percent; color of the worker, 21 percent; and sex of the worker, 47 percent.

55. See, for example, the philosophy expressed in the first issue of *Personnel* (June 1919), p. 9.

56. E. F. Wonderlic, "Personnel as a Control Function," *Personnel* 14 (August 1937), p. 31.

57. Guy B. Ford, "The Many Hats of the Personnel Manager," *Manager's Forum* 2 (February 1975), p. 1. The same situation apparently occurred with the wage guidelines suggested by the Carter administration. See, for example, Ralph E. Winter, "Rough Guidelines: Wage Price Program Costs TRW $1 Million, plus Many Headaches," *Wall Street Journal,* (May 12, 1980), pp. 1, 32.

58. Harold B. Bergen, "Basic Factors in Present-Day Industrial Relations," *Personnel* 14 (November 1937), p. 46.

59. Giblin, "Evolution of Personnel," p. 25.

60. Herbert E. Meyer, "Personnel Directors Are the New Corporate Heroes," *Fortune* (February 1976), pp. 84–88, 140.

61. Frank O. Hoffman, "Identity Crisis in the Personnel Function," *Personnel Journal* 57 (March 1978), p. 130.

62. *P-H/ASPA Survey: The Personnel Executive's Job* (Englewood Cliffs, N. J.: Prentice-Hall, 1977), p. 21.

63. "Interview with Robert L. Berra," in *Personnel Administration Today: Readings and Commentary,* ed. Craig Eric Schneier and Richard W. Beatty (Reading, Mass.: Addison-Wesley, 1978), p. 51.

64. Meyer, "Personnel Directors," p. 87.

65. Ross A. Webber, "Staying Organized," *Wharton Magazine* 3 (Spring 1979), p. 16.

66. Allen R. Janger, *The Personnel Function: Changing Objectives and Organization* (New York: Conference Board, 1977), p. 52.

67. George Ritzer and Harrison M. Trice, *An Occupation in Conflict: A Study of the Personnel Manager* (Ithaca: New York State School of Industrial and Labor Relations, Cornell University, 1969), p. 67.

68. Thomas H. Patten, "Personnel Management in the 1990's," in *Management of Human Resources,* ed. Edwin L. Miller, E. L. Burack, and Maryann Albrecht (Englewood Cliffs, N.J.: Prentice-Hall, 1980), p. 69.

69. Steven Langer, "Personnel Salaries: A Survey, Part I," *Personnel Journal* 59 (December 1980), p. 984.

70. Dalton E. McFarland, *Company Officers Assess the Personnel Function,* (New York: American Management Association, 1967), p. 31.

71. Donald E. Klinger, "Changing Role of Personnel Management in the 1980's," *Personnel Administrator* 24 (September 1979), p. 42

72. Jack W. English, "The Road Ahead for the Human Resources Function," *Personnel* 57 (March/April 1980), p. 38.

73. Lawrence A. Appley, "Management Is Personnel Administration," *Personnel* 46 (March/April, 1969), p. 8.

74. George S. Odiorne, "Personnel Management for the 1980's," in *PAIR Policy and Program Management,* ed. Dale Yoder and H. G. Heneman, Jr. (Washington, D.C.: Bureau of National Affairs, 1978), p. 151.

75. Giblin, "Evolution of Personnel," p. 30.

76. Mary Anne Devanna, Charles Fombrun, and Noel Tichy, "Human Resources Management: A Strategic Perspective," *Organizational Dynamics* 9 (Winter 1981), p. 53.

77. Fred K. Foulkes and Henry M. Morgan, "Organizing and Staffing the Personnel Function," *Harvard Business Review* 55 (May/June 1977), p. 149.

78. Hoffman, "Identity Crisis," p. 130.

79. Foulkes and Morgan, "Organizing and Staffing," p. 150.

80. Robert Firth, "Top Management Philosophy for the Personnel Function, at Xerox," in *Top Management of the Personnel Function,* ed. William B. Wolf (Ithaca: New York State School of Industrial and Labor Relations, Cornell University, 1980), p. 34.

81. *Aspects of the Personnel Function: Structure, Use of Electronic Data Processing, and Professional Activities* (Washington, D.C.: Bureau of National Affairs, 1979), p. 7. For additional information on this topic, see Charles J. Coleman, "The Personnel Director: A Cautious Hero Indeed," *Human Resources Management* 18 (Winter 1979), pp. 14–20. Among other things, this article reported that personnel directors spend almost 12 percent of their time with higher management officials.

82. Janger, *Personnel Function,* p. 37.

83. Fred K. Foulkes, "The Expanding Role of the Personnel Function," *Harvard Business Review* 53, (March/April 1975), p. 75.

84. Melville Dalton, *Men Who Manage* (New York: John Wiley, 1959), p. 75.

85. R. M. MacIver, *Society: Its Structure and Changes* (New York: Ray Lang Inc., 1931), p. 256; Karl Mannheim, *Systematic Sociology* (London: Routledge and Keagan Paul, 1957), p. 25; and Elton Mayo, "Positive Interaction and the Problem of Collaboration," *American Sociological Review* 4 (June 1939), p. 336.

86. Ferdinand Toennies, *Community and Society* (New York: Harper and Row, 1957), p. 41; Max Weber, *Basic Concepts in Sociology* (New York: Citadel Press, 1962), p. 75; and Robert K. Merton, *Social Theory and Social Structure* (Glencoe, Ill.: Glencoe Free Press, 1959), p. 195.

87. Dale Henning and Wendell L. French, "The Mythical Personnel Manager," *California Management Review* 3 (Summer 1961), pp. 33–45.

88. For a variety of possible strategic approaches, see Charles J. Coleman and Joseph M. Rich, "Why Not Fire the Personnel Manager?" *Human Resource Management* 14 (Summer 1975), p. 21.

89. Edward Gross, "Sources of Lateral Authority in Personnel Departments," *Industrial Relations* 3 (May 1964), p. 129.

90. Jeff Harris, "Personnel Administrators: The Truth about Their Backgrounds," *MSU Business Topics* 17 (Summer 1969), p. 28.

91. *Ibid.,* p. 26; and Ritzer and Trice, *Occupation in Conflict,* p. 16.

92. See, for example, Andrew F. Sikula, "The Values and Value Systems of Industrial Personnel Managers," *Public Personnel Management* 2 (July/August 1973), p. 309.

93. John Sussman, "Profile of the Successful Personnel Executive," *Personnel Administrator* 25 (February 1980), p. 46; Harris, "Personnel Administrators," p. 24.

94. "Selection and Performance Criteria for a Chief Human Resources Executive . . . a Presidential Perspective," *Personnel* 54 (May/June 1977), p. 13.

95. Robert Dubin, *Human Relations in Administration* (Englewood Cliffs, N.J.: Prentice-Hall, 1962), p. 193. The negative effect of the educational level of one participant in line-staff relationships is described in Dalton, *Men Who Manage,* p. 87.

96. Robert Townsend, *Up the Organization,* (New York: Alfred A. Knopf, 1970), p. 44.

97. Ross A. Hennigar, "People Management in the 1980's; A CEO's View," *Personnel Journal* 59 (November 1980), p. 898.

98. Jerome E. Blood, ed., *A Look at Personnel through the President's Eye* (New York: American Management Association, 1965), p. 1.

99. Meyer, "Personnel Directors," p. 87. One current estimate of top personnel executives' salaries is $150,000 a year in annual wages plus perquisites that could represent as much as an additional 30 percent. Isadore Barmash, "Personnel Chief Has New Role," *New York Times* (April 21, 1981), p. D-2.

100. *P-H/ASPA Survey: The Personnel Executive's Job* (Englewood Cliffs, N.J.: Prentice-Hall, 1977), p. 9. In 1977, the staff operating budget was about 3.5 percent of the total payroll.

101. Harris, "Personnel Administrators," p. 28.

102. Jack L. Rettig and Robert F. McCann, "Job Satisfactions of Personnel Managers," *Personnel Administrator* 23 (September 1978), p. 26

103. "Selection and Performance Criteria for a Chief Human Resources Executive . . . a Presidential Perspective," *Personnel* 54 (May/June 1977), p. 21.

104. For a typology of this variation, see Robert Harschnek, Jr., Donald G. Peterson, and Robert Malone, "Which Personnel Department Is Right for You?" *Personnel Administrator* 28 (April 1978), p. 59.

105. John D. Ingalls, "The Decline and Fall of Personnel," *Training and Development Journal* 34 (January 1980), p. 30.

Chapter 3

Understanding Organizations, Jobs, and Employees

There is a common misconception in the U.S. that the theories behind participatory management have been imported from Japan. This could not be further from the truth. American psychologists have led the way in research in motivational theory, alienation, the impact of different management styles and the need for—or lack of—clearly delineated hierarchies to make things work.

Organizations achieve goals through directing their members' activities, which are in turn grouped into various jobs. The people who hold these jobs work to meet their personal, social, and economic needs. A basic knowledge of *organizations, jobs,* and *employees,* then, is important for an understanding of the personnel function, which operates within the organizational structure to better match jobs and individuals, to create a motivational climate to ensure that employees' performance will be productive, and to ensure that employees will be rewarded for that performance. Exhibit 3.1 illustrates the interrelationship of the organization, jobs, and individual jobholders in developing a motivational climate for improving performance and job satisfaction.

Within the organization, there exists an organizational philosophy (or culture), formal and informal groups, goals and structures, and managerial (leadership) styles. Organizational conflicts can occur within groups and between groups and individuals. Organizations attempt to prevent conflicts and improve organizational processes through such efforts as organizational development. Organizations are composed of activities combined into jobs, which may be designed to enhance motivational potential, performance, and job satisfaction. These jobs are held by individuals who differ in many respects, such as in motivation, abilities, personalities, attitudes, and capacities to learn. These differences affect how much the individual is willing or able to contribute to the organization's effectiveness and determine the degree to which the organization will want to employ the individual.[1] This chapter discusses these basic concepts for understanding organizations, jobs, and individuals.

Organizations

In General, an organization serves both societal and individual needs; but it has more specific roles as well. For example, an organization "is a vehicle for accomplishing goals and objectives, . . . is a mechanism having the ultimate purpose of offsetting those forces which undermine human collaboration, . . . tends to minimize conflict and to lessen the significance of individual behavior which deviates from values that the organization has established as worthwhile, . . . increases stability in human relationships by reducing uncertainty, (and) . . . enhances the predictability of human action because it limits the number of behavioral alternatives available to an individual."[2]

An organization is designed to achieve some end, and the activities and efforts of its employees are directed toward this end. The end toward which organizational processes are directed is usually defined in terms of *goals,* which can be categorized into five types:

Societal goals, which represent the goods produced and services provided to enhance the general welfare, to maintain order, and to generate and maintain cultural values.

Exhibit 3.1

Interrelationship of Organization, Job, and Individuals

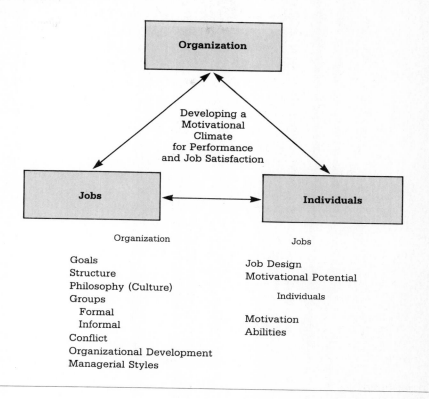

Organization

Goals
Structure
Philosophy (Culture)
Groups
  Formal
  Informal
Conflict
Organizational Development
Managerial Styles

Jobs

Job Design
Motivational Potential

Individuals

Motivation
Abilities

Constituent goals, which identify client and customer groups for which services are provided or goods are produced.

System goals, which provide specificity for the direction of the overall organization and its workforces and include growth, profits, market share, and market penetration.

Product goals, which characterize the goods or services produced on the basis of quality, quantity, styling, availability, uniqueness, and innovativeness.

Derived goals, which provide guidance for generating other goals, including community services, investment, plant-location policies, and employee relations.[3]

These goals may to some extent be independent, but a substantial amount of interrelatedness and interdependency exists. Goals reflect the character of the organization, the personalities and managerial philosophy of its top executives, the history of the organization and the environment in which it operates, external influences and societal norms, and the technology of its industry. Such goals are granted varying degrees of importance and are likely to conflict at times. However, their establishment is critical to the organization they serve.

Structure

An organization starts with an idea formulated by its founder, the *strategic apex* or top manager. He or she hires people to perform the work of the organization. This group is called the *operating core.* As the organization grows, intermediate managers between the chief executive and the workers are added to form the *middle management* group. Then the organization finds it must employ two kinds of staff personnel: First come the analysts, who design systems for formal planning and control of the work; next comes the *support staff,* which provides indirect services—public relations, legal counsel, personnel activities, and so on[4]—to the rest of the organization.

Organizational structure helps coordinate the work, which has been divided into positions and jobs, and the activities of the employees who do the work. In the simplest of cases, coordination is achieved by direct supervision—the top manager (owner of a small business) gives the orders and directs the employees' activities. However, as organizations grow, coordination depends more and more on standardization of work, skills of employees, and output. At this point, organizations may be subdivided into operating units, often with autonomous operating responsibilities, and with professional support staffs and sophisticated specialists who form a configuration of line and staff responsibilities.[5] Such organizations are designed and built around the following dimensions:

Division of labor Subdivision of work into basic elements to achieve continuous, reliable, and predictable performance in the interests of efficiency.

Departmentalization Grouping of similar activities by function (sales, finance, personnel), by product, or by area. Groups report to a central authority.

Scalar chain of authority Systematic ordering of positions and duties in a hierarchy of authority.

Unity of command Establishment of areas of responsibility and chains of command that allow every member to know who to report to and who reports to him or her.

Span of control Establishment of the number of persons one manager can effectively supervise.

Line and staff Classification of employees by function. Generally, *line* employees are directly involved in accomplishing the work of the organization, while *staff* employees facilitate the work by advising and assisting the line.[6]

These structural dimensions are not absolute, particularly in today's high-technology environment.[7] Unlike work in the time of F. W. Taylor, much work today is not easily measured in output units. Instead, abstractions and judgments (for example, interpreting computer printouts or anticipating future innovations in equipment, products, and markets) are emphasized. Organizational structure often has to be flexible[8] to respond to a more complicated environment as well as employees who have self-concepts, views, and frustrations, not just skills and abilities.[9] Two examples of structural flexibility are *matrix organizations* and *Theory Z management.*

In recent years, matrix organizations have been used in large companies in connection with such subgroups and reporting systems as project teams, program management, and task forces. In matrix organizations, individuals continue to report to their functional departments, but they also report temporarily on a part-time or full-time basis to the project or task-force leader. In other words, one individual reports to two managers. While the popularity of matrix organizations continues to grow, it is still too soon to tell how well they work.[10]

Theory Z is a label given to a model of successful companies which have integrated the positive characteristics of traditional American firms and those of successful Japanese firms. Based on successful companies like Kodak, IBM, Proctor and Gamble, Cummins Engine, and Levi Strauss in the United States and Sony, Toyota, Nippon, and Matsoshita Electric Co., seven characteristics of Type Z organizations have been identified (see Exhibit 3-2).

Some of Theory Z's characteristics, such as its emphasis on consensual decision making and individual responsibility, blur the previously cited dimensions of organizational structure such as departmentalization, scalar chain of authority, and unity of command. Type Z organizations also recognize employees bring more than skills and abilities to the job, since these organizations emphasize social and family relationships[11] and express a commitment to the idea that corporate employees are "ends in themselves."[12]

Some companies, such as Westinghouse, are experimenting with Theory Z concepts in hopes of achieving a dramatic improvement in productivity.[13] While it is too early to measure the effect of Theory Z concepts, initial indicators have been promising.

Philosophy and Culture

Within organizations, management philosophy develops that enables employees to understand organizational goals and methods for achieving these goals. This philosophy facilitates the integration of the individual into the organization and more closely links the individual

Exhibit 3.2	**Characteristics of Type Z Organizations**		
	Traditional American Model	Typical Japanese Model	Type Z Model
	Short-Term Employment	Lifetime Employment	Long-Term Employment
	Individual Decision Making	Consensual Decision Making	Consensual Decision Making
	Individual Responsibility	Collective Responsibility	Individual Responsibility
	Rapid Evaluation and Promotion	Slow Evaluation and Promotion	Slow Evaluation and Promotion
	Explicit, Formalized Control	Implicit, Informal Control	Implicit, Informal, Control with Explicit, Formalized Measures
	Specialized Career Paths	Nonspecialized Career Paths	Moderately Specialized Career Paths
	Segmented Concern	Holistic Concern	Holistic Concern, Including Family

Source: William G. Ouchi and Alfred M. Jaeger, "Type Z Organization: Stability in the Midst of Mobility," *Academy of Management Review* 3 (April 1978), pp. 305–314. Used by permission of the Academy of Management. For additional study and references, see Richard T. Pascale and Anthony G. Athos, *The Art of Japanese Management* (New York: Simon and Schuster, 1981).

with organizational goals.[14] In other words, an organization develops a culture, which includes a common set of beliefs about the organization shared by its members. It tells what tasks and goals are important and how people will behave at work; it establishes a pattern for company actions.[15] The personnel function can facilitate the linking between the organization and the individual by conducting adequate orientation and development, ensuring proper placement, and helping to resolve employee problems.

Some of the most successful corporations have clearly demonstrated that the corporate culture can be a major strength when it is consistent with corporate strategies. For example, IBM created a corporate culture characterized by shared beliefs that the customer should be given the best service possible, that all employees should be respected and treated with dignity, and that the company should strive to accomplish every task in a superior manner. Delta Air Lines focuses on customer service provided by a high degree of employee teamwork. Digital Equipment Corporation emphasizes innovation. Its philosophy allows employees both freedom and responsibility. Digital's employees set their own hours and working style but are expected to perform well under these conditions.[16]

Some organizations recognize that they must change because their cultures prevent them from meeting competition or adapting to changing economic and social conditions. Pepsi-Cola was once content to be second to Coca-Cola, but its new corporate culture emphasizes striving for first place. American Telephone and Telegraph Company is trying to change from a service-oriented operation to one with a greater marketing orientation. Its new direction is to encourage employees to be entrepreneurs, problem solvers, and innovators.[17]

Groups

Types and Significance Groups are the intermediaries between the tops of large organizations and individual employees. While they may not appear in an organization chart, they play an important role in shaping the organization's behavior. Groups may be formal or informal, and both types serve important organizational purposes. While formal groups exist within the formal organization structure, informal groups develop in work situations outside the formal structure.

An informal group represents a response by employees to a need to associate with others. It may be composed of employees in one or more plant departments or offices. The informal group may be organized around some interest, such as a bowling team, or around a common cause, such as might occur with older employees who feel passed over in promotion decisions.[18]

Whether formal or informal, groups affect individuals and organizations in the following ways:

They discipline, mold, and change employees' behaviors.

They serve as important decision-making mechanisms.

They bargain, negotiate, compete, conflict, and cooperate with one another.

They provide a communication network within the organization.

They influence morale, learning, and development of employees within the organization.[19]

Group behavior can range from productive to destructive.

Groups also have at their command a kind of awesome power to induce members to conform to their standards. Group members are rewarded by being accepted, included, and praised if they abide by group norms, but are rejected, excluded, and ridiculed if they do not conform. How wonderful to be warmly accepted and included by others, and how terrible to be an outcast—rejected and ridiculed.[20]

The establishment of informal groups is inevitable. Such groups serve vital employee needs and are present in all organizations. Management must therefore recognize the existence of these groups and create a climate to ensure that their contributions to the organizations are positive. For example, management can listen to suggestions presented by the group leader, prevent rumors by promptly releasing accurate information, build employee confidence by designing effective development and reward systems, and help resolve problems that surface at the workplace.[21]

Group Conflict and Conflict Management Within and between groups, conflicts are likely to occur. Such conflicts appear when the organization has limited resources that must be allocated among operating units, when the various units have different goals; when a competitive reward system exists; and when misperceptions and misunderstandings arise concerning one group's role in relation to others'. Conflict management involves the process of recognizing signs of conflict, determining when conflict might be healthy, and preventing or resolving unnecessary or harmful conflict. In other words, conflict management attempts to make groups more effective while fulfilling the organization's needs as well as the needs of the group's members.

In cases where intergroup conflict occurs, whether in labor-management disputes, sales-production disagreements, or quality control–production conflicts, the same phenomena tend to occur. *Within* each competing group, certain characteristics emerge: members become closely knit and close ranks; leadership style becomes more centralized and autocratic; the group becomes highly structured; and group leaders demand greater loyalty and conformity from members. *Between* competing groups, one group views the other as the enemy; perceptions become distorted; members develop stereotypes; hostility toward the other group grows; interaction and communication between groups decrease; and group members listen only to others in their own group and listen for only positions that support theirs.[22]

In dealing with conflict, management must not react too quickly. While conflict can result in breakdowns in coordination and efficiency, it also indicates that critical questioning of the status quo in terms of existing goals, policies, and procedures is taking place. In this regard, conflict offers potential for creativity, innovation, and organizational change. One executive has commented that conflict is "a sign of a healthy organization—up to a point. A good manager doesn't try to eliminate conflict, he tries to keep it from wasting the energies of his people."[23]

Even so, conflict management is an important managerial activity, and skills for dealing with conflict are essential.[24] Managers need to understand sources of and means to resolve conflict in their dealings with other managers and employees. The personnel function is no exception, since many, if not all, its activities can involve conflict. For example, conflict can occur when a personnel department institutes changes such as the following:

Supervisors will no longer be allowed to discipline (suspend or discharge) employees without consulting the personnel department.

The policy of having reserved parking spaces based on employee seniority will be discontinued and parking will be on a first-come, first-served basis.

Managers will be limited to giving wage increases no larger than 8 percent, and each department's increase must average 4 percent.

The personnel representative can help reduce unnecessary or harmful conflict between or within groups by encouraging management to take the following actions:

Emphasize total organizational effectiveness and the role of each organizational unit as a contributor to it.

Design a system by which rewards are given and performance is measured in terms of contribution to the total effort.

Create opportunities for frequent interaction and communication among groups.

Facilitate joint problem-solving and provide rewards for organizational units that give help to other units.

Rotate organizational members among groups to enhance their understanding and empathy for one another's problems.

Avoid win-lose situations by not placing groups in the position of competing for organizational rewards.[25]

These recommendations are not foolproof; unnecessary or harmful conflict may still occur. Attention then shifts to resolving conflict productively. Conflict resolution relies on the following strategies:

Competition. Attempting to attain one party's goals at the expense of the other party's by use of authority, threats, and arguments. "Put your foot down where you mean to stand."

Collaboration. Attempting to satisfy the concerns of both parties by discussion and reasoning. "Come let us reason together."

Compromise. Seeking to find a middle ground that partially satisfies both parties, with each making some sacrifice by bargaining, sharing, and splitting the difference. "You have to give some to get some."

Avoidance. Neglecting both parties' concerns by postponing or sidestepping conflicting issues. "Let sleeping dogs lie."

Accommodation. Satisfying another's concerns while neglecting one's own by yielding and moving toward the other's position. "It is better to give than receive."[26]

While managers may practice different approaches in different situations, the outcomes will be viewed by those involved as either satisfying both parties' concerns or in some way dividing satisfaction between the two parties. Satisfaction of both parties (a win-win solution) is more likely reached by the collaborative approach, while varying degrees of satisfaction (various degrees of win-lose situations) are reached by the remaining approaches. Competition represents the extreme position of taking; accommodation represents the extreme position of giving; and compromise and avoidance represent intermediate approaches.[27] Regardless of the approach used, all parties must continue to be conscious of the primary objectives of the organization.

Organization Development Conflicts within organizations and organizational ineffectiveness can be reduced by organization development (OD), a process designed to improve the organization's functions and reduce conflict by enabling organization members to better manage their groups and organization culture. OD is designed to eliminate destructive conflict and to better match the needs of the organization with those of its individual members. The process includes various structured interventions that involve organizational units (target groups or individuals) who engage in activities that aim to improve organizational effectiveness. OD interventions include:

Diagnostic (fact-finding) activities designed to ascertain the state of the organization, the status of the problems, or the "way things really are" by data-collection methods such as interviews, questionnaires and surveys (discussed in Chapter 20 under personnel research), and meetings.

Team-building activities designed to enhance the effectiveness of the operational unit by identifying skills needed to accomplish tasks, allocate resources for task accomplishment, and clarify roles of and relationships among groups.

Survey-feedback activities based on diagnostic activities. Various organizational units work with the data produced by the surveys to design action plans for the respective units.

Process consultation activities designed to help employees understand the human processes that occur within organizations and teach skills (such as communication, leadership roles, problem solving, sensitivity training, and group interaction) helpful in diagnosing and managing these processes.[28]

Among the interventions in which the personnel function is involved are group and individual goal setting, career planning, training and development, compensation, and collective bargaining. Because many of the interventions are personnel-related, it seems only logical that personnel representatives are expected to be agents of positive organizational change.[29]

Leadership (Managerial) Styles

Leadership (managerial) styles represent a "manager's ability to influence subordinates to perform specific tasks for the purpose of goal accomplishment."[30] While the purpose of leadership in an organization is to influence employees' behaviors to contribute to organizational performance, different styles of leadership are effective under different circumstances.

Theory X and Theory Y As defined by Douglas McGregor, Theory X and Theory Y are management styles based on the assumptions managers make about employees. For example, subscribers to Theory X believe that employees are lazy, dependent, resistant to change, and lacking in ambition; they prefer to be led and dislike responsibility. Consequently, managers who subscribed to Theory X typically use coercion and threats, close supervision, and tight controls over employees' behavior.

On the other hand, subscribers to Theory Y believe that employees are not inherently passive but have become so as a result of their organizational experiences. McGregor believed that motivation, potential to develop, and capacity to assume responsibility are all present in people and that management can help employees recognize and develop their potential. Finally, management can arrange organizational conditions and methods of operation so that people can achieve their own goals *best* by directing *their own* efforts toward organizational objectives.[31]

The Theory Y approach creates opportunities, releases potential, encourages growth, and provides guidance. It focuses on many of the modern managerial concepts discussed in connection with personnel activities throughout this book. Some examples covered in later chapters are performance-based compensation, employee involvement in performance appraisal, quality of work efforts, and career planning and development.[32]

Managers may use a particular style in leading employees toward organizational objectives; however, group effectiveness depends not only on leadership style but also on employees' and leaders' characteristics and on the situation.[33] In other words, no single style is always effective. For example, an employee-centered manager who develops trust with employees, shows respect for employees' interests, and considers their ideas tends to be very effective with highly motivated employees. However, less-motivated employees usually require that their manager schedule work in detail, prescribe definite standards of performance, and establish and adhere to specific rules and regulations. No set of leadership behaviors, then, has been identified as improving employee performance in *all* situations.

Today, most explanations of managerial style and leadership are situational in nature. Fred Fiedler was the first to develop the idea that group performance depends on the interaction of the leader's behavior, the quality of the interpersonal relationship between the leader and the group members, the degree to which the job can be structured, and the authority vested in the leader's position.[34]

Another situational approach, the path-goal theory, explains leadership in terms of the leader's impact on the subordinate's motivation, ability to perform, and job satisfaction.[35] Here, various leadership behaviors are used in certain situations; but the focus is on how the leader influences the subordinate's perceptions of his or her work goals, personal goals, and paths to goal attainment. The role of the leader is to increase motivation to perform, provide greater job satisfaction, and be accepted by the subordinate. The leader's behavior is motivational to the extent that it helps subordinates cope with environmental uncertainties, threats from others, or sources of frustration. Such behavior consequently increases subordinates' satisfaction in the job and enhances employees' motivation to the extent that it increases their expectations that effort will lead to valued rewards.[36]

Job Design

Within every organization, work activities are subdivided into jobs and positions. Jobs are designed to include the content, methods, and relationships that satisfy the "technological and organizational requirements as well as the social and personal requirements of the job holder."[37] A *job* refers to a group of positions identical with respect to their major or significant task and sufficiently alike to justify their being covered by a single analysis (for example, personnel representative). A *position* consists of the tasks and duties for any individual (for example, an interviewer for hourly employees). For each position in the organization, there are *duties* which describe a large segment of the work performed by the employee holding the position. These duties represent a distinct grouping of activities (for example, to maintain a list of and process applicants for plant positions). More specifically, a job *task* refers to a discrete unit of work performed by an employee and comprises a logical, necessary step in the performance of a duty (for example, to evaluate and score each application for a specific position).[38] The duties and tasks of the job are determined by a process called *job analysis,* covered in Chapter 4; and a related topic, quality of work, is discussed in Chapter 17.

In the traditional organization based on principles of scientific management, work is designed to emphasize simplicity, specialization, minimal wasted effort, minimal training, and smooth workflow. In these organizations, workers are closely supervised to assure that work is properly done. More recently, behavioral scientists have influenced job design by emphasizing the importance of psychological and social aspects of jobs and individual employee-job relationships. Numerous organizations have found that implementing job design projects has resulted in improvement in both the quality of worklife and organizational productivity. Thus, jobs can serve organizational purposes as well as enhance employees motivation potential and job satisfaction.[39]

Motivational Potential of Jobs

Jobs should be designed to help employees achieve high performance, job satisfaction, and internal motivation and to reduce turnover and improve attendance. Job designers thus seek to include in jobs characteristics that enhance the jobs' potential to motivate employees. Such job characteristics have been identified by Hackman and Lawler[40] as *core job dimensions.* They are:

Skill variety The degree to which a job requires a variety of skills and talents, thereby providing a challenge to the job holder.

Task identity The degree to which the employee is required to complete the whole job—for example, assemble the entire product—or complete an identifiable piece of the work—for example, assemble an important component of a product.

Task significance The degree to which the job has a substantial impact on the lives or work of other people in terms of their well-being.

Autonomy The degree to which the job provides substantial freedom, independence, and discretion to the jobholder in terms of scheduling the work and determining the procedures to be used in performing it.

Feedback The degree to which performing the work required by the job results in the jobholder's receiving direct and clear signals about the effectiveness of his or her performance.[41]

Because employees' motivation, abilities, personalities, and goals differ and jobs' motivational potential varies, personnel representatives and other managers should take special care in staffing activities to properly match employees' needs with what is needed on the job. Since not every employee wants challenge and responsibility, the personnel representative must be conscious of potential consequences of matches and mismatches between employees and jobs. For example, if the job is high in motivational potential and the employee has a desire for challenge and responsibility, the result should be high performance, job satisfaction, and low turnover and absenteeism. On the other hand, if the employee does not want challenge and responsibility but is placed on a job high in motivational potential, the employee will probably be confused and overwhelmed, performance will be low, absence will be frequent, and the employee will eventually quit.

Similarly, if the job is simple, routine, and low in motivational potential, an employee seeking challenge and responsibility will feel underutilized, will be dissatisfied, will be frequently absent, and will seek other employment. However, some employees who do not want responsibility or challenging work may be motivated to be high performers in such a job if their pay is tied to their performance level and pay is important to them.[42]

Personnel representatives can serve a key role in helping to match the applicant with the organization. For example, personnel representatives should not only determine whether the employee is qualified for a particular job (in terms of ability, experience, so on) but also should help the job applicant decide whether he or she can perform the job and will find it satisfying. Also, the personnel representative can give a more realistic picture of the job in order to achieve congruency between what the employee needs and expects and what the job actually can provide. In fact, showing serious applicants the results of job satisfaction surveys, data on turnover and grievances, and job descriptions of employees and supervisors may benefit the employee as well as the organization.[43]

Job Satisfaction

Job satisfaction, another important consideration of job designers and analysts, refers to an employee's own evaluation of his or her job in terms of supervision, coworkers, pay, promotions, and the work itself. This evaluation is actually a comparison between the employee's expectations about these job-related factors and his or her actual experiences on the job.[44]

Job satisfaction does not cause employees to work harder; research has found only a slight positive relationship between job satisfaction and performance. Job satisfaction is generally considered more the result of job performance than its cause. The reasoning is that high performance usually leads to rewards, such as recognition, higher pay, and promotion. It is these subsequent rewards that are considered causes of job satisfaction.

Despite the evidence that job satisfaction does not cause higher performance, it can still increase organizational effectiveness, because satisfied employees are less likely to be absent, to be tardy, or to quit. Because losing an employee can cost as much as ten times his or her monthly salary (for highly skilled and technical employees), efforts to increase job satisfaction are considered excellent investments for improving the economic effectiveness of the organization.[45]

Job satisfaction is more closely related to membership behavior such as tenure, turnover, absenteeism, and tardiness than to employee effectiveness, such as quantity and quality of production, performance ratings, and the like. As noted above, the relationship between job satisfaction and productivity is weak; however, this relationship becomes stronger when production is under the employee's control, when rewards are contingent on positive performance, and when workers are capable and involved in their work. Again, it has been shown that performance effectiveness and subsequent rewards have been more the cause of job satisfaction than job satisfaction has been the cause of performance effectiveness.[46] Personnel representatives, by conducting job satisfaction surveys and by effectively designing jobs, can contribute to organizational and individual effectiveness by facilitating the efforts of operating managers and employees throughout the organization.

Employees

The final major component illustrated in Exhibit 3.1 is the employee, who is a member of society, of the organization for which he or she works, of a family, of social groups, and so on. Primarily, though, he or she is an individual. All individuals are similar in some ways. They are motivated; their behavior is purposeful and is directed toward satisfying their needs and goals. However, they are different in ways that affect their behavior within organizations. These differences include:

Biographical variables: age, sex, race, education, experience.

Attitudes: values toward work, motivation, work ethics, sources of satisfaction and dissatisfaction.

Life and career stages: exploration, trial, establishing themselves, advancement, maintenance, and decline.

Organizational commitment.

Psychological and personal variables: emotions, personality, amount of control over work activities.[47]

Because individual employees do differ, especially in ability to perform and motivation, personnel representatives and other managers have to understand these individual differences so they can staff the organization properly and design a climate to motivate employees to perform at higher levels. Motivating employees is one of the most consistent challenges any manager faces.

[Managers must be] concerned with motivation because it affects performance. Performance is the target; motivation can be one means for getting there. From one managerial perspective, "performance" might mean maintaining or improving on a certain level of productivity. From another perspective, performance means the human factor—having employees who are reasonably satisfied. At yet a higher level, the human performance factor involves personal (and team) growth or development. Employees acquire knowledge and skills which enable individuals and the organization to adapt to and undertake changes in job tasks and programs.[48]

While there are many motivation theories (equity theory, for example, is covered in Chapter 10), the following section will discuss a few that seem to have had the greatest impact on organizational behavior and the personnel function.

Motivation

Needs Approach A. H. Maslow's theory of motivation, introduced forty years ago, is still covered in most management and organizational behavior books. Maslow developed what is now called the hierarchy of needs approach to understanding human motivation, which considers humans to have the following needs:

1. *Physiological* needs for food, water, air, shelter, and so on.
2. *Safety* needs for security from assault.
3. *Social* needs for affection, belonging, relations with others.
4. *Esteem* needs for self-respect, high self-evaluation, respect from others, confidence, recognition, reputation, usefulness.
5. *Self-actualization* needs for doing what one is best fitted for, self-fulfillment, reaching one's capacity, achieving one's potential, becoming what one is capable of becoming.

Maslow explained that these needs are arranged in hierarchical order and that the average person established priorities for satisfying the needs. For example, the first order of needs—physiological needs—provides the primary motivation for human behavior if these needs are not satisfied. While "man does not live by bread alone," getting bread is the primary motivator when there is none. Once the physiological needs are reasonably satisfied, a new set of needs— safety needs—dominates the individual's need structure and causes him or her to seek protection, security, and safety. Then, when safety needs are reasonably satisfied, the next order, social needs, emerges. Subsequent advancement toward satisfying esteem needs and then self-actualization needs may follow.

   The fact that the five sets of needs are presented in step-wise form gives the impression that one need must be totally satisfied before the next higher need motivates behavior; however, that is not the case. The point is that the individual's needs and their subsequent satisfaction move in the direction from the first order, physiological needs, to the highest order, self-actualization needs. It is important to recognize that all individuals have partially satisfied their basic needs and have partially unsatisfied needs at the same time.[49] They differ mainly in the degree to which their needs have been satisfied.

Herzberg's Motivation-Hygiene Theory Herzberg developed a motivation-hygiene theory which remains popular especially among personnel practitioners and has had a major impact on job design. Originally based on a study of accountants and engineers who were asked when they felt exceptionally good about their jobs and when they had negative feelings about them, Herzberg identified five factors—achievement, recognition, work itself, responsibility, and advancement—which were strong determinants of job satisfaction and which led to superior performance and effort. The work itself, responsibility, and advancement were considered of greatest importance, because these factors had a more lasting effect on attitudes.

Herzberg also identified hygiene factors—company policy and administration, supervision, salary, interpersonal relations, and working conditions—that did not motivate employees to perform at higher levels but potentially could lead to incidents that cause job dissatisfaction. In other words, hygiene factors did not motivate employees to perform at higher levels; however, unsatisfactory levels of hygiene factors could result in job dissatisfaction.[50]

Herzberg's theory has drawn attention to the work itself as a major factor in motivation and satisfaction. The theory is simple and believable; further, it is relevant to job design and actual organizational changes. The difficulties scholars have had with this theory include: its lack of clear differentiation between the motivation and hygiene factors in particular work settings; its failure to account for individual differences (not all employees want challenge and responsibility); and serious measurement problems. Still, the theory continues to be widely used and is well known throughout U.S. industry.[51]

Expectancy Theory Because theories of employee motivation have been based on a premise that employees and situations are similar, researchers continue searching for a better explanation of motivation. A theory frequently called expectancy theory, drawn from the work of Victor Vroom, takes into account individual differences among employees.[52] Like other theories of motivation, the expectancy theory is based on certain assumptions about people:

A number of forces within the individual and the environment determine behavior.

Individuals make conscious decisions about their behavior, such as going to work, working hard, and producing at a high level.

Individuals differ in terms of their needs and goals as well as what kind of rewards they want.

Individuals tend to do things and exhibit behaviors they perceive as leading to the rewards they want.

Individuals tend to avoid behaviors they perceive as leading to unwanted outcomes.

Based on these general assumptions, the following propositions have been formulated to serve as the foundation of the theory:

Relationship of performance and outcome Individuals believe certain behaviors are linked to certain outcomes. In other words, an employee expects that if he or she behaves in a certain way, such as being a productive employee, he or she will receive a reward, such as a salary increase.

Valence Outcomes (rewards) have varying degrees of value, worth, and attractiveness for different individuals. For example, some employees value promotions while others value time off for recreation. A pension program has value for older employees; to younger employees, cash payments are more important. Certain outcomes (such as suspensions) are negative, and behavior leading to those outcomes is to be avoided.

Effort and performance expectancy Individuals believe that certain behaviors are associated with an expectancy or probability of success. This expectancy represents an individual's perception of how much effort to put forth to achieve such behavior and the probability of his or her successfully achieving it. For example, an employee on a wage incentive plan has a strong expectancy that if he or she can perform at a pace above standard, the result will be a substantial pay bonus.

According to the expectancy theory, motivation is greatest when the following conditions are present:

The individual believes that the behavior will lead to certain outcomes (performance-outcome expectancy).

The individual believes that these outcomes have positive value for him or her (valence).

The individual believes that he or she is able to perform at the desired level (effort-performance expectancy).

Based on these propositions, individual employees determine the various levels and types of behavior that have the greatest motivational force for them; the employees perform on the job in accordance with their expectancies and valences.

Exhibit 3.3 displays a model of the expectancy theory of motivation. As shown, motivation provides the force that causes employees to put forth the necessary effort. Because effort alone is not enough, it must

Exhibit 3.3   Model of
Expectancy Theory
of Motivation

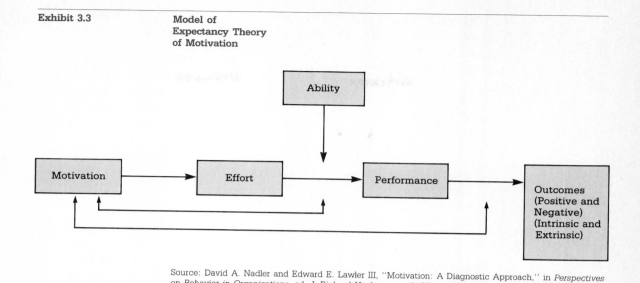

Source: David A. Nadler and Edward E. Lawler III, "Motivation: A Diagnostic Approach," in *Perspectives on Behavior in Organizations,* ed. J. Richard Hackman et al. (New York: McGraw-Hill, 1977), p. 29. Reprinted by permission of the authors.

be combined with the individual's abilities (mental and physical ability, skills, training, experience, and so on). Effort with ability produces the performance that provides the rewards or outcomes. These outcomes can be external (extrinsic)—from supervisors, coworkers, wages, and so on—or internal (intrinsic)—from feelings of personal achievement, accomplishment, personal contribution, and so on. The perceived equity of the rewards produces job satisfaction, which, as we noted earlier, is considered more the result of good performance than its cause. Personnel representatives and other managers play a critical role in facilitating the linkage between the components of the expectancy theory. Through proper staffing, maximum performance can be assured; through training, skills can be improved or developed; through an effective performance-based reward system, the relationship of performance and outcomes such as wages, promotion, and so on can be made clear.

**Developing a
Motivating
Climate**

As indicated, innumerable features of physical and social working environments have a substantial impact on the organization and the individual. Research has found that the following features can be associated with superior performance: (a) organization-wide factors, (b) work-group factors, (c) supervision factors, and (d) individual job factors.

The organization-wide factors that create a positive motivational climate and higher performance include fewer levels of authority;

smaller-sized organizations; mutual trust between management and employees; employees' sharing in earnings; adequate resources and technology; flexible work schedules; and flexible incentives, benefits, and opportunities. Work-group factors include clear and congruent goals; shared norms for good performance; worker cohesiveness; autonomy and self-determination; interchangeability of jobs among employees; and earnings related to group productivity. Supervision factors refer to supportive, considerate, and facilitative supervisors; effective communication; and participation in decision making. Individual job factors include clear, difficult, attainable goals; full utilization of employees' skills and abilities; work offering variety; social contacts, sense of contribution, and feedback; freedom to carry out responsibilities; and rewards linked to performance and job responsibilities.

The personnel function has an important role in creating a positive motivational climate and contributing to individual and organizational effectiveness. One objective of the following chapters of this book is to present ways the various personnel activities help build a motivational climate and facilitate organizational and individual achievement of mutual objectives. Therefore, we will not detail such activities here. However, a few examples of how such personnel activities contribute to motivation and effectiveness follow:[53]

Job design By designing job content that will maximize autonomy, variety, challenge, significance, and feedback in the work itself and by tailoring the design to such aspects as needs and abilities of workers and technology of the workplace. Design factors may include *job enlargement,* which increases the variety of job duties, or *job enrichment,* which increases the complexity and challenge of the job by increasing the responsibility of the employee (see Chapter 17).

Employment By recruiting, selecting, and placing employees to match individual needs with job and organizational needs (see Chapters 5–7).

Promotion and career opportunities By providing career guidance and promotional opportunities to assure that employees' potential is achieved (see Chapter 7).

Training and development By improving abilities and enhancing skills so that each employee can maximize his or her potential and make a greater contribution to the organization (see Chapter 9).

Performance appraisal By setting goals that focus on a limited number of specific outcomes and furnishing individualized coaching, counseling, and performance information feedback (see Chapter 8).

Compensation By designing pay plans that link compensation to duties, responsibilities, qualifications, and performance (see Chapters 10–11).

Preservation of effective employee-management relationships By providing benefits in appreciation for service to the organization, a safe workplace, and equitable treatment of employees (see Chapters 12–15).

Issue: **Can U.S. Organizations Meet the Challenges of**
                        Slower Productivity Growth and Foreign Competition?

An issue for the 1980s is whether U.S. organizations will be able to meet
foreign competition from countries with higher productivity growth and to
compete effectively with foreign firms that sell products in the United
States. In the last twenty years, the U.S. productivity growth rate has
averaged less than 2 percent, while Germany, France, and Italy have averaged over 4 percent and Japan over 7 percent. Certain basic industries—auto, steel, and electronics—have experienced increased difficulty
in competing effectively; and the U.S. balance of payments is frequently
unfavorable.

Much of the blame has been placed on unfair competition, government
regulations, inflation, tax laws, labor costs, capital shortage, imported oil,
monetary and fiscal policies, and outdated plants. However, one important
contributing factor has been management. While U.S. management has
much to be proud of in terms of accomplishments over the years (for example, U.S. workers remain the highest producers in the world), some
fundamental management problems appear to affect the ability of the
United States to remain competitive and retain its leadership in the world
economic community.[54] One executive, when asked about the major challenge facing U.S. business in the 1980s, responded:

**The major problem will not be inflation, not regulation, and not even
new technology. Instead, the major challenge will be how we respond
to the fact that, for the first time ever, there is someone else who
knows how to manage better than we do—and that is the Japanese.[55]**

In U.S. industry today, a powerful movement is underway to reexamine
and if necessary, to alter, traditional managerial assumptions and approaches. Executives now realize that the business system they have
studied and mastered is no longer the "world beater" it once was. They
are seeking alternatives that are more flexible and participative than the
rigid organizations they grew up with. These alternatives include approaches pioneered by Elton Mayo, Douglas McGregor, Rensis Likert,
Chris Argyris, and others. They call for participatory management, concern for quality of worklife, job enrichment, collaboration between unions
and management, and work reform. These concerns involve new initiatives and recognition of the valuable inputs of those doing the work—the
employees.[56]

While Japanese management offers U.S. managers much to consider, Japanese management cannot automatically be transferred to the United
States. U.S. management must determine what works here and what
works in Japan and then try to use these factors to design organizations
and jobs that will be successful.

Successful Managerial Practices

These challenges call for U.S. managers to identify factors and practices that lead to success. One study by a Stanford professor, T. J. Peters, examined the management practices of thirty-seven companies frequently identified by organizational analysts as the best-managed U.S. firms. Peters named eight attributes common to these firms:

Bias toward action The firms avoid analyzing products to death and avoid complicated procedures for developing new ideas; they concentrate on a few well-defined goals for their managers.

Simple form and lean staff Activities are kept to small, manageable groups and staffs are kept small to avoid bureaucracies.

Closeness to the customer The firms are driven by concern for customers, not concern for technology, product, or strategy. Their constant contact with customers provides insights that direct the company; and new product ideas reflect input from customers.

Productivity improvement via consensus Productivity improvements are achieved by motivating and stimulating employees, providing autonomy, letting employees set their goals, and rewarding employees for performance.

Autonomy to encourage entrepreneurship The firms authorize their managers to act as entrepreneurs, make decisions, start programs on their own, and take reasonable risks.

Stress on a key business value A single-minded focus on a value becomes a culture for the company, such as reducing cost and improving productivity at Dana, calling on customers at IBM, and developing new products at 3M and Hewlett-Packard; this culture gives direction to the entire organization.

Sticking to what they know best The firms never acquire any business they do not know how to run and never leave their bases. The companies have identified their strengths and built on them. They have resisted the temptation of attractive expansions into areas where they do not have corporate skills or know-how.

Simultaneously loose and tight controls The firms control a few variables tightly while allowing flexibility and looseness in others; for example, 3M uses return on sales and number of employees as a control but gives considerable leeway in day-to-day operations.

The successful companies achieve better-than-average growth by being able to change quickly and keeping their eyes on their customers, competitors, and financial reports. They have learned success takes perseverance, time, repetition, simplicity, plant visits, memos, and systems; and they have learned that ignoring their rules for success will cause them to slowly lose vitality, growth, and competitiveness.[57]

Back to the Basics: Production

One reason for U.S. problems has been the nation's own success. In the last twenty-five years, the U.S. economy has moved from a product orientation to a service orientation. The fast-growing service industries have provided more jobs and more opportunity. Thus, the younger generation, especially those with exceptional talent, have been attracted to the service sector. Today, even people who work in manufacturing want to perform jobs similar to those in the service sector. Few young, highly trained people want to work in factories. Twenty-five years ago, the young, talented engineers worked with the design and facilities personnel and trained employees worked with the design and facilities personnel and trained employees to perform better. During those times, strong vitality on the production side was coupled with ingenious capability on the design side. Some authorities believe those days must return.[58]

Some top executives foresee a new "era of the manufacturing executive" or "new pragmatism." Whatever the movement is called, U.S. companies are refocusing on making a better product at a better price. New initiatives in technology, inventory control, and material handling are being tried. Seeking employee input for ideas on increasing quality and efficiency—an approach long advised by behavioral scientists—is becoming a way of life. Increased use of microelectronics, robotics, and automation is considered inevitable.[59]

Changes Abroad

Structural changes within Japan may help U.S. firms compete with Japanese firms. Ironically, many of these changes seem to mirror those that have characterized U.S. society. Japan has experienced a decline in number of manufacturing workers from 14.4 million in 1973 to 13.7 million in 1980. As the United States did earlier, Japan seems to be developing an oversupply of white-collar employees who want service-oriented jobs and an undersupply of skilled employees willing to work in production jobs. Another change is the increase in "job hopping," especially in the high-technology industries. Surprisingly, this change has resulted from two Japanese traditions: lifetime employment and a seniority-based pay system. Talented younger personnel have grown impatient with slow promotions and pay increases based primarily on seniority.[60]

Summary

Understanding organizations, jobs, and individual employees is important to understanding the personnel function. Organizations formulate goals to give direction and are structured in such a way that the goals will be achieved. Every organization develops a philosophy of management or an organizational culture, which includes a common set of beliefs about the organization and guides the behavior and activities of its employees.

Within organizations at the intermediary levels are formal and informal groups. Both play an important role in organizations. They have leaders, have structure, and serve organizational purposes. Within and between groups, conflict can occur, usually because of limited resources, differences in goals, or a competitive reward system. While conflict may be destructive, efforts can be made so that it will be constructive. Organization development is one alternative to reduce conflict within and between groups.

The Theory Z model is one method being used to increase organizational success. Deriving characteristics from traditional U.S. and successful Japanese firms, Theory Z is based on the following concepts: long-term employment; consensual decision making; individual responsibility; slow evaluation and promotion; implicit, informal controls with explicit, formalized measures; moderately specialized career paths; and holistic concern for employees.

Managerial styles are important in leading employees in organizational settings. After years of study, researchers have concluded that success in leadership depends on the interaction of leadership styles, employees' perceptions and needs, acceptance of the leader, and the situation.

Because the work of the organization is divided into jobs, job design is an important organizational process. Jobs are designed to maximize performance, job satisfaction, and motivation and reduce turnover and absenteeism. Providing skill variety, task identity, task significance, autonomy, and feedback enhances the motivational potential of the job. Proper matching of employees' expectations from jobs with their actual experiences improves job satisfaction.

The individual employee must be considered in terms of individual differences and motivation. Theoretical approaches to motivation include the needs approach, motivation-hygiene theory, and expectancy theory. The personnel function can facilitate the development of a motivational climate in a number of ways.

An important contemporary issue is lower productivity growth in the United States coupled with intense foreign competition. This issue must be faced now and in the future.

Discussion Questions

1. Examine your last job for its motivation potential in terms of skill variety, task identity, task significance, autonomy, and feedback.
2. Assess the last organization by which you were employed in terms of its motivational climate.
3. Compare an organization with which you are familiar with the Theory Z model.

4. What is a corporate culture? How can it affect an organization?

5. Within a campus organization, identify (a) the informal groups, (b) intergroup and intragroup conflicts, and (c) ways to make these groups and conflicts constructive forces.

6. Why has it taken so long for behavioral scientists to have a major effect on organizational change?

7. In your opinion, what must U.S. organizations do to meet the challenges of slower productivity growth and foreign competition?

Notes

1. Louis E. Davis, "Individuals and the Organization," *California Management Review* 22 (Spring 1980), pp. 5–14.

2. William G. Scott, "Organization Theory: An Overview and an Appraisal," *Journal of the Academy of Management* 4 (April 1961), p. 7.

3. Charles Perrow, *Organizational Analysis: A Sociological View* (Belmont, Calif.: Brooks/Cole Publishing Company, 1980), pp. 133–136.

4. Henry Mintzberg, "Organization Design: Fashion or Fit," *Harvard Business Review* 59 (January/February 1981), pp. 103–116.

5. *Ibid.*, p. 104.

6. Arthur G. Bedeian, *Organization: Theory and Analysis* (Hinsdale, Ill.: Dryden Press, 1980), pp. 52–66.

7. Davis, "Individuals and the Organization," pp. 5–14.

8. Dennis Briscoe, "Organizational Design: Dealing with the Human Constraint," *California Management Review* 23 (Fall 1980), p. 72.

9. *Ibid.*

10. Bedeian, *Organizations,* pp. 67–69.

11. William G. Ouchi and Alfred M. Jaeger, "Type Z Organization: Stability in the Midst of Mobility," *Academy of Management Review* 3 (April 1978), pp. 305–314; and Nina Hatvany and Vladimir Pucik, "Japanese Management Practices and Productivity," *Organizational Dynamics* 9 (Spring 1981), pp. 5–21.

12. L. K. O'Leary, "Theory Z," *Bell Telephone Magazine* 60 (No. 3, 1981), p. 8.

13. Jeremy Main, "Westinghouse's Cultural Revolution," *Fortune,* June 15, 1981, p. 82.

14. William G. Ouchi and Raymond I. Price, "Hierarchies, Clans, and Theory Z: A New Perspective on Organization Development," *Organizational Dynamics* (Autumn 1972), pp. 40–42.

15. Edwin L. Baker, "Managing Organizational Culture," *McKinsey Quarterly* (Autumn 1980), pp. 51–53.

16. "Corporate Culture," *Business Week,* October 27, 1980, pp. 148–150.

17. *Ibid.*

18. Scott, "Organization Theory," p. 13.

19. Harold J. Levitt, *Managerial Psychology* (Chicago: University of Chicago Press, 1978), pp. 189–190.

20. William G. Dyer, "Group Behavior," in *Organizations and People,* ed. J. B. Ritchie and Paul Thompson (St. Paul, Minn.: West, 1980), p. 182.

21. Scott, "Organization Theory," p. 14.

22. Edgar Schein, *Organizational Psychology* (Englewood Cliffs, N.J.: Prentice-Hall, 1970), pp. 96–99.

23. Robert Townsend, *Up the Organization* (New York: Alfred A. Knopf, 1970), p. 39.

24. Kenneth W. Thomas and Warren H. Schmidt, "A Survey of Managerial Interests with Respect to Conflict," *Academy of Management Journal* 19 (June 1976), pp. 315–318.

25. Schein, *Organizational Psychology,* pp. 102–103.

26. Thomas and Schmidt, "A Survey of Managerial Interests," pp. 315–318.

27. *Ibid.*

28. Wendell French and Cecil H. Bell, Jr., *Organization Development: Behavioral Science Interventions for Organization Improvement* (Englewood Cliffs, N.J.: Prentice-Hall, 1978), p. 97.

29. Harold L. Schneider, "Personnel Managers Look to the 80's," *Personnel Administrator* 24 (November 1979), pp. 52–54.

30. Arthur G. Bedeian and William F. Glueck, *Management* (Hinsdale, Ill.: Dryden Press), to be published in 1983.

31. Douglas McGregor, "The Human Side of Enterprise," in *Leadership and Motivation,* ed. W. G. Bennis and E. H. Schein (Cambridge, Mass.: MIT Press, 1966), pp. 5–16.

32. *Ibid.*, p. 15.

33. Fred Fiedler, "Validation and Extension of the Contingency Model of Leadership Effectiveness," *Psychological Bulletin* 76 (August 1971), pp. 128–148.
34. Bedeian and Glueck, *Management.*
35. Robert J. House and Terence R. Mitchell, "Path-Goal Theory of Leadership," *Journal of Contemporary Business* 3 (Fall 1974), p. 85.
36. *Ibid.,* p. 84.
37. Richard W. Woodman and John J. Sherman, "A Comprehensive Look at Job Design," *Personnel Journal* 56 (August 1971), p. 385.
38. Ernest J. McCormick, *Job Analysis* (New York: American Management Association, AMACOM, 1979), p. 19.
39. J. R. Hackman, Edward E. Lawler, and Lyman Porter, *Perspectives in Behavior in Organizations* (New York: McGraw-Hill, 1977), p. 225.
40. J. R. Hackman and Edward E. Lawler, III, "Employee Reactions to Job Characteristics," *Journal of Applied Psychology* 55 (July 1971), pp. 267–283. Also see J. Richard Hackman and Greg R. Oldham, *Work Redesign* (Reading, Mass.: Addison-Wesley, 1980) for details and expected future developments.
41. *Ibid.*
42. John P. Wanous, "Who Wants Job Enrichment?" *S.A.M. Advanced Management Journal* 41 (Summer 1976), p. 16.
43. Edward E. Lawler III, "For a More Effective Organization: Match the Job to the Man," *Organizational Dynamics* 3 (Summer 1974), p. 25.
44. Raymond A. Katzell, "Work Attitudes, Motivation, and Performance," *Professional Psychology* 11 (June 1980), pp. 409–412.
45. Lawler, "For a More Effective Organization," p. 25.
46. Katzell, "Work Attitudes," p. 414.
47. Briscoe, "Organizational Design," pp. 71–80.
48. Curtis W. Cook, "Guidelines for Managing Motivation," *Business Horizons* 23 (April 1980), p. 62.
49. A. H. Maslow, "A Theory of Human Motivation," *Psychological Review* 50 (July 1943), pp. 370–396.
50. Frederick Herzberg, *Work and the Nature of Man* (New York: World Publishing Co., 1966), pp. 96–98.
51. J. Richard Hackman, "Work Design," in *Improving Life at Work,* ed. J. Richard Hackman and J. Lloyd Suttle (Santa Monica, Calif.: Goodyear Publishing Company, 1977), pp. 106–109.
52. This theory is explained in many books and articles. The authors recommend David Nadler and Edward E. Lawler III, "Motivation: A Diagnostic Approach," in *Perspectives on Behavior in Organizations,* ed. Hackman, Lawler, and Porter, pp. 26–29.
53. Katzell, "Work Attitudes," pp. 416–418.
54. Robert H. Hayes and William J. Abernathy, "Managing Our Way to Economic Decline," *Harvard Business Review* 58 (July/August 1980), pp. 65–66.
55. William G. Ouchi, "Organizational Paradigms: A Commentary on Japanese Management and Theory Z Organizations," *Organizational Dynamics* 9 (Spring 1981), p. 43.
56. Charles G. Burch, "Working Smarter," *Fortune,* June 15, 1981, pp. 68–73.
57. Thomas J. Peters, "Putting Excellence into Management," *Business Week,* July 21, 1980, pp. 196–205.
58. "Shinto: Why the U.S. Can't Compete in Japan," *Business Week,* December 14, 1981, p. 44.
59. "Business Refocuses on the Factory Floor," *Business Week,* February 2, 1981, pp. 91–92.
60. "A Changing Work Force Poses Challenges," *Business Week,* December 14, 1981, pp. 116–118.

The Fulgham Research Institute in Houston has grown rapidly over the last few years, because its professional staff has successfully secured large research grants to study cancer resulting from water and air pollution. In the last five years, total employment has grown from 75 to 175. The present workforce comprises twenty managers, seventy-five professional and technical employees, and eighty other employees.

In the past, the institute has operated almost as three separate units. The director of cancer research has managed his division, the director of pollution research has managed her division, and the office manager has managed the rest. Now the overall director, Dr. Donna Fulgham, and the members of the institute's board have become concerned with the operational framework of the institute. The institute has recently been informed of a pending EEOC charge of race and sex discrimination and has been told that the Teamsters Union is contacting employees about joining.

Because of the uncertainty of federal grants, a base for the institute's funding, it is questionable whether the institute can attract an established personnel professional. However, there is no question that the institute must respond to the union campaign and the EEOC charge.

Thus, Dr. Fulgham called the two research directors and the office manager for a meeting to choose a personnel director. The name of John Spellings was recommended by both research directors. Spellings was a chemical engineer who had worked in both research divisions, had experience with computers, and had recently handled administrative work on several grants. He was thirty-four years old and had been employed by the institute as a promising chemist when he graduated from college. After about five years, his interest in chemical research became less enthusiastic, and his last four research proposals had not been funded. Spellings was well liked by employees of the institute; he headed the United Appeal program, coordinated the recreation activities, and often helped employees with personal and job-related problems. Dr. Fulgham and the two research directors agreed that personnel work was not difficult like the "hard" sciences and believed John could do the work. The office manager responded that they misunderstood the personnel function, adding that a clear indicator of their misconception was the presence of the EEOC charge and the union campaign.

Dr. Fulgham decided she wanted each person to vote on Spellings as personnel manager. The vote was three to one, with the office manager casting the negative vote.

Questions

1. Assess the institute's personnel philosophy and the views toward personnel exhibited by the research director.
2. What are the qualifications necessary for the personnel manager at the institute?
3. What can John Spellings do to succeed?

JoAnn Martin is a personnel manager for one of Ajax Corporation's many production facilities. The only other individual in the department is a secretary who also handles employee benefit claims; therefore, JoAnn is responsible for all personnel functions. Her immediate boss is the plant manager of operations, although she is requested to perform corporate personnel functions from time to time.

It is Monday, the first of the month. JoAnn has returned to the facility from a college recruiting trip the previous Thursday and Friday. This recruiting function is coordinated by the corporate college recruiting manager, although many campus recruiting activities are performed by JoAnn and other plant personnel managers.

Ms. Martin arrives at the office early Monday morning and looks at the following list of messages received by the secretary in her absence:

1. Mr. Smith [the corporate college recruiting manager] wants to know if you can recruit at Knowledge University [out of state] this Wednesday and Thursday. There are two full recruiting schedules each day [over twenty students have signed up each day for campus interviews], and one of the college recruiters had to cancel the trip because of an emergency at his facility. Mr. Price [the corporate vice-president of personnel] will be the other recruiter.

2. Ms. Johnson [an extremely popular employee at the facility] had a sudden heart attack and passed away. Funeral arrangements are incomplete because of out-of-town relatives, but it looks like the funeral will be Wednesday morning.

3. Mr. Parks's [the assistant plant manager] daughter, Jenny, has received scholarship offers from three universities and would like you to advise her which of them might be best.

4. June [an hourly employee who single-handedly ran last year's United Way Campaign] wants to meet with you to discuss this year's United Way campaign, which officially starts the eighth of this month. She figures this meeting will not take more than three hours.

5. Robert Edwards [secretary of the local union and a notorious "cry-baby"] has several potential employee grievances he would like to discuss with you.

6. Walter Simms [the plant manager] would like a progress report on the new

management development program for first-line supervisors scheduled to begin the fifteenth of this month.

7. Jean Scan [manager of assembly operations at the facility] received the plant manager's O.K. to add six new hourly employees to her department. She would like these individuals to report to work by the eighth of this month.

8. Dr. Edith Jones [professor of management at the local liberal arts college] would like you to talk to her class on the ninth of the month. She says the topic and approach are up to you but the length of the class is two hours.

Questions

Assume you are JoAnn Martin. Present a detailed strategy for handling these messages. In what order would you make the calls? Which of the requests would you accept? All of them? Be prepared to defend your decisions. Also include what additional information you would need to help you make your decision. Finally, tell what insights you have obtained into the personnel function.

Quality Manufacturing Company makes electronic calculators sold in chain retail stores throughout the United States. In recent times, its profits have dwindled because of high labor costs, foreign competition, and the increasingly questionable reliability of its products.

Several of its largest customers have complained about the defective products received from Quality. The president of the company has called a meeting of various departments in the organization. Each department was assigned the responsibility of determining the reasons for the problem of defective products. Excerpts from the managers' explanations include the following:

Sales Manager: Our sales team can sell every product we make if it is reliable. Our customers say our product has declined in quality, and several have come to believe we cannot deliver what we promise.

Production Manager: We produce the best product on the market. Our inspectors check every calculator. If there are defects, they must occur after the product leaves us—either in the shipping department or in transporting the products. We could produce even more if personnel would send us employees who take pride in their work and can produce what we demand.

Accounting Manager: We have to issue credit to customers who discover the calculators do not work when they are received. It has been our policy to credit their account and to ask them to return the defective products. The problem is that the percentage of sales that goes to credit for defects has increased too much over the last three years.

Personnel Manager: We are recruiting the best-qualified employees for the wages we offer. I realize that the quality is not what it used to be— but neither is anything else.

Questions

1. What kinds of organizational conflict appear here?
2. Do these reactions to problems seem typical to you?
3. Devise a plan of action for the company.
4. Describe what each department might do to improve the company's competitive position.

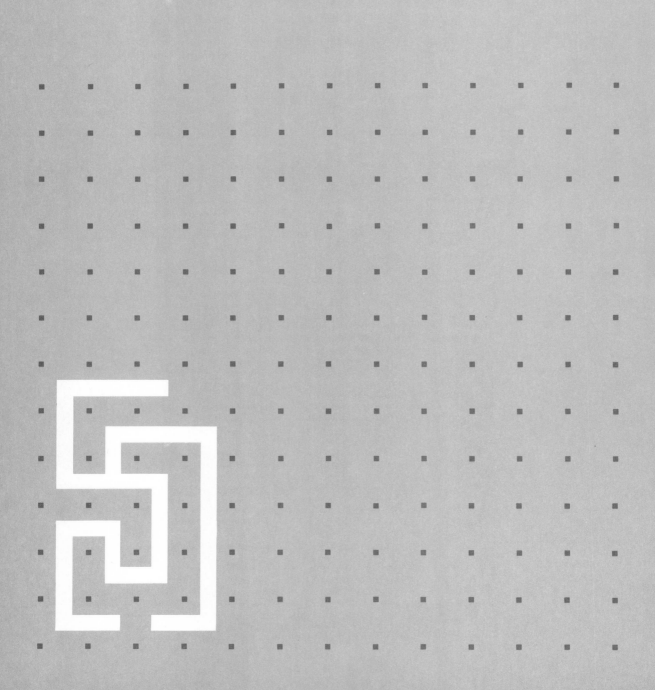

Part Two

Determining Employment Needs and Staffing

Determining employment needs and staffing from outside and inside the organization are vital personnel activities, since the quality of employees in the organization will determine the degree to which organizational objectives are achieved. The four chapters in Part 2 explain these important functions.

Chapter 4 introduces various methods and uses of job analysis and human resource forecasting. Chapter 5 explains recruiting activities and affirmative action plans. Staffing from outside the organization, including staffing concepts, selection procedures, fair employment considerations, and selection methods, are discussed in Chapter 6. Chapter 7 describes internal staffing activities, such as promotions, transfers, and layoffs, and devotes special attention to assessment centers and career development planning.

Chapter 4

Job Analysis and Human Resource Forecasting

Virtually every aspect of human resource administration is affected by the movement of personnel into, within, and out of the organization. Effective management of such movement and its impacts first requires mechanisms for systematically identifying and analyzing it.

Herbert G. Heneman III, and Marcus G. Sandver, "Markov Analysis in Human Resource Administration: Applications and Limitations," *Academy of Management Review* 2 (October 1977), p. 535.

In a sense, this chapter connects Chapter 3 with the remaining chapters of the book. We noted in the previous chapter that jobs are important in understanding employees' behavior and the organization's structure. Job analysis, which is discussed in some detail in this chapter, represents a fundamental starting point for the study of the other personnel functions described in the rest of the text. This discussion also suggests that all managers, regardless of their particular organizational positions, should be well versed in job analysis techniques, since accurate job analyses will likely increase their departments' effectiveness as well as help them avoid problems associated with equal employment opportunity legislation.

The chapter also describes human resource forecasting and its potential advantages to the organization. This function is relatively new; and the chapter concludes by presenting a related issue: what challenges and prospects are faced by a new personnel function such as human resource forecasting?

Job Analysis

Definition and Significance of Job Analysis

Job analysis represents a fundamental starting point for human resource forecasting as well as other personnel activities.[1] It represents the collection, ordering, and evaluation of information related to work or workers.[2] Two general forces, *competition* and *equal employment opportunity legislation,* have made job analysis a significant organizational consideration. Organizations faced with domestic and foreign competition must ensure that employees are working on necessary jobs in an efficient manner. Job analysis can uncover obsolete jobs, as suggested by the following:

Any organization, especially an older one, may unknowingly have sick jobs, for the natural course of a job is for it to die at some time—unless steps are taken to prevent this from happening.

Jobs tend to die especially as a company or an organization grows in size, be it a government organization, a church, or a hospital.[3]

Eliminating such jobs can streamline an organization, which in turn should improve its competitive position.

Equal employment opportunity legislation has also demanded a thorough analysis of individual job components.[4] One judge noted in a related employment test validation case:

The cornerstone of the construction of a content valid examination [an examination based on qualifications really needed in the job] is the job analysis. Without such an analysis to single out the critical knowledge, skills, and abilities required by the job, their importance to each other, and the level of proficiency demanded as to each attribute, a test constructor is aiming in the dark and can only hope to achieve job relatedness by blind luck.[5]

In 1978, the federal agencies that enforce equal employment opportunity laws confirmed that job analysis is a fundamental prerequisite for proving that employment practices are free of discrimination. The *Uniform Guidelines of Employee Selection Procedures* state:

There should be a job analysis which includes an analysis of the important work behavior(s) required for successful performance and their relative importance and, if the behavior results in work product(s), an analysis of work product(s). Any job analysis should focus on the work behavior(s) and the tasks associated with them. If work behavior(s) are not observable, the job analysis should identify and analyze those aspects of the behavior(s) that can be observed and the observed work product(s). The work behavior(s) selected for measurement should be critical work behavior(s) and/or important work behavior(s) constituting most of the job.[6]

Many organizations, especially those that have lost EEO cases, are now placing more emphasis on job analysis than ever before. But job analysis is not a casual process that can be relegated to a clerk. "It is not accomplished by rummaging around the organization; it is accomplished by applying highly systematic and precise methods."[7] In too many cases, organizations have not taken job analysis seriously. causing one management consultant to conclude:

In many ways, job analysis is analogous to the group of blind men who came in contact with an elephant. They may have sensed the beast was ponderous, but each was able to describe it only from a narrow perspective. Jobs generally are complex configurations of task-related behaviors. An analyst could spend a week or more studying most jobs and not run out of new information to record. Moreover, as with the blind men, the analyst's perspective is critically important in determining the results of job analysis.[8]

Not only must the organization take the job analysis process seriously, but it must be careful in its selection of a job analyst. Characteristics shown to lead to success in this position include:

A good grasp of the nature and functions of organizations in modern society.

A capacity to study the interaction among the cultural, technological, and behavioral variables that shape jobs and their outcomes within organizational situations.

An ability to relate to persons at all levels, from assembly-line operators to professionals.

A working knowledge of existing methods and statistical tools.[9]

Exhibit 4.1   **Job Analysis Worksheet**

Identifying Information

Employee Name _____

Organization/Unit _____

Title _____   Date _____

Brief Summary of Job

(Job analyst asks employee to summarize job in a few sentences, highlighting major duties and responsibilities.)

Task Statements

[Employee is asked (I) what he or she does; (II) how he or she does it; (III) why it is done; (IV) what the output is; (V) what tools and procedures are used; (VI) how much time it takes; and (VI) the frequency and difficulty of the task.]

I.	V.
II.	VI.
III.	VII.
IV.	

Skills, Knowledge, and Abilities Required

1. Knowledge:
(Employee is asked to specify the subject matter areas, facts, or principles and the level, degree, and breadth of knowledge required.)

2. Skills Required:
(Employee is asked to describe the manual skills needed.)

3. Abilities Required:
(Employee is asked to list written and oral language, mathematical, problem-solving, interpersonal, and physical abilities required.)

Methods of Job Analysis

Although many different job analysis methods exist, all focus on:

1. Eliciting information from a source—for example, by observing and interviewing a job holder or by having that individual report similar information on a questionnaire.

2. Organizing and presenting the information in a usable format, such as a job description or job specification.

Four of the most common job analysis methods are *interview, observation, questionnaire,* and *participant log.* While one method may be sufficient, the methods are usually combined to improve the quality of the job analysis.

Interview   The interview involves talking with the job holder, supervisors, and others qualified to provide job-related information. Job hold-

Exhibit 4.1 | **Continued**

| Physical Activities | *(Employee is asked to describe the frequency and degree of physical activities, such as lifting, climbing, reaching, carrying, pushing, kneeling, and sitting, required.)* |

| Environmental Conditions | *(Employee is asked to describe the frequency and degree to which the following occur: excessive noise, inadequate ventilation, heat, smoke, smell, cramped quarters.)* |

Analysis of Task

Tasks	Percent of Time[a]	Level of Difficulty[b]
I.		
II.		
III.		
IV.		
V.		
VI.		
VII.		

[a] Must equal 100%

[b] S = Simple
SD = Slightly Difficult
D = Difficult
VD = Very Difficult

Adapted from U.S. Civil Service Commission, *Job Analysis: Developing and Documenting Data* (Washington, D.C.: United States Civil Service Commission, 1973), 9–11.

ers may be interviewed at their work site and asked questions similar to those on the job analysis worksheet shown in Exhibit 4.1. At the beginning of the interview, the job analyst should explain the reason for the interview so that the job holder will not fear that the job is being eliminated. Other considerations that concern job analysis interview questions are found in Exhibit 4.2.

Single interviews are preferable for gathering data about desk jobs and other jobs that involve little observable physical activity. Group interviews, on the other hand, are preferable where there are several levels of a single occupation. For example, a senior electrician, the electrician's helper, and the apprentice electrician are employed in the electrician trade, but each job has distinct duties and responsibilities. Supervisors who have a thorough knowledge of the jobs in their departments also are nearly always interviewed to verify other information (sometimes they are the only source.)[10]

The interview is the simplest but the least controlled job analysis method. The results are usually limited to use in the preparation of job descriptions and job specifications, the planning of career objectives, and the setting of performance objectives. The effectiveness of the interviews depends on the interviewer, on the quality of the support-

Exhibit 4.2	**Do's and Don'ts for** **Job Analysis Interviewers**

1. Don't take issue with the worker's statements.
2. Don't take sides on issues concerning employer-employee grievances or conflicts.
3. Don't show any interest in the wage classification of the job.
4. Be polite and courteous throughout the interview.
5. Don't "talk down" to the worker.
6. Don't be influenced by your personal likes and dislikes.
7. Be impersonal. Don't criticize or suggest any changes or improvements in organization or methods of work.
8. Talk to the worker only with permission of his supervisor.
9. Verify job data, especially technical or trade terminology, with foreman or department head.
10. Verify completed analysis with proper official.

Source: Ernest J. McCormick, *Job Analysis: Methods and Applications* (New York: American Management Association, 1979), p. 39. Copyright © 1979 by American Management Associations. All rights reserved.

ing interviews (with supervisors and other employees), and on the ability of the job holder to make meaningful responses.[11]

Observation When observation is used, the job analyst actually watches the job holder do the work and records relevant activities. Certain jobs lend themselves to the direct observation method—for example, the jobs of drill press operator, forklift operator, assembly worker, and janitor. The entire work cycle involved in these jobs can be observed in a short time. Also, while the job analyst observes the work, he or she can clarify any points not understood. Job holders unaccustomed to writing will feel relieved to know they do not have to explain their job in writing.[12]

The observation method allows the analyst to study work activities in depth; however, the accuracy of the results depends on the analyst's perception of the job. Further, thorough observation of complex jobs takes considerable time, thereby increasing the cost of the process.[13]

Questionnaire The questionnaire method provides a set of questions about the work for the job holder and supervisor to complete. The questionnaire's format may include a checklist of duties, behaviors, and responsibilities or may have open-ended, general questions, such as "What are your assigned duties on this job?" The itemized responses provide quantitative data that allow further analysis. With such analysis, an organization may be more readily able to prove the validity and reliability of the job analysis results. Exhibit 4.3 lists some

Exhibit 4.3	Common Job Analysis Questionnaires	
	Functional Job Analysis	Functional job analysis characterizes a job in terms of three principal job dimensions—data, people, and things—which are then assessed on their relative complexity.[a]
	Management Position Description Questionnaire (MPDQ)	MPDQ provides job information about managerial activities, responsibilities, demands, and restrictions. Thirteen job dimensions, such as planning, control, coordination, and autonomy of action, are produced.[b]
	Position Analysis Questionnaire (PAQ)	PAQ consists of a 194-item checklist of job elements that characterize employees' work behaviors and attributes. Elements include information input, mental processes, work output, job context, interpersonal activities, and miscellaneous aspects.[c]
	Task Analysis (U.S. Department of Labor)	Task analysis studies workers' functions, workers' traits, and work fields such as machines, tools, equipment and work aids, materials, products, and services.[d]
	Threshold Traits Analysis	Threshold traits analysis consists of a checklist of thirty-three traits that encompass physical, mental, learned, motivational, and social elements of a job.[e]

Sources:
[a] Sidney A. Fine and W. W. Wiley, *An Introduction to Functional Job Analysis* (Kalamazoo, Mich.: Upjohn Institute for Employment Research, 1971).
[b] Pat Pinto and Walter W. Tornow, "The Development of a Managerial Job Taxonomy," *Journal of Applied Psychology* (August 1976), pp. 410–418.
[c] Ernest J. McCormick, *Job Analysis* (New York: American Management Association, AMACOM, 1979).
[d] U.S. Department of Labor, Manpower Administration, *Handbook for Analyzing Jobs* (Washington, D.C.: Government Printing Office, 1972).
[e] Felix M. Lopez, Gerald A. Kesselman, and Felix E. Lopez, "An Empirical Test of a Trait-Oriented Job Analysis Technique," *Personnel Psychology* 34 (Summer 1981), pp. 479–502.

types of questionnaires as well as the job information each questionnaire captures.

Participant Log The participant log requires the job holder to log his or her tasks or duties as they are performed over a prescribed period of time. When the participant changes tasks, he or she records the nature of the new task along with the time of the change. While this method is comprehensive, busy job holders do not like to record such information over a long period of time. To gain cooperation and still obtain useful data, analysts often collect random records. Once the tasks have been recorded, they must be rewritten and reviewed by the job holder.[14]

**Uses
of Job
Analysis**

Job analysis serves the informational needs of a wide variety of management functions. First and foremost, job analysis provides information used in writing job descriptions and job specifications. *Job descriptions* are written portrayals of the work activities performed on a particular job. They include duties and responsibilities and may include other job-related information, such as working conditions, tools, and equipment (see Exhibit 4.4). *Job specifications* detail the qualifications necessary for adequate performance of the job. These qualifications normally include statements about skills, knowledge, abilities, physical characteristics, and other relevant personal characteristics.[15]

Job Descriptions Job descriptions serve several important organizational purposes. They establish a rational basis for salary structures, because the pay systems of most firms are tied to employees' duties and responsibilities. Job descriptions help to clarify relationships between jobs and to avoid overlap and gaps in responsibility. They are useful to help employees acquire a greater understanding of their jobs and the content of other jobs, thereby helping employees to visualize how the jobs fit together. In addition, job descriptions can be used in restructuring the organization and reassigning duties and responsibilities. Finally, they serve as a basis for employees' orientation, training, and performance appraisals.[16]

The most exhaustive compilation of job descriptions is the *Dictionary of Occupational Titles (DOT)*, which contains job information on 12,099 occupations and an additional 16,702 occupational titles. The information includes a listing of tasks performed; type of work; complexity of the work in relation to data, people, and things; and traits required of workers, such as aptitude, interests, training time, and physical demands.

Job Specifications Job specifications, which contain the employee qualifications for jobs, must be carefully determined. Special caution must be given when height, weight, age, sex, and other physical qualifications are included to assure that they are bona fide occupational requirements. In few cases may these qualifications be justified as a basis for employment.

The most important use of job specifications is in staffing activities. As will be discussed in Chapters 6 and 7, job specifications and employees' qualifications should match. Once employees are on the job, these specifications provide information to workers who want promotions or transfers. Where the employee's present qualifications fall short, training to upgrade them may be available. Finally, because organizations must pay more for highly qualified employees, job specifications serve as a basis for compensation plans.

Exhibit 4.4	**Example of a Job Description for a Management Position**

Alpha Electric Public Utility

Job Description

Exhibit A

Job Title:	Division Personnel Supervisor	**Rate Range:**	Negotiable
Location:	Operating Divisions	**FLSA Code:**	A-Administrative
Reports to:	Division Vice President (Line)	**Dept. No.**	24-Employee Rel.
	Vice President-Emp. Rel. (Staff)	**Job No.**	28Q

Job Summary

The job of Division Personnel Supervisor has responsibility, within the geographic division, for the performance of a variety of personnel related functions. Serves in a line capacity to the Division Vice President and in a staff capacity to the Vice President of Employee Relations. Administers group medical and health and accident insurance programs; coordinates employee appraisal and employee awards programs; directs the employee identification program; assists in coordination of the equal employment opportunity program; interviews, screens, and investigates applicants for employment; responsible for payroll record preparation and the completion of a six-month probationary period review on all new employees; assists in the administrative aspects of the salary administration program; handles distribution of general notices, general orders, and similar material for division distribution.

Specific Duties & Responsibilities

(1) Administers group medical insurance program within the division. Assists employees with insurance problems and the filing of claims, distributes insurance forms, and prepares necessary change in status cards for further processing in the general office.

(2) Administers group health and accident and group life insurance programs within the division. Serves as liaison between the employee and the general office insurance department. Pays claims incurred under the health and accident program. Assists survivors of deceased employees in obtaining death benefits.

(3) Coordinates the management appraisal and employee performance review programs. Works under direction of the division vice president relative to receiving, scheduling, completing, and returning of appraisal forms required in the maintenance of the two programs.

(4) At the direction of the Division Vice President coordinates the division equal employment opportunity program and assists in developing the division affirmative action plan for approval by the Division Vice President. Annually makes a "review and analysis" to assure that the division is meeting its requirements under the plan. Assists division supervision in the selection and placement and upgrading of minority employees. Assists the general office staff in the preparation of that portion of the annual EEO-1 Report pertaining to the division.

Exhibit 4.4   **Continued**

(5) Directs the division employee identification program. Coordinates the photographing of employees in accordance with requirements of the Company's security program using the Polaroid Land Identification System. Maintains proper schedules for issuing of renewals.

(6) Coordinates the employee awards program within the division. Distributes information to aid employees in the selection of service award emblems, award watches, and retirement plaques. Assists the Division Vice President as required in the presentation of these awards.

(7) Interviews and screens all job applicants within the division where feasible, makes referrals, personal history investigations, schedules physical examinations, explains Company policy and benefit programs to new employees. Prepares or has prepared all records relating to employment.

(8) Responsible for the accurate preparation of all major change in status cards, employment authorizations, extensions of sick leave, request for workman's compensation, progress increase lists, and employee termination records originating in the division.

(9) Responsible for seeing that a detailed review on every new employee is made near the end of the six-month probationary period in order to ascertain the employee's qualifications for continued employment.

(10) Distributes general notices, general orders, and other communications received from the general office to appropriate division personnel.

(11) Handles the administrative aspects of the division salary administration program. Maintains a merit ledger reflecting disbursements and account balance. Assures that merit recommendations forwarded to the general office for approval are on proper effective dates. Applies Company promotional policy on exempt and non-exempt intra-division promotional moves. Assures that Company policy regarding physical examinations has been complied with relative to merit and promotional recommendations prior to submission of the major change in status or other appropriate record. Assures that all employment offers are consistent with Company policy relative to job requirements and applicant's education and related experience.

(12) Performs such other duties and responsibilities as assigned by the Division Vice President.

Exhibit B

10. An Assistant Division Superintendent now spends about 50% of his time on duties to be assigned the Division Personnel Supervisor. The Supervisor of Customer Accounting devotes about 25% of his time to divisional personnel work and the Vice President, his secretary and members of the division staff are now performing other duties to be reassigned.

Exhibit C

11. a. Relieving the Assistant Division Superintendent of duties relating to divisional personnel administration will double his time available for primary duties of an operating engineer. He will be assigned the general responsibility for all functions relating to existing transmission line operation; new transmission line construction other than major projects; and will coordinate all major project activities relating to the new 230 KV and 500 KV lines planned or under construction in this division. He is presently responsible for coordinating and preparing the operating and construction budgets, construction and maintenance of all general structures

Exhibit 4.4	Continued

and has the general responsibility for additions, operation and maintenance of all automotive vehicles and equipment.

b. The Supervisor of Customer Accounting spends approximately 25% of his time on functions related to personnel administration that will be reassigned to the Division Personnel Supervisor.

This will permit the Accounting Supervisor to devote more time to follow up on audit reports on local offices, to correct deficiencies and to develop more efficient work practices in these field offices. He will also have more time to examine routine accounting reports, detect areas needing attention and take steps to increase employee efficiency. He will also be assigned more responsibility to collect delinquent retail electric accounts and this should reduce amounts that have to be charged off as uncollectable.

Exhibit D

12. The Vice President and his staff will be relieved of detailed duties relating to personnel administration and can devote more time to overall general administrative duties.

Source: Used by permission.

Job analysis information and subsequent job descriptions and job specifications are the foundation of other personnel activities. For example, human resource planning depends on accurate job descriptions to determine workloads and outputs as well as on job specifications to determine whether present employees are qualified to fill vacant or newly created jobs.

Other examples include the following:

Staffing Job analysis data help identify the skills and knowledge required to perform the job, and this information serves as the basis for tests, interviews, and other selection procedures that will be used in staffing.

Orientations Job descriptions guide new employees in learning their duties and responsibilities.

Performance Job analysis data serve as the basis for determining the performance standards used to measure success in jobs.

Training Information from job analysis provides input in the design of training programs.

Compensation Job descriptions and job specifications serve as the foundation for determining the value of jobs in organizations.[17]

Considerations in Job Analysis Implementation

While numerous considerations affect implementation of job analysis in specific organizations, a few seem to apply to nearly all organizations. A key decision that precedes all others relates to the intended purpose of job analysis, which will affect the method of analysis used. For example, task analysis may be best for writing job descriptions; however, the position analysis questionnaire may be better for test design. In selecting the particular method of job analysis, the organization must not overlook practicality factors—costs, resources available, time, number of respondents, and capabilities of persons chosen to conduct job analysis.

Ideally, the decision about which method or methods to use should be based primarily on the purposes for which the organization needs to conduct the job analysis. Realistically, however, practicality is likely to play an equally important part in the decision, especially for smaller organizations with limited resources.[18]

Another consideration is the degree of accuracy desired of the information obtained. Because the quality of the information depends on employees' responses, job analysts' perceptions, and supervisors' expectations, the results may be open to doubt. Also, the end product may have questionable reliability, or consistency. For example, if different job analysts produce different results or if different results are produced at different times, the information may lack reliability.

Care must be taken in analyzing jobs—such as those of managers, professionals, and technicians—whose duties vary from day to day. When jobs vary substantially over time, the job analyst must look for patterns and analyze the jobs over a long period.

Where there are many employees with the same job title, analysis must be representative. While sampling is appropriate, the key is accurate representation. Where duties and skills differ among people with the same job title, a change in job titles for some may be appropriate.

Care should be taken to recognize inadvertent exaggeration, either by the job holder or the supervisor. Both realize that pay is tied to job descriptions and job specifications; the job analyst thus must be aware that employees' or supervisors' responses may be self-serving.

Finally, because we live in a dynamic world and most industries and organizations are constantly changing, organizations should design maintenance features into their job analysis procedures. Many organizations automatically review a job when a vacancy occurs; others periodically conduct job analysis at prescribed times.[19]

Human Resource Forecasting

Human resource, or employee, forecasting is a common practice in many organizations; however, there is little agreement over related definitions and methods. For example, one survey of eighty-three re-

Dimensions
and
Significance
of Human
Resource
Forecasting

spondents found seventy-three position titles reported for the human resource forecasting.[20] This confusing situation is further complicated by the fact that several different forecasting methods and statistical techniques are used. We will discuss employee forecasting in general terms, since most organizations apparently disregard the more sophisticated statistical forecasting models.[21] Readers interested in seeking additional knowledge in this area are encouraged to examine the sources cited in related notes at the end of the chapter.[22]

Employee forecasting represents two broad activities:

A regular *monitoring* activity, through which the workforce and its relationship to the business can be better understood, assessed, and controlled; problems can be highlighted; and a base can be established from which to respond to unforeseen events.

An *investigatory* activity, by which the implications for the workforce of particular problems and change situations—for example, the restructuring of the business—can be explored and the effects of alternative policies and actions investigated.[23]

These activities can, in turn, help the organization, since they examine:[24]

How well utilization of employees compares with organizational objectives.

Alternative forms of work organization and job structuring.

Wastage levels according to employee category, such as job classification, length of service, age, and so forth.

External labor markets and the availability of employees.

Career progressions for employees.

Organizations also rely on employee forecasting to protect their *investments in human resources*. For example, annual salaries of inexperienced college graduates with bachelor's and master's degrees average over $26,000 and $28,000, respectively, with specific amounts depending on the particular degree and industry.[25] Fringe benefits and other costs such as those for office space, secretarial support, and time spent by other managers can easily push a firm's investment to over $60,000 a year.[26] There is little chance that a newly hired employee can contribute half this figure to the organization in terms of his or her first year's job efforts. An organization hiring these individuals one year, laying them off the next year because of poor human resource forecasting, then rehiring new replacements the third year is incurring large, unnecessary costs.

Massive layoffs (of auto workers in recent times, for example) can pose three additional economic costs to the organization:

1. *Loss of other valuable employees,* who leave the firm fearing they too will be laid off in the near future.[27]
2. *Lowered morale* among the remaining employees, which can reduce an organization's productivity.[28]
3. *Difficulty in finding suitable replacements* for future job openings. Recently, demands have increased for certain employees, such as salesworkers, managers, administrators, and professionals.[29] A shortage of 129,000 qualified candidates for engineering vacancies is expected to occur between 1981 and 1985.[30] Organizations that have had publicized employee layoffs will likely be at a competitive disadvantage in recruiting such scarce employees.

Proper employee forecasting can also help organizations withstand sudden and dramatic technological advancements. Some firms have had to postpone plans because they did not have the number and type of employees needed to react to technological shifts in terms of expansion and diversification.[31]

Considerations Involved in Human Resource Forecasting

Any successful employee forecasting attempt starts with the job analysis activities discussed earlier in the chapter. Job analysis should provide a specific, realistic anchor to four general considerations often involved in employee forecasting:

1. Workforce composition and capabilities.
2. Information obtained from organizational executives concerning financial, sales, and production objectives as well as anticipated organizational changes.
3. Unit employee forecasts.
4. External influences.

Organizations interpret this information differently. They apply different techniques in evaluating it; and some organizations entirely disregard one or more of its facets. Employee forecasting efforts are therefore extremely varied, with no two organizations likely using identical processes.

Workforce Composition and Capabilities The composition of the workforce and its ability to carry out organizational objectives are necessary considerations in employee forecasting. An analysis should be made of the organization's workforce by age distribution and job category. Age distribution can provide useful information; findings in this area might suggest that many employees are approaching retirement, either in the company as a whole or in specific areas.

Also helpful are historical trends related to the proportions to each other of various employee categories normally needed in the operation.[32] Examples of such information include the following:

The number of secretaries and clerical employees compared with the number of managers.

The number of personnel representatives compared with the number of hourly employees.

The number of production inspectors compared with the number of assembly-line employees.

Some organizations are fortunate in having productivity benchmarks that specifically determine the number of employees needed per job classification. The number of hospital nurses, technicians, and orderlies, for example, usually depends on the number of hospital beds. Employee projections can be accurately made according to the estimated number of beds to be served by hospital staff in the future. However, many organizations have productivity measures but fail to consider them in any systematic employee forecasting efforts.

Trend information offers useful clues for employee forecasting, although it has some limitations:

The emphasis on numerical projections results in a lack of attention to necessary future managerial and professional qualities, to the level at which these qualities will be needed, or to the education and experience quotients that lead to the possession of these qualities. In addition, the lack of attention to qualitative problems may lead to the neglect of the career development of current managerial and professional personnel.[33]

Thus, employee forecasting often also includes a qualitative audit of employees, particularly those at the professional and managerial levels. *Employee audits and successor charts* vary in design and in the information they seek to obtain, although they typically contain indicators of an employee's present and potential performance, age, and possible replacements. Figure 4.1 presents an example of how such information can be arranged.

Employee audits are most useful, since they indicate whether sufficient replacements exist in the present workforce to fill various organizational positions. If not, the organization needs to consider instituting appropriate training programs to prepare some employees for higher-level positions or recruiting from outside sources. In some cases, a review of this information might suggest ways to prevent needless employee buildups that might result in future layoffs.

In Figure 4.1, for example, assume that Commercial Sales Representative B (R. Purdy) gets a job with another organization and, further, that sales reductions are estimated for the foreseeable future. The employee audit would suggest that this vacancy should not be filled in the short term, since the replacement hired for the position

Figure 4.1

A Succession Chart with
Information Obtained from
a Manpower Audit

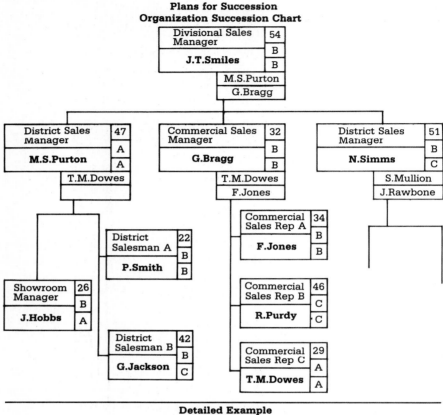

Plans for Succession
Organization Succession Chart

Detailed Example
Covering One Post
From a Management Succession Chart

Source: John Bramham, *Practical Manpower Planning* (London: Institute of Personnel Management, 1975),
pp. 76, 77. Reprinted by permission.

might eventually have to be laid off (through no fault of his or her performance) if sales continue to decline. Perhaps a better alternative would be to assign the responsibilities of Commercial Sales Representative B to the remaining sales representatives.

Employee audits do, however, involve two potential problems. First, much of the information obtained is superficial and subjective,[34] particularly if several of the managers supplying the information have differing views about what constitutes performance and potential. More specifically, one manager might assign a grade of B to an employee's performance, while another might assign that same employee an A. Second, the audit needs to be continually updated, or employees may suffer because of out-of-date evaluation. Consider, for example, the situation of N. Simms (district sales manager) in Figure 4.1. If the employee audit were not updated over a five-year period, then at the end of this period Simms would be fifty-six years old with relatively little chance to be promoted, whatever his actual accomplishments during the period.

Information Obtained from Top Executives Information from top executives concerning organizational objectives (financial, sales, production, and so on) and anticipated changes are also necessary in employee forecasting. However, obtaining this executive input is often difficult, and the results can be inconclusive. Some executives might be reluctant to disclose confidential information, such as the elimination of a particular production facility or the merger of two departments in an organization, fearing that employee morale would be drastically lowered if this information were publicized in advance.

Unanticipated events can also have serious implications for employee forecasting. For example, the Federal Drug Administration might ban a drug produced by a pharmaceutical company, making several hundred employees' jobs obsolete. In spite of such problems, however, employee forecasting efforts should include an organizational analysis.

Unit Employee Forecasts Unit employee forecasts are conducted by personnel representatives and managers of organizational departments. In essence, unit forecasts are based on the following four sources of departmental information:

1. *Number of employees required* in various job classifications for the next two years. This figure also must include a reasonable estimate of the overtime to be worked during the forecast period as well as estimates of employee absenteeism.[35]
2. *Estimated yearly attrition* (voluntary quits, deaths, retirements, and so forth) for which replacement is needed.
3. *Total employees needed* (attrition replacements plus expansion) for the next two years.

4. *Sources of employee replacements* (existing employees who will be upgraded, those who will transfer in from other departments or divisions, those who will return from military or educational leave, those to be recruited at the trainee level, those to be recruited at the experienced level, and so forth).

External Influences External influences include the community's labor supply and the demand by other organizations on this supply. Analyses of external variables can range from reviewing labor force projections published by the government, trade groups, and news media to conducting sophisticated statistical tests based on available data.[36] Related considerations include:

Local supply of manpower according to skill.

Local and regional unemployment trends.

Economic activity at both local and national levels.

Activity of competitors and other firms (especially where expansion or contraction is involved).

Total local and national labor force.

Educational trends.[37]

Another external influence pertains to social trends, which are often affected by various governmental activities, including legislation. One of the more widespread and publicized current social trends is equal employment opportunity for females and minorities. This trend has implications for employee forecasting,[38] particularly when affirmative action plans, discussed in Chapter 5, are involved.

Issue:

What Challenges and Prospects Are Faced by a New Personnel Function Such as Human Resource Forecasting?

Chapter 1 noted that personnel functions are often performed by a variety of participants. However, personnel representatives are often charged with planning and implementing a new personnel function or activity such as human resource forecasting. While the following discussion pertains specifically to challenges and prospects associated with human resource forecasting, it contains implications for other new personnel activities as well.

Exhibit 4.5 suggests many potential barriers to effective human resource forecasting. Such barriers can be grouped into three categories: (1) lack of clear definition and methods; (2) presence of unpredictable events that can dramatically affect forecasting efforts; and (3) inadequate attention or capability of organizational officials. Examples of the first two categories can be found earlier in the chapter; therefore, only the third will be discussed here.

Many organizations give personnel representatives major if not entire responsibility for employee forecasting efforts.[39] However, effective implementation of this function requires the active participation and cooperation of top executives and other organizational managers. These individuals are often unconcerned about employee forecasting efforts; in some cases, they even engage in counterproductive "games" such as the following:[40]

"Stone tablets," which describes the situation in which past policy decisions are not to be questioned, regardless of their applicability to current conditions.

"Empire player," the manager who spends to the limit of his or her budget—and beyond, if possible—in order to obtain larger budgets in the future.

"Musical chairs," a situation in which reorganization is used as an excuse for poor performance. Employees are moved into new and unfamiliar positions. Taking time to learn the new jobs can serve as an excuse for lowered departmental or organizational output.

These challenges should not discourage organizations from conducting employee forecasts. Indeed, this personnel function has major importance for the organization and its employees. We have previously discussed some of the many organizational advantages of employee forecasting. Employees should also benefit from the organization's ability to stabilize its job needs.

Employee forecasting therefore reflects both organizational and employee goals. An organization does not want to lose its investment in employees

Exhibit 4.5

**Practitioners' Attitudes toward
Human Resource Forecasting and Planning
Response Categories and Percentages**

Attitude Statement	Strongly Agree or Agree	Undecided	Disagree or Strongly Disagree
Human resource planning suffers from lack of understanding of what human resource planning is.	72.4%	5.7%	21.9%
Human resource planning suffers from lack of data in forecasting human resource demand and supply.	62.8	9.3	27.9
Human resource planning suffers from lack of involvement by top management.	60.9	1.1	37.9
Changes in government policy often frustrate planning efforts.	50.6	14.1	35.3
Human resource planning suffers from lack of readily applicable planning techniques.	50.6	4.6	44.8
Human resource planning suffers from non-existence of corporate plan.	45.9	8.2	45.9
Human resource planning suffers from lack of personnel qualified for planning.	42.6	8.0	49.4
Human resource planning is seen as an interference by line managers.	23.3	17.4	59.3

Note: Figures are based on responses from eighty-seven firms.
Source: Harvey Kahalas, Harold L. Pazer, John S. Hoagland, and Amy Levitt, "Human Resource Planning Activities in U.S. Firms," p. 62. Reprinted by permission of the publisher from *Human Resource Planning*, Volume 3, November 2 (1980). Copyright 1980 by The Human Resource Planning Society.

who are performing well, and employees do not want to be removed from the organization for reasons beyond their control. Challenges should not discourage forecasting efforts, particularly when the disadvantages of the alternative—no attempt at employee forecasting—are considered.

Summary

Job analysis represents the collection, ordering, and evaluation of information related to work or workers. A job analysis should clearly indicate employees' duties and responsibilities. Organizations faced with foreign and domestic competition can benefit from job analysis, which can indicate whether employees are working on necessary jobs in an efficient manner. Job analysis can also become important in complying with equal employment opportunity legislation. For example, many employment tests must be derived from a careful job analysis to ensure that the test is not discriminatory.

All job analysis methods elicit information from a source and present that information in a desired format, such as a job description or job specification. Four of the more common job analysis methods are interview, observation, questionnaire, and participant log. Job descriptions are written statements of the work activities performed on the job, including duties, responsibilities, and working conditions. Job specifications set out the qualifications necessary for adequate performance of the job. This and other information obtained through job analysis can be used in many personnel functions and activities, such as selection procedures, training, and performance appraisals.

Human resource forecasting, or employee forecasting, assesses how well utilization of employees compares with organizational objectives and what number and type of employees are needed for the organization now and in the future. This function should help the organization protect its investment in human resources and adapt to sudden technological changes.

Employee forecasting uses job analysis results, then assesses the composition of the workforce and its capability to carry out organizational objectives. Information is also obtained from top executives concerning organizational objectives and anticipated changes. Additional information (unit forecasts) gathered from department managers concerns the number of employees required in various job classifications, estimated yearly attrition, total employees needed, and sources of employee replacements. Employee forecasting also considers external conditions, which refer to the community's labor supply and the demand by other organizations on this supply.

Human resource forecasting is relatively new; therefore, few if any specific forecasting techniques have been proven applicable for all organizations. Other problems include lack of clear definition and methods; unpredictable events, which can dramatically affect forecasting efforts; and inadequate attention or capability of organizational officials. These challenges should not discourage employee forecasting efforts, since this function offers tremendous advantages to the organization.

Discussion Questions

1. Assume you are responsible for a job analysis of the position bearing the title "university professor." Which job analysis method would you use, and why? Prepare a job description for this position similar in format to Exhibit 4.4.

2. Fully explain several reasons why job analysis is important to the organization in general and to the personnel function in particular.

3. Explain specifically the contention that organizations have significant investments in human resources, and indicate the many problems organizations may face when they must lay off employees.

4. Fully discuss one step in employee forecasting—namely, determining workforce composition and capability. Indicate several problems that could occur in this step and your recommendations for minimizing these problems.

5. Explain how information obtained from executives and other departmental managers is necessary yet inconclusive in the employee forecasting function. Your answer should include a consideration of unit forecasts and managerial games.

Notes

1. Jai Ghorpade and Thomas J. Atchison, "The Concept of Job Analysis: A Review and Some Suggestions," *Public Personnel Management,* 1980, no. 3, p. 134.
2. U.S. Department of Labor, *Job Analysis for Human Resource Management: A Review of Selected Research and Development* (Washington, D.C.: Government Printing Office, 1974), p. 2.
3. Robert N. Ford, *Why Jobs Die and What to Do About It* (New York: American Management Association, 1979), p. 15.
4. "Job Analysis: A Symposium," *Employee Relations Law Journal* 4 (Spring 1979), p. 524.
5. Kirkland *v.* New York State Department of Corrections, 374 F. Supp. 1361 (S.D.N.Y.) 1974.
6. "Uniform Guidelines on Employee Selection Procedures Adopted by EEOC, Civil Service Commission, Departments of Labor and Justice," *Government Employee Relations Reporter* (Washington, D.C.: Bureau of National Affairs, 1978), p. 13. For other examples of the legal implications of job analysis techniques, see Erich P. Prien, "The Function of Job Analysis in Content Validation," *Personnel Psychology* 30 (Summer 1977), pp. 167–174; and Gerald A. Kesselman and Felix E. Lopez, "The Impact of Job Analysis on Employment Test Validation for Minority and Nonminority Accounting Personnel," *Personnel Psychology* 32 (Spring 1979), pp. 91–108.
7. Ghorpade and Atchison, "Concept of Job Analysis."
8. Howard W. Risher, "Job Analysis: A Management Perspective," *Employee Relations Law Journal* 4 (Spring 1979), p. 537.
9. Ghorpade and Atchison, "Concept of Job Analysis."
10. Bureau of Intergovernmental Personnel Programs, *Job Analysis* (Washington, D.C.: Civil Service Commission, 1973), pp. 23–27.
11. Risher, "Job Analysis," p. 537.
12. Bureau of Intergovernmental Personnel Programs, *Job Analysis.*
13. Risher, "Job Analysis."
14. Bureau of Intergovernmental Personnel Programs, *Job Analysis.*
15. Ernest J. McCormick, "Job Information: Its Development and Applications," in *Staffing Policies and Strategies,* ed. Dale Yoder and H. G. Heneman, Jr. (Washington, D.C.: Bureau of National Affairs, 1974), pp. 4–39.
16. Conrad Berenson and Henry O. Ruhnke, *Job Descriptions* (Santa Monica: Personnel Journal, 1976), pp. 13–15.
17. U.S. Department of Labor, *Job Analysis for Human Resource Management: A Review of Selected Research and Development* (Washington, D.C.: Government Printing Office, 1974), pp. 2–4.
18. Ronald A. Ash and Edward L. Levine, "A Framework for Evaluating Job Analysis Methods," *Personnel* 57 (November/December 1980), p. 58.
19. Thomasine Rendero, "Consensus: Job Analysis Practices," *Personnel* 58 (January/February 1981), pp. 4–11.
20. James W. Walker and Michael N. Wolf, "Patterns in Human Resource Planning Practices," *Human Resource Planning* 1:4 (1978), p. 191, as cited in Harvey Kahalas, Harold L. Pazer, John S. Hoagland, and Amy Levitt, "Human Resource Planning Activities in U.S. Firms," *Human Resource Planning,* 1980, no. 2, p. 53.
21. *Ibid.,* p. 64; and Charles R. Greer and Daniel Armstrong, "Human Resource Forecasting and Planning: A State-of-the-Art Investigation," *Human Resource Planning,* 1980, no. 2, p. 69.
22. For related starting points, see Richard C. Grinold and Kneale T. Marshall, *Manpower Planning Models* (New York: North-Holland, 1977); David J. Bartholomew and Andrew F. Forbes, *Statistical Techniques for Manpower Planning* (New York: John Wiley & Sons, 1979); and Herbert G. Heneman III, and Marcus G. Sandver, "Markov Analysis in Human Resource Administration: Applications and Limitations," *Academy of Management Review* 2 (October 1977), pp. 535–542.
23. R. J. Cason, "Re-Evaluating Company Manpower Planning in the Light of Some Practical Experiences," in *Manpower Planning and Organization Design,* ed. Donald T. Bryant and Richard J. Niehaus (New York: Plenum Press, 1977), p. 552.
24. *Ibid.,* pp. 556–557.
25. College Placement Council, *CPC Salary Survey: Formal Report Number 1* (January 1981), pp. 2, 8.

26. For examples of acquisition, learning, and separation costs, see Clark E. Chastain, "Evolution of Human Resource Accounting," *University of Michigan Business Review* 31 (June 1979), pp. 16–23.

27. Amanda Bennett, "Bailing Out: Many Employees Quit Jobs at Ailing Chrysler: Recovery May Suffer," *Wall Street Journal,* February 8, 1980, pp. 1, 18.

28. See, for example, Amanda Bennett, "Sad Survivors: In Auto Slump, Those Who Keep Their Jobs Often Suffer Anyway," *Wall Street Journal,* July 27, 1981, pp. 1, 12.

29. *Employment and Training Report of the President* (Washington, D.C.: Government Printing Office, 1980), p. 6.

30. Bill Roeder, "Periscope," *Newsweek,* September 14, 1981, p. 21.

31. Kahalas, Pazer, Hoagland, and Levitt, "Human Resource Planning," p. 54.

32. Glenn A. Bassett, "Elements of Manpower Forecasting and Scheduling," *Human Resource Management* 12 (Fall 1973), p. 36.

33. Eric W. Vetter, *Manpower Planning for High Talent Personnel* (Ann Arbor, Mich.: Bureau of Industrial Relations, 1967), p. 13.

34. For a further discussion of this situation, see F. James Staszak and Nicholas J. Mathys, "Organization Gap: Implications for Manpower Planning," *California Management Review* 17 (Spring 1975), pp. 32–38.

35. Bassett, "Elements of Manpower Forecasting," p. 36.

36. See, for example, Richard B. Freeman, "An Empirical Analysis of the Fixed Coefficient 'Manpower Requirements' Model, 1960–1970," *Journal of Human Resources* 15 (Winter 1980), pp. 176–199.

37. John Bramham, *Practical Manpower Planning* (London: Institute of Personnel Management, 1975), p. 81.

38. See, for example, William D. Torrence, "Manpower Planning and Reductions in Force: Competitive Status Seniority and EEOC Compliance," *Personnel Journal* 54 (May 1975), pp. 287–289; Richard J. Niehaus, *Computer-Assisted Human Resources Planning* (New York: John Wiley & Sons, 1979), pp. 56–123; A. Charnes, W. W. Cooper, K. A. Lewis, and R. J. Niehaus, "Equal Employment Opportunity: Planning and Staffing Models," *Human Resource Planning,* 1978, no. 2, pp. 103–112; and James Ledvinka and R. Lawrence LaForge, "A Staffing Model for Affirmative Action Planning," *Human Resource Planning,* 1978, no. 3, pp. 135–149.

39. Guvenc G. Alpander, "Human Resource Planning in U.S. Corporations," *California Management Review* 22 (Spring 1980), p. 97.

40. Louis Fried, "Games Managers Play," in *Organizations and Human Resources: Selected Readings,* ed. Herbert G. Hicks (New York: McGraw-Hill, 1972), pp. 292–293.

Chapter 5

Recruiting Employees

The demand seems for "instant" people in much the same way you would go to the local hardware store and order a pound each of six, eight, and ten penny nails.

Roger H. Hawk, *The Recruitment Function* (New York: American Management Association, 1967), p. 18.

Organizations must recruit potential employees to fill many of the employment openings estimated through human resource forecasting. Most readers will experience the recruiting function firsthand when they are interviewed by a company recruiter on the college campus. Once hired by an organization, many will also do some college recruiting, even if they do not work full time in the personnel department. A discussion of college recruiting can also furnish insights into the personnel department in terms of related program planning, interactions with other managers, and problems in establishing effectiveness measures.

The chapter begins by discussing two major influences on recruiting: sources of employees and affirmative action plans. Affirmative action is discussed early in the book, since it, along with other equal employment opportunity principles, affect many of the personnel functions discussed in the remainder of the book. The rest of the chapter concerns college recruiting, which is also the subject of the chapter's issue: "How can the college student improve his or her chances with the campus recruiter?"

Influences on Recruiting

Sources of New Employees

New employees can be recruited from a variety of sources, as indicated in Exhibit 5.1. A review of this exhibit suggests two general conclusions:

The most frequently used recruitment sources for each employee group are not always the most effective.

There is no clear agreement over the most effective recruiting source for any employee group.

This inconclusiveness probably reflects the notion that each recruiting source offers both advantages and disadvantages, an idea reflected in the following discussion of many of these sources. However, the personnel representative should attempt to systematically determine which recruiting source is best for employment openings at his or her organization.[1]

Internal Sources *Employees already working for the organization might refer prospective job applicants.* This source can be particularly effective if employees who are good performers make the recommendations, since people show a general tendency to make friends with people similar to them.[2] Employees tend to be selective in making recommendations, since they know the referred employee's performance will reflect on them. Applicants referred through this process tend to have a more realistic picture of the organization's strengths and weaknesses. Referrals have limitations, however. Existing employees cannot refer applicants for all positions available at any given time. Also, employees might be embarrassed, even bitter toward the organization, if their referrals do not receive employment offers.

Exhibit 5.1

**Sources Used for Recruitment by
Employee Group and Their Perceived Effectiveness**

Source	Office/ Clerical N-184	Plant/ Service N-155	Sales N-96	Employee Group Professional/ Technical N-182	Management N-181
	First number in each entry indicates percent of respondents who use source. Figure in parentheses indicates percent who consider source effective.				
Employee Referrals	92%	94%	74%	68%	65%
	(20%)	(5%)	(17%)	(67%)	(7%)
Walk-Ins	87%	92%	46%	46%	40%
	(24%)	(37%)	(5%)	(7%)	(2%)
Newspaper Advertising	68%	88%	75%	89%	82%
	(39%)	(30%)	(30%)	(38%)	(35%)
Local High Schools or Trade Schools	66%	61%	6%	27%	7%
	(2%)	(2%)	(0%)	(0%)	(0%)
U.S. Employment Service	63%	72%	34%	41%	27%
	(5%)	(6%)	(0%)	(1%)	(1%)
Community Agencies	55%	57%	22%	34%	28%
	(1%)	(3%)	(0%)	(1%)	(2%)
Private Employment Agencies	44%	11%	63%	71%	75%
	(10%)	(2%)	(23%)	(25%)	(27%)
Career Conferences/Job Fairs	19%	16%	19%	37%	17%
	(0%)	(1%)	(2%)	(2%)	(1%)
Colleges/Universities	17%	9%	48%	74%	50%
	(1%)	(1%)	(8%)	(15%)	(2%)
Advertising in Special Publications	12%	6%	43%	75%	57%
	(0%)	(0%)	(3%)	(5%)	(8%)
Professional Societies	5%	19%	17%	52%	36%
	(0%)	(1%)	(1%)	(0%)	(2%)
Radio and TV Advertising	5%	8%	2%	7%	4%
	(0%)	(1%)	(0%)	(0%)	(1%)
Search Firms	1%	2%	2%	31%	54%
	(0%)	(0%)	(2%)	(5%)	(17%)
Unions	1%	12%	0%	3%	0%
	(0%)	(2%)	(0%)	(0%)	(0%)

Note: *N* refers to number of companies. Percentages are based on number of companies providing data for each employee group. Columns may add to more than 100 percent because of multiple responses or less than 100 percent because of nonresponses.

Source: Adapted by permission from Mary Green Miner, *Personnel Policies Forum No. 126: Recruiting Policies and Practices,* July 1979, pp. 2, 5, copyright 1979 by The Bureau of National Affairs, Inc., Washington, D.C.

Labor unions, particularly in the construction industry, can represent a second internal recruiting source. This source is not commonly used in manufacturing industries, where union officers consider managers responsible for hiring decisions. Further, many managers might be suspicious of union referrals, believing such applicants to be committed to union rather than company goals.

External Sources *School referral sources* are found at many high schools and universities. These services are often used in recruiting full-time employees. In addition, many organizations use them in recruiting summer employment candidates, who eventually may become full-time employees. This strategy can be effective, since: (a) summer employees have a realistic picture of the organization when they apply for full-time employment, and (b) employers have a chance to observe summer employees' job performance before extending a permanent employment offer.

Walk-ins are applicants who apply at the organization's employment office. Many are unaware of what specific employment opportunities exist; therefore, an immediate match with available openings (both in terms of required skills and number of vacancies) is unlikely. However, this employment source is relatively inexpensive, and applications can be filed and acted upon when appropriate openings occur. This source, if handled properly, can also offer public relations advantages; walk-in applicants who are treated well will likely inform their friends and relatives, which could increase the pool of potential applicants.

Advertising through the mass media (newspapers, special publications such as trade journals, radio, television, and so on) might be used when an intense labor shortage or a critical need for certain employment openings exists. This source can save recruiting time spent by organizational members. Applicants responding to advertisements usually send resumes (summaries of educational background and work experience) to the personnel department, which sends "no interest" letters to applicants who do not meet job criteria, thereby saving interview time. Advertising is one of the more selective recruiting sources, since the employment opening is clearly indicated and individuals who respond to the advertisement should have related qualifications. However, advertising is relatively expensive and responses to it are unpredictable.

Private employment agencies and *search firms* are often used to help fill difficult positions, often at the executive level. These sources are similar, although employment agencies tend to represent the job applicant, while search firms are hired by the organization. Search firms are often more familiar with the job opening and selection standards, although they require more financial commitment from the organization, since they are often hired on a retainer basis. An employment agency, in contrast, receives a fee only when its recommended applicant is hired.[3] In many cases, these fees, for an executive, are one-third of the first year's salary.[4] In spite of their expense, use of these sources has increased sharply over the years,[5] largely because they keep applicant files more extensive than those kept by organizations and based on information from an extensive system of contacts.[6]

Public employment agencies at both the local and state level typically match job openings with a computerized listing of job applicants. They also administer various job-related tests, such as typing tests, which can serve as a useful prescreening function. Some states, such as New York, require employers to place a job order with the state agency before it is given to others. Employees may also be required to contact employers under the Vietnam Veteran Reemployment Act. A government agency cannot supply competent applicants in every case, and an employer is not required to hire an applicant from the agency.[7] However, this recruitment source charges no fee to the applicant or the employer. This advantage, coupled with various legal regulations, should result in steady, even increased, use of public employment agencies.

Leasing can be an effective method of recruiting employees for a limited project. Organizations can contact a leasing firm, which sends the required number of employees—ranging from secretaries to engineers—to complete a temporary project, usually for six months or less. Some employees like the variety of assignments offered by this situation and the possibility of earning more money than they could being employed full time by one employer.[8]

Organizations will likely pay a higher hourly rate under this arrangement; yet, this rate may be offset by reduced benefit costs. In many cases, managers have more flexibility in removing leased employees from the organization (either because of performance problems or poor business conditions). Leasing can also enable managers to examine employees on a trial basis before a permanent employment offer is extended.

Career conferences and job fairs can be arranged by either private or public organizations. Here, many organizations agree to send a recruiter to a specific place during a certain period. A large number of applicants are also invited to attend this session and informally talk about employment opportunities with a variety of company recruiters. In many ways, this recruiting source is the least predictable, which probably accounts for its low effectiveness rating in Exhibit 5.1.

Colleges and universities represent a potentially significant recruiting source; their advantages and disadvantages will be discussed later in the chapter.

Affirmative Action Plans

The influence of legislation on personnel activities has been noted in previous chapters. A variety of laws are aimed at providing equal employment opportunities to women and minorities. This situation can pose problems to the employer, as explained below:

EEO compliance efforts are made inordinately difficult by the fact that there are no less than six major federal laws related to EEO as well as various and differing state and local laws. In addition, there are numerous federal, state and local agencies which enforce these laws and these agencies frequently have varying compliance requirements.[9]

As the number of requirements has increased, so has their complexity. One author has noted that the first affirmative action decision by the Secretary of Labor focused simply on employers' intent to hire minorities, while subsequent interpretations have included sophisticated statistical analysis of minority employees.[10]

Affirmative action plans (AAPs) represent an important component (in some cases, an extension) of equal employment opportunity (EEO) laws, since these plans obligate an employer to follow certain guidelines to ensure that a balanced and representative workforce will be achieved.

Nondiscrimination alone is not affirmative action. To be truly affirmative, a company must take specific steps to remedy the present effects of past practices. . . . A company has to go out of its way to recruit, select, train and promote women, minorities, veterans, and handicapped persons until they are equitably represented in the work force. Under EEO, a company may adopt a policy of neutrality and hope or assume this will happen. Under the affirmative action guidelines, the company is required to make sure it will happen.[11]

Although not all employers are required to have AAPs, many organizations do have them, usually for one of the following three reasons:[12]

1. Employers doing business with the government at local or state levels may be required to have AAPs. Executive Orders 11246 and 11325 require all employers who have federal government contracts or subcontracts that provide $50,000 or more in a twelve-month period to have a written affirmative action program. The Office of Federal Contract Compliance Programs (OFCCP) monitors AAPs, and firms that violate the intent and/or practice of affirmative action can be barred from receiving federal contracts. At one time, the OFCCP was criticized for lax enforcement, since few companies had received its sanction.[13] Recently, however, it has become more aggressive. For example, in 1979, the OFCCP scheduled AAP audits for a large cross-section of government contractors, ranging from Disneyland to Harvard University.[14] Subsequent investigations resulted in federal contracts being withdrawn from major companies such as Prudential[15] and Uniroyal.[16]

2. Court-ordered remedies may be directed at employers found guilty of unlawful discrimination. The Equal Employment Opportunity Commission (EEOC), while often involved in employment discrimination court cases, is seldom involved in

AAP considerations. Judges, however, might order companies found guilty of employment discrimination to implement appropriate AAPs.

3. AAPs may be voluntarily implemented by employers not in the first two categories. This action might be attributed to a sense of social responsibility. It might also reflect a desire to avoid losing possible discrimination suits, since some courts have tended to regard the absence of AAPs as an indication for employment discrimination.

Affirmative action programs typically emphasize a strong organizational commitment and procedures for effectively communicating that commitment to organizational members. Such plans affect nearly all personnel activities (training, performance appraisals, wage and salary considerations, seniority systems, and so forth); these effects are discussed in subsequent chapters of this book. The following influences of AAPs on recruiting activities will be discussed in the remainder of this section:

Analysis of workforce composition.

Establishment of employment goals.

Assessment of recruiting activities.

Analysis of Workforce Composition Workforce composition must be analyzed to determine whether an organization's employment policies are discriminatory. Employers with 100 or more employees and all government contractors must file annual employment data on the following job categories: officers and managers; professionals; technicians; sales workers; office and clerical workers; craftsmen (skilled); operative (semiskilled); laborers (unskilled); and service workers. "The figures are broken down for male and female employees, for total minority employees, and for four minority groups: Black, Hispanic, Asian or Pacific Islander, American Indian or Alaskan native."[17]

These figures can reveal possible employment discrimination when minority or female employees are either *underutilized* or *concentrated* in a particular job category. A common example of underutilization is the scarcity of females and minorities among officers and managers; a concentration of female employees typically occurs in the office and clerical job category.

Deciding whether employees are underutilized or concentrated hinges on a judgment of what representation in a certain category they might reasonably be expected to have, based on their numbers in the relevant labor market. As might be expected, organizations and the courts sometimes have major differences of opinion over what might be "reasonably expected" and over what constitutes the "relevant labor market."[18] Employers often defend their workforce composition in the courts with sophisticated statistical analyses.[19]

Some organizations may be able to justify concentrations of certain employees and exclusion of others (such as females and minorities) on the basis of *bona fide occupational qualifications* (BFOQ). For example, some hospitals and universities have successfully contended in the courts that various job openings for medical technicians and professors require certain educational levels and that certain minority groups are underrepresented in these jobs because they have not proportionately attained these educational levels. Organizations do not have wide discretion in establishing BFOQs, since the EEOC and the courts have defined the concept in rather narrow terms. One airline failed to adequately demonstrate to the courts that female flight attendants were better qualified than males to minister to the "unique psychological needs of its passengers."[20] Other employers have had difficulty in establishing that female job applicants should be disqualified because of difficult lifting or other physical job requirements.

Controversy notwithstanding, workforce analysis suggests recruiting goals concerning what kinds of job applicants should be hired. This influence on recruiting activities is discussed later in the chapter.

Establishment of Employment Goals Setting goals regarding female and minority employment is at first glance a relatively straightforward affair. Employers voluntarily establish recruitment goals to correct the previously mentioned problems of underutilization or concentration. *Quotas,* on the other hand, are mandatory standards, usually imposed by the courts as a remedy for judicially determined employment discrimination.[21] Yet various forms of equal employment legislation place goals and quotas in direct conflict. Legislation and judicial orders can require that an organization set goals for hiring minorities and women while simultaneously stipulating that it offer equal employment opportunity without reference to race, color, religion, national origin, or sex. "This seems to make the creation of goals illegal if in meeting them, *preference* is to be given minorities and women."[22] Some have contended that this confusing situation has offset any potential benefit of affirmative action programs.[23] Another problem often raised in the courts is *reverse discrimination,* where female and minority applicants are selected over white males to comply with an affirmative action program.[24] The Supreme Court has approached the reverse discrimination issue in two major cases. The first case involved Allan Bakke, a white male refused admission into the University of California Medical School at Davis. The university had reserved 16 out of 100 places in each entering medical-school class for minorities. Bakke contended that this action represented reverse discrimination, since the university rated him better qualified than some of the minority applicants admitted under the special program.

The Supreme Court voted to affirm a lower-court decision ordering the medical school to admit Bakke but voted to overturn a lower-court ruling that race can't be a factor in admissions decisions.[25] One observer of civil rights legislation noted that "the Bakke case shows that it is possible for a Supreme Court decision to be highly controversial without really deciding anything."[26] Many personnel representatives believed that the Bakke decision would have little or no effect on company-sponsored affirmative action plans.

More direct judicial implications were found in the 1979 Supreme Court decision *Steelworkers* v. *Weber et al.*, which involved an AAP negotiated by the United Steelworkers of America (USWA) and Kaiser Aluminum and Chemical Corporation in 1974. A portion of this AAP concerned a program to train production workers to fill craft openings. Trainees were chosen on the basis of seniority, but at least 50 percent were to be black until workforce composition in those job categories approximated that of the local labor force. Mr. Weber, a white employee, was not allowed into the training program, although minority employees with less seniority were admitted. He contended this practice discriminated against white employees.

The Supreme Court disagreed with Weber, ruling that an employer can voluntarily institute programs to remedy past injustices to minorities in traditionally segregated areas of the workforce even if the programs adversely affect nonminority employees. The Court did not specifically distinguish the line of demarcation between permissible and impermissible affirmative action plans, although it noted that Kaiser's AAP was permissible in part for the following reasons:

[The plan] does not unnecessarily trammel the interests of white employees, neither requiring the discharge of white workers and their replacement with new black hires, nor creating an absolute bar to the advancement of white employees since half of those trained in the program will be white. Moreover, the plan is a temporary measure, not intended to maintain racial balance, but simply to eliminate a manifest racial imbalance.[27]

Thus, nonminority employees might have to endure temporary, but not too severe, setbacks in their employment.

Two implications of this decision are that it will probably reduce reverse discrimination suits[28] and that it will probably have limited practical impact on AAPs.[29] However, employers cannot totally disregard Weber in AAP formulation. Economic recessions might make layoffs necessary;[30] and it is uncertain how the Weber decision should be applied to layoff decisions, since the Court indicated that AAPs could not force white employees to pay too high a price, such as give up their jobs to minority employees who have less seniority with the company.[31]

Assessment of Recruiting Activities Recruiting activities must be assessed to ensure that adequate numbers of female and minority candidates are hired to comply with the employer's AAP. Two general approaches to this task are *avoiding a variety of discriminatory recruiting activities* and *making concentrated efforts to locate minority employees.* Examples of the first approach include the following:

Not having improperly trained recruiters or interviewers who exhibit bias against females or minorities in the initial recruiting interview.[32]

Not turning away female or minority job applicants for fraudulent reasons (for example, indicating there is no job opening when there is).

Not relying on recruiting sources that are discriminatory in results if not in intent. Two such sources are referrals from present employees—if the employer's workforce is predominantly white males—and employment agencies that do not have an adequate base of minority applicants.[33]

The second approach is marked by imagination and activity. Extensive efforts must be made to communicate job vacancies to the female and minority community. Related activities could include establishing employment offices in predominantly minority areas, conducting job fairs sponsored by community agencies or schools, and placing ads in newspapers, magazines, radio stations, and so forth that cater predominantly to the female or minority market. To be effective, such activities require much time and decision making. For example, placing advertisements in minority publications at first glance seems like a straightforward task. However, one book lists nearly 100 periodicals with a predominantly black audience.[34]

Many affirmative action activities yield impressive but not immediate results. The coordinated efforts of many companies to increase the number of black engineers is a case in point. Related activities include engineering orientation sessions with high-school students, summer employment programs, and financial aid incentives to engineering schools. These efforts have no doubt contributed to the increase in black engineering graduates; for example, the proportion of bachelor's degrees from engineering schools awarded to minority students increased from 2.9 percent in 1973 to 4.1 percent in June 1980.[35]

Recruiting practices can include more than attracting minority applicants to the company. Affirmative action activities can also affect newly hired employees. Such activities include:

Explanation of tuition refund and training programs during the new employee orientation procedure.

Institution or support of a transportation or car-pooling service if the employer's facility is not adequately served by public transportation.

Institution of a job rotation program in an effort to broaden employees' work skills.[36]

College Recruiting

Establishing and Maintaining a College Recruiting Program

Establishing and maintaining a college recruiting program is a difficult and time-consuming task. Three main considerations are involved: determining the number of new college graduates to be hired, selecting and scheduling universities, and selecting and training recruiters.

Number of New Graduates to Be Hired The number of new college graduates to be hired is largely determined by employee forecasting estimates and the extent to which other recruiting sources, such as advertising and employment agencies, will be used to fill positions. The recruiting department must obtain this information well in advance so that campus interviews will yield an appropriate number of candidates. Of course, interviews with several students are needed to fill a single position. Recruitment planners must establish an applicant base much larger than the number of employees to be hired (see Exhibit 5.2). This base is usually estimated from the company's past experiences or, if the recruiting function is new, from experiences of other companies.

Selecting and Scheduling Universities The second consideration, selecting and scheduling universities is affected by the number of employees to be hired plus other considerations. When a college recruiting program is starting up, universities are often selected on the basis of academic reputation, recommendations of other managers and executives (who usually suggest their alma maters), and ability to get on the recruiting schedule (a problem at some of the more popular schools, which have three-year waiting periods for companies that have not previously recruited there). These considerations seldom are successful; for example, many companies that recruit at "prestige" schools find it difficult to hire graduates there because of intense competition. It is also difficult to convince students at universities in some regions (say California, Arizona, or Florida) that they would benefit from working in a different, unfamiliar locale (say, Anchorage, Alaska). For these and other reasons—transportation costs, for example—some companies limit their recruiting schedules to nearby colleges or to colleges that have programs (such as in welding or packaging engineering) suited to their employment needs.

Exhibit 5.2   **Campus Recruiting Yield Pyramid for XYZ Company**

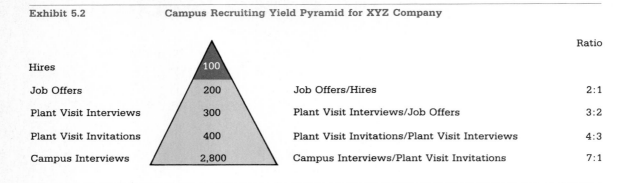

		Ratio
Hires	100	
Job Offers	200	Job Offers/Hires	2:1
Plant Visit Interviews	300	Plant Visit Interviews/Job Offers	3:2
Plant Visit Invitations	400	Plant Visit Invitations/Plant Visit Interviews	4:3
Campus Interviews	2,800	Campus Interviews/Plant Visit Invitations	7:1

Affirmative action requirements might also affect selection. The Equal Employment Opportunity Commission recently stated: "The identification by race and sex of minority and female students for the purpose of referring only such students to an employer would constitute discriminatory action."[37] Consequently, placement officials at universities cannot "earmark" certain minority candidates for employer attention, and employers may need to recruit at universities that have large numbers of minority students.

Regardless of the selection criteria used, many college recruiting managers have learned to avoid including too many universities on their recruiting schedule and instead perform a thorough job at a limited number of schools that have proven themselves productive.[38]

Selecting and Training Recruiters A third consideration involves selecting and training college recruiters. Personnel representatives are usually involved in college recruiting activities, although other organizational members (managers of sales, production, accounting, and other functions) often visit two or three colleges a year to interview prospects for specialized positions.

College recruiters, regardless of their backgrounds, must be prepared for their campus visits. Training programs include video tapes of practice interviews, role-playing workshops, seminars, and on-the-job training (participating in campus interviews with experienced campus interviewers). Recruiters should find out how the job to be filled fits into the overall operation of the company and the types of problems to be solved, decisions to be made, and projects to be undertaken by the person filling the position. The recruiter should also meet with the line supervisor to determine required and preferred job qualifications from which interview questions can be designed.[39]

Planning and establishing the recruiting function requires many other efforts, such as designing recruiting literature, following up recruiter recommendations, monitoring recruiting (and recruiter) effectiveness, and so forth.

Campus Recruiting Activities

Campus recruiting activities include prescreening, campus interviews, and post-interview activities. These activities result in the companies and the applicants determining together the suitability of the applicant for the job.

Prescreening Prescreening, a campus visit by a company representative in advance of the scheduled recruiting trip, is intended to uncover and encourage qualified applicants to sign the company's interview schedule. Related activities include examining graduating students' resumes at the placement office and obtaining professors' opinions of various graduating students. Prescreening expenses may be justified, since, if appropriate students do not sign up on the interview schedule, then subsequent recruiting activities at that university grind to a halt, a particularly serious situation if the company visits that campus only once a year.

Prescreening's success is not guaranteed, however. The Educational Rights and Privacy Act has given students access to their academic files, including job references written by college professors. Some professors, fearing legal suits, are less than candid in their remarks (for example, they overstate students' positive qualities and fail to mention negative qualities).[40] Such lack of candor would, of course, minimize the effectiveness of a prescreening visit.

Campus Interviews The campus interview is often a hectic affair, particularly when as many as twenty students are on the college recruiter's daily interview schedule. With so many students on the recruiting schedule, the interview is usually limited to a half-hour, from which ten minutes are usually deducted from time actually spent interviewing (for example, five minutes of "small talk" at the beginning of the interview to put the applicant at ease and five minutes at the end of the interview for the recruiter to evaluate the applicant). Twenty minutes is a very short period in which to sell the company and evaluate the applicant.

The short interview places an equally difficult burden on the applicant. The applicant's difficulties increase when recruiters use the *negative, or knockout, interview approach,* described below by two college recruiters:

Each campus interview is a series of decisions that I make during the progress of the interview. I may knock out of consideration a young man when he first walks in the door, or I may be impressed favorably. If I'm impressed favorably, I'll look further at his résumé. If this looks good, I'll go on to asking him about his interests, and so on. At any stage of the interview I may find that the things I'd discovered up to then were offset by some other facts which are so negative we couldn't fit him into our organization. When I make this discovery I begin backing away from any evidence of enthusiasm as gracefully as possible.

Campus interviewing is really just a series of steps which try to discover major flaws or "knockout blows" on the candidate. If you don't find any, you invite him in for further talks. If you find them, that's it then and there, except you aren't too abrupt about it.[41]

One author has suggested several possible reasons for the knockout interviewing approach, including the following:[42]

Interviewers are cost oriented and believe hiring an incompetent person costs more than occasionally overlooking a qualified person.

Some jobs are easily performed by a large percentage of candidates. The recruiter needs some way to reject candidates, even through small negative facts.

Recruiters often receive criticism when they have suggested employees who turn out to be unsuccessful in the organization. Recruiters are therefore more sensitive to negative than positive characteristics.

In a short interview, it is easier and perhaps more efficient for the recruiter to uncover applicants' flaws than to establish and develop their strong points. However, this practice shifts the burden to the applicant, who typically has to demonstrate why he or she is an outstanding prospect. (Ways the college student can deal with this situation are discussed in this chapter's issue.)

Post-Interview Activities After the campus interview, the recruiter must evaluate the interviewed student. Recruiters seldom have the authority to extend a plant visit invitation, much less a job offer, to students during the campus interview. They do have significant authority in a negative sense; that is, they determine which students will not go any further in the college recruiting procedure.

Assuming the company is interested in an interviewed student, the next step in most cases is an invitation to the applicant to make an expense-paid visit to the company's facilities. These visits vary widely in format; however, they typically include:

A plant tour, in which the applicant is given an extensive look at the company's facilities and operations.

Several individual interviews with the applicant's prospective boss and work associates.

An extended lunch, allowing the applicant to obtain informal insights into the company's objectives and personnel.

An interview with a personnel representative, who answers questions the applicant might have regarding company policies such as career progression and company benefits.

After the visit, company representatives meet to determine whether the applicant should be extended a job offer. An affirmative decision does not always result in that applicant being hired, however, since the applicant may decline the job offer.

Policy Issues Involved in College Recruiting Programs

College recruiting activities, like other personnel activities, are strongly influenced by policy considerations. Three such considerations include: the need for a college recruiting program; selection criteria used by campus recruiters; and evaluation of the recruiting program's effectiveness.

Need for a College Recruiting Program Companies should consider the relative merits and problems of a college recruiting program before commiting necessary funds. College recruiting offers a useful and continuous source of applicants, and recruited students often bring current academic knowledge and enthusiasm to the job. College recruiting does have its disadvantages, however; the turnover of college graduates in industry averages 50 percent during the first three years of employment and 75 percent in the first five years.[43] Some managers might contend that these statistics reflect problems in college recruiting or unrealistic job expectations in the college graduate. Some companies might divert time and expenses to other recruiting sources that attract employment candidates who have had their unrealistic expectations blunted by a few years of industrial experience.

If the organization decides to become involved with college recruiting, it must consider the total expenditures needed for the program's effective implementation. The recruiting procedure has been described here in relatively simple terms: visiting a college campus once or twice a year and following up on prospective applicants with job offers when appropriate. This approach to college recruiting may be sufficient for filling many employment openings, particularly when student applicants are abundant. Some companies may, however, experience shortages of applicants in certain areas, such as specialized engineering graduates,[44] minority graduates, or Master of Business Administration (MBA) graduates.[45]

Recruiting for these positions usually requires more than intermittent campus visits; often, an extensive *college relations program* at selected universities is needed. College relations programs include campus recruiting activities but are much broader in scope. Their objectives are to provide a continuous relationship between company officials and university members such as students, placement officers, and professors. These objectives are often accomplished through one or more of the following activities:[46]

Lectures presented by company officials to campus organizations.

Donations of company equipment for use in engineering or science laboratories.

Social visits between professors and placement officers on occasions other than recruiting trips.

Invitations to professors and their classes to visit nearby company facilities.

Another significant college relations activity is *co-op education,* whereby a student might, say, work a semester, then attend classes for a semester. The student receives several advantages, including income to subsidize educational expenses. He or she can also benefit from the blend of academic principles and industrial experience. In addition, the student is better prepared to judge employment offers upon graduation (even a bad co-op experience can teach the student to avoid certain entry-level positions).

Selection Criteria The abilities college recruiters look for in interviews can be grouped under the following general categories:

Job knowledge and related technical skills.

Interpersonal abilities to get along, motivate, and work with people.

Desirable work characteristics such as assumption of responsibility, imagination, flexibility, dependability, and stability under pressure.

These abilities are typically inferred from selection criteria such as those in Exhibit 5.3. These factors, derived from past performance, are considered important because "The single most important indicator of how an employee will perform in the future appears to be how he or she has performed in the past."[47]

The exhibit suggests that, at least in terms of weighted averages, no criteria are clearly agreed upon as most important. This lack of agreement is caused in part by differences in the way recruiters define criteria and perceive their relative importance. Consider, for example, the criterion related to personal appearance. This criterion includes physical mannerisms such as nervousness. Some recruiters regard a nerv-

Exhibit 5.3   **Criteria Used to Evaluate College Graduates**

Criterion	Percent of Respondents Who Rank Criterion Number 1	Weighted Average
Interest in Job and Company	26	4.0
Previous Work Experience	21	4.5
Work Motivation	19	4.1
College Grades	10	6.1
Maturity	8	4.5
Personal Achievements	6	5.9
Personality	5	6.1
Oral Expression	2	6.4
Future Career Goals	2	6.9
Test Scores	2	10.3
Appearance	0	7.9
Extracurricular Activities	0	9.5

Note: Results are based on responses from 188 personnel executives who were asked to rank the criteria from 1 (most important) to 12 (least important). The lower the weighted average, the higher the average ranking.

Source: Adapted by permission from Mary Green Miner, *Personnel Policies Forum No. 126: Recruiting Policies and Practices,* July 1979, p. 14, Copyright 1979 by The Bureau of National Affairs, Inc., Washington, D.C.

ous applicant negatively, while others see nervousness as a positive sign that indicates the student really wants a job with the company. Recruiters in each company need to reach some consensus on the definition and priority of recruiting criteria.

One important evaluation criterion pertains to grades. Consider, for example, two inescapable attributes of a straight-A student. This person might not be extremely intelligent, highly motivated, or even hard working. However, he or she has *identified what each professor expects* and has *delivered it in outstanding fashion.* These qualities are, of course, applicable and desirable in most employment positions. Recruiters also look for trends in grade point averages (for example, higher grades in the junior and senior years than in the freshman and sophomore years) and for high grades in certain courses strongly related to the employment opening. Applicants' abilities (job knowledge, interpersonal skills, and work characteristics) can also be specifically illustrated in many other recruiting criteria in Exhibit 5.3, such as previous work experience, extracurricular activities, personal achievements, and test scores.

Evaluation of the Recruiting Program's Effectiveness Problems for personnel representatives and related effectiveness measures for their activities have been mentioned in Chapter 1 and can be further illustrated here. Consider the following recruiting effectiveness ratios:

1. Plant visit acceptances compared with plant visit invitations.
2. Job offers extended to applicants compared with applicant plant visits.

3. Job offers accepted by applicants compared with job offers extended to applicants.

While each of these effectiveness measures seems to make sense, each involves difficulties for the college recruiter. The first ratio is easiest for the recruiter to meet, particularly if he or she oversells job opportunities or the attractiveness of the plant visit location to the student. And recruiters would no doubt contend that this ratio is a most valid measure of their effectiveness, since only candidates who visit the plant location can receive job offers. "People we have been unable to attract will never be viable contenders, no matter how desirable they may be."[48] A recruiter who has only 25 percent of his or her recommended applicants accept plant visit invitations is probably neither conveying a favorable impression nor adequately selling the organization and its job potential.

College recruiters assume more accountability when the second effectiveness measure, the ratio of job offers to plant visits, is used. This measure includes recruiters' job-selling skills as well as their ability to successfully match job requirements with available applicants. However, a job recruiter held accountable for this measure might become over-cautious, inviting only exceptional candidates. Such candidates may receive offers from several organizations, thereby reducing the chance that a particular organization will be able to hire them.

Other managers believe that the third recruiting effectiveness measure, the ratio of acceptances to offers, is best, since the purpose of college recruiting is to fill employment vacancies. College recruiters would raise objections to being held accountable for this measure, since they had only a half-hour with the applicant while management officials had some eight hours during the location visit to persuade the applicant to join the organization.

Some contend that all these recruiting effectiveness measures are too narrow. They believe a broader and more realistic perspective includes not only attracting and selecting competent newcomers but managing to *retain* them as well. Under this approach, successful recruiting occurs only when the college applicant remains with the firm for a period of time (say, five years) and performs well in assigned jobs. This method of assessing effectiveness could include several measures pertaining to job satisfaction, organizational commitment, absenteeism, and voluntary turnover.[49] Though this method appears sound, college recruiters might contend that holding them accountable for such results would be impractical. Controversy notwithstanding, some effort must be made to evaluate whether college recruiting activities justify their costs, which include direct costs such as travel and indirect costs such as recruiters' and managers' pay for time spent interviewing.[50]

Issue:

How Can the College Student Improve His or Her Chances with the Campus Recruiter?

Many readers may find the question of how to deal with the campus recruiter the most significant issue discussed in this book. The campus recruiting schedule has already been described as a hectic affair for recruiter and student alike, since eighteen or more students may be interviewed in an eight- or nine-hour period. As noted earlier, further complications occur when the campus recruiter uses the knockout approach.

To deal with this situation, *a college student must successfully differentiate himself or herself from the other students interviewed by the campus recruiter*. However, this task is not easily accomplished. Successful differentiation is related to several considerations:

1. Making Efficient Use of Scarce Interview Time The ability to use time efficiently improves with experience; so a student is well advised to sign up for as many interviews as possible. Experience also enables the student to anticipate a wide variety of recruiters' questions, some of which are presented below:

What do you consider a fair starting salary?

What are your strengths and weaknesses?

Where do you expect to be in an organization five years from now?

Which courses did you like most and least? Why?

How did you become interested in our company?

Explain how your campus activities and summer work experience have prepared you for your career in _____?

When do you anticipate having children?

Students might believe, with some justification, that some of these questions are unfair or even illegal. However, their responses to such questions can strongly affect recruiters' evaluations.

At the same time recruiters are evaluating applicants, applicants must attempt to assess potential employers. Students should enter the interview with several questions such as the following:

What are the specific responsibilities of the job for which I am being interviewed?

What qualifications, education, ability, and interests are considered necessary to do the job satisfactorily?

Where is the job site located?

Does the job require travel; if so, how much?

What is the general salary range for the job?

What are my future career opportunities with the company?

Does the company promote from within?

What professional and management development assistance does the company provide?

Does the company provide opportunities to gain broad professional and managerial experience in several functions and locations?

What advanced degree or specialized education does the company consider important for my future progress?[51]

2. Researching the Company to Be Interviewed Recruiters, like all of us, are egotistical to some degree. They like to think that applicants have spent time researching the company (after all, they have spent time traveling to the campus).

There is one thing that charms a corporate recruiter as nothing else: an intelligent interest in his company. An enthusiastic "I've always wanted to work for Exxon" doesn't carry much weight (especially when, as happened last year, the recruiter works for Mobil). But the M.B.A. who has tutored himself or herself in the company's strengths or even better, weaknesses, generally gets an express ticket to see the brass at headquarters.[52]

Information on most companies can be found in such financial directories as Standard and Poor's, Dun and Bradstreet, Moodys, and Value Line, which can be found in university libraries. The student should also read the company's recruiting material, which can be found in the college placement office.

A student unfamiliar with the organization's products or services makes a poor impression:

When I was a recruiter for a manufacturer of large motors, I interviewed hundreds of people in such fields as accounting, personnel, sales, and data processing. Often an interview would be going along smoothly and then, halfway through, the candidate would hit me with "What do you make?" It always floored me.

[The employment lobby was full of company literature, and my office was next to the manufacturing area.] If [the candidate] came through the plant to get to my office, as some candidates did, he could see blue curls and steel from milling machines and shavers all over the place. Obviously it wasn't a dairy, but whenever a candidate asked what was made, I always had a sadistic urge to answer "ice cream," and follow that up with "Figure that out, imbecile."[53]

3. Articulating Goals and Explaining How Educational Background and Work Experience Correspond to the Employment Opening Many students do not clearly communicate to the recruiter what job responsibilities and activities they want. When asked to describe an ideal position, they respond with vague answers such as "management with responsible and challenging activities" or "opportunity to enter a sales, accounting, or production training program." Recruiters faced with these answers often conclude that the college student has no idea what he or she wants to do and therefore will be unable to earn his or her salary, at least in the short run.

Students who have a clear idea of their short-run job objectives will be viewed favorably, particularly if they show how their activities and part-time work experiences logically support their objectives. Many college recruiters who have nontechnical backgrounds ask engineering graduates to describe their senior engineering projects; students who can explain these projects in understandable and enthusiastic terms are viewed favorably by recruiters.

Recruiters are a varied bunch of individuals; what pleases one recruiter might be viewed as a knockout factor by another. Applicants can learn from unsuccessful interviews; however, they can also do themselves a disservice if they regard these interviews as failures and try to become all things to all people.

Summary

Employees can be recruited from a wide variety of internal and external sources, such as employee referrals, labor unions, school referrals, walk-ins, advertising, employment agencies, and leasing. There is little agreement over the relative effectiveness of these sources; each has unique advantages and disadvantages that depend on the particular position to be filled.

Equal employment opportunity legislation has influenced recruiting, since organizations are charged with taking affirmative action to ensure that minorities and females are employed at all organizational levels. These legal requirements suggest that the organization's workforce should be analyzed to determine if female and minority employees are either underutilized or concentrated in a particular job category. Such situations might have to be corrected through recruiting efforts, which in some cases could legally exclude white male employees. Organizations have to eliminate discriminatory recruiting practices and take specific steps such as recruiting at schools and advertising in publications that give access to the female and minority community.

A college recruiting program involves the following considerations: the number of new college graduates to be hired by the company; the selection and scheduling of universities; and the selection and training of campus recruiters. Campus recruiting activities include prescreening, campus interviews, and location visits. These activities result in the company and the applicant deciding whether the applicant is suitable for the job vacancy.

College recruiting, like other personnel functions, is influenced by policy considerations. A first consideration pertains to the need for a college recruiting program. Some organizations might not have such a program, believing that other recruiting sources are more effective. Some, on the other hand, have determined that college relations activities are worth the added expense, since these activities provide a continuous relationship between company officials and members of the university community. Remaining policy considerations pertain to criteria used in evaluating students and effectiveness measures to evaluate the success of the college recruiting program.

Discussion Questions

1. Assume you need to recruit a production engineer (undergraduate degree in mechanical engineering with at least three years' industrial experience in resolving mechanical problems with equipment used to manufacture a product). Briefly define three possible recruiting sources. Also explain why one of your recruiting sources would be better than the others in this situation. (Your answer should indicate the relative advantages and disadvantages of each source.)

2. Explain how equal employment opportunity legislation and the concept of affirmative action can have specific implications for the employee recruiting function and related activities.

3. Define *reverse discrimination* and describe its status today in light of the Bakke and Weber Supreme Court decisions.

4. Define the following terms: *prescreening, college relations,* and *knockout approach*. Explain the relationship of these concepts to the college recruiting program.

5. "The effectiveness of the college recruiting program is easily determined; simply count the number of college students who were recruited into the organization during the year." Assess the validity of this statement, describing a variety of recruiting effectiveness measures and the controversies they can cause between personnel representatives and other organizational members.

6. Assume you are one of two students on a campus recruiter's

interview schedule. Both of you have the same academic major and grade point average. Based on the recruiter selection criteria and the issue discussed in this chapter, develop a complete strategy for increasing your chances to be selected over the other student.

Notes

1. For an example of this verification effort, see James E. Breaugh, "Relationships between Recruiting Sources and Employee Performance, Absenteeism, and Work Attitudes," *Academy of Management Journal* 24 (March 1981), p. 145.

2. Laurence Lipsett, Frank P. Rodgers, and Harold M. Kenter, *Personnel Selection and Recruitment* (Corvallis, Oregon: Continuing Education Book, 1972), p. 18.

3. Wayne J. Bjerregaard and Mark E. Gold, "Employment Agencies and Executive Recruiters: A Practical Approach," *Personnel Administrator* 26 (May 1981), p. 129.

4. Herbert E. Meyer, "Headhunters Cast a Wider Net," *Fortune,* September 15, 1981, p. 66.

5. Bjerregaard and Gold, "Employment Agencies," p. 127.

6. Richard R. Conarroe, *Executive Search* (New York: Van Nostrand Reinhold, 1976), pp. 29–30.

7. Ruth W. Stidger, *The Competence Game: How to Find, Use, and Keep Competent Employees* (New York: Thomond Press, 1980), p. 16.

8. "Labor Letter," *Wall Street Journal,* October 28, 1980, p. 1.

9. James M. Higgins, "A Manager's Guide to the Equal Employment Opportunity Laws," *Personnel Journal,* 55 (August 1976), p. 406.

10. Arthur B. Smith, Jr., "The Law and Equal Employment Opportunity: What's Past Should Not Be Prologue," *Industrial and Labor Relations Review* 33 (July 1980), p. 502.

11. Francine S. Hall and Maryann H. Albrecht, *The Management of Affirmative Action* (Santa Monica, Calif.: Goodyear Publishing, 1979), p. 26.

12. Richard Peres, *Dealing with Employment Discrimination* (New York: McGraw-Hill, 1978), p. 142.

13. See, for example, James C. Hyatt, "Toothless Tiger? All Sides Criticize Law Barring Job Bias by Federal Contractors," *Wall Street Journal,* November 11, 1975, pp. 1, 35.

14. Bureau of National Affairs, *Daily Labor Report,* November 23, 1979, p. 3.

15. "Labor Agency Blocks Prudential from U.S. Work," *Wall Street Journal,* July 29, 1980, p. 4.

16. Bureau of National Affairs, *Daily Labor Report,* April 16, 1980, p. 2.

17. Mary Green Miner and John B. Miner, *Employee Selection within the Law,* (Washington, D.C.: Bureau of National Affairs, 1978), p. 62. See also James M. Higgins, "The Complicated Process of Establishing Goals for Equal Employment," *Personnel Journal* 54 (December 1975), pp. 631–637.

18. Howard R. Bloch and Robert L. Pennington, "Measuring Discrimination: What Is a Relevant Labor Market?," *Personnel* 57 (July/August 1980), pp. 21–29.

19. See, for example, Michael O. Finkelstein, "The Judicial Reception of Multiple Regression Studies in Race and Sex Discrimination Cases," *Columbia Law Review* 80 (May 1980), pp. 737–754; Edward L. Bode, "Auditing Affirmative Action through Multiple Regression Analysis," *Labor Law Journal* 31 (February 1980), pp. 115–117; John S. Grady, "Statistics in Employment Discrimination," *Labor Law Journal* 30 (December 1979), pp. 748–753; and J. P. McGuire, "The Use of Statistics in Title VII Cases," *Labor Law Journal* 30 (June 1979), pp. 361–371.

20. For a more complete discussion of this topic, see Frederick S. Hills, "Job Relatedness vs. Adverse Impact in Personnel Decision Making," *Personnel Journal* 59 (March 1980), pp. 211–215, 229.

21. James Ledvinka, "Goals or Quotas? Numerical Hiring Standards in Equal Employment Law," *Interchange* 2 (Fall 1974), p. 1.

22. Clement J. Berkowitz, *The Job Analysis Approach to Affirmative Action* (New York: John Wiley & Sons, 1975), p. 8. See also G. C. Pati and P. E. Fahey, "Affirmative Action Program: Its Realities and Challenges," *Labor Law Journal* 24 (June 1973), p. 353.

23. See, for example, Thomas Sowell, "A Dissenting Opinion about Affirmative Action," *Across the Board* 13 (January 1981), pp. 64–72; and Butler D. Shaffer and J. Brad Chapman, "Hiring Quotas—Will They Work?," *Labor Law Journal* 26 (March 1975), pp. 152–162. For a review of the literature concerning controversial dimensions of affirmative action programs, see Nijole V. Benokraitis and Joe R. Feagin, *Affirmative Action and Equal Opportunity: Action, Inaction, and Reaction,* (Boulder: Westview Press, 1978), pp. 172–191.

24. See for example, Gopal C. Pati and Charles W. Reilly, "Reversing Discrimination: A Perspective," *Labor Law Journal* 24 (January 1978), pp. 9–25; and Judith M. Janssen, "The Use of Racial Preferences in Employment: The Affirmative Action/Reverse Discrimination Dilemma," *Vanderbilt Law Review* 32 (April 1979), pp. 783–818.

25. Laurence H. Tribe, "Perspectives on Bakke: Equal Protection, Procedural Fairness, or Structural Justice?" *Harvard Law Review* 92 (February 1979), pp. 864–877.

26. Thomas Sowell, "Racism, Quotas and the Front Door," *Wall Street Journal,* July 28, 1978, p. 8.

27. Bureau of National Affairs, *Daily Labor Report,* June 27, 1979, p. D-1.

28. See, for example, "Address by Professor Alfred W. Blumrosen Analyzing Supreme Court Decision in Weber *v.* Kaiser Aluminum," in Bureau of National Affairs, *Daily Labor Report,* July 2, 1979, pp. F-1–F-4; and George P. Sape, "Use of Quotas after Weber," *Employee Relations Law Journal* 6 (Autumn 1980), p. 239.

29. See, for example, Bureau of National Affairs, *Daily Labor Report,* April 2, 1979, pp. 2–3.

30. See, for example, Amal Nag, "Slipping Back: Recession Threatens to Erode Job Gains of Women, Minorities," *Wall Street Journal,* January 7, 1980, pp. 1, 14.

31. Burt Neuborne, "Observations on Weber," *New York University Law Review* 54 (June 1979), pp. 546–559.

32. See, for example, Benson Rosen and Thomas H. Jerdee, "Effects of Applicants' Sex and Difficulty of Job on Evaluations of Candidates for Managerial Positions," *Journal of Applied Psychology,* no. 4, 1974, pp. 511–512; and Stephen L. Cohen and Kerry A. Bunker, "Subtle Effects of Sex Role Stereotypes on Recruiters' Hiring Decisions," *Journal of Applied Psychology,* no. 5, 1975, pp. 566–572.

33. Alfred W. Blumrosen, *Black Employment and the Law* (New Brunswick, N.J.: Rutgers University Press, 1971), p. 239.

34. Robert Calvert, Jr., *Equal Employment Opportunity for Minority Group College Graduates: Locating, Recruiting, Employing* (Garrett Park, Md.: Garrett Park Press, 1972), pp. 109–114.

35. "Labor Letter," *Wall Street Journal,* April 14, 1981, p. 1. See also "A Push for Black Engineers," *Business Week,* February 14, 1977, pp. 124–129.

36. Kenneth E. Marino, "Conducting an Internal Compliance Review of Affirmative Action," *Personnel* 57 (March/April 1980), p. 29.

37. Stephen J. Wilhelm, "Is On-Campus Recruiting on Its Way Out?" *Personnel Journal* 59 (August 1980), pp. 302–303.

38. Richard L. Brecker, "10 Common Mistakes in College Recruiting—Or How to Try without Really Succeeding," *Personnel* 52 (March 1975), p. 23.

39. Dawn C. Holinbonich, "Current Issues in College Recruiting" (Unpublished paper), p. 2.

40. Liz Roman Gallese, "Campus Concern: Student Job Referrals Hit Snags, Due to a Privacy Law," *Wall Street Journal,* January 14, 1977, p. 1, 16.

41. George S. Ordiorne and Arthur S. Hann, *Effective College Recruiting* (Ann Arbor: Bureau of Industrial Relations, University of Michigan, 1961), p. 123.

42. John P. Wanous, *Organizational Entry* (Reading, Mass.: Addison-Wesley, 1980), p. 109.

43. B. Scanlon, "Some Further Views on Changes in Hiring Practices: The Last Decade," *Personnel Journal* 59 (June 1980), p. 480. For related insights, see Charles A. O'Reilly III, and David F. Caldwell, "The Commitment and Job Tenure of New Employees: Some Evidence of Postdecisional Justification," *Administrative Science Quarterly* 26 (December 1981), pp. 597–616.

44. F. Brendler, "College Recruiting Practices,"*Personnel* 56 (March/April 1979), pp. 4–12.

45. Charles W. Stevens, "Sitting Pretty: Job Offers are Lavish in Competition to Hire Business-School Grads," *Wall Street Journal,* February 11, 1980, pp. 1, 25. More recently, there have been fewer openings for MBAs; see, for example, John Curley, "New MBAs Are Scrambling for Jobs as Recession Brings Drop in Hiring," Wall Street Journal, March 8, 1982, p. 29.

46. For examples of company college relations programs, see: "GM's Earnest Effort to Recruit," *Business Week,* December 4, 1978, p. 114; and Warren D. Robb, "How's Your CRP?," *Personnel Administrator* 25 (June 1980), pp. 101–106.

47. Arthur A. Witkin, "Commonly Overlooked Dimensions of Employee Selection," *Personnel Journal* 59 (July 1980), p. 573.

48. Erwin S. Stanton, *Successful Personnel Recruiting and Selection* (New York: American Management Association, AMACOM, 1977), p. 49.

49. Wanous, *Organizational Entry,* pp. 38, 45.

50. David L. Chicci and Carl M. Knapp, "College Recruitment from Start to Finish," *Personnel Journal* 59 (August 1980), p. 657.

51. Howard M. Mitchell, "What Should You Ask the Company Interviewer?" *S.A.M. Advanced Management Journal* 41–42 (Winter 1977), pp. 59–61.

52. Sam Andrews, "How to Charm the Campus Recruiter," *MBA* 8 (November 1974), p. 50.

53. Reprinted from *Job Hunting Secrets and Tactics,* p. 130, by Kirby W. Stanat with Patrick Reardon by permission of Westwind Press, a division of Raintree Publishers, Inc. Text copyright © 1977, Kirby Stanat and Patrick Reardon.

Chapter 6

Staffing from Outside the Organization

Companies can no longer afford the luxury of making poor personnel selection decisions. Organizational goals are clearly affected every time a personnel selection decision is made. . . . Maximizing the effectiveness of these decisions directly affects training time, turnover, absenteeism, safety, and satisfaction—in addition to job performance.

Elliott Pursell, Michael A. Campion, and Sarah R. Gaylord, "Structured Interviewing: Avoiding Selection Problems," *Personnel Journal* 59 (November 1980), p. 907.

Every organization ultimately depends on the skills and abilities of its employees. Staffing, which includes all the methods of matching skills with tasks (selection, placement, promotion, transfer, and the like), plays a key role in determining whether the organization will be effective. The concept of staffing is based on the fact that individuals differ in how they can perform various jobs. Employers, in striving to achieve organizational objectives, seek to employ or promote individuals who will perform most effectively in their jobs and reject those who are less likely to perform effectively.[1]

Staffing includes selection from applicants outside of the organization and promotion, transfer, demotion, and layoff decisions from within the organization. This chapter will discuss staffing from outside the organization; the next chapter will discuss staffing from within the organization.

As suggested in Chapter 2, in the early days of industrialization, labor was considered a commodity and staffing the organization was relatively simple. The foreman would go to the place where people seeking work were assembled; would employ those who looked the strongest; and would send the rest home. Later, as staffing became more sophisticated, decisions were based on recommendations from employees and references from friends or previous employers. Then came conversations about the job (now called interviews), application forms, and finally tests. As the procedures become more advanced, however, the objective of the employers remains the same—to find out more about applicants in hopes of employing "someone better."[2]

Therein lies the focus of this chapter. Not only will the general concepts of staffing be presented and explained, but specific steps and methods in the selection procedure will be discussed. The methods most commonly utilized will be presented in greater detail. Finally, the effectiveness of the various methods used in selection will be analyzed.

Staffing Concepts and Procedures

Staffing concepts are the foundations on which most staffing systems are based, whereas staffing procedures are systematic sequences of steps established to accomplish staffing objectives. Staffing concepts generally apply to all organizations and include staffing objectives; staffing criteria; validation procedures, discussed later in the chapter; and basic strategies for an effective staffing program. Staffing procedures are designed for a specific organization to accomplish its objectives; these procedures vary in accordance with the job and organizational needs.

Staffing Concepts

Staffing Objectives Assessing people is an important managerial responsibility. Personnel managers more specifically have been involved with the problem of "picking winners" from among job applicants. Often, they have become frustrated if top management has not recognized the complexities of the staffing process, which are complicated by legal and administrative regulations and technicalities placed on employers in the last decade.[3] Top management must understand the high costs of errors in an employment decision—errors such as failing to hire a promising prospect or hiring someone who later fails to meet standards. On the other hand, it is easy to get top management's attention when the EEOC brings a major class action suit against the organization on behalf of minorities who believe they have been excluded from employment because the organization does not have a fair and equitable employment and promotion policy.

With these considerations in mind, organizations strive to meet several general objectives:

To select employees who are most likely to meet the desired standards of performance.

To maximize the utilization of human resources, especially women, minorities, and older workers, without endangering profits through increased labor costs.

To place employees in positions that will allow them to utilize their abilities, interests, and motivations in a manner most personally rewarding and beneficial to them[4] and allow them to contribute positively to the organization.

These objectives provide direction for establishing criteria for selecting employees and for developing procedures and methods to meet the objectives.

Staffing Criteria Any decision that involves hiring or promoting an employee contains an implicit prediction that the individual selected or promoted will succeed. In other words, each selection decision involves the process of predicting what will be a successful match between individual attributes and job requirements. To make effective personnel selection decisions, the organization must first obtain the best predictive information available about the applicant as well as complete data about the requirements necessary for successful job performance. Information about applicants can be obtained from a variety of sources, such as application forms, tests, interviews, references, and the like, which compose steps in the selection procedure. Information about the job is obtained from thorough job analysis (described in Chapter 4). Job analysis data must be used to determine specific criteria for the job, such as scores on job-related tests; educational requirements; training, experience, and skills necessary to perform the job; and interviewers' assessments of the personal qualifications needed. While recruiters will attempt to seek out applicants whose personal qualifications meet the requirements for the jobs available, only careful examination of the applicant's qualifications at each step in the selection procedure will ensure that the final decisions are based on sound, objective, and defensible evidence.[5]

Staffing Strategies Organizations usually develop a number of strategies for their staffing activities. As a general policy, for positions above entry level up to first-line management, qualified candidates from inside the organization are usually considered first (promotion from within, discussed in the next chapter). However, if no current employee is qualified or interested or if the vacancy exists at the entry level, selection must be made from outside applicants. Within these broad strategies exist a number of specific approaches to selecting employees.

One approach, the *successive hurdle approach,* subjects applicants to a succession of selection methods designed to measure the applicant's qualifications for the job. Each method is considered a hurdle that must be passed before the applicant can progress to the next. Applicants judged to be qualified at each successive step in the procedure are considered qualified for the job. This approach is common in organizations where employment decisions are designed for specific jobs and not much flexibility exists in terms of placing applicants in the organization.

A second approach, called the *compensatory approach,* allows applicants to proceed through the entire selection process, securing measures and assessments of their qualifications at each step. Instead of screening out the applicant when he or she does not meet the minimum standard at a step, the employer obtains a composite score of assessments at each step in the procedure. If the applicant is deficient in any one area or scores low in one or two assessments, the low score can be offset by higher scores in other areas. In other words, the applicant can compensate for low assessments in areas of weakness. This approach provides for better utilization of the total human resources available to the organization, because it provides a more thorough assessment of each applicant. Still, most organizations, especially small to medium-sized firms, do not have a large variety of vacancies at any one time and cannot afford the expenses of allowing all applicants to proceed through the entire process before making a final assessment.

An interesting selection strategy used by Japanese companies is a variation of these two methods. They select the "best" person available, provide essentially a life-time employment contract, then locate the appropriate position in the organization to maximize the individual's contribution. As Chairman Akio Morita of SONY has described:

I know it's hard for Westerners to believe [but] I want to be able to utilize each person's unique abilities for the utmost. . . . So we have to find the right position for each person.[6]

This placement approach may require changes in the structure of jobs in the organization, usually in terms of expanding duties and responsibilities as the employee is able to accept additional assignments. While this approach to human resource utilization has been extremely effective in Japan, a question remains whether it can be transferred to North America, where there exist cultural differences, different traditions at the workplace, and differing commitments of employees and employers to each other.

A final strategy consists of a succession of selection decisions. The applicant is considered initially for the specific vacancy that needs to be filled first. If qualified, he or she is placed on the job. If not qualified or not interested, then he or she is considered for the next most important job in the organization's priority of needs. This process continues until the applicant is hired and placed on the job or rejected.[7]

Selection Procedures

An important consideration in the design of an overall staffing program is the establishment and administration of the selection procedure to meet the organization's staffing objective. This objective is usually to employ the most qualified person available who is willing to work under the relevant employment conditions (wage, hours, conditions, climate, opportunities, and the like). The organization attempts to maximize the probability that it will make the right selection or, better yet, minimize the probability that it will make a wrong decision.

Considerations Based on Position to Be Filled It is important to note that there is not a single selection procedure for any one organization; instead, several procedures usually exist within the same organization. For example, an organization will probably have separate selection procedures for clerical, production, and managerial jobs. Just as examples, below are described typical procedures to select an hourly employee such as a production employee and a typical procedure to select a management trainee from college student applicants.

Selecting Hourly Employees A personnel requisition may activate the selection procedure, which usually includes the following sequence. The procedure starts with an applicant's filling out a short application form that highlights personal data, work history, skills and training, and references. Then an interviewer in the personnel department conducts a preliminary interview, probably for about fifteen minutes, in which the applicant is told about the organization, present vacancies, pay, and personnel policies. Tests, such as work sampling and manual dexterity tests, may be given to assess the applicant's current level of proficiency for a particular job. Before the applicant is called back for an interview with the immediate supervisor, a reference check will be conducted to determine the accuracy of the information already obtained and to secure additional assessments to be used in the screening process.

The data collected and information from the applicant will be assessed and one or two of the applicants will be referred to the immediate supervisor, who will interview them more thoroughly before a final decision is made. This interview will involve topics closely related to the job and will allow the supervisor and the applicant to exchange ideas and information. Allowing the supervisor to interview the applicants and to make the final decision is important in order to obtain a commitment from the supervisor, who will be ultimately responsible for the training and performance of the new employee. When the supervisor makes the final decision, it will be sent to the personnel department, which will process the application and employment records. The applicant will then be offered the job and, after accepting it and passing a physical examination, will be placed on the job.

Selecting a Management Trainee The selection of a management trainee from college student applicants is considerably more deliberate than the selection of hourly employees. A mistake at this level could cost considerable time in training and money in lost salaries, whereas the right decision could help enfuse vitality into an organizational unit and ultimately give new directions to the organization.

Selection procedures begin after the recruiting efforts (described in Chapter 5) have been completed and application forms (resumes) have been reviewed. The candidates considered most qualified based on campus interviews, recommendations, grades, and so on will be invited to the organization's facilities for a visit. While the personnel department may coordinate the activities, the immediate supervisor for the job in question plays a key role in the selection process. One- to two-hour interviews with persons with whom the candidate would work are held. These interviews may be one-on-one or in groups and usually are not as structured as the campus interview.

Before or after the interviews and the visit to the organization's facilities, contact will be made with the persons the candidate has given as references. An attempt will be made to obtain a more thorough assessment of the candidates's experience, accomplishments, interpersonal skills, and the like. Organization members will provide their assessments to the immediate supervisor, and a selection decision will be made. If the applicant accepts the job offer and passes the physical examination, a new management trainee will be employed.

Obviously, organizations use many varieties of selection procedures, which tend to vary in accordance with legal factors, organizational needs, levels of jobs, and types of jobs. The main point is that selection procedures are designed to meet predetermined staffing objectives taking into consideration the nature of the job; the urgency of filling the vacancy; the labor market conditions; the number of applicants; and the time, costs, and risk factors involved in selecting the most-qualified applicant who is willing and able to work under the employment arrangements offered.

Fair Employment Considerations

Legal Background

In 1964, Congress passed the Civil Rights Act, which included Title VII, a section that prohibits employment discrimination based on race, color, sex, religion, and national origin. Title VII is administered by the Equal Employment Opportunity Commission (EEOC), which adopted a set of guidelines to advise employers on employment practices considered acceptable under the law. The guidelines were controversial and not widely accepted by employers. The Supreme Court in 1971 issued a landmark decision, *Griggs v. Duke Power Co.,* that gave the guidelines much notoriety. The case involved an employer whose job requirements—test scores and high-school education—led to its employing a disproportionately low number of minority workers. Using the guidelines as the basis for its decision, the Court held that employment practices that have an *adverse impact* on minority applicants (or current employees) must be demonstrated to be relevant to the job. As the Supreme Court specifically stated:

Congress did not intend by Title VII . . . to guarantee a job to every person regardless of qualifications. In short, the Act does not command that any person be hired simply because he was formerly the subject of discrimination, or because he is a member of a minority group. Discriminatory preference for any group, minority or majority, is precisely and only what Congress has proscribed. What is required by Congress is the removal of artificial, arbitrary, and unnecessary barriers to employment when the barriers operate invidiously to discriminate on the basis of racial or other impermissible classification.

. . . The Act proscribes not only overt discrimination but also practices that are fair in form, but discriminatory in operation. The touchstone is business necessity. If an employment practice which operates to exclude Negroes cannot be shown to be related to job performance, the practice is prohibited.[8]

In 1972, Congress confirmed this interpretation when it amended Title VII by enacting the Equal Employment Opportunity Act, which broadened coverage and gave additional authority to the EEOC (to sue on behalf of a complainant). Three years later, in *Albermarle v. Moody,* the high court made it clear that the EEOC guidelines were to be considered the law of the land regarding employment practices.[9]

The guidelines have been developed and changed by the federal administrative agencies responsible for enforcing the laws that cover employment discrimination. The most recent revision occurred in 1978, when four federal agencies—EEOC, Civil Service Commission (now Office of Personnel Management), and Departments of Labor and Justice—agreed to use one set of guidelines, the Uniform Guidelines on Employee Selection Procedures.[10] These guidelines incorporated previous standards, federal EEO agency interpretations, and major court decisions. In addition, in their attempt to clarify the complex provisions of these guidelines, the agencies published "Questions and Answers,"[11] which provides interpretations of questions frequently asked by personnel professionals.

While many employers initially believed that Title VII applied only to selection of new employees, the broad definition of a selection procedure and subsequent court use of the guidelines quickly changed this belief. According to the guidelines, a selection procedure is:

Any measure, combination of measures, or procedures used as a basis for *any employment decision.* Selection procedures include the full range of assessment techniques from traditional paper and pencil tests, performance tests, training programs, or probationary periods and physical, educational, and work experience requirements through informal or casual interviews and unscored application forms.[12] (Emphasis added.)

In other words, the law and the guidelines cover initial selection, promotion, transfers, interviewing, assessment centers, and any other type of staffing activities or practices (promotion, transfer, and other internal staffing processes will be covered in Chapter 7).

Role of Adverse Impact in Selection

While some employers have interpreted the guidelines as making them guilty of employment discrimination until proven innocent, this interpretation is not correct. The guidelines state that a selection procedure that has no adverse impact on minority employees generally does not violate the law. Thus, where there is no adverse impact, the guidelines do not require the employer to prove its selection procedures are valid and reliable. However, where adverse impact does exist, legitimate job-related reasons for it must be shown.

Adverse impact exists when members of a certain race, sex, age, or ethnic group are hired or promoted at a substantially lower rate than other applicants or employees (usually white males). Before 1978, considerable confusion was caused by courts' using different percentages to compute adverse impact. However, the Uniform Guidelines adopted a rule of thumb, the 80-percent rule, to be used by federal EEO agencies for such computations. Exhibit 6.1 illustrates its use. If male applicants are hired at a 60 percent rate based on a certain interview, then the percentage of female applicants hired based on the *same* type of interview must be at least 48 percent [60 percent times 80 percent (rule of thumb) equals 48 percent]. A lower percentage would be considered to show adverse impact on female applicants. In other words, the interview would have resulted in a disproportionately low percentage of female applicants being hired.

Once the presence of adverse impact is determined—or, in legal lan-

Exhibit 6.1	Determining the Presence of Adverse Impact		
		Number Interviewed	Number Hired	Selection Rate

	Number Interviewed	Number Hired	Selection Rate
Number of Female Applicants	50	20	40%
Number of Male Applicants	100	60	60%

Rule of thumb: If the selection rate for minority groups is less than 80 percent that for the majority group, then adverse impact is present.

Using the data above: 60% × 80% = 48%.

The female selection rate (40%) is less than 48%; therefore, adverse impact is present.

guage, once a *prima facie* case of employment discrimination has been established—the burden of proof shifts to the employer, who must show that job-related selection techniques were used. (See Exhibit 6.2.) The organization may choose to modify or eliminate the employment procedures that produced the adverse impact; or it may attempt to justify the use of the selection technique by showing a clear relationship between assessments from the selection techniques and actual job performance (as determined by performance ratings).

The employer may decide to continue its current practices and wait for the EEOC or minority applicants or employees to initiate legal proceedings. While this alternative does not seem attractive, it is surprising how many employers have chosen this route over the years and then waited until the court has ordered them to take certain steps to correct their employment practices.

Typical examples of failure to meet the guidelines are:

Using tests or interviews that have not been validated.

Using subjective performance appraisals as the criteria for showing job-relatedness between test scores and job performance.

Using tests for entry-level jobs which have been validated only for upper-level jobs or for entry-level jobs at another plant location.

Validating tests by using only white employees and not including black employees in the study.

Validation techniques will be further discussed later in the chapter. Needless to say, there was much employer resistance to the guidelines and to federal agencies' and courts' interpretations and uses of them. In general, employers complained not so much that validation of selection procedures were inappropriate or infeasible but that compliance with the guidelines would be inconvenient and expensive and

Exhibit 6.2

Legal Procedure in EEOC Cases

1. Initial burden of proof is on PLAINTIFF (complainant).

   Must show adverse impact:
      80% rule.
      Statistics.
   Must show an individual case of discrimination.
   Must show intent to discriminate by employer.

2. If plaintiff is successful, burden of proof shifts to EMPLOYER.

   Must eliminate discriminatory employment practices.
                     Or:
   Must show validity of employment practices.
   Must articulate a nondiscriminatory reason for employment decisions.

3. PLAINTIFF may rebut evidence presented by employer.

For more detailed coverage, see: Stephen A. Rubenfeld and Michael D. Crino, "The Uniform Guidelines: A Personnel Decision-Making Perspective," *Employee Relations Law Journal 7* (Summer 1981), pp. 105–121.

would limit an important managerial prerogative. In fact, however, a sizable proportion of companies had never conducted a validation study of their selection procedures (less than one-fourth of employers with less than 1,000 employees and less than half of employers with less than 10,000 employees).[13]

Selection Methods

Application Forms and Resumes

One of the most commonly used selection methods is the application form. In fact, it has been estimated that over a million are received by organizations each year in the United States.[14] As illustrated by the application form in Exhibit 6.3, the types of information usually supplied by job applicants are previous employment, educational record, military service record, personal references, and medical history. The information requested by application forms should be restricted to fairly obvious job-related items that can be easily justified and do not offend any applicant.[15] Questions about matters such as race, color, age, sex, national origin, religion, and handicaps are omitted unless the employer is convinced that such data are bona fide occupational qualifications. Items such as hair and eye color, marital status, maiden name, age of children, and date of high school graduation, which may be less obviously related to EEO considerations, should be given careful analysis before they are included on the application form. Somewhat surprisingly, a recent study of the Fortune 500 firms revealed that 98.7 percent of these firms included one or more items on their application forms that could be considered potentially inappropriate (that is, items that did not appear job-related, were not necessary for making an employment decision, or were clearly questionable from a legal view).[16]

Resumes are sources of biographical data and are similar in content to application forms. However, they cannot be controlled for EEO considerations because the job seeker chooses the content. Resumes include items that allow the applicant to present a favorable representation of his or her objectives, experience, background, and activities. (Exhibit 6.4 gives suggested content for resumes based on a study of 205 personnel managers.)

A few organizations have weighted and scored the data on application forms or resumes in an attempt to predict job performance from the scores. Researchers have concluded that weighted applications present an attractive alternative to the employment tests that have been attacked by the courts and federal EEO agencies. (However, weighted application forms must also be nondiscriminatory.) Applicants are receptive to completing application forms, since most expect to be required to do so. Many find that reporting information on an application form makes them less anxious than taking a written test that will be scored, recorded, and stored in the employer's file. Finally, if the application form's content and the weights given to it are based on job analysis, they can be valid predictors of job performance.[17]

The utility of application forms depends on the accuracy of the information furnished by the applicant. However, since applicants want to be hired, some may stretch the truth, especially concerning such information about previous employment as duration of employment, position held, duties, reasons for leaving, and salary (which is often overstated).[18] One of the authors received an application form from a female prospect that indicated she had spent four years in a Catholic convent. Her subsequent job behavior on the assembly line appeared inconsistent with this background, and investigation revealed that she had spent those four years in the state prison. To reduce falsification of information, many employers require that the applicant sign a statement providing for immediate dismissal if application information proves false. A few employers have gone so far as to use lie detector tests.[19]

With such potential for basing employment decisions on inaccurate information, one may be surprised that a study of 250 organizations found that 16 percent never verified educational background, 44 percent never verified police records, 25 percent never verified personal references, and 29 percent never verified military records.[20]

Psychological Tests

A psychological test is an objective, standardized measure of behavior used frequently in personnel management. Not all such tests are practical for employment purposes; some have been developed for other

Exhibit 6.3   **Typical Application Form**

```
                              OMEGA ENTERPRISES
                           Application For Employment

        Date_____

        Name_____
              (First)        (Middle)      (Maiden name, if any)      (Last)
        Social Sec. No._____Phone_____ _____

        Address_____How Long?_____
                  (Street)            (City)          (State)
        Previous Address_____How Long?_____
                         (Street)           (City)      (State)
        Ht._____ Wt._____ Marital Status_____

        No. of Dependents_____ Ages of Dependents_____

        In case of emergency notify: _____
                                     (Name)            (Address)        (Phone)
        ============================================================================

                                    EDUCATION

        Circle highest grade completed: Grade School  1 2 3 4 5 6 7 8  High School  1 2 3 4
                                        College 1 2 3 4
        Other_____Last school attended_____
                                                        (Name)          (Address)
        Were you graduated?_____Year_____ List degrees or honors_____

        _____ List special courses taken that might help you

        in the work applied for_____

        ============================================================================

                                 MILITARY STATUS

        Have ever served in the US Armed Forces?_____Branch_____Dates: From_____to_____

        Rank at discharge_____Type of discharge_____

        ============================================================================

                                 PHYSICAL HISTORY
        How much time have you lost from work due to illness in the past three years?_____

        Have you ever been injured on the job?_____If so, nature and degree of injury_____

        _____Have you received Workman's Compensation?_____

        When?_____List any physical limitations (such as eysight, limb impairment, diabetes)__

        _____Date of last physical examination_____

        Doctor's name and address_____
```

uses, such as career counseling and selection for training. The value of tests in any employment setting depends on the degree to which the test score serves as a predictor of job performance. For a test to have value to an employer, it must meet three requirements: standardization, reliability, and validity.

Standardization is uniformity of procedure in the administration as well as the scoring of the tests. *Reliability,* which often is confused with validity, refers to the consistency of the test—that is, whether the test produces consistent scores for the same person retested with the same test or an equivalent form of the test. Reliability also refers to the internal consistency of test items. For example, applicants should give similar responses to similar questions. *Validity* is the degree to which the test is capable of achieving the purposes for which it is intended. This means that a person who has the ability to perform at a

Exhibit 6.3   **Continued**

HISTORY OF EMPLOYMENT

Account for all past employment. Use additional sheets if neccessary.

(List Present Employer First)

Dates	Employers	Type of Business	Your Position	Rate of Pay
From	Name			
To	Address			
Reason for leaving				
From	Name			
To	Address			
Reason for leaving				
From	Name			
To	Address			
Reason for leaving				
From	Name			
To	Address			
Reason for leaving				
From	Name			
To	Address			
Reason for leaving				

REFERENCES

Name_____ Phone_____

Address_____

Name_____ Phone_____

Address_____

Name_____ Phone_____

Address_____

TO BE READ AND SIGNED BY APPLICANT

This certifies that this application was completed by me and that all entries on it and in it are true and complete to the best of my knowledge.

It is agreed and understood that the answers to the foregoing questions are true and correct, and that any misrepresentations of information given above shall be considered an act of dishonesty.

It is agreed and understood that the employer or his agents may investigate the applicant's background to ascertain any and all information of concern to applicant's record, whether same is of record or not, and applicant releases emplyers and persons named herein from all liability for any damages on account of his funishing such information.

The applicant agrees to furnish such additional information and complete such examinations as may be required to complete his employment file.

It is agreed and understood that this application for employment in no way obligates the employer to employ the applicant.

It is agreed and understood that if hired, the employee may be on a probationary period during which time he may be discharged without recourse.

_____
(Applicant's Signature)

APPLICANT DOES NOT WRITE BELOW

Interviewed by_____Date_____

Comments_____

Test results:_____

Reviewed by_____Reviewed by_____

Assigned to_____Department or location_____

Classification_____Rate of Pay_____Reporting Date_____

high level should score high on a test which assesses the person's ability. In other words, test validation considers what a test measures, such as ability or job knowledge and how well the test measures it. Thus, a test is considered valid when there is a close relationship between the test score and job performance measures. Validity is discussed in more detail later in the chapter.

Types of Tests Tests can be categorized in many ways; the following classifications focus on how tests are used in an employment setting:

Aptitude tests, or cognitive ability tests, measure ability or capacity to learn as well as ability to perform a job that has been learned. Such tests include the general intelligence tests that measure five cognitive abilities: verbal, numerical, perceptual, spatial, and reasoning.

Psychomotor ability tests measure abilities related to strength, coor-

Exhibit 6.4

**Checklist of Item Content
in Resume Construction**

Clusters of Resume Content	Resume Items[a]
1. Personal Data	Current Address
	Permanent Address
	Date of Availability for Employment
2. Job and Career Objectives and Goals	Specific Job Objectives
	Specific Career Goals
3. Previous Experience	Past Work Experiences (Include Description of Duties)
	Tenure on Previous Jobs
	Military Experience
4. Educational and Academic Background	Major in College
	Minor in College
	Grades in College Major
	Grades in College Minor
	Colleges and Universities Attended
	Overall Grade Point Average
	Class Standing
	Years in Which Degrees Were Awarded
	Awards and Scholarships Received
	Sources for Financing College Studies (Percent of Money Earned for College)
5. Physical Health	Specific Physical Limitations
	Overall Health Status
6. Professional Activities	Membership in Professional Organizations
	Offices Held in Professional Organizations
7. Miscellaneous	Salary Requirements
	Travel Limitations
	Specific Skills
	Spouse's Willingness to Relocate
	References
	Job Location Requirements

[a] Includes only those items rated by the 205 personnel managers as being important in the resume.

Source: Hubert S. Feild and William H. Holley, ''Resume Preparation: An Empirical Study of Personnel Managers' Perceptions,'' *Vocational Guidance Quarterly* 24 (March 1976), p. 236. Used by permission.

dination, and dexterity. Sets of psychomotor abilities that may be measured are finger dexterity, manual dexterity, wrist-finger speed, aiming, and arm movement speed.

Job-knowledge tests measure how much the individual knows about the kind of work involved in the position for which the applicant is being considered. These tests consist of a series of questions that truly differentiate experienced, skilled workers from the less experienced ones and are usually designed for specific jobs in designated organizations, such as a welder, electrician, or other trades.

Vocational interest tests measure interest patterns of applicants in relation to interest patterns of people successful in specific jobs. These tests reveal areas of interests, preferences, and occupations in which an individual is most interested and most likely to be satisfied. Used mostly for counseling and vocational guidance, the Strong Vocational Interest test shows the similarity of interests between successful persons in numerous occupations and those of the person taking the test. The Kuder Occupational Interest Survey shows interest groupings, such as persuasive, literary, clerical, artistic, mechanical, scientific, and computational.[21]

Work sample tests require job applicants to perform tasks like those performed on the job. Examples of work sample tests are typing, shorthand, and filing tests. These tests have considerable "face validity" in that they appear to the applicant to be closely related to the job being sought.

Personality tests measure such characteristics as emotional adjustment, interpersonal relations, motivation, interests, and attitudes. These tests include *self-report inventories,* such as those asking the individual to accurately describe himself or herself by identifying characteristics from a list, and *projective tests,* relatively unstructured tests in which the individual projects himself or herself into a situation.[22]

Of the tests described above, personality tests lag far behind aptitude, psychomotor ability, job knowledge, and work sampling tests in terms of usefulness in selection and placement. Frequently characterized by low reliability and validity and limited objective data, personality tests should be used only by a qualified professional. Even then, the user organization may have difficulty justifying their job-relatedness if challenged in an EEO suit.[23]

Validation Processes Validation is a highly technical, complex procedure for demonstrating that a selection technique—for example, a test or an interview—accurately predicts job performance. It is perhaps easiest to understand in relation to tests; thus, it is discussed here. Three methods can be used for validation: (1) *criterion-related, or empirical, validity;* (2) *content validity;* and (3) *construct validity.*

In the criterion-related approach, a selection procedure can be justified by a demonstration that a statistically significant relationship (a validity coefficient) exists between scores on a test, interview, or the like and measures of job performance. For example, Figure 6.1 shows a close relationship between test scores and performance. Content validity is demonstrated when the selection procedure is shown to representatively measure significant parts of the job requirements, such as a filing and typing test for a clerical employee. Construct validity involves identifying the psychological traits (constructs) that underlie successful performance on the job—for example, leadership ability for a management position.[24]

Measuring construct validity is a relatively new procedure in the field of personnel selection. Thus, the discussion below will focus on criterion-related, or empirical, validity and content validity, because

Figure 6.1

Figure 6.1

Relationship of Performance and Test Scores

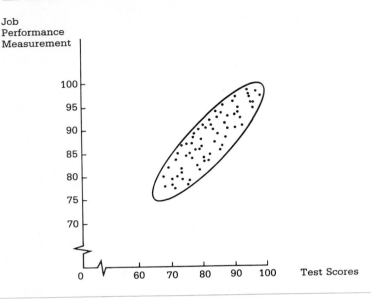

they have more practical value for employers at the present time. Empirical validation is the preferred procedure, for reasons that will become readily apparent in the next section; however, content validation has become popular with small and medium-sized organizations and large organizations with only a few employees in each separate job class.[25]

Criterion-Related, or Empirical, Validation Criterion-related validity consists of two types: concurrent and predictive.[26] The second type is preferred by the EEOC; but both types are generally disliked by employers because of the cost, time, and effort they require.

In *concurrent validity* studies, the selection instrument being tested is administered to current employees; and results are measured against these employees' performance. In *predictive validity* studies, the selection instrument is administered to job applicants; and results are filed and later measured against the performance of the applicants who were hired. (Here, the selection instrument is not used in the hiring decision; it is administered only so that its validity can be tested.) Exhibit 6.5 outlines the steps in measuring predictive and concurrent validity.

Each type involves advantages and disadvantages. Concurrent va-

Exhibit 6.5   **Steps in Empirical Validation of Employment Tests**

Predictive Validity		Concurrent Validity
Conduct job analysis.	Same	Conduct job analysis.
Determine qualifications that can be measured by tests and select the test.	Same	Determine qualifications that can be measured by tests and select the test.
Determine criteria for success on the job.	Same	Determine criteria for success on the job.
Administer test to applicants but do not use test in hiring; instead, store test scores until performance is measured.	Different	Administer test to current employees; obtain performance measures or production records of current employees from personnel files.
Correlate test scores with performance criteria and compute validity coefficients.	Same	Correlate test scores with performance criteria and compute validity coefficients.

lidity studies can be completed in a short time and usually allow cost savings in the short run. However, current employees' scores on tests (or other selection instruments) are likely to be unrealistically high because of their job experience. Further, current employees represent only applicants who have performed well enough to keep their jobs. This means the concurrent validation study's results are based on a restricted sample—a narrow range of performance scores. Another narrowing influence is the composition of the present workforce, which may not reflect the racial, ethnic, or sexual composition of the labor market, creating the possibility of problems with the EEOC. Finally, results can be influenced by employees' and supervisors' attitudes and the organizational climate; for example, employees may not be motivated to take the procedure seriously, since the results will not affect their jobs.

Predictive validation is the preferred method in terms of statistical purity, or lack of contamination by the kinds of factors described above. Scores are not affected by organizational climate or the like. All applicants are trying to score high; and their scores are not raised by job experience. The sample includes a wider range of subjects. However, where job turnover and applicant flow are low, using predictive validation takes too long to be practical. Further, companies may have to keep poor performers on the job longer than they ordinarily would to show that their low test scores correspond to subsequent unsatisfactory performance.[27]

In general, empirical validation methods involve two problems. First, in organizations with low turnover or few employees in each job category, the sample size is too small for the study to be meaningful. Second, often it is difficult to find performance criteria that are objective and free of bias.[28]

Content Validation The popularity of content validation has grown quickly in the last few years, partly because of the problems associated with the empirical validation methods. Content validation, like the other models, begins with the job analysis. Because tests are designed to predict how applicants for a specific job will perform on that job, the first step may be to determine the knowledge, skills, or behaviors the job requires. For example, if reading skills are critical to successful performance, a job analysis should help to determine exactly what materials are read on the job and their relative importance. On one job, materials to be read might include: safety materials (50 percent), work procedures (30 percent), and operations manuals (20 percent). Test items would then be based on these job-related reading materials. An applicant might be directed to read a paragraph on safety procedures and then asked to respond to a series of questions on the content, such as "What do you do when ammonia touches a person's skin?"

Cut-off scores (discussed later in the chapter) will then be set. When a cut-off score is established, the employer is concluding that anyone who scores above it is qualified for the job.

After the test is designed, it should be administered to a representative group to determine its usefulness as a selection device. The results should be analyzed in terms of pass-fail percentages, comparison between race and sex groups to determine whether adverse impact is present, and assessment of the test's reliability.[29] Some organizations may wish to conduct a concurrent or predictive validation study to ensure that the test meets empirical validation standards.

Administering the Testing Program Once the organization has determined that the test it has chosen is valid and reliable, other decisions concerning the testing program must be made. These decisions apply to giving the test and determining cut-off scores.

Giving the Test An initial administrative consideration concerns who will give the test. Some of the more complex tests may require the services of a test professional. Others, like a ten-minute typing test, do not require skilled interpretation; responsibility for these tests can be assigned to a personnel technician. Employing a consultant or a testing service is another option that may be considered by organizations that give only a few tests; however, large organizations that give many tests to applicants as well as employees probably will employ a full-time testing specialist.

Another consideration is the testing environment, which includes physical and emotional aspects. Tests should be given in an environment that is quiet, separate, well-ventilated, and free of interruptions. Thorough and clear directions should be provided. The person who gives the test must realize that applicants are almost always nervous, since they realize their test results will strongly influence their employment possibilities. Test administrators should attempt to reduce this anxiety.

Determining Cut-off Scores A major decision in a testing program is the determination of cut-off scores. Applicants who score above the cut-off point are considered qualified to proceed in the selection process; those who score below the cut-off point are considered unqualified. Establishing cut-off scores involves varying the probabilities of making a correct selection decision. While there are no guarantees that any decision will prove accurate, the general rule is that applicants with higher scores on a valid test will perform better on the job than those with lower scores. As you will recall, a valid test indicates a clear relationship between the test score and job performance. The dots on the graph in Figure 6.2 demonstrate such a relationship between test scores and job performance measures.

To establish the cut-off score, the organization must consider several factors, including the desired probability of making a correct decision, labor market influences, legal considerations, wages paid for the job, number of applicants, and reasons applicants want to work for the employer. If labor market conditions are characterized by low unemployment and few persons looking for jobs, the cut-off score may have to be relatively low in order to qualify the needed number of applicants. During periods with high unemployment and many applicants, the cut-off score may be adjusted upward so that only the better applicants will proceed in the selection process. If the company is considered a good employer and has a reputation as a good place to work, it may consistently have a large number of applicants; consequently, its cut-off scores may also be adjusted upward.

The employer must also determine whether it wants to hire the most qualified applicant or only a qualified applicant. In the latter case, it might use a score above a certain point to indicate that the applicant is qualified, though not necessarily the most qualified among the applicants. If the organization wants to improve the probability of making a correct selection decision, it may increase the cut-off score. Figure 6.2 shows a graph reflecting an organization's testing strategy. When the cut-off score was set at A, or 80, fourteen of twenty applicants (probability of 0.7) were allowed to proceed in the selection process and later performed at an acceptable level on the job. However, when the organization wanted to improve the chances of making a correct selection decision, it increased the cut-off score from A to B, or

Figure 6.2

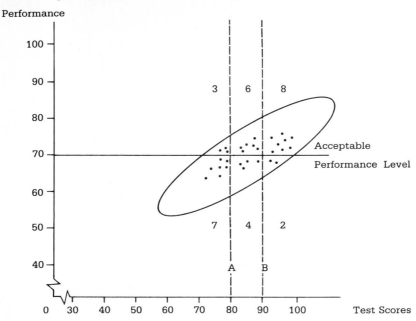

Determining Cut-off Scores

from 80 to 90, at which point eight of ten applicants (probability of 0.8) were allowed to proceed in the selection process and later performed at an acceptable level on the job.

Some organizations may construct tables (like the one in Exhibit 6.6) that combine test score cut-offs and expected performance levels. In the example, a person who scores 90 or above has an 80 percent chance of being a successful performer. A score of 80–89 would yield a lower probability (60 percent) of successful performance.

Within the context of costs of recruiting, legal regulations, testing, interviewing, labor market conditions, desired performance level, wages paid to attract applicants, and attractiveness of the employer, the organization must determine the utility of the test it plans to administer.

Employment Interviews

Interviews are the most widely used method of selecting employees, and the use of interviews has been gaining in popularity since increased pressures have been brought by the courts and the EEOC on users of written tests.[30] An employment interview involves observing representative samples of candidates' behavior for selection purposes

Exhibit 6.6   **Performance Expectancy Table**
                                   and Bar Chart

Test Score	Chances in 100 of Being Successful Performer
90–100	80
80–89	60
70–79	30

Test Score   **Chances in 100 of Being Successful Performer**

Test Score	
90–100	80
80–89	60
70–79	30

based upon questions from an individual or a group of individuals.[31] Nearly all employees that are finally hired are interviewed at least once, and a majority of organizations consider the interview the most important step in the selection procedure.[32]

Although the interview is frequently criticized as lacking structure, it provides the employer a unique opportunity to assess the applicant's qualifications. The interview provides direct observation of certain aspects of the applicant's behavior, such as communication skills, physical appearance, and mannerisms, which are not obtainable by other methods. During the interview, information about the applicant can be obtained that will fill in the gaps left in results from other sources. In addition, because the interview is a two-way process, the interviewer can inform the applicant about the job, the company, and the company's expectations of employees.[33] While the primary purpose of an interview is to assess the applicant's qualifications, it can also be used to sell the organization to the applicant. On the other hand, an interviewer may take the view that the applicant ought to be exposed to a realistic job preview to avoid false expectations and to prevent a mismatch between organizational needs and individual needs.[34]

The interview has been criticized by researchers for its lack of validity and reliability and for bias, stereotyping, and prejudice on the part of interviewers. However, its continued use and importance seem to indicate that employers have either rejected the research or have decided to focus on the positive features of the interview.[35] Either way, it seems reasonable to conclude that instead of concentrating on the failures of the interview, researchers should focus on how to make it more effective as a valid and reliable selection method, especially since employers will continue to use it in employee selection.

Types of Interviews A variety of types of interviews are available, and more than one type may be used in the selection of any applicant. Among the most common types are the structured interview; the non-structured, or discussion, interview; the multiple, or group, interview, and the stress interview.

Structured Interviews The structured interview involves a predetermined pattern of questions that will be asked the applicant. Exhibit 6.7 presents an example of a structured interview guide. When more than one interviewer is used in the selection procedure, the structured interview is more likely to provide consistency among these interviewers. It is also more likely to be valid, provided the questions are drawn directly from job analysis information. The main drawback is lack of flexibility; simply responding to specific questions from the interviewer may not enable the applicant to exhibit his or her "real" personality, communication skills, and other attributes.

Nonstructured, or Discussion, Interviews Nonstructured interviews are based on the nondirective techniques used by counselors, psychologists, and psychotherapists. There are no set questions and no predetermined order in which topics are to be covered. This type of interview is highly applicant-oriented; in fact, the direction and content of the interview are usually determined by the content of the answers given by the interviewee. In some cases, the interviewer may ask only one formal question—for example: "In view of your personal background (family life, interest, and so forth), what interests you about this company?"

This type of interview usually yields more information about the applicant's opinions and reactions than the other types, but the information may not be job related. In addition, the interview responses are very difficult to score objectively. For this type of interview to be useful for selection, it must be conducted by a skilled interviewer, usually with training and experience. Even then, it is difficult to show that the final assessment is reliable and valid.

Multiple, or Group, Interviews Group interviews may occur when several managers interview one applicant in a small group or as part of a panel or when a group of applicants react to each other rather than to an interviewer. The inclusion of several managers at one interview is expensive and does not utilize their time very well. Also, these interviews are stressful to applicants and difficult to control. However, in

Exhibit 6.7   **Structured Interview Guide**

Name of Applicant _____ Date _____
Position Applied for _____ Department _____
Interviewer _____

I. Work and Military Experience

   1. How did you originally get your job with the company?
   2. Would you describe your duties and responsibilities in the job?
   3. Would you describe a typical work day?
   4. What were some things you particularly enjoyed in your job?
   5. What was less enjoyable?
   6. What were some of your major accomplishments in the job?
   7. What were some of the problems or setbacks you experienced in the job? How did you attempt to handle them?
   8. How would you describe your boss? What were his or her major strengths and limitations?
   9. What do you feel you gained from your experience in this job?
   10. Why did you leave this job (company)?

II. Education

   11. Why did you select the college you attended?
   12. What was your major field of study? Why did you select it?
   13. What courses did you like best? Why?
   14. What courses did you like least? Why?
   15. In what course did you make your best grades? Worst grades?
   16. How much effort did you devote to your studies?
   17. Did you participate in any extracurricular activities? Why or why not? Did you hold any positions in them?
   18. How did you spend your summers while in college?
   19. How was your education financed?
   20. Do you have any plans for further education?

III. Background Information

   21. How do you spend your spare time (reading, social activities, sports, community affairs, etc.)?
   22. Do you or your family have a geographical preference? Are there any areas in which you or your family would not particularly care to relocate?
   23. What is your attitude toward job-related travel? How much would you be willing to do?
   24. Which aspects of our community appeal to you as a place to live? Which are less appealing?

IV. Job Related Topics

   25. What type of relationship do you think should exist between a manager and his or her subordinates?
   26. In what type of work environment are you most comfortable?
   27. What is your reaction to working under pressure?

Exhibit 6.7	Continued

28. What do you consider to be your strong points?
29. In what areas do you think you could use some improvement?
30. What factors in a job are most important to your job satisfaction?
31. What motivates you to put forth your maximum effort?
32. Why did you decide to seek a position with our company?
33. In what ways do you believe you can make a contribution to our company?
34. What do you see yourself doing five years from now?
35. What are your long-range career goals? How do you plan to achieve them?
36. If you joined our company, what training or experience do you think you would need in order to make a maximum contribution?
37. Looking into the future, what changes and developments do you anticipate in your field?
38. Are there any additional aspects of your qualifications for the job opening which you would like to discuss?

the selection of high-level executives, the group setting may be the most appropriate to allow the applicant and the interviewers to assess the social interaction and determine the "chemistry" of the group. When several applicants are involved in a discussion without the active participation of an interviewer, the assessment may be highly subjective unless the group is given specific direction for the discussion.

Stress Interviews The stress interview subjects the applicant to stressful situations; for example, the interviewer may deliberately and frequently interrupt the applicant; remain silent for long periods of time; adopt a hostile, unfriendly posture; or ask stressful questions in an attempt to intimidate and pressure the applicant (see Exhibit 6.8). Observation of the applicant's reaction by a trained and experienced interviewer can help in assessing personality characteristics that only reveal themselves when tension is present and in determining how the applicant may react in stressful situations. This interview technique may be too threatening to some applicants and may cause applicants to form a negative impression of the organization; in addition, conflicts initiated in the interview can continue after the applicant is hired. However, the technique has been used for selection of people to fill high-pressure jobs, such as police work, airline piloting, firefighting, and military leadership.[36]

Conducting the Interview[37] Conducting the interview necessitates adequate *preparation.* An initial preparatory step involves securing an appropriate physical setting, one that is comfortable and free of interruptions. Since the purpose of the interview is to assess the qualifications of the applicant, the physical setting should allow the applicant to be able to demonstrate those qualifications as well as possible.

An important part of preparation is planning for the interview itself. The interviewer should determine ahead of time what type of inter-

Exhibit 6.7   **Continued**

Interview Evaluation Form

Name of Applicant _____ Date _____
Position Applied for _____ Department _____
Interviewer _____

Instructions

Two ratings are required for each of the factors listed below: (1) an importance rating, and (2) a degree rating.

The importance rating indicates how important each factor is to overall successful performance on the job for which the candidate is being considered. The degree rating indicates the degree to which the candidate possesses each factor. Use the rating scales in the boxes below when making your ratings.

If any of the factors which are listed are not relevant to the job for which the candidate is applying, do not assign ratings to them. Also, if there are factors which are relevant to the job which are not listed, add them to the list and rate them as discussed above.

To obtain a total score, multiply the importance rating by the degree rating for each factor and sum the results.

Importance Ratings	Degree Ratings
5 = Very Important	5 = High Degree
4 = Above Average Importance	4 = Above Average Degree
3 = Average Importance	3 = Average Degree
2 = Below Average Importance	2 = Below Average Degree
1 = Slight Importance	1 = Slight Degree

Factors	Importance Rating	Degree Rating	Result
1. Appropriate Work Experience, Knowledge, and/or Skills			
2. Appropriate Educational Background			
3. Ability to Assume Responsibility			
4. Leadership Ability and Potential			
5. Diligence (Hard Worker)			
6. Ability to Plan Ahead			
7. Maturity			
8. Ability to Interact with Others			
9. Ability to Handle Job Stress			
10. Oral Communication Skills			
11. Relocation and/or Travel Flexibility			
12. _____			
13. _____			
14. _____			

Total Score =

Source: Developed by William F. Giles, Auburn University. Used by permission.

view will be used and should review the job description as well as other information already available on the applicant, such as that from test scores, application form, and so forth. The interviewer should also discuss the job vacancy with the immediate supervisor, determine

| Exhibit 6.8 | **Example of a**
Stress Interview |

Question (by interviewer): Assume that tomorrow either you or your child must die. However, you have a choice as to which will die. Whom will you pick?

Answer: Well, I guess I would pick myself.

Question: Why?

Answer: Well, I don't know, it just seems like the thing to do. After all, I am older and have led a rather full life and, furthermore, I am reasonably well insured and my son would be fairly well taken care of financially.

Question: You mean you were the dupe of an insurance salesman who sold you something that you didn't need?

Answer: No! I bought the kind of insurance I need. After all, my insurance salesman is my brother-in-law, and he took careful pains to design a well-planned program for me.

Question: How can you justify buying insurance on the basis of nepotism?

Answer: I didn't buy it on the basis of nepotism! I bought what I needed from my brother-in-law.

Question: Isn't buying from your brother-in-law nepotism?

Answer: Not necessarily. It simply meant that I bought from someone that I could trust.

Question: You mean that most insurance salesmen are untrustworthy?

Answer: No. Simply that they don't always have your best interests at heart in selling you an insurance program.

Question: If someone doesn't have your best interests at heart, isn't he untrustworthy?

Answer: Not necessarily. I just don't understand what you mean.

Source: Reprinted from pp. 16–17 of *Interviewing Skills for Supervisory Personnel* by Lawrence L. Steinmetz, copyright © 1971, by permission of Addison-Wesley Publishing Company, Reading, MA.

what additional information is needed from the applicant, and anticipate what additional information (such as promotion opportunities, educational reimbursement policy, insurance program, and so forth) the applicant might request or need to know. Also, the interviewer will probably want to outline a general format for the interview, to include:

Opening the interview (small talk, purpose of interview).

Giving information about company and jobs available.

Determining applicant's interest in jobs available.

Discussing application and clarifying and expanding on qualifications.

More specifically discussing company policies and specific job.

Giving time to allow applicant to ask questions.

Informing applicant about the next steps in the selection procedure and when he or she will be contacted.

Closing the interview.

Careful Preparation Is Needed to Avoid Interview Errors Such as this

"Retirement plan? I wouldn't worry about that. You'd be out of your mind to work here that long."

Source: *Wall Street Journal*, July 25, 1981.

Before the interview takes place, the interviewer should schedule enough time so that the objectives of the interview will be accomplished. The interview should be open and friendly but business-like. Also, the interviewer should attempt to relieve the tension and anxiety usually present in applicants so that the interview will accurately reflect the applicant's qualifications. While there are numerous recommendations on how to conduct an interview, the following suggestions are appropriate for nearly all interviews:

The interviewer should control the interview by keeping the interview flowing and keeping it pertinent to job-related information.

Questions should be worded so that they will not be answered "yes" or "no." Instead, the candidate should be given an opportunity to talk.

The interviewer should be an attentive and interested listener. Neither his or her manner nor words should imply criticism or impatience.

The interviewer should not show approval or disapproval by word or expression, because the applicant may tend to slant toward what will win approval from the interviewer; however, showing mild general approval will encourage applicants to keep talking.

The interviewer should avoid any inquiries that could involve EEO considerations or that might be interpreted as showing a discriminatory attitude (see Exhibit 6.9).

Once the interviewer has asked all the essential questions and obtained the information sought and after the interviewee has been given an opportunity to ask for additional information or to provide information voluntarily, the interview should be closed in a friendly manner. Customarily, the interviewer immediately writes down facts, opinions, and assessments from the interview. This information will be useful for follow-up interviews and will provide helpful insights for other interviewers who may be involved in them.

Problems with Interviewing As noted earlier, the interview is not only widely used, but it is the most important step in many selection systems. However, using the interview as a predictor of job success involves several serious problems. First, interviewers are often not prepared for the interviews and frequently have received little or no training. "More importantly, few give serious though to what information they seek to acquire in the interview or how they will go about obtaining it."[38] An untrained, ill-prepared interviewer can not only damage the selection process but also can cause serious harm to the organization's reputation and public image.

In addition to training and preparation, the interviewer needs detailed knowledge of the job. This knowledge does not come from a personnel requisition or job description form. Rather, it comes from personal observation and discussion with supervisors concerning how the job fits into the overall operation and what typical problems, projects, and reports the job involves.[39]

A second category of problems in interviewing involves interviewers' errors, which, of course, affect the validity and reliability of the interview.

In *stereotyping,* a common error, the interviewer forms a preconceived notion about the candidate based on physical characteristics or behaviors that have nothing to do with job qualifications. For example, such an interviewer might conclude that an applicant is not a good accountant because he wears flashy clothes, has a beard, and seems outgoing.

Another error can occur as a result of the interviewer's perceptions of the candidate's interests. For example, the interviewer may believe that an applicant is mostly interested in the job's intrinsic factors, while the applicant is primarily interested in the extrinsic factors.[40]

Exhibit 6.9	**Guide to Preemployment Inquiries that Involve EEO Considerations**		
Subjects	Permissible Inquiries	Inquiries to be Avoided
Marital Status	Whether applicant can meet specified work schedules	Child-care arrangements; number and age of children
	Anticipated absences	Questions concerning pregnancy
Age	Inquiry as to whether applicant's age is less than company's retirement age	Requirement that all applicants state date of birth
Sex	Inquiry limited to bona fide occupational qualifications (very limited use)	State sex on applicant form
Race	(same as above)	Applicant's race Color of eyes, skin, hair, etc.
Birthplace	After employment, can you submit proof of U.S. citizenship?	Birthplace of applicant, parents, relatives
Military Service	Education and experience in military related to job	Type of discharge
Photograph	May be asked for after employment for identification purposes	Require photograph on application form
Education	Academic, vocational, or professional education, school attended, language skills	Questions about racial, religious, and nationality-related schools
Conviction, Arrest, and Court Record	Inquiry to convictions *related* to job	Any inquiry *not* related to the specific job
References	Names of references	Applicant's pastor or religious reference
Credit Rating	None	Any reference to charge accounts, credit, car ownership, etc.

Source: Clifford M. Koen, Jr., "The Pre-employment Guide," *Personnel Journal* 59 (October 1980), pp. 826–828. Reprinted with the permission of *Personnel Journal*, Costa Mesa, California; all rights reserved.

A *halo error* occurs when one trait or characteristic is generalized to other traits and characteristics. For example, an applicant who exhibits self-confidence and composure in an interview may be characterized as a person who will be able to analyze problems, write reports, and present the findings to upper management.

Another error, the *contrast error,* occurs when an interviewer is overly influenced, either positively or negatively, by the interviews of previous candidates. For example, if an applicant with acceptable qualifications follows a particularly strong candidate, the second applicant may be considered less than qualified and rejected from employment.

Finally, errors that involve *excessive leniency or strictness* and *central tendency* may be made. Central tendency occurs when the interviewer does not differentiate among applicants but gives all applicants an average rating. Excessive leniency and strictness occur when the ratings are limited to the extreme ends of a rating scale.[41]

Equal Employment Opportunity Implications for Interviewing Like testing and other selection techniques, interviews are considered part of the employment procedure and therefore are covered under the Uniform Guidelines. Whenever interview assessment leads to adverse impact on various groups, the employer may be called upon to present validation data. Unless interviews can be supported by such data, such as by showing a relationship between interview performance and subsequent job performance, the employer may be vulnerable in an EEO complaint or court suit. Vulnerability may result from failure to develop questions from job analysis, lack of standardization in interviews, and subjectivity in the decision-making process. In other words, the interview questions must help the employer measure the skills and knowledge required to perform the job, and the assessment must be objective and made under standardized conditions.

Because the nonstructured interview especially may encounter EEO-related problems (unless it is conducted by a skilled interviewer), the structured interview has been recommended in many sources. Such interviews take place under standardized conditions, and the questions do not vary much from interview to interview. The questions should be specific and should be written down to guide the interviewers; and each interviewer should be trained. Structure in the interview does not restrict probing or clarifying answers; these techniques are proper when related to task performance. Structure does not prevent establishing rapport and exchanging the pleasantries common in most interviews. However, the interview results should be based on job-related data, not personal feelings. While it is impossible to objectify all information in an interview, it is possible to reduce subjectivity by improving the structure of the interview.[42]

Reference Checking

Reference checking involves collecting and using information concerning applicants' past performance, health, character, personal activities, and education that can be supplied by persons other than the applicant.[43] Reference checks are conducted on the premise that past behavior is a predictor of future performance and the more clues an employer can obtain about past behavior of applicants the greater the likelihood an accurate hiring decision will be made. Nearly all employers conduct reference checks on at least some of their applicants; and the higher the position in the organization, the greater the likelihood that a thorough reference check will be done.[44]

The major problem with reference checks is that persons given as references, partly because of the possibility of being sued, are usually reluctant to reveal information that will reduce the chances than an applicant will obtain employment. Also, applicants seldom voluntarily name a reference who will give anything other than a favorable recommendation. Further, the passage of the Family Education Rights and Privacy Act of 1974 (the Buckley Amendment), which allows students to see letters of reference written about them unless they waive such right, has led to the writing of many bland letters which do not seem to disclose anything about the applicants.[45] Since only a few employees have exhibited poor performance and work habits on previous jobs, the chances may not be high that the organization will obtain useful information from a reference check. Thus, organizations may have to assess the benefits and costs of conducting reference checks in various situations.

Reference checking is usually done by the personnel department, either by mail questionnaires or telephone interviews. Telephone interviews are preferable, because they are quick and cost-effective and because more information can be obtained through the two-way communication. Direct questions from a structured questionnaire or telephone format usually yields appropriate information. Types of information sought include reasons for leaving previous job, eligibility for rehire, dates of employment, job held, last salary, and overall performance rating.[46] The questions asked should be direct and should be structured in such a way that useful information will be obtained. Information beyond the propriety of the job in question and information unreasonably difficult to gather should not be sought.[47]

Written references to general inquiries may be of little value, because they seldom give unfavorable information. However, some letters can be analyzed for their content and length. A letter that includes only factual information and does not favorably mention the applicant's work is commonly interpreted as negative. The length of a letter also may be revealing, longer letters generally are considered more positive. Letters describing the applicant in terms of specific observed behaviors are usually more helpful than general descriptions that are not job-related.

Attention must be given to the sources of information. For references to serve as useful indicators of future performance, the people who give them must have observed the applicant on the job, must be competent to make evaluations, must be willing to be candid, and must express the evaluations either orally or in writing. Like other types of assessments, references are likely to involve errors in perception and memory; and it cannot be taken for granted that records of a previous employer are always accurate. At times, a potential employer may even receive a positive recommendation from a present employer who hopes a marginal employee will be hired away. Thus, employers must look for consistent evaluations and recommendations. When questionable information surfaces, additional investigation should be conducted.[48]

When the employer wants a thorough reference investigation, usually for a high-level position, it may employ a professional firm to perform a reference audit. Because hiring the wrong person in an executive position will cost thousands of dollars, an in-depth reference audit may be justified. In such cases, supervisors, peers, and subordinates of the prospective candidate will be interviewed to obtain accurate job-related information. This approach, however, may be limited when the candidate does not want his present employer to know that he or she is seeking another position.

Examples of questions asked during a reference audit include the following: What were the candidate's major responsibilities (give in order of importance)? How would you evaluate the candidate's performance (quality and quantity, comparison with those in similar positions)? How would you characterize the candidate's interpersonal relationships (with staff, peers, superiors)?[49]

Roles of the Personnel Department and Other Managers in Selection

The personnel department and other managers work together to achieve the organization's selection objectives, and both carry out separate but related activities that involve staffing from outside the organization.

The personnel department provides leadership and expertise in the development of staffing policies and selection procedures. Members of the personnel department usually coordinate selection activities—for example, by setting up the interview schedules for management trainee prospects visiting from colleges; making the appropriate introductions; and ensuring that the schedule is carried out. The personnel department is also involved in administering the selection methods, such as conducting preliminary interviews, giving and scoring pre-employment tests (when qualified), contacting references for assessments, and completing background investigations. These activities are considered assessment activities to determine which applicant or applicants will be referred to the immediate supervisor for a final interview.

The personnel department is nearly always assigned the responsibility of maintaining employment-related records, such as application forms, test scores, and letters of reference, and filing the appropriate government reports, such as those required by the EEOC. Finally, the personnel department assesses the effectiveness of the organization's selection strategies, policies, and procedures in terms of its stated objectives. Its members conduct validation studies when qualified or serve as liaisons with consultants employed to perform the studies. Personnel representatives attempt to measure the relative effectiveness of each step in the selection procedure in terms of costs and benefits and examine the overall degree to which selection procedures contribute to organizational effectiveness.

Managers throughout the organization contribute to this personnel activity. Without their efforts and inputs, overall objectives related to personnel management could not be achieved. Managers in other departments play important roles in at least three areas related to selection of employees. First, their role is vital in determining job qualifications. The immediate supervisor knows the jobs in his or her department much better than the personnel staff; therefore, when determining job qualifications, the personnel department relies heavily on supervisors' inputs. Second, the immediate supervisor interviews the applicants screened and recommended by the personnel department. When the applicant is being considered for a managerial position, the activities may include not only interviewing but entertaining the prospect. Third, and most critical to the success of the organization, the supervisor usually makes the final decision.

| Issue: | **How Much Do Various Selection Methods Help Firms Pick the Most Qualified Employee?** |

Each of the selection methods discussed in this chapter is designed and utilized to help the organization select the most qualified applicant for the vacant position and to place the new employee in the position in which he or she will be most productive and satisfied. In probability statistics language, these methods are intended to increase the probability that the selection decision will be correct or to reduce the probability that the decision will be wrong. To examine the relative effectiveness of these methods, we can analyze the results of some research investigating each method.

The first selection predictor to be considered is biographical data, which several leading personnel researchers consider the best predictor available.[50] This assessment may explain why application forms must be completed by nearly all job applicants. The basic information, experience, education, and references included among the biographical information of the applicant have been shown to be successful predictors of job performance. You may wonder why organizations do not rely completely on biographical data and save the time, money, and effort they spend on testing, interviewing, and the like. One problem has been that some types of the personal data that are important parts of any application form may have adverse impact on minority applicants. It is also difficult to demonstrate that certain types of personal information are job related. Still, most research has supported the general conclusion that biographical data are valid predictors of job performance for a wide variety of jobs, such as bus drivers, custodial workers, managers, salespersons, clerical employees, and scientific and engineering personnel.[51]

Analysis of the interview as a predictor of job success has not been optimistic. In fact, several major reviews of interview research in the last two decades have concluded with essentially the same results.[52] The following, though not a complete listing of the criticisms, provides a representative sample: interviews are highly subjective, not valid, and not reliable; interviews are prone to form sex-role stereotypes; more attractive applicants are evaluated more favorably in interviews; positive information is underweighted and negative information is overweighted; applicants more similar to the interviewer are more likely to receive favorable evaluations.[53]

While most of the findings about interviews have been negative, several have led to recommendations that could be useful in improving the effectiveness of the interview. First, it has been found that interviews can be used to accurately assess intelligence, skill in interpersonal relations, and motivation to work.[54] Where these characteristics are important to specific jobs, the interview can be quite useful. Second, interviews are improved when they are structured and when the interviewer is trained, knows the job requirements thoroughly, and focuses on these requirements during the interview. Third, the candidate must be allowed to talk so that a larger sample of behavior and more information can be obtained. This reduces the possibility that the interviewer will make a judgment based on a quick first impression.[55] Since the interview will always play an important role in employee selection, the organization's obvious choice is to determine ways to make the interview better. Finally, it should be noted that the interview serves multiple purposes in addition to predicting job success, including allowing an exchange of information between the employer and the prospective employee, providing a public relations outlet, and promoting the organization as a good place to work.

Testing is the most sensitive of the selection methods; but it is difficult to draw specific conclusions about the entire field of testing, since there are more than 3,000 measures to be obtained from testing and nearly 2,500 different types of tests.[56] Because government agencies have closely scrutinized testing in employee selection in the last decade, many organizations have abandoned it. Some organizations have successfully validated their tests; however, despite interest and efforts in the profession, progress in validation has been disappointing.[57]

The degree to which tests have been shown to be job related (reliable and valid) depends greatly on the type of test. General intelligence tests have been held to be culturally biased and not to be predictive of job performance; however, they seem to be better able to predict managerial success.[58] Mechanical aptitude, manual dexterity, and clerical aptitude tests have generally been demonstrated valid. Personality tests have been very difficult to validate for employment purposes, because it is extremely difficult to show job-relatedness. Interests tests have been used mostly for career counseling and guidance; thus, the Uniform Guidelines have not required that they be validated.[59] In short, it seems that any conclusion made about employment testing must relate to the specific test and its specific use.

Reference checks—or, more broadly, background investigations—have been shown to have some predictive value; however, the level of validity is low. Persons who have had close contact with an applicant and have frequently observed his or her performance in a job similar to the one for which he or she is applying should provide the most useful information about the applicant; however, personnel managers who read letters of reference every day rarely find even the mildest form of negative information in them. Employers who have been threatened with suits for giving unfavorable references—or who have heard of other employers being sued for that reason—may be reluctant to provide an accurate assessment and may only provide factual information, such as wage rate, dates of employment, reasons stated for leaving and so on.[60] In addition, applicants who have no employment record are at a distinct disadvantage with this method.

Summary

The objectives of staffing are to select employees likely to meet performance standards, to maximize human resource use, and to utilize employees so that their maximum contribution will be obtained. Job analysis is used to determine the qualifications necessary for the job and provide criteria against which the applicant's education, experience, test scores, and the like will be compared. The major selection strategies include the successive hurdle approach, which requires the applicant to successfully qualify at each step in the selection procedure, and the compensatory approach, which allows the applicant to complete the entire process to obtain a total score.

Fair employment considerations are a major factor in employment decisions. The Uniform Guidelines establish acceptable principles for fair employment, define the selection procedure broadly, and specify the meaning of adverse impact.

Various selection methods are used for employment purposes. Biographical data from application forms and resumes have been useful in predicting job success. Various types of tests—aptitude, psychomotor, job knowledge, work sample, personality, and vocational interest—are also used, subject to the requirements of standardization, reliability, and validity. The validation process applies to all selection methods. The most appropriate types for organizational purposes are empirical (predictive and concurrent) and content. Elements of a testing program include giving the tests, determining cut-off scores, and comparing scores to an expectancy table for selection purposes.

Types of interviews include structured, nonstructured, group, and stress. Considerations in conducting the interview include adequate preparation, general format, interviewer behaviors, and follow-up. Some problems in interviewing are lack of preparation and training of interviewers and interviewers' errors. Because interviews are used in making employment decisions, EEO implications are important. The final selection method presented, reference checks, are often conducted, especially for higher-level management applicants. However, reference persons rarely give adverse information. To be more systematic, organizations can use mailed questionnaires or telephone interviews and ask direct and structured questions about the applicants.

The personnel department and other organizational managers work together to achieve the organization's selection objectives.

Discussion Questions

1. Why is predictive validation more acceptable to the EEOC than concurrent or content validation?

2. Assess the following statement: "Interviews have been proven invalid and unreliable in most cases. Other methods which are valid and reliable should be used and interviews eliminated."

3. Think of a time when you took a preemployment test or were

interviewed as a prospective employee. How did the methods used compare with the recommendations presented in this chapter?

4. Evaluate the various selection methods in terms of their use in selecting college graduates for management trainee positions.

5. Are employers guilty of employment discrimination until they prove their innocence? Explain.

6. Are the effort, time, and resources employers invest in selection methods worthwhile?

Notes

1. L. E. Albright, "Staffing Policies and Strategies," in *Staffing Policies and Strategies,* ed. Dale Yoder and H. G. Heneman, Jr. (Washington, D.C.: Bureau of National Affairs, 1974), p. 4-7
2. R. M. Guion, "Recruiting, Selection, and Job Replacement," in *Handbook of Industrial and Organizational Psychology,* ed. M. D. Dunette (Chicago: Rand McNally, 1976), pp. 777–778.
3. Albright, "Staffing Policies," p. 4-118.
4. *Ibid.,* pp. 4-117–4-118.
5. *Ibid.,* pp. 4-22–4-23.
6. "SONY: A Diversification Plan Tuned to the People Factor, "*Business Week,* February 9, 1981, p. 89
7. Guion, "Recruiting, Selection, and Job Replacement," p. 780
8. *Griggs v. Duke Power Company,* 401, U.S. 430 (1971).
9. James Ledvinka and Lyle F. Schoenfeldt, "Legal Developments in Employment Testing: Albemarle and Beyond," *Personnel Psychology* 31 (Spring 1978), pp. 1–2.
10. "Uniform Guidelines on Employee Selection Procedures," *Federal Register* 43 (August 25, 1978), pp. 38290–40223.
11. "Adoption of Questions and Answers to Clarify and Provide a Common Interpretation of the Uniform Guidelines on Employee Selection Procedures," *Federal Register* 44 (March 2, 1979), pp. 11996–12009.
12. "Uniform Guidelines," p. 38308.
13. Ledvinka and Schoenfeldt, "Legal Developments," pp. 4–13; F. S. Hills "Job Relatedness v. Adverse Impact in Personnel Decision Making," *Personnel Journal* 59 (March 1980), pp. 211–215.
14. Albright, "Staffing Policies," p. 4-20.
15. Ernest C. Miller, "An EEO Examination of Employment Applicants," *Personnel Administrator* 25 (March 1980), pp. 63–81.
16. "Application Forms," in *Personnel Management* (Washington, D.C.: Bureau of National Affairs, 1980), p. 201:240.
17. Larry Pace and Lyle Schoenfeldt, "Legal Concerns in Use of Weighted Applications," *Personnel Psychology* 30 (Summer 1977), pp. 159–166.
18. Irwin L. Goldstein, "The Application Blank: How Honest Are the Responses?" *Journal of Applied Psychology* 55 (May 1971), pp. 491–492.
19. George M. Beason and John A. Belt, "Verifying Applicants' Background," *Personnel Journal* 55 (July 1976), pp. 345–348.
20. Staff of Bureau of National Affairs, *Selection Procedures and Personnel Records* (Washington, D.C.: Bureau of National Affairs, 1976), p. 5.
21. C. Harold Stone and Floyd L. Ruch, "Selection, Interviewing, and Testing," in *Staffing Policies and Strategies,* ed. Dale Yoder and H. G. Heneman, Jr. (Washington, D.C.: Bureau of National Affairs, 1974), pp. 4-138–4-142.
22. Anne Anastasi, *Psychological Testing* (New York: Macmillan, 1976), pp. 18–19
23. Stone and Ruch, "Selection, Interviewing, and Testing," p. 4-142.
24. "Uniform Guidelines," p. 38292.
25. Dwight R. Norris and James A. Buford, Jr., "A Content Valid Writing Test: A Case Study," *Personnel Administrator* 25 (January 1980), pp. 40–43.
26. Robert D. Gatewood and Lyle F. Schoenfeldt, "Content Validity and the EEOC: A Useful Alternative for Selection," *Personnel Journal* 56 (October 1977), p. 520.
27. Gerald Bassford, "Job Testing—Alternatives to Employment 'Quota,' " *Business Horizons* 17 (February 1974), p. 42.

28. Norris and Buford, "Content Valid Writing Test, pp. 42–43.
29. Gatewood and Schoenfeldt, "Content Validity," pp. 521–524.
30. Susan Krug, *The Oral Interview as a Selection Technique: Some Suggested Formats and Guidelines for Structuring the Interview Process* (Chicago: U.S. Civil Service Commission), p. 2
31. Richard D. Arvey, "Unfair Discrimination in the Employment Interview: Legal and Psychological Aspects," *Psychological Bulletin* 86 (July 1979), p. 736.
32. Staff of Bureau of National Affairs, *Selection Procedures,* p. 11.
33. "Employment Interviews," in *Personnel Management* (Washington, D.C.: Bureau of National Affairs, 1977), p. 201:221.
34. John Wanous, "Tell It Like It Is at Realistic Job Interviews," *Personnel* 52 (July/August 1975), pp. 50–60.
35. Robert L. Decker, "The Employment Interview," *Personnel Administrator* 26 (November 1981), pp. 71–73.
36. "Employment Interviews," p. 201:226.
37. R. A. Fear, *The Evaluation Interview,* 2d ed. (New York: McGraw-Hill, 1973), pp. 59–122.
38. Jack Bucalo, "The Balanced Approach to Successful Screening Interviews," *Personnel Journal* 57 (August 1978), p. 420.
39. *Ibid.,* p. 421
40. William F. Giles and Hubert S. Feild, "Accuracy of Interviewers' Perceptions of the Importance of Intrinsic and Extrinsic Job Characteristics to Male and Female Applicants," *Academy of Management Journal* 25 (March 1982), pp. 148–157.
41. Krug, *The Oral Interview,* pp. 23–27
42. Robert D. Gatewood and James Ledvinka, "Selection Interviewing and EEO: Mandate for Objectivity," *Personnel Administrator* 21 (May 1976), pp. 15–18.
43. Edward L. Levine and Stephen M. Rudolph, *Reference Checking for Personnel Selection: The State of the Art* (Berea, Ohio: American Society for Personnel Administration, 1977), p. 5
44. *Ibid.,* p. 138.
45. Wayne Cascio, *Applied Psychology in Personnel Management* (Reston, Va.: Reston Publishing Co., 1982), pp. 190–191.
46. "Checking References," in *Personnel Management* (Washington, D.C.: Bureau of National Affairs, 1979), p. 201:251.
47. *Ibid.,* p. 201:252.
48. Levine and Rudolph, *Reference Checking,* pp. 140–141.
49. Peter A. Rabinowitz, *Reference Auditing: An Essential Management Tool* (Wellesley Hills, Mass.: Barthodi & Company, n.d.).
50. William A. Owens and Lyle F. Schoenfeldt, "Toward a Classification of Persons," *Journal of Applied Psychology* 63 (October 1979), p. 596; Cascio, *Applied Psychology,* p. 202; James J. Asher, "The Biographical Stem: Can It Be Improved?" *Personnel Psychology* 25 (Summer 1972), pp. 251–269.
51. Richard R. Reilly and Georgia T. Chao, "Validity and Fairness of Alternative Employee Selection Procedures" *Personnel Psychology* 35 (Spring 1982) pp. 5–14.
52. Edwin E. Ghiselli, "The Validity of a Personnel Interview," *Personnel Psychology* 19 (Winter 1966), pp. 389–394.
53. Marvin Dunnette and Walter C. Borman, "Personnel Selection and Classification Systems," in *Annual Review of Psychology,* ed. Mark R. Rosenzweig and Lyman W. Porter (Palo Alto, Calif.: Annual Reviews, 1979), pp. 504–509.
54. Richard R. Reilly and Georgia T. Chao, "Validity and Fairness of Alternative Employee Selection Procedures," (unpublished paper, American Telephone and Telegraph Company, 1980), pp. 19–20.
55. Neal Schmidt, "Social and Situational Determinants of Interview Decisions: Implications for the Employment Interview," *Personnel Psychology* 29 (Spring 1976), pp. 97–98.
56. Dunnette and Borman, "Personnel Selection," p. 479.
57. Phillip Ash and Leonard P. Kroeker, "Personnel Selection, Classification, and Placement," in *Annual Review of Psychology,* ed. Mark R. Rosenzweig and Lyman W. Porter (Palo Alto, Calif.: Annual Reviews, 1975), pp. 481–507.
58. Edwin E. Ghiselli, "The Validity of Aptitude Tests in Personnel Selection," *Personnel Psychology* 26 (Winter 1973), pp. 461–477.
59. Helen LaVan and Peter F. Sorenson, "Legal and Effectiveness Issues in the Personnel Selection Process," in *Management of Human Resources,* ed. E. L. Miller, E. H. Burack, and M. Albrecht (Englewood Cliffs, N.J.: Prentice-Hall, 1980), p. 346.
60. Reilly and Chao, "Validity and Fairness," p. 43.

Organizations face increasing demands to systematize and rationalize their policies and procedures regarding the career mobility of employees. Changes in government regulations, the nature of the economy, and the demographic composition of the labor force are examples of external pressures on management to increase human resources management and career planning. Internal pressures are created by employees and potential employees with rising expectations, who demand more from organizations than just a job: some want to know details about their career within the organization.

John C. Anderson, George T. Milkovich, and Anne Tsui, "A Model of Intra-Organizational Mobility," *Academy of Management Review* 6, no. 4 (October 1981), p. 529. Reprinted by permission of the Academy of Management.

Much daily personnel work is spent in changing the placement of individuals already in the organization. The external labor market exists outside the organization (as discussed in Chapter 1), and all employees must initially come from the external labor market (as discussed in Chapter 6). The internal labor market—employees present in the organization—serves as the mechanism through which the organization adjusts its personnel to changing conditions,[1] such as new product lines, expanded facilities, new markets, altered goals and functions, and so forth. Proper placement of these personnel allows them to be more productive and increases the likelihood that they will be satisfied with their jobs, resulting in less turnover and lower absenteeism.

This chapter discusses internal staffing decisions and the means by which they are made. An important part of internal staffing activities—career planning and development—is also explained. The chapter concludes with a discussion of several issues in internal staffing.

Organizational Assignments

The personnel changes that occur most commonly within organizations are promotions, transfers, demotions, and layoffs (layoffs will be discussed later in the chapter).

Promotions are upward moves that involve increases in responsibility and in wages. Promotions are used to reward employees for past performance. In fact, one personnel expert has claimed:

Promotion, of course, is the most potent motivating force in our industrialized society, for it means prestige as well as money. Any weakening of this incentive for improving productivity can only have a negative influence that must be offset in some way.[2]

Promotions also offer opportunities and experience for employees who are likely to move further up the organization, as well as placing employees where they are most productive and can contribute most to the organization.

Transfers are horizontal moves that involve no changes in level or in pay. Transfers occur at the organization's request or at the individual's; their usual purpose is to better match the person's capabilities to the position's responsibilities. Transfers also provide an opportunity for training for an employee, staffing a new department, or opening up a clogged promotion line. Employees may request a transfer for other reasons, such as to avoid conflicts with their present supervisor, move to a job where upward mobility will be improved, or move to a different geographic location.[3]

Promotion and transfer systems operate similarly; however, employees who are promoted must meet standards of the higher job level, while those transferred must meet only the standards of their present level. The criteria used for making promotion and transfer decisions and the operation of the systems should be fair and understandable.

However, promotions and transfers must be compatible with the organization's needs for efficiency and effectiveness. In addition, a requirement that has emerged in recent years is compliance with affirmative action and equal employment opportunity regulations.[4]

U.S. organizations in the 1980s will be facing a new problem—the lack of enough promotional opportunities (and in some cases transfers), to distribute among a growing number of qualified employees. From 1980 to 1990, the number of persons between the ages of thirty-five and forty-four (considered the age group of prime middle-manager candidates) will increase by 42 percent. Meanwhile, the number of available middle-manager jobs will increase by 21 percent. The gap between number of positions and number of people qualified to fill them is expanded by the trend toward delayed retirement of executives and by new technologies such as desk-top computers that increase manager's productivity. Being able to adjust to this problem will require much imagination. Some companies are already preparing for such adjustments. General Electric has established task forces to allow new assignments and challenges to employees affected by the problem. Prudential rotates managers to improve performance and "recharge" those who cannot move up as fast as their qualifications should allow.[5] Other companies are "buying" early retirement for executives by increasing their pension benefits. Others are making cosmetic changes for younger managers—for example, changing job descriptions to read "considerable responsibility" instead of "some responsibility" and improving the physical environment of the work place.[6]

Demotions are moves from a job with more responsibility and pay to one with less responsibility and pay. Such moves usually are traumatic for the organization and the individual. Often, demotions cause great personal embarrassment, disappointment, and, consequently, lower performance. Because of their potential for damage to the organization and the individual, such job changes are made with great care. In fact, they are frequently avoided, if possible, or are made in a way that allows the employee to save face (for example, the employee may be told he or she is being moved to a job that may lead to better things in the future).

Demotions are difficult to study because they are infrequent and are difficult to identify. An investigation of 6,332 job changes revealed that only 3 percent of the affected employees viewed their job change as a demotion (in terms of decreased responsibilities). However, corporate estimates show that downward moves involve 9 percent of job changes. The 6-percent difference lies in the eye of the beholder. While top management may view a job change as a demotion, the employee may argue that the move was lateral—partly because, as mentioned, top management is reluctant to directly tell the employee that he or she is being demoted.[7]

Some demotions may be necessary because the employee was promoted too early and proved unable to perform at the higher level. While no promotion decision can be made with assurance of the employee's success at the higher level, the problem of failure can sometimes be handled by including in the promotion a probationary period and an understanding that the employee can return to his or her former job after this period. Under such arrangements, the demoted employee will be better able to rationalize to coworkers the return to the former job and will be able to more readily accept the situation in his or her own mind. Organizations should be prepared with various ways to relocate those who were promoted prematurely or mistakenly placed, especially when these employees have had records of acceptable performance on previous jobs with less responsibility and when face saving will facilitate acceptance of the demotion decision.[8]

Policies and Procedures for Promotions and Transfers

Because policies and procedures for promotions and transfers are similar and such decisions are made considerably more frequently than demotion decisions, the following discussion will focus on promotions and transfers.

Promotion-From-Within Policies

A promotion-from-within policy gives present employees first consideration when a vacancy occurs. Only when no present employee is qualified for the vacancy does the organization turn to the outside labor market. Obviously, present employees favor promotions' being made from within.[9] This policy also demonstrates to employees that they will be rewarded if they work to qualify themselves for higher positions. In return, the employees usually give enthusiasm to their jobs and loyalty to their company.[10] The organization gains from promoting employees who have had experience within the organization, understand and respect the employer's values and traditions, know the way the organization operates, and know its internal social structure and informal groups.[11] Promotion from within is also cost-effective, as long as it produces qualified applicants; it reduces not only recruiting and selection costs but also turnover costs, since present employees should have realistic assessments of the organization's problems and prospects and so should be less likely to quit.

On the other side of the coin, promoting only from within may have a negative impact on the organization. First, new ideas may be needed and excessive promotion from within may lead to stagnation in the work group. Second, present employees, though qualified, may not necessarily be the most qualified when compared with applicants from the external labor market. Complete reliance on promotion from within provides only a limited number of applicants from which to choose. (On the other hand, of course, bringing in an outsider when there are equally qualified employees available for promotion can cause ill feelings within the organization.) Third, promotion from within may cause competition within work groups, and excessive competition may not be healthy for the organization. Conceivably, a promotion could occur in a work group having two or more highly (perhaps equally) qualified employees. Those disenchanted individuals not receiving the promotion might subsequently reduce their work output or even leave the organization for another job. Finally, organizations must guard against managers who decide which employee they want to promote and then write the qualifications specifically for the chosen individual, not for the vacant job itself.

Job Posting   Job-posting systems are commonly associated with promotion-from-within policies and open promotion systems (systems that allow anyone in the organization to apply for any opening). Job posting is required by about 80 percent of the collective bargaining agreements in unionized firms;[12] and a recent study of large nonunion firms indicates that 65 percent have job-posting procedures. Job posting involves announcing vacancies on the company bulletin board or in the company newsletter. The title of the job, its duties and responsibilities, the qualifications necessary, the wage schedule, and other pertinent information are posted. Employees who are interested and who meet the posted qualifications can sign the list of those who want to be considered for the opening. In accordance with the promotion criteria and policies in existence, the employee who best meets the qualifications published will be chosen for the open position.

Job posting has several advantages. First, it helps to discover talent and qualified persons within the organization that might not have been identified if the organization relied solely on supervisory recommendations. Although some supervisors may not intentionally attempt to hide talented performers and keep them in their own departments, they may simply not be aware of employees' interests and qualifications. Job posting informs employees of areas for advancement opportunities and allows them a chance to let management know they are interested in advancement. Not to be overlooked is the fact that job posting helps the organization meet its equal employment opportunity commitments.[13]

Using job-posting procedures also involves negative features. Paperwork within the organization is increased, because the personnel department must keep track of all job bidders and must seriously consider every application. Those who are not promoted after bidding for the vacancy will expect to be told why they were not promoted and what they should do to increase their chances for promotion in the future. Each step takes time and therefore increases costs. Also, job-posting systems may increase movement from job to job within the firm and thus create instability within the organization, unless the number of times an employee can make a job change within a certain period is restricted by policy.[14] Finally, some managers do not like the reduction of their freedom to move employees when and where they believe the employees are needed. Job posting offers employees greater choice, but some managers prefer that employees' choices be limited.

Selection Procedures Once the job vacancy is announced, either through job posting or directly to supervisors, candidates may apply by bidding or may be recommended by management. Deliberations over which candidate will be chosen begin with attempts to match the job specifications and the applicants' qualifications. While the basic consideration is the candidates' ability and willingness to do the job at the announced wage rate, many other factors must be considered as well. Sources of information on current employees are usually readily available from personnel records or can soon be obtained.

To facilitate the process of gathering these data, skills inventories such as the one shown in Exhibit 7.1 have been developed. While small organizations usually maintain such inventories in manual systems, larger ones use computerized systems for speed and efficiency. For each employee, information such as age, sex, race, employment and salary data, education, skills, training, years and types of experience, foreign language ability, organizational memberships, performance ratings, preference in future assignments, and potential is maintained. When an opening occurs, the manager of the department in which the vacancy exists specifies the knowledge, skills, and experience requirements and sends this information to the personnel department. A computer search will be conducted and a list of all qualified individuals wil be sent to the manager. In accordance with the procedures and policies in existence, employees who are qualified will be considered for the vacancy.

For the skills inventory to be effective, the information must be updated on a regular basis, typically biannually. This updating indicates to employees that management is sufficiently interested in them to ensure that promotions and other personnel changes will be based on current information. The system also must be fairly simple and easy to administer, and employees should understand how it works. However, it must be sufficiently detailed so that a computer run based on four or five variables will not generate the names of hundreds in the company. Also, top management must support the concept with resources. Under a promotion-from-within policy, the skills inventory search takes place before recruiting outside the organization is attempted.[15]

After the data are collected and considered, the final decision is usually made by the department head or supervisor for the position being filled. Several selection strategies are available. First, every candidate can be carefully and thoroughly evaluated and a meaningful compari-

Exhibit 7.1   Managerial Skills Inventory

Employee Name	Department	Years of Education	Age	Sex	Race	Years with Company	Years in Present Position	Assessment Center Score (100 Maximum)	Last Performance Appraisal (100 Maximum)	Managerial Level (6 Maximum)	Potential Rating (10 Maximum)	Current Salary
Sidney Bolton	Sales	13	41	M	W	10	3	83	96	3	9	$32,500
Robert Boyce	Production	15	35	M	W	5	2	78	86	4	7	39,600
Ann Fulton	Finance	17	50	F	W	20	10	82	90	5	9	42,500
Charles Hastings	Transportation	16	32	M	W	2	2	88	82	3	8	32,750
David Hunt	Legal	19	26	M	W	1	1	91	92	3	9	34,600
William Ikerd	Accounting	16	45	M	W	15	2	80	80	3	8	25,000
Grace Jackson	Accounting	18	48	F	W	10	5	96	96	2	9	44,600
Larry Tate	Sales	16	55	M	W	25	5	90	85	5	8	38,450
Marcia Fulgham	Transportation	16	40	F	N-W	15	15	92	94	4	7	31,000

son of their qualifications can be made. While this approach is comprehensive and may lead to the best final decision, it is time consuming and costly. Second, all candidates can be screened quickly according to certain basic qualifications; then a more thorough assessment can be made of only a few top candidates. While this alternative is the most frequently used and the least costly, it allows some qualified candidates to be overlooked. Another alternative is to evaluate candidates one by one until a qualified person is identified. This strategy is also less costly; but it enables the organization only to select a qualified person, not to select the most-qualified person. Further, many applicants may believe they were treated unfairly when this method is used. A final alternative involves the situation in which the employer already has in mind one candidate who seems qualified. Other candidates are compared with this candidate. While this strategy is operable, it promotes favoritism and results in half-hearted searches for qualified applicants.[16]

Peer Ratings and Nominations

Often-neglected techniques that can be used for promotion decisions are peer ratings and peer nomination. Peers or coworkers often have the best opportunity to observe each other's job behaviors and activities, which can be more revealing and realistic than tests, interviews, and situational exercises.[17] Peer ratings, or buddy ratings, have been used extensively in the military, and their effectiveness as a predictor of future performance has been impressive.[18]

In nonmilitary settings, peer ratings have been equally impressive. On some occasions, they have been judged a better predictor of job performance than supervisor evaluations used in promotion decisions. Indeed, they have been called "superior to all other measures available at the time of rating."[19] Peer ratings are considered simple to administer and very practical, and employees do not seem to object to completing the ratings.

A typical demonstration of the effectiveness of peer ratings involves two studies of employees promoted after nomination by their peers. One study found that only 39 percent of employees rated low by their peers were doing a good or excellent job six months after their promotion, whereas 75 percent rated high by their peers were performing at a comparable level. A second study showed that, of the employees receiving a below-average number of promotion nominations, only 36 percent were later rated successful. Almost twice as many of the employees receiving an above-average number of nominations were rated successful.[20]

Although these studies show impressive results from peer ratings, organizations must be cautious in their implementation. First, peer ratings can be used only when there is sufficient interaction within the work group for the members to be qualified raters. If there is little or no contact between peers on the job, ratings will be based on uninformed judgments. Second, organizations should be cautious of influences on ratings of friendships, prejudices (sex, race, age, and so on), differences in educational levels, degrees of acquaintance on and off the job, and physical appearance.[21] There may also be a tendency for peer ratings to be motivated by self-interest—that is, raters may agree to evaluate each other favorably. Finally, peer ratings may be completed in a half-hearted fashion if the raters don't feel responsible or accountable for this activity.

Assessment Centers

Because employers have not been satisfied with traditional procedures for making promotion decisions, particularly on promotions from line positions to supervisory positions, they have sought better techniques. One technique used by the British and German armies for selection of officers is called the assessment center. It was developed and applied to organizational purposes in the late 1950s by the American Telephone and Telegraph Company. Now, after more than twenty years of experience with and application of the method, it is estimated that as many as 200,000 persons in 2,000 organizations have participated in assessment center evaluations.[22]

Although the term *assessment center* suggests a physical place for assessing personnel, the assessment center is actually more a methodology for making staffing decisions. This methodology includes multiple assessment techniques developed by experts in psychological and individual assessment, evaluations of observed behavior demonstrated in simulation exercises that take place during a one- to three-day period, and judgments based on pooled information from the assessors and scores from the various techniques. (See Exhibit 7.2 for a more detailed definition of assessment centers.) The job dimensions, characteristics, and qualities evaluated are based on analysis of relevant job behaviors.[23]

Assessment Center Procedures While the specific details of simulation exercises vary in accordance with the nature of the job and organization, several types of exercises are usually administered at assessment centers. One standard exercise is the *in-basket method,* which requires that the assessee spend thirty minutes processing the contents of a hypothetical manager's in-basket—memos, reports, complaints from customers, directives from higher management, and the like. During this exercise, managerial skills such as organizational analysis, decision making, and ability to delegate and assign priorities are assessed.

Role playing is a technique frequently used in assessment centers. Here, the assessees are given specific roles in a job-related situation. For example, one assessee may be given the role of a union grievance

Exhibit 7.2   **Assessment Center Defined**

An assessment center consists of a standardized evaluation of behavior based on multiple inputs. Multiple trained observers and techniques are used. Judgments about behavior are made, in part, from specially developed assessment simulations.

These judgments are pooled by the assessors at an evaluation meeting during which assessment data are reported and discussed and the assessors agree on the evaluation of the dimensions and any overall evaluation that is made.

The following are the essential elements which are necessary for a process to be considered an assessment center.

Multiple assessment techniques must be used. At least one of these techniques must be a simulation. A simulation is an exercise or technique designed to elicit behaviors related to dimensions of performance on the job requiring the participants to respond behaviorally to situational stimuli. The stimuli present in a simulation parallel or resemble stimuli in the work situation. Examples of simulations include group exercises, In-Basket exercises, interview simulations, Fact Finding exercises, etc.

Multiple assessors must be used. These assessors must receive thorough training prior to participating in a center.

Judgments resulting in an outcome (i.e., recommendation for promotion, specific training or development) must be based on pooling information from assessors and technique.

An overall evaluation of behavior must be made by the assessors at a separate time from observation of behavior during the exercises.

Simulation exercises are used. These exercises are developed to tap a variety of predetermined behaviors and have been pretested prior to use to ensure that the techniques provide reliable, objective and relevant behavioral information for the organization in question. The simulations must be job-related.

The dimensions, attributes, characteristics, qualities, skills, abilities or knowledge evaluated by the assessment center are determined by an analysis of relevant job behaviors.

The techniques used in the assessment center are designed to provide information which is used in evaluating the dimensions, attributes or qualities previously determined.

The following kinds of activities *do not* constitute an assessment center.

1. Panel interviews or a series of sequential interviews as the sole technique.
2. Reliance on a specific technique (regardless of whether a simulation or not) as the sole basis for evaluation.
3. Using only a test battery composed of a number of pencil and paper measures, regardless of whether the judgments are made by a statistical or judgmental pooling of scores.
4. Single assessor assessment (often referred to as individual assessment)—measurement by one individual using a variety of techniques such as pencil and paper tests, interviews, personality measures or simulations.
5. The use of several simulations with more than one assessor where there is no pooling of data; i.e., each assessor prepares a report on performance in an exercise and the individual reports (unintegrated) are used as the final product of the center.
6. A physical location labeled as an "assessment center" which does not conform to the requirements noted above.

Source: Reprinted from "Standards and Ethical Considerations for Assessment Center Operations," pp. 35–38 of the February 1980 issue of *Personnel Administrator,* copyright 1980, The American Society for Personnel Administration, 30 Park Drive, Berea, OH 44017, $26 per year.

committee member representing an employee who has been denied a promotion, while another assessee plays the role of the supervisor who denied the promotion. During this exercise, the two assessees discuss the promotion denial and try to conclude with an agreement in the best interest of the company and the aggrieved employee. Both assessees are evaluated on their communication skills and persuasive ability in addition to their ability to compromise in an effort to reach the correct result.

Leaderless group discussions, another common technique, involve a small group of assessees—about six—who are given a topic (for example, the importance of productivity and motivation in an organizational setting) for discussion but are given no structure, direction, or leadership. The group members are expected to discuss the subject in the presence of the assessors, who judge their communication skills, persuasive ability, leadership characteristics, and skill in interpersonal relations.

In addition to simulation exercises, the candidates may take paper-and-pencil tests to assess mental ability and knowledge; take part in a comprehensive interview concerning their backgrounds, future plans, and aspirations for supervisory responsibility; and write papers about their personal and career goals.

Assessments are made by a group of trained assessors whose organizational positions are at least one level above the positions pursued by the assessees. Ideally, none of the assessors should be personally acquainted with the assessees; this should allow the assessors to concentrate on the results of the assessment sessions without being influenced by prior interactions. The assessors independently evaluate each activity and rate the assessees on the characteristics, such as decision making, leadership, communication, and interpersonal relations, that are considered important for the position sought. The assessors then meet as a group and discuss each assessee. The group often concludes with an overall rating, such as (a) more than acceptable, (b) acceptable, (c) less than acceptable, and (d) unacceptable for promotion.[24] The assessees are usually given the results orally as well as in a written report. In the majority of cases, specific developmental recommendations are made to the candidates ready for promotion and also to those who need further training and experience before they will be considered suitable for promotion.[25]

Evaluating the Assessment Center Technique Wide acceptance of the assessment center by the personnel profession is one indicator of its effectiveness. However, its effectiveness must be compared with its cost, which typically is about $1,500 per candidate.[26]

The assessment center method has several distinct advantages over the more traditional approaches, such as relying on performance ratings or seniority. Its most common use is in the assessment of nonsupervisory employees for promotion into supervisory positions. In this type of promotion, past performance may not be an effective indicator of future performance, because nonsupervisory and supervisory positions require different types of skills. Since assessment center techniques are based on managerial skills, they expose all candidates for promotion to a common set of standard measurements of their ability to perform in a managerial position. In addition, since these exercises are closely related to the tasks of a manager, they have considerable face validity—that is, they appear to examine relevant job qualifications.

One of the most important studies to evaluate the results of an assessment center is the Bell System's evaluation of the work it did in the 1950s and 1960s. Between 1956 and 1960, 422 employees were evaluated by assessment center techniques, and their success in the organization was followed for eight years. The results of the assessment center evaluations were filed away and not revealed to any management personnel who would make relevant promotion decisions during this time. Eight years later, 78 percent of those who had been assessed as having qualifications to be promoted had already reached middle management. Of those who had not been promoted, 95 percent had been assessed as not being promotable eight years before.[27]

Results of research by proponents of assessment centers have been favorable. One study of sixty-three organizations using assessment centers indicated that their estimated savings were more than four times their costs.[28] Further, proponents of assessment centers claim that well-designed assessment center techniques can be defended on the basis of their content validity. By 1980, twelve different court decisions had endorsed the content validity of various assessment centers.[29]

Other research, however, is not as positive. One researcher stated that multiple assessment measures are not needed, the interview that is an integral part of the process has dubious validity, and the situational exercises that are relied on heavily are only in the initial stages of development as predictors of job performance. The researcher concluded that "The absurdity is that most of the procedures used to predict future job success are the very ones experience has demonstrated do not work."[30]

Other studies also give less than optimistic evaluations. John Hinrichs conducted an eight-year follow-up of an assessment center and concluded that simple and inexpensive predictions based on managerial review of the personnel files did as well as the assessment center.[31] A second study gave more credit to the staff at the assessment center than to the assessment center itself. The researcher hypothesized that the assessment center is able to work because the staff members learn to make judgments based on their knowledge of the organization and of the preferences of higher-level managers.[32]

A final problem involves the negative effects on assessees who are told that their performance at the center was unacceptable and the necessity for the organization to set policies on how long the unsuccessful candidate must wait before being assessed again.

Validation Problems of Promotion Decisions

Promotion decisions come under the general heading of employment procedures, and are subject to the federal EEO agencies' Uniform Guidelines. Therefore, organizations that have promoted a disproportionately low number of minority employees may be required to show validity for their promotion decisions. Management may wish to follow employees' progress through the organization to determine which predictors are most effective in foretelling job success. For example, if performance ratings in first-line supervisory positions are closely correlated with performance in middle management, performance ratings can be considered valid predictors of job success for middle management. Further, if general laborers are given the opportunity to train for apprenticeships, their scores on various skill training tests may be correlated with later performance to determine whether these training tests are valid predictors of job performance.

While the validation strategies discussed in Chapter 6 are appropriate here, there are several reasons why validation of promotion decisions is difficult. First, the numbers of people promoted into similar positions are likely to be too small and to occur too infrequently to make a predictive validity study feasible. Next, promotion decisions are made on the basis of diverse types of information, such as performance ratings, assessment center scores, evaluations of potential, and so on. Also, organizations may want to base their promotion decisions on job dimensions that may not be important in the job at the present time but may be expected to become important in the near future. For example, candidates for promotion to a senior marketing position might be given credit for foreign language proficiency because the company is considering an expansion of its marketing activities to foreign countries. Further, certain jobs may be used as stepping stones for "fast-track" employees who are expected to be of future value in higher positions in the organization. It might be necessary for a prospective marketing executive, for example, to receive brief exposure to personnel and production operations. This individual's present qualifications for such positions might be lower than those of other applicants. However, under the circumstances, the company might ignore this discrepancy, focusing instead on long-range potential. Finally, those who are promoted usually include only the high performers from the level below; so the validation study would be based on a restricted sample.

**Career
Planning
and
Development**

An important personnel activity that relates to internal staffing has emerged in the last several years—career planning and development. These activities involve the personnel department in its role of helping employees establish or reexamine their career objectives and then providing opportunities for them to achieve their objectives. While career planning and development are essentially employee-centered, a growing number of organizations are recognizing that such activities are essential to the effectiveness of an overall internal staffing system.

**Career
Stages**

Careers develop over people's working lives and can be divided into at least five stages, which occur at different ages for different people. Recognition and understanding of these stages helps the personnel department to determine how its staff can facilitate a person's advancement and adjustment to the various stages.

Pre-work career exploration involves people's examining their needs and personal goals and evaluating the alternatives and educational choices available. In this stage, which usually occurs when people are between sixteen and twenty-one, individuals rely on family members' and vocational counselors advice, test results, and personal interest to determine their directions.

Career establishment begins with the individual's entry into the world of work, ideally in a position that matches organizational needs with the individual's needs. This stage involves the individual's entry into the organization, socialization on the job, recognition for effective work, possible promotions and transfers, and achievement of full acceptance by the work group.

The advancement stage is characterized by upward movement in the organization. In this stage, the individual is not so concerned with fitting into the organization as with moving up in the organization. Those who are successful realize job satisfaction and self-fulfillment. Many remain in this stage for a long period. On the other hand, the less successful never reach the advancement stage but instead move to the next stage.

The *maintenance stage* begins when people detect cues that they are nearing the limit of their advancement; their careers are beginning to level off, and/or their need to compete is declining. In this stage, people seek other means of personal gratification, such as helping younger employees or engaging in community- and society-oriented activities.[33]

The *disengagement stage* may occur at various ages, depending on the person's degree of success in previous stages. Those who are not very successful may begin to disengage after they reach a mid-career crisis in their forties or fifties; they may merely go through the motions of their jobs until they reach retirement. Successful employees may continue to be active and make productive contributions to their organizations until their last day on the job and may resist retirement. Others may develop new and productive careers.[34]

Career Planning and Development Considerations

Some believe that fate, luck, or chance accounts for a great deal of what happens in careers.[35] However, many believe that careers can be logical and well planned. Researchers like to trace people's careers in an attempt to identify reasons for success and failure. Four principal categories that fit most employees have been identified:

The *learners,* or *comers,* who have high potential for advancement but presently perform below standard.

The *stars,* who have high potential for continued advancement and do outstanding work on a fast-track career path.

The *solid citizens,* who presently perform at a satisfactory level but have little chance for advancement.

The *deadwood,* who have little potential for advancement and whose performance is presently unsatisfactory because of lack of motivation or ability or because of personal difficulty.

While the deadwood is viewed as the organizational problem that must be dealt with in the short run, the real challenge for the organization is to prevent the solid citizen from becoming deadwood and to create opportunities for the comers and stars to reach their potential.[36]

To meet these challenges, organizations are willing to invest resources in career planning and development activities. Pressures to establish formal career planning and development programs have come from several sources: highly talented job prospects who give preference to employers who can demonstrate that opportunities exist in their organizations; women and minority employees, mid-career employees, and college recruits who ask for career-planning assistance; affirmative action plans and court-approved settlements of employment discrimination suits that require career development programs for women and minorities; and organizational growth and staff requirements that necessitate individual career planning to meet organizational needs.

While interest in career planning and development is growing, organizations also have certain fears about committing resources to these activities. For example, upper management may believe that career planning could raise employees' expectations unrealistically high and consequently cause greater employee turnover when expectations are not met. (In fact, however, effective career planning should cause the individual to be more realistic about career expectations.) Also, career counseling adds burdens on supervisors who are already fully engaged. Likewise, the programs require company resources—for training, tuition reimbursement, executive time, and so on—that are often

Exhibit 7.3   **Typical Career Paths (Ladders)**

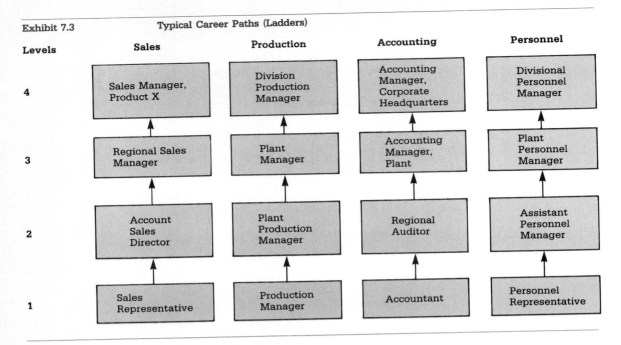

Levels	Sales	Production	Accounting	Personnel
4	Sales Manager, Product X	Division Production Manager	Accounting Manager, Corporate Headquarters	Divisional Personnel Manager
3	Regional Sales Manager	Plant Manager	Accounting Manager, Plant	Plant Personnel Manager
2	Account Sales Director	Plant Production Manager	Regional Auditor	Assistant Personnel Manager
1	Sales Representative	Production Manager	Accountant	Personnel Representative

scarce. Finally, career planning activities lead to demands for more organizational information, such as that concerning vacancies, salary levels, and career opportunities, which the organization may be reluctant to provide.[37] (Of course, in an open, trusting environment, much of this information is already provided.)

Within the general framework of career planning, organizations as well as individuals are frequently faced with questions concerning the most appropriate career ladders for promising executive candidates. Some organizations allow employees to specialize and move up within their specialties. In such cases, the career path is similar to those in Exhibit 7.3. Other organizations may prefer broad-based experience among their executives and provide a wider range of experiences for executives as they move up the organizational ladder. As shown in Exhibit 7.4, to reach the top, the president of such an organization may have started in production, moved to sales, to accounting, to personnel, and to finance before becoming assistant to the president and finally president. While these broad-based experiences provide knowledge in each of the organization's functional areas, movement up through one functional area allows the development of greater expertise, which may be needed by an organization that wants to focus its attention on a specific area.

Consideration must also be given to the increasing number of *dual career families,* in which both husband and wife have careers. While traditional personnel policies and practices have not had to face this issue and many organizations have yet to determine their policies

Exhibit 7.4   **Broad-Based Career Path**

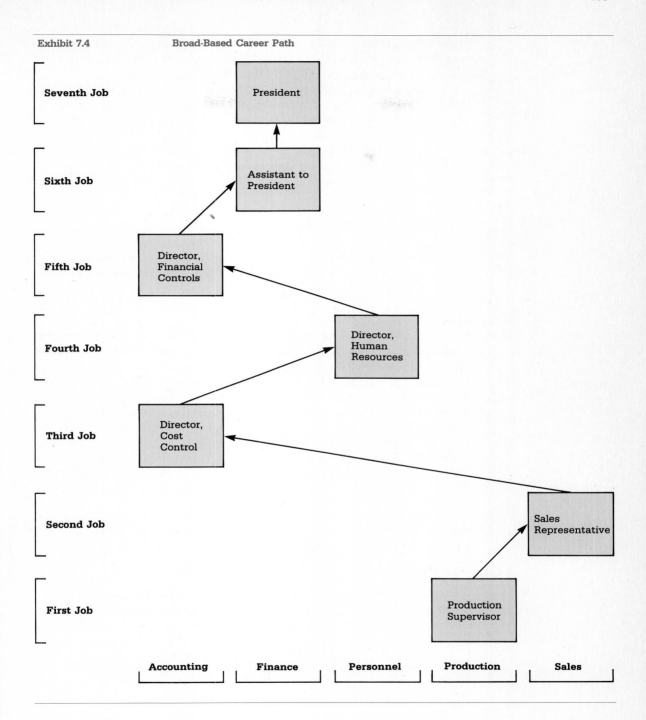

regarding it, dual career families are becoming commonplace. During recent years, the number of dual career families has risen substantially, and most experts expect the rise to continue.

Difficulties occur in career development when one spouse will not relocate or even accept a promotion unless both careers in the family are improved. The dual career issue will definitely have an impact on organizations' policies and practices regarding recruiting, scheduling, career advancement, promotions, and relocation; and organizations will have to determine their attitude and policies to accommodate this new organizational reality.

[While] some companies may try to resist this trend by selecting more passive or easily socialized people, [the more progressive] corporate response . . . is to develop more flexible management policies and practices so that the potential for growth of the [self-directed] employee is not only tolerated but utilized for increased corporate, as well as personal, success.[38]

Career Planning and Development Activities

Career planning and development activities occur at two levels: the organizational level and the individual level. Organizational career planning focuses on future organizational needs, career paths, assessment of employees' potential, and interconnection between organizational needs and individuals' opportunities and desires for advancement. Individual career planning focuses on the individual employee's needs, skills, abilities, and desires for the future. It involves employees' awareness of their abilities and interests, their plans to achieve their goals, and the designing of career paths for their advancement.[39]

For a formal career planning and development program to be effective, the individuals involved need to know and understand the following:

His or her interests, values, achievements, objectives, abilities and skills, and competencies.

His or her work and future in the organization.

Ways of obtaining information within the organization, such as through skill inventories, job posting, getting nominated for promotions, and organizational politics.

The external labor market, the status of job opportunities, the probabilities of the closing out and opening up of new opportunities, the impact of new technology or policies, and so on.

The opportunities available for personal and professional growth.

The dimensions and personal impact of career stages.

The organization needs to have the following:

Knowledge about itself, such as current demographics of its human resources, implications for human resources of organizational plans and business trends, societal and environmental impact, and so on.

Information about individual employees, their abilities, interests, goals, performance levels, past contributions, and the like.

Ways to communicate career-related information to employees—open-position listings, self-nomination procedures, catalogues of educational programs, and opportunities for career discussions.[40]

A Model Program To give the reader a better indication of the content of a comprehensive career planning and development program, a model that includes four major components is outlined below:

I *Announcement of the Program:*

Notices on bulletin boards, articles in internal company publications, announcements at staff meetings, and distribution of pamphlets.

Notices that include discussion of the general purpose and philosophy of the program and activities of the individuals involved.

Encouragement of employees to consider their own situations and determine whether the program is appropriate for them.

II *Pre-Workshop Activities:*

Orientation to provide more detailed information so employees can determine whether to proceed.

Activities for those who decide to continue, including: writing a brief history about themselves that includes education, work experiences, influences on their worklife, reasons for choosing their present career, preceived past accomplishments, and so on; listing their assessments of their skills and abilities, strengths and weaknesses, and areas of desired development; completing a questionnaire on career concerns and values related to work, family, and nonwork activities; considering their long-range career goals and plans for attaining these goals.

Identification by each participant of three to five people who can provide information about his or her strengths, weaknesses, behaviors, potential, and the like and who will be willing to anonymously evaluate the participant.

A series of personality, interests, and value inventories administered and scored for use later in the workshop.

III *Workshop Activities:* (These activities involve about fifteen participants and four professionals at an off-work site for about four days.)

Session 1: Introduction and orientation; get-acquainted exercises designed to build trust and openness; small-group activities to consider factors that affect careers; exercises in which participants draw their lifelines and explain the ups and downs and trends of their lives, write introductions for themselves ten years in the future, and list long-range career goals.

Session 2: Assessment of skills such as decision making, oral and written communication, leadership, and ability to plan, develop, and control the work of others; involvement in individual and group exercises such as leaderless group discussions and role playing; assessment of needs for achievement, affiliation, and power and values related to family, leisure, and work; assessment of activities intermixed with feedback on results and discussion.

Session 3: Integration of self-assessment with other assessments; lectures on career development (patterns of adult development, vocational choices, models of career growth); small-group discussions for sharing preliminary career plans and brainstorming for potential career paths.

Session 4: Lecture on applied behavioral analysis, self-behavior modification, and steps in career planning; planning of intermediate steps for career growth; formulation of action plan for implementing career development plan; sharing of plans and feedback on feasibility of plans and obstacles to implementation; presentation and discussion of plans for follow-up activities.

IV *Follow-up Activities:*

Regular meetings for assessing progress toward goals.

Publications, such as newsletter or round-robin letter written by participants.

Continued coaching by the employees' immediate supervisors.

Continued association among employees involved in program.

Demonstrations of organizational support, such as job posting, training, professional development committees, and career counselors or mentors.[41]

**Staffing
during
Declines
in Employment**

One message for the 1980s and thereafter is that structural changes in the U.S. economy and consequently in the U.S. workforce will continue. Job obsolescence will be brought about by technological changes, and personnel reallocation will be brought about by plant closings and realignment of U.S. and world markets. Many workers at all levels will find that skills they developed over several decades are no longer required. "The highly specialized human resources within many troubled firms are discovering that they are looking at obsolescence. Personal obsolescence."[42]

**Avoiding
Layoffs**

Between 1976 and 1979, 42 percent of U.S. companies found it necessary to lay off employees. Less senior employees are usually laid off first, and organizations face a strong possibility that these workers will not return to their former jobs but will find employment elsewhere. This situation can cause organizations to lose their investment in training new employees and to lose young, aggressive employees who in the future must operate the company. To deal with this problem, companies have looked for and in some cases found ways to avoid layoffs, especially during the initial stages of declines in economic activity. Alternatives include; reducing hours of work for all employees, building inventories, offering voluntary leaves of absence, using vacations and early retirement, and asking employees to accept wage concessions to reduce labor costs. Some companies have planned ahead for the inevitable times of economic decline by hiring only temporary employees; using overtime, at least in the short run; selling from built-up inventories; extending delivery time; and subcontracting excess work during upswings.[43]

Naturally, both advantages and disadvantages are involved in these layoff avoidance programs, and they must be considered in light of their benefits and costs. The major costs include extra payroll costs, such as for early retirement; pay for temporary workers while they are being trained; and pay for overtime during expansion. Other problems include possible loss of sales because of extended delivery time and financial costs of carrying extra inventories. Finally, if technological advances are delayed to avoid layoffs, productivity increases may be lost.

The benefits include higher morale; lower unemployment insurance costs; savings on recruiting, selection, and training; less resistance to technological change; and favorable image in the community.[44] In addition, some nonunion companies use the layoff avoidance program to help maintain their nonunion status.

**Layoffs—
Methods
and Programs**

Even with programs to avoid them, layoffs still occur; and they are costly to the employer and traumatic to the individuals laid off:

> Layoffs, as a particular kind of crisis, dramatize issues imbedded in normal work relations. Subordinates feel a one-sided dependency upon hierarchical powerholders and a concomitant sense of individual helplessness that at times approaches terror. . . .
>
> In the factory, where individualism and meaningful specialization on the job are repressed, it is almost impossible not to see oneself as a commodity—a commodity that is replaceable on the labor market, a commodity whose human qualities are irrelevant to its disposition.[45]

Before employees are laid off, they are usually informed about the benefits, such as unemployment benefits, to which they are entitled; the effect of layoff on company benefits, such as group insurance; and recall rights and notification procedures relevant when a job becomes available.

Some organizations allow *bumping,* a system permitting one employee, usually with longer service, to displace another employee with less service. This system provides job security to long-service employees. Because bumping on a companywide basis would create havoc with operations, it is usually limited—for example, bumping by senior employees may be permitted only on jobs for which no training is required or which the senior employee has already held in the past.[46] Companies must be careful when they use bumping. One company, Lockheed, claims to have lost $15 million in two years because of a complicated seniority system that allowed layoff-threatened employees with more than six years' service to take junior employees' jobs. Studies showed that one layoff caused a chain reaction of an average of five job switches, causing serious problems with employees' learning their jobs.[47]

Two general programs often associated with layoffs are financial supplements and outplacement services. Some employers have such programs to help employees until they become eligible for unemployment compensation. Because most states have a one- or two-week waiting period before unemployment benefits take effect, a week's pay or more is often given when a layoff begins. Supplemental unemployment benefits (SUB) are negotiated with unions to supplement state unemployment benefits. Although the amount of payment varies, most plans allow the laid-off employee 60 to 80 percent of regular pay. Qualification and duration of benefits usually depend on the length of employment prior to the layoff. The SUB plans are normally financed by employers' contributions to a fund administered by a trustee or a joint union-management committee. However, some plans allow establishment of individual accounts from which employees may draw during layoffs, disability, or other financial emergencies. In other words, this fund serves as a form of forced savings plan.[48]

Some companies have provided outplacement services to employees whose layoffs are permanent. Because typical employees may experience job hunting only two or three times in their lives, they frequently need guidance and help to find jobs when they are terminated. In outplacement programs, employees are taught how to apply for jobs, prepare resumes, and be interviewed. Other services include job fairs arranged by the company; use of the company's WATS line, copying facilities, office space, and career counselors; and provision of resume booklets prepared by the employers and mailed to other employers who may have openings.

Organizations perform such services because they are committed to maintaining their public images as good employers. In addition, if they are successful, they can receive savings in their unemployment taxes by reducing the time their employees receive unemployment compensation.[49] One study of outplacement programs at Sears and American Can estimated a saving of $14.50 for every dollar invested in the program. This estimate was based on the experience that 70 percent of the participants found jobs within 60 to 180 days after the layoff.[50]

After a temporary layoff, employees are usually recalled in reverse order of their layoff. Thus, the factors—seniority, ability, and so on—used in determining whom to lay off are also considered in determining whom to recall. In some cases, special consideration may be given to employees essential for startup operation after a shutdown.

Some companies limit recall rights to six months, because some employees tend to lose their skills after a long layoff; and the better employees find other jobs, leaving only the less desirable with first preference on the recall. Other considerations should include establishing procedures for maintaining contact with employees; determining how the employees will be recalled, such as by letter or radio announcement; and setting a time limit during which employees must report to accept reemployment.[51]

Legal Considerations in Layoffs

Employers have been taken to court over layoff and recall decisions based on seniority. When employers, under affirmative action programs, are hiring minorities at a greater rate than in the past, their company seniority lists frequently feature white males toward the top and minorities at the bottom. When layoffs occur, the employer using the last-hired, first-fired policy lays off the newly hired minority employees first.[52] This common layoff procedure was challenged in the courts as being unfair and discriminatory to minority employees; and it was not until recently that the issue was settled by the Supreme Court. The Court has upheld seniority systems (1) that were instituted prior to the enactment of the Civil Rights Act of 1964, that were adopted in "good faith" (non-discriminatory) after 1964, and (3) where evidence must be presented to show that there was no "intent to discriminate" against minority employees in the administration of layoff policy.[53] In cases where a company has continued discriminatory acts after 1964, the seniority system loses its status as a bona fide seniority system; and proper adjustment must be made. Minority employees who suffered under such discriminatory practices must be restored to their rightful place in the organization and may receive back pay for the time during which they were discriminatorily laid off.[54] Many large companies are concerned that layoffs of minorities and women will leave them with a workforce in which these groups are underrepresented, making them vulnerable to EEO suits. Because unions have shown little willingness to give up their hard-fought seniority provisions for the sake of keeping the newest employees on the payroll, companies are trying to transfer these newly hired employees to other departments and plants. With unions on one side and federal EEO agencies on the other, companies face a real dilemma. As Thomas Hourihan, vice-president of human resources, Norton Co., says, "It's Catch-22 . . . you're damned if you do and damned if you don't."[55]

Role of the Personnel Department and Other Managers in Internal Staffing Processes

The staff of the personnel department and managers throughout the organization serve important functions in internal staffing processes. The personnel department coordinates staffing activities and plays an essential role in formulation of policy and procedures. Where assessment centers, peer nominations, skills inventories searches, and early identification programs are operable, the personnel department is usually an important part of the planning and administrative structure. The personnel department helps line managers in their assessment of candidates' qualifications and tries to minimize the time they must spend in the screening process. Since personnel records are an important responsibility of the personnel department, especially where skills inventories are established, the personnel department must be sure the proper records are maintained and appropriate government (EEO) reports are sent. Finally, where a career planning and development program exists, the personnel department usually designs and administers it.

Line managers usually make the final decisions in internal staffing matters within the limits of established policies and procedures. They serve as staff members of the assessment center when the organization has one. They help to identify employees who have managerial abilities and potential; and throughout the year they appraise the performance of their employees—a valuable input for promotion decisions. Line managers help determine the qualifications necessary for vacant positions; and when the position changes in duties and responsibilities, the appropriate changes are made by the immediate supervisor. Finally, line management serves as a resource for the personnel department in formulating policies and procedures for internal staffing processes.

**Issues
in Internal
Staffing**

Internal staffing involves activities that force organizations to face the following issues: Should seniority or ability be the basis for promotion decisions? Should organizations try to identify leaders early in their careers? When is a promotion really a promotion?

Issue: ## Should Promotions be Based on Seniority or Ability?

In making promotion decisions, organizations attempt to act in the best interests of the organization and the individuals involved. Organizations want productive employees in every position and want to reward employees for past performance. Employees want to be rewarded for past performance and want to be given a fair chance at higher-level positions. Thus enters the controversy involving the use of seniority versus ability as the basis for promotion decisions.

Relying on seniority has several features that appeal to organizations as well as to some individuals within these organizations. First, seniority is objective and easy to measure. Once seniority is defined, it is easy to administer; and grievances by employees who are denied promotions can be dramatically reduced, because everyone is treated the same. The senior candidate receives the assignment regardless of the supervisor's likes, dislikes, and personal biases. Second, using seniority demonstrates gratitude from the organization for employees' loyalty and long service. Employees realize that the longer they remain with the employer, the greater their job security and thus the less their anxiety and need to change jobs. One feature that cannot be overlooked by nonunion firms is that basing promotions on seniority takes away an important part of the sales pitch of unions conducting organizing drives. Also, the organization will save money that it invests in developing assessment centers, designing tests, validating peer nominations, and so on; it simply promotes on the basis of seniority. Finally, the firm may avoid EEO suits by reliance on seniority if no employment discrimination has occurred after the passage of the Civil Rights Act of 1964 and if the promotion system was established with no intention of discriminating against women and minorities.

Reliance on seniority, however, also has several negative features. First, while past performance is considered an excellent predictor of future performance, this principle applies to situations in which the nature of the jobs are similar. If promotions to higher-level jobs require skills not needed in the lower-level jobs, past behavior may not accurately predict future behavior. Second, using seniority has a discouraging effect on aggressive, talented, new employees. It may dampen their motivation to achieve on the job; even more likely, they may not accept employment with a firm when they discover that it relies heavily on seniority in promotion decisions. Third, reliance on seniority, though it may allow for the promotion of a qualified candidate, may not allow the organization to select the most qualified candidate for a position. Fourth, relying on seniority does not allow new blood to flow into higher-level positions. Frequently, organizations need a boost, a change in direction, new ideas, or an opportunity for fast-track employees (discussed earlier in the chapter) to move quickly in and out of a variety of organizational positions. Basing promotions on seniority precludes these considerations. Last, promotion based on seniority does not provide an opportunity for promising black and female employees to move up the organizational hierarchy and does not add to the firm's reputation as an equal opportunity employer.

Issue:

Should Organizations Try to Identify Leaders Early in Their Careers?

During the 1980s, a generation of senior executives who entered the business world after World War II will be retiring, leaving U.S. industry with a crucial shortage of management leaders. Because the cost of an executive search averages $50,000 in addition to the costs of temporary disruptions and adjustments, some firms have espoused the career advancement concept often referred to as the *crown prince* syndrome. These firms have attempted to identify early in their careers individuals with high potential for advancement and provide them with developmental experiences and special courses as they advance in the corporate structure.[56]

Some organizations call similar efforts early identification programs. NCR Corporation of Dayton, Ohio, screened 4,000 white-collar employees and identified 828 with high performance. Each of them completed a biographical questionnaire and a psychological test called the Strong Campbell Interest Inventory. The results were used to determine whether the employees' backgrounds and interests were similar to those of successful NCR managers. This group was then narrowed to about 100 people, who were given more tests and interviews. From this group, the organization selected twenty-four who were considered the promotables. While none of these individuals know they have been singled out, NCR is making a special effort to provide them with a series of managerial jobs that will broaden their experiences. Douglas Yaeger, assistant vice-president for management development, states: "We're trying to find people very early on who have strong potential for general management.[57]

This approach has the obvious advantages of narrowing the number of persons to receive management development and reducing the costs of administering a development program. A negative feature of the approach arises when the firm proves to have made a mistake in identifying members of this narrow group. In such a case, an expensive search for a replacement must take place, because too few employees have been prepared for promotion to higher-level positions.[58] Another negative consequence occurs when employees who are productive find out they have not been chosen to be among the crown princes and subsequently leave the organization.

Issue:

When Is a Promotion Really a Promotion?

An organizational reassignment usually involves some change in pay, working conditions, and status. A promotion occurs when these variables are increased; a transfer, when they remain the same; and a demotion, when they are decreased. This rather simplistic explanation is probably more applicable to changes in hourly positions than to changes in salaried positions. Usually, everyone in the facility knows the wages and conditions associated with hourly positions (a situation seldom found at the salary level). Finally, the hourly employee (unlike the typical salaried employee) usually has the option of turning a new assignment down. The hourly employee therefore has the freedom to determine whether or not a new assignment really represents a promotion.

Defining a reassignment in terms of promotion, transfer, or demotion becomes much more complicated for the salaried employee. Consider, for example, the following new assignments that could be offered a salaried or managerial employee. In each case below, try to determine whether the change from *Job a* to *Job b* represents a promotion, demotion, or lateral transfer.

Case 1

Job a. Industrial relations manager, Parkersburg, West Virginia, production facility (one of seventeen plants in one division of the company). Reports to plant manager. Responsible for all personnel and labor relations activities (training, employment, wage surveys, grievances, safety, and so forth) pertaining to the facility's 1,400 hourly and salaried employees. Supervises five exempt employees and two secretaries.

Job b. Divisional manager of training. Reports to the division's general manager of personnel. Responsible for devising and implementing appropriate training programs for division's 12,000 hourly and salaried employees. Job represents a 20-percent increase in pay and is located in New York corporate headquarters. Has supervisory responsibilities for one secretary.

Case 2

Job a. District sales representative for all of Company X's consumer products sold to distributors, who in turn sell products to retail stores. Reports to regional sales manager.

Job b. Brand manager for one of Company X's consumer products. Responsible for coordinating nationwide production and promotional efforts for this product. Responsible for advertising coupons. Makes sure production facilities mark appropriate discounts on packages. Also makes sure production scheduling is timed so that sufficient quantities of product are available in store after advertising campaign. Reports to manager of marketing.

Case 3

Job a. Vice-president, production, in Company X's largest division (largest in sales, profits, and employees). Reports to the executive vice-president of the division.

Job b. Executive vice-president of Company X's smallest division, which has had a steady decline in profits. Reports to the president of that division.

These examples suggest several general problems in defining a promotion. For one, there are too many variables involved in a new assignment. Exhibit 7.5 indicates several job-related variables suggested by these examples; but this exhibit is far from exhaustive. No exact equation concerning the variables can be formulated, since in many cases it is necessary to compare unlike qualities (for example, level in the organization compared with number of employees supervised). Any new assignment probably increases some variables while decreasing others. This situation is complicated further when the applicant for the new assignment adds to the equation non-job-related variables (such as pulling his or her children out of their present school, leaving a familiar and pleasant living environment for an unfamiliar one, forcing his or her spouse to give up his or her present job, and so forth).

Another problem is the many uncertainties involved in a new job assignment. Often, the motives behind the promotion are unclear. For example, in Case 3, it is difficult to know whether top corporate officers are giving the individual the opportunity of a lifetime to turn the division around or are placing the individual in a position from which he or she will be let go if the division is subsequently disbanded or sold.

Exhibit 7.5   **Job-Related Variables Usually Associated with a Promotion**

Increase in pay (adjusted for possible changes in cost of living).
Access to higher-level company officials.
Job title.
Title and position of new supervisor.
Number of people supervised.
Nature of work (reviewing, coordinating, planning versus directing).
Authority at least equal to responsibility for implementing activities.
Promotional opportunity after new assignment is completed.
Scope of duties.
Potential impact on the organization in terms of dollars generated or saved, number of employees affected by actions, ability to make a significant change in organization's policies and related activities.

There is ample opportunity for these problems to occur; a recent *Fortune* study of the top 1,300 U.S. corporations indicated that nearly 300,000 executive transfers take place yearly at an average cost approaching $20,000.[59] Another survey revealed two interesting facts: (1) 51 percent of the responding companies indicated that an employee's refusal to accept a move would seriously jeopardize his or her future with the organization; and (2) 25 percent of these companies reported that the number of employees declining relocation had increased over the previous year.[60] Even employees accepting a new assignment might do so with some serious reservations or negative afterthoughts. A survey of 1,000 midwestern executives found that two-thirds of them believed their companies did not plan their transfers well.[61]

New assignments, particularly those involving relocation, can therefore offer many problems for both the organization and the employee. Here is yet another personnel area in which the concern of the employee might at least partially be reflected in organizational policies and actions. Perhaps many companies should more thoroughly consider the implications of the new assignment before offering it to the employee—and in some cases pressuring him or her to accept.

The following diagram shows various values of new assignments to the organization and the employee:

New Job Assignment

		Value to the Organization	
		Minimal	High
Value to the Employee	Minimal	1	2
	High	3	4

If, after careful analysis, the new assignment is found to fall into the first or fourth categories, the implications are obvious—type 1 assignments should be minimized and type 4 assignments stressed. More difficult to deal with are type 2 and type 3 job assignments. With type 2 assignments, the employee's supervisor should explain to the employee why the assignment is necessary to the organization; and the employee should have some reasonable assurances of future rewards or benefits if he or she takes the assignment. Supervisors should actively seek type 3 assignments for their employees—often a difficult task, since the supervisor will have to convince other organizational officials that the move might eventually benefit the organization. Further, few supervisors like to remove outstanding employees from their own operations.

In any event, personnel representatives and other organizational members must realize that potential assignments require serious attention, particularly since they often have serious impacts on employees.

Summary

Internal staffing includes promotions, transfers, demotions, and layoffs. These job changes have to be deliberate, because they affect both employees and the organization. Methods used in promotions include job posting and bidding, peer ratings and nominations, and assessment centers as well as the traditional method of supervisors' recommendations. Typical assessment center techniques include in-basket exercises, role playing, leaderless group discussions and paper-and-pencil tests. While the assessment center has grown in popularity and has been accepted by the courts as being content valid, several researchers have recently questioned the value of assessment center techniques.

Career planning and development activities combine self-examination and organizational opportunities. Individuals advance through various career stages—prework career exploration, career establishment, advancement, maintenance, and disengagement—and organizations need to understand these stages. To facilitate career advancement and maximize individuals' contributions to the organization, many firms are providing career planning and development opportunities. Some organizations have initiated these activities willingly; others have been pressured by young, talented employees, women and minority groups, midcareer employees, and federal EEO agencies. Organizations must consider many factors in the design of these programs: investments of resources and time; costs; possibility of creating unrealistic expectations; choice of career paths (specialized or broad based); and concerns of dual-career families.

Staffing during declines in employment usually means layoffs. Various methods used by organizations to stabilize employment include hours reduction, leave and vacation adjustments, wage reductions, overtime, subcontracting, and temporary workers. Layoffs involve considerations such as use of seniority or bumping, recall procedures, and layoff-related activities such as financial supplements and outplacement services. Like other staffing decisions, layoffs must be consistent with EEO regulations.

The personnel department and other managers play important roles in internal staffing matters. Finally, some issues related to promotion decisions involve seniority versus ability as the basis for promotion decisions, the crown prince syndrome, and the difficulty of identifying a promotion.

Discussion Questions

1. Assess promotion-from-within policies and job-posting systems in light of equal employment opportunity concerns.

2. Since peer ratings have proven so successful in predicting success in higher-level jobs, why do organizations use this method so infrequently?

3. Project present trends into 1990 and assess the possibilities for career growth, taking into consideration limited promotional opportunities in middle management and the growing number of two-career families.

4. Assess the career planning and development activities of an organization with which you are familiar.

5. In what ways can an organization move a manager aside in order to open up promotional opportunities within the organization?

6. What are the costs and savings of the various methods of layoff avoidance?

7. Of the three cases in the chapter's final issue, which are truly promotions?

Notes

1. Richard D. Conner and Robert L. Fjerstad, "Internal Personnel Maintenance," in *Staffing Policies and Strategies,* ed. Dale Yoder and H. G. Heneman, Jr. (Washington, D.C.: Bureau of National Affairs, 1974), pp. 4-204—4-205.

2. Arch Patton, "The Coming Promotion Slowdown," *Harvard Business Review* 59 (March/April 1981), p. 46.

3. Conner and Fjerstad, "Internal Personnel Maintenance," p. 4-221.

4. Fred K. Foulkes, *Personnel Policies in Large Nonunion Companies* (Englewood Cliffs, N.J.: Prentice-Hall, 1980), p. 143.

5. Earl C. Gottschalk, Jr., "Promotions Grow Few as 'Baby Boom' Group Eyes Managers' Jobs,' *Wall Street Journal,* October 23, 1981, p. 1, 24.

6. Patton, "Coming Promotion Slowdown," pp. 46—52.

7. John Veiga, "Do Managers on the Move Get Anywhere?" *Harvard Business Review* 59 (March/April 1981), pp. 20—21.

8. Conner and Fjerstad, "Internal Personnel Maintenance," p. 4-226.

9. Foulkes, *Personnel Policies,* p. 124.

10. Fred K. Foulkes, "How Top Nonunion Companies Manage Employees," *Harvard Business Review* 59 (September/October 1981), p. 93.

11. Conner and Fjerstad, "Internal Personnel Maintenance," p. 4-209.

12. Staff of Bureau of National Affairs, *Employee Promotion & Transfer Policies* (Washington, D.C.: Bureau of National Affairs, 1978), p. 1.

13. Foulkes, *Personnel Policies,* p. 125

14. Dave R. Dahl and Patrick R. Pinto, "Job Posting: An Industry Survey," *Personnel Journal* 56 (January 1977), pp. 40—42.

15. Conner and Fjerstad, "Internal Personnel Maintenance," pp. 4-214—4-216.

16. Manual London, "What Every Personnel Director Should Know about Management Promotion Decisions," *Personnel Journal* 57 (October 1978), p. 554; Stephen A. Stumpf and Manual London, "Management Promotions: Individual and Organizational Factors Influencing the Decision Process," *Academy of Management Review* 6 (October 1981), p. 542.

17. Richard R. Reilly and Georgia T. Chao, "Validity and Fairness of Some Alternative Employee Selection Procedures," *Personnel Psychology* 35 (Spring 1982), pp. 19—24.

18. London, "What Every Personnel Director Should Know," p. 554.

19. Arie Lewin and Abram Zwany, "Peer Nominations: A Model, Literature Critique, and a Paradigm for Research," *Personnel Psychology* 29 (Autumn 1976), p. 428.

20. Eugene Mayfield, "Peer Nominations—a Neglected Selection Tool," *Personnel* 48 (July/August 1971), pp. 39–40.

21. Lewin and Zwany, "Peer Nominations," pp. 431–433.

22. Wayne F. Cascio and Val Silbey, "Utility of the Assessment Center as a Selection Device," *Journal of Applied Psychology* 64 (April 1979), pp. 107–118.

23. Richard A. Dapra and William C. Byham, "Applying the Assessment Center to Selection Interviewing," *Training and Development Journal* 32 (April 1978), p. 44.

24. "Standards and Ethical Considerations for Assessment Center Operations," *Personnel Administrator* 25 (February 1980), pp. 35–38.

25. Walter Wikstrom, "Assessing Management Talents," *Conference Board Records* 4 (March 1967), pp. 39–44.

26. "How to Spot the Hotshots," *Business Week,* October 8, 1979, p. 67.

27. Wikstrom, "Assessing Management Talents," pp. 39–44.

28. Stephen L. Cohen, "The Bottom Line on Assessment Center Technology," *Personnel Administrator* 25 (February 1980), pp. 50–57.

29. Stephen L. Cohen, "Validity and Assessment Center Technology: One and the Same," *Human Resources Management* 19 (Winter 1980), p. 8. To investigate this controversy more fully, see: George F. Dreher and Paul R. Sackett, "Some Problems with Applying Content Validity Evidence to Assessment Center Procedures," *Academy of Management Review* 6 (October 1981), pp. 551–560; Stephen D. Norton, "The Assessment Center Process and Content Validity: A Reply to Dreher and Sackett," *Academy of Management Review* 6 (October 1981), pp. 561–566; Paul Sackett and George Dreher, "Some Misconceptions about Content-Oriented Validation: A Rejoinder to Norton," *Academy of Management Review* 6 (October 1981), pp. 567–568.

30. Ann Howard, "An Assessment of the Assessment Centers," *Academy of Management Journal* 17 (March 1974), pp. 115–134.

31. John Hinrichs, "An Eight Year Followup of a Management Assessment Center," *Journal of Applied Psychology* 63 (September/October 1978), pp. 596–601.

32. Richard Klimoski and William J. Strickland, "Assessment Centers—Valid or Merely Prescient," *Personnel Psychology* 30 (Autumn 1977), pp. 353–361.

33. Edgar H. Schein, *Career Dynamics* (Reading, Mass.: Addison-Wesley, 1978), pp. 41–42.

34. Douglas T. Hall, *Careers in Organizations* (Pacific Palisades, Calif.: Goodyear, 1976), pp. 54–55.

35. "Plotting a Route to the Top," *Business Week,* October 12, 1974, p. 127; Daniel Seligman, "Luck and Careers," *Fortune,* November 16, 1981, pp. 60–72.

36. Thomas P. Ference, James A. F. Stoner, and E. Kirby Warren, "Managing the Career Plateau," *Academy of Management Review* 2 (October 1977), pp. 602–612; Janet P. Near, "The Career Plateau: Causes and Effects," *Business Horizons* 23 (October 1980), pp. 53–57.

37. J. W. Walker, "Does Career Planning Rock the Boat?" *Human Resource Management* 17 (Spring 1978), pp. 2–7.

38. Francine S. Hall and Douglas T. Hall, "Dual Careers—How Do Couples and Companies Cope with the Problems?" *Organizational Dynamics* 6 (Spring 1978), p. 77.

39. Elmer H. Burack, "Why All of the Confusion about Career Planning?" *Human Resource Management* 16 (Summer 1977), pp. 21–23.

40. Sharon L. Connelly, "Career Development: Are We Asking the Right Questions?" *Training and Development Journal* 33 (March 1979), p. 10.

41. Phillip G. Benson and George C. Thornton, III, "A Model Career Planning Program," *Personnel* 55 (March 1978), pp. 30–39.

42. Tom Jackson, "Industrial Outplacement at Goodyear, Part 2: The Consultant's Viewpoint," *Personnel Administrator* 25 (March 1980), p. 430.

43. Staff of Bureau of National Affairs, *Layoff and Unemployment Compensation Policies* (Washington, D.C.: Bureau of National Affairs, 1980), pp. 2–4.

44. Foulkes, *Personnel Policies,* p. 118.

45. Richard M. Pfeffer, "When the Niceties Go," *New York Times,* April 30, 1975, p. 41.

46. "Layoff," *Personnel Management* (Washington, D.C.: Bureau of National Affairs, 1980), pp. 207:401–207:417.

47. "Why Lockheed Strike Is a 'Holy War,'" *Business Week,* December 19, 1977, p. 31.

48. "Layoff," pp. 207:405–207:406.

49. Conner and Fjerstad, "Internal Personnel Maintenance," p. 4-235.

50. Tom Bailey, "Industrial Outplacement at Goodyear, Part I: The Company Position," *Personnel Administrator* 25 (March 1980), pp. 42–45.

51. "Layoffs," p. 207:407.

52. William H. Holley, Jr., and Hubert S. Feild, "Equal Employment Opportunity and Its Implications for Personnel Practices," *Labor Law Journal* 27 (May 1976), p. 285.

53. *International Brotherhood of Teamsters et al.* v. *U.S.,* 45 L. W. 4566 (1977); *Patterson* v. *American Tobacco Co.* 28 EPO 32, 561 (1982).

54. Marvin J. Levine, "The Conflict between Negotiated Seniority Provisions and Title VII of the Civil Rights Act of 1964: Recent Developments," *Labor Law Journal* 29 (June 1978), pp. 352–363,

55. Amal Nag, "Slipping Back: Recession Threatens to Erode Job Gains of Women, Minorities," *Wall Street Journal,* January 7, 1980, p. 1.

56. Marion Kellogg, "Executive Development," in *Training and Development,* ed. Dale Yoder and H. G. Heneman, Jr. (Washington, D.C.: Bureau of National Affairs, 1977), p. 5–109.

57. Bernard Wysocki, "Talent Hunt: More Companies Try to Spot Leaders Early, Guide Them to the Top," *Wall Street Journal,* February 25, 1981, p. 1.

58. T. J. Murray, "Where Are Tomorrow's Top Managers?" *Dun's Review* 114 (December 1979), pp. 98–100.

59. "Locating the Company's Relocation Program," *Financial Executive* 46 (February 1978), pp. 26–33.

60. "Managers Move More but Enjoy It Less," *Business Week,* August 23, 1976, pp. 19–20. See also another survey, which indicated that 42 percent of the employees turned down a transfer, a tenfold increase over the previous year: "More Employees Say No to Transfers," *Industry Week,* August 2, 1976, pp. 23–24.

61. William F. Glueck, "Managers, Mobility, and Morale," *Business Horizons* 17 (December 1974), pp. 68–70.

1. Grace Lowrey, an accountant with one of the "Bight Eight" accounting firms, worked in Oakland, California. She had an accounting degree from the University of California at Berkeley and five years' experience as an accountant; and she was interested in moving into a management position. A friend who worked at Western Pacific in Oakland told Grace that an accounting manager's position had been announced in Western Pacific's house publication. Grace immediately applied. When she was interviewed, she noticed that the department was composed of all males; but she believed she was most qualified among the people considered candidates for the position.

Two weeks after her interview, Bill Smith, an inside candidate, was promoted to the management position. Grace was notified that the company had selected him based on a promotion-from-within policy.

Grace filed a complaint with the EEOC. What do you believe will be the outcome? Explain.

2. The Delta Corporation decided that it needed better-qualified supervisors to cope with the ever-growing, complex problems in its organization. Its answer was a presupervisory training program. The program was advertised widely in company publications and promoted throughout the company. On the date applications were due, twenty nonwhite and sixty white employees volunteered for the program. Using performance appraisals and ratings by supervisors, the company chose a class of fifty trainees—ten nonwhite and forty white.

As soon as the class started, the company was notifed by the EEOC that a charge had been filed against it. Does adverse impact exist? If so, what must the Delta corporation do to prove that it did not discriminate against nonwhite applicants in selecting members for the presupervisory training class.

3. Two years later, the Delta Corporation was trying to determine whether the presupervisory training program had been effective in supplying qualified supervisors. It conducted in-house study that showed five nonwhite and thirty white trainees had been promoted since their successful completion of the training program.

Does adverse impact exist? If so, what must the company do to prove that its internal staffing decisions are nondiscriminatory?

1. Hastings Oil Company, which has an affirmative action plan, has expressed an interest in promoting a female to a supervisory position. The company has never had a female supervisor. During an interview, the personnel director pointed out to Gladys Mathews, a candidate, that she would face problems if she was promoted and that she should be aware of them while she considered the promotion. Then, he promised her the next promotion if she refused the present one. A week after the interview, Larry Tate, a white male, was promoted. Two weeks later, the company was notified that an EEOC charge had been filed against it.

What is your assessment of this situation?

2. William Ikerd, with excellent experience and references, answered an ad for a first-line supervisor. During the initial interview, it was revealed that Ikerd was fifty-two years of age. The interviewer said something like this: ''I was afraid of that. You have impressive credentials for this job. Don't misunderstand me, but you are probably over-qualifed for this position. Our company has been trying to develop a more youthful, aggressive, forward-looking image. I'd like to hire you, but you know top management—my hands are tied.'' Two weeks later, Ikerd was informed that his application had been rejected.

What is your analysis of this interview? Are there problems?

3. David Hunt, personnel director, believed Nancy Smith was an excellent prospect for a personnel interviewer position. During an interview with her immediate supervisor, Hunt discovered that Smith had three school-aged children. Later, he asked Smith: ''What do you plan to do with your children when school is out or when they are sick?'' She replied: ''That's a personal question!'' He responded: ''I guess I'm too sensitive about this issue, but my last assistant gave me a lot of problems staying home with her children.'' The interview was completed, but Smith's application was rejected.

What potential problems exist?

In an interview with Robert Boyce, the employment manager of a medium-sized electric utility company, the following question was asked: "What selection procedures for employing hourly workers are used by your company?" The employment manager replied that applicants fill out an application form that includes personal data, experience, education, references, and so on. The applications are filed in accordance with the job categories that interest the applicants. "We tell all applicants that their applications will be active for only 60 days unless they inform the company that they wish to continue as active applicants," he continued. "When a job is vacant, we retrieve the application forms, study them, compare them with the job specifications, and invite the three most-qualified applicants for an interview."

The next question was: "If you rely on the interview, how do you avoid EEOC charges?" Boyce replied: "That's easy. We call in the three most-qualified candidates during the same week so that we can make a valid comparison of qualifications and suitability. We maintain no records of the interview; so the EEOC cannot say we use the interview to discriminate."

Questions

1. Assess the selection strategy used by this company.
2. According to EEOC guidelines, is the company safe from EEOC charges?
3. What recommendations would you make to the employment manager?

Using the Incident Method in an Assessment Center to Make Promotion Decision

You are a supervisor in a production department of a local furniture manufacturing plant. The leadperson (assistant supervisor) has decided to transfer to another department, and this transfer will create a vacancy. In accordance with your company's promotion-from-within policy and related procedures, the job vacancy has been posted for two weeks; and proper notification has been given to employees in the company newsletter. On the final date for bidding on the vacancy, three members of your department applied.

Your class assignment is to obtain enough information on the candidates and on the company situation to make a qualified decision. You are to ask specific questions, and your professor will respond to them by giving the appropriate answers. If you ask the correct questions, you will obtain all the available data and will be able to make an informed decision. However, if you ask the wrong questions or an insufficient number of correct questions, your decisions will not be based on complete information.

Once you have decided which employee should be promoted, you must justify your answer orally to the professor. The assessment of your performance will be based on: inquisitiveness, creative questioning, logical reasoning, persuasive ability (communicating your decision and the reasons for it), and systematic decision making.

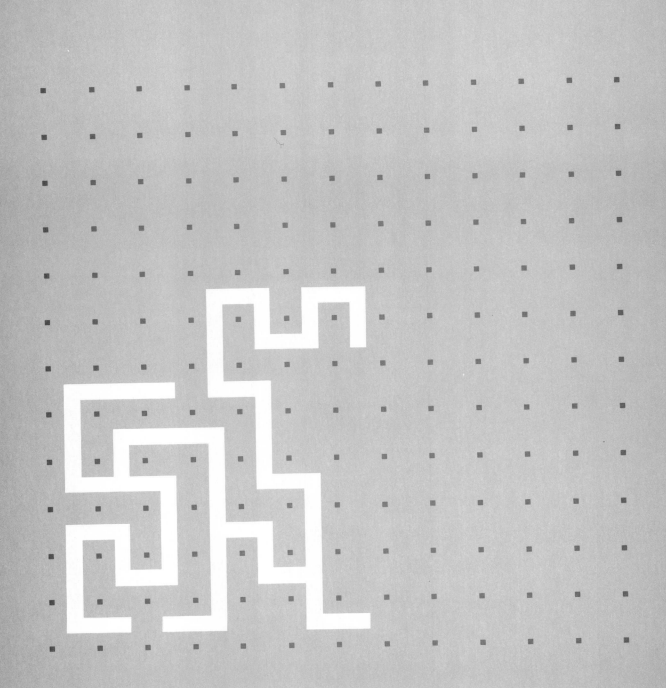

Part Three

Measuring and Developing Employee Potential

Throughout an employee's career, his or her performance will be appraised. Further, each employee will attempt to realize his or her potential; and the organization will attempt to develop employees' skills and abilities so that their contribution to the firm will be enhanced. Chapter 8 introduces the performance appraisal and explains the elements of a comprehensive performance appraisal system. Chapter 9 discusses training and development activities, including determination of training and development needs of both individuals and organizations, training and development processes and methods available to managers and employees, and evaluation of training and development activities.

Chapter 8

Performance Appraisal

In recent years a great deal of management attention has been directed towards the development of valid and equitable performance appraisal systems. The momentum . . . has come from companies vitally concerned with finding new ways to enhance the performance of their employees. However, performance appraisal programs have at least two audiences: they should provide management with information on wage and salary decisions, promotions and dismissals, and training and development needs, and provide employees with feedback as to how well they are doing their job, specifying their strengths and weaknesses.

We receive appraisals throughout our lives. In fact, we may conclude that we live in a society in which some form of appraisal is occurring almost at every moment. This chapter pertains to a specific type of appraisal—appraisal of job performance.

This personnel activity received national publicity in 1979 when the White House instructed its managers to use a numerical scale to appraise their subordinates on such nebulous traits as confidence, maturity, flexibility, loyalty, and brightness. Although the form allowed space for the manager to list the employee's strengths and weaknesses, some believed it placed personnel theory in the nineteenth century. The Carter White House was not alone in its problems with performance appraisal; the subject has been attacked from nearly every angle. Appraisals have been labeled as overly subjective, cumbersome, illegal—a nuisance at least and an evil at worst. In fact, the search for an effective performance appraisal system has been compared to the search for the Holy Grail.[1]

This chapter will present the elements of a comprehensive performance appraisal system. These elements include the purpose, content, method, and frequency of appraisal; the choice of appraisers; and performance feedback. Also discussed are sources of errors and the components of an effective system. The chapter concludes with the discussion of a controversial issue concerning the relationship of pay to performance.

Elements of the Performance Appraisal System

Performance appraisal has plagued the personnel professional for years, possibly because too much has been expected from performance appraisal systems. As will be shown later, organizations want appraisals to serve many purposes; they want to base salary increases on performance, use appraisals to reinforce effective behavior and eliminate ineffective activities, use them as a development tool, use them to provide a realistic assessment of employees' potential for advancement, and use them as a valid defense in an employment discrimination suit if one should occur.[2]

Realistically, an organization has no choice about whether to appraise employees' performance. Personnel decisions, such as salary adjustments and promotions, must be made; and there should be some rational basis for these decisions. With the exception of the smallest firms, organizations typically use formal appraisal systems which include forms, procedures, and policies.

While numerous factors must be considered in the design and administration of performance appraisal systems, the following six questions provide a framework for most organizations:

1. What are the purposes of performance appraisal?
2. What is to be appraised?
3. How is it to be appraised?
4. Who will appraise?

5. When is appraisal performed?

6. When and how should feedback be given?[3]

Purposes
of Appraisal

One of the first decisions to be made in the design of a performance appraisal system concerns the purposes for which the system is intended. Most decisions about design usually flow from this determination. Common purposes include serving as a basis for salary decisions and promotion decisions and helping in employee planning and development.

The organization's perception of the purposes of performance appraisals may differ from that of individual employees. While the organization essentially uses performance appraisals as a basis for personnel decisions and for developmental efforts, individuals view appraisals as a means of receiving feedback on their performance, satisfying their psychological needs for success, learning how to avoid unfavorable evaluations, and obtaining higher pay and promotions.

Among these various purposes, possible conflicts can occur, as shown in Exhibit 8.1. For example, two of the organization's purposes for appraising performance may conflict—if a low score on a performance appraisal justifies a low wage increase, how can the performance appraisal feedback be used for developmental purposes? Conflicts between the organization's purposes and the employee's can lead to adversary relationships between supervisors and employees. When performance is outstanding, promotions and salary increases are abundant, the supervisor is adequately prepared, and plenty of time has been allowed, performance appraisals provide the basis for a pleasant experience. Unfortunately, during times of limited resources, lack of opportunities, and time pressures and stress on supervisors, appraisals are difficult.[4]

**Content of
Appraisal**

At the beginning of the process to design a performance appraisal program, the organization must determine what performance measures will be used. Some measures are objective, such as production, costs, and return on investment. Others are based on behaviors, objectives, or traits. Behavior-based procedures define performance in terms of observable physical actions or behaviors; objectives-based procedures define performance in terms of job-related end results; and trait-oriented procedures define performance in terms of personal characteristics observed in the employee's work activities.[5]

Because the courts and EEOC have mandated that appraisals be based on objective criteria obtained from job analysis, organizations have attempted to develop more objective performance measures. However, subjectivity enters the appraisal of all jobs.[6] For example, a secretary's job cannot be measured completely in objective terms. One can measure the speed at which a secretary can type, take dictation,

Exhibit 8.1   **Conflicts in Purposes of**
                                   Performance Appraisal

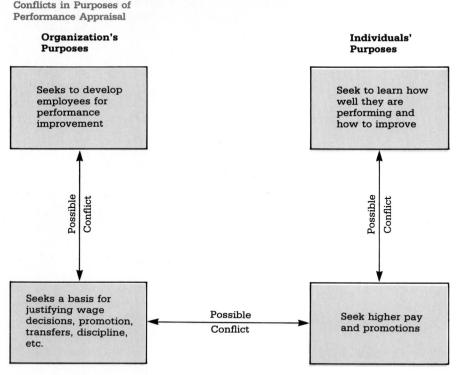

and transcribe. However, the secretary may type twenty letters one day, none the next. Also, the speed of taking dictation partly depends on the dictating ability of the supervisor.

A manager's performance is frequently appraised according to objectives agreed upon in discussions with supervisors. But should the production supervisor be held accountable if the units produced are 20 percent less than the planned objective because overall business slumped and there was no demand for the product? How do you account for the fact that a supervisor may set low objectives so the objectives can be easily achieved? On a machine operator's job, it would seem that performance could be easily measured objectively. However, such performance depends on a machine that must be operational and parts that must be ready to be processed. Further, the standard is determined on the basis of what the normal operator produces, taking into account allowances for fatigue, personal time, breaks, and the like. Are these determinations completely objective?

While judgment and subjectivity are part of every appraisal process, organizations must continue to strive to reduce errors of judgment and increase objectivity. Whatever the procedure chosen, the content of the appraisal must be job-related and derived from proper job analysis (covered in Chapter Four). On some jobs, it may be most appropriate to appraise the performance of an employee from the product or results produced. However, where such products are inaccessible or difficult to measure, behavior or traits exhibited on the job may be selected.[7] Because organizations vary in terms of what they expect from the appraisals and how they plan to use them and because jobs vary in terms of observable and measurable job dimensions, a number of methods have been designed to meet these numerous purposes and job conditions. The methods described in the following section are those which are most commonly used and widely accepted.

Methods of Appraisal

After the purpose and content of performance appraisal have been determined, the next step is to match the method to the established purposes (or uses). A variety of performance appraisal methods exist, and selection among them should be based on the organization's objectives. The more common methods are: graphic scales, essay appraisals, comparative methods, critical incident technique, forced choice method, behaviorally anchored rating scale (BARS), and management by objectives (MBO).

Graphic Scales The most commonly used method for appraising employee performance is the graphic scale. Introduced in 1922, this method uses a scale to denote a range of performance from unsatisfactory to outstanding for each of a number of job dimensions (see Exhibit 8.2). The rater judges the employee's performance on these job dimensions, sometimes totaling the ratings to obtain an overall score for the appraisal. In an attempt to assure that the dimensions are job-related and that the overall score reflects performance on the specific job, weights may be given to each job dimension.[8]

Essay Appraisal The essay, or narrative, appraisal is a written summary of an individual's performance based on guidelines provided the appraisers. For example, a supervisor may be asked to describe how an employee has performed during the past year by discussing his or her strengths, areas for improvement, quantity and quality of work, potential for advancement, and so on. Although the guidelines provide some structure to the appraisals, the supervisor retains much flexibility of expression. However, this method is time consuming, impractical for evaluating large groups of employees, overly subjective, and difficult to administer.[9]

Comparative Methods Comparative methods include appraisals in which supervisors compare employees against one another, such as by rating them from best to worst. Employees may be compared on one measure relating to overall performance or on a number of specific traits, behaviors, or job characteristics. Comparison methods are classed into three

Exhibit 8.2   **Performance Appraisal Using Graphic Scale**

Department of Personnel

NAME   POS. NO.

BLACKEN in the space provided with a no. 2 pencil *only*.
Read each of the descriptions carefully;
they are not necessarily in order.

Performance Review Form

JOB KNOWLEDGE   N/A ☐

☐ Knows job reasonably well.	☐ Lacks some basic knowledge and expertise.	☐ Knows job well.	☐ Reasonable knowledge and expertise.	☐ Occasionally requires assistance.

ATTITUDE   ☐

☐ Poor job interest.	☐ Attitude varies with personal mood.	☐ Constantly motivated to do an excellent job.	☐ Conscientiously motivated to do a good job.	☐ Reasonably conscientious about doing a satisfactory job.

PLANNING AND ORGANIZATION   ☐

☐ Plans and organizes work satisfactorily.	☐ Extremely effective in organizing work unit and planning future objectives	☐ Lacks some basic organizational and planning skills.	☐ Occasionally, plans and organization lack detailed consideration.	☐ Usually plans and organizes work well.

EMPLOYEE DEVELOPMENT   ☐

☐ Generally counsels employees on self-development and training needs.	☐ Offers sound advice for improvement and development.	☐ Occasionally counsels employees.	☐ Apathetic about employee recognition and self-development.	☐ Frequently counsels employees on self-development.

DIRECTING AND CONTROLLING   ☐

☐ Rarely delegates.	☐ Delegates occasionally.	☐ Usually delegates well.	☐ Delegates effectively.	☐ Generally delegates.

EXPRESSION   ☐

☐ Expresses himself clearly and effectively.	☐ Sometimes unable to express subject matter clearly.	☐ Does not communicate effectively on most subjects.	☐ Usually clear in expression for most situations.	☐ Reasonably clear in expression.

SUPERVISORY RELATIONS   ☐

☐ Always considerate of employees' feelings, fair to all.	☐ Usually shows interest in employees.	☐ Occasionally shows interest in employees.	☐ Generally shows interest in employees' feelings and situations.	☐ No interest in employees.

INITIATIVE   ☐

☐ Constantly finds and pursues appropriate new opportunities.	☐ Lets things go along unless forced to innovate.	☐ Does not initiate many innovations himself/herself	☐ Modifies procedures and activities appropriately on occasion.	☐ Often finds better ways of dealing with things.

SUMMARY EVALUATION   ☐

☐ Results achieved consistently exceeded the requirements of the job.	☐ Results achieved exceeded the requirements of the job at times.	☐ Results achieved met the requirements of the job.	☐ Marginal performance, must improve.	☐ Inadequate performance, on notice.

My immediate supervisor and I have discussed this evaluation. ☐

I have checked by agreement or disagreement with each area reviewed and I understand those areas in which I need improvement. ☐

NAME _____

Exhibit 8.3   **Ranking Method**

Employees		Overall Rank
Abbott	Best	1
Doe	Next Worst	6
Green		3
Jones		4
Johnson		5
Smith	Worst	7
Walker	Next Best	2

categories: (1) ranking, (2) paired comparison, and (3) forced distribution.

Ranking entails placing the employees in order of overall performance. Supervisors are asked to select the best and worst performers, to select the next best and next worst, and then to rank the remainder within these extremes (see Exhibit 8.3). The shortcoming of the method is that ranking overall performance does not reveal employee's strengths and weaknesses in various components of the jobs and does not indicate the distance between ranks. In some cases, the top three performers may be equally outstanding while the fourth may be below average.

The *paired comparison,* or person-to-person, method requires that each employee be compared, one at a time, with every other employee. The appraiser then selects the better employee in each comparison, and the final rank is determined by the number of times the employee was rated higher than the other employee being appraised (see Exhibit 8.4). While this method is simple for a small number of employees, it is prohibitively time consuming and cumbersome for larger numbers. For example, a seven-employee department requires twenty-one comparisons, but an eleven-person department requires fifty-five. The problem mounts when comparisons involve several job behaviors or characteristics.

The *forced distribution* approach is founded on the principle of the bell-shaped curve, or normal statistical distribution, which requires the rater to assign a specific proportion of employees to predetermined performance categories, such as those indicated in Exhibit 8.5. While forced distribution attempts to eliminate the problems of inflated ratings and the tendency of raters to give everyone high ratings, it has limited application to small departments and is overly rigid.[10] For instance, consider two departments in an organization: Department A has a high proportion of employees who are better-than-average performers, and Department B has a high proportion of average performers. A forced distribution approach in this situation completely distorts

Exhibit 8.4	**Paired Comparison—Quantity of Production**								
		A	D	G	JS	JN	S	W	Score	Rank
	Abbott (A)		X	X	X	X	X	X	6	1
	Doe (D)						X		1	6
	Green (G)	X			X	X	X		4	3
	Jones (JS)	X				X	X		3	4
	Johnson (JN)	X					X		2	5
	Smith (S)								0	7
	Walker (W)	X	X	X	X	X			5	2

Note: X means that the individual's performance is better than the individual's with which it was compared. For example, Abbott's is better than Doe's, Green's, Jones's, Johnson's, Smith's, and Walker's, while Doe's is better only than Smith's.

a comparison between these departments' employees' performance. In other words, it cannot be assumed that departments throughout organizations always have the same proportion of outstanding, above average, below average, and unsatisfactory performers.

A variation of this technique is the *nomination* method, which requires the supervisor to select a certain number of employees who are outstanding performers and an equal number who are inadequate. The remaining employees are not differentiated but are listed as satisfactory.[11]

Critical Incident Technique The critical incident technique requires the rater to record incidents of an employee's behavior that represent less than satisfactory or outstanding performance (see Exhibit 8.6).[12] Usually, the appraisal form lists categories for classifying and recording the incidents, such as productivity, quality of work and so on. These recorded incidents provide the basis for appraisal and feedback.

Although the critical incident technique continues to be useful as a research method, its popularity as a method of performance appraisal has waned. This waning popularity is due partly to the tedious chore of recording the observations, the tendency of supervisors to delay feedback, and employees' possible resentment and lack of influence on or knowledge of the standards by which they are appraised.[13]

Exhibit 8.5	**Forced Distribution**

Instructions: Assign the employees in your department ratings in accordance with their overall performance using the following distribution as the guide:
10 percent: Outstanding
20 percent: Above Average
40 percent: Average
20 percent: Below Average
10 percent: Unsatisfactory

Exhibit 8.6   **Critical Incident Performance Record**

Performance Indicators	Incidents of Less than Satisfactory Performance	Date	Incidents of Outstanding Performance	Date
Productivity				
Quality of Work				
Initiative and Ingenuity				
Dependability				
Personal Development				
Use of Work Time				
Others (Specify)				

Forced Choice Method Dissatisfied with what it considered lenient performance ratings, the personnel research section of the U.S. Army devised the forced choice method during World War II. This method groups statements related to a particular job and requires raters to select from a group of three to five statements one statement or more that best describes the employee's job-related behavior (see Exhibit 8.7). Each statement is given a weight according to its relevance to the particular job. The rater is not given the weightings and so cannot show favoritism. The employee receiving the highest overall score is judged the best performer, and so on. While this method seems to be a job-related, bias-free approach, it has serious problems. It is not well accepted by raters; the preformulated statements greatly reduce their flexibility, and they have difficulty using the statements to provide feedback. Further, the scale is complicated and costly to develop; and its results have proved to be no more valid than those of the graphic scale.[14]

Behaviorally Anchored Rating Scale (BARS) BARS, a recently developed method or appraisal, incorporates elements of a rating scale and the critical incident approach. The requirements for effective performance

| Exhibit 8.7 | **Forced Choice Appraisal** |

From each group of descriptive statements below, mark *MD* beside the statement *most descriptive* of the employee's behavior and mark *LD* beside the statement *least descriptive* of the employee's behavior.

I.   _____Becomes dogmatic about authority.
    _____Careless in attention to duty.
    _____No one ever doubts his/her authority.
    _____Well adjusted in all phases of company activities.

II.   _____Follows directions closely.
    _____Inclined to "gold-brick."
    _____Criticizes unnecessarily.

III.   _____A go-getter who always does a good job.
    _____Cool under all circumstances.
    _____Doesn't listen to suggestions.
    _____Drives instead of leads.

IV.   _____Always criticizes, never praises.
    _____Carries out orders by "passing the buck."
    _____Knows job and performs it well.
    _____Plays no favorites.

V.   _____Constantly seeks new ideas.
    _____Businesslike in manner.
    _____Apparently not physically fit.
    _____Fails to use good judgment.

Source: Adapted from Elaine F. Gruenfeld, *Performance Appraisal: Promise and Peril* (Ithaca, N.Y.: NYSSILR, Cornell University, Key Issues no. 10, 1981), p. 10. Used by permission.

in a specific job or job category are identified and anchored at one end of the rating scale. Ineffective performance is identified and anchored at the opposite end. Within these extremes and along the continuum scale, specific definitions, examples of job behaviors, or critical incidents are described. The rater determines which description or example of job behavior best identifies the employee's performance and scores the performance for each behavior on the appraisal form. Exhibits 8.8 and 8.9 show such scales for a manager and a personnel representative.

BARS has several advantages over other methods. Persons who will use it are usually extensively involved in its development, and the development process provides an important learning experience for them. The feedback that the method provides employees is usually specific and job related, and the review sessions focus on behaviors that contribute to successful performance.[15]

While BARS appears to eliminate the errors commonly associated with the graphic scale, its development requires considerable time, effort, and commitment of resources.[16] Separate forms must be developed for unrelated jobs, creating significant costs for organizations that have a large variety of jobs and only a few employees in each

Exhibit 8.8

**Managers' Performance Appraisal
Using BARS**

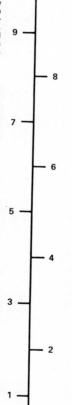

| WestPoint Pepperell | **PERFORMANCE PLANNING AND REVIEW SYSTEM** (SALARIED EMPLOYEES) | APPENDIX G: RATING SCALES/GENERAL EFFECTIVE: 2-26-79 SUPERSEDES: (New) | PAGE: G-16 |

REPRESENTING THE ORGANIZATION TO THE PUBLIC

The individual represents the Company formally in community affairs in an effective and professional manner.

The individual has projected a very positive image of the Company to those in the community with whom he/she has worked. He/she has made an obvious contribution to the community as well. His/her sense of service to the community and loyalty to the Company is surpassed by only a very few employees. He/she could be trusted as a Company spokesman under any condition.

— 9

— 8

The individual has been a real asset in cementing and maintaining a good relationship with the community and its activities or services. He/she has deliberately and consistently worked to present a positive image of the Company. He/she has made a contribution to the community's welfare through his/her actions. He/she would only require guidance as a Company spokesman in a few extreme situations.

— 7

— 6

The individual has been a willing representative of the Company in those community activities in which he/she was asked to participate. He/she presented a positive attitude toward the community and took care to present a positive image of the Company. He/she requires little supervision as a Company spokesman under most conditions.

— 5

— 4

The individual has presented the appearance of grudging participation in the public relations activities. This person has not shown an appreciation for the importance of good community relations. He/she presents a negative image of the Company, either on purpose or unwittingly through his/her acting.

— 3

— 2

The individual has presented a very negative image of the Company and its employees. He/she would not be a candidate for any future participation in community relations. He/she could never be trusted as a Company spokesman.

— 1

Code 022679-G-G-16

Source: Courtesy of WestPoint Pepperell, West Point, Georgia.

Exhibit 8.9   **Personnel Representative's Performance**
Appraisal Using BARS

West Point Pepperell	PERFORMANCE PLANNING AND REVIEW SYSTEM (SALARIED EMPLOYEES)	EFFECTIVE: 2-26-79 SUPERSEDES: (New)	PAGE: P-15

SELF DEVELOPMENT

The individual makes planned and organized effort to prevent technical and/or professional skills becoming obsolete. The individual treats all job situations as developmental and growth experiences and is always aware of personal skill deficiencies and makes conscious efforts to improve.

Could be expected to have obtained an advanced degree or certification and continues to maintain current knowledge on professional matters through professional associations, journals, and workshop attendance. — 9

— 8 — Could be expected to belong to a professional PIR, training, or safety association and subscribe to personnel-oriented periodicals in an effort to keep current of changes and issues in his/her profession.

Could be expected to attend training courses for line managers, as well as those pertinent to his/her own professional field, so as to gain a better understanding for the problems and perspectives of those for whom staff support was being provided. — 7

— 6 — Could be expected to read professional literature extensively in an attempt to prevent becoming an obsolete resource of information on human resource management, training, safety, etc.

Could be expected to be involved in a deliberate, professional reading program. — 5

— 4 — Could be expected to say or believe that it was a knack for getting along with people that got him/her started in the PIR field and between that and a human relations course he/she had taken, he/she was well-prepared to perform his/her job duties and responsibilities.

Could be expected to comment that "if you keep your eyes and ears open, all you ever have to learn about PIR work can be found on your job." — 3

— 2 — Could be expected to consistently decline enrolling in professionally-developing PIR courses or seminars.

Could be expected to have read no professional (PIR) periodicals or made any attempt to attend a professionally-developing meeting, seminar, or training course in the past year. — 1

Code 022679-G-P-15

Source: Courtesy of WestPoint Pepperell, West Point, Georgia.

category. Also, developing and preparing the rating scales requires fairly sophisticated statistical analyses, and unless the organization already employs someone with skills for such analysis, a consultant must be hired, resulting in greater costs.[17] Thus, although BARS is intuitively appealing, its limitations are serious.[18] In fact, one review involving a comparison of BARS to the graphic scale has concluded that it is "difficult to justify the increased time investment in the BARS development procedure."[19]

Nevertheless, BARS has several features that may appeal to large organizations with the technical capability and commitment to develop the system. First, employees realize that performance is measured on the basis of actual job behaviors. Second, the appraisal instrument is used by people actually involved in its development; therefore, employees are more closely identified with the system and more willing to accept its use. Third, the process of developing the scales helps identify valid predictors for selection and promotion decisions and gathers data for training. Finally, discussion and development of job performance scales by employees and managers should improve communication and understanding.[20]

Management by Objectives Management by objectives (MBO), or results-oriented, appraisal is a popular and apparently effective approach to appraising managerial performance. MBO assumes that performance can be measured best by comparison of actual results with plans (see Exhibit 8.10). MBO essentially entails three phases. First, objectives (or goals) for a predetermined period of time are established, usually by mutual agreement between the supervisor and the employee. These objectives must coincide with those of the department and the overall organization. During the subsequent period, frequent discussions about progress, problems, obstacles beyond the employee's control, and so on must occur to make the system work. Finally, at the end of the period, actual results are compared with the predetermined objectives; and objectives for the next period are established.

MBO has several appealing features, particularly with regard to managerial performance appraisal. It sets objectives in advance, allowing managers to direct or prioritize their activities in a way that will affect their appraisals. Because the system requires setting objectives, it highlights the planning function, causing managers to think ahead, anticipate obstacles, and develop a mind-set oriented toward the future. In addition, the appraisal is obviously job related, because the objectives essentially define the most important elements of the job. MBO enhances appraisal feedback; since objectives have been established before the appraisal interview, the discussion can focus on problems, ways to improve, resources and assistance needed, and future objectives.[21]

Exhibit 8.10   **MBO Approach to Performance Appraisal**

KEY SPECIFIC OBJECTIVES							(Name)
PERFORMANCE PLANNING			PERFORMANCE ASSESSMENT				
Column A	Column B		Column C				Column D
KEY SPECIFIC OBJECTIVES	PERFORMANCE REQUIREMENTS		RATING				PERFORMANCE ASSESSMENT COMMENTS (OPTIONAL)
List the key specific objectives to be accomplished by the senior executive during the appraisal period. These may include managerial, organizational and/or individual responsibilities. Key objectives should be realistic and as specific as possible. Asterisk (*) any critical element(s).	Specific statement(s) of what accomplishments, results, or actions are necessary for assessment or performance as successful. Use interim milestones or intermediate results for longer term objectives.	OUTSTANDING	HIGHLY SUCCESSFUL	SUCCESSFUL	MINIMALLY SATISFACTORY	UNSATISFACTORY	Indicate the rationale for the rating. Other significant general comments on results achieved, behaviors observed that affect job performance or factors beyond the senior executives control may be included here.

Signatures / Optional

Supervising Official _____ (date)

Executive _____ (date)

_____ (date)

_____ (date)

Page 1 of _____

Source: Courtesy of NASA Headquarters.

MBO, like other appraisal systems, has its problems. MBO is more than a performance appraisal method, since it offers a means by which management can make decisions and give directions for the organization. The process must work at all levels of the organization and must be coordinated and integrated among these levels. The sales manager, for example, cannot be expected to establish an objective of increasing sales volume by 15 percent if the production facilities are already producing at capacity. Another problem occurs when the system is not monitored closely, allowing some managers to establish unrealistically low objectives so they can attain them easily and receive bonuses, salary increases, and other rewards. On the other hand, when unrealistically high objectives are set in an attempt to challenge the manager to perform at a higher level, frustration and disappointment result if the objectives are not reached.[22] Some employees might also *bank* under MBO—that is, achieve extra output in one period but list this output in the next reporting period. Banking allows employees the option of working at levels below their capacities.

Organizations using MBO must also be conscious of the overemphasis on objectives of some managers, who may achieve their objectives in the short run but leave the department with low morale, high turnover, and other problems in the longer run. Pressures on managers to meet goals can cause them to behave unethically. Managers at H. J. Heinz Company resorted to deceptive bookkeeping to meet profit goals. A plant manager at Dorsey's glass-container plant overreported production to assure that an aging plant would not be closed. A classic example occurred in a General Motors assembly plant, where three managers increased the speed of the assembly line in violation of the General Motors–United Auto Workers labor agreement in order to meet production goals (UAW later won a $1 million back-pay settlement, and the three managers were transferred).[23] To avoid such problems, it is necessary for objectives to emphasize not only results but also managerial processes—such as developing employees and handling grievances—by which results are achieved.[24]

MBO requires considerable time, training, commitment from the top of the organization, and resources to be effective. Research has shown that the following principles are important:

1. Setting specific goals is more likely to lead to higher performance than telling the employee to "do their best."
2. Employee participation in setting goals tends to lead to higher goals than unilaterally set goals.
3. Higher goals tend to lead to high performance.
4. Feedback is critical to reinforce goal setting, maintain employee interest, revise goals, and continue employee efforts.
5. Employees will set high goals if they are evaluated on performance rather than simply on goal attainment.
6. Employees should not be evaluated on factors over which they have no influence or control.
7. Employees must not be threatened by job loss that results from higher performance.[25]

Combining BARS and MBO Because the objectives-oriented appraisal system is criticized for its overemphasis on the short run and for overlooking managerial processes and because BARS is criticized for its failure to include measurable results, attempts are now being made to integrate MBO and BARS. This approach would entail identifying common, results-oriented job dimensions and designing behavior-based measurements along these dimensions. For example, a manager's job might include several dimensions under the following headings: (a) administrative activities, such as planning, organizing, and controlling; (b) interpersonal skills, such as communication, leadership, and motivation; and (c) technical skills, such as report writing. Also, each manager's performance would be appraised on performance effectiveness measures—cost reduction, production increase, waste control, quality of output, number of grievances, and the like. With a growing interest in both behavior-oriented and objectives-oriented appraisals, there is reason to believe that this combination of the two approaches will grow in popularity.[26]

One personnel executive says of his firm's system:

Integrating BARS, a modified BARS, and MBO considers that three elements must be combined to provide a minimally comprehensive appraisal. First, there must be a clear understanding of the job: its responsibilities, relationships, and priorities. Second, there must be a clear and mutual understanding of specific goals or objectives. At WestPoint Pepperell, three categories of goals are identified: Routine, Project, and Self-Development. In addition to setting appropriate work objectives, priorities of those objectives are established to avoid confusion when rating the effectiveness on an overall met expectations/did not meet expectations rating. Finally, an appraisal of job-related skills, abilities, and activities is conducted. Goals may be achieved not so much due to the rated individual's actual contribution, but rather to that of a favorable business environment or subordinates' effort. Another case where MBO fails in appraisal is when an objective is not achieved, and was, due to the individual's work environment, probably unachievable as the rating period progressed. Comments can explain the discrepancy, but an appraisal of job-related skills that had been brought to bear upon the effort provides a more complete picture. Finally, an appraisal of the performance element along with the results element can provide a useful vehicle for personal development discussion, particularly where some work objectives were not achieved.[27]

Choosing Appraisers

The ideal appraiser is one who has observed the performance of a job, can determine what is important about it, and can report judgments without error or bias. The absence of one or more of these characteristics leads to questionable performance appraisals.[28]

Typical appraisers are supervisors, peers, subordinates, and employees themselves. Each type has its own merits, and organizations may use them separately or in combination. *Supervisory appraisals* are the most common, and subordinates seem to favor them. Supervisors are usually the ones most knowledgeable about the job requirements from the organizational view, and they are in a position to observe and judge an individual's performance. *Peer appraisals* are useful when the supervisor is unable or less qualified to observe certain job behaviors and employee characteristics.[29] Such appraisals have been particularly valuable in identifying leadership potential.[30] However, careful watch should be maintained to avoid inflation of ratings, since peers may tend to agree to give each other high ratings.

Subordinate appraisals have been used in situations where the focus is supervisory development. The subordinates are asked to respond anonymously to such questions as: "Are you kept informed in the matters that concern you." "Does your supervisor provide you with an environment that should bring out your best performance?" "Does your supervisor exhibit work behaviors that set the example for the department?" Responses are given to a third party, totaled, and fed back to the supervisor for consideration. Since the objective is improvement of supervision, the supervisor usually meets with a personnel professional to discuss the results of the responses. For this approach to be effective, the supervisors must be receptive to it. On the other hand, the supervisor is already being appraised indirectly by subordinates, because the appraisal of a supervisor's performance is usually the results of the employees' work.[31]

Self-appraisals have received increased attention since the development of MBO systems, since self-appraisal is built into the MBO process. While self-ratings may be inflated and may place too much emphasis on getting along with others in the department, self-analysis—introspection—can be valuable if seriously performed.[32] Because employees respond more positively to appraisals that are consistent with their own, the key may be in providing sufficient appraisal data so that employees can develop their own appraisals.[33] Advocates attest that self-appraisal results in more satisfying and constructive appraisal interviews, less defensiveness, and greater improvement in subsequent job performance.[34]

Because raters in different positions can appraise different dimensions of a job more accurately,[35] organizations sometimes use more than one type of rater. *Multiple raters* are likely to observe employees' performance with varying frequency. For example, peers usually have frequent contact with each other, while supervisors observe employees' performance intermittently. Further, different rater groups may have different expectations of employee performance. Generally, supervisors are less lenient and have high expectations; peer appraisals and self-appraisals are typically less critical.[36]

A combination of approaches brings together the benefits of each, provides a wealth of information useful for development and decision making, and pulls certain theories about appraisals together. However, administering more than one approach must be justified in terms of cost-benefit considerations.

**Frequency
of Appraisal**

Although performance appraisal must be a continuous process, formal systems require that appraisers periodically fill out the appropriate forms, discuss the appraisals with employees, and make decisions based on the appraisals. Most firms conduct appraisals annually, either on the employee's anniversary date or during a predetermined period for all employees. Using the anniversary date allows the supervisor to stagger the appraisals throughout the year and avoid a mad rush to complete all forms and discussions during a single period. Also, since a merit increase is usually given on the employee' anniversary date, the decision concerning such an increase can be made at the time of the appraisal. Some organizations, which focus on setting objectives, planning, and coordination between departments, must complete their appraisals during the same time period. In these organizations, appraisals are usually conducted at the beginning and ending of the planning period.

Some personnel professionals have concluded that conducting only an annual appraisal is too inflexible; they believe more meaningful and timely feedback should be provided frequently, such as after a major project is completed. Others have proposed that periodic progress reviews throughout the appraisal period should be held to discuss the changing conditions of the job.[37] There is substantial evidence to suggest that reducing the intervals between appraisals improves the accuracy of the appraisals, upgrades the effectiveness of their administration, and makes the appraisal process less liable to attack for race, sex, and age discrimination.[38]

**Sources
of Error
in
Performance
Appraisal**

The performance appraisal process is not error free; indeed, it requires careful monitoring and assessment by the personnel department. This section discusses general sources of errors that may be found in performance appraisals.

Errors in the administration of performance appraisal systems can be categorized under four headings: (a) attitudes of higher management officials, (2) tendencies and perceptual inaccuracies of raters, (3) characteristics and interactions of raters and people being rated, and (4) format of appraisals.

**Attitudes
of Higher
Management
Officials**

Performance appraisal systems, like other personnel activities, need the support and encouragement of top management. Many times, top management gives pro forma support to the inauguration of appraisal programs, perhaps by signing a cover memo describing the program or making a "kick-off" speech to managers attending a training session in performance appraisal techniques.

However, executive support may be reduced during the administration of the program. Relatively few companies reward raters for their abilities in administering appraisals. Few managers are promoted for the high-quality, in-depth appraisals they give their subordinates. Indeed, one personnel executive has noted that "compensation systems tend not to reward managers for effective development and effective performance of their subordinates."[39]

Managers charged with implementing appraisals often uncover executive attitudes toward this activity that range from indifference to belief that performance appraisals are nothing more than time-consuming paper-work chores. Faced with this situation, managers may devote less time to appraisals, concentrating instead on tasks perceived to be more important. Managerial reluctance in administering performance appraisals may also be due to a belief that employees' behavior cannot be changed by a few performance appraisals.

The personnel department must enlist the aid of upper management to ensure that performance appraisals are taken seriously. Unfortunately, in some companies, this aid comes only when management fears or receives negative consequences from improper performance appraisals—namely, employment discrimination suits.[40] On the other hand, top management will support performance appraisal when the appraisal process demonstrates that it facilitates accomplishment of organizational objectives.

Tendencies and Perceptual Inaccuracies of Raters

Inaccuracies can result when appraisers exhibit certain systematic tendencies and perceptions of the appraisal process. Some appraisers, for example, seem to believe that nearly all employees are average performers; thus, they are reluctant to give very good or very bad ratings. These appraisers commit what is called a *central tendency error* when they rate nearly all employees as average. Similarly, when supervisors are required to supply written justification for any ratings other than average, some will take the easier route and give nothing but average ratings. The end result is that all employees receive an average rating, even though some may deserve an excellent rating and others may need drastic improvement.

Appraisers who give nothing but favorable ratings commit a *leniency error*.[41] Leniency may be due to several causes. Some raters are reluctant to discuss performance appraisals, particularly critical ones, with their subordinates. Some may feel threatened by a situation in which the subordinate can ask questions and discuss "anything on his mind."[42] Raters' apprehension over performance appraisals is increased when they must make judgments (in some cases, imprecise judgments of personality traits) beyond their perceived competence.

The conventional approach, unless handled with consummate skill and delicacy, constitutes something dangerously close to a violation of the integrity of the personality. Managers are uncomfortable when put in the position of "playing God." The respect we hold for inherent value of the individual leaves us distressed when we take the responsibility for judging the personal worth of a fellow man. Yet the conventional approach to performance appraisal forces us, not only to make such judgments and to see them acted upon, but also to communicate them to those we have judged. Small wonder we resist![43]

Now its one thing for an executive to react to another person's personality when "sizing him up." We do that all the time. But it is quite another thing for a manager to delve into the personality of a subordinate in an official appraisal that goes into the records and affects his career. The latter amounts to quackery—to a pretension to training or knowledge which is not in fact possessed. . . . Where does one draw the line, for example, between intelligence and common sense, or between self-confidence and aggressiveness?[44]

Such uncertainties can be minimized by giving lenient performance ratings. A similar situation was found in universities during the height of the Vietnam War. Students who received low grades often lost their student draft deferments and were likely to be drafted into military service. Many professors raised grades for students in this situation.

Leniency may also be due to the rater's desire to be regarded as a good manager. Some raters assume that poor performers in their department reflect negatively on their ability to manage. Higher-level managers in the organization may share this view, especially if an employee has received poor performance ratings two years in a row. In this situation, managers may believe that the employee's supervisor (the rater) has failed to properly develop the employee.

Since lenient ratings do not differentiate among levels of employee performance, they cause high performers to become disenchanted with appraisals.[45] Such appraisals also lose their effectiveness as a basis for personnel decisions.

Halo errors occur when raters allow their assessment of the employee's performance on one performance dimension, such as cooperation with peers, to unduly influence their assessment of each separate dimension on the rating scale. Appraisal forms usually include many job dimensions; and raters should judge each dimension (trait or behavior) separately and independently.

Other rater-related errors include overemphasizing the employee's most recent behavior; varying the ratings to meet a specific purpose, such as a salary increase; or showing a bias toward the person being rated.[46]

Rater's perceptions may also cause errors. Some raters use themselves as the norm by which to judge others. Obviously, raters' using themselves as the standard for comparison interferes with the accuracy of the ratings and may cause extreme variance in standards across departmental lines.

Characteristics and Interaction of Raters and People Being Rated

When the rater and the employee being rated share common backgrounds and are similar in age, race, sex, or education or have family connections, the rater may tend to inflate the ratings. Conversely, dissimilarites may cause the rater to give lower ratings. A rater may falsely conclude that an employee with much seniority is a poor performer, since a good performer would already have been promoted to a higher position. (In fact, an employee may stay in a position for a number of reasons.) Age, education, and personality of employees are other factors that can affect their ratings.[47]

Interaction (or lack of it) between raters and employees being rated can influence ratings and can raise the issue of lack of validity. For example, ratings can be invalid if higher-level supervisors rate individuals several levels lower without having observed their performance. Further, when the rater and employee being rated have known each other for a long time, the ratings may be affected.

Format of Appraisals

The final source of error is the appraisal format, or the rating scale itself. Performance factors—such as communication with customers, cooperation with coworkers, and use of work time—may not be well defined. The form may not provide space to explain ratings, and the scale may not allow enough variation to distinguish adequately between poor and excellent performers. Errors can be caused by the number of factors rated. When less than five job dimensions are used, insufficient data are obtained; when more than nine are used, differentiating among them is difficult.[48]

The appraisal form might also fail to take into account factors beyond the control of the employee being rated. For example, a university professor is appraised equally for teaching, research, and public service. If he or she has no opportunity to perform public service functions because of teaching and research obligations, the tasks and therefore the weights should be realigned.

Since jobs are multidimensional, they contain a wide variety of different tasks—some of which defy quantitative measurement. Still, rating of irrelevant behaviors or traits and equal weighting of job dimensions can lead to erroneous appraisals.

Important Components of an Effective Performance Appraisal System

Although there are many reasons for success of performance appraisals and just as many reasons for failure, several components are fundamental to such a system's effectiveness. An important part of any comprehensive performance appraisal system is continuous monitoring and assessment. After introducing a new system or revising an

existing one, the personnel department usually establishes a procedure for assessing the system's effectiveness. This assessment may
include feedback from managers and employees, analysis of appraisals
for rating errors (leniency, central tendency, halo error), examination of
rating tendencies, analysis of interrelations between raters' and rated
employees' characteristics and ratings given, and investigation of possible legal problems.[49]

Some organizations computerize appraisal results and assess possible trends in rating tendencies, such as inflation trends over time. The
computer can help identify problems associated with raters' and rated
employees' characteristics, such as race, sex, age, length of service,
and level of job. With the decreasing cost of computer storage and the
vastly improved ability of personnel professionals to use computer
technology, more organizations will seek this approach to assess and
monitor their appraisal systems.[50]

Reliability and Validity

The appraisal system must provide consistent, reliable data in order to
successfully defend the organization against legal challenges and to
provide accurate bases for personnel decisions.[51] Thus, the separate
appraisals of equally qualified appraisers should generally agree on
the performance of individual employees (this is called *inter-rater reliability*). If the appraisals disagree, the system must be using unreliable
measures or ratings from appraisers that are not equally qualified.

Appraisals must also be valid—that is, measure what they are supposed to measure. An appraisal used to make judgments about employees' potential for higher-level jobs should be valid for that specific
purpose. If the requirements for the higher-level job coincide with
those of a current job, current performance appraisals may be valid
predictors of how the employee will perform in the higher-level job.
However, if the job requirements differ, the current performance appraisal is invalid for estimating potential. Of course, the appraisal
could still be valid for the purpose of obtaining information about current performance. Thus, the validity of the appraisal is meaningful only
in terms of its intended purpose; it may be valid for one purpose and
invalid for another.

Job Relatedness

The issues of reliability and validity draw attention to the necessity of
measuring performance criteria that are relevant and important to the
particular job. Appraisal should be based on observable job behavior
or measurable elements of the job.[52] To assure that job relatedness
receives proper attention, the EEOC guidelines require that performance criteria represent major critical work behaviors based on careful
job analysis. The following comments about one firm's appraisal methods illustrate the EEOC's and courts' requirements:

The analyst did not verify the description by making an on-site inspection of the employee who actually performed the job. . . . The former procedure was flawed insofar as it created the possibility of inconsistent descriptions, over- or under-inflation of job duties or requirements, and was associated with the lack of employee awareness of the evaluation procedure. . . . The criteria actually employed . . . were not developed by professional consultants, but rather adapted from a commercially-available method of job analysis from which [the firm] borrowed what [it] believed to be pertinent to [its] needs.[53]

Standardization

Because appraisals are used to make judgments for personnel decisions, such as promotions and compensation, and appraisal data are used to make comparisons among employees, appraisal systems must be standardized in form and administration. Lack of standardization in forms, appraisers, procedures, and so on raises the question of whether differences in performance appraisals result from the system and its administration rather than from differences in employees' performance.

Effective Administration

An appraisal system may meet the tests of reliability, validity, job relatedness, and standardization; but if it is too difficult and costly to administer, it does not meet the test of practicality.[54] A system must accomplish the purposes for which it was designed, comply with legal requirements, and operate in an efficient manner. Moreover, the benefits of the system must be greater than the costs of designing and administering it.

Another important administrative requirement is that specific instructions for the completion of appraisals be provided to raters. Apparently, some courts have the view that such instructions are a prerequisite to conducting systematic, unbiased appraisals. For example, in a case involving a promotion, which the employer lost, the judge noted that one important reason for his decision was that "there were no written guidelines for evaluating the potential of supervisory personnel."[55] On the other hand, in a case in which the employer was able to defend its appraisal system, the judge concluded that "detailed written instructions were provided to supervisors, and applicants were rated on specifically described attributes, rather than on vague, general standards."[56]

Legality

Because the EEOC guidelines include performance appraisals as an employment practice on which personnel decisions may be based, organizations want to be certain that their appraisal system meets all legal requirements. In cases where employees or groups of employees can establish that decisions based on performance appraisals have had adverse impact on them, the employer must prove the validity and reliability of the performance appraisal system. The characteristics of the appraisal system—reliability, validity, job relatedness, standardization, and administration—are scrutinized carefully by the EEOC and the courts to determine if employment discrimination has occurred. In addition, they consider race-, sex-, and age-related biases; the degree of subjectivity of the ratings; the quality of the job analysis; the consistency with which the rater has observed employees' performance; and any discriminatory decisions based on performance appraisals.[57]

Training of Appraisers

The final component necessary for an effective performance appraisal system is well-trained appraisers. Without adequate training for appraisers, the chances of achieving the stated objectives of the appraisal system will be lessened, and the program may be doomed to failure.[58] Perhaps surprisingly, a recent survey confirmed what previous studies had already suggested—that a majority of organizations (large and small) have no performance appraisal training whatever for supervisors.[59] The majority seem to believe that training is not needed or that it is too costly in comparison with its benefits. Research had indicated, however, that training is needed for several reasons: (a) observing and appraising employees' behavior is not an inherent human skill, (b) experience in appraising employees' performance is not necessarily a good teacher, and (c) managers who are appraisers have in nearly all cases an enormous effect on their organizations and the individuals in them, and this impact may be adverse.[60] Moreover, training reduces rating errors and results in more valid and reliable appraisals.[61]

The content of the training program varies according to the organization's needs. Training during the implementation stage of a new program should cover the objectives, uses, forms, procedures, and policies of the new program. In addition, training should create awareness of purposes and of causes for rating errors and should include feedback interviews and role-playing sessions with video taping for self-examination.[62] Training for new supervisors should be part of their overall orientation to the organization and should include a general overview of the performance appraisal program followed by more specific training in skill areas.

Most training programs try to improve the raters' "judgments"—that is, their ability to determine what information is needed, obtain that information, and assess it. Pertinent questions to raters might include the following:[63]

Does the rater know more about his or her poorest employee than about his or her best?

Does the rater fail to note the good qualities of the worst employee and the bad qualities of the best employee?

Does the rater know as much about his or her average employees as about his or her best and worst employees?

Is the "best" employee rated high simply because the rater knows the employee best?

If the supervisor's answer to any of these questions is yes, he or she should benefit from training.

The Performance Appraisal Interview

The performance appraisal (feedback) interview is considered by many personnel professionals to be the most critical, and potentially the most productive, part of the appraisal process. Nearly all organizations require that the supervisor discuss the appraisal results with the employee being appraised. These discussions are designed to achieve the following objectives:[64]

Let employees know where they stand.

Help employees do a better job by clarifying what is expected of them.

Plan opportunities for development and growth.

Strengthen the supervisor-subordinate working relationship by developing a mutual agreement on expectations.

Provide an opportunity for employees to express themselves on performance-related issues.

The structure of the appraisal interview may take many forms, depending on the purposes, circumstances, individuals, and problems to be addressed. However, a general framework can be presented whose content is closely in line with the objectives listed above.[65]

Preparation for the Interview

Before the interview, the supervisor should be aware of possible problems and should try to anticipate the employee's reaction. For example, an appraisal interview may be limited by communication failures—the employee may not be able to express himself or herself well; the supervisor may overestimate the employee's ability to absorb information; or the employee may not concentrate on the interview. Problems may arise when too great a difference exists between the employee's perceptions of reality and objective reality; the appraiser must be aware that perceptions may be distorted by the employee's needs, feelings about the supervision, and attitudes toward the job. Further, employees tend to behave in ways appropriate for satisfying their personal needs; an unexpected low appraisal that leads to a low wage increase may cause frustration, repressive behavior, anxiety, and fears.

To prepare for the interview, the supervisor should review the appraisal period, analyze supporting data and documentation, list items to be discussed, and arrange for a quiet interview setting, free of distractions and interruptions. In addition, the employee being appraised should be notified in advance so that he or she can adequately prepare for the interview, because a better-prepared employee can contribute more to the interview and to a discussion of job-related problems.[66]

Content of the Interview

While the interview can take many forms and can range in emphasis, its content should include at least the following: The appraiser should first help the appraisee feel at ease, perhaps with small talk and personal conversation to relieve anxiety and create an atmosphere of cordiality. Then, the employee should be told the purposes of the interview and assured that the discussions are to be two-way, informal, and positive. During the session, the supervisor can facilitate the discussion by showing interest, listening attentively, periodically summarizing what has been discussed, acknowledging insightful analysis and self-criticism, allowing the employee to discuss concerns, and probing when necessary to come to grips with the causes of problems. Ideally, criticism should be minimized, although the employee must be told when the supervisor is not satisfied with the employee's progress and performance. If employees must be given negative information about their performance, they are more receptive when they are allowed to participate in the interview, when plans and objectives are the focus of the discussion, and when the evaluation is based on factors relevant to their work.[67] Disagreements over the performance appraisal between the supervisor and employee should be resolved before the close of the interview or listed to be discussed on a predetermined date.

Close of the Interview

As the interview comes to an end, the employee should be asked if other issues need to be discussed. If not, the supervisor should summarize what they have agreed upon to assure a common understanding and set of expectations. Finally, a plan for resolving problems should be formulated and expectations (goals and plans for future) should be developed.

Assessment of the Interview

As previously mentioned, raters might not like to furnish feedback, because they may wish to avoid negative face-to-face discussions with employees. Still, most organizations require appraisal interviews, because they have the potential for being an effective motivational and developmental tool. On the other hand, an untrained, unskilled interviewer may do more harm than good.[68] Thus, the effectiveness with which the supervisor conducts the appraisal interview is a key factor in determining whether the appraisal process contributes toward motivating behavioral changes.[69]

Experience and research have led to several conclusions about the effectiveness of the appraisal interview. First, performance feedback must be given more frequently than once a year. It is a well-established fact that performance feedback associated immediately with an act is more effective than delayed discussion.[70] This, of course, does not mean that periodic, summary performance appraisal interviews are not important; the two types of feedback serve different purposes. Also, the more involved employees are and the greater their opportunities to state their views of the issues in the interview, the more positive their feelings are about being helped by the interview.[71]

The content of the performance appraisal interview and the employee's perception of the process have enabled researchers to draw conclusions about its effectiveness. For example, setting specific objectives during the interview results in significantly more performance improvement than simply discussing general objectives or criticizing past performance without reference to specific objectives.[72] Further, interviews in which the content of the discussion is balanced between the strengths and weaknesses of performance have shown the greatest positive effects. A General Electric study in the 1960s showed that criticism has negative effects on performance; however, a more recent study has revealed that where only the favorable results are reviewed, the employee may tend to get "too rosy" a picture of performance and perhaps to believe that further improvement is neither possible nor desirable. Finally, when employees perceive the results of their appraisal interviews to be instrumental in their performance they are more positive about the interview process and more highly motivated to improve their performance.[73]

Role of the Personnel Department and Other Managers in the Appraisal Process

The personnel department has an extensive role in each phase of the performance appraisal program. The department usually spearheads the overall design of the program, which includes the use of appraisals, forms, procedures, policies, training, implementation, and administration. Although upper management makes the final decision concerning the composition of the program, the personnel department usually presents the program proposal to upper management for consideration, alteration, and final acceptance. Once the appraisal program is accepted, the personnel department takes the lead in its introduction, orientation to its use, and its implementation. The program's purposes and uses must be explained, the forms presented, supervisors trained, and employees oriented. Throughout the implementation phase and thereafter the personnel department must be available to answer questions and to help line managers and employees. The department must continue throughout the system's use to coordinate the system, send out forms when appraisals are due, and follow up to assure that appraisal interviews are conducted in a timely manner.

Such systems also involve an enormous amount of record keeping, because data from the appraisal forms must be recorded for use in other personnel activities. For example, records of identifiable training needs will be filed for future reference, notice of employees' potential will be recorded for future job openings, and evaluations of overall performance may be used as a basis for merit pay increases and other forms of recognition. A final responsibility of the personnel department involves its role in monitoring the system for rating errors, recognizing raters' tendencies and omissions, and assessing the system's overall effectiveness. Every three to five years, the personnel department should analyze and assess the effectiveness of the program, compare results with objectives, determine whether overall benefits justify costs, make adjustments when needed, and introduce proposals to improve the program for upper management's consideration.

The success of a performance appraisal system also depends on its effective administration by line management throughout the organization. No appraisal program, regardless of how well it is constructed, can be effective unless managers throughout the organization put forth the conscientious effort necessary to appraise employees. Even when appraisals by other groups, such as peers and subordinates, are involved, managers must set the example and carry out their responsibilities in accordance with the design of the appraisal program.

Line managers play a vital role by conducting the appraisal interview. How well this interview is conducted not only determines in large part whether the employee will take affirmative steps after the interview but also goes a long way in reassuring the employee that the system is fair, that he or she has input, and that decisions about him or her are based on deliberate considerations.

The last responsibility of line managers is to provide assistance to the personnel department in its assessment of the system's effectiveness. Because line managers have daily contact with employees, they are sources of valuable data that can be used to determine the program's effectiveness. If line managers believe the program is not meeting its objectives, they will be the first to lose confidence. Later, they will withdraw support, openly or by poor administration. Thus, for a viable, dynamic program, to be maintained, continuous feedback from line management to the personnel department is essential.

Issue:	**Should Performance Appraisals Be Related to Pay?**

The foundation of an effective performance appraisal program has been established in this chapter. However, the issue regarding the relationship of performance appraisals to pay is still the subject of controversy and differing opinions. At first glance, this issue seems to offer little ground for controversy. Few would argue against high performers' receiving wage increases higher than those of low performers.

Paying employees on the basis of their performance . . . is the way to get performance motivation in organizations. Not only does this approach make sense intuitively, it has a solid theoretical base. Expectancy theory postulates that if people want more pay and believe that working harder will result in their getting more pay, they'll work harder and perform better in order to get more pay. The theory has been tested in actual and experimental situations and found to explain a significant amount of the variability in employee effort and performance.[74]

On the other hand, other questions may be asked:

Should oil company executives be paid huge bonuses because OPEC has substantially increased prices and subsequently profits to oil companies increased?

Should top motion picture executives receive huge bonuses when they produce a movie which captures the public's fancy?

Should computer company executives receive huge bonuses from enormous sales when the market for computers is so strong?[75]

Some may call such bonuses the result of luck and circumstances; others call them payment for performance.

Even if the pay-for-performance policy is accepted, the *strength* of the relationship must be determined. Several interrelated factors can dilute or even subvert this relationship: the firm's profitability; inflation; varied, possibly conflicting, uses of performance appraisals; supervisory actions; and ineffective performance appraisals.

The firm's annual profit picture determines the amount of money available for wage increases. In profitable years, even poor performers might get wage increases, distorting the relationship between performance appraisals and pay. During bad years, even high performers will not receive pay increases regardless of how well they have performed.

In other cases, the relationship between performance appraisal and pay might be distorted when managers make salary increase decisions and then complete performance appraisals to justify their salary decisions.

Some might contend that limited money for merit raises should not disrupt the purity of the pay-for-performance relationship. In other words, good performers should receive their wage increases, however skimpy; and poor performers should receive no increase. Yet, other personnel concerns suggest that even marginal performers should receive some wage increase. As will be discussed in Chapter 10, one function of wage and salary programs is to retain the existing workforce by maintaining external pay equity. During periods when the inflation rate is around 10 percent, employees receiving no increase will probably seek employment elsewhere. The resultant cost of recruiting, selecting, and training of new employees must be compared with the advantages of strictly applying the pay-for-performance policy. In some cases, the benefits of retaining marginal employees through wage increases might outweigh the costs of recruiting and training replacements.[76]

Another concern is that the distribution of a limited amount of money for wage increases according to performance appraisal scores might heighten competition among employees. While such competition can stimulate creativity and growth, excessive competition may have negative results, since much of an organization's effectiveness depends on the unity and integration of individual employees' efforts.

Further complications result from the diverse purposes of performance appraisals:

Is performance being evaluated to develop and upgrade the individual's skills? Or is performance being assessed to provide a basis for rewarding him? Behavioral scientists warn us that the two evaluations do not mix well.[77]

The performance appraisal's effect on salary will probably overshadow its developmental aspects. While the supervisor is talking about development, performance improvement, and goal setting, the employee is wondering: "Did I get a raise? If so, how much?" Some have suggested that development and salary justification should be dealt with separately (possibly in two different interviews).[78] However, separate treatment doubles the time and effort required.

My experience in the United States clearly indicates that top management simply will not spend the time necessary to examine an individual's performance on two separate occasions, once to reward him and again to speed his development. Only reward—that is, compensation and promotion—carries a priority high enough with the top executive

group to ensure a reasonable time commitment on their part to performance evaluation.[79]

One reason the pay-for-performance concept may not work in industry is the reluctance of managers to penalize poor performers. A Conference Board study of 493 firms concluded that:

It seems clear to many personnel executives that pay and performance will never truly be linked when the consequences of an honest low rating must be firing or early retirement. Unless a manager perceives himself to be really free to pick and choose among a variety of rewards, punishments and remedies to follow up his performance rating, he will continue to lump everyone under the protection of an average-to-above-average rating. Declining white-collar productivity and homogeneous salary treatment seem to be the twin products of failure to find solutions in this vital area.[80]

Another reason for this reluctance is that many managers question the validity and accuracy of performance appraisals. As this chapter pointed out, requirements for a successful performance appraisal system include accurate job-related measures, valid appraisals, good administration, skilled feedback, and trained managers. As one executive concludes, "I have never seen any organization meet these criteria."[81]

Another barrier to application of the pay-for-performance policy is the presence of a union. When the union succeeds in obtaining an across-the-board wage increase for bargaining-unit employees, the ability of the company to use a pay-for-performance policy is limited, especially when it has a policy to maintain a 10 percent differential between employees and supervisors. In such cases, the employees and the supervisors will receive increases that are not necessarily related to performance. In addition, to maintain internal equity, employees not covered by the labor agreement must also receive wage increases. Further, competitive firms give employees wage increases so that external equity can be maintained.[82]

Most employees would prefer to work under a merit pay plan, because they believe they will do well under such a plan. However, since almost everyone views his or her performance as above average, almost everyone expects an above-average increase. Giving everyone about the same increase does not solve this problem, because the majority will be dissatisfied with average treatment. Thus:

The manager appears to be in a damned-if-you-do, damned-if-you-don't situation. . . . He must either abandon the idea of pay as a potentially effective motivator or use a merit pay plan and accept the probability that the majority of employees will be dissatisfied with their salary treatment.[83]

Summary

The elements of an appraisal system include purposes, content, methods, appraisers, frequency, and feedback. Purposes include forming the basis for personnel decisions, such as those involving wages and promotion, and serving developmental aims, such as identifying training needs and improving performance. The content of appraisals includes measures, traits, behaviors, and objectives. Popular methods are graphic scales, BARS, MBO, and others, each with its own advantages and disadvantages. Raters may include supervisors, peers, subordinates, and the employees themselves. The frequency with which appraisals should be conducted is also an issue of importance.

Sources of errors are management attitudes, perceptions and tendencies of raters, characteristics and interactions of raters and employees being rated, and format of appraisals. The components of an effective performance appraisal system are validity and reliability, job relatedness, standardization, legality, and training.

The feedback process—the performance appraisal interview—involves preparation, content, and closing. Performance feedback must not be merely an annual event, but a continuing process.

The various roles of the personnel department include designing the program and monitoring and maintaining the system. Roles of other managers, keys to the success of the program, include completing the appraisal and conducting the interview.

A controversial issue in performance appraisal involves whether—and to what extent—performance appraisals should be related to pay.

Discussion Questions

1. On what occasions might some of the many purposes of performance appraisals be in conflict?

2. Which method is most appropriate to appraise performance for the following jobs?
   a. Managers.
   b. Professionals.
   c. Clerical employees.
   d. Sales personnel.
   e. Accountants.
   f. Hourly production workers.

3. What can an organization do to improve its chances of having objective appraisals?

4. How can performance appraisals conflict with equal employment opportunity regulations?

5. What can a supervisor do to make the performance appraisal interview more constructive?

6. Under what conditions can pay be effectively related to performance appraisals?

7. Why is BARS attractive to federal EEO agencies?

Notes

1. Harry B. Anderson, "Formal Job Appraisals Grow More Prevalent but Get More Criticism," *Wall Street Journal,* May 23, 1978, p. 1.

2. "Appraising the Performance Appraisal," *Business Week,* May 19, 1980, pp. 153–154.

3. William J. Kearney, "Performance Appraisal: Which Way to Go," *MSU Business Topics* 25 (Winter 1977), p. 57. Also see Bruce McAfee and Blake Green, "Selecting a Performance Appraisal Method," *Personnel Administrator* 25 (June 1977), pp. 61–63.

4. Michael Beer, "Performance Appraisal: Dilemma and Possibilities," *Organizational Dynamics 8* (Winter 1980), p. 27; Ralph F. Catalanello and John A. Hooper, "Managerial Appraisal," *Personnel Administrator* (September 1981), pp. 75–81.

5. Michael Keeley, "A Contingency Framework for Performance Evaluation," *Academy of Management Review* 3 (July 1978), pp. 428–438.

6. Michael J. Kavanagh, "The Content Issue in Performance Appraisal: A Review," *Personnel Psychology* 24 (Winter 1971), pp. 653–654.

7. Gary P. Latham, Larry L. Cummings, and Terence R. Mitchell, "Behavioral Strategies to Improve Productivity," *Organizational Dynamics* 9 (Winter 1981), pp. 6–10.

8. Donald G. Patterson, "The Scott Company Graphic Rating Scale," *Journal of Personnel Research* 1 (August 1922), pp. 362–366.

9. Robert I. Lazer and Walter S. W. Wikstrom, *Appraising Managerial Performance* (New York: Conference Board, 1977), p. 95.

10. *Ibid.,* pp. 116–120.

11. Jack Smith, Edward Niedzwiedz, Melissa Davis, and Cheryl Kniesner, *Handbook of Job Proficiency Criteria: A GLAC Research Report* (Columbus, Ohio: Ohio Department of State Personnel, 1974), pp. 33–35.

12. John C. Flanagan, "The Critical Incident Technique," *Psychological Bulletin* (July 1954), pp. 327–358.

13. Thomas N. Baylie, Carl Kujawski, and Drew Young, "Appraisal of 'People' Resources," in *Staffing Policies and Strategies,* ed. Dale Yoder and H. G. Hendman, Jr. (Washington, D.C.: Bureau of National Affairs, 1974), p. 4-191.

14. *Ibid.,* p. 4-192.

15. *Ibid.,* p. 4-189–4-191.

16. Walter C. Borman and Marvin D. Dunnette, "Behavior-Based versus Trait-Oriented Performance Ratings: An Empirical Study," *Journal of Applied Psychology* 60 (October 1975), pp. 561–565.

17. BARS can be divided into behavioral observation scales and behavioral expectation scales. See G. P. Latham and K. N. Wexley, "Behavioral Observation Scales for Performance Appraisal Purposes," *Personnel Psychology* 30 (Summer 1977), pp. 255–268.

18. Paul O. Kingstrom and Alan R. Bass, "A Critical Analysis of Studies Comparing Behaviorally Anchored Rating Scales (BARS) and Other Rating Formats," *Personnel Psychology* 34 (Summer 1981) pp. 263–265.

19. Frank Landy and J. L. Farr, "Performance Rating," *Psychological Bulletin* 87 (January 1980), pp. 72–107.

20. William J. Kearney, "The Value of Behaviorally Based Performance Appraisal," *Business Horizons* 19 (June 1976), p. 82.

21. Lazer and Wikstrom, *Appraising Managerial Performance,* pp. 88–94.

22. Jack Bucalo, "Personnel Directors . . . What You Should Know Before Recommending MBO," *Personnel Journal* 56 (April 1977), pp. 176–178, 202.

23. George Getschow, "Overdriven Execs: Some Middle Managers Cut Corners to Achieve High Corporate Goals," *Wall Street Journal,* November 8, 1979, pp. 1, 34.

24. Harry Levinson, "Appraisal of What Performance?" *Harvard Business Review* 54 (July/August 1976), pp. 30–34.

25. Latham, Cummings, and Mitchell, "Behavioral Strategies," p. 20.

26. Craig E. Schneier and Richard W. Beatty, "Combining BARS and MBO: Using an Appraisal System to Diagnose Performance Problems," *Personnel Administrator* (September 1979), pp. 51–55.

27. Earl Ingram III, manager, personnel research and development, WestPoint Pepperell, personal correspondence, March 4, 1981. Reprinted Courtesy of WestPoint Pepperell, West Point, Georgia.

28. Marion G. Haynes, "Developing an Appraisal Program," *Personnel Journal* 57 (January 1978), pp. 18–19.

29. A. A. Bolton, district staff manager, Chesapeake & Potomac Telephone Co., personal correspondence, February 10, 1982.

30. Allen I. Kraut, "Prediction of Managerial Success by Peer and Training-Staff Ratings," *Journal of Applied Psychology* 60 (January/February 1975), pp. 14–19.

31. Levinson, "Appraisal of What Performance?" p. 44.

32. Herbert H. Meyer, "Self Appraisal of Job Performance," *Personnel Psychology* 33 (Summer 1980), pp. 291–295.

33. Lloyd Baird, "Self and Supervisor Ratings of Performance: As Related to Self-Esteem and Satisfaction with Supervision," *Academy of Management Journal* 20 (June 1977), p. 299.

34. Glenn A. Bassett and Herbert H. Meyer, "Performance Appraisal Based on Self-Review," *Personnel Psychology* 21 (Winter 1968), pp. 421–430; Herbert H. Meyer, "Self-Appraisal of Job Performance," *Personnel Psychology* 33 (Summer 1980), pp. 291–295.

35. R. J. Klimoski and M. London, "Role of the Rater in Performance Appraisal," *Personnel Psychology* 59 (Winter 1974), pp. 445–451.

36. Craig E. Schneier, "Multiple Rater Groups and Performance Appraisal," *Public Personnel Management* 6 (January/February 1977), pp. 15–16.

37. Lazer and Wikstrom, *Appraising Managerial Performance,* pp. 23–24.

38. Robert C. Ford and Kenneth M. Jennings, "How to Make Performance Appraisals More Effective," *Personnel* 54 (March/April 1977), pp. 51–56.

39. Elizabeth M. Fowler, "Management: Challenges for Corporate Appraisals," *New York Times,* October 21, 1977, p. D–5.

40. Anderson, "Formal Job Appraisals," pp. 1, 23.

41. Smith, Niedzwiedz, Davis, and Kniesner, *Handbook,* pp. 25–30.

42. Ludwig Huttner and Thomas R. O'Malley, "Let Them Know!" *Personnel Psychology* 15 (Summer 1962), pp. 185–186.

43. Reprinted by permission of the Harvard Business Review. Excerpt from "An Uneasy Look about Performance Appraisals," by Douglas McGregor, *Harvard Business Review,* May–June 1957, p. 90. Copyright © 1957 by the President and Fellows of Harvard College; all rights reserved.

44. Reprinted by permission of the Harvard Business Review. Excerpt from "Positive Programs for Performance Appraisals," by Alva Kindall and James Gatza, *Harvard Business Review,* November–December 1963, pp. 159–165. Copyright © 1963 by the President and Fellows of Harvard College; all rights reserved.

45. Randall G. Sleeth, "The Mediocrity Paradox," *Personnel Administrator* 24 (September 1979), p. 63.

46. Michael C. Gallagher, "More Bias in Performance Evaluation," *Personnel* 55 (July/August 1978), pp. 35–40.

47. H. S. Feild and W. H. Holley, "Subordinates' Characteristics, Supervisors' Ratings and Decisions to Discuss Appraisals' Results," *Academy of Management Journal* 22 (June 1979), pp. 315–321.

48. William I. Sauser, Jr., "Evaluating Employee Performance: Needs, Problems, and Possible Solutions," *Public Personnel Management* 9 (January/February 1980), pp. 11–18.

49. W. H. Holley, H. S. Feild, and N. J. Barnett, "Analyzing Performance Appraisal Systems: An Empirical Study," *Personnel Journal* 55 (September 1976), pp. 457–459, 463.

50. M. E. Schick, "The 'Refined' Performance Evaluation Monitoring System: Best of Both Worlds," *Personnel Journal* 57 (January 1980), pp. 47–50.

51. Hubert S. Feild and William H. Holley, "The Relationship of Performance Appraisal System Characteristics to Verdicts in Selected Employment Discrimination Cases," *Academy of Management Journal* 25 (June 1982), pp. 392–406.

52. Lazer and Wikstrom, *Appraising Managerial Performance,* p. 47.

53. *Greenspan* v. *Automobile Club of Michigan,* 22 FEP 195 (1980).

54. W. H. Holley and H. S. Feild, "Performance Appraisal and the Law," *Labor Law Journal* 26 (July 1975), pp. 423–430; Gary Lubben, Duane Thompson, and Charles Klasson, "Performance Appraisal: The Legal Implications of Title VII," *Personnel* (May/June 1980), pp. 11–21.

55. *Hill* v. *Western Electric Co.,* 12 FEP 1182 (1976).

56. *Frink* v. *U.S. Navy,* 16 FEP 67 (1977).

57. Patricia Linenberger and Timothy J. Keaveny, "Performance Appraisal Standards Used by the Courts," *Personnel Administrator* 26 (May 1981), pp. 89–94; Lawrence S. Kleinman and Richard L. Durham, "Performance Appraisal, Promotion and the Courts," *Personnel Psychology* 34 (Spring 1981), pp. 103–121; Giovanni B. Giglioni, Joyce B. Giglioni, and James A. Bryant, "Performance Appraisal: Here Comes the Judge," *California Management Review* 26 (Winter 1981), pp. 14–23.

58. Alan H. Locher and Kenneth S. Teel, "Performance Appraisal—a Survey of Current Practices," *Personnel Journal* 56 (May 1977), p. 247.

59. N. B. Winstanley, "Performance Appraisal: Another Pollution Problem," *Conference Board Record* 9 (September 1972), pp. 59–63; Gary P. Lathan, K. N. Wexley, and E. D. Pursell, "Training Managers to Minimize Rating Errors in the Observation of Behavior," *Journal of Applied Psychology* 60 (October 1975), pp. 553–555; W. C. Borman, "Effects of Instruction to Avoid Halo Error on Reliability and Validity of Performance Evaluation Ratings," *Journal of Applied Psychology* 50 (October 1975), pp. 556–560.

60. H. John Bernardin and C. S. Walter, "Effects of Rater Training and Diary-Keeping on Psychometric Error in Ratings," *Journal of Applied Psychology* 62 (January/February 1977), p. 68.

61. "Training Managers to Rate Employees," *Business Week,* March 17, 1980, p. 178.

62. Theodore Purcell, "Observing People," *Harvard Business Review* 33 (March/April 1955), p. 100.

63. Lazer and Wikstrom, *Appraising Managerial Performance,* pp. 30–32.

64. Stephen Carroll and Henry Tosi, *Management by Objectives* (New York: Macmillan, 1973), pp. 90–102.

65. Ronald J. Burke, William Weitzel, and Tomara Weir, "Characteristics of Effective Employee Performance Review and Development Interview: Replication and Extension," *Personnel Psychology* 31 (Winter 1978), p. 916.

66. John Miner, "Management Appraisal: A Capsule Review and Current References," *Business Horizons* 11 (October 1968), pp. 88–89.

67. Robert L. Dipboye and Rene de Pontbriand, "Correlates of Employee Reactions to Performance Appraisals and Appraisal Systems," *Journal of Applied Psychology* 66 (April 1981), pp. 248–251.

68. Herbert H. Meyer and W. B. Walker, "A Study of Factors Relating to the Effectiveness of a Performance Appraisal Program," *Personnel Psychology* 14 (Autumn 1961), pp. 296–298.

69. Herbert H. Meyer, "The Annual Performance Review Discussion—Making It Constructive," *Personnel Journal* 56 (October 1977), p. 508.

70. Martin M. Greller, "Subordinate Participation and Reactions to the Appraisal Interview," *Journal of Applied Psychology* 60 (October 1975), p. 546.

71. Ronald J. Burke and Douglas S. Wilcox, "Characteristics of Effective Employee Performance Review and Development Interviews," *Personnel Psychology* 22 (Autumn 1969), p. 302.

72. H. H. Meyer, E. Kay, and J. R. P. French, "Split Roles in Performance Appraisal," *Harvard Business Review* 43 (January/February 1965), pp. 123–219.

73. Douglas Cederblom, "The Performance Appraisal Interview: A Review, Implications, and Suggestions," *Academy of Management Review* 7 (January 1982), pp. 219–227.

74. David Belcher, "Pay and Performance," *Compensation Review* 12 (Third quarter 1980), p. 14.

75. Graef S. Crystal, "Pay-for-Performance—Even if It's Luck," *Wall Street Journal,* November 2, 1981, p. 16.

76. Frederick S. Hill, "The Pay-for-Performance Dilemma," *Personnel* 56 (September/October 1979), pp. 25–26.

77. Arch Patton, "Does Performance Appraisal Work?" *Business Horizons* 16 (February 1973), p. 84.

78. Meyer, Kay, and French, "Split Roles," pp. 123–129.

79. Patton, "Does Performance Appraisal Work?"

80. David A. Weeks, *Compensating Employees: Lessons of the 1970s* (New York: Conference Board, 1976), p. 70.

81. N. B. Winstanley, "Comment on Patten's 'Pay for Performance or Placation,'" *Personnel Administrator* 23 (May 1978), pp. 50–51.

82. William J. Kearney, "Pay for Performance? Not Always," *MSU Business Topics* 27 (Spring 1979), pp. 5–16.

83. Herbert H. Meyer, "The Pay-for-Performance Dilemma," *Organizational Dynamics* 4 (Winter 1975), pp. 45–46.

Chapter 9

Training and Development

Much leadership and management training today reflects vague or confused theoretical foundations, resulting in somewhat aimless training efforts. The seasoned eye can usually detect the implied theoretical base (or often several of them) underlying a particular training design and its published agenda. Frequently the program design and its parts are drawn, with no one seemingly aware of it, from fragments of theory buried in three pervasive theories of leadership dominating this century: trait, behavior and contingency theories. But these fragments seem selected casually, at random (cafeteria style) or for personal reasons (hunch, personnel preferences, good-old-boy network, etc.) rather than by conscious design based on the integration of clear program goals and subordinated, explicitly chosen, means.

Reprinted from ''A Reappraisal of Leadership Theory and Training,'' by James Owens, p. 75 of the November 1981 issue of *Personnel Administrator,* copyright 1981, the American Society for Personnel Administration, 30 Park Drive, Berea, OH 44017, $26 per year.

Training and development activities help new employees learn how to perform their jobs and help current employees improve job performance and prepare for higher-level positions. *Training* usually refers to the formal learning procedures organizations use to guide employees' specific behavior so that it will contribute to the organization's objectives. Where learning does not pertain to specific behaviors or where it pertains to concepts and principles that the learner will apply to a variety of situations, it is usually referred to as *development.*[1]

Training and development activities are common in every organization; it is estimated that over $100 billion is spent each year in such efforts.[2] More than a million managers each year participate in formal management courses.[3] American Telephone & Telegraph alone enrolls 15,000 managers in its in-house management education program; and one three-day course offered by the American Management Association, "Improving Managerial Skills for the New or Prospective Manager," attracts 3,000 participants at $450 each.[4]

Training can contribute to the attainment of organizational objectives and can be cost-effective. However, several obstacles that can blunt the effectiveness of training efforts must be overcome. First, training cannot be considered an end in itself; it must be considered a means to an end. Second, managers must evaluate training and development activities in terms of what they cost and how much they contribute to organizational effectiveness in terms of returns over costs. Finally, managers must realize that training and development efforts are intended to manage the learning process.[5]

This chapter presents the fundamentals of training and development activities from a general perspective. It starts with the new employee's entrance to the organization, then focuses on the components of a training and development system. The final section highlights several important issues concerning training and development.

Organizational Entry, Orientation, and Socialization

Organizational entry involves the activities of employees joining the organization.[6] One such activity is orientation, which attempts to help the new employee learn more about the organization, job, and fellow employees and work associates. Orientation programs launch the assimilation process (also called *organizational socialization* and *learning the ropes*[7]) whereby the organization's performance requirements are meshed with the new employee's expected rewards, including job satisfaction.

Orientation programs attempt to create a favorable impression of the organization and provide more specific information about the tasks of the job and its relationship to the organization as a whole.[8] These activities are becoming increasingly important because of high voluntary turnover (quits) of new employees, particularly those who were not given a realistic picture of the job and the work environment. Turnover results in lost investments in training and increased expenses for recruiting and selecting replacements. An effective orientation program can increase employee job satisfaction, morale, and productivity; reduce turnover, conflict, and tension; and improve creativity.[9]

The personnel department and the immediate supervisor of the new employee share the responsibility for orientation. Generally, the personnel department explains company-wide personnel policies; but the major tasks rest with the immediate supervisor, who conducts a detailed briefing about specific job procedures, introduces the new employee to co-workers, and so on. Orientation programs vary in formality, length, and content; however, most programs cover certain basic elements. For example, the personnel department usually verifies the terms of employment and sees that the employee receives identification cards, tools, uniforms, handbooks, parking stickers, and the like. The supervisor then tries to reduce the employee's anxiety about the new job and make the new employee feel at home in the immediate work group.

Before the employee arrives at work, the immediate supervisor usually informs the work group; prepares the work station, equipment, and supplies; and chooses an experienced employee to assist in the new employee's adjustment. Once the new employee arrives, the supervisor tries to make him or her feel at ease before explaining the details of the job. For instance, a tour of the department and introduction to other employees are common activities. The supervisor also shows the employee what the job entails and how it fits with what others do and answers questions. Some organizations assign a sponsor to the new employee to help in the adjustment. Most often, the assigned sponsor will have common interests and background with the new employee. More importantly, the sponsor must be genuinely interested in the adjustment of the new employee.

Some organizations use an orientation checklist, which prescribes each action to be taken, when it should occur, and who should perform it. An example of such a checklist is presented in Exhibit 9.1.

Most orientation programs have two major focal points: the *employee* (benefits and services, training programs, and promotional opportunities) and the *organization* (products, services, objectives, history, and relationships among departments). Written materials, such as employee handbooks and brochures describing the benefits program and the safety program, are provided; and films on topics like motivation or the free enterprise system and filmed messages from the president of the organization may be shown. The personnel department coordinates these formal orientation activities with the assistance of the training and development directors and line management. Speakers for the various topics covered in such a program may include representatives from personnel and training departments, key company officials, line managers, and safety supervisors.[10]

Exhibit 9.1   **Orientation Checklist**
                         DUN & BRADSTREET, INC.
                         INTRODUCTION CHECKLIST

See General Personnel Instruction
4C-18. Numbers following some
items refer to reference material in
"Welcome to Our Company"

NAME OF EMPLOYEE _____

WHEN TO BE DONE	INITIAL WHEN DONE	WHAT IS TO BE DONE	SUGGESTED PERSON TO HANDLE
Day before Employee arrives	_____	Prepare Supervisor for arrival; have Supervisor review application blank.	Dept. Head
	_____	Prepare future immediate associates.	Supervisor
	_____	Have desk cleaned out and supplies ready.	Supervisor
	_____	Have instructional materials ready.	Supervisor
	_____	Have initial work ready.	Supervisor
	_____	Arrange for first-day luncheon companion.	Supervisor
1st Day On Arrival (Estimated time - numbers 1 - 9: 30 minutes)	_____	1. Have employee fill out duplicate application form and withholding certificate if not done previously.	Dept. Head
	_____	2. Give the new employee a copy of the booklet, "Welcome to Our Company". If not done previously, review the function of Dun & Bradstreet along the lines of pages 3-5 in the booklet.	Dept. Head
		3. Briefly review the job - give its title.	Dept. Head
		a. Sketch the duties.	
		b. Stress its importance - how it fits in with other jobs.	
		c. Where the work originates.	
		d. What employee and others in department do with it.	
		e. Where it goes.	
	_____	f. Relation of job with others in the department - with others in the office	
	_____	4. Give assurance that employee will learn quickly - that we recognize there is much to learn - that employee will have adequate and friendly supervision.	Dept. Head
	_____	5. Explain who immediate Supervisor will be - something about her or him. Stress importance of Supervisor in all employee - employer relationships "your instructor, your supervisor, your representative in Management".	Dept. Head
		6. Review compensation.	Dept. Head
		a. Amount per week or month.	
		b. When is pay day.	
		c. Mention briefly deductions required by law; these will be explained on pay day. ("Welcome" booklet 10-12)	
		1. Federal Withholding (Income) Tax.	
		2. State or City Income Tax (if any)	
		3. Federal Old Age Benefits (Social Security)	
		4. State Disability Insurance (if any)	
		5. State Unemployment Insurance (if any)	
		d. Explain policy on payment for short-term absences.	
		e. Salaries are confidential.	

BE BRIEF,   CLEAR,   NON-TECHNICAL!   LISTEN PATIENTLY!   ENCOURAGE QUESTIONS
4C-22(29577)

◇12-80   Published by The Bureau of National Affairs, Inc.

Organizational socialization incorporates the orientation but extends the process to the point at which the employee is transformed into a productive, participating member of the workforce. The socialization process includes three phases. The first involves what the new employee has learned in previous experiences. The next occurs when the new employee encounters the "real" organization; this phase may cause the employee to adjust values, learn new skills, and change attitudes. In the final phase, which is longer lasting, changes take place, new skills are mastered, new roles are successfully performed, and satisfactory adjustment is made to the work group's value structure and norms. Ideally, the end product of the socialization process will be that the employee carries out his or her assignments dependably, remains with the organization, and cooperatively contributes to the organization's objectives beyond his or her assigned tasks and required duties. In addition, it is hoped that the employee will be satisfied with and involved in the job and will be internally motivated to perform effectively.[11]

Training and Development Systems

Once an employee is selected for the job, attention is directed toward the employee's development. If the employee already possesses the skills necessary to perform the assigned tasks, no immediate training may be necessary. In such cases, the focus is on performance improvement and possibly on developing skills for advancement. In cases where the new employee has the aptitude and motivation to learn but not the skills, job-oriented training must be provided. Many alternatives and many combinations of training and development activities are available. What follows are the basic components of a comprehensive training and development system, which include: (a) assessment of training needs, (b) training and development methods, and (c) evaluation of training and development efforts.

Assessment of Training Needs

Even though vast amounts of money are spent each year on training and development at all levels of organizations, training needs are seldom carefully and systematically analyzed. Before buying a new piece of equipment, management carefully and deliberately specifies the production requirements and potential benefits; but little analysis is commonly done prior to training. In other words, managers want to make certain they get their money's worth in purchasing equipment; however, when spending funds and investing time of employees in training, they tend to be less systematic.

Assessment of training needs is usually a reaction to a crisis, such as excessive waste, low productivity, or morale problems, and frequently is not coordinated with other functions of the organization. Training decisions often are based on informal requests from management, talks with supervisors, and observation of employees. While these approaches are appropriate on occasion, training needs can be systematically determined. Such an approach includes analysis at three levels: organizational, operational, and personnel (individual).

Organizational Analysis

Organizational analysis determines where training efforts in the organization are needed or where training has the highest potential to contribute to organizational objectives and goals. Organizational effectiveness measures—such as labor costs; production efficiency; quality; and rates of accidents, turnover, and absenteeism—should be considered in the assessment of training and development needs. Also assessed is the organization's climate—the feelings, opinions, beliefs, and attitudes of organizational members. Training content, organizational climate, and managerial style must be consistent. For example, if training instructors recommend that employees participate in decision making, the organizational climate and supervisory style must reinforce the training. Promoting employee participation in a centralized, autocratic organization would cause conflict.

Operations Analysis

Operations analysis involves determining for each job the type of behavior required of the job holder and the standards of performance that must be met to achieve the desired results. While operations analysis is similar to job analysis, it is employee-centered, not job-centered, and is concerned with behavior needed on the job and expected levels of performance. This process should yield specific training objectives and criteria for judging training effectiveness.

Individual Analysis

Individual analysis determines what behaviors should be developed in a specific employee and focuses on the individual trainee. It is important here to take into consideration individual differences, because identical training for all employees in a given job category without regard to individual differences not only wastes the company's resources but also can negatively affect the behavior of employees already adequate for the job tasks. The organization needs to identify the employees whose performance can be improved by training and development experiences, determine what behavioral change can help these employees perform in a satisfactory manner, and determine their deficiencies in terms of the specific skills, knowledge, and attitudes needed to be effective on the job.[12]

During the assessment of individuals, several questions should be asked:

1. Is performance lower than it should be because of a skill deficiency? If so, what costs and benefits are involved in train-

ing? What are the appropriate techniques? Will the skill be improved by training? Can the skill be improved?

2. Has the individual been discouraged by a motivational barrier, such as an ineffective reward system, a lack of opportunity to apply learning, deficient feedback, or punishment for performing well (for example, being given more work)? If so, can the barrier be removed?[13]

Other Considerations in Assessment of Training Needs

Attention must also be given to work group performance and internal processes that involve groups. These processes often affect the results of training on the job as much as the training itself. Support from the work group provides necessary reinforcement of the principles and behaviors presented in the training sessions. A truly successful training program is one that is continuously implemented at the workplace.

Assessment of training needs should also be integrated with other human resource activities. The data sources, measurements, and data collection techniques used in assessment can also be used in other personnel activities. For example, operational analysis can be coordinated with job analysis, the writing of job descriptions, and the determination of job specifications. The results can be useful in many activities, such as recruiting, selection, and compensation. Further, data from groups and individuals can be useful for group training and organizational development efforts.[14]

Finally, the training analyst must consider five criteria to ensure that training will be related specifically to organizational objectives and needs.

Employee involvement can create the necessary enthusiasm for training and help satisfy employees' desire to participate in decisions that directly affect their careers. Employees have a legitimate need to know why they have been selected for training.

Management involvement is also necessary, since management either directly or indirectly absorbs the costs of the training. Further, managers should have information about employees' performance deficiencies and training needs so that they can attempt to create a reinforcing work climate to which the employee can return after training.

Two related criteria are the *time* required for the program and the program's *costs,* which must be considered in relation to the program's benefits. Proposed training efforts must also be *relevant and quantifiable.* Upper management, which approves the amount of funds to be spent on training and development activities, is pragmatic.[15] These managers want documented reasons for training and measurable training results; they are seldom convinced by emotional pleas and subjective opinions.

Exhibit 9.2 analyzes various methods used in assessing training needs in terms of the criteria mentioned above.

Exhibit 9.2   **Analysis of Training Needs Assessment Methods**

Methods	Criteria[a]				
	Employee Involvement	Management Involvement	Time Requirement	Cost	Relevant, Quantifiable Data
Committees	−	0	0	−	−
Assessment Centers	+	−	+	+	+
Surveys (Attitudes)	0	−	0	0	−
Group Discussions	+	0	0	0	0
Employee Interviews	+	−	+	+	0
Exit Interviews	−	−	−	−	−
Management Requests	−	+	−	−	−
Observation	0	−	+	+	0
Performance Appraisal	0	+	0	−	+
Questionnaires	+	+	0	0	+
Skills Tests	+	−	+	+	+

[a] + = High, 0 = Moderate, − = Low.

Source: Adapted from John W. Newstrom and John M. Lilyquist, "Selecting Needs Analysis Methods," *Training and Development Journal* 33 (October 1979), p. 56. Copyright 1979, Training and Development Journal, American Society for Training and Development. Reprinted with permission. All rights reserved.

Training and Development Methods

Principles of Training and Learning

Training and development activities are varied in their objectives, approach, setting, content, and intended audience. However, certain common principles should guide these activities:

The developmental activities should be spaced over a period of time (*distributed learning*) so as to enhance training effectiveness. This principle allows the trainee to digest what has been presented and to consider how it can be implemented on the job.

Rewards (praise, recognition, possibility for promotion) should be designed into the program. The training should explicitly answer the question on most trainees' minds: "What's the pay off for attending this session? What's in it for me?" Trainers unable to answer this question should seriously ask themselves whether the sessions should be conducted.

Feedback improves the developmental process because it lets the trainee know what progress he or she has made and what mistakes need correction. Trainers can observe trainees and give evaluative feedback so that trainees can implement what has been learned.

Trainees must be *motivated*. It is fundamental to productive human behavior and employee development that trainees must want to learn.

The learning that takes place in training situations should be *transferred* to on-the-job activities and behavior. Thus, it is imperative that the trainer not only explain concepts but explain how the concepts can be implemented on the job.

Trainees must be given an *opportunity to practice* on the job what has been learned in training sessions. For example, training in performance appraisal should occur before the annual performance reviews. Supervisors should attend training sessions that deal with completing appraisal forms and conducting reviews with employees. Then, they should apply what they have learned. These actions should be followed by additional sessions to probe supervisors' reactions and assessments of the new approaches.

Trainees *learn from many sources*—trial and error, modeling (imitating behaviors of others[16]), and communications from people knowledgeable about various subjects. No single training method or experience has a monopoly on employee development. However, organizations can facilitate the learning process by implementing effective training and development activities.

Training should take into account *individual differences* of trainees—differences in intelligence, motivation, aptitudes, interests, and so on. Most employees will improve their skills with increased training time, although there is a point at which too much training can cause information overload or boredom. Employees assimilate training at different rates. Some employees, particularly those who have not had related job experience, may require more training than others.

After an organization has determined its training and development needs, it must consider its objectives, its capability for securing support and training resources, the learning principles upon which training and development activities are based, and the expected returns and costs of the various needs identified. Based on this analysis and the conclusions drawn from it, the appropriate method or methods should be chosen. Of course, each organization has resource personnel who can be called on for certain training activities. On other occasions, the activities call for resources outside the organization. In other words, many combinations of training activities may be found in organizations, depending on their objectives, resources, and training and development methods. What follows are descriptions of some of the more common training and development methods:[17]

On-the-Job Training and Development Methods

On-the-job training, clearly the most common type of training, is designed to maximize learning while allowing the employee to perform the job. However, the following description is probably typical of many on-the-job training situations:

Who trained you to do your present job? Probably no one. Probably like most of us, you worked it out by yourself. Because you were ambitious and highly motivated you observed the good and bad practices of others doing similar work, and read all you could, and got some good coaching from senior members of your profession, and perhaps even learned something at school.

The point is that you weren't "trained" by your employer. You learned to do your job by your own initiative. And that is the way most people in business and industry learn their jobs, including the industrial worker who theoretically gets "trained" by his supervisor. Actually the amount of actual useful learning that occurs as a result of "training" is minor compared to the amount picked up in ingenious subtle ways by the employee himself. We don't train our employees; they learn in spite of us.[18]

Job Instruction Job instruction training occurs when the trainer explains the job to the trainee, allows the trainee to perform the tasks, observes the trainee's performance, and then gives feedback in terms of ways to improve performance.[19] Exhibit 9.3 outlines these steps in such a procedure on a pocket card for supervisors.

Job Rotation Job rotation is a technique designed to give the trainee knowledge and experience of operations in various parts of the organization. The trainee moves through various training positions in the organization, receiving instructions and feedback from the supervisor in each department. While this method is considered essential in many organizations, it is expensive and may fail if supervisors are unprepared or have no interest in or time for training.

On-the-Job Coaching When on-the-job coaching is used, the supervisor acts as a tutor, instructing the employee on how to perform a task and providing assistance to facilitate learning. To assure effective results, the coach should be trained and prepared for the training activities, and the proper environment (adequate time, freedom from interruptions) should be established. In addition, trainees should be given ample opportunity to practice what they learn and should be properly rewarded for using new knowledge and skills on the job.

Exhibit 9.3	Pocket Card for Supervisors

How to Train

Step 1—Prepare the Employee for Instruction
Put him at ease.
Explain the job and its importance.
Get him interested in learning job.
Step 2—Present the Job
Follow your breakdown.
Explain and demonstrate ONE STEP at a time. Tell why and how.
Stress KEY POINTS.
Instruct clearly and patiently.
Give everything you will want back but no more.
Step 3—Tryout Performance
Have him do the job.
Have him tell why and how and stress KEY POINTS.
Correct errors and omissions as he makes them. Encourage him.
Get back everything you gave him in step 2.
Continue until YOU know He knows.
Step 4—Follow Through
Put him on his own.
Encourage questions.
Check frequently.
Let him know how he's doing.
If the Learner Hasn't Learned, the Trainer Hasn't Taught

Source: Courtesy of Lee Holley, management consultant, Atlanta, Georgia.

Committee or Project Assignments Committee or project assignments may involve one trainee or a group of trainees who are given a real organizational problem to solve. The trainees are required to do a considerable amount of data gathering and analysis before recommending a solution. The solution and justifications for it are presented to higher management and a critique of the trainees' performance is conducted.

Apprenticeship Apprenticeship is primarily an on-the-job method, although the trainee is expected to attend classes off the job, usually at night. At work, the trainee, or apprentice, is assigned to an experienced journeyman (skilled craftsman) for a fixed period of time; in addition, as mentioned, he or she is required to successfully complete a program of classroom instruction. By combining classwork and practice on the job, apprenticeship maximizes one of the key learning principles—practicing what one learns. However, it has been criticized for specifying a fixed period for all apprentices and thus not taking into consideration individual rates of learning and progress.[20]

Off-the-Job Training and Development Methods

Off-the-job activities are used to support and facilitate the learning and development that take place on the job. Such activities are intended to achieve objectives that cannot be reached by relying solely on on-the-job activities. The methods considered the most common and effective are business games, case studies, conference method, in-basket technique, incident method, sensitivity training, lecture method, auto-instructional techniques, role playing, behavioral modeling, and vestibule training.

Business Games A business game is a simulation of an organizational unit, a company, or an industry. The simulation is based on established relationships derived from organizational and economic principles and studies of the operations of a unit, company, or industry. These established relationships dictate how various combinations of inputs (raw materials, human resources, machines and equipment, and the like) interact with wage rates, product prices, advertising, research and development, and the like to affect the organization's outcomes, sales, profits, net worth, and so on. (See Exhibit 9.4 for a typical business game decision form.) The participants make business decisions based on the information they are given. Their decisions are entered into a computer and participants are able to see the results of their decisions. The primary objectives are to learn decision-making skills; to learn how an organization or industry operates; to identify the interrelationships within an organization; and to gain an appreciation of how a decision in one organizational unit affects other units. Business games can mirror real life in organizations, thereby allowing considerable transfer of training to the job. They are also intrinsically motivating and create substantial involvement and interest. However, games are not without problems. Trainees may become overly involved with "winning" by attempting to figure out the programmed relationships established for the game. Also, the realism of the game situation is diminished because of the fixed set of relationships programmed into the game. Finally, members within each of the competing groups may let the more aggressive members make most of the decisions, thereby reducing some members' training experiences.

Case Studies In case studies, conditions and problems in a simulated organizational setting are described on paper to the trainee. Trainees are expected to identify reasons for the problems and offer solutions to them. Frequently, trainees work through the steps of problem identification and analysis, development of alternative solutions, and selection of the most appropriate solution. Then, the solution and its justification are presented to the group, where they will be discussed and defended. (Examples of cases are included at the end of each section of this book.)

Advocates of this method believe that working through cases helps trainees develop or improve several skills—for instance, it enhances abilities to carry out logical, systematic analysis; forces decisions to be made based on incomplete information; develops decision-making

Exhibit 9.4

Firm Name _____

Team Number _____

Team Members _____

Decisions:

  Production

    Volume _____

    Inventory _____

  Research and Development _____

  Price _____

  Promotion _____

  Dividends _____

  Bonds Issued _____

  Stock Issued _____

  Environmental Costs _____

  Employees Hired _____

skills; involves active participation; and promotes interest among the trainees. Critics, however, have pointed out several deficiencies, including the possibility that the case will be overly artificial, thereby diminishing the learning experience. In addition, the method relies heavily on the discussion leader, who, without proper skill, can allow the discussions to stray from the subject matter.

Conference Method The conference, or discussion, method combines presentation of information with participation in small groups. The leader provides guidance and feedback, but no instruction. With the objectives of developing problem-solving and decision-making capabilities and learning about new and complex materials, the learner actively participates in discussions with other group members. The discussions are oriented toward specific problems or new areas of knowledge selected by the leader or by the participants. For example, a tire manufacturer had a plant characterized by low employee morale, serious labor-management problems, and low productivity. After many attempts to correct these conditions had failed, the plant manager as a last effort decided to implement a program of group discussions within and across departments. Middle and upper management was excluded—the supervisors would hold the meetings and lead the discussions. The supervisors were trained in how to be effective conference leaders. Conferences subsequently were held throughout the plant; and many problems were identified and resolved by supervisors and employees working together.

Designed primarily to offset negative reactions to lectures (which will be discussed later), the conference method engenders considerable involvement and provides an opportunity for two-way communication. On the other hand, it is limited to small groups and, without effective leadership, suffers from frequent disorganization. Thus, the success of this method depends heavily on the conference leader, who must be sure that those present have an opportunity to participate, that divergent views are presented, that feedback is not unduly negative, and that discussions proceed toward the stated objectives. Some organizations change conference leaders so that more than one person can learn from the experience of conference leadership.

In-Basket Technique The in-basket technique is a simulation exercise designed to develop decision-making, problem-solving, and organizing ability by placing the trainee at the desk of a manager. The trainee is presented with a description of the manager's job and an in-basket containing correspondence, memos, requests from other departments, customer complaints, operating statements, and the like. The purpose of the exercise is to introduce the trainee to a realistic workday in the life of a manager and determine how well the trainee performs in this situation. The trainee works through the in-basket by making decisions, determining which material will be given first priority, making recommendations, drafting communications, and giving advice. At the end, a follow-up discussion is held to evaluate how well the trainee performed and to make recommendations for improving the trainee's managerial skills.

An expansion of this technique is the Kepner-Tregoe approach, in which four managers operate as members of one organization. Each manager has a desk and an in-basket containing problems interrelated with those of other members of the network. Trainees may use the telephone and hold conferences; however, a premium is placed on organization and speed. The heart of this training method is the critique, wherein the objectives of the training are reinforced.

The Incident Method The incident method closely resembles the case method; however, the trainees are given only a sketchy outline of a particular incident. To get additional information necessary to resolve the problem presented in the incident, the trainees must ask the trainer questions. When the trainees have sufficient information or when they can think of no more questions, they develop a solution based on the information given and their analyses of it. (See an example of the incident method on page 220 of the cases for Part II.) At the conclusion, the trainer tells the trainees all the information that would have been available if all the right questions had been asked. Finally, the solution based on all the information is compared with the trainees' solution, and appropriate learning principles are discussed. At this point, the role of the trainer is critical, because trainees tend to become more concerned with finding the solution to the incident than with focusing on the principles to be learned from the exercise.

Sensitivity Training/Laboratory Method Sensitivity training stresses participant involvement and is directed toward changing behavior in interpersonal relations. It is a unique and most controversial learning experience based on the premise that knowledge alone does not change behavior. The objectives of sensitivity training are:

To help trainees gain self-awareness by helping them understand how and why they act as they do and how they affect others.

To help trainees gain insight into why others act as they do.

To help trainees increase their tolerance and understanding of others.

To provide a setting in which trainees can try new ways of interacting with others and receive feedback.

While this training may be supplemented with short lectures, group exercises, role-playing, and other experiences, the core activity centers on the *T-group.*

T-groups are set up in various ways. For example, there may be *stranger* groups—composed of trainees from different organizations—or *family* groups—composed of people from the same organization. Some programs may last for a few hours, whereas others may extend to one or two weeks. The T-group members (usually no more than fifteen) discuss topics that pertain to an industrial problem. They are also involved in relatively unstructured projects, such as the selection of five items to take on a hypothetical trip to the moon.

The major emphasis is on the interpersonal relations among the members as they carry out assigned projects; for example, one member might be extremely ''bossy'' while another member is distant from the group. Subsequent discussions examine group members' actions, their reactions to each other, the defenses they use to protect their self-images, their abilities to communicate, and their capacities for leadership. This examination is carried out through group members' honest and open appraisal of each other's behavior. The trainer during this time serves as a resource person and often as a role model for the group—that is, he or she expresses himself or herself openly and honestly, does not become defensive when the group criticizes, and demonstrates his or her acceptance of others' behavior.

The T-group exercise is a highly engaging experience that has been applied in a variety of organizations. However, it is expensive, involves only small numbers of trainees at any one time, and exposes the trainees to considerable psychological stress. In fact, mental breakdowns and severe traumas have been recorded.

Lecture Method The lecture method, the most common method of instruction and job training, is familiar to all those who have attended a formal education program. In the purest form, the lecture consists of a one-way presentation of prescribed information. It remains a common method because it allows a substantial amount of material to be imparted to a large group in a relatively short time. If the lecturer is skilled, the lecture can be presented in a highly organized and systematic manner. Rarely does the effective lecturer actually do all the talking; rather, he or she invites dialogue, audience response, and active participation. Successful lecturers inject questions, change the pace of their presentations, and use body language to enrich their presentations.

Critics of lectures have noted a number of deficiencies. Foremost, the learning is not self-controlled and individualized and does not provide reinforcement to participants. Trainees differ in abilities, interests, and motivation; and the lecture is not sufficiently flexible to meet these individual differences. Finally, the lecture has limited potential for use in skill training, where hands-on experience is essential.

Auto-Instructional Techniques Two self-instruction training techniques are *programmed instruction* and *computer-assisted instruction.* Programmed instruction presents material in a series of carefully planned steps, provides learning at the individual's pace, and provides immediate feedback to the learner. The *linear* approach to programmed instruction requires the learner to respond correctly at each step of the program before proceeding to new, more difficult material. For example, in a basic management course, the trainees will be expected to master the principles of planning before they are expected to make an employee forecast. The *branching* approach does not require errorless performance, but incorrect answers lead the learner to additional background information that must be mastered before the correct response can be selected. For example, suppose the trainee is required to make an employee forecast based on a 20-percent increase in sales.

If the trainee makes the forecast by simply adding 20 percent, the answer may be incorrect. The correct answer may require the consideration of overtime in the short run, lack of machines, selling from inventories, and so on. The trainee who does not consider these factors will be required to read additional materials and answer questions on them before returning to the original forecasting problem.

Advocates of programmed instruction praise its advantages because it incorporates many important principles of learning—trainee involvement; individualized, self-paced instruction; knowledge of results; challenge and interest; and careful organization of material. In addition, it reduces training time by about one-third and is particularly effective for high- and low-ability trainees, since they can proceed at an individual pace appropriate to their learning abilities.[21] With so many of the major learning principles satisfied, this approach should receive wide acceptance. However, the method is costly unless large numbers of employees can use the program; and it cannot be used in situations in which the training objectives include facilitation of social interaction.

Computer-assisted instruction is an extension of the programmed instruction methodology. The learning program is stored in the computer, and learning occurs through interaction between the trainee and the computer. While this type of instruction allows self-control, provides feedback and knowledge of results, and increases trainee motivation, it also is costly to design, must be justified by large numbers of trainees, and has yet to demonstrate any significant improvement in learning over the non-computer-assisted program instruction technique.

Role Playing Role playing is a simulation technique that requires trainees to act out prescribed roles. For example, in a training program on conducting interviews, one trainee may be assigned the role of a job applicant and another given the role of the interviewer. The focus of the exercise usually is on human relations aspects of a manager's job. The exercise attempts to promote understanding and problem solving. Its success depends on the ability of the trainees to adopt their prescribed roles and to react as if they were truly in a work situation. The trainees try various solutions to the problems with which they are presented and obtain immediate feedback on their approaches to handling supervisory problems and communication skills. Role playing has been effective in changing attitudes of employees toward their supervisors and the supervisors' attitudes toward subordinates. In addition to being highly involving, it provides practice in personal interaction that closely corresponds with real-life situations.

On the negative side, role playing is time consuming and expensive. The number of persons that can be actively involved is limited; however, the entire group can be divided into numerous role-playing sessions to gain greater participant involvement. Other problems can surface: the trainees may overact and forget the learning objectives, the trainer may lose control over the content of the sessions, and the trainees may believe the exercise is unrealistic and childish.

Behavioral Modeling Behavioral modeling is a process in which trainees learn about desirable as well as undesirable work behaviors from a role model on the job or from models who act out the behaviors on film or video tape. The trainee first is exposed to the modeled behavior—for example, effective interviewing or handling of employee grievances. After the trainee has observed these behaviors, he or she practices them. Next, feedback on the trainee's performance is given to reinforce the desired behavior and provide recommendations for improvement. The final phase involves transfer of the newly learned behaviors to the job.[22] Behavioral modeling as a training method has been shown to result in a positive reaction from trainees, a measurable increase in their knowledge of interpersonal skills, improvement in their behavior, and an increase in their performance levels.[23]

Vestibule Training/Simulators Vestibule training programs are carried out in special training centers where trainees use the same equipment and procedures they would use on their regular jobs. While such training permits ideal learning conditions—immediate reinforcement, knowledge of results, opportunity to practice, and sequenced learning—it is very costly except to large organizations that train many employees at one time.

In training centers where trainees must use very expensive equipment, such as flight or space equipment, or when trainees are exposed to dangerous materials, such as weapons and explosives, simulators are frequently used. Simulator training for corporate pilots is estimated to cost $40 million per year. The pilot simulators are ground-based cockpit mockups that duplicate electrically the inflight actions of the planes they represent. Costs of these simulators can amount to as much as $10 million each.[24]

Categorizing Training and Development

The preceding discussion has categorized training and development methods according to whether they are used on the job or off the job. However, there is some overlap between the two. Exhibit 9.5 shows which methods are used on the job, which are used off the job, and which are used both on and off the job.

Training and development methods can also be categorized by the type of employees who are likely to be involved in them. Exhibit 9.6 divides the various methods according to whether they are used primarily for training employees, for training both employees and managers, or for training managers.

Exhibit 9.5

Training and Development Methods
Categorized by Use on the Job and off the Job

On the Job	On and Off the Job	Off the Job
Job Instruction Training	Apprenticeship	Business Games
Job Rotation	Behavioral Modeling	Case Studies
Coaching	Vestibule Training/	Conference Method
Committee or Project	Simulators	In-Basket Technique
Assignments		Incident Method
		Laboratory Method/
		Sensitivity Training
		Lecture Method
		Programmed Instruction
		Computer-Assisted Instruction
		Role Playing

Frequency of Use of Training and Development Methods

The training and development methods described above are used by numerous organizations, but they are not used with the same frequency. Exhibits 9.7 and 9.8 show the results of two surveys that sought information about the frequency of use of various training methods. As you can see, planned on-site training and lectures, demonstrations, and group discussions are popular on-the-job training methods, while group discussions and lectures are popular off-the-job methods.

In-House versus Outside Training and Development Programs

Organizations have many factors to consider in selecting the training and development activities that will best meet their needs. Just as important is their determination of whether to set up an in-house program or to send employees outside the organization for training. Each alternative has advantages. For example, in-house programs can be

Exhibit 9.6

Training and Development Methods
Categorized by Type of Employee Trained

Employees	Employees and Managers	Managers
Apprenticeship	Coaching	Business Games
Job Instruction Training	Committee or Project	Case Studies
Vestibule Training/	Assignments	Conference Method
Simulators	Job Rotation	In-Basket Technique
	Programmed Instruction	Incident Method
	Computer-Assisted Instruction	Laboratory Method/
	Behavioral Modeling	Sensitivity Training
		Lecture Method
		Role Playing

Exhibit 9.7	**Frequency of Various On-Site Training and Development Methods**		

	Percent of Organizations Using Particular Method		
	Production or Operations (Responses from 297 Organizations)	Office and Clerical (Responses from 435 Organizations)	Lower-Level Exempt (First-Line Supervision) (Responses from 442 Organizations)
Planned on-the-Job	74	73	61
Lecture, Demonstration, Group Discussion	45	59	76
Self Study with Training Manual	33	38	37
Programmed Instruction	27	36	43
Job Rotation	28	28	34
Role Playing	9	22	42
Case Method	7	15	41
Apprenticeship	52	9	7

Source: Harriet Gorlin, *Personnel Practices I: Recruitment, Placement, Training, Communication* (New York: The Conference Board, 1981), p. 41. Excerpted by permission.

specifically designed for the organization, and the cost per trainee can be lowered, whereas tuition per participant for an outside program is high ($500 for two days, in some cases), and the program content can be quite general and not company-oriented. Some organizations favor in-house programs because they are convenient and easy to attend. However, they also are frequently interrupted; and trainees often leave the sessions to tend to problems that occur in their departments during the time set aside for training. In-house programs assume that trainees know more about the company than any instructor from outside. However, an in-house instructor known by the trainees often has problems establishing credibility (it is sometimes difficult to be an expert in one's own back yard).

Other considerations about outside programs include uncertainty about the quality of the instructors, especially in new programs, and uncertainty about whether trainees will attend the sessions.[25] To deal with these problems, organizations may send only one participant to a new outside program and then ask this participant to evaluate the program's content and the instructors and advise the organization on whether additional personnel should attend. This trainee must objectively evaluate the training program in terms of its advantages and disadvantages—a difficult task. Few trainees who have spent two weeks in a program at a cost of thousands of dollars have the courage to indicate that it was a complete waste of time. Many organizations now require trainees to write a report or make an oral presentation describing the content of the outside programs they attend so the

Exhibit 9.8

**Training Methods Used for
Initial Off-the-Job Training
and Extent Used**

Methods	Number of Respondents	Number of Respondents Reporting Various Percentages of Program Time to a Given Method				
		0% to 20%	21% to 40%	41% to 60%	61% to 80%	81% to 100%
Group Discussions	141	36	69	32	4	
Lecture	137	74	35	23	4	1
Case Study	124	100	22	2		
Role Playing	106	99	6	1		
Business Games	51	48	3			
Programmed Instruction	38	35	1	2		
Laboratory (Sensitivity) Training	18	15	2	1		

Source: Walter S. Wikstrom, *Supervisory Training* (New York: The Conference Board, Inc., 1973), p. 15. Adapted by permission.

training experience can be shared and the organization can ensure that the trainees attend the sessions. Evaluation also helps the outside programs' instructors and coordinators, who continuously try to improve their programs and rely on inputs from participants for making the program content more appropriate and useful.

Evaluation of Training and Development Activities

Evaluating training activities is necessary because of the large expenditures involved (trainees' time as well as funds devoted to the programs).[26]

As the amount of money being expended on these programs increases and resources become more limited, the training/development budgets come under the gun. Better evaluation instruments are going to be demanded. No great strides have been made in this area, though substantial research is being conducted.[27]

Upper management also needs to know whether training programs not directly related to the production and distribution of goods and services are contributing to organizational effectiveness. Recently, the courts and the Equal Employment Opportunity Commission have questioned certain practices related to training, such as trainee selection and presupervisory training, as possible sources of employment discrimination.[28] In spite of these reasons for evaluation, training directors and personnel managers have revealed that 75 percent of their firms have no formal method of evaluating the effectiveness of their training activities.[29]

Training evaluations take various approaches and are of variable quality. Evaluations are misleading when they employ only a single criterion, such as a favorable impression, to measuring effectiveness. Evaluations that only concern outcomes ignore process measures, such as measures of benefits derived from the interaction between trainees that takes place during the training. Selection of the criteria for evaluation should be deliberate and should represent more than a value judgment by the people directly responsible for training activities.[30]

Criteria for Evaluation

Four categories of training criteria commonly selected for evaluation are: reactions, learning, on-the-job behavior, and results. *Reactions* include the trainees' feelings and opinions about the program and whether they were satisfied with the training. Management needs honest, meaningful reactions from the participants, because these assessments will be the first indication of the success or failure of the program. *Learning* includes the knowledge and skills acquired from the training and changes in attitudes that may have resulted from the training. Changes in *on-the-job behavior* that result from the training program are usually determined by the supervisors, peers, subordinates, or participants. This criterion is more difficult to measure than reaction and learning, and sufficient time must elapse to allow for any behavioral changes that result from training to take place. *Results* include changes in such tangible factors as quantity and quality of production, accidents, turnover, and costs.[31]

While these criteria are separately defined and used, they are highly interrelated. If trainees reacted favorably, they probably learned more. If they learned more, they probably changed their on-the-job behavior. If their behavior changed, their performance on the job probably improved. Negative reactions to the training do not necessarily reduce learning, worsen behavior, or lower performance; however, negative reactions certainly do not improve learning, behavior, or performance.

These criteria can be arranged in order of the value of the information obtained through their evaluation, the frequency with which they are used, and the difficulty of assessing them (see Exhibit 9.9). For example, trainees' reaction is the easiest to measure, the most frequently used, but the lowest in value in terms of information obtained. On the other hand, results provide the information of highest value but are relatively difficult to measure and are used less frequently.[32]

For accuracy and credibility, "hard," results-oriented measures are preferred; however, less rigorous measures are not without value and are easier to obtain. The conclusion about the present practice of managerial use of criteria is fairly clear: Managers have typically doubted that the benefits of the more sophisticated measures warrant the costs involved and they continue to employ the easiest evaluation measures, such as trainee opinion and reaction.[33]

Exhibit 9.9   **Characteristics of Four Commonly
                                    Used Evaluation Criteria**

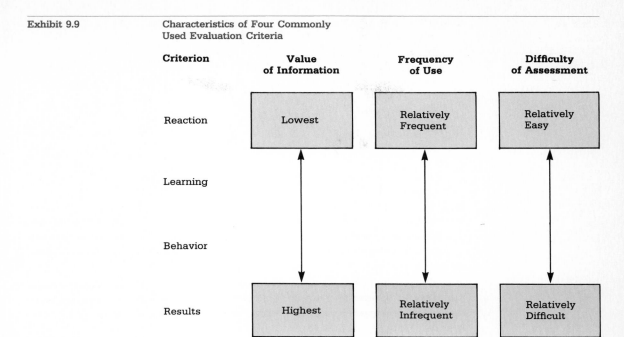

Criterion	Value of Information	Frequency of Use	Difficulty of Assessment
Reaction	Lowest	Relatively Frequent	Relatively Easy
Learning			
Behavior			
Results	Highest	Relatively Infrequent	Relatively Difficult

Source: John W. Newstrom, ''Catch-22: The Problem of Incomplete Evaluation of Training,'' *Training and Development Journal* 11 (November 1978), p. 23. Copyright 1978, Training and Development Journal, American Society for Training and Development. Reprinted with permission. All rights reserved.

**Evaluation
Design**

The previously discussed measures are used in each of the evaluation designs. Each design is affected by many potentially conflicting influences, such as the evaluator's abilities and skills, the need for accuracy, the time and costs involved, and the expectations and requirements of higher management. Often the evaluation design represents a compromise among these influences. For example, the individuals responsible for evaluation may desire accuracy and thoroughness but may not have the time or skills necessary to achieve them.

Exhibit 9.10 summarizes three types of evaluation designs. Many companies rely on the *after-only design* for training evaluation. Questionnaries for assessing trainees' reactions after the training are used, as are supervisors' observation of trainees' behavior and changes in job performance. This design yields the lowest level of accuracy and also raises the question of whether influences other than training may have caused changes in behavior or performance.

Another evaluation design is the *before-and-after design*. Here, learning, behavior, and results are measured before and after the training to help determine whether change occurred as a result of the

Exhibit 9.10   **Evaluation Designs**

Design	Pretest Measure	Stimulus	Posttest Measure
I. After Only	No Measure Taken	Training	Measure Taken
II. Before and After	Measure Taken	Training	Measure Taken
III. Before and After with Experimental and Control Groups			
Experimental Group	Measure Taken	Training	Measure Taken
Control Group	Measure Taken	No Training	Measure Taken

training. While this approach allows the evaluators to conclusively state whether any change took place before or after the training, the evaluators cannot conclusively state that the change can be attributed exclusively to a specific training activity.

To increase the confidence with which the evaluators can point to training as the cause for a change in performance, the *before-and-after design with experimental and control groups* can be used. The experimental group includes the participants in the training activities. The control group is equal in number and has similar personnel, work loads, working conditions, and the like; but it is not exposed to the training. By comparing measures from both groups before and after the training, evaluators can determine whether training had any effect. For example, if the performance of the experimental group increases after the training and the performance of the control group does not, it can be concluded that training caused job performance to improve.

However, questions arise among evaluators concerning the validity of such conclusions. For example, was the change due to trainees' motivation's being heightened when they were singled out for special attention and consideration (called the *Hawthorne effect*)? Does the fact that the trainees know they are being rated or will be rated after they return to their jobs stimulate them to better performance? Does taking a pretest measure of what trainees know about a topic alert them to the topic and cause them to concentrate and learn more in the training sessions? Is higher performance on the job after training a short-run effect that will fade out? To obtain the answer to these questions, more sophisticated designs will have to be used and greater evaluation skills will have to be employed.[34]

Organizations must be cautious about using evaluation results obtained in another organizational setting, even though the training programs may seem identical. Organizations have many important differences, such as in organizational climate, trainees' characteristics, and organizational support. Managers in each organization should develop skills in evaluation so they can accurately evaluate their own programs in terms of costs and benefits.[35] Further, evaluators should not overlook the positive features of training that are difficult to measure. For instance, the recognition of being selected, improved job satisfaction, and renewed feelings of self-worth and value to the organization are important considerations to the individual employee.[36]

Perceived Effectiveness of Training Methods in Meeting Specific Training Objectives

Because training and development activities involve such a significant investment of resources, training directors, personnel managers, and top management are interested in the effectiveness of various training methods. While an effective way to determine the effectiveness of a specific training activity is to measure on-the-job results by use of before-and-after measures with experimental and control groups, the opinions of training directors provide useful considerations. A recent survey of 200 firms disclosed the perceived effectiveness of nine training methods in achieving six training objectives (see Exhibit 9.11). The survey shows that the case method was rated best for developing problem solving skills and gaining participants' acceptance. The conference (discussion) method was considered most effective for knowledge acquisition; and programmed instruction, for knowledge retention. Role playing and sensitivity training (T-groups) were considered best in achieving behavioral objectives, such as changing attitudes and developing interpersonal skills. At the low end of the scale of effectiveness were television lectures, movie films, and lectures with questions.[37]

Role of the Personnel Department and Other Managers in Training and Development Activities

The personnel department plays a key role in training and development activities. Large organizations' personnel departments usually include a training and development unit with a staff of specialists, whereas in small organizations, the personnel manager may be responsible for these activities as part of the overall personnel function. In a few organizations, primarily very small firms, each department handles its own training.

Where the personnel department conducts training and development activities, it has several major responsibilities: (a) it determines training needs of individuals and identifies departments in the organization in which training is needed and can be productive; (b) it designs programs to meet organizational and individual needs and selects employees who would gain from these activities; and (c) it assesses the effectiveness of these activities and programs. In addition to these specific responsibilities, the personnel department is responsible for representing the entire human resource development activities to

Exhibit 9.11   **Perceived Effectiveness of Nine
Training Methods For Six Objectives**

Training Objectives

Method	Knowledge Acquisition Mean	Rank	Changing Attitudes Mean	Rank	Problem-Solving Skills Mean	Rank	Interpersonal Skills Mean	Rank	Participant Acceptance Mean	Rank	Knowledge Retention Mean	Rank
Case Study	3.35	4	2.63	5	3.89	1	2.69	5	4.40	1	3.04	4
Conference (Discussion) Method	3.72	1	2.93	3	2.91	5	2.89	4	3.45	5	3.26	2
Lecture (with Questions)	2.57	8	2.35	7	2.47	7	1.72	8	2.79	8	3.15	3
Business Games	3.27	5	2.75	4	3.68	2	2.93	3	3.57	2	2.98	7
Movie Films	2.98	6	2.41	6	2.06	9	2.00	6	3.50	4	3.00	5
Programmed Instruction	3.49	3	2.21	8	2.85	6	1.81	7	2.69	9	3.87	1
Role Playing	3.59	2	3.63	2	3.33	3	4.06	1	3.55	3	3.00	5
Sensitivity Training (T-Group)	2.74	7	3.65	1	3.00	4	3.80	2	2.86	6	2.57	9
Television Lecture	2.43	9	2.20	9	2.15	8	1.67	9	2.81	7	2.76	8

Note: Rating scale: 5 = highly effective; 4 = quite effective; 3 = moderately effective; 2 = limited effectiveness; 1 = not effective.

Source: Reprinted from "Evaluating the Effectiveness of Training Methods" by John W. Newstrom, p. 58 in the January 1980 issue of *Personnel Administrator,* copyright 1980, the American Society for Personnel Administration, 30 Park Drive, Berea, OH 44017, $26 per year. A similar study was conducted in 1972 by S. J. Carrol, F. T. Paine, and J. J. Ivancevich, "The Relative Effectiveness of Training Methods—Expert Opinion and Research," *Personnel Psychology* 25 (Autumn 1972), pp. 495–509.

upper management. In this role, it is also held accountable for funds and resources used in these efforts. By demonstrating success in developing human resources, the personnel department will receive more support and funds from top management; and a more receptive, reinforcing climate for training and development activities will be created and maintained.

Like other personnel activities, training and development objectives cannot be achieved without the efforts and willing cooperation of line management. Line managers help determine training needs in their departments and identify individuals who can gain from the programs. They provide support for development activities and quite often participate as instructors in training sessions. After a program is completed, their role in assessing its effectiveness is essential, because they frequently collect the data used in the assessment and make judgments about whether the trainees have gained from the programs.[38]

Issues in Training and Development

What Effect Will Equal Employment Opportunity Considerations Have on Training and Development Activities?

Several issues in training and development will face management in the 1980s. Those to be discussed here are: equal employment opportunity; fads in training; and problems in obtaining top management commitment and support for training and development activities.

Recently, training decisions have been interpreted by the EEOC and the courts as falling under Title VII of the Civil Rights Act when the selection for training activities adversely affects members of minorities. Adverse impact has occurred when personnel were selected for on-the-job training, formal training programs, and apprenticeship classes. In addition, employment decisions relating to training that may be subject to EEO suits involve the use of education requirements, test scores, age limits, and experience requirements as prerequisites for admittance to training classes.

Under special circumstances, the courts have already allowed or ordered quotas of minorities for training classes and have required companies to provide training to help minorities become eligible for better positions (for example, see Chapter 5's discussion of the Weber case). In out-of-court settlements of EEO suits, companies have agreed to offer more management development programs to women and minorities to help them qualify for promotions that may become available.[39] With more EEO investigations of selection and promotion practices, EEO issues will continue to be important in personnel management.

Are Training and Development Fads Harmful or Helpful?

Another problem is the susceptibility of training to fads. It has been said that the training and development literature is not only voluminous, nonempirical, poorly written, and dull, and also faddish to an extreme. These fads follow a characteristic pattern. First, a new technique appears and collects a group of advocates. The technique then is extended and modified through additional demonstrations at several industrial locations. Next is the backlash, in which a few critics say the technique does not work and is not backed by empirical data. Then, the technique is replaced by a new technique that appears on the horizon; and the cycle begins again.[40]

One reviewer concluded after surveying the training literature:

The training field is dominated by a fads approach. Children go from yo-yos to hoola hoops to skate boards, and training directors move from sensitivity training to organization development to behavioral role modeling. Probably, each of these techniques has a place . . . , but analysts never seem to find out very much about their approach before they are off examining another type of program.[41]

An individual experienced in training has admitted:

I think we have to face the reality that a good many of us have been guilty of pushing the latest fad rather than truly looking at the needs or the performance requirements of our organization and using them as indicators of what is required to strengthen performance.[42]

On the other hand, Malcolm Knowles claims to have learned how to cope with fads:

"Fad" is not a bad word to me, as it is to some people. I know there is likely to be some useful outcome from every fad. And I don't have to feel guilty about being identified with a fad. I think that a fad mobilizes the energy of its adherents, particularly in the early stages of its evolution, that is necessary for the creative development of its theory and technology to its full potential. The people I feel sorry for are the ones who got ideologically so committed to a fad that they couldn't move beyond it.[43]

Fads may be a way of life in training and development. However, personnel representatives must maximize the opportunities offered by fads, while at the same time minimizing fads' counterproductive aspects.

How Can Personnel Representatives Gain Commitment and Support for Training and Development Activities from Top Management?

A final issue pervades nearly all training and development activities: The difficulty of gaining commitment and support from top management. As stated earlier, one of the reasons for this lack of commitment is that top management wants to see objective results in terms of measured benefits and costs, and such results are not provided. Another reason is articulated by Theodore Levitt, who says:

We can teach about management, but we cannot teach management. We can teach what a manager does, but not by teaching enable someone to do it; a person can learn to manage, but not necessarily be taught to manage.

A manager may come away from a seminar more aware of his behavior, more knowledgeable about alternative styles and interpersonal practices, and even sincerely determined to behave and operate differently. But there is no evidence whatever that he can, or has ever been able to, successfully change his fundamental behavior.[44]

In spite of Levitt's skeptical assessment, training and development activities can be valuable; however, they must be judged in terms of their benefits and costs; training departments must be viewed as profit or cost centers; and trainers must be held accountable for training results in terms of economy and productivity. If these occur, training and development activities will become an essential, integral part of an effective organization and these activities will receive support from top management officials. Maintaining this support will depend on the training and development activities' contribution to the organization's objectives.

Summary

Organizational entry involves the activities of employees joining the organization. Orientation involves formalized approaches that help the employee in his or her assimilation into the organization. Socialization extends the process to the point at which the employee is transformed into a productive, participating member of the workforce. Training and development systems in organizations include assessment of training needs, training and development methods, and evaluation of training and development efforts. The first phase of the training and development system, assessment of training needs, includes three levels of analysis—organizational, operations, and personnel.

When training and development methods are chosen, important learning principles—such as distributed learning, rewards, feedback, motivation, transfer, opportunity to practice, variety of learning sources, and individual differences—must be taken into consideration. Methods must be designed and selected to meet certain objectives and return benefits to the organization and the individual. The methods may involve on-the-job as well as off-the-job training. They may be in-house or outside programs, and they may be designed for various levels of employees in the organization.

Evaluations of training and development activities usually are based on reactions, learning, behavior, and results. Evaluation designs include the after-only design, the before-and-after design, and the before-and-after design with experimental and control groups. In addition, there are several problems with evaluation, such as the "Hawthorne effect."

As with other personnel activities, the personnel department and other managers have important, interdependent roles in training and development. Issues in training and development include equal employment opportunity considerations, fads, and top management support.

Discussion Questions

1. Distinguish among organizational entry, orientation, and socialization.

2. Compare the various methods for assessment of training needs according to the criteria used to judge their effectiveness.

3. Since the objective of sensitivity training is to improve interpersonal skills, and since managers need these skills, why do you think sensitivity training is used so infrequently?

4. If lectures have so many shortcomings, why are they so commonly used in higher education?

5. Compare the relative advantages and disadvantages of in-house training programs and outside training programs.

6. How can the personnel department gain and maintain support for training from top management?

7. How can a company show that it is an equal opportunity employer through its training activities?

Notes

1. William McGehee, "Training and Development Theory, Policies, and Practices," in *Training and Development,* ed. Dale Yoder and H. G. Heneman, Jr. (Washington, D.C.: Bureau of National Affairs, 1977), pp. 5-1–5-7.
2. T. F. Gilbert, "The High Cost of Knowledge," *Personnel* 53 (March/April 1976), pp. 11–23.
3. William J. Kearney, "Management Development Can Pay Off," *Business Horizons* 18 (April 1975), p. 81.
4. Roger Rickels, "More Executives Take Work-Related Courses to Keep Up, Advance," *Wall Street Journal,* March 3, 1980, pp. 1, 23.
5. McGehee, "Training and Development," pp. 5-5–5-7.
6. John P. Wanous, "Organizational Entry: Newcomers Moving from Outside to Inside," *Psychological Bulletin* 84 (July 1977), pp. 601–618.
7. M. R. Louis, "Surprise and Sense Making: What Newcomers Experience in Entering Unfamiliar Organizational Settings," *Administrative Science Quarterly* 25 (June 1980), pp. 227–230.
8. Diana Reed-Mendenhall and C. W. Millard, "Orientation: A Training and Development Tool," *Personnel Administrator* 25 (August 1980), pp. 40–41.
9. J. P. Kotter, "The Psychological Contract: Managing the Joining-Up Process," *California Management Review* 15 (Spring 1973), pp. 91–93.
10. "Induction & Orientation," in *Personnel Management* (Washington, D.C.: Bureau of National Affairs, 1977), pp. 201:311–201:332.
11. Daniel C. Feldman, "The Multiple Socialization of Organization Members," *Academy of Management Review* (April 1981), pp. 309–311.
12. McGehee, "Training and Development," pp. 5-1–5-34.
13. M. L. Moore and P. Dutton, "Training Needs Analysis: Review and Critique," *Academy of Management Review* 3 (July 1978), pp. 533–544; R. F. Fraser, J. W. Gore, and C. C. Cotton, "A System for Determining Training Needs," *Personnel Journal* 57 (December 1978), pp. 682–685, 697; William McGehee and Paul W. Thayer, *Training in Business and Industry* New York: John Wiley & Sons, 1961), pp. 24–26.
14. Moore and Dutton, "Training Needs Analysis."
15. J. W. Newstrom and J. M. Lilyquist, "Selecting Needs Analysis Methods," *Training and Development Journal* 33 (October 1979), pp. 52–56.
16. Charles C. Manz, "Vicarious Learning: The Influence of Modeling on Organizational Behavior," *Academy of Management Review* 6 (January 1981), pp. 105–113.
17. Descriptions of the training and development methods are taken from the following excellent sources, unless otherwise noted: John P. Campbell, Marvin D. Dunnette, Edward E. Lawler III, and Karl E. Weick, Jr., *Managerial Behavior, Peformance, and Effectiveness* (New York: McGraw-Hill, 1970), pp. 233–252; John R. Hinrichs, "Personnel Training," in *Handbook of Industrial and Organizational Psychology,* ed. M. D. Dunnette (Chicago: Rand McNally, 1976), pp. 829–860; Max Foster, "Training and Development Programs, Methods, and Facilities," in *Training and Development,* ed. Dale Yoder and H. G. Heneman, Jr. (Washington, D.C.: Bureau of National Affairs, 1977), pp. 5-35–5-56.

the instructors. The instructors said they could be ready to teach in two weeks, and dates were established. Six classrooms were provided by the university. The classrooms were located so the groups could easily rotate among them.

During the first two days, the following comments from members of Groups III, IV, V, and VI were heard:

Performance appraisal: "That's not the way we do it in the plant."

Motivation: "I'll bet you won't be covering this topic the same way with Group I."

Communication: "Nobody in the plant's upper management ever listens to us."

Decision making: "Why are we here? We don't ever make decisions at the plant."

Group I liked its first session, cases in management, because the cases were similar to situations faced at the plant. Its members became a little suspicious when the communication instructor continued to emphasize the importance of upward communication, suggestions from employees, and open-door policies and the value of employee grievances. The group became even more skeptical of the program when the performance appraisal instructor proposed that employee participation in goal setting and self-appraisals were useful in achieving higher performance. Then, when the motivation instructor advocated employee participation and involvement, intrinsic motivating factors, job enrichment, and employee incentives, the plant manager asked: "Are you telling this to every group?" To the surprise of the plant manager, the instructor said yes.

The plant manager left the room, found the corporate training director, and asked whether each instructor was covering each topic in the same way with every group. The director replied: "I assume so." The plant manager then called a meeting of the instructors, Group I, and the corporate training staff for the end of the day.

Questions:

1. What went wrong with this management development program?
2. How does this company's approach compare with the training and development system outlined in the chapter?
3. Now that two days of classes have been completed, what should be done?
4. After the program has been completed, what should the members of Group I consider?
5. What should the corporate training and development staff consider?
6. How do you account for the comments from Groups III, IV, V, and VI?

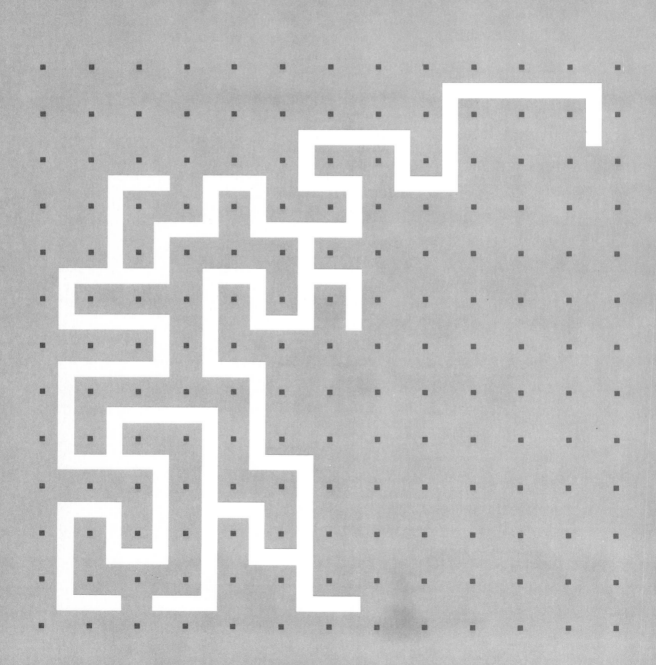

Part Four

Preserving Effective Employee-Management Relationships

Earlier chapters have discussed selecting and developing employees for an organization. Additional ongoing personnel efforts are necessary to ensure that this workforce continues to contribute to the organization's objectives on a daily basis. Of major significance are compensation systems, which are introduced in Chapter 10. The chapter considers various factors, including job evaluation, that influence wage and salary decisions. Chapter 11 describes wage incentives and compensation administration issues, while Chapter 12 considers various objectives and types of employee benefits.

Employees' contribution to the organization can also be affected by the physical characteristics of the work environment and the presence of a union. Chapter 13 discusses organizational and legal dimensions of safety and health programs. Chapter 14 introduces the reader to historical and legal aspects of labor unions as well as considerations prompting nonunion employees to join unions. Two major labor-management activities, labor agreement negotiation and contract administration, are discussed in Chapter 15.

Chapter 10

Compensation: Basic Plans

Perhaps in no other personnel administration field is so much money spent with so little objective information as the field of wage and salary administration.

William R. Marshall, *Administering the Company Personnel Function* (Englewood Cliffs, N.J.: Prentice-Hall, 1976), p. 130.

Compensation includes *wages* (usually determined as an hourly rate of pay) and *salaries* (usually determined as a weekly, monthly, or yearly rate of pay). Wages and salaries are important to everyone. They represent income to employees, costs to employers, and a basis for taxes for the government. Compensation plays an important role in economic decisions, serves as a factor in allocation of resources, influences individuals' decisions in selecting careers and occupations and choosing to move from one employer to another, influences employers' decisions on plant location and purchase of machines and equipment, and causes unemployment when labor costs become so high that workers are priced out of particular labor markets.[1] Because employers have limited resources, their major goal in wage and salary matters is to get the maximum possible returns on the resources they use. Related objectives include:

1. Attracting and retaining a workforce adequate in number and skill mix at affordable levels.
2. Motivating employees by consistently informing them of what various levels represent in terms of pay expectations.
3. Ensuring that employees believe they are fairly rewarded for their efforts.
4. Controlling compensation costs while accomplishing related objectives.[2]
5. Complying with government regulations covering wage-related matters.
6. Portraying the organization as a good place to work.

Employers try to achieve these wage and salary objectives within the context of interconnected external and internal labor markets. These markets are influenced by such factors as employers' competitive pay positions, their ability to pay, comparable wages and labor market forces, cost of living, pay equity, performance and productivity, collective bargaining agreements, legal considerations, and job evaluation.[3] This chapter will focus on components of basic wage and salary programs and Chapter 11 will cover incentives for employees and administration of the compensation system.

Influences on Determining Wages and Salaries

There is no single basis for the wages and salaries paid employees; they are based on several interrelated influences. While most of these influences are at work in most organizations, they vary in degree of importance, depending on the company's objectives and the role it wants wages and salaries to play in its organizational strategy.

The Organization's Competitive Pay Position

Organizations differ in their competitive pay positions, and an organization's desired position is a major determinant of its wage levels. Generally, organizations choose from four overall competitive pay positions: (a) to be among the national leaders, (b) to be among the leaders in the area or industry, (c) to stay competitive with local wage rates, and (d) to institute compensation policies that are conservative but not too far behind other firms. Being a national leader is usually reserved for the largest and most prestigious firms in the country (approximately 6 percent of the total). These firms plan to keep their wages 5 to 10 percent above the going rate. About 23 percent of firms are identified as area or industry leaders, while half choose to stay competitive with local rates. Just less than 20 percent want to follow the leaders but stay slightly behind them. These positions also can be differentiated by industry; more manufacturing and retail firms want to lead, while banks, insurance companies, and public utilities primarily want to remain competitive.[4]

The Organization's Financial Resources

Financial resources or limitations must be considered a vital factor in wage determination. The availability of financial resources determines the organization's competitive pay position regardless of its desired role. Organizations that cannot pay competitive wages will not be able to recruit and retain qualified personnel. Moreover, firms that lack financial resources and have no prospects for improvement cannot reward their more productive employees.[5]

Emphasizing ability to pay as a wage-determining criterion has been criticized as impractical by labor economists. First, in years when profits are nonexistent or inadequate, wages supposedly would be cut—until recently considered an unlikely possibility. Second, placing too much weight on ability to pay would adversely affect the relationship of wages, costs, prices, and profits. Because profits must be shared with stockholders and reinvested for growth and expansion, returning a disproportionately high share of profits to workers in the form of wages would change the relationship between costs, prices, and profits. Third, wages are supposedly paid to workers in accordance with their relative value and contribution to the organization, not simply because financial resources are available. Finally, wage decisions are made in advance of wage payments, and there is no necessary relationship between profits of the past and profits of the future. Because profits are volatile, wages dependent on profits and ability to pay also would be volatile.[6]

Employees have traditionally disregarded their employers' arguments regarding inability to pay. Consider, for example, an individual earning $35,000 a year from a firm employing several hundreds or even thousands of employees. This individual believes his performance has at least equalled that of the previous year and realizes that inflation over the last year has made serious inroads into his income. This employee is not likely to believe that management cannot pay him a "modest" 10-percent wage increase, particularly since management could obtain such funds from denying pay increases for "less deserving" employees.

Ability to pay has nonetheless become increasingly significant under governmental wage guidelines or companies' economic difficulties. Some companies, particularly in the airline, automobile, steel, rubber, and construction industries, have directly used the lack of ability to pay as an argument to constrain wage increases or to reduce wages in order to retain their competitiveness.

Comparable Wages and Labor Market Forces

Wage comparisons among firms can strongly influence wage determination; organizations want to pay enough to remain competitive in securing and retaining qualified employees, but they do not want to pay too much. To obtain comparable wage data, 93 percent of U.S. organizations rely on wage surveys.[7]

Wage comparisons can become quite complicated and can lead to incorrect conclusions, because job duties and responsibilities, methods of payment, regularity of employment, and fringe benefits can vary from job to job. It is difficult to obtain standard measures, identify comparable firms, determine the size of the labor market, and account for industrial differentials.

Since the 1950s, the Bureau of Labor Statistics, several professional consulting groups, the American Management Association, and others have engaged in surveying wages and salaries; and such surveys are "ten times more valid today than they were 20 years ago."[8] Accurate survey data are based on clear and complete descriptions of positions, standard reporting and statistical analysis, and adequate identification of responding organizations. The high degree of accuracy that has been achieved may be causing other problems, however; for instance, one compensation specialist says:

> The problem is the surveys today may be becoming far too valid and that, in fact, they are becoming causal. Rather than only reporting what salaries are, surveys now determine what pay will be.[9]

He adds the following caution about reliance on survey data:

> Salary surveys are the major information input into salary-level decisions made by modern managers. These surveys have been around long enough so that we all take their methods of reporting for granted. By habit, we make decisions using information that may be neither valid nor reasonable. Assuming that survey reporting methods remain unchanged, the charge of "no validity" against the survey results will disappear. The world of salaries will be painted by surveys. It will, however, not be a world of reason.[10]

Cost of Living

The cost of living must be considered in wage and salary administration. The term usually refers to the consumer price index (CPI) as determined by the Bureau of Labor Statistics. The CPI measures changes in prices of a fixed market basket of goods and services purchased by the average U.S. family. The Bureau of Labor Statistics computes CPI for most major cities, but the most commonly accepted indicator of variations in the cost of livng is the all-cities CPI.[11]

Employers and employees keep a cautious eye on effects of cost of living on wages. As one personnel professional has said, "Any year that an employee's salary is not increased is really a relative reduction in his salary in relation to inflation."[12] It is essential that wage increases equal cost of living increases so that workers can maintain their real incomes. However, as income increases, the progressive tax laws place the income-earner in a higher tax bracket, causing a loss in earning power (so-called bracketflation). The Conference Board calculated that a family of four earning $21,000 in 1975 would have to earn $34,000 (62 percent more) in 1981 to maintain the same purchasing power, not only because of higher prices but also because the family would move to higher income tax brackets.[13]

More than 5 million employees are covered by automatic COLA (cost of living adjustment), or escalator, clauses, which adjust their wages by a predetermined formula (usually a 1-cent-per-hour increase for each 0.3 rise in the CPI, adjusted quarterly).[14] When Social Security recipients, military retirees, and civilian service personnel are included, an estimated 50 million or more U.S. citizens have their incomes automatically adjusted by some cost of living formula.[15]

One compensation specialist has claimed that:

> Inflation is here to stay. . . . It is a problem that will not go away in the near future [yet] we in the U.S. had not learned to deal with the inflation problem, at least as it affects our compensation programs. It occurred to me that most of the people in the U.S. had at least until recently not mentally accepted the continuing problem that inflation presents. We have all assumed that given a few more months, the rate of inflation will diminish and then somehow it will magically go away or at least become significantly less important. I am convinced today that we do acknowledge the continuing problems of inflation, so it is time that we think about the ramifications of inflation on our compensation programs.[16]

A related consideration is the wide variation in cost of living among geographic areas. For example, an employee who is promoted and moves from Atlanta to San Francisco may find that he or she will face a house value increase of nearly 100 percent. Similar problems would be faced if the move was from Orlando, Portland, Tucson, or Austin to New York, Chicago, Minneapolis, or Los Angeles.[17] On the other side of the coin, it may be that "Within ten years we are likely to take for granted situations in which executives transferred from, say, San Francisco to Tucson will expect a salary *cut* that is based on cost-of-living differentials."[18]

However, overemphasis on the cost of living influence can cause several problems for management:

Cost of living adjustments are usually unrelated to the productivity and profitability of the firm; therefore, management gets little if anything in return for cost of living increases in wages and salaries.

Changes in the cost of living are unpredictable and beyond management's control; quarterly cost of living adjustments can seriously disrupt budgeting considerations.

Cost of living adjustments are taken for granted by employees who have received them before. These employees believe that merit considerations should be added on top of cost of living adjustments.

Pay Equity

Organizations seek to develop and maintain a wage and salary program that is both internally and externally equitable. Equity theory states that employees will determine the fairness of their pay and other rewards by comparing their contributions to the organization with the rewards they receive from the organization. They then compare this relationship with the contribution-reward relationships of others. Comparisons within the organization determine internal equity, and comparisons with employees in other organizations determine external equity. Inequity occurs when rewards do not balance with inputs.[19] Examples of such inequity include: (a) when an employee perceives that he or she is doing work more difficult and more important than the work of others who are paid more, (b) when supervisors realize that their pay is less than their subordinates', (c) when nonunion employees in one plant hear that their pay is less than that of employees in a comparable unionized plant, and (d) when new employees with no experience are hired at salary levels nearly equal to those of experienced, high-performing employees in the same department.

Organizations must attempt to design and administer their compensation programs equitably. Because employees act on the basis of their perceptions, beliefs, and expectations, employers must be sure that employees *understand* the system and are clearly *informed* about employment terms and that the company's actions support its stated policies.[20] In other words, "Pay intentions and actions must not only be fair and give consistent signals of what the organization is trying to do, but employees must believe that they are fair and receive and accept the signals."[21]

Productivity and Performance

Most organizations tend to subscribe to the philosophy that employees should be paid in relation to their productivity and performance.

In fact, one survey revealed that nearly 90 percent of the 493 firms surveyed subscribed to this philosophy.[22] This topic is so important that much of the next chapter covers wage incentive systems which are designed to closely tie pay to performance and productivity. It is mentioned here to note its importance in wage and salary administration.

Collective Bargaining

Labor negotiations result in agreements that prescribe the wages of employees covered. Nonunion employers closely monitor union activities and wage settlements and pay close attention to wages of the so-called sensitive employee groups, such as truck drivers and skilled employees. In fact, nonunion employers tend to make their wages conform with union wage settlements to remain competitive and also to reduce the risk that their employees will want to join unions.[23] Thus, unions have an impact not only on wages in unionized sectors but in nonunion sectors as well.

A recent study that compared wage differentials between heavily unionized sectors and lightly unionized sectors disclosed that wages in heavily unionized sectors rose about 0.5 percent per year faster than wages in lightly unionized sectors. While this differential was small on an annual basis, the difference was over 10 percent for the years studied (1935–1976). Part of the explanation for the wage differential comes from the tendency for heavily unionized sectors to be those with (1) higher wages, (2) fewer females, (3) higher capital intensity, (4) lower quit rates and presence of seniority clauses in labor agreements, and (5) wages relatively insensitive to real business-cycle conditions because of multiyear labor agreements with automatic wage increases.[24]

Legal Influences

Wage and salary administration has been influenced substantially by legislation. While some states have enacted legislation for wage regulation, the following discussion highlights only major laws at the federal level.

Davis-Bacon Act The Davis-Bacon Act of 1931 was a depression-era act passed to help maintain wages at a level that would allow workers to purchase products, thereby putting more money in circulation and helping to end the existing economic depression. This law requires federal government contractors performing construction work for $2,000 or more to pay the *prevailing wage* (which includes fringe benefits) of the labor market in which the construction takes place. It authorizes the Secretary of Labor to determine in advance the wages acceptable on federal projects. The Department of Labor determines the prevailing wage by determining the wage paid to the majority of workers in various job classifications. Since wage data are maintained by labor organizations, critics of this law contend that unions are able to keep wages high because they represent the largest number of construction workers in most areas and are able to send wage data on short notice to the wage specialists in the Department of Labor.[25] Since the law's enactment, forty-one states have passed "little Davis-Bacon Acts," and seventy-seven federal laws now require Davis-Bacon Act wage determination.[26]

Walsh-Healy Act The Walsh-Healy Act of 1936 extended the authority of the Secretary of Labor to determine the prevailing wage in all industries having federal government contracts for goods and services worth $10,000 or more. The prevailing wage rates were to be determined much as under the Davis-Bacon Act; but this law further requires that employers pay all employees time and one-half for working over eight hours in any work day.

Fair Labor Standards Act In 1938, Congress passed the Fair Labor Standards Act, which regulates wages as well as hours (and also regulates child labor). This act covers most firms in interstate commerce. It requires the payment of overtime (one and one-half the regular wage) for any hours over forty per week and the payment of a minimum wage of $3.35 (as of 1981). This law is administered by the Wage and Hour Administration in the Department of Labor and receives complaints from workers as well as initiating its own investigations of employers' records and practices.

Laws Administered by the EEOC Three laws, the Equal Pay Act of 1963, Title VII of the Civil Rights Act of 1964 (now Equal Employment Opportunity Act of 1972), and the Age Discrimination in Employment Act of 1978, are now administered by the Equal Employment Opportunity Commission. The Equal Pay Act of 1963 prohibits pay discrimination between men and women who perform jobs that require equal skill, effort, and responsibility and who work under similar conditions. The Civil Rights Act of 1964 is broader in that it prohibits employment discrimination (including compensation discrimination) related to race, color, religion, sex, and national origin. The Age Discrimination in Employment Act prohibits employment discrimination (including compensation discrimination) against employees between the ages of forty and seventy.

Wages of women and minorities average about 60 percent those of white males, and the wage gap has not shown any improvement over the last twenty years. In a public EEOC hearing on job segregation and wage discrimination in April 1980, then Chairperson Eleanor Holmes opened by stating:

Wage discrimination is likely to be one of the central legal and industrial relations issues of the 1980's. It clearly affects both minorities and women, although its most obvious effects have been on women who hold jobs in a very few categories of work that have most often never been held by any other group of workers.[27]

This problem is so significant that a thorough discussion of it will be presented at the end of this chapter under the issue relating to comparable worth.

Economic Stabilization Act In 1970, Congress passed the Economic Stabilization Act, which authorizes the president to establish wage and price controls or guidelines. This authority was used by President Nixon, who placed a ninety-day freeze on wages, followed by a 5.5 percent limit on pay increases and then by a voluntary compliance period, which was lifted in 1974.[28] President Carter established a voluntary pay and price program in 1978, placing the pay standard at 7 percent. Exceptions for pay inequities, acute labor shortages, and productivity-improving work-rule changes were created for special incidents; and the Carter administration later adjusted the pay standard to permit increases up to 10.5 percent in any year as long as the increases averaged 9.5 percent.[29]

Wage guidelines can cause negative consequences for companies adhering to them. For example, when the inflation rate is higher than the wage increase allowed by the guidelines, employees are displeased. If competitive firms do not abide by the guidelines, then external equity becomes a problem.[30]

Tax Laws Not to be overlooked in wage and salary administration are the tax laws. For instance, as employees earn more through merit, cost of living, or other adjustments, the progressive tax laws place them in higher tax brackets. As employees earn more and see an increasing percent of their earnings going to pay taxes, they tend to seek tax shelters, deferred payments, and other means of compensation that are difficult to tax (free transportation to work, fees to private clubs, free lunches at work, and the like). The various laws covering capital gain tax, stock options, and deferred payments have considerable influence on the composition of the salary package provided top executives. The Economic Recovery Tax Act of 1981 recently adjusted rules for tax-sheltered individual retirement accounts, incentive stock options, and employee withdrawals from company-matched profit-sharing plans and reduced slightly the problem of bracketflation.

Job Evaluations

A major determinant of wages and salaries within organizations is job evaluation, a systematic method used to determine the relative value of jobs in terms of such compensable factors as responsibility, skill, effort, and working conditions. Because of its importance in determining wages and salaries and because it is an important personnel management technique, job evaluation will be more thoroughly discussed below.

Job Evaluation

Job evaluation is the process of determining the relative importance and worth of jobs for pay purposes. The process entails comparing jobs with other jobs inside and outside the organization and determining their positions in the wage structure. Job evaluation is used for wage determination in organizations employing most of the U.S. labor force.

While job evaluation systems vary in complexity and formality, such systems include two fundamental principles. First, the process *establishes minimum acceptable qualifications for the job.* For example, most colleges hiring a secretary for the management department would prefer to hire an individual with a college degree in that discipline along with other useful skills such as statistical analysis and computer programming. These qualifications, however desirable, would be unrealistic. Few individuals with these skills would even consider applying for the job; such individuals would likely require and receive higher wages at higher levels in the organization. Further, governmental agencies such as the Equal Employment Opportunity Commission monitor job evaluation systems to ensure that artificially high job qualifications do not harm minorities' chances for employment.

Second, the evaluation process *considers the job, not the employee performing the job.*[31] Job evaluation is completely different from employee performance evaluation, discussed in Chapter 8; the former determines the relative worth of jobs to the company; the latter evaluates the performance of employees on the job.

While job evaluation systems vary according to the jobs covered, the organization's needs, and the designer of the system, five basic types of job evaluation systems can be identified: ranking, job classification, market pricing, point system, and factor comparison. Two of the systems, *ranking* and *job classification,* are considered nonquantitative, while the *point system* and *factor comparison* methods are quantitative. The ranking and factor comparison methods compare jobs with other jobs, and the classification and point systems compare jobs with predetermined rating scales. The fifth method, *market pricing,* consists of determining the prevailing labor market wage for jobs within the organization and paying employees according to these rates. The point system is the method most commonly used (see Exhibit 10-1). These methods will be described in more detail later in the chapter.

Preliminary Steps of Job Evaluation

The first steps for each of the job evaluation methods are the same: to conduct an organizational analysis, analyze the jobs covered, write job

Exhibit 10.1   **Job Evaluation Methods**

	Frequency of Use (N = 172)
Point System	53 (31%)
Factor Comparison	33 (19%)
Classification	24 (14%)
Ranking	14 (8%)
Market Pricing	12 (7%)

Source: Reprinted by permission from *Job Evaluation Policies and Procedures*, p. 4, copyright 1976 by The Bureau of National Affairs, Inc., Washington, D.C.

descriptions, and determine job specifications. The organizational analysis examines the authority and responsibility of each job and assesses the authority and responsibility relationships between jobs. Any changes likely to be made in the organizational structure ought to be made before the jobs are analyzed. Making changes in job content after the job evaluation study has been completed will necessitate reevaluation.

Job analysis, job descriptions, and job specifications are the foundations of job evaluation systems. As you recall from Chapter 4, job analysis focuses on the content of the jobs; job descriptions are written summations of the jobs' duties and responsibilities; and job specifications are the qualifications an employee must possess to be able to perform the jobs.

Before a job evaluation method is selected, two preliminary decisions must be made: the designer of the system must be chosen and the organization members who will be involved in evaluation must be identified. The decision as to who will design the system depends in large part on the resources and personnel available within the organization. Large organizations usually have the resources and qualified personnel to perform all the necessary tasks. A national survey revealed that in-house systems were developed by 47 percent of the organizations polled. Among organizations that needed assistance, consultants were employed to design a system, to modify a standard system for the organization, or to work jointly with personnel in the organization to develop a system.[32] Consultants can provide expertise and ensure objectivity. Where a sophisticated system is desired, the expertise of consultants may be necessary in the initial stages.[33]

Within the organization, job analysts and wage and salary administrators from the personnel department are usually the key individuals in analyzing jobs; writing, updating, and maintaining job descriptions and job specifications; and administering the wage and salary system. Frequently, organizations establish wage and salary committees of five to seven people. These committees usually try to achieve broad representation and include persons that employees know, respect, and trust. One or two positions on the committee may be used for rotation of departmental supervisors so they can gain experience and training. One position may be allotted for a representative of the particular division whose jobs are currently being reviewed and evaluated. These committees are considered essential in many organizations, because they help win support of employees and managers and provide insights into jobs that cannot be gained by job analysis alone.

The role of the union must also be considered before the job evaluation plan is initiated. If the organization does not involve the union in the program's development, the topic will certainly be discussed at the bargaining table. Because the wage issue is a mandatory subject for bargaining, the results of a job evaluation plan and the wage structure derived from job evaluations will later be the subject of negotiations. Thus, the union *will* be involved in wage determination; the only question is when. The more successful programs are joint ones in which the union is represented throughout the development process. On some occasions, the union does not want to be actively involved; however, union officials want to be kept informed of progress and to understand how the plan is developed and operated. Unions generally like the idea of establishing job hierarchies, and information gained through establishing a job evaluation plan can be used in contract negotiations.[34] Thus, while unions still maintain that collective bargaining is the process for wage determination, an informed union negotiator considers job evaluation concepts and processes useful tools in negotiations.[35]

Once the organization has made proper preparation, it should select the job evaluation system that fits its purposes. Before taking any action that affects employees, management should inform them about the program, explain how it works, and tell them their wages will not be lowered even though some realignments may take place. In other words, management should try to prevent anxiety and insecurity among workers whose jobs are being evaluated.

Ranking Method

The ranking method simply involves ranking the jobs from lowest to highest in terms of one dimension, such as overall importance to the organization. This method is used primarily by small organizations that lack resources for a sophisticated program but want some form of hierarchical order for jobs.[36] The method ranks the whole job, rather than various factors such as skill or effort. This method is not held in high regard by the personnel profession, because it is subjective and can easily be manipulated. Another disadvantage is that the persons who rank the jobs must have thorough knowledge of all the jobs in the organization, and this knowledge is infrequently found. Still, the method is simple and easy to understand.

The methods used in ranking the jobs are the *card-sorting method*

Exhibit 10.2	**Results of Card Sorting Ranking Method**	
	Score	Rank
	4	Tool and die maker ranks higher than executive secretary, electrician, file clerk, and janitor.	1
	3	Electrician ranks higher than executive secretary, file clerk, and janitor.	2
	2	Executive secretary ranks higher than file clerk and janitor.	3
	1	File clerk ranks higher than janitor.	4
	0	Janitor ranks lowest.	5

and the method of *paired comparison*. The card-sorting method uses full job descriptions written on small cards. The person evaluating the jobs places the cards in order, from jobs of least value to jobs of most value (See Exhibit 10.2). Any differences in ranking among rankers will be resolved by discussion and group decision.

The paired comparison requires that each job be compared with all other jobs. The job valued more than all other jobs being considered will receive the highest score and therefore the highest rank; the job receiving the next highest score will receive the second highest rank; and so forth.[37] For example, assume that an organization wants to rank the following jobs: executive secretary, electrician, tool and die maker, file clerk, and janitor. Exhibit 10.3 gives examples of comparisons that might be made between these jobs.

Job Classification System

The job classification system involves defining a number of job classes or grades of jobs and then fitting the jobs into the classes provided.[38]

Exhibit 10.3	**Results of Paired Comparison Ranking Method**						
		Tool and Die Maker	Electrician	Executive Secretary	File Clerk	Janitor	Job Ranks Higher Than This Number of Jobs	Overall Ranking
	Tool and Die Maker		X	X	X	X	4	1
	Electrician			X	X	X	3	2
	Executive Secretary				X	X	2	3
	File Clerk					X	1	4
	Janitor						0	5

Exhibit 10.4	**Examples of General Definitions of Grade Levels in the Federal Government Compensation Plan**

	Examples of Jobs
Grade GS–1	Laundry Worker
	Janitor (Light)
Grade GS–6	Truck Driver (Medium)
	Sewing Machine Operator
	Stockroom Attendant
Grade GS–10	Automotive Mechanic
	Welder
	Electrician
	Machinist
Grade GS–15	Instrument Maker

Grade GS–1

Grade GS–1 includes those classes of positions the duties of which are to perform, under immediate supervision, with little or no latitude for the exercise of independent judgment—

A. the simplest routine work in office, business, or fiscal operations; or

B. elementary work of a subordinate technical character in a professional, scientific, or technical field.

Grade GS–6

Grade GS–6 includes those classes of positions the duties of which are—

A. to perform, under general supervision, difficult and responsible work in office, business, or fiscal administration, or comparable subordinate technical work in a professional, scientific, or technical field, requiring in either case—

1. considerable training and supervisory or other experience;

2. broad working knowledge of a special and complex subject matter, procedure, or practice, or of the principles of the profession, art, or science involved; and

3. to a considerable extent the exercise of independent judgment; or

B. to perform other work of equal importance, difficulty, and responsibility, and requiring comparable qualifications.

Grade GS–10

Grade GS–10 includes those classes of positions the duties of which are—

A. to perform, under general supervision, highly difficult and responsible work along special technical, supervisory, or administrative lines in office, business, or fiscal administration, requiring—

1. somewhat extended specialized, supervisory, or administrative training and experience which has demonstrated capacity for sound independent work;

2. thorough and fundamental knowledge of a specialized and complex subject matter, or of the profession, art, or science involved; and

3. considerable latitude for the exercise of independent judgment; or

B. to perform other work of equal importance, difficulty, and responsibility, and requiring comparable qualifications.

Exhibit 10.4   **Continued**

Grade GS–15   Grade GS–15 includes those classes of positions the duties of
                             which are—

A. to perform, under general administrative direction, with very
   wide latitude for the exercise of independent judgment, work
   of outstanding difficulty and responsibility along special technical, supervisory, or administrative lines which has demonstrated leadership and exceptional attainments;

B. to serve as head of a major organization within a bureau involving work of comparable level;

C. to plan and direct or to plan and execute specialized programs
   of marked difficulty, responsibility, and national significance,
   along professional, scientific, technical, administrative, fiscal,
   or other lines, requiring extended training and experience
   which has demonstrated leadership and unusual attainments
   in professional, scientific, or technical research, practice, or
   administration, or in administrative, fiscal, or other specialized
   activities; or

D. to perform consulting or other professional, scientific, technical, administrative, fiscal, or other specialized work of equal
   importance, difficulty, and responsibility, and requiring comparable qualifications.

Source: Excerpted from Donald J. Treiman, *Job Evaluation: An Analytical Review* (Washington, D.C.:
National Academy of Science, 1979), pp. 136–139.

Here, an idealized structure is predetermined and categories are differentiated on the basis of factors—for example, skill, responsibility,
effort, and working conditions—considered important on all jobs. Each
job is then placed in a particular class or grade. Exhibit 10.4 includes a
sample of selected job classifications in the federal government. As
the exhibit shows, what the laundry worker and janitor do on the job
closely fits the general description for Grade GS–1. The corresponding
wage schedule is shown in Exhibit 10.5. At step 1 in this schedule, the
laundry worker and janitor will earn $6,561. The duties and responsi-
bilities of medium truck drivers, sewing machine operators, and stock-
room attendants more closely match the general definition for Grade
GS–6; thus, the pay for these positions, at step 1, is $11,712.

   The job classification system is not complex and can be easily understood by workers. Job classifications can be changed easily as job
duties and responsibilities are changed. However, this method is
suited only for larger organizations, which have sufficient resources
and sufficient numbers of jobs to warrant using the system. It is
very popular with governments at all levels, even though the trend is
moving away from evaluating the whole job in the manner described above in favor of evaluating the components of each job. The
federal government now evaluates jobs in the federal service on the
basis of compensable factors and points before the GS levels are
finalized.

Exhibit 10.5		Federal Government General Schedule								
					Annual Rates and Steps					
Grade	1	2	3	4	5	6	7	8	9	10
GS–1	$6,561	$6,780	$6,999	$7,218	$7,437	$7,656	$7,875	$8,094	$8,313	$8,532
GS–2	7,422	7,669	7,916	8,163	8,410	8,657	8,904	9,151	9,398	9,645
GS–3	8,366	8,645	8,924	9,203	9,482	9,761	10,040	10,319	10,598	10,877
GS–4	9,391	9,704	10,017	10,330	10,643	10,956	11,269	11,582	11,895	12,208
GS–5	10,507	10,857	11,207	11,557	11,907	12,257	12,607	12,957	13,307	13,657
GS–6	11,712	12,102	12,492	12,882	13,272	13,662	14,052	14,442	14,832	15,222
GS–7	13,014	13,448	13,882	14,316	14,750	15,184	15,618	16,052	16,486	16,920
GS–8	14,414	14,894	15,374	15,854	16,334	16,814	17,294	17,774	18,254	18,734
GS–9	15,920	16,451	16,982	17,513	18,044	18,575	19,106	19,637	20,168	20,699
GS–10	17,532	18,116	18,700	19,284	19,868	20,452	21,036	21,620	22,204	22,788
GS–11	19,263	19,905	20,547	21,189	21,831	22,473	23,115	23,757	24,399	25,041
GS–12	23,087	23,857	24,627	25,397	26,167	26,937	27,707	28,477	29,247	30,017
GS–13	27,453	28,368	29,283	30,198	31,113	32,028	32,943	33,858	34,773	35,688
GS–14	32,442	33,523	34,604	35,685	36,766	37,847	38,928	40,009	41,090	42,171
GS–15	38,160	39,432	40,704	41,976	43,248	44,520	45,792	47,064	48,336[a]	49,608[a]
GS–16	44,756	46,248	47,740[a]	49,232[a]	50,724[a]	52,216[a]	53,708[a]	55,200[a]	56,692[a]	
GS–17	52,429[a]	54,177[a]	55,925[a]	57,673[a]	59,421[a]					
GS–18	61,449[a]									

[a] Basic pay is limited by sec. 5308 of title 5 of the United States Code to the rate for level V of the Executive Schedule. In addition pursuant to sec. 304 of the Legislative Branch Appropriation Act, 1979, funds are not available to pay a salary in this schedule at a rate which exceeds the rate for level V of the Executive Schedule in effect on September 30, 1978, which is $47,500.

Note: The rates in this General Schedule are effective on the first day of the first pay period beginning on or after October 1, 1978, and they were prescribed by the President in Executive Order 12087 (October 7, 1978) pursuant to subch. 1 of ch. 53 of this title.

Source: "Introduction to Pay under the General Schedule," *Federal Personnel Manual* (Washington, D.C.: Office of Personnel Management, 1981), p. 531–533.

Market Pricing

The market pricing approach to wage determination simply involves the organization's paying the average of what other organizations in the labor market pay employees in comparable jobs. As one personnel manager said, "We pay what we have to in order to hire 'em and pay what we have to to keep 'em." This approach obviously relies heavily on wage survey data, trade reports, and government studies.

Organizations that use the market pricing plan want to maintain their competitive position; however, they must be aware that they are letting other organizations determine their pay structures. As one wage and salary specialist said:

Perhaps it is the unspoken idea that others surely know more about proper salary administration than we do. [That makes] many firms believe that the pooling of pay data within a survey discloses that magic *going rate* that is necessary to attract and retain employees in the job.[39]

Point System

The point system, the most commonly used job evaluation system, is a quantitative method for establishing pay relationships and developing a wage structure. By use of job descriptions, job specifications, a predetermined rating scale, and a wage survey, a point value for each job is determined. The points are used to construct a wage curve, which will serve as the basis for wage rates, wage ranges, and wage classes.[40] This method represents a systematic way for determining the wage structure and enables the organization to logically show its employees how their wages are determined by use of the rating scale and of compensable factors such as job requirements, effort, responsibility, and job conditions. The point system is discussed in detail in the appendix to this chapter.

Factor Comparison

The factor comparison method relies heavily on accurate job descriptions and job specifications. It is similar to the point system in that it evaluates jobs by use of compensable factors; however, it is considerably different in design. Its design involves ranking certain benchmark jobs according to compensable factors to which dollar weightings will be assigned. The final result is a measurement scale that is used for all jobs throughout the organization. A more detailed description of this process is presented in the appendix to this chapter.

While the factor comparison system, like the point system, has the advantage of being custom designed for a particular organization, it is difficult to explain to employees and costly and time consuming to develop.

Job Evaluation for Managerial Employees

The ultimate responsibility for organizational performance rests with the chief executive officer, although this responsibility is shared throughout the organization. In the United States, the chief executive officer's earnings average sixteen times the average earnings of a production worker. The job of a steelworker may be hard, dirty, and potentially dangerous, and the pay may reflect these considerations. However, the total responsibility of a typical steelworker is limited to performing one particular job well. The chief executive officer's job responsibilities, measured in sales, assets, people employed, and so on, is greater by several magnitudes.[41] Still, it is debatable how much an executive is really worth. Twenty-six U.S. executives earned more than $1.4 million in 1981, and four earned more than $3 million.[42]

One critic has written the following about executive compensation:

As everyone knows, public and stockholder mistrust of large corporations is widespread and appears to be growing . . . [One] cause of unrest . . . stems from stockholders' and public's suspicion of top-level salaries, contracts, consulting fees, fringe benefits, and other payment policies. . . .

Stockholders and the knowledgeable public agree that sound, honest, and imaginative management should be well rewarded. Substantial salaries, fringe benefits, savings and investment plans, and profit-sharing plans covering large groups of employees, including executives, are quite acceptable.

Stockholders and the public resent, however, the prospect that key executives are becoming a privileged class, receiving special contracts or bonuses along with their extensive perquisites and often spectacular salaries—regardless of the performance of their companies. The rewards should not be, as a judge once termed them, "a misuse or waste of corporate funds, or a gift to a favored few." Executive compensation practices that undermine public trust must be changed, or capitalists themselves will become a major force undermining capitalism.[43]

Another critic, who is concerned that laws will be passed to limit executive salaries, has expressed similar concern:

Few people object on principle to executives' being paid well, as long as that pay is visibly related to both their responsibilities and the quality of their performance.

Many people, however, have real trouble understanding just what any corporate executive can possibly be *doing* to earn a seven-figure pay package. They are beginning to suspect that complicated executive pay schemes are frequently rigged to reward top managers handsomely—regardless of performance.[44]

Managerial salaries often have been associated with scale of operation—the larger the size, the higher the managers' salaries[45] and productivity.[46] Their salaries also have been associated with job complexity, in terms of the nature and magnitude of the responsibility vested in the job, and with employers' ability to pay, in terms of total profit and rate of return.[47] However, each organization pays its managerial personnel in accordance with its compensation objectives as outlined at the beginning of the chapter.

At the first level of management, organizations attempt to structure pay grades so that the median of the supervisors' salary range is 10 to 25 percent above the salaries of the highest-paid workers supervised. In addition to paying a base salary, more than half of the organizations pay supervisors for scheduled overtime, even though the law (the Fair Labor Standards Act) does not require overtime payments for supervisory personnel. Supervisors also may qualify for incentives and bonus pay opportunities.[48]

While organizations may design their own compensation plans for management personnel, several established firms specialize in such plans. These firms help organizations determine the base salary and design incentive systems and benefit packages for management personnel. The Compensation Institute's Phoenix plan uses twenty-eight compensable factors[49] (see Exhibit 10.6); Hay uses three compensable factors: know-how, problem solving and accountability.[50] (See Exhibit 10.7 for the dimensions of "problem solving" and its relationship to "know-how.") Sibson determines base salary according to the market value of the job, its relationship to other positions in the organizations, and the individual's value to the organization based on experience and long-term performance.[51]

Some organizations emphasize competitiveness of salaries. These firms rely completely on survey data and have no job evaluation systems. Some organizations conduct surveys and then establish an internal wage structure from these data. Others develop an internal wage

---

Exhibit 10.6	**Sample of Compensable Factors for the Phoenix Plan**

Job Related Experience Required (Years)
Formal Training Time Required
Frequency of Review of Work
Utilization of Independent Choice
Frequency of Reference to Guidelines
Frequency of Work Transferred through Supervisor
Interpretative/Analytical Complexity
Time Spent Processing Information
Time Spent in Planning
Contact with Public
Contact with Customers/Suppliers
Impact on Department Budget
Persuasion/Selling/Directing of Others
Training of Staff
Physical Stress Experienced
Time Spent Working under Deadlines
Time Spent in Hazardous Conditions
Travel Outside Work Location
Salary Grade to which this Position Reports
Salary Grade of Positions Supervised
Management Responsibility
—Revenue Size
—Asset Size
—Employee Size
—Budget Size
—Payroll Size
—Supervisors Reporting to Position

Source: David J. Thomsen, *The Phoenix Plan* (Los Angeles: Compensation Institute, 1980), pp. 11–30.

Exhibit 10.7	Hay Guide Chart Profile for Problem Solving

PROBLEM SOLVING

		THINKING CHALLENGE					
		1. REPETITIVE	2. PATTERNED	3. INTERPOLATIVE	4. ADAPTIVE	5. UNCHARTED	
A.	STRICT ROUTINE	10% / 12%	14% / 16%	19% / 22%	25% / 29%	33% / 38%	A
B.	ROUTINE	12% / 14%	16% / 19%	22% / 25%	29% / 33%	38% / 43%	B
C.	SEMI ROUTINE	14% / 16%	19% / 22%	25% / 29%	33% / 38%	43% / 50%	C
D.	STANDARDIZED	16% / 19%	22% / 25%	29% / (33%)	38% / 43%	50% / 57%	D
E.	CLEARLY DEFINED	19% / 22%	25% / 29%	33% / 38%	43% / 50%	57% / 66%	E
F.	BROADLY DEFINED	22% / 25%	29% / 33%	38% / 43%	50% / 57%	(66%) / 76%	F
G.	GENERALLY DEFINED	25% / 29%	33% / 38%	43% / 50%	(57%) / 66%	76% / 87%	G
H.	ABSTRACTLY DEFINED	29% / 33%	38% / 43%	50% / 57%	66% / 76%	87% / 100%	H

KH	PS	AC	TOTAL
152	50		

SUPERVISOR KEY PUNCH

KH	PS	AC	TOTAL
304	200		

ACTUARIAL SPECIALIST
RESEARCH ASSOCIATE

KH	PS	AC	TOTAL
700	400		

AREA MANAGER

Note: Compensable factors are:
1. KH = know-how, the knowledge (practical, specialized, or technical knowledge) and skills (motivational and other managerial skills) needed for satisfactory performance.
2. PS = problem solving, which involves the degree of freedom and type of mental activity (complexity and originality) involved in the thinking process required on the job.
3. AC = accountability, the measurable effect in terms of dollar magnitude, freedom to act, and impact on end results.

Source: Courtesy of Hay Associates.

structure based on ranking, classifications, or points and then conduct a salary survey to make adjustments to the external labor market.

One approach to market pricing is Ellig's Selective Pricing, which was designed by Pfizer, Inc., after the company became dissatisfied with its formalized job evaluation system, which covered all positions below the level of board of directors.

In the Pfizer system, the division presidents review all the managerial jobs and agree on the jobs that will be evaluated. Next, they agree on the outside companies that will be surveyed; and where possible, available survey data are obtained. Then, the group of presidents and compensation specialists complete the tasks internally.

We set up 35 to 40 magnetic boards with horizontal and vertical grid lines. We put the salary grades on a vertical axis and show total compensation at the midpoints. We add magnetic strips with the job titles on them; in many cases, we color code these by function, so that it's a little easier for the individual to identify research jobs, marketing jobs, and so forth. We will identify the jobs that are in the existing structure and for which market data are available—use a star or whatever. Now we have an organizational chart that shows the relative position of jobs that might otherwise be considered to be on the same level.

When we meet with the division head, we review first the market data to see whether a particular position should have its salary range increased through an upgrading process so that the range can be raised faster than the simple repricing of the structure would allow. Or we may have had an unusual situation earlier that led to our paying a premium to a given job that is no longer necessary. Data processing jobs are a good example. This review process lasts anywhere from a couple of hours for a very small operation to several days for a very large one. The division president reviews all jobs up to his own.

After we have completed the review with the division president, the organization and compensation structure beyond a certain compensation level automatically comes before an employee compensation committee for review. That committee reviews the evaluation of every job up to the jobs of the executives who are on the board of directors; those jobs, the inside directors, are reviewed by a committee consisting of the outside directors.[52]

Another method, used by the American Management Association's Executive Compensation Service (ECS), which has been surveying compensation levels for twenty years, is called EVALUCOMP. This method starts with outside data and then follows with a systematic assessment of internal relationships. In other words, it combines direct market pricing with a systematic ranking to design the managerial compensation system.[53]

Using wage and salary surveys has become common practice in determining management compensation. As one compensation specialist has claimed:

The advent of the computer had led to the availability of more sophisticated data. One data exchange provides the executive-compensation decision maker with index-related data that he can use to determine the appropriate level of executive compensation for specific kinds of organizations. This service provides information on the levels of compensation offered to specific executives, and identifies the variables that influence the compensation paid by various organizations.[54]

Some contend that using market data first and then internally evaluating jobs allows the organization to avoid conflicts between internal and external rates. If an organization designs the internal salary structure first and attempts to place all jobs in their appropriate classifications within the salary range, invariably two or three jobs will be priced outside the internal salary structure. This can happen as a result of favoritism to a particular employee or as a result of seniority. The favored or senior employee may have received salary adjustments greater than those the value of the job justifies. Making the necessary adjustments may cause conflicts. On the other hand, reservations about the direct market pricing method also exist.

In almost any industry and for almost any kind of job, you obtain an incredibly wide range of data. If you really know the jobs and you really know the companies in the survey, you can interpret the data on the basis of your knowledge of each company's philosophy and other related factors. But there is still too great a tendency to deal with competitive data as if they were "facts" and to gear one's program to the competitive marketplace; much more weight needs to be given to what's happening in your business, its profit economics, relative competitive position, and dynamics.[55]

Issue:	Do Traditional Job Evaluation Systems Discriminate against Females? The "Comparable Worth" Controversy.

As previously indicated, job evaluation determines the relative importance of jobs irrespective of employees' performance in them. A problem can occur, however, if those jobs considered less important are heavily populated by females. As previously mentioned, Eleanor Norton, former EEOC Chair, has said that wage discrimination will be the central EEO issue of the 1980s. She also asked the controversial question that is the focus of this section:

Do the forces that have determined that certain jobs and job categories are predominantly minority or female also simultaneously determine that the economic value of those jobs is less than if they were white or male jobs?

Have women and minorities whom we know have been deprived of initial hiring opportunities in many job categories also been paid less than they would have been but for discrimination?[56]

The concept of equal pay for equal work dates back to the World War II period, but it was not until 1963 that Congress passed the Equal Pay Act.[57] Under this act, employers are prohibited from discriminating on the basis of sex in the amounts they pay employees. In other words, if an employer pays an employee of one sex less than an employee of the other sex, it must justify the wage differential on the basis of skill, responsibility, effort, working conditions, merit, seniority, or production. In 1964, Congress passed a more inclusive law, the Civil Rights Act, which prohibits employment (including pay) discrimination on the basis of race, color, religion, sex, or national origin.

In spite of these laws, efforts to achieve wage equality for women who do the same or virtually the same work as men have not resulted in reducing the wage gap between sexes. In 1955, women's wages averaged 63.9 percent of men's; in 1978, they averaged 58.9 percent. Part of the explanation is that nearly 80 percent of the women in the workforce work in what has been called the "pink ghetto"—low-paying secretarial, clerical, and service jobs. Half of all working women are employed in jobs that are at least 70 percent female, and 25 percent work in jobs that are 95 percent female.[58] Other explanations include the following: Males tend to work full-time during their entire post-college careers, whereas females tend to enter and exit the job market more frequently; a large percentage of females work part-time; and women often make a conscious choice to permit family obligations to interfere with their career objectives, preventing them from optimizing their earning.[59]

One example of wage differentials between female-predominant and male-predominant jobs comes from Montgomery County, Maryland, in the suburbs of Washington, D.C.:

A state pays librarians with masters degrees, whose jobs involve a fair amount of skill, effort, and responsibility, decidedly less ($11,000) than State liquor-store clerks ($18,500) who essentially make change. . . . State librarians are almost always women, and liquor-store clerks are almost always men. One would want to inquire what there is about the librarian's job that makes it worth several thousand dollars less than the State liquor-store clerk's job. I don't think market forces will explain it! I think it is easier to find State liquor-store clerks than librarians.[60]

In response to this phenomenon, a legal theory called the theory of comparable worth has been developed; it holds that traditional female jobs draw pay less than the pay for traditional male jobs of comparable worth and that such wage discrepancy is discriminatory and therefore illegal.

Most secretaries earn less than most carpenters, nurses less than police officers, telephone operators less than machine operators. The recently asserted legal theory of "comparable worth" argues that the pattern of lower pay for traditional "women's" work is illegal wage discrimination.[61]

The comparable worth issue is controversial; indeed, it becomes emotional with certain groups. Proponents of the theory point to wage data that show a wage differential of over 40 percent and employment data that reveal that females are disproportionately overrepresented in lower-paying jobs. Based on these data, they infer that sex discrimination occurs.

Proponents of comparable worth theory also argue that job evaluation systems inherently discriminate against female-dominated jobs. Their analysis of the available job evaluation systems shows, for example, that:

Assembly line jobs requiring visual scanning for defects are usually held by women. Most evaluation systems do not value this skill; a bias-free system would include a factor for sensory decisions. Female jobs tend to have greater demands of interpersonal skills than male jobs, but such skills are not highly valued in many job evaluation systems. In addition, to the extent that a system builds in marketplace factors, it merely builds in historical bias.[62]

Proponents also list the following concerns about job evaluation in the wage-setting process:

Job analysis and evaluation systems tend to be subjective and judgmental and permit considerable latitude in interpretation.

Accuracy of job descriptions is questionable, because frequently employees are not involved in the job description process.

The reliability of the job evaluation process is questionable, and there is too much variation between scores given to compensable factors.

A common step in job evaluation systems is to conduct a wage survey. This survey secures the existing wages rates in the labor market, which are based on tradition and therefore include built-in sex bias.[63]

E. Robert Livernash, a compensation expert, has responded to the criticism of job evaluation as a wage-setting mechanism by stating:

There is simply no known technique by which job "worth" in any intrinsic sense can be measured. [There exists] the necessity of basing relative rates of compensation on a combination of market rates and job evaluation and . . . a failure to do so will lead not only to highly arbitrary and controversial results, but also to an administrative quagmire.

. . . Anyone who has worked in the development and administration of job evaluation systems is very much aware of the subjective nature of skill and responsibility requirements, as well as the difficulty of making comparative judgments as to working conditions and physical effort. When rating jobs with distinctively different types of skill, the rater is consciously and unconsciously guided by market rates.[64]

Some have argued that the remedies to wage discrimination against females would upset labor market forces, although others contend that action affecting wage-setting "is no more and no less an interference with market forces than regulating recruitment, selection, or other employment practices."[65] One judge has said the effect of acting on the comparable worth theory could be to disrupt "the entire economic system of the United States of America."[66] Labor economist George H. Hildebrand has also taken a strong stand:

Economic theory tells us that if comparable worth is put into effect (1) unemployment rates for females will rise, (2) unemployment of females also will rise, (3) the major victims will be the poorest female workers, (4) welfare dependency will grow, (5) female youngsters will be larger losers of job opportunities, and (6) there will be some withdrawal of discouraged women workers from the labor force.[67]

In addition, employers have estimated that to raise the average pay of 27.3 million working females to the average of the males would cost $150 billion per year. Since the earnings gap is about 40 percent, it would require that:

Employers would have to increase female employees' pay about 66 percent to equalize the earnings of men and women. To erase the earnings gap by raising women's pay by 66 percent, in effect correspondingly decreasing men's pay, would create an economic and social upheaval of the most radical proportion.[68]

The final argument against the comparable worth theory is the absence of any legislation that supports the approach. The Equal Pay Act does not cover wage differentials in jobs unless the jobs are very similar.[69] In addition, the Bennett Amendment to the Civil Rights Act states that:

It shall not be an unlawful practice under this Title for any employer to differentiate upon the basis of sex in determining the amount of the wages or compensation paid or to be paid to employees of such an employer if such differentiation is [based on differences in skill, effort, responsibility, working conditions, seniority, or performance].[70]

The Supreme Court has ruled that the Bennett Amendment does not restrict the coverage of the Civil Rights Act when sex-biased wage discrimination is claimed. In the same case, Justice Brennan emphasized the narrowness of the decision and specifically pointed out that the controversial concept of comparable worth was not the question before the Court.[71] However, the court has approved use of the comparable worth theory as an argument in sex discrimination cases. Then, in 1982, two of the most widely-publicized cases were settled in out-of-court settlements, thereby delaying a more definitive resolution of the issue of comparable worth.[72]

Summary

The fundamentals of a wage and salary system start with wage and salary objectives, such as to attract, retain, and motivate employees. Important influences on wage and salary determination include the competitive position of the organization, its ability to pay, comparable wages and labor market forces, cost of living, pay equity, performance and productivity, collective bargaining agreements, legal influences, and job evaluation.

Job evaluation serves as the foundation of most wage and salary systems. The most common methods are ranking, job classification, market pricing, point system, and factor comparison. The point system, discussed in the appendix, is the most commonly used method. Proper job analysis and current job descriptions and specifications are important to each method. Because there is a relationship between wages paid and the number and complexity of the job duties and responsibilities, as well as the personal qualifications needed for performing the job, special attention to job analysis, job descriptions, and job specifications is imperative.

While the compensable factors for managerial jobs are different from those for hourly employees' jobs, the principles on which managerial pay is established are essentially the same. At the first level of management, the pay of employees in the department plays a major role in the determination of supervisors' pay. For middle management, several methods—the Phoenix plan, the Hay system, and others—have been developed. Additional compensation may be provided through various incentive plans, which will be discussed in the next chapter.

An important and controversial issue in compensation is whether traditional job evaluations discriminate against females and the jobs they have traditionally held. The final decision awaits the Supreme Court's interpretation.

Discussion Questions

1. Evaluate the effectiveness of each job evaluation method in reaching the wage and salary objectives stated at the beginning of the chapter.

2. Discuss the interrelationship between the various influences that determine wages and salaries in organizations.

3. Why do some people consider job evaluation systems biased against females?

4. Why do the compensable factors used in evaluating managerial jobs differ from those used in evaluating hourly employees' jobs? Could this difference result in problems?

5. What arguments can you make to justify the fact that twenty-six executives in the United States earn more than 1.4 million dollars a year? What argument can you make against such salaries?

6. Do wage surveys have too much influence in wage determination? Do they help to maintain the status quo of wage differentials between jobs?

7. Is the job evaluation process: (a) scientific, (b) systematic, (c) nonsystematic? Explain.

8. Would you rather be employed by a company with or without a job evaluation system? Why?

Notes

1. Jules Bachman, *Wage Determination: An Analysis of Wage Criteria* (Princeton, N.J.: D. Van Nostrand, 1959), pp. 1–7.

2. David W. Belcher, "Wage and Salary Administration," in *Motivation and Commitment,* ed. Dale Yoder and H. G. Heneman, Jr. (Washington D.C.: Bureau of National Affairs, 1975), p. 6-76.

3. *Ibid.*

4. David A. Weeks, *Compensating Employees: Lessons of the 1970's* (New York: Conference Board, 1976), p. 8.

5. *Ibid.,* p. 9.

6. *Ibid.,* p. 9.

7. Staff of Bureau of National Affairs, *Wage and Salary Administration* (Washington, D.C.: Bureau of National Affairs, 1981), p. 3.

8. Reprinted, by permission of the publisher, from David J. Thomsen, "Unmentioned Problems of Salary Administration," *Compensation Review,* Second Quarter 1977 (New York: AMACOM, a division of the American Management Associations, 1977), p. 14.

9. *Ibid.*

10. *Ibid.,* p. 19

11. Janet L. Norwood, "The CPI Controversy," *Labor Law Journal* 31 (March 1980), pp. 131–138.

12. William R. Marshall, *Administering the Company Personnel Function* (Englewood Cliffs, N.J.: Prentice-Hall, 1976), p. 137.

13. Margaret Yao, "Inflation Outruns Pay of Middle Managers, Increasing Frustration," *Wall Street Journal,* June 9, 1981, p. 1.

14. Douglas R. LeRoy, "Scheduled Wage Increases and Cost-of-Living Provisions in 1981," *Monthly Labor Review* 104 (January 1981), p. 12.

15. Robert J. Thornton, "A Problem with the 'COLA' Craze," *Compensation Review* 9 (2d quarter, 1977), p. 42.

16. Reprinted from "Inflation and Salary Administration," by Howard Risher, p. 33 of the May 1981 issue of *Personnel Administrator,* copyright 1981, the American Society for Personnel Administration, 30 Park Drive, Berea, OH 44017, $26 per year.

17. Rufus E. Runzheimer, Jr., "How Corporations Are Handling Cost-of-Living Differentials," *Business Horizons* 23 (August 1980) pp. 38–40.

18. *Ibid.,* p. 38.

19. Robert H. Finn and Sang M. Lee, "Salary Equity: Its Determination, Analysis, and Correlates," *Journal of Applied Psychology* 56 (July 1972), pp. 283–284.

20. David W. Belcher, "Pay Equity or Pay Fairness?" *Compensation Review* 11 (2d quarter 1979), p. 32.

21. Belcher, "Wage and Salary Administration," pp. 6-76–6-78.

22. *Ibid.,* p. 6-78.

23. Fred K. Foulkes, *Personnel Policies of Large Non-Union Companies* (Englewood Cliffs, N.J.: Prentice-Hall, 1979), pp. 157–166.

24. Daniel J. B. Mitchell, "Union and Wages: What We've Learned Since the 50's", *California Management Review* 12 (Summer 1980), pp. 56–64.

25. Robert S. Goldfarb and John F. Morrall III, "The Davis-Bacon Act: An Apraisal of Recent Studies," *Industrial and Labor Relations* 34 (January 1981), pp. 191–193.

26. John P. Gould and George Bittlingmayer, *The Economics of the Davis-Bacon Act* (Washington, D.C.: American Enterprise Institute for Public Policy Research, 1980), pp. 5–9, 84–89.

27. Equal Employment Opportunity Commission, *Hearings before the United States Equal Employment Opportunity Commission—on Job Segregation and Wage Discrimination* (Washington, D.C.: Government Printing Office, 1980), p. 4.

28. Bruce R. Ellig, "Compensation Management: Its Past and Its Future," *Personnel* 54 (May/June 1977), pp. 32–34.

29. Lucretia D. Tanner and Janice D. Murphy, "The Voluntary Pay Standard: A Review," *Labor Law Journal* 32 (March 1981), pp. 158–163.

30. Mitchell L. Marks and Phillip H. Mirvis, "Wage Guidelines: Job Attitudes and Behavior," *Industrial Relations* 20 (Fall 1981), p. 295.

31. Donald J. Treiman, *Job Evaluation: An Analytic Review* (Washington, D.C.: National Academy of Science, 1979), p. 1

32. *Job Evaluation Policies and Procedures* (Washington, D.C.: Bureau of National Affairs, 1976), p. 4.

33. Belcher, "Wage and Salary Administration," pp. 6-93–6-94.

34. *Ibid.;* Harold D. Janes, "Union Views on Job Evaluation: 1971 vs. 1978," *Personnel Journal* (February 1979) pp. 80–85.

35. John Zalusky, "Job Evaluation: An Uneven World," *American Federationist* 88 (April 1981), pp. 11–20.

36. Treiman, *Job Evaluation,* p. 2.

37. *Ibid.*

38. Belcher, "Wage and Salary Administration," p. 6-99.

39. James Carey, "Participative Job Evaluation," *Compensation Review* 9 (4th quarter, 1977), p. 31.

40. Belcher, "Wage and Adminstration," p. 6-101.

41. Hugh Parker, "The Effective Manager—What Is He Worth?" *Compensation Review* 8 (4th quarter 1976), p. 49.
42. "No Sign of Recession in Pay at the Top" *Business Week,* May 10, 1982, pp. 76–77.
43. Reprinted by permission of the Harvard Business Review. Excerpt from "Are Corporate Executives Overpaid?" by John C. Baker, *Harvard Business Review* 55, no. 4, July–August 1977, p. 51. Copyright © 1977 by the President and Fellows of Harvard College; all rights reserved.
44. David Kraus, "Executive Pay: Ripe for Reform," *Harvard Business Review* 58 (September/October 1980), p. 36.
45. William J. Baumol, *Business Behavior, Value, and Growth,* rev. ed. (New York: Macmillan, 1961) pp. 45–52, 140–144.
46. David R. Roberts, *Executive Compensation* (Glencoe, Ill.: Free Press, 1959), p. 50.
47. Narash C. Agarwal, "Determinants of Executive Compensation," *Industrial Relations* 20 (Winter 1981), pp. 36–45.
48. Ernest C. Miller, "Setting Supervisors' Pay and Pay Differentials," *Compensation Review* 10 (3rd quarter 1978), pp. 13–16.
49. David J. Thomsen, *The Phoenix Plan* (Los Angeles: Compensation Institute, 1980), pp. 11–30.
50. *Fact Sheet* (Philadelphia: The Hay Group, 1980).
51. *Sixteenth Annual Study of Executive Compensation* (Princeton, N.J.: Sibson & Co., 1980), p. 98.
52. Reprinted, by permission of the publisher, from "How Companies Set Top- and Middle-Management Salaries . . . A Compensation Review Symposium," *Compensation Review,* First Quarter 1977 (New York: AMACOM, a division of American Management Associations, 1977), pp. 37–38.
53. *Ibid.,* p. 38.
54. Jay R. Schuster, "Executive Compensation," in *Motivation and Commitment,* ed. Dale Yoder and H. G. Heneman, Jr. (Washington, D.C.: Bureau of National Affairs, 1975), p. 6-143.
55. "How Companies Set Top- and Middle-Management Salaries," p. 41.
56. Eleanor H. Norton, *EEOC Hearings on Job Segregation and Wage Discrimination* (Washington, D.C.: Government Printing Office, 1980), p. 8.
57. Lawrence Lober, "Job Segregation and Wage Discrimination under Title VII and the Equal Pay Act," *Personnel Administrator* 25 (May 1980), p. 34.
58. Rosselle Pekelis, "Equal Pay: Comparability vs. Identical Work," in *Proceedings of NYU 33rd Annual National Conference on Labor,* ed. Richard Adelman (New York: Matthew Bender, 1981), pp. 368–369.
59. James A. Buford, Jr., and Dwight R. Norris, "A Salary Equalization Model: Identifying and Correcting Sex-Based Salary Differences," *Employee Relations Law Journal* 6 (Winter 1981), p. 408.
60. Eleanor Norton, *Washington Report,* May 19, 1980, p. 7.
61. Bruce A. Nelson, Edward M. Opton, Jr., and Thomas E. Wilson, "Wage Discrimination and Title VII in the 1980s: The Cases against 'Comparable Worth,'" *Employee Relations Law Journal* 6 (Winter 1980), p. 380.
62. Rosselle Pekelis, "Equal Pay," p. 377.
63. Elaine Wegner, "Does Competitive Pay Discriminate?" *Personnel Administrator* 25 (May 1980), pp. 38–43, 66.
64. E. Robert Livernash, "An Overview, "in *Comparable Worth: Issues and Alternatives,* edited by E. Robert Livernash (Washington, D.C.: Equal Employment Advisory Council, 1980), pp. 3, 9. Copyright 1980 by Equal Employment Advisory Council. Reprinted with permission of the publisher.
65. Ruth G. Blumrosen, "Wage Discrimination and Job Segregation: The Survival of a Theory," *University of Michigan Journal of Law Reform* 14 (Spring 1980), p. 5.
66. *Lemons v. City and County of Denver,* 17 FEP 909 (1978).
67. George H. Hildebrand, "The Market System," in *Comparable Worth: Issues and Alternatives,* ed. E. Robert Livernash (Washington, D.C.: Equal Employment Advisory Council, 1980), p. 106.
68. Nelson, Opton, and Wilson, "Wage Discrimination and Title VII in the 1980s," pp. 388–390. Also see Bruce A. Nelson, Edward M. Opton, Jr., and Thomas E. Wilson, "Wage Discrimination and 'Comparable Worth' Theory in Perspective," *University of Michigan Journal of Law Reform* 13 (Winter 1980), pp. 233–301.
69. Nelson, Opton, and Wilson, "Wage Discrimination and Title VII in the 1980s," p. 381.
70. 42 U.S.C. 2000–2(h) (1965).
71. *County of Washington, Oregon v. Gunther,* 49 USLW 48 (1981).
72. "Settlement of Two Comparable Worth Cases," *Labor Relations Reporter,* May 22, 1982, p. 109 LRR 254.

Establishing a Wage Structure by the Point System and by the Factor Comparison System

Point System

After the organization has completed its organizational analysis and job analysis and has on hand current job descriptions and job specifications, two preliminary decisions must be made; they concern the compensable factors and the point rating scale that will be used. The compensable factors are selected and weighted on the basis of past experience within the organization and knowledge of compensation practices outside the organization. The criteria for choosing the compensable factors are:

1. *Acceptability* to the employees and managers.
2. *Applicability* to the group of jobs that will be evaluated.
3. *Ratability* in that the job content and requirements vary sufficiently so that jobs with different requirements, responsibilities, and so on will be assigned different points.
4. *Distinctiveness* so that each factor will represent a separate element of job content, without overlap, and each factor will be clearly defined.
5. *Ease of administration* so the plan will be cost effective in comparison with the benefits derived.[1]

The compensable factors vary according to the organization's needs, the nature of the jobs, variations in complexity and sophistication of the system, and the importance placed on various aspects of the jobs. Exhibit 10A.1 shows four compensable factors: job requirements, effort, responsibility, and job conditions. Each of these factors is divided into subelements. For example, the job requirements factor is divided into education, experience, and job complexity. These compensable factors represent the content for plant and office jobs and would not be appropriate for managerial and executive positions. For managerial positions, such compensable factors as know-how, problem-solving skills, accountability, interpersonal skills, and the like might be selected.

Once the compensable factors have been selected, their relative weights and degrees must be determined. (The *degree* refers to the amount of the factor required.) In our example in Exhibit 10A.1, the relative weights can be inferred from the points given to the various degrees. For example, education and experience are considered equally important; so the points are the same at each degree.

| Exhibit 10A.1 | Compensable Factors for Plant and Office Jobs | | | | | |

| | | Degrees | | | | |
Compensable Factors	1	2	3	4	5
Job Requirements					
Education	15	30	45	60	75
Experience	15	30	45	60	75
Job Complexity	10	20	30	40	50
Effort					
Physical	15	30	45	60	75
Mental	10	20	30	40	50
Responsibility					
Machines and Equipment	5	10	15	20	25
Parts and Materials	5	10	15	20	25
Personnel	10	20	30	40	50
Job Conditions					
Working Conditions	10	20	30	40	50
Hazards	5	10	15	20	25

Responsibility for personnel is considered twice as important as responsibility for machines and equipment.

Next, the number of degrees must be determined and points assigned to each degree. In the example, as you have already noted, five degrees for each compensable factor were selected, and points were assigned according to the weights given each factor.

The next step is a critical one: Each degree for every compensable factor must be defined. Of utmost importance is defining each degree in such a way that it will be clearly differentiated from all other degrees. Exhibit 10A.2 displays samples of definitions for two compensable factors: education and experience.

The job evaluation committee must now select *benchmark jobs* that will be used to establish the foundation of the program and later to form the basis for evaluating jobs throughout the organization. These jobs must be:

Representative—varying from low to high in value and selected from jobs throughout the organization.

Definable—capable of being clearly defined to minimize error, inconsistency, and controversy.

Noncontroversial—having a current wage considered correct so as to assure acceptance.

Although ten to fifteen benchmark jobs are usually selected, our presentation will use only six: janitor, keypunch operator, assembler, executive secretary, machinist, and electrician.

Exhibit 10A.2		Definitions of Compensable Factors and Degrees for Plant and Office Jobs
	Factor: Education	This factor measures the educational level or equivalent required to perform at various levels of complexity.
	Degree 1:	Ability to read and write, add and subtract, and carry out nontechnical instructions (less than high school education).
	Degree 2:	Ability to read and write, do simple arithmetic, maintain records, and interpret and give nontechnical written and oral instructions (high school education).
	Degree 3:	Ability to read and interpret fairly complex material, compute statistical data, and perform on fairly technical machines (two years of trade school or junior college with no specialty or apprenticeship program).
	Degree 4:	Ability to read and interpret complex materials, compute fairly complex mathematical and statistical problems, operate sensitive machines, interpret complex drawings, and resolve difficult problems (two years of college with a specialty in a specific subject).
	Degree 5:	Possession of comprehensive knowledge and understanding of complicated subjects (such as engineering, accounting, or the like); ability to use higher-level mathematics, statistics, and computer science; ability to solve nonroutine, complex problems (college degree in area of work).
	Factor: Experience	This factor measures the length of time required to learn the job tasks so as to perform in a minimally acceptable manner.
	Degree 1:	Less than three months.
	Degree 2:	Three months to six months.
	Degree 3:	Six months to one year.
	Degree 4:	One year to three years.
	Degree 5:	Over three years.

The job evaluation committee is now ready to retrieve the written job descriptions and job specifications. The committee will be asked to study thoroughly the job descriptions and job specifications for each of the benchmark jobs. While each member may work independently at first, final decisions are made by the committee as a whole.

The committee assigns points to the benchmark jobs with the help of the job descriptions and specifications and the definitions of each degree for each compensable factor. For example, Exhibit 10A.3 shows the points assigned for the compensable factors of education and experience. This procedure is continued until each of the benchmark jobs has been evaluated. Then, the points are totaled, and the total points give an indication of the relative worth of the benchmark jobs. The total points, as well as the wage rates, for the benchmark jobs in our example are given in Exhibit 10A.4. Once the total points have been determined, a graph representing each job's points and wage rate should be constructed (see Figure 10A.1). If there is more than one wage rate for any of the benchmark jobs (because of differences in

Exhibit 10A.3   Points Assigned for Education
                            and Experience

Benchmark Jobs	Education		Experience	
	Degree	Points	Degree	Points
Janitor	1	15	1	15
Keypunch Operator	2	30	1	15
Assembly Worker	1	15	1	15
Machinist	2	30	2	30
Executive Secretary	3	45	5	75
Senior Electrician	3	45	5	75

seniority, merit, and the like), the committee may decide to use the midpoint of the current rates or the entry-level wage rate for each job.

The graphic relationship of the benchmark jobs forms a wage curve. The curve's slope can be determined by two methods: the least-squares method or the eyeball method. The former is a statistical method that determines the slope of the curve accurately and provides a formula in the form of a regression equation. The eyeball method is a less sophisticated method used by some organizations to visually center the wage curve on all the wage rates on the graph.

Because one of the objectives of wage and salary administration is to provide external equity in pay, the organization's next task is to compare its wages with those of other organizations. Wage survey data are used to determine the labor market wages in comparable organizations. Nearly all organizations use wage survey data in establishing their wage structure. In fact, one source shows that 79 percent of organizations conduct their own surveys, 79 percent receive wage data from government and private consultants, and 75 percent obtain industry wage survey data.[2]

Exhibit 10A.4   Total Points and Wage Rates for
                            Benchmark Jobs

Benchmark Jobs	Total Points	Current Wage Rate
Janitor	130	$4.00
Assembly Worker	180	4.75
Keypunch Operator	210	5.25
Machinist	260	6.25
Executive Secretary	310	6.80
Senior Electrician	340	8.20

Figure 10A.1   **Wage Curve for Benchmark Jobs**

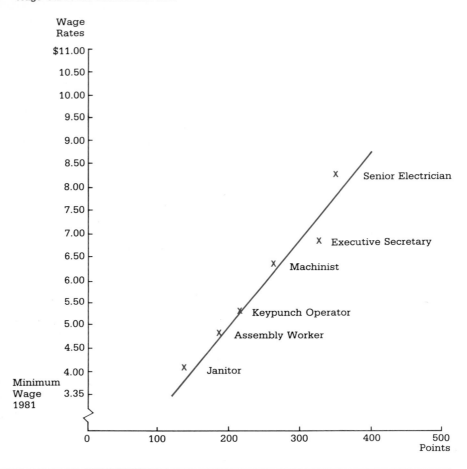

To assure accuracy of the wage data obtained, job descriptions and job specifications should be given to the wage analysts at the organizations surveyed to ensure that the jobs to be compared are the same. Careful attention should be given to variations in benefits, seniority, and working conditions to assure comparability. If the job content varies, even though the job title is the same, the data received will not be relevant. If such data are used, the basis on which the organization establishes its wage structure will be faulty.

For our example, assume that ten firms in the relevant labor market have been identified as employing persons in our firm's benchmark jobs. The organization has gained their cooperation and participation in its wage survey by offering to share the results with them. Thus, it

Exhibit 10A.5

Wage Survey Data

Benchmark Jobs	Total Points	Current Wage Rates for Comparable Firms	Comparison with Company Wage Rate
Janitor	130	4.20	+0.20
Assembly Worker	180	5.05	+0.30
Keypunch Operator	210	5.40	+0.15
Machinist	260	6.50	+0.25
Executive Secretary	310	6.90	+0.10
Senior Electrician	340	8.40	+0.20

obtains the wage data shown in Exhibit 10A.5. The data show that wage rates in the labor market range from 10 cents to 30 cents more an hour than the rates in our organization.

The wage data from the other organizations should be drawn on the organization's wage curve graph in order that a comparison between the organization's wage curve and the wage curve for the labor market can be made (see Figure 10A.2). As indicated on the graph, the company curve is below the curve for the labor market. In other words, the company is generally paying below the going wage rate. This may cause problems in recruiting new employees and higher than normal turnover. If neither of these problems exists, it may be that our company offers advantages—such as better supervision, better working climate, better promotion opportunity, or the like—that cannot be computed in a wage survey. However, if our company wants to be competitive, a slight upward adjustment would be proper.

Let us assume the organization in our example has decided to make such an adjustment. The resulting *adjusted wage curve* will become its new wage curve and will provide the basis for wage classes and wage ranges. Based on the adjusted wage curve, the organization will establish a wage class for every fifty points and will allow a variation in the wage ranges of 10 percent above and below the adjusted wage curve (see Figure 10A.3). Wage classes, point ranges, and wage ranges are placed in a table (see Exhibit 10A.6).

Now that the wage structure has been established, the job evaluation committee can evaluate all the remaining jobs and determine the wage class and range to which each will be assigned. A wage and salary manual is then written to explain how the system works and how it will be administered.

On occasion, a job may be assigned points that would place it above the wage range for its class. These jobs have *red-circled wage rates,* which means that the company is presently paying too much for the job according to its value as determined by the job evaluation system. For example, the dot in Figure 10A.3 represents the job of timekeeper, which was assigned 228 points, placing it in Class III. However, the

Figure 10A.2

Wage Curves for Labor Market and Organization

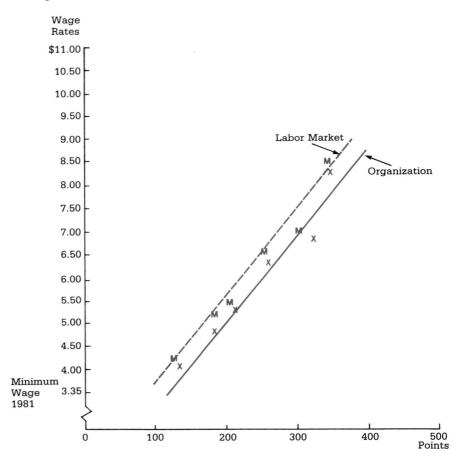

job's current wage rate is $6.70 per hour, although the maximum wage rate for Class III jobs is $6.14.

There are several reasons for the existence of these red-circled rates, such as favoritism, or the presence in these jobs of long-time employees or of employees transferred from higher-paying jobs who were allowed to keep their previous wage rate. Organizations vary in their approach to this problem, but rarely do they lower the wage rate. Usually, they follow one of two approaches. They may freeze the wage rate until the wage curve and consequently the wage ranges are adjusted upward to include the red-circled job. Alternatively, they may assign additional tasks and responsibilities to increase the value of the

Figure 10A.3   **Adjusted Organization Wage Curve,**
                          Wage Ranges, and Wage Classes

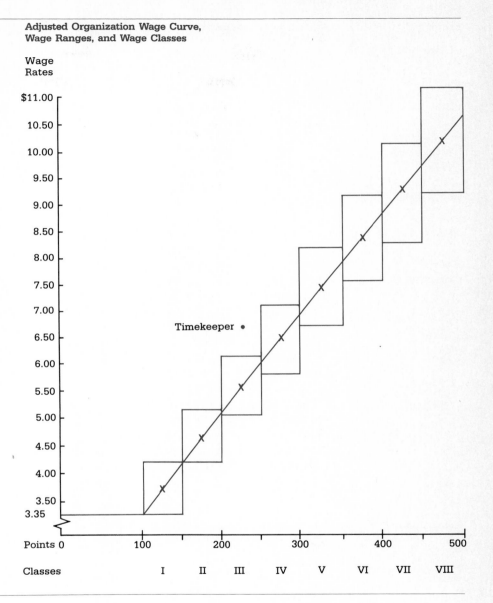

job and the points assigned for it; then the job can be moved into a
higher wage class and wage range.

When a job has been undervalued in the past and its current wage
rate falls below the minimum level of the wage range for its assigned
class (called a *blue-circled rate*), an automatic increase is usually given.

Exhibit 10A.6   **Wage Classes and Ranges for**
                          Benchmark Jobs

		Wage Range		
Class	Points	Starting	Midrange	Maximum
I	0–149	$3.37	$3.75	$4.13
II	150–199	4.23	4.70	5.17
III	200–249	5.04	5.60	6.16
IV	250–299	5.83	6.48	7.13
V	300–349	6.66	7.40	8.14
VI	350–399	7.51	8.35	9.19
VII	400–449	8.28	9.20	10.12
VIII	450–500	9.18	10.20	11.22

Factor Comparison

After the job descriptions and job specifications have been updated, the organization must determine the compensable factors (see Exhibit 10A.7 for definitions) and benchmark jobs for the design of the system. To help show how the factor comparison system differs from the point system, we will use compensable factors (job requirements, mental effort, physical effort, responsibility, and working conditions) and benchmark jobs (janitor, assembly worker, keypunch operator, machinist, executive secretary, and senior electrician) similar to those used in the description of the point system.

Next, the job evaluation committee will rank the benchmark jobs for each compensable factor (see Exhibit 10A.8). For example, the senior electrician has the highest ranking in terms of job requirements. This rank is justified by the educational preparation required (apprenticeship program, experience, and job preparation), whereas the low rank-

Exhibit 10A.7   **Definitions of Compensable Factors in**
                          the Factor Comparison System

Job Requirements:	This factor measures education, job knowledge, and experience required.
Mental Effort:	This factor measures independent action, exercise of judgment, mental application, attention, and concentration required.
Physical Effort:	This factor measures the physical exertion (difficulty and duration) required and the physical strain of working in the position.
Responsibility:	This factor measures responsibility for equipment, materials, safety, work of others, and information processes.
Working Conditions:	This factor measures physical surroundings and conditions that make the job disagreeable (presence of hazards; exposure to dust, dirt, fumes, noise; and the like).

Exhibit 10A.8 **Ranking of Benchmark Jobs According to Compensable Factors**

Rank	Job Requirements	Mental Effort	Physical Effort	Responsibility	Working Conditions
1	Senior Electrician	Senior Electrician	Assembly Worker	Executive Secretary	Janitor
2	Executive Secretary	Executive Secretary	Machinist	Senior Electrician	Machinist
3	Machinist	Machinist	Janitor	Machinist	Assembly Worker
4	Keypunch Operator	Keypunch Operator	Senior Electrician	Keypunch Operator	Senior Electrician
5	Assembly Worker	Assembly Worker	Keypunch Operator	Assembly Worker	Keypunch Operator
6	Janitor	Janitor	Executive Secretary	Janitor	Executive Secretary

ing assigned the janitor reflects the relatively small amount of education and experience required to perform janitorial tasks. The job evaluation committee will proceed with this factor-by-factor ranking until all the benchmark jobs are ranked by each compensable factor.

The next step is to assign dollar weightings to each of the compensable factors according to its relative worth to the organization. Using the members' combined expertise, the job evaluation committee weights each compensable factor according to its contribution to the total worth of the benchmark jobs. The job evaluation committee must answer the following question for each benchmark job: How much of the current wage for this job is being paid for (a) job requirements, (b) mental effort, (c) physical effort, (d) responsibility, and (e) working conditions?

The result of this process is a measurement scale that will be used for all jobs throughout the organization. Thus, the *accuracy* of this step must be emphasized. It is *absolutely essential* that the benchmark jobs are being paid properly. Exhibit 10A.9 demonstrates the results of assigning dollar weights to the benchmark jobs. You may wish to refer back to Exhibit 10A.8 to see how the ranking by factors corresponds to the assigned dollar weightings.

After the measurement scale has been completed by the job evaluation committee, it can be used to evaluate the remaining jobs in the organization. These jobs will be compared factor by factor using the benchmark jobs as guides. When this process is complete, wage classes and wage ranges can be set up. The organization may conduct a wage survey in order that external equity can be achieved. Policies

Exhibit 10A.9   **Measurement Scale for Evaluating Jobs by Factor Comparison**

Job Requirements	Mental Effort	Physical Effort	Responsibility	Working Conditions
$3.00—	$2.50—	$1.50—	$2.00—	$1.00— Janitor
				Machinist,
2.80—	2.30—	1.40— Assembly Worker	1.90 Executive	0.95— Assembly Worker
			1.85 Secretary	
2.60— Senior Electrician	2.10— Senior Electrician	1.30—	1.80—	0.90—
2.40— Executive Secretary	1.90— Executive Secretary	1.20— Machinist, Janitor	1.70— Senior Electrician	0.85—
2.20—	1.70—	1.10— Senior Electrician	1.60—	0.80—
2.00—	1.50—	1.00— Keypunch Operator	1.50—	0.75—
1.80—	1.30—	0.90—	1.40—	0.70— Senior Electrician
1.60— Machinist	1.20— Machinist	0.80—	1.30— Machinist	0.65—
1.40— Keypunch Operator	1.10— Keypunch Operator	0.70—	1.20— Keypunch Operator	0.60—
1.20—	0.90—	0.60—	1.10—	0.55— Keypunch Operator
1.00—	0.70— Assembly Worker	0.50—	1.00—	0.50—
0.80— Assembly Worker	0.50— Janitor	0.40—	0.90— Assembly Worker	0.45—
0.60— Janitor	0.30—	0.30— Executive Secretary	0.80—	0.40—
0.40—	0.10—	0.20—	0.70— Janitor	0.35— Executive Secretary

Dollar Allocation to Compensable Factors

Benchmark Jobs	Job Requirements	Mental Effort	Physical Effort	Responsibility	Working Conditions	Current Wage
Janitor	$0.60	$0.50	$1.20	$0.70	$1.00	$4.00
Assembly Worker	0.80	0.70	1.40	0.90	0.95	4.75
Keypunch Operator	1.40	1.10	1.00	1.20	0.55	5.25
Machinist	1.60	1.20	1.20	1.30	0.95	6.25
Executive Secretary	2.40	1.90	0.30	1.85	0.35	6.80
Senior Electrician	2.60	2.10	1.10	1.70	0.70	8.20

and procedures for administering the program must also be established.

Notes for Appendix

1. Henry A. Sargent, "Using the Point Method to Measure Jobs," in *Handbook of Wage and Salary Administration,* ed. Milton Rock (New York: McGraw-Hill, 1972), pp. 2–32.
2. *Job Evaluation Policies and Procedures* (Washington, D.C.: Bureau of National Affairs, 1976), pp. 6–10.

Chapter 11

Compensation: Incentives and Administration

It is apparent that rising labor costs have wreaked havoc on previously sound company pay structures and incentives, causing salary compression at many levels of the organization, undermining merit pay plans, and impairing recruiting efforts. If coping with inflation were not enough of a task, the recent focus on pay equity issues has required many wage/salary administrators to reexamine their methods of job evaluation and pricing and, in many cases, to undertake formal systems and procedures where none had been used.

After the basic wage and salary system has been established as described in Chapter 10, many organizations design incentive systems for certain employee and managerial groups. These incentive systems are intended to strengthen the links between pay and performance. This chapter presents the major types of incentive plans—individual, group, and company-wide. Next, the chapter explains how the wage and salary system is typically administered. Important administrative tasks include maintaining the system and keeping it up to date, resolving problems, and making proper wage adjustments. The chapter also includes a discussion of the personnel department and other managers in relation to the compensation system. Finally, the chapter presents a controversial issue that has a major impact on the motivational aspects of compensation systems: Should wages and salaries be secret or open?

Incentive Systems

Monetary incentives are based on the assumption that money plays an important role in employees' performance. Organizations using incentive plans assume further that performance can be measured and controlled by the employee and that pay can be tied to various levels of performance. Incentive plans can be established in numerous ways: for individuals or groups, for example, and for various organizational positions, such as production, sales, or executives. For any of these incentives to be effective, the employees covered must believe the following:

1. That higher levels of performance will lead to higher pay (see Chapter 3's discussion of expectancy theory).
2. That pay is important.
3. That greater effort will lead to higher performance.
4. That higher performance will not hurt them (for example, that it will not result in an increase in production standards).
5. That other rewards—such as promotions, better opportunities for advancement, and so on—will also result from higher levels of performance.[1]

If any of these beliefs are not present, the incentive system will not achieve its motivational potential. It is important that managers and personnel representatives create conditions in which these beliefs will be fulfilled and reinforced through actual practice.

Experts in the design of incentive plans contend that the incentive itself should allow payments between 15 percent and 35 percent above the base wage for a typical forty-hour week. Below 15 percent is considered too low to motivate workers effectively, and above 35 percent is considered excessive. In fact, workers often believe that consistent earnings of more than 35 percent above standard will cause management to reduce the incentive or change the standard. This belief itself causes employees to hold back their production to a level they believe management will tolerate.[2]

Incentives for Production Employees

Incentive plans for plant employees have been declining for the past several years (about 20 percent of such employees are now covered under individual plans and 12 percent under group), and very few office workers are covered under such plans. In Europe, incentive plans have been increasing. Over 50 percent of production employees in many countries are covered by such plans; surprisingly, the highest percentage covered is in the U.S.S.R.[3] In the United States, incentive plans are not widespread in unionized plants; but they are quite common in certain manufacturing plants (80 percent in basic steel, over 70 percent in footwear and men's clothing, over 60 percent in hosiery).[4]

While numerous varieties of incentive plans exist, individual incentive plans can be classified as either *piecework* plans or *standard hour* plans. Under a piecework plan, individual employees are paid a set "price" per unit of their output; and the more productive employees receive pay in direct proportion to their productivity. Normally, the rate is established in such a way that the average experienced operator working with normal efficiency can earn well above the amount that he or she would have earned under a hourly wage rate. For example, a seamstress in a garment factory may be paid $0.20 per collar completed. If the seamstress completes 1,500 collars in a forty-hour week, earnings for the week will be $300. A variation of the piecework plan designed by Frederick Taylor includes differential piece rates for different levels of performance. The seamstress who sewed 1,500 collars in the example above would under this plan be paid $0.20 per unit for the first 1,000 collars but would be paid $0.25 for the next 500, for a total of $325 [(1,000 × $0.20) + (500 × $0.25)]. The graduated rate provides an even greater incentive to produce more.

The standard hour plan, which is based on time, has many variations. The standard, usually expressed as 100 percent, refers to the amount of work of a specified quality that an average, experienced employee can produce in an hour working with normal effort (time is allowed for rest, personal needs, and minor delays). Employees are not paid according to the time that they work; they are paid according to the work accomplished in that time. When employees exceed the production standard, they receive additional compensation based on a predetermined formula.[5] For example, assume that employees on a TV transmitter assembly line have a production standard of sixty transmitters per hour and are paid at a rate of $7.50 per hour. If an employee assembles 3,000 transmitters in a forty-hour week, fifty hours' worth of work (3,000 ÷ 60) will have been performed in the forty hours, according to the standard. Thus, the employee will receive pay of $375 (50 × $7.50) for the forty-hour week. Under a variation of this plan, called the Halsey gain-sharing plan, the employee receives pay for a percentage, typically 50 percent, of the savings in time. For example, the employee in the example above saved ten hours, because he or she produced fifty hours' worth of work in forty hours. His or her earnings will equal pay for forty hours actually worked plus pay for 50 percent of the ten hours saved, or \$337.50 [(40 × \$7.50) + (10/2 × \$7.50) = \$337.50].

Individual incentive pay plans have the advantage of paying employees in relation to their performance. When individual performance cannot be accurately measured or when the company places a premium on teamwork and cooperation, group incentives are used. Group incentive plans often are similar in nature to individual plans except that they focus on group performance. They may be established on the basis of a plant-wide productivity plan—such as the Scanlon Plan, which is discussed later in the chapter—or designed on the basis of some form of profit sharing, also discussed later.

Experience with incentive plans has shown that they result in greater output per hour, lower cost per unit, and higher earnings per employee. Some believe that a large part of these results is due to the prerequisites for a successful incentive plan, such as improved methods, existence of standards, employee control of production, positive reinforcement, and employee trust.

Experience with incentive plans has also shown that they involve problems, mostly because the preconditions of a successful program have not been met. For example, employees may restrict their output because they believe the standard will be increased if their output is too high. Employees are reluctant to increase output when they fear that management will increase the standards. They will have to increase their efforts to maintain their past earnings. Consequently, they hold production to a level that seems safe although it is lower than their maximum. Employees in groups unofficially set production standards which are acceptable to group members as well as management. Because of fear, employees produce less than they could and the incentive system does not work as well as it should.

Another problem is that precise performance measures can be established only for certain types of work—work that is relatively standardized, repetitive, and stable over time. In some cases, management may lack the commitment to continue supporting the pay-for-performance relationship. Finally, employees may not trust management. As suggested they may believe not only that rates will be increased but that peers will reject them and that they will work themselves out of a job by producing more. They may also believe the performance standard is beyond their control (for example, when the pace is controlled by machine).[6]

Unions vary in their opinions of wage incentives; generally, they do not favor incentives. In the apparel industry, piecework pay is traditional and has been accepted by unions for many years. On the other hand, the machinists openly oppose incentives and attempt to negotiate provisions in labor agreements to prevent their installation. Unions' concerns typically include the difficulty of developing and administering the standards, the possibility that the standards will be increased, and the possibility that the standards will cause numerous grievances.[7]

Incentives for Executives

Companies often build in bonuses and incentives to provide additional rewards for executives with above-average performance. In some cases, the incentives are related to short-term performance as measured by sales volume, inventory management, year-end profits, and so on. Longer-term performance is assessed in terms of absolute financial standards, such as earnings growth, stock price, and total return to shareholders over a three- to ten-year period. Generally, short-term performance is rewarded by payment of annual cash bonuses, and long-term performance is rewarded through some form of stock-related capital accumulation program. Nearly 80 percent of large companies have both, while 94 percent have annual bonus plans and 91 percent have some form of long-term incentive plan.[8]

Stock Options and Rights *Stock options* offer executives the right to buy a number of shares in the firm at a specific price. *Stock appreciation rights (SARS)* allow the holder to receive stock or cash equal to the appreciated value of the stock between the time the right is granted and the time it is exercised.[9] Such plans were the backbone of most incentive programs in the 1950s and 1960s; but more recently, their popularity has declined, because the options did not pay off when the stock market was in a slump. In 1970, sixty-one of the largest hundred companies used stock options as their only long-term incentives; but ten years later, none of them relied completely on options.[10]

The Economic Recovery Tax Act of 1981 has restored some of stock options' attractiveness, because it allows taxes on gains to be postponed to the time the stock is sold. Nevertheless, many companies prefer to use stock appreciation rights, which allow more flexibility, and performance plans.

Performance Plans Performance plans pay executives cash or stock bonuses based on the company's growth statistics as measured by earnings per share of stock, return on assets, return on shareholders' equity, increases in capital spending, and other measures. Their purpose is to provide rewards to executives for meeting growth targets up to six years away. These plans have grown in popularity in recent years, and now forty-one of the largest hundred firms have adopted them. This popularity has resulted from companies' efforts to attract and retain high-performing executives.

Honeywell, using growth in earnings per share, started its performance plan in 1978 with forty-one participating executives. These executives were to receive 130 percent of their allotted number of performance shares for a 17-percent growth rate, 100 percent for a 13-percent growth rate, and nothing for a 9-percent growth rate. Earnings rose 27 percent in 1978 and 22 percent in 1979, and Honeywell paid out $1.6 million in performance shares. Champion International Corporation measures its executives' performance by comparing the company's earnings per share growth to the average growth of fifteen competitors. If the performance of Champion is better than the industry average, its executives receive a performance payment.[11]

The happy thing about the true performance bonus is that it marries so well the interests of the recipient and of the shareholders. For if the bonus plan is skillfully designed, no executive will get any extra pay unless the shareholders, too, have a much better-than-average year. And if the company rings up a truly superlative year, the stockholders should hardly begrudge a bonus—even one in six figures—to the executive chiefly responsible. The (person) who performs has a right to the payoff.[12]

Incentives for Salespeople

Sales incentives are designed to provide rewards to salespeople who contribute toward particular sales goals of the company. These goals may range from improved service to clients to profit optimization from increased sales volume.

While most salespeople are paid a straight salary, the salary can be modified by various incentive programs. One method, the *commission,* simply relates pay directly to sales volume by paying the salesperson a predetermined percent of each dollar of sales. Because pay is directly tied to performance, this is a high-risk, high-return incentive plan. The rate may vary from 1 to 25 percent, and it may also vary among products, customers, and levels of sales volume. *Bonus* plans reward sales above a given quota. When the sales quota is reached, the salesperson has justified the base salary; he or she is then paid for sales above the quota according to a set formula, such as 5 percent of all sales above the quota.

Each company designs its sales incentive program to encourage sales while controlling costs. At the same time, it offers salespersons the opportunity to earn high incomes while providing a base salary to reduce financial uncertainty.[13]

Scanlon Plan

Begun by a former local union president, Joe Scanlon, and based on Douglas McGregor's Theory Y management, the Scanlon Plan has become widely accepted in compensation circles. The Scanlon Plan is a group incentive plan, but more importantly it is an innovative process for total organizational development.

Exhibit 11.1 shows how a company Scanlon Plan operates. The Scanlon ratio, the foundation of the plan, is the average monthly payroll costs divided by the average monthly sales value of production for the

Exhibit 11.1	**Operation of a Company Scanlon Plan**
	(January 1983)

Scanlon Ratio (to be used for 1983)

Average Sales Value of Production for the Year 1982 = $200,000

Average Payroll Costs for the Year 1982 = $80,000

$$\text{Scanlon Ratio} = \frac{\$\,80,000}{\$200,000} = 40\%$$

Bonus Money for Distribution (for January 1983)

Actual Sales Value of Production = $200,000

Anticipated Payroll Costs for $200,000 in Sales Value = $80,000

Actual Payroll Costs for $200,000 in Sales Value = $60,000

Labor Cost Savings = $20,000

Distribution of Labor Cost Savings of $20,000

25% to Company for Production Improvement = $5,000

75% to Employees = $15,000

   20% of $15,000 to Reserve Account = $3,000

   80% of $15,000 to Immediate Distribution = $12,000

Bonus to Each Employee (Determined as a Percentage of Present Pay)

$$\frac{\text{Bonus Money Available}}{\text{Actual Payroll Cost}} = \frac{\$12,000}{\$60,000} = 20\%$$

Example: An employee who earns $1,500 in January 1983 will receive $1,800 ($1,500 × 1.20), of which $300 is a bonus.

previous year. In the exhibit, this ratio is 40 percent ($80,000 ÷ $200,000). In January 1983, sales continued at $200,000; according to the Scanlon ratio of 40 percent, payroll costs for this month should have been $80,000. However, because of efficiency, better performance, better utilization of the workforce, and so on, actual payroll costs were only $60,000—a labor cost savings of $20,000. This $20,000 became bonus money. Seventy-five percent, or $15,000, was shared by the employees; and 25 percent was invested to improve production. Part of the employees' share went into a reserve account to offset any deficits in future months; money in this account is distributed at the end of the year. The remainder of the employees' share was paid directly to the employees as bonuses.

The Scanlon Plan is based on four critical principles:

Employees must identify with the organization's objectives, the need for change, and the roles of the various groups—customers, investors, managers, themselves, and so on.

All employees must be able to influence decisions within the company.

All employees must have the opportunity to realize an equitable return for their ideas, energy, competence, and commitment.

Management must develop increasing professional competence and establish systems that allow participation of all elements within the organization.[14]

A review of research on experiences with the Scanlon Plan reveals several important elements that affect its success. Positive measures of employee participation as perceived by the employees, managerial attitudes, number of years the plan is used, and employee expectations of subsequent success seem to be associated with successful plans. Also, there is strong evidence to indicate that a high-level executive must take a leading role if the plan is to succeed. On the other hand, company size and technology in the workplace were not associated with success.[15]

Lincoln Electric Plan

One of the most widely recognized and successful plans in the world is the Lincoln Electric Plan, based primarily on the managerial philosophy of James F. Lincoln. The plan, used at Lincoln Electric in Cleveland, Ohio, includes the following components:

1. A basic hourly rate or salary based on responsibilities is paid to some employees; but the majority of pay is based on straight piecework. Basic compensation approximates the Cleveland, Ohio, average and is adjusted quarterly by the Cleveland area consumer price index.
2. A year-end bonus (not guaranteed and not a gift) is paid based on the contribution of each employee to the company's success as determined by a performance rating on output, quality, dependability, ideas, and cooperation. In 1980, a year-end incentive bonus of $43,249,000 was shared by 2,637 eligible employees. That means an average bonus of $16,400.83 above the basic compensation was paid.

In addition, the company provides guaranteed employment (no layoffs since 1958), promotion from within, a retirement plan, group life insurance, an employee stock purchase plan (75 percent of the employees own 45 percent of the company's stock), and other benefits.[16] While the plan has been an amazing success, it has proven difficult to replicate because of the uniqueness of the company's philosophy and its employees.

Profit Sharing

Profit sharing is any procedure in which the employer makes payments, directly or indirectly, to employees from profits of the business. Direct payments are made in the form of cash, usually in the month of March, based on the profits from the previous year. Indirect payments may be made in the form of deferred payments into a trust that will be held for the employee until a specified time, such as retirement, or under defined circumstances, such as serious illness or college for children. These plans are widely applied in the United States and have been deemed highly desirable in that they are said to strengthen the capitalistic system. Profit sharing seeks to instill a feeling of partnership between employees and employers while improving efficiency, performance, and employee relations. In other words, profit-sharing plans are usually adopted for the very practical business reason of improving organizational effectiveness.

Many companies, such as Proctor and Gamble, Sears, Eastman Kodak, Texas Instruments, Xerox, and Zenith, have used profit sharing successfully for years.[17] Indeed, profit sharing has been one of the fastest-growing incentive methods; new plans doubled every five years between 1951 and 1976. Approximately 50 percent of all companies with twelve or more employees have developed some form of profit sharing. The amount employees receive ranges from 10 to 50 percent of their annual base salary rate; the majority of companies pay from 10 to 15 percent.[18]

Of the firms with profit-sharing plans, one-third provide for immediate cash payments; but there has been a steady growth in the use of deferred plans. Some plans allow both cash payments and deferred investments. Eastman Kodak allows each employee each year to select the proportions in which his or her share will be allocated to cash and deferred investment.[19]

In spite of their success, profit-sharing plans have faced several problems. One difficulty arises when the value of employees' profit-sharing accounts declines. In fact, two companies, Marriott and Tappan, were sued by retirees who claimed that the trustees violated their fiduciary duties when they invested too much of the profit-sharing assets in the companies' stock, which declined substantially.[20] The other problem is that there may be no clear relationship between employees' efforts and the company's profitability. Because profits and losses may be tied closely to managerial decisions—such as entering new markets or introducing new products—or to overall economic conditions, employees may not perceive their extra efforts as contributing directly to greater profits. When this happens, the relationship of effort and reward is weakened and the plan loses its effectiveness.

In smaller companies, employees may more closely identify their efforts with the profits of the firm; and some companies are able to closely incorporate the interests of the employees with the economic interests of the company. One example is the Woodward Governor Company of Rockford, Illinois, which has established a corporate partnership (Cor-Par) between shareholders and workers wherein both groups are rewarded by the firm's performance. Figure 11.1 illustrates how the revenues are shared.

Figure 11.1   **Cor-Par Plan of Woodward Governor Company**

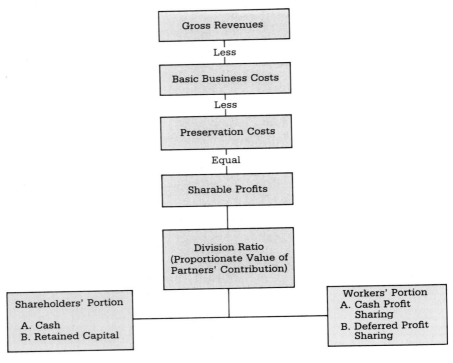

Notes:

Basic Business Costs:
Basic business costs include all costs of materials and services, insurance, taxes, compensation for the workers and compensation for the shareholders.

Base compensation for each worker member is determined yearly as a result of the member evaluation process.

Base compensation for each shareholder member is equivalent to a stated rate of interest applied to each shareholder member's share of the book value (net worth) of the company at the beginning of the fiscal year. At the discretion of the board of directors, the base compensation may be distributed by the payment of cash dividends or by reinvestment in the company.

Preservation Costs:
Preservation costs are the expenses of providing those services which contribute to the well-being of the worker membership and to the maintenance of adequate facilities and capital. These expenses can vary according to economic circumstances. Included in preservation costs are provisions for seniority recognition, personnel maintenance and development, and retirement.

Division of Sharable Profits:
Sharable profits are determined by subtracting the basic business and preservation costs from gross revenues. Sharable profits, if any, are divided annually between the worker and shareholder members according to their respective capital values. The net worth of the company and the total base salaries of the worker members are used to determine the relative capital values.

Shareholder Members' Portion of Profit Sharing:
The shareholders' portion of sharable profits is, at the discretion of the board of directors, paid in additional dividends and/or retained for reinvestment.

Worker Members' Portion of Profit Sharing:
The worker members' portion of sharable profits is allocated among plants on an equitable basis. These amounts are distributed to the workers as cash and/or deferred profit sharing. The division is determined by the board of directors.

Source: Reprinted by permission from *Constitution: Philosophy and Concepts of Human and Industrial Association in the Woodward Company,* rev. ed. (Rockford, Ill.: Woodward Governor Co., June 1978), pp. 7–8.

Employee Stock Ownership Plans

An employee stock ownership plan (ESOP) provides employees an opportunity to become shareholders in the company that employs them. Of course, employees can always buy stock in the stock market; but ESOPs create additional incentives by providing discount prices on shares or by matching employees' payments for stock. These plans provide a method, not necessarily related to profits, for employee participation in ownership.

The motivation for introducing an ESOP is similar to that for introducing profit sharing—to create a sense of common identity and purpose among employers and employees. These plans provide sources of funds that in some cases have helped employees retain their jobs in economically troubled companies. Employees have expressed some reservations about ESOPs, because they expose the employees to a double risk when the company has economic difficulty. The employees may lose not only their jobs but also the assets they have invested in company stock shares.[21]

ESOPs are similar to traditional stock bonus plans; however, they require that investments be made in the employer's stock, while stock bonus plans allow investments in others' stock. All distributions to employees must be made in the form of stock and must not be based on profits. ESOPs require the employer to make contributions to qualified tax exempt trust funds on behalf of employees for the purchase of the stock. The ESOP is a legitimate business expense for the employer; and the employee does not pay tax on the employer's payment into the fund until he or she receives the stock. ESOPs have become increasingly popular; it was estimated that there were 423 such plans in 1977 and as many as 5,000 in 1982.[22]

Some ESOPs have been extended to a point where the trust fund owns the company. Since the early 1970s, an estimated fifty companies that were facing extinction were bought by employees using loans, government assistance, and their ESOPs. The federal government has encouraged these takeovers, because they save federal payments in unemployment compensation, food stamps, and welfare outlays while preserving the tax base and the welfare of the local community.

While there has not been a thorough evaluation of employee-owned companies, the present assessment seems mixed.

The record of plants bought by their employees with government help has been mixed. Some have been profitable, others have lost money; some have shown productivity gains, others have not. In few, if any, has the vibrant glow of co-ownership transformed the shop floor into a showcase of participatory democracy. And profitability has often had little or no connection with the form of ownership.[23]

Administering the Wage and Salary System

After the basic wage and salary system has been designed, attention turns to its administration, which includes five important activities:

1. Adjusting wages and salaries.
2. Keeping the system up to date.
3. Communicating information about compensation policies and plans.
4. Dealing with pay inequities.
5. Controlling labor costs.

Adjusting Wages and Salaries

Usually wages and salaries are adjusted at some predetermined point during a fiscal year. While in the past, nearly all these adjustments have been increases, recently employees at well-known companies such as Chrysler, Ford, Uniroyal, and Firestone have made wage concessions or have postponed cost-of-living increases. When wages are adjusted upward, the adjustments are usually based on four types of increases: (a) a general increase given to all employees, (b) merit increases paid to employees in relation to some measure of job performance, (c) a cost-of-living adjustment (COLA) based on the consumer price index (CPI), and (d) an increase based on longevity or seniority. Exhibit 11.2 displays the frequency of use of the various forms of increases for various employee groups. Exhibit 11.3 shows the frequency with which general increases are made.

Merit Increases Merit increases present special problems. Organizations that attempt to administer a merit system usually establish guides for merit increase decisions. Exhibit 11.4 shows how a merit increase range can be related to levels of performance. Exhibit 11.5 relates individual performance to organizational performance to determine merit increases. It is important to recognize that merit increases

---

Exhibit 11.2   **Frequency of Use of Four Types of Pay Increases in 1979**

Employee Group	Number of Companies	Type of Increase (Percent)			
		General	Merit	COLA	Longevity
Hourly Union Employees	159	93%	7%	50%	31%
Hourly Nonunion Employees	173	74	39	17	25
Nonexempt Salaried Employees	198	29	96	12	8
Exempt Salaried Employees	208	19	99	10	1
Top Management	207	11	98	3	1

Source: Adapted by permission from Charles A. Peck, *Compensating Salaried Employees during Inflation: General vs. Merit Increases* (New York: Conference Board, 1981), p. 9. Also see a similar study by the staff of the Bureau of National Affairs: *Wage and Salary Administration* (Washington, D.C.: Bureau of National Affairs, 1981), p. 9.

Exhibit 11.3

Frequency of General Wage Increases

Employee Group	Number of Companies	Frequency of Adjustment (Percent)		
		Once a Year	Two or More Times a Year	After More Than a Year
Hourly: Union	217	49%	34%	17%
Hourly: Nonunion	231	37	25	39
Nonexempt Salaried	272	15	18	66
Exempt Salaried	249	11	12	78
Officers	155	13	5	83

Source: Adapted by permission from David A. Weeks, *Compensating Employees: Lessons of the 1970's* (New York: Conference Board, 1976), p. 33.

do not reflect performance exclusively; the organization must be able to pay the amount that will compensate employees for their merit. On the other hand, when performance declines, employees' pay is rarely reduced. In fact, in actual practice, companies tend to dismiss poor performers rather than reduce their pay.[24]

Pay increases are considered important organizational rewards. Thus, a pay increase should be large enough to be meaningful; but just how large an increase should be is a difficult question.[25] Research has indicated that the individual employee's values and perceptions of pay help provide the answer. For instance, if pay is important to the employee and if pay increases are related to successful performance, a pay increase will be meaningful and will provide a positive motivational impact. Also, if the pay level (as determined by effort, training, and experience) and the pay increase are reasonably close to the employee's own assessment of where he or she should be in the pay structure, the employee will be satisfied with his or her pay.[26] (It may

Exhibit 11.4

Example of Performance Levels Related to Merit Increase Ranges

		Merit Increase Range (Percentage)
	Outstanding	10 to 12%
	Very Satisfactory	7 1/2 to 10%
Employee's Performance Is	Satisfactory	5 to 7 1/2%
	Marginally Satisfactory	3 to 5%, Not to Exceed Midpoint of Range
	Unsatisfactory	None

Source: Courtesy of Hay Associates, New York City. Published in Charles A. Peck, *Compensating Salaried Employees during Inflation: General vs. Merit Increases* (New York: Conference Board, 1981), p. 17.

Exhibit 11.5	**Example of a Matrix Method for Determining Individual Incentive Awards**

Organization Performance (Percent of Goal Reached)	Rating: Score:	Individual Performance and Incentive Award (As a Percent of Salary)				
		Poor Below 80	Marginal 80–90	Good 90–100	Superior 110–130	Outstanding Over 130
80		0	5	20	30	60
90		0	10	25	40	80
100 (Target)		0	15	30	50	100
110		0	20	35	60	120
120		0	25	40	70	140

Source: Adapted, by permission of the publisher, from "Individual Performance in Incentive Compensation," by F. Dean Hildebrandt, Jr., *Compensation Review* Third Quarter 1978, © 1978 by AMACOM, a division of American Management Associations, p. 31. All rights reserved.

be that a person, given a range of job choices, selects the organization that has a compensation system congruent with his or her needs.[27])

Although the merit principle is widely held in industry, one executive has claimed that "the way many merit pay programs are structured, they neither adequately reward meritorious performance or motivate people to perform well.[28] A study of large nonunion firms revealed that "it is probably fair to say that the merit principle . . . results in nearly everyone moving in an automatic or nearly automatic manner to the top step."[29] Thus, nearly all employees eventually reach the top step of their pay range if they perform well enough to keep their jobs.

Supervisors usually claim they want a pay system that allows them considerable discretion; however, discretion often is not used when it is available. Supervisors tend to treat all employees the same and try to give them as much of a wage increase as they can. This behavior is understandable, because supervisors have to live with employees on a daily basis. Explaining pay differentials based on performance is difficult and often results in arguments, hard feelings, and grievances. Such problems are especially acute when performance measures are not objective or when inflation rates exceed wage increases. In cases where the organization cannot afford a general increase but allows only merit increases, the supervisor often avoids conflicts by giving increases based less on performance than on seniority, automatic progression, and equal treatment. Still, higher performers may receive recognition in other ways: greater promotional opportunities, better and more interesting assignments, and praise from supervisors.[30]

Keeping the System Up to Date

An important requirement of an effective wage and salary system is to keep the system current. Regardless of how well the system is designed, it must be continuously evaluated, updated, and adjusted.

Wage surveys should be administered at least once a year to make sure that external equity is maintained. A mechanism must be built into the procedure to advise job analysts and compensation specialists of job content changes, so that the jobs can be analyzed and reevaluated. If reorganization or any realignment of reporting procedures that might affect job duties and responsibilities occurs, the jobs affected must be studied again.

Most large organizations take advantage of computerized payrolls and human resource information systems to monitor their compensation programs. Reports can be obtained by organization units; positions; salaries; performance levels; dates of last increase; and compa-ratios, which are employees' actual salaries divided by the midpoint of the salary range. For example, a compa-ratio of 80 indicates a salary at the lowest end of the salary range; a ratio of 100, a salary at the midpoint; and a ratio of 120, a salary at the high end (see Exhibit 11.6).

In view of these problems, the personnel department has an opportunity to help the organization by fostering the pay-for-performance concept through training and design of performance measures. By objectively defining performance measures and training supervisors in performance appraisal, the personnel department can ensure that the purposes of the merit pay plan will be achieved. Training in performance feedback, goal setting, and handling grievances also will help reduce some of the problems that arise in wage administration. Compa-ratio reports are valuable tools in keeping the system up-to-date. For example, when the average compa-ratio is substantially higher than 100, the compensation specialist should determine whether an increase in the midpoints of the wage ranges (and the wage curve) is appropriate. Exhibit 11.7 demonstrates how such adjustments help maintain the currency of the system. The only difference between the two tables in the exhibit is in the columns showing the midpoints of the salary levels and the compa-ratios. The changes keep the midpoints from being too high.[31]

Communicating Information about Compensation Policies and Plans

Communication about compensation is based on the premise that employees want to know how they are paid and why they are paid as they are. As one personnel executive said:

Employees do want to know that there is a logical system in establishing the relative worth of their position and that they are being paid for performance. Whether publishing all salaries on the bulletin board would motivate superior effort is debatable. Not establishing credibility for your salary system through good communication, however, is the pitfall that demotivates.[32]

The basic objective of compensation communication is to increase employees' awareness that the organization seeks to create internal

Exhibit 11.6   **Computerized Compensation Report**

COMPA-RATIO REPORT

INTERNATIONAL MULTIFOODS CORPORATION

SALARY REPORT PAGE

JOB TITLE	NAME	HIRE DATE	BIRTH DATE	LAST INCR DATE	AMT	SALARY	C	SALARY RANGE MINIMUM	MID-POINT	MAXIMUM	COMPA RATIO	HAY PTS
DIRECTOR OF MARKETING	HANSON, ANNE T.	06 25 69	02 36	03 81	4 100	36 700		30 400	38 000	45 600	97	750
MARKETING MGR - SPECIAL PRODUCTS	O'CONNOR, TIMOTHY S.	05 01 76	01 44	01 81	2 400	26 100		22 500	28 100	33 700	93	523
MARKETING MGR - BROKER/DISTRIBUTOR	SIMPKINS, JOHN Q.	03 25 73	07 40	10 80	2 500	28 500		22 500	28 100	33 700	102	523
MARKETING ASSISTANT	CYZMZEWSKY, JAN O.	10 15 80	12 54			19 500		18 000	22 500	27 000	87	290
SECRETARY	SCHUMACHER, PHYLLIS L.	06 12 79	04 56	06 81	75	1 050	6	900	1 060	1 250	99	

THE COMPA-RATIO FIGURE SHOWN IN THE RIGHT HAND COLUMN IS THE RATIO OF
THE EMPLOYEE'S CURRENT BASE SALARY TO THE MIDPOINT OF THE SALARY RANGE.

DEPARTMENT: Marketing
LOCATION: Lewiston
DIVISION: Industrial Products
DATA AS OF: 6/1/81
COPIES TO: PQT, IFG, ABL

Source: Courtesy of International Multifoods Corporation, Minneapolis, Minnesota.

equity, ensure external competitiveness, and reward individual performance. Organizations can accomplish these objectives by:

Writing down and communicating the company's compensation philosophy and policies.

Telling employees how salary actions consistently and equitably reflect that philosophy and those policies.

Find out what employees need to know and what they simply want to know out of curiosity.

Train supervisors in compensation-related subjects.

Communicate to each employee what percentage of his or her pay increase is based on merit and what percentage is based on other factors, such as seniority, cost of living, and so on.

Exhibit 11.7   **Salaries before and after Adjustment**

Before Adjustment

Name	Title	Current Salary	Performance Level	Midpoint	Compa-Ratio	Date of Last Increase
Atkinson	Office Manager	$20,400	3	$16,000	127.5	12/82
Fulgham	Account Executive	22,000	4	17,200	129.9	9/81
Jackson	Credit Manager	20,800	2	16,000	130.0	5/80
Spelling	Programmer	16,200	4	14,200	114.1	9/81

After 25-Percent Increase in Midpoint of Salary Ranges

Name	Title	Current Salary	Performance Level	Midpoint	Compa-Ratio	Date of Last Increase
Atkinson	Office Manager	$20,400	3	$20,000	102.0	12/82
Fulgham	Account Executive	22,000	4	21,500	102.3	9/81
Jackson	Credit Manager	20,800	2	20,000	104.0	5/80
Spelling	Programmer	16,200	4	17,750	91.3	9/81

Establish a vehicle (such as a company newsletter) to answer frequently asked questions about compensation matters.

In years past, disclosure of wage and salary information was considered unwise. Managerial objections went something like this: "Most employees can't begin to understand the complexity of a modern salary administration program, so why start something you can't finish?"[33] On the other hand, the purpose of communicating compensation matters is not to make compensation experts of employees; the "purpose is to stimulate positive employee feelings that management's approach to salary administration is rational, fair, and systematic."[34]

Dealing with Pay Inequities

Pay inequities exist when an employee perceives that he or she is not receiving the amount of pay deserved, regardless of the reason. For an organization, the question is not whether inequities exist but rather how extensive they are and what is being done about them. While there are numerous inequity problems, one of the most common is wage compression.

Wage compression is a continuing decline in the wage differential between more highly valued jobs, such as electrician, and jobs of lower value such as assembly worker. It is usually caused by a higher percentage wage increase at lower-level positions than at higher-level positions. Wage compression occurs in situations such as the following: (a) minimum wages are increased for entry-level jobs, but a comparable increase is not given other hourly employees; (b) unions negotiate a 10-percent increase for their members, but supervisors and employees not represented by the union do not receive a comparable adjustment; (c) new employees (from other firms or college graduates) start at salary levels equal to those of employees in comparable positions with several years' experience.[35] Problem (a) above resulted from legislation; problem (b) from wage negotiations, and problem (c) from labor market forces. While the logical solution is to give wage increases to all deserving employees in order to maintain an equitable differential, the reality is that frequently the organization does not possess the financial resources to implement such a solution.

As indicated by problem (c) above, labor market conditions cause real, as well as perceived, inequities. When a job evaluation study assigns a job to a specific grade based on compensable factors, its purpose is to achieve internal equity. However, when a wage survey is conducted and it is determined that the assigned wage is out of line with the market wage, the company may face problems of turnover and inability to recruit employees who can get better pay elsewhere. What often has occurred in such situations is that labor market forces of supply and demand have resulted in a few skills' being in short supply relative to the demand for them; consequently, the wage rates for people with these skills have been bid upward beyond the rate determined on the basis of job evaluation and internal equity. This type of problem is very visible on college campuses, as witnessed by the wide differential between salaries of faculty members who teach business, engineering, law, or medicine and those of faculty members who teach English or history.

Usually, shortages correct themselves over a longer period of time, because school counselors direct students toward fields of study in high demand. If a sufficient number pursue such careers, a surplus may be created after a few years. However, the compensation specialists have to deal with the problem in the present time by explaining the predicament to employees and working with recruiters to resolve the problem.[36]

Two compensation specialists have suggested ways to deal with the wage compression problem:

The only solution to compression that has ever worked will have to be applied and that is paying more at certain levels of the organization to relieve compression and maintain motivation.[37]

I think salary compression has become a way of life. The thing we have to do is communicate this fact to our people so they understand that their perception that salary differentials are becoming smaller is correct, and that this is because of societal changes that we are all going to have to live with.[38]

Controlling Labor Costs

Control of labor costs occurs at three levels of management. First, the level of wages and benefits is primarily controlled by top management through policy and budgets. Second, control of the wage and salary structure (to preserve internal and external equity) is usually delegated to compensation specialists or shared with industrial engineering in cases where wage incentives are used. Third, control of individual wage and salary rates is usually delegated to the individual manager, who makes decisions within established guidelines.

Control of labor costs can be exercised in various ways; however, four common ways are:

1. *Approval* Compensation decisions must receive approval from top management, a compensation review committee, or staff specialists before being finalized.
2. *Budgetary controls* Limits in total payrolls for organization units are set, and decisions must conform with this budget.
3. *Statistical controls* Controls are developed from reports on relationships of payroll to other organizational indexes—such as sales, output, and indirect labor—and historical statistical reports showing trends and relationships over time.
4. *Influence* Decisions are made according to carefully developed policies and procedures known and understood by managers who are informed, trained, and accountable.[39]

Role of the Personnel Department and Other Managers in the Compensation System

Members of the personnel staff and other management representatives share key roles in wage and salary administration. Personnel representatives usually are responsible for designing the wage and salary system and maintaining its currency. These responsibilities include the preliminary steps of performing job analysis, writing job descriptions, and determining job specifications. With the assistance of other managers, the personnel department will choose one of the job evaluation systems and determine the monetary value for each job. In this phase, personnel representatives conduct the wage survey and handle the mechanics of pricing the wage and salary structure. In addition, personnel representatives usually write the first draft of the statement of program objectives, policies regarding wage and salary adjustments, and procedures for maintaining the system. Once top management has approved the objectives, policies, and procedures, the personnel department administers the program. In day-to-day activities, personnel representatives help other managers carry out compensation-related tasks; they also monitor the system to assure that the objectives are achieved and the policies and procedures followed.

Compensation activities provide significant potential for the personnel function to contribute to organizational effectiveness. As one personnel executive has explained:

I think our role as compensation or personnel executives is changing. Now, and in the future, we will need to design systems and tools for management. Approaches to establishing objectives, measuring performance against objectives, and planning compensation will have to be designed for management's use more effectively than we have done in the past. The other great challenge is that once we have these tools—good, practical tools—we will have to communicate the results of their use to our employees. . . . We must all work to avoid having an employee for whom we have high hopes for the future walk in one day and say, "I have found a more promising position with another company." If that happens, our effectiveness as compensation executives will have gone down the drain because we didn't communicate effectively. I think we have to try to do a better job of communicating inside the organization, to our line managers and employees.[40]

Other manager's, too, have responsibilities that greatly affect the overall wage and salary program. First, a representative group of managers is needed in the initial wage-determining process, because these managers know about the jobs in their departments. While the personnel staff conducts the job analysis and writes the job descriptions and specifications, other managers must be involved throughout, because they are most familiar with the activities in their departments. Other management officials have a critical role in keeping the system up-to-date. Since line management has authority to change job content, line managers must notify the compensation specialist of any such changes so that job descriptions and specifications can be adjusted. Where the job content undergoes a major change, the wage rate may also be adjusted. Other managers are instrumental in determining the merit increases of employees under their supervision. The supervisors observe behaviors and performance on a daily basis; therefore, they should be the ones who make decisions about pay raises, within the guidelines established by top management. Finally, management officials throughout the organization help to determine whether the objectives of the wage and salary system are being achieved and, if not, what should be done to achieve these objectives. They can observe the effects of pay levels, incentives, general increases, benefits, profit sharing, or any other elements in the compensation package; thus they represent valuable resources in building and maintaining a dynamic compensation program.

Issue:	## Should Salaries Be Secret or Open?

A controversial issue in the compensation field is the subject of secrecy. In only 25 percent of 183 companies surveyed by the Bureau of National Affairs did managers have a general knowledge of the salaries of other managers at their own or higher levels. Sixty-two percent of these companies made available information on salary ranges, but not on individual salaries.[41] Several reasons are offered for organizations' preferences for secrecy in pay policies. First, one's salary is considered a personal matter that should not be disclosed to others. Second, secrecy in pay prevents much quibbling among managers, who might spend too much time making salary comparisons with other managers. Third, in situations where salaries are extremely competitive, it may be difficult to explain and justify salary differentials.[42] Last, in some organizations, in which inequities exist for many reasons, such as favoritism and poor administration, openness would cause havoc among employees.

E. E. Lawler conducted several studies on the effects of secrecy in pay plans in private and public organizations.[43] His results showed that managers generally did not have a clear picture of what other managers in their organizations earn; thus, the policy of secrecy was working. However, his studies revealed some important perceptions about pay. First, managers underestimated the pay of their superiors. Second, they overestimated the pay of their subordinates. Third, they overestimated the pay of managers at their own level.

These findings, then, revealed that managers had inaccurate pictures of what others earned. They felt their own pay was too close to that of their superiors and subordinates. Part of their dissatisfaction with pay can be explained by the unfavorable comparison of their own pay to what they perceived that others made. Thus, one effect of secrecy in pay policies is to increase dissatisfaction with pay.

Another aspect of secrecy involves performance feedback and rewards. Where secrecy exists, managers tend to overestimate the average size of the raise given to their peers. Thus, each manager's raise seems smaller by comparison than it actually is; and high-performing managers get the impression that superiors evaluated their performance more negatively than they actually did. This misperception has a negative effect on motivation.

Often, managers use secrecy to avoid giving subordinates accurate evaluations of their performance. For example, a manager who wants to avoid an unpleasant task can capitalize on the secrecy policy and tell each employee that he or she has been given as large a raise as possible and that each employee's performance has been satisfactory. The supervisor has rewarded good performance with high pay and has not caused any unhappiness among poor performers. However, the good performer cannot be sure that he or she is being rewarded, because no comparison between his or her reward can be made with the rewards of others; thus, the potential to reinforce high performance with pay is reduced. The poor performer, on the other hand, believes that he or she has been rewarded for the type of performance that has been demonstrated; thus, poor performance is reinforced. Eventually, of course, rumors will spread about the amounts of all employees' raises. The end result will be dissatisfaction and lack of trust in superiors from both high performers and poor performers.

When asked about the secrecy issue, Lawler, who has become the leading advocate of an open pay policy, replied:

I think that a high level of openness about how pay is determined, about what people are paid, about how their performance is measured, and about the outcomes of those measures is a necessary condition for a highly productive work group. Now that is not to say you have to make each individual's salary public. But what I would say is that if you aren't going to make the details of your pay programs public, you ought to realize that you are losing motivational power. The reason for that is basically that in order for pay to be an incentive at any level of the organization, people have to see the relationship between their performance and their pay, and they have to trust the organization will reward them if they perform well.

Based on all the research that I have done, and all that I have read, I am forced to conclude that you do not build trust, you do not build a clear perception of the relationship between performance and pay, by keeping it a secret. Secrecy destroys trust, openness builds it. When all is said and done, I think secrecy about pay serves mainly the needs of the people who are making the pay decisions: Secrecy protects them from getting into uncomfortable interpersonal situations in which they will have to justify their decisions to the people who are subject to them. With openness, they are asked to be accountable for their decisions.[44]

While the research suggests that openness will produce greater satisfaction and make pay a more effective motivator, the transformation from secrecy to openness can create problems. Openness may be very threatening to low-salaried managers. Disclosure will inform others that these managers' salaries are low and consequently that their services are not valued highly by upper management. Openness may alert some managers to the fact that they are underpaid, whereas under secrecy, they may have been satisfied with their pay. This problem is particularly likely to occur in organizations suffering from internal inequities and inconsistencies in the pay system. Openness may also disclose that the overall salary structure is low in comparison with comparable firms. This lack of external equity may lead to dissatisfaction and turnover. Moving from secrecy to open-ness may cause employees to become dissatisfied with their performance ratings and with the rating supervisor. Under the open system, not only will the employee know the evaluations and salary increases, but others in the organization will know them as well. This will increase pressure on supervisors.[45] Finally, openness may cause supervisors to deviate from the practice of making raises contingent on performance to avoid unpleasant-ness in future interactions with those who would receive low salary in-creases under such a system. Supervisors may inadvertently try to avoid conflict by averaging out performance appraisals as well as salary in-creases.[46]

While the issue of secrecy versus openness in compensation administra-tion will be debated for some time, the appropriate answer will depend on the organization, its past practices, its employees, and its organizational climate. Behavioral science research can help identify the organizations in which open pay policies could enhance job satisfaction, motivation, and productivity; however, wholesale adoption will be very slow in coming. A gradual approach, starting with the release of pay ranges and median sal-aries, is the recommended first step.[47] More importantly, setting the orga-nization's house in order—providing internal and external equity, assuring valid and objective performance appraisal, and training supervisors in compensation administration and performance appraisal—is a fundamen-tal prerequisite.

Summary

Organizations attempt to relate pay to performance by using incentive plans. Based on certain preconditions, such as employees' believing that higher pay and pay's being important to the individual employee, organizations design incentive plans to meet their established objec-tives. These plans may include individual piecework rates, a standard hour plan, or various combinations. Under certain circumstances, such as when the company wants to emphasize teamwork and cooperation, group incentive plans may be designed. Executive incentives may be tied more closely to profits and performance objectives; salespersons may be paid on a commission basis or may receive bonuses. In organi-zations with incentive plans, various combinations of plans for differ-ent types of employees may be used.

The administration of the wage and salary system includes five im-portant areas: adjusting wages and salaries, keeping the system up to date, communicating information about the system, dealing with pay inequities, and controlling labor costs. Wage adjustment activities may include making general, merit, longevity, and cost-of-living ad-justments. The system must be kept up to date, and information about policies and plans must be communicated so that employees will be informed of how they are paid and how the system works. Dealing with pay inequities includes the difficult task of attempting to deal with wage compression problems. Labor costs can be controlled in various ways; four common methods involve approval for wage changes, budgets for salary limits, statistical reports for analysis, and influence of top management.

The personnel department and other managers in the organization share the responsibilities involved in dealing with compensation matters. A controversial issue in compensation policy is whether pay should be secret or open.

Discussion Questions

1. Evaluate unions' arguments against wage incentives.

2. Why do companies find it so difficult to design and administer merit pay plans and other pay-for-performance policies?

3. Why might the Scanlon Plan seem so attractive to employees?

4. Would the Lincoln Electric Plan be successful in an organization with which you are familiar?

5. What are the advantages and disadvantages of profit-sharing plans?

6. Since employees already have the option of buying stock in the company that employs them, why are ESOPs attractive?

7. If a company has a secret pay plan and wants to move to an open system, what must it do first?

Notes

1. David W. Belcher, "Wage and Salary Administration," in *Motivation and Commitment,* ed. Dale Yoder and H. G. Heneman, Jr. (Washington, D.C.: Bureau of National Affairs, 1975), p. 6-110.
2. *Ibid.,* p. 6-112.
3. Bureau of Labor Statistics, *Major Collective Bargaining Agreements: Wage-Incentives, Production-Standards, and Time-Study Provisions* (Washington, D.C.: Government Printing Office, 1979), p. 3.
4. Herbert G. Zollitsch, "Productivity, Time Study, and Incentive-Pay Plans," in *Motivation and Commitment,* ed. Dale Yoder and H. G. Heneman, Jr. (Washington, D.C.: Bureau of National Affairs, 1975), p. 16–63; Norma W. Carlson, "Time Rates Tighten Their Grip on Manufacturing Industries," *Monthly Labor Review* 105 (May 1982), pp. 15–17.
5. Bureau of Labor Statistics, *Major Collective Bargaining Agreements,* p. 3.
6. Belcher, "Wage and Salary Administration," pp. 6-112–6-114.
7. Charles W. Brennan, *Wage Administration* (Homewood, Ill.: Richard D. Irwin, 1963), pp. 54–56.
8. David Kraus, "Executive Pay: Ripe for Reform?" *Harvard Business Review* 58 (September/October 1980), pp. 42–44.
9. "A Clearer Look at Executives' Pay," *Business Week,* September 15, 1980, p. 46.
10. John Curley, "More Executive Bonus Plans Tied to Company Earnings, Sales Goals," *Wall Street Journal,* November 20, 1980, p. 29.
11. *Ibid.*
12. John Perlman, "Payoff in Performance Bonuses," *Dun's Review* 103 (May 1974), p. 55.
13. Robert Sibson, *Compensation* (New York: AMACOM, American Management Associations, 1974), pp. 139–150.
14. Carl F. Frost, "The Scanlon Plan: Anyone for Free Enterprise?" *MSU Business Topics* 28 (Winter 1978), p. 26.

15. J. Kenneth White, "The Scanlon Plan: Causes and Correlates of Success," *Academy of Management Journal* 22 (June 1979), pp. 310–312.

16. *The Lincoln Electric Company Incentive Management System* (Cleveland, Ohio: The Lincoln Electric Company 1981), pp. 1–6.

17. Geoffrey W. Latta, *Profit Sharing, Employee Stock Ownership,, Savings, and Asset Formation Plans in the Western World* (Philadelphia: Industrial Research Unit, University of Pennsylvania, 1979), pp. 2–5.

18. Zollitsch, "Productivity, Time Study, and Incentive-Pay Plans," p. 6-67.

19. Latta, *Profit Sharing,* p. 11.

20. *Ibid.,* p. 19.

21. *Ibid.,* pp. 6–7

22. Irwin Ross, "What Happens When the Employees Buy the Company," *Fortune,* June 2, 1980, p. 109; "ESOPs: Taking Stock," in *Bulletin to Management* (Washington, D.C.: Bureau of National Affairs, 1982), p. 8.

23. Ross, "What Happens When the Employees Buy the Company."

24. Charles A. Peck, *Compensating Salaried Employees during Inflation: General vs. Merit Increases* (New York: Conference Board, 1981), p. 14.

25. Linda A. Krefting and Thomas A. Mahoney, "Determining the Size of a Meaningful Pay Increase," *Industrial Relations* 16 (February 1977), p. 83.

26. Lee Dyer, Donald P. Schwab, and Roland D. Theriault, "Managerial Perceptions Regarding Salary Increase Criteria," *Personnel Psychology* 29 (Summer 1976), pp. 233–242.

27. Linda A. Krefting, "Difference in Orientations toward Pay Increases," *Industrial Relations* 19 (Winter 1980), pp. 85–86.

28. Myles H. Goldberg, "Another Look at Merit Pay Programs," *Compensation Review* 9 (3d quarter 1977), p. 20.

29. Fred K. Foulkes, *Personnel Policies in Large Non-Union Companies* (Englewood Cliffs, N.J.: Prentice-Hall, 1980), p. 179.

30. *Ibid.,* pp. 183–189.

31. Richard Traum and Russel C. Buzby, "Using the Computer to Monitor a Salary Program: A Case Study History," *Compensation Review* 7 (1st quarter 1975), pp. 39–45.

32. William R. Marshall, *Administering the Company Personnel Function* (Englewood Cliffs, N.J.: Prentice-Hall, 1976), p. 138.

33. Bruce R. Ellig, "Pay Inequities: How Many Exist within Your Organization?" *Compensation Review* 12 (3d quarter 1980), pp. 42–43.

34. "Emerging Problems in Administering Management Compensation Programs . . . A Compensation Review Symposium," *Compensation Review* 9 (2d quarter 1977), p. 58.

35. *Ibid.*

36. David W. Belcher, *Compensation Administration* (Englewood Cliffs, N.J.: Prentice-Hall, 1974), pp. 574–581; Ellig, "Pay Inequities," p. 39.

37. "Emerging Problems in Administering Management Compensation Programs," p. 50.

38. *Ibid.*

39. Belcher, "Wage and Salary Administration," p. 6-120.

40. Statement by Jeremiah Reen, director of Compensation and Benefits, GTE International, in group discussion in "Emerging Problems in Administering Management Compensation Programs . . . A Compensation Review Symposium," *Compensation Review,* Second Quarter 1977 (New York, AMACOM, a division of American Management Associations, 1977) p. 58.

41. Staff of Bureau of National Affairs, *Wage and Salary Administration* (Washington, D.C.: Bureau of National Affairs, 1981), p. 23.

42. Mary G. Miner, "Pay Policies: Secret or Open? And Why," *Personnel Journal* 53 (February 1974), pp. 110–115.

43. Edward E. Lawler III, "The Mythology of Management Compensation," *California Management Review* 9 (Fall 1966), pp. 11–22; E. E. Lawler III, "Secrecy and the Need to Know," in *Managerial Motivation and Compensation,* ed. H. L. Tosi, Robert House, and Marvin D. Dunnette (East Lansing: Michigan State University, 1972), pp. 455–496.

44. "Administering Pay Programs . . . An Interview with Edward E. Lawler III," *Compensation Review,* First Quarter 1977 (New York: AMACOM, a division of American Management Associations, 1977), pp. 13–14.

45. Charles M. Futrell and Omer C. Jenkins, "Pay Secrecy versus Pay Disclosure for Salesmen: A Longitudinal Study," *Journal of Marketing Research* 15 (May 1978), pp. 214–219.

46. Robert Peters and Robert Atkin, "The Effect of Open Pay Systems in Allocations of Salary Increases," in *Academy of Management Proceedings,* ed. R. C. Huseman (Athens, Ga.: University of Georgia, 1980), pp. 293–297.

47. Miner, "Pay Policies," pp. 110–115.

Chapter 12   Employee Benefits

Both employers and unions acknowledge that the average
employee usually does not fully appreciate the value of the
benefits he receives over and above what he sees in his pay
envelope. Both are on the alert for ways in which to bring home to
the employee the value of these benefits, which usually are so
substantial today as to make the term "fringe" benefits a
misnomer.

Staff of Bureau of National Affairs, *Bulletin to Management* (Washington, D.C.: Bureau of National Affairs, January 7, 1971).

The relationship between employees' benefits and wages is both close and complicated. Employers place limits on total compensation costs (direct wages plus benefits); therefore, a large wage increase will probably restrain the amount of increase in benefits, and vice-versa. Yet no clear-cut method has been agreed upon for distinguishing between various wage payments and benefits. Chapters 10 and 11 discussed two forms of wage payments— direct pay for time worked and incentive wages related to productivity and profits. This chapter will discuss the remaining financial payments received by employees.

First discussed are the extent, objectives, and types of employee benefits in industry. Next, benefits are placed into four general categories—payment for time not worked; health and welfare benefits; retirement benefits; and miscellaneous services. Since employee benefits can be costly, the chapter's issue concerns the effectiveness of benefits in accomplishing organizational objectives.

Extent, Objectives, and Types of Employee Benefits

Exhibit 12.1 illustrates the tremendous increase in employer-paid benefits over the past twenty years. A comparison between figures reported by 186 companies in 1959 and 1980 reveals that benefit dollars per year per employee have increased by 600 percent. Also increasing at a steady pace is the proportion of benefit costs to total payroll costs. Simply put, employee benefits have increased faster than wages and currently, on the average, represent 40 percent of payroll costs.[1]

Exhibit 12.1	Comparison of Employee Benefits in 1959 and 1980 for 186 Companies											
Item	1959	1961	1963	1965	1967	1969	1971	1973	1975	1977	1979	1980
All Industries (182 Companies)												
1. As Percent of Payroll, Total	24.7	26.6	27.4	27.7	29.2	31.1	33.1	35.3	37.9	40.0	41.3	41.4
a. Legally Required Payments (Employer's Share Only)	3.5	4.0	4.5	4.2	4.9	5.3	5.6	6.6	7.0	7.6	8.1	8.1
b. Pension, Insurance, and Other Agreed-upon Payments (Employer's Share Only)	8.5	8.9	9.1	9.4	9.7	10.4	11.5	12.2	13.4	14.5	15.1	15.2
c. Paid Rest Periods, Lunch Periods, etc.	2.2	2.6	2.6	2.6	2.9	3.1	3.2	3.3	3.8	3.8	3.8	3.8
d. Payments for Time Not Worked	8.4	8.9	9.1	9.3	9.5	10.1	10.6	10.8	11.3	11.6	11.8	11.9
e. Profit-Sharing Payments, Bonuses, etc.	2.1	2.2	2.1	2.2	2.2	2.2	2.2	2.4	2.4	2.5	2.5	2.4
2. As Cents per Payroll Hour	62.0	70.8	79.2	85.9	100.6	118.4	141.4	174.0	219.7	260.4	330.6	355.2
3. As Dollars per Year per Employee	1,282	1,461	1,637	1,782	2,084	2,467	2,927	3,640	4,553	5,368	6,871	7,633

Source: Reprinted by permission from *Policies and Practices: Personnel Management* (January 1982), p. 267:188, copyright 1982 by The Bureau of National Affairs, Inc., Washington, D.C.

Exhibit 12.2   **Benefit Program Objectives**

Objective[a]	Actual Rank	Mean Ranking[b]	Frequency Cited as #1 Objective
Attract Good Employees	1	2.4	152 (48%)[c]
Increase Employee Morale	2	3.8	35 (11%)
Reduce Turnover	3	3.9	32 (10%)
Increase Job Satisfaction	4	4.3	37 (12%)
Motivate Employees	5	4.5	19 (6%)
Enhance Organization's Image among Employees	6	5.0	23 (7%)
Better Use of Compensation Dollars[d]	7	5.2	28 (9%)
Keep the Union out	8	5.9	13 (5%)

[a]Two other objectives mentioned by respondents were: (1) maintaining a favorable position in relation to competitors (N = 12) and (2) enhancing employee security (N = 10).
[b]For instance, "attract good employees" was chosen as the number one goal by 152 respondents, but because many others ranked it lower than number one, the *mean* ranking was 2.4, making it the most prevalent.
[c]These are the percentages of the entire sample (N = 354) which ranked a particular goal number one.
[d]This objective refers to an organization's "saving" money by taking advantage of group-funding mechanisms and tax-savings provisions of the IRS code.

Source: Richard C. Huseman, John D. Hatfield, and Russell W. Driver, "Getting Your Benefit Programs Understood and Appreciated," *Personnel Journal* 57 (October 1978), p. 562. Reprinted with the permission of Personnel Journal, Costa Mesa, California; all rights reserved.

Some of this cost is due to legally required benefits, which have slowly but steadily increased over the twenty-year period. There is no doubt that benefit policies are influenced by government legislation and regulations.[2] Yet, employers cannot currently contend that government policies are responsible for organizations' total benefit expenses. Exhibit 12.1 indicates that government requirements accounted for only 20 percent of employer's benefit expenses in 1980.

Thus, we must assume that benefits serve organizational objectives; or they would not be voluntarily assumed by employers. Employee benefits are commonly instituted to accomplish various organizational goals, as illustrated in Exhibit 12.2. The objectives cited in the exhibit are universal, although some companies might structure benefit programs according to their unique market situations. One author has suggested that entrepreneurial and growth companies may emphasize direct pay instead of benefits, while stable or stagnant companies are likely to have a compensation program oriented toward security-type benefit plans.[3] Few benefits are paid by all organizations; Exhibit 12.3 shows the distribution of benefits among companies found in one study.

Compounding the differences in benefit plans are the almost unlimited number of benefits that can be selected. This situation is illustrated in Exhibit 12.4, which illustrates the variety of benefits found in one company, and Exhibit 12.5, which lists some of the more unusual benefits offered by various companies in the United States.

Exhibit 12.3   **Percent of Companies Paying Employee Benefits, 1980**

Type of Benefit	Percent of Surveyed Companies Having Benefit
1. Legally required payments (employer's share only):	
a. Old-Age, Survivors, Disability, and Health Insurance (FICA taxes)	100%
b. Unemployment Compensation	98
c. Workers' compensation (including estimated cost of self-insured)	96
d. Railroad Retirement Tax, Railroad Unemployment and Cash Sickness Insurance, state sickness benefits insurance, etc.	9
2. Pension, insurance, and other agreed-upon payments (employer's share only):	
a. Pension plan premium and pension payments not covered by insurance-type plan (net)	87
b. Life insurance premiums, death benefits; hospital surgical, medical and major medical insurance premiums, etc. (net)	100
c. Short-term disability	40
d. Salary continuation or long-term disability	46
e. Dental insurance premiums	44
f. Discounts on goods and services purchased from company by employees	18
g. Employee meals furnished by company	21
h. Miscellaneous payments (compensation payments in excess of legal requirements, separation or termination pay allowances, moving expenses, etc.	24
3. Paid rest periods, lunch periods, wash-up time, travel time, clothes-change time, get-ready time, etc.	80
4. Payments for time not worked:	
a. Paid vacations and payments in lieu of vacation	97
b. Payments for holidays not worked	96
c. Paid sick leave	80
d. Payments for State or National Guard duty; jury, witness, and voting pay allowances; payments for time lost due to death in family or other personal reasons, etc.	73
5. Other items:	
a. Profit-sharing payments	22
b. Contributions to employee thrift plans	22
c. Christmas or other special bonuses, service awards, suggestion awards, etc.	48
d. Employee education expenditures (tuition refunds, etc.)	51
e. Special wage payments ordered by courts, payments to union stewards, etc.	30

Note: N = 983 employers.

Source: Reprinted by permission from *Policies and Practices: Personnel Management* (January 1982), 267:183, copyright 1982 by The Bureau of National Affairs, Inc., Washington, D.C.

Exhibit 12.4   **Illustration of the Variety of Benefits Found in One Organization**

Source: Reprinted by permission from *Bulletin to Management*, January 7, 1971, copyright 1971 by The Bureau of National Affairs, Inc., Washington, D.C.

All these benefits can be grouped into four general categories: *payment for time not worked, health and welfare benefits, retirement benefits, and miscellaneous services*. In the following sections, each of these categories will be briefly described and representative benefits will be discussed to illustrate related issues and problems.

Payment for Time Not Worked

Holidays

One current survey found that a large majority of companies allow ten or more paid holidays.[4] Several holidays are observed by most companies; they include New Year's Day, Memorial Day, Independence Day, Labor Day, Thanksgiving, and Christmas. Some companies also offer paid holidays applicable to their particular regions—for example, Patriots' Day, observed in Massachusetts, or Mardi Gras, observed in the New Orleans area.

Administrative problems can occur in the process of determining which holidays should be observed and scheduling work during holidays. An increasingly popular practice is to give employees a number

Exhibit 12.5	**Examples of Unusual Benefits Offered by Various Companies**

Employees are given first chance to buy company used cars (Allison Division, General Motors).

Dogwood trees are sold to employees for 25 cents each (Goodyear Tire and Rubber Company).

City employees are allowed to use city equipment to plow driveways on their own time (Bath, Maine).

Readers' Digest editors receive one-week, all-expense-paid trip anywhere in the United States to help them generate story ideas.

Employees receive subsidized college course on how to be better parents (New England Life Insurance Company).

Postage for letters from employees to their congresspersons is paid by the company (United Life Insurance).

Male and female employees are eligible for up to two years' (mostly unpaid) child-rearing leave (U.S. Labor Department).

Dog training programs are set up for employees' dogs (Goodyear Aircraft Corporation).

World Series scoreboards are placed in centrally located positions (General Electric Company).

Free transportation to polls is provided on election day (Kentucky Utilities Company).

Free carpeting was given to company's flood disaster victims (Thermoid Company).

Source: Information obtained from the following sources: J. H. Foegen, "The Next Employee Benefit— Grand Paternity Leave?" *Human Resource Management* 19 (Fall 1980), p. 25; J. H. Foegen, "Employee Benefits: Imagination Unlimited," *Labor Law Journal* 29 (January 1978), p. 38; Bureau of National Affairs, *Personnel Policies and Practices,* no. 439, p. 245:137; and "Labor Letters," *Wall Street Journal,* September 13, 1977, p. 1; October 28, 1980, p. 1; and December 23, 1980, p. 1.

of *floating holidays;* here, the employee selects several days to be used as paid holidays. One analyst believes that "one reason companies have gone to floating holidays is because the logical ones are pretty well used up."[5] This practice also considers employees' unique preferences. Some may wish to take a holiday for religious or ethnic observances (Yom Kippur, Martin Luther King's death, and so forth), while others may wish to celebrate their own birthdays or anniversaries.

The number of paid holidays tends to increase each year, a situation that can cause serious work scheduling problems for companies that require continuous operations (a steel mill or a public utility, for example). In these companies, employees typically work during holidays at a premium rate (usually two and one-half times their hourly rate including holiday pay). Thus, holidays are thought of as premium pay days instead of days away from the workplace.

Vacations

The existence of employee vacations has remained fairly consistent over the past thirty years; for example, one study has found that since

1949, approximately ninety-three percent of the negotiated labor agreements have provided for vacations.[6] Currently, most companies provide the following:

Two weeks of vacation after one year's service.

Three weeks of vacation after two year's service.

A maximum of five weeks of vacation after thirty years' service.[7]

In general, U.S. companies appear to lag behind some of their European counterparts, whose governments (with the exception of the United Kingdom) establish the legal minimum for vacation length. In no case is the legal minimum less than two weeks a year. Poland's employees typically receive a month's paid vacation after a few years' service, and West Germany's employees are usually paid more money when they are on vacation to cover extra travel and lodging expenses.[8]

Vacation policies often are related to the perceived costs and benefits of vacations to the company. Obviously, paid vacations cost the company money, such as wages paid to the vacationing employee and premium pay for vacation replacements. Some believe that these costs contribute to inflation, which hurts companies, employees, and consumers alike.[9]

A contradictory view finds vacations essential to increased productivity and employees' well-being. Vacations, in this view, are a primary mechanism for relaxation, which in turn should help in the "restoration and recuperation of mind and body."[10] However, some employees, particularly at the managerial level, are reluctant to take vacations that would require their being away from work for extended periods of time. They might feel guilty about leaving unfinished work behind or apprehensive that their work cannot be performed—or can be too easily performed—by others in their absence. Vacation anxieties over facing new experiences, conflicts, and pleasures might even exist.[11] Therefore, even if vacations offer employees the potential for self development, some employees might not automatically benefit from a vacation.

One survey of over 10,000 individuals revealed several interesting attitudes concerning vacations, including the following:

Few underwent remarkable transformations while on vacation. For example, workaholics only transferred their compulsions to a new locale; they brought their briefcases along in order to catch up.

Forty-six percent of the respondents believed they received exactly as much vacation as they deserved; 42 percent believed they deserved more.

People with six weeks off were less bored with work.

Eleven percent of the respondents said they often felt depressed after vacations.

Physical and mental tensions (anxiety, digestive problems, headaches, fatigue, irritability, and so forth) were substantially reduced when respondents were on their vacations.[12]

Paid Leaves

Companies grant a variety of paid leaves, such as leaves for jury duty, funerals of relatives, educational activities, and maternity. One highly publicized paid leave is the *sabbatical,* which gained popularity after the United Steelworkers Union negotiated such a leave into many of its labor agreements in 1963. Sabbaticals differ from vacations in that they are usually much longer (ranging from several months to a year) and are not given to all employees. Eligibility is often based on length of service or the intended purpose of the sabbatical.

The sabbatical is intended to allow one to broaden one's horizons or to carry out some worthwhile project such as writing a book or heading up a community building campaign.[13] The major purpose of a sabbatical is self-development, a need well articulated by a prominent industrial executive:

[Typical successful business persons] will probably have read their last poem when they leave college. There will be no creation of art that will move them to tears. There will be no shocking condition in the world or tragic event that can cause consuming anger in them or raise genuine righteous indignation. . . . Their capacity to feel will be slowly extinguished and only the appetites will remain.[14]

A successful sabbatical can result in better job adjustment in at least two ways. First, some employees might realize through the sabbatical that they have chosen the wrong occupation or career and make appropriate adjustments within or outside the company. Second, other employees might return from their sabbaticals with better knowledge of themselves and a new perspective on their work and colleagues.[15] Sabbaticals also force organizations to promote subordinates or seek outside replacements for those on leave. An organization cannot afford to rely totally on any employee; therefore, sabbaticals encourage needed employee planning and development.[16]

At first glance, you might assume the sabbatical would be eagerly accepted by employees and employers; however, this is not always the case. One survey found that some 45 percent of 272 firms had some type of formal or informal sabbatical program.[17] However, some executives believe that sabbaticals reduce managerial control; for example, one executive has said that "when people discover how neat it is to sit back and relax, they might have a lethargy syndrome or lack of enthusiasm upon return to work."[18] Even IBM, probably the industrial leader in number of sabbaticals given employees, does not publicize this benefit in its recruiting efforts.

Many employees are reluctant to accept sabbaticals because of job insecurities (such as a fear of being permanently replaced while on sabbatical) and uncertainty over what to do with a large block of unstructured time.[19] These apprehensions can be reduced by administrative policies. First, sabbaticals' purposes can be defined. Some sabbaticals are totally unstructured; for example, one executive used his sabbatical to play all of the world's most famous golf courses.[20] However, most companies prefer structured sabbaticals that relate to or extend the employee's job expertise, such as sabbaticals used to achieve more formal education or perform a social service. Xerox Corporation, for example, encourages social service sabbaticals for such diverse projects as "rehabilitation of alcoholics, training parents and teachers of migrant children, serving aboard the S.S. Hope, or helping to save water-threatened art and architecture in Venice."[21]

Employees who take sabbaticals also need some form of guarantee that their career won't be jeopardized. Xerox, for example, indicates in its sabbatical program that "the returning employee is guaranteed either the same job or one that offers the same pay, responsibility, status, and opportunity for advancement.[22]

Health and Welfare Benefits

A wide variety of benefits could be included in this category. However, this section focuses on two representative areas: (1) employee benefits pertaining specifically to health and (2) workers' compensation programs.

Health Insurance: Rationale and Alternatives

Health insurance has often been controversial; presidents of the United States and presidential candidates have debated it.[23] Few can argue, however, that health costs have soared in recent years; and a substantial portion of the expenses have been absorbed by employers. Health care costs increased 157 percent nationally for companies from 1970 to 1978, a year when employers paid about $42 billion on group health insurance premiums and $12.6 billion in workers' compensation expenses.[24] Major employers' price tags for medical expenses will represent at least 11 percent of payroll costs by 1990.[25] Placing this situation in another perspective, General Motors currently spends far more on health care than on steel or rubber.[26] There are several reasons for increased health costs. One reason is that new and expensive hospital equipment must continually be purchased. The health care industry has undergone tremendous—and costly—technological change. For example, just five pieces of mandatory hospital equipment cost approximately $2 million, and equipment for intensive-care and cardiac-care units currently averages $100,000 per bed.[27]

A second reason for increasing cost is that the health care industry determines to a large extent its own supply, demand, and prices.[28] There are relatively few incentives for cost reduction, since in many cases, doctors are paid on a fee service basis, hospitals are reimbursed for costs, and consumers have most of their medical expenses paid by insurance.[29]

A third significant cost factor is the extensiveness of employer-paid health coverage. A major survey conducted by the Department of Labor found that nearly 70 percent of all private-sector employees were covered by some form of sponsored insurance plan. Health insurance that paid at least a portion of hospital and surgical expenses was included in 97 percent of the sponsored plans; disability benefits were included in 36 percent, and short-term disability benefits in 21 percent.[30] The number of U.S. workers covered by private dental plans rose from 2 million in 1965 to 70 million in 1980.[31]

Companies have reduced health insurance costs through several innovative practices.[32] Some companies sponsor physical fitness programs or pay employees for practices such as losing weight or quitting smoking.[33] Other programs screen employees for potential or existing health problems such as high blood pressure.[34] An example of an extensive health screening program is found at Control Data Corporation, whose employees receive an individualized and confidential health risk profile based on a questionnaire, medical history, and blood tests. This profile is computer-analyzed and compared against health risks for the population as a whole to determine the specific above-average risks that each individual will face in the next ten years. The employee is offered a choice of activities, such as education and exercise, to reduce this risk.[35]

Another health insurance innovation is the *health maintenance organization* (HMO), which is usually run by a group of doctors located at one facility. Patients pay a flat annual fee in advance to cover the cost of subsequent care, which is available twenty-four hours a day, seven days a week. Currently, there are nearly 240 HMOs in the United States, nearly a third of them in California. Employers providing employee health insurance were legally required by the 1973 HMO Act to offer employees the choice of an HMO where one existed.[36]

Since there are many locations without HMOs, many employers are not involved with this innovation. However, some companies, notably R. J. Reynolds, Deere & Company, and Gillette, have actively initiated HMOs and have been rewarded by subsequent health cost reductions. HMOs' emphasis on preventive health care has in some cases dramatically reduced the number of days employees have had to spend in a hospital.[37] The presence of an HMO in a community also tends to lower the fees charged by other doctors in the area.[38] Further, HMO patients, when compared with the general public, appear to be more pleased with their health care service.[39]

HMOs are not always successful, however. They require sound management techniques and an adequate number of patients who are educated and enthusiastic about their potential benefits.[40] This last requirement is not easily met, since employees accustomed to their existing health insurance often see little reason for change. Some even believe that HMOs smack of socialized medicine.[41]

Workers' Compensation

Prior to 1911, employees were seldom able to receive financial compensation for injuries caused by industrial accidents. Employees seeking legal redress for their injuries ran into one or more of the following employers' legal defenses.

1. *Contributory negligence.* If the worker, even in a minor way, contributed to the injury through negligence, he or she could not collect.
2. *The fellow-servant doctrine.* The injured employee could not collect if a fellow worker's negligence contributed to the injury.
3. *Assumption of risk.* If the injury was caused by an inherent hazard of the worker's occupation and if the worker could be expected to know of the hazard, he or she could not recover. Under the law, the worker had knowingly assumed the risks of the occupation.[42]

New Jersey passed the first workers' compensation law in 1911, and many other states quickly adopted similar legislation. The general goals of most such programs are tied to the following benefits for injured employees.

Medical payments. In the large majority of states, all medical payments arising from work-related accidents are made by the employer or the employer's insurance carrier.

Temporary total disability payments. Temporary total disability payments are given to injured employees who do not work while recovering from their injuries. Most states require a waiting period (3.7 days average) before employees are eligible for the funds, which in many cases amount to two-thirds of lost wages.

Permanent total disability payments. Most state plans furnish compensation payments for life to employees who can no longer work because of an on-the-job injury.

Death payments. The dependents of an employee killed in a work-related accident receive compensation that in a majority of states is not subject to time limits as long as legal dependency continues.

Permanent partial disability payments. An employee receives permanent partial disability payments when a work-related accident results in the loss or loss of use of part of the body. Payments are based on a schedule that states how many weeks of compensation are due given the extent of the injury. These payments represent a large portion of total workers' compensation expenses and in almost all states are made whether or not the employee suffers income loss results from the accident.[43]

The preceding description of workers' compensation benefits is very general. Coverage, procedures, and payments vary widely among state plans: "For example, in 1980, payments for the loss of an arm varied from $6,750 in Massachusetts to $105,957 in Illinois.[44] This variation has produced extensive controversy, and attempts have been made over the years to standardize state workers' compensation plans under federal legislation.[45] Controversy notwithstanding, workers' compensation costs have increased over the years for employers, some much more than others.

Workers comp is the nation's second largest insurance expense. It now costs the average employer $2.70 for every $100 paid in salaries, compared with $1.10 in 1970. High risk industries have an even more acute problem. In mining, for instance, rates are as high as $60 for every $100 in wages.[46]

Retirement Benefits

Many benefits can enhance an employee's retirement income. Two major retirement benefits will be discussed here: social security and private-sector pension plans.

Social Security

The Social Security Act of 1935 has provided financial assistance to individuals in a variety of situations, although the most publicized pertains to retirement income.[47] Indeed, a major role of social security is to help the elderly, who are restricted from improving their retirement situations in a number of ways—physically, by the job market, and by uncertainty about the future. No major changes have been made in the content of the programs since 1935; "policy makers have confined themselves to tinkering with benefit and payroll tax levels."[48]

Financing social security benefits typically falls equally on employers and employees; each makes a payroll tax payment identical to the other's. From 1937, when these payments were first collected, through 1977, a total of $743 billion was collected in contributions and interest; and $707 billion was paid out in benefits and administrative expenses,

Exhibit 12.6

**Effect of 1977 Amendments Concerning
Social Security Payment Changes**

	Maximum Annual Pay Which Is Taxable	Tax Rate	Maximum Tax (Both employees and employers pay this amount.)	Increase from Previous Social Security Tax Schedule
1977	$16,500	5.85%	$ 965.25	—
1978	$17,700	6.05%	$1,070.85	—
1979	$22,900	6.13%	$1,403.77	$ 260.32
1980	$25,900	6.13%	$1,587.67	$ 353.47
1981	$29,700	6.65%	$1,975.05	$ 595.35
1982	$32,400	6.70%	$2,170.80	$ 696.60
1983	$34,800	6.70%	$2,331.60	$ 762.90
1984	$37,200	6.70%	$2,492.40	$ 810.30
1985	$39,900	7.05%	$2,812.95	$1,017.45
1986	$42,600	7.15%	$3,045.90	$1,072.20
1987	$45,600	7.15%	$3,260.40	$1,151.25

Source: Barnet N. Berin, "From the Pony Express to the Pension Express," *Across the Board,* June 1978, p. 46. Updated by the author. Used by permission of The Conference Board and the author.

leaving a balance of less than $40 billion in the trust funds at the end of December 1977.[49] This situation prompted Congress to increase the social security tax payments made by employers and employees. Exhibit 12.6 indicates the effect of the 1977 social security revisions.

The figures presented in the exhibit are of real concern to employers and employees, since each group makes identical social security payments. Even greater concern is focused on the future stability and financing of social security, which is complicated and unpredictable.[50] One almost certain prediction is that funding costs will increase. In 1980, the combined social security payments of employers and employees represented slightly over 12 percent of taxable payroll; conservative estimates place this figure at nearly 17 percent in 2010 and 25 percent in 2030.[51] A major reason for increased costs is that the ratio of active employees to retired workers has been reduced over the years. In 1940, when the first social security pension checks were received, 35 million taxpayers contributed to social security, and benefits went to 222,000 individuals—a ratio of 150 workers to 1 retiree. This ratio had dropped to 14 to 1 in 1950, 5 to 1 in 1960, and almost 3 to 1 in 1980.[52] Additional complications can occur when unemployment reduces the number of individuals paying social security taxes and when increased life spans extend the period during which people receive social security payments.

Controversy over the purpose, fairness, and administration of social security programs will likely increase over the years.[53] Employers and employees will be financially affected by related decisions.

Pensions

Private and public pension plans apply to many employees and retirees.[54] Pension plans have been fairly common since 1935 and have grown substantially during the years following World War II.[55] Unfortunately, the history of pensions has often been accompanied by frustration and loss among employees. For example, in 1964 Studebaker closed its automobile facility in South Bend, Indiana, and terminated its pension plan. According to pension standards at that time, the company made every fair and reasonable effort to divide its remaining pension fund assets among its employees. However, some 4,000 employees between the ages of forty and sixty received only 15 percent of their vested benefits; and nearly 3,000 Studebaker employees under the age of forty received nothing at all.[56]

Studebaker's experience was not unique; indeed, all private-sector pension plans before 1974 had at least the potential for serious problems, as described below:

No government regulation requires an employer to contribute enough money to cover all claims. Nor is there any guarantee that your employer will continue to fund the pension plan at all. Except under certain union-negotiated plans, employers usually reserve the right to alter, modify, or terminate the plan at any time. Another clause in the pension contract may give the employer the right to suspend, reduce, or discontinue contributions at any time—if business is falling off, for example, or if profits are down. No government regulation requires an employer to continue a plan. All an employer is required to do is pay out all the funds to employees when the plan is terminated. An employer is not responsible for claims that cannot be met because the pension fund does not have enough money.

Furthermore, employees have little protection when their pension funds are lost or mismanaged.[57]

Thus, employees could not be guaranteed any pension benefits even though a pension plan was in effect and they contributed to it.

This situation was dramatically altered in 1974 with the passage of the Employee Retirement Income Security Act (ERISA), which applies to private-sector pension plans (federal, state, and local government pension plans are exempt from ERISA's provisions). ERISA was designed to protect "the interests of participants in employee benefit plans and their beneficiaries . . . by establishing standards of conduct, responsibility, and obligations for fiduciaries of employee benefit plans, and by providing for appropriate remedies, sanctions, and ready access to the Federal courts."[58] ERISA does not require employers to establish pension plans, but it affects pension plans under its coverage in the following ways:

It requires pension plans to offer liberal eligibility standards (membership at age twenty-five after only one year of service).

It requires fairly liberal standards for vesting pension rights (100 percent after ten years' of service), so that employees who leave their jobs will continue to be eligible for accumulated benefits. (Vesting will be explained later in the chapter.)

It requires employers to disclose the full details of pension plan operations, including investments, in periodic reports to federal authorities and to supply employees with full information on plan operations.

It requires periodic actuarial valuations of pension plan operations and the use of actuarially determined methods of funding past-service liabilities

It includes actuaries, consultants, investment managers, and plan administrators as fiduciaries with legally enforceable responsibilities to beneficiaries of pension plans.

It sets up a Pension Benefit Guaranty Corporation to insure plan members against losing their vested benefits if their plans are abandoned.

It revised the tax laws to encourage the self-employed and others not in pension plans to save for retirement.[59]

Since ERISA's passage, many employers have terminated their pension plans. By the end of 1978, a total of 23,756 termination notices had been filed; nearly one out of every four pension plans existing when ERISA was passed had been terminated.[60] This situation may have been caused by a number of circumstances:

Confusion among employers over ERISA, which was several hundred pages (some 75,000 words) in length.

Provisions that the Pension Benefit Guaranty Corporation would collect premiums from employers and could "slap a lien on an employer for up to 30 percent of the company's net worth in order to replenish the insurance fund."[61]

Several other ERISA regulations that affect pension plan administration.

This last reason is explained in the remaining discussion of pension plans' major components—eligibility, vesting, formulas, funding, and payments method. ERISA provisions and other legal considerations will be cited when appropriate.

Eligibility Eligibility provisions tell who can be covered by the pension plan. Before ERISA, many plans excluded employees hired after the age of fifty-five, the rationale's being that it took too much money to purchase retirement benefits for someone already so near retirement. Many other companies excluded younger employees, especially those under the age of thirty, and employees having only a few years' service with the company. Under ERISA, full-time employees who joined the firm between the ages of twenty-four and sixty and who have completed at least one year's service are eligible for the company's pension plan.

Vesting   Vesting provisions indicate when the people in the pension plan gain legal rights to their benefits. Employees who belong to the organization's pension plan will not receive their benefits if they leave the organization before their pensions are vested. Before ERISA's enactment, employers had a great deal of flexibility in determining vesting arrangements. Three general practices could occur:[62]

Stringent requirements could be placed on vesting (twenty-five years' service and retirement at age sixty-five could be required, for example).

Pension benefits could be *backloaded*—for example, a plan might credit a monthly pension benefit of $2 for each year of service up to age sixty and $30 for each year of service from ages sixty to sixty-five. This practice minimized the effects of vesting provisions; a fifty-five-year-old employee might be fully vested but receive minimal pension benefits.

An employee's vested privileges might be canceled if he or she violated competitive activity clauses (by setting up his or her own company or working for a competitor).

ERISA provisions have greatly reduced the employer's flexibility in establishing employees' pension vesting rights. Now, employer pension plans must follow one of the three following vesting schedules:

1. *Ten-year vesting.* 100 percent vesting is achieved after ten years' service.
2. *Graded vesting.* 25 percent vesting is achieved after five years' service. This percentage increases by 5 percent per year to 50 percent vesting after ten years' service and thereafter increases by 10 percent a year to 100 percent vesting five years later.
3. *Rule of forty-five.* Fifty percent vesting is achieved when a participant's age and years of service add up to forty-five. The percentage increases by 10 percent a year to 100 percent vesting five years later.[63]

ERISA has also placed severe limitations on backloading and has indicated that vested benefits are nonforfeitable, even if an employee violates a competitive activity agreement or is convicted of criminal conduct.

Formulas Pension formulas indicate how the retirement benefit is determined. The benefit is most commonly an annuity, or an income that starts when the employee retires and continues for the rest of the employee's life. The amount of pension benefits received by the employee usually is determined by the employee's earnings, length of service, or both. The employee's earnings can be determined in a variety of ways, such as the employee's average annual earnings over his or her career with the company, the employee's average earnings over the last five years of employment, or the employee's annual salary at the time of retirement. The proportion of earnings actually received in yearly pension benefit payments is usually adjusted by length of company service.

One benefits specialist estimates that a decent monthly pension should total 1.6% of your final monthly salary for each year of service. In other words, 30 years' service should give you a pension of 48% (30 multiplied by 1.6) of your last salary, plus Social Security benefits.[64]

Funding Funding pension plans can become quite complicated, particularly in terms of related ERISA provisions.[65] Consideration must be given to the way in which the pension plan will be funded and the length of time it will take for the plan's unfunded liabilities to be paid off. There are many things which can affect pension plan funding (sources of assets balanced by liability payments). Two of the most important factors are:

The typical increase in employees' salaries each year, which causes related increases in pension benefits.

The rate at which the pension plans' assets earn interest.

Pension plan funding is also affected by the proportions of employer and employee contributions. One recent survey found that nearly 80 percent of company pension plans were funded entirely by the employer, while the remainder were funded by some combination of employer and employee contributions.[66] Problems have sometimes occurred with relation to employees' contributions to pension plan funding. For example, some pension plans have required female employees to contribute more to pension funds than males. The practice was based on the rationale that females have a greater life expectancy and will receive more pension benefits. However, the Supreme Court held in 1978 that employers cannot require females to contribute more to pension funds than males.[67]

Payments Payment of pension benefits may at first glance appear to be a routine aspect of pension plan administration—the pension administrators simply send pension benefit checks to employees for a given period of time. However, as a rule, personnel activities are complicated, and pension plan payments are no exception. For example, the Supreme Court recently decided that the amount of pension payments due an employee can be reduced by the amount of compensation that the employee receives under state law as compensation for a disabling work-related injury or disease.[68] An increasing number of employers also find themselves in divorce court as the court determines whether the employee or the employee's former spouse should receive pension payments.

The problem stems from the growing realization by divorce lawyers that one of the richest assets a couple may have is the pension due the working member of the pair. More and more divorce settlements earmark a share for the nonworking member. And as [one] divorce lawyer points out: "The only way you can make such an arrangement is to make the employer a party to the litigation."[69]

Another payment consideration concerns how much of the pension benefits should be paid to employees at one time. ERISA provisions offer tax advantages to many employees who receive their pension benefits in one lump sum. Employers are naturally concerned about employees' receiving a single large pension settlement, particularly employees who are in poor health at retirement time. Managers fear that employees in poor health at retirement will ask for lump-sum settlements in order to safeguard their dependents. Companies often screen applicants to determine if lump-sum pension payments would be appropriate. "Texaco, for example, requires just two things of each applicant for a lump sum: a physician's certificate of good health and a letter from the applicant's accountant or attorney declaring that it is in the employee's best interest to receive a lump sum."[70]

Miscellaneous Services

Miscellaneous services represent a wide variety of employer-sponsored activities. Many of them can be categorized as social events, such as company sports leagues, dances, parties, and picnics. These occasions, while they may appear insignificant in terms of organizational efforts and objectives, can be important for the personnel representative:

1. These events can have a major impact on the personnel representative's reputation. Managers as well as academicians talk about employees' morale; however, they often define this concept differently. Many managers believe that a good

gauge of employee morale is how employees behave at a social event. Happy faces, excitement, employees at all organizational levels mingling with each other, employees staying late—all are measures of a successful social event, for which the personnel department will receive much of the credit. On the other hand, an event marked by boredom, low participation, and dissension might reflect negatively on the personnel department's abilities.

2. Planning and scheduling these events requires much more time and effort than other organizational members appreciate. Related activities include arranging for the facilities, mailing out invitations, receiving employee contributions for the facilities, determining which employees are eligible to participate, deciding how funds should be allocated between prizes and food and drinks, and so on.

These considerations and several others can be applied to the case entitled "Scheduling a Company Golf Tournament" at the end of Part 4.

Three other services that have received recent publicity are company day-care centers, legal aid, and employee assistance programs (employee assistance programs are discussed in Chapter 17).

Day-Care Centers Some companies have recently instituted corporate day-care centers for employees' preschool children during the work week. This is usually a far cheaper alternative than at-home babysitters or other day-care services, since the employer pays for at least a portion of the expenses. Corporate day-care centers have had mixed results. Having one may help recruit employees who have younger children, and it may reduce absenteeism. However, use of the day-care center may be limited if its location is inconvenient; and users may lose contact with their former babysitters and have to stay home when their children are sick. There is also some evidence to suggest that middle-level employees have little interest in this service. One researcher of women's benefits has commented, "The midlevel women who would have the most clout in pushing the company to start a center are old enough so that their children are in school."[71]

Legal Aid Widespread need exists for legal counseling in such areas as divorce, real estate, traffic violations, wills, taxes, consumer problems, and so forth. One author has suggested that "at least 140 million Americans are denied access to adequate legal services because of prohibitive costs and the very real difficulty of finding the 'right' lawyer at an affordable price."[72] Some community-based legal services have been offered in populated areas but are usually limited to those individuals with very low income levels; consequently, many employees are not eligible for them. Many such employees want employer-sponsored prepaid legal insurance plans.[73]

Increased interest, however, has not resulted in substantial employer involvement in this area. A recent survey found that only 6 of 672 responding companies had some type of sponsored legal service plan.[74] Evidently, employees' enthusiasm for this benefit is outweighed by its costs to the employer. It will be interesting to see if continued employee interest in legal aid will prompt employers to implement this benefit in the near future.

Issue:

How Can Employee Benefits Help Accomplish Organizational Objectives?

As previously mentioned, benefits are intended to serve several organizational objectives, including attracting, retaining, and motivating employees. Benefits also cost the company money, and personnel representatives as well as other managers should ask if benefits' expenses are justified in terms of organizational advantages. Unfortunately, research into the motivational impact of employee benefits has been relatively skimpy. However, empirical findings do suggest that:

Recent MBA graduates place benefits far behind other factors (opportunity for advancement, salary, geographic location, and so forth) in deciding which company they will join. This finding may be due to the fact that many MBA students are unaware of the tremendous cost implications of various benefits.[75]

Benefits appear to play a large role in retaining low-skilled manufacturing employees but a very small role in retaining professional and managerial employees.[76]

These findings, coupled with the little research available, suggest that personnel managers have little basis for believing that benefits accomplish organizational objectives. This issue, therefore, quickly turns to procedures management might take to ensure that benefits accomplish organizational objectives. Such procedures fall into three general and interrelated areas: determining appropriate benefits, communicating benefit programs to employees, and monitoring benefit plans to determine their cost-effectiveness.

In planning benefit programs, the firm should *avoid* three commonly used techniques:[77]

Basing the company's benefit package on those offered by competitors.

Determining the additional amount that the company can spend on benefits and simply ask for a package of benefit improvements that can be supported by the expenditure.

Relying on the opinion of a key organizational official (the president or a board member, for example).

These planning techniques seldom consider changing employee lifestyles or the unique benefits sometimes required and used by employees at a particular company.[78] However, designing and implementing employee-tailored benefit plans is far from easy. One design aid is employee input, an option organizations seldom use.[79] Surveys of employees, for example, can yield the following valuable information for the benefit planner:

A ranking of the relative importance of benefits to employees as a group and a similar ranking for individual categories of employees within the group.

Identification of the benefits most in need of improvement, in order of priority.

Identification of the new benefits most valued by employees, in order of merit.

Exposure of deficiencies in design, administration, and communication of benefit plans.

Cost-effective allocation of contributions through the determination of highly valued low-cost benefits and lesser-valued high-cost benefits.

Knowledge of whether employees would prefer a change in the relative proportions of direct compensation and benefits and, if so, in what direction and to what extent.[80]

There are problems with employee benefit surveys, particularly when they raise employees' expectations. Employees who do not see their preferences implemented by the company will likely view the survey as meaningless. Yet, aggregate employee responses in a particular company might suggest a unique benefit structure for that company. For example, benefit surveys conducted at two companies revealed opposite findings concerning employees' vacation preferences. Employees at one company had a strong negative reaction to more vacation and holiday time and appeared willing to give up some of this benefit for other forms of pay and benefits.[81] Employees at another company, however, strongly preferred increased vacation time over any other suggested benefit.[82]

Differences may also occur within a particular company. Some companies handle this situation by offering a *cafeteria* benefits program, which allows each employee some flexibility in selecting his or her benefits. To establish a cafeteria benefit plan, a firm carries out a complete costing of benefits, then establishes a benefit account for each employee based on his or her pro-rata share. If, for example, a company employing 100 people spent $100,000 a year on benefit costs, each employee's pro-rata share would be $1,000, which could be distributed over various benefit categories. When this approach issued, the number of employees electing each benefit option is fewer, making the underlying actuarial assumptions less favorable and the benefits more costly. However, the higher cost of a particular benefit is offset by the employee's ability to concentrate expenditures on those benefits regarded as most desirable.[83] The company might also modify this plan by requiring certain minimum amounts to be spent on certain benefits or by giving employees additional benefit credit for length of service in the organization.

The major advantage of cafeteria benefit plans is reflected in the experience of one company, American Can:

Young single employees take more time off. So do married women, who usually want the same number of vacation days as their husbands, who tend to have more time off because they have been working longer. Those with young families tend to choose more medical and life insurance coverage. Older employees are more concerned with savings, first for their children's education and later, as their children leave home, for their retirement.[84]

Employees under the cafeteria benefit program do not see their benefits go to waste, a situation that can occur when, for example, a husband and wife working for different companies pay double for the standard medical and insurance benefits but cannot collect twice.[85] This program, with its emphasis on choice, also enables employees to become knowledgeable about benefit costs and preferences, an awareness that could result in increased satisfaction and productivity.[86]

Promising as it may seem, the cafeteria benefit plan is an example of a personnel technique that inspires more discussion than implementation. One personnel consultant has noted that, while more than 150 articles have been written on this subject, very few major organizations currently implement such a plan.[87] TRW and Educational Testing Service, as well as Alaska's state employees, are currently under cafeteria benefit plans. Some managers are fearful of implementing this approach because of legal restrictions suggested by ERISA and Internal Revenue Service Codes.[88] Other managers believe that offering cafeteria benefits would result in an "administrative nightmare," since a company with 10,000 employees could conceivably have 10,000 different benefit plans. Another problem may arise because employees need to know benefits' costs to choose the ones they want, but employers need to know how many employees will choose each benefit to determine the benefits' costs. Further, this type of plan is limited to companies already having a fairly rich benefit program, because there must be sufficient benefits to be converted into options.[89] Also involved are communication difficulties which, as discussed below, are found to some extent in all benefit programs but which tend to be increased under a cafeteria plan.

Benefits, in order to attract, retain, and motivate employees, must be communicated to them.[90]

Far too many employees see only the net amount of their wages as all they have coming to them. In a period of high inflation, with un-

employment at unprecedented levels, how can they know they are more secure employed at one particular company rather than another if their employers do not engage in a sincere, on-going program of informing them of the many unseen benefits which are provided in their behalf? Many managers either do not know how to approach their employees with this information or they, too, are overlooking the importance of these benefits.[91]

The advantages of benefit communication are obvious; yet evidence suggests that organizations are not doing a very effective job in this area. One survey found that many employees were aware of only a small portion of their company's benefits, while another survey found that 90 percent of the companies surveyed spend less than $15 a year per employee on benefit communication activities.[92] These findings seem to support each other—an unfortunate situation, since (as Exhibit 12.1 showed) it is not unusual for employers to spend over $7,000 a year for each employee's benefit package. Benefit communication can take several forms. Perhaps most common are periodic statements indicating to the employee the dollar amount the organization paid for his or her benefit package.[93] However, more complicated communication efforts are sometimes needed. Such a situation is illustrated in Exhibit 12.7, a hypothetical response to an employee's question concerning benefit entitlements.

Finally, benefit programs can be made more effective if they are monitored for extent of use or, in some cases, abuse. For example, one benefit offered by nearly all large corporations is some form of college tuition reimbursement program for employees. However, one current survey estimates that only a very small number of eligible employees ever use the program.[94] Reviewing the use of this program might result in modifications (better publicity, for example) or in elimination if the benefit is deemed ineffective. Additional monitoring of benefit usage might also indicate that a disproportionate share of the benefits are used by marginal, or even poor, performers. If this is found to be the case, then appropriate adjustments could be made—tying benefits to hours worked or even to job performance, for example.[95]

Summary

Employee benefit costs have increased dramatically over the years. Some of this increase is due to inflation and legal requirements; however, employers are voluntarily assuming many employee benefit costs, presumably because employee benefits offer organizational advantages such as attracting good employees, increasing employees' morale, and reducing turnover.

The tremendous number of employee benefits can be grouped into four general categories: payment for time not worked, health and wel-

Exhibit 12.7   **Personnel Manager's Letter of Reply to an Employee's Benefit Inquiry**

Dear Confused Employee:

In response to your questions about an untimely death and the monies that would thereby be payable, I refer you to your Group Life Insurance booklet, your Pension Plan text, your Savings Plan booklet, your Voluntary Accident Insurance pamphlet, the Travel Accident Policy, our company Policy Manual, Section III: "Lump-sum Death Benefit," and the Social Security program, including supplements.

As for your personal benefits, I shall have to confine my answers to the prospect of your immediate demise, which takes into account that you are 39 years of age, have a wife who is now expecting, have 17 years of service and are earning $18,000 per year.

First, our group life insurance plan will pay $36,000 to your mother, who is still the named beneficiary under the plan. Unless you have assigned the policy, this amount will be subject to estate taxes. The state of your residence does not levy estate taxes on this benefit, so be sure you don't move to one that does or your wife may have to pay taxes on your mother's benefits.

Our Pension Plan will pay $7,230 to your wife, this being the total contribution you have made in the 14 years you have contributed to the plan since you first became eligible at age 25, plus interest at three percent. (Don't be alarmed at the three percent. The fund really does earn more than that to assure you a pension at retirement.)

If you could hang on for another five and a half months, you will have 15 years of service, and your wife will get a monthly pension income of 15 percent of your average final five years' pay, discounted 25 percent as though you had taken a joint and survivor option, or about $1,500 per year. This will be paid so long as she does not remarry. It is all right if she lives common law.

The government will also help by paying your wife a monthly Social Security benefit equal to three quarters of your primary insurance amount and when the child is born, he or she will be entitled to a benefit equal to 50 percent of your primary insurance amount. (See the attached calculation sheet for determining your primary insurance amount.)

We have covered most situations, so I will end now with the wish that if you must die, it should occur within the precise circumstances I have described otherwise I will have to start all over again.

(signed) Personnel Manager

Source: Carson E. Beadle, "Revitalizing Employee Benefit Programs," *Risk Management* 26 (November 1979), pp 64–66. Reprinted by permission from the November 1979 issue of Risk Management.

fare benefits, retirement benefits, and miscellaneous services. Payment for time not worked includes payments for holidays, vacations, and leaves such as sabbaticals. Each raises administrative issues, such as those involving number of paid holidays, length of vacations and paid leaves, purpose of sabbaticals, and eligibility.

Health care costs have increased 157 percent nationally for companies from 1970 to 1978, and one estimate indicates that major employers' price tags for medical expenses will represent at least 11 percent of payroll costs by 1990. Organizations have responded to this situation with some innovative practices, such as physical fitness and health screening programs and health maintenance organizations. State governments have instituted various workers' compensation programs, which typically provide medical payments to injured employees, temporary and permanent payments for total disabilities, payments to survivors, and permanent payments for partial disabilities.

Two major types of retirement benefits are social security and pensions. Both employers and employees contribute to social security through tax payments. The 1977 amendments concerning changes in social security payments increased the maximum possible tax payments for each year through 1987. Until 1974, private employer-sponsored pension plans were marked by uncertainty; employees could never be sure that they would eventually receive pensions, particularly if the company closed its production facilities. This situation was dramatically altered in 1974 with the passage of the Employee Retirement Income Security Act (ERISA), which applies to private-sector pension plans. ERISA, while it does not require employers to have pension plans, does strongly affect existing plans, since it liberalizes eligibility and vesting standards and requires employers to disclose full details of pension plan operations to federal authorities and employees. The Pension Benefit Guaranty Corporation, established under ERISA, ensures that employees will not lose their vested pension plan rights if the plans are abandoned.

Miscellaneous services include a wide variety of employer-sponsored activities, such as social events, day-care centers, and legal aid. These activities require considerable time of personnel representatives and can affect their reputations in the organization.

There has been little research to demonstrate whether employee benefits help accomplish organizational objectives. Communicating information about benefits to employees and offering cafeteria benefit plans may increase the effectiveness of the benefits. Also important are control mechanisms to determine the extent to which various benefits are being used (or, in some cases, abused) by employees.

Discussion Questions

1. Explain why holidays, vacations, sabbaticals, and cafeteria benefit plans often receive mixed reactions from employees and cause administrative difficulties for employers.

2. Discuss several reasons for increased health care costs and several innovative responses to this problem, including health maintenance organizations.

3. Discuss the following components of pension plans: eligibility, vesting, formula, funding, and payments. Indicate ERISA's influence when appropriate.

4. Explain possible organizational advantages of benefits. Then discuss difficulties employers face in determining whether these advantages have been achieved. Finally, suggest two ways in which organizations might improve the effectiveness of em-

ployee benefits, indicating related advantages and disadvantages.

5. Explain how company social functions (a Christmas party, for example) can affect the personnel representative.

Notes

1. It should be noted that this figure varies widely among the reporting companies.
2. See, for example, Patricia A. Dreyfus, "Benefits Are Better Than Ever," *Money* 10 (May 1981), p. 99; Edward E. Burrows, "Sex, Civil Rights, and Fringe Benefits," *Financial Executive* (June 1973), pp. 76–86; "Executive Prerequisites: The Impact of New Disclosure and Tax Rules," *Business Week,* April 3, 1978, pp. 103–105; Edward E. Scharff, "The Battle over Taxing Fringe Benefits," *Money* 7 (October 1978), pp. 52–55; Ernest Griffes, "Retirement Age Legislation," *Personnel Administration* 23 (August 1978), p. 14.
3. Niels H. Nielsen, "The Art of Compensation and Benefit Plan Design," *Compensation Review* 10 (Third Quarter 1978), pp. 53–56.
4. Bureau of National Affairs, *Compensation* (BNA Policy and Practice Series no. 837, 1981) p. 335:302.
5. "More Firms Giving Workers Voice in Holiday Schedules," *Industry Week,* April 12, 1976, p. 17.
6. John Zalusky, "Vacations–Holidays: Tools in Cutting Work Time," *American Federationist* 84 (February 1977), pp. 3–4.
7. "More Time Off . . . ," *New York Times,* May 25, 1980, section 3, p. 15.
8. Charles McLaughlin, "2 Weeks Aren't Enough," *New York Times,* September 1, 1980, p. 13.
9. See, for example, J. H. Foegen, "Time Off with Pay: An Illusive Reward," *Supervisory Management* 23 (June 1978), p. 29.
10. Arthur L. Svenson, "The Nine-Month Year," *S.A.M. Advanced Management Journal* 38 (July 1973), p. 24.
11. C. Richard Williams, "Are Vacations against Policy, or Does It Seem So?" *Advertising Age,* July 9, 1979, pp. 53–54.
12. Carin Rubenstein, "PT's Report on How Americans View Vacations," *Psychology Today* 13 (May 1980), pp. 62–66, 71–76.
13. Michael J. Ashby, "And in the Seventh Year Thou Shalt Rest," *C A Magazine* 112 (May 1979), p. 57.
14. The quotation is from Irwin Miller in Richard B. McAdoo, "Sabbaticals for Businessmen," *Harpers,* May 1962, p. 39, and was obtained from Angelos A. Tsaklanganos, "Sabbaticals for Executives," *Personnel Journal* 52 (May 1973), p. 365.
15. *Ibid.*
16. Ashby, "And in the Seventh Year," p. 58.
17. Jon M. Healy, "The Sabbatical—Executive Style," *Dun's* 103 (March 1974), p. 75.
18. Marilyn Much, "Few Firms Offer the Ultimate 'Perk,'" *Industry Week* November 13, 1978, p. 84.
19. For case studies of the problems faced by managers when they plan and take sabbaticals, see Robert A. Dods, "Is There a Sabbatical in Your Future," *Business Quarterly* 45 (Winter 1980), pp. 30–36; Eli Goldston, "Executive Sabbaticals: About to Take Off?" *Harvard Business Review* 51 (September/October 1973), pp. 57–68.
20. Healy, "The Sabbatical—Executive Style," p. 75.
21. *Ibid.,* p. 76.
22. Goldston, "Executive Sabbaticals," p. 60.
23. See, for example, "Cradle and Grave," *Economist,* June 23, 1979, pp. 63–64.
24. Bruce Jacobs, "Can Innovation Curb Health Care Costs?" *Industry Week,* September 1, 1980, p. 80.
25. Quentin I. Smith, "Health Care Coverage and Costs: A Major Challenge for Innovative Managers," *Management Review* 69 (December 1980), p. 38.
26. K. Per Larson, "Taking Action to Contain Health Care Costs, Part I," *Personnel Journal* 59 (August 1980), p. 640.
27. "Unhealthy Costs of Health," *Business Week,* September 4, 1978, p. 58.
28. Larson, "Taking Action," p. 64.
29. Alain C. Enthoven, "Consumer-Centered vs. Job-Centered Health Insurance," *Harvard Business Review* 57 (January/February 1979), p. 142.
30. *Personnel Management—Policies and Practices,* report bulletin 4 (Englewood Cliffs, N.J.: Prentice-Hall, August 3, 1981), p. 1. This nationwide survey covered 2,400 plans sponsored by employers, employee organizations, and union-management boards.

31. "Labor Letter," *Wall Street Journal,* June 10, 1980, p. 1; Bureau of National Affairs, *Daily Labor Report,* July 19, 1979, p. 3. For additional information on dental and vision plans, see Donald R. Bell, "Dental and Vision Care Benefits in Health Insurance Plans," *Monthly Labor Review* 103 (June 1980), pp. 22–26; and "Dental and Vision Care Benefits," *Personnel Journal* 59 (August 1980), pp. 677–681.

32. Joann S. Lublin, "Seeking a Cure: Companies Fight Back against Soaring Cost of Medical Coverage," *Wall Street Journal,* May 10, 1978, pp. 1, 23.

33. Robert Levy, "Fitness Fever," *Dun's Review* 116 (November 1980), p. 115; C. Higgens and B. Phillips, "Keeping Employees Well," *Management Review* 59 (December 1979), pp. 53, 55.

34. See, for example, George A. Zeppenfeldt and John Tuckman, "Hypertension Insurance: Screening Workers on the Job," *Risk Management* 27 (October 1980), pp. 72–74.

35. Putting a Lid on Corporate Health Care Costs," *Dun's Review* 116 (September 1980), p. 98.

36. For an overview of the rationale and implementation of this legislation, see James F. Doherty, "HMO's: The Road to Good Health Care," *American Federationist* 86 (June 1979), pp. 7–12.

37. For example, a typical group of 1,000 R. J. Reynolds employees under HMO plans spend only 436 days in the hospital on the average, compared with 900 days for the general population. K. Per Larson, "Taking Action to Contain Health Care Costs, Part II," *Personnel Journal* 59 (September 1980), p. 737.

38. "A Bright Prognosis for the Once-Frail HMOs," *Business Week,* October 27, 1980, p. 113.

39. Mary Zippo, "American Attitudes toward Health Maintenance Organizations," *Personnel* 58 (January/February 1981), p. 38.

40. For some administrative considerations relating to HMOs, see Edmund Faltermayer, "Where Doctors Scramble for Patients' Dollars," *Fortune,* November 6, 1978, pp. 114–120; Judson Goodway, "Rx Health Maintenance Organization," *Across the Board* 15 (December 1978), pp. 21–31.

41. "A Bright Prognosis," p. 113.

42. Nicholas Askounes Ashford, *Crisis in the Workplace: A Report to the Ford Foundation* (Cambridge: MIT Press, 1976), p. 388.

43. This description is slightly modified from that found in John E. Logan, "A Review of Recent Trends and Events in Workers' Compensation," *Business and Economic Review* 27 (April/May 1981), pp. 7–8.

44. *Ibid.*

45. See, for example, Albert Kutchins, "The Most Exclusive Remedy is No Remedy at All: Worker's Compensation for Occupational Diseases," *Labor Law Journal* 32 (April 1981), pp. 213–228; Robert J. Paul, "Workers' Compensation—an Adequate Employee Benefit?" *Academy of Management Review* 1 (October 1976), p. 114.

46. From advertisement by INA, *Wall Street Journal,* August 4, 1981, p. 11.

47. Related programs include retirement insurance; survivors' insurance; disability insurance; hospital and medical insurance for the aged and the disabled; black lung benefits; supplementary security income; unemployment insurance; and public assistance and welfare services.

48. W. Kip Viscusi and Richard Zeckhauser, "The Role of Social Security in Income Maintenance," in *The Crisis in Social Security: Problems and Prospects,* ed. Michael J. Boskin, (San Francisco: Institute for Contemporary Studies, 1977), p. 51. For a discussion of the origin of social security, see Roy Lubove, *The Struggle for Social Security, 1900–1935* (Cambridge: Harvard University Press, 1968).

49. Robert M. Ball, *Social Security Today and Tomorrow* (New York: Columbia University Press, 1978), p. 44.

50. For insights into financing considerations of social security, see A. Haeworth Robertson, "The Cost of Social Security: 1976–2050," *Industrial Management* 20 (January/February 1978), pp. 18–22; Ball, *Social Security Today and Tomorrow,* pp. 43–77.

51. A. F. Ehrbar, "How to Save Social Security," *Fortune,* August 25, 1980, p. 34.

52. "The Social Security Act—Then and Now," *Personnel* 56 (July/August 1979), p. 48.

53. For related controversial dimensions, see Rita Ricardo Campbell, "The Problems of Fairness," in *The Crisis in Social Security: Problems and Prospects,* ed. Michael J. Boskin (San Francisco: Institute for Contemporary Studies, 1977) pp. 125–145; Abraham Ellis, *The Social Security Fraud* (New Rochelle, N.Y.: Arlington House, 1971); A. Haeworth Robertson, "A Debate on Social Security, I," *Across the Board* 17 (June 1980), pp. 32–48; Henry Aaron, "A Debate on Social Security, II," *Across the Board* 17 (July 1980), pp. 22–29; William Flanagan, "How Uncle Screws Us All," *Esquire,* January 30, 1979, pp. 79–80.

54. In 1977, for example, about 48 million persons were covered by major private-sector pension plans, and about 15 million persons were covered by government pension plans. Barnet N. Berin, "From the Pony Express to the Pension Express," *Across the Board* 15 (June 1978), p. 43.

55. For example, "in 1940, some four million American workers were covered by private pen-

sion plans with assets totaling $2.4 billion. By 1960, those assets had grown to $52 billion, with more than 21 million participants." Harrison A. Williams, Jr., "Development of the New Pension Reform Laws," *Labor Law Journal* 26 (March 1975), p. 135.

56. James Gollin, *The Star Spangled Retirement Dream* (New York: Charles Scribners' Sons, 1981), pp. 140–141.

57. Ralph Nader and Kate Blackwell, *You and Your Pension* (New York: Grossman Publishers, 1973), pp. 9–10.

58. Bruce M. Scott, "How Will ERISA Affect Your Pension Plan?" *Personnel Journal* 56 (June 1977), p. 300.

59. Gollin, *Star Spangled,* pp. 140–141.

60. *Ibid.,* p. 152. See also Richard S. Soble, "Bankruptcy Claims of Multiemployer Pension Plans," *Labor Law Journal* 33 (January 1982), pp. 57–63.

61. Gollin, *Star Spangled,* p. 153. See also Raymond J. Donovan, "Effective Administration of ERISA, *Labor Law Journal* 33 (March 1982), pp. 131–136.

62. Jack L. Treynor, Patrick J. Regan, and William W. Priest, Jr., *The Financial Reality of Pension Funding under ERISA* (Homewood, Ill.: Dow Jones–Irwin, 1976), p. 9.

63. *Ibid.,* p. 98.

64. "Fringe Benefits and Inflation," *Business Week,* April 28, 1980, p. 130. See also Robert Frumkin and Donald Schmitt, "Pension Improvements since 1974 Reflect Inflation, New U.S. Law," *Monthly Labor Review* 102 (April 1979), pp. 32–37.

65. For a discussion of pension funding considerations, see Dan M. McGill and Donald S. Grubbs, Jr., *Fundamentals of Private Pensions* (Homewood, Ill.: Richard D. Irwin, 1979), pp. 239–321; C. L. Trowbridge and C. E. Farr, *The Theory and Practice of Pension Funding* (Homewood, Ill.: Richard D. Irwin, 1976).

66. *Pension Plans and the Impact of ERISA,* PPF survey no. 119, (Washington, D.C.: Bureau of National Affairs, October 1977), p. 4.

67. Roger B. Jacobs, "The *Manhart* Case: Sex-Based Differentials and the Application of Title VII to Pensions," *Labor Law Journal* 31 (April 1980), pp. 232–246. The case was *City of Los Angeles, Department of Water and Power v. Manhart.*

68. Bureau of National Affairs, *Daily Labor Report,* May 18, 1981, p. 1. The case was Alessi *v.* Raybestos-Manhatten, Inc.

69. "Pensions Land in Divorce Court," *Business Week,* November 7, 1977, p. 104.

70. John Perham, "The Dilemma over Lump-Sum Pensions," *Dun's Review* 117 (June 1981), p. 76.

71. Suzanne Seixas, "Fringe Benefits: Yours vs. the Best," *Money* 6 (July 1977), p. 38.

72. Stephen F. Gordon, "The Case for Company Sponsored Prepaid Legal Services," *Personnel Administrator* 25 (July 1980), p. 79.

73. For a discussion of the various types of legal aid plans and related constraints, see Guvenc G. Alpander and Jordan I. Kobritz "Prepaid Legal Services: An Emerging Fringe Benefit," *Industrial and Labor Relations Review* 31 (January 1978), pp. 172–182; R. A. Pitchford, "Prepaid Legal Services: A Case Study," *Risk Management* 27 (July 1980), p. 70.

74. Gordon, "The Case for Company Sponsored Legal Services," p. 80.

75. Richard D. Huseman, John D. Hatfield, and Richard B. Robinson, "The MBA and Fringe Benefits," *Personnel Administrator* 23 (July 1978), p. 58.

76. Vincent S. Flowers and Charles L. Hughes, "Why Employees Stay," *Harvard Business Review* 51 (July/August 1973), pp. 54–55. It should be noted, however, that some companies have implemented employee benefits (such as "money market" programs) that underwrite a portion of the company's operations. This benefit can offer direct financial advantages to the company. See, for example, Amanda Bennett, "Ford Offers Workers a Plan That Aids Firm," *Wall Street Journal,* March 29, 1982, pp. 21, 24.

77. Darrel J. Croot, "Employee Benefits—How Objectives Are Set and Achieved," *Financial Executive* 41 (October 1973), pp. 108–109.

78. See, for example, "New Benefits for New Lifestyles," *Business Week,* February 11, 1980, pp. 111–112.

79. One study, for example, found that only 29 percent of the surveyed companies formally provided for employee input into their benefit programs. Larger organizations were more likely than smaller organizations to follow this practice. H. Wayne Snider, "Employee Benefits Administration Examined," *Risk Management* 28 (January 1981), p. 32.

80. William L. White and James W. Becker, "Increasing the Motivational Impact of Employee Benefits," *Personnel* 57 (January/February 1980), p. 35.

81. Nielsen, "Art of Compensation and Benefit Plan Design," p. 55.

82. Vivian C. Pospisil, "Reshaping Employee Benefit Plans," *Industry Week,* April 5, 1975, p. 38.

83. William B. Werther, "Variable Benefits: A New Approach to Fringe Benefits," *Arizona Business* 22 (November 1975), p. 19.

84. Gerard Tavernier, "Pick and Choose . . . How American Can Manages Its Flexible Benefits Program," *Management Review* 69 (August 1980), p. 11.

85. John Perham, "New Life for Flexible Compensation," *Dun's Review* 112 (September 1978), p. 66.

86. Deborah Randolph, "More Workers Are Getting a Chance to Choose Benefits Cafeteria-Style," *Wall Street Journal,* July 14, 1981, p. 33.

87. David J. Thomsen, "Introducing Cafeteria Compensation in Your Company," *Personnel Journal* 56 (March 1977). This article also cites a representative sample of sources pertaining to cafeteria benefit plans.

88. For a further discussion of these legal considerations, see Robert W. Cooper, "Cafeteria Benefit Plans: The Revenue Act of 1978—the New Ground Rules and Some New Issues," *CLU Journal* 34 (April 1980), pp. 29–39.

89. "Companies Offer Benefits Cafeteria-Style," *Business Week,* November 13, 1978, p. 121.

90. S. Travis Pritchett, "Can Employee Benefits Also Be Employer Benefits?" *CLU Journal* 31 (April 1977), pp. 44–45.

91. Mathew W. Jewett, "Employee Benefits: The Need to Know," *Personnel Journal* 55 (January 1976), p. 18.

92. William H. Holley, Jr., and Earl Ingram, II, "Communicating Fringe Benefits," *Personnel Administrator* 18 (March/April 1973), p. 22; Richard C. Huseman, John D. Hatfield, and Russell W. Driver, "Getting Your Benefit Programs Understood and Appreciated," *Personnel Journal* 57 (October 1978), p. 563.

93. For related insights into benefit techniques, see Huseman, Hatfield, and Driver, "Getting Benefit Programs Understood"; Jeffrey C. Claypool and Joseph P. Cangemi, "The Annual Employee Earnings and Benefits Letter," *Personnel Journal* 25 (July 1980), pp. 563–565.

94. "Labor Letter," *Wall Street Journal,* August 12, 1980, p. 1. This survey estimated that of the 1.6 million eligible employees surveyed, only 4 percent of white-collar employees and 1 percent of blue-collar employees used the plan.

95. See, for example, various techniques discussed in the following articles: Clarence R. Deitsch and David A. Dilts, "To Cut Casual Absenteeism: Tie Benefits to Hours Worked," *Compensation Review,* 13 (First Quarter 1981) pp. 41–46; Edward A. Weinstein, "Vacation Pay: Theory vs. Practice," *CPA Journal* 49 (May 1979), pp. 35–39; Richard March Hoe, "Performance Based Employee Benefit Plans," *CLU Journal* 34 (January 1980), pp. 50–55; Patrick M. Towle, "Calculating Sick Leave and Vacation with an Hourly Accrual System," *Personnel Journal* 58 (May 1979), pp. 303–305.

. . . to assure so far as possible every working man and woman in the Nation safe and healthful working conditions and to preserve our human resources.

.

Preamble of the Occupational Safety and Health Act

Perhaps more than any other personnel concern, safety and health interest managers and employees alike. All want to work in a safe environment; accidents and health problems result in human as well as organizational costs. Having mutual safety and health objectives does not ensure complete agreement, however, since controversy often occurs when these objectives are implemented.

The first section in this chapter explains the relationship between safety and health and discusses causes, measurements, and trends related to accidents. The next section examines various influences that may have increased companys' interest in safety, including the Occupational Safety and Health Act. A third section discusses various organizational techniques for improving safety. Finally, as noted in the analytical framework discussed in Chapter 1, legislation represents a significant influence on many personnel functions. Safety is no exception, as seen in the concluding issue: "What Are the Legal Rights of Employers and Employees in Safety Activities?"

Safety and Health in Perspective

Material written on the subject of safety and health ranges from the detached to the dramatic. An example of the dramatic approach is found in the introduction to *Muscle and Blood:*

This book is about the continuing carnage which can be found hidden just beyond the most modern factory facade of shining steel and brick. To the age-old problems . . . dirt, disease, and injuries . . . even more serious perils have been added. Since World War II countless new chemicals have been developed, and employers have rushed to put the new chemicals to use, with little regard for their toxic properties.[1]

The preceding quotation illustrates several dimensions of this topic. First, the quotation brings to mind the sometimes interrelated terms *safety* and *health.* Many believe these terms are nearly identical and use them interchangeably. This chapter tends to follow the same practice; but some distinctions between the two terms should be made. *Safety* typically refers to the avoidance of accidents that can cause injury. Naturally, safe practices contribute positively to the employee's health. However, *health* also includes physical conditions other than injuries; these conditions may not be easily detected. It is sometimes difficult, if not impossible, to determine whether an employee's illness, disease, premature aging, or deteriorating health was caused by workplace conditions or other circumstances.

Both safety and health are affected by the hazards described in the *Muscle and Blood* quotation. There is an almost endless variety of potential hazards—noise, dust, fires, explosions, electrocution, toxic materials, carcinogens, health stress, stationary and moving equipment, and so forth. Companies do not have identical types or amounts of safety and health hazards, since they use different technologies. Yet, all companies have the potential for such problems. Even at Disney World—which supports an extensive safety program, including safety training, a large medical staff, and two full-time fire stations—safety problems can occur:

One reported incident involved an employee costumed as Donald Duck. While mingling with the crowd, she was overcome by heat fatigue and fell to the ground. Almost immediately, several children pounced upon her, delighted to have a beloved cartoon character playing possum with them. Luckily, a nearby attendant rescued the worker from possible injury.[2]

Causes of Accidents

Accidents result from *unsafe acts, unsafe conditions (mechanical or physical hazards),* or a *combination of unsafe acts and unsafe conditions.* However, though all accidents can be placed in one of these three categories, the categories represent only a starting point. Using them in a superficial manner would overlook many factors that contribute to accidents. Consider, for example, a common industrial accident: an employee's falling off a stepladder. A safety investigation might determine that the cause was a defective ladder (an unsafe condition), and the correction would be to replace the ladder. Yet, a more complete safety investigation might reveal the following contributing factors: inadequate safety inspections; poor job training; and failure of the supervisor to examine job conditions before the job was performed.[3] Contributing factors may be found in *employees' characteristics* and in the *relationship between the work environment and employees' abilities.*

Employees' Characteristics Employees' characteristics can represent a major contributing factor to accidents. One author contends that unsafe acts account for 50 to 90 percent of all industrial accidents.

Simple inattentiveness, conscious disregard of safety equipment, and slovenly housekeeping form the greatest threats to worker safety. . . . Unsafe attitudes and lack of interest in safety need to be corrected before a further reduction in the accident rate can occur.[4]

Psychological interpretations of employees' characteristics have generally attempted to isolate the *accident-prone* employee—the one who has significantly more accidents than others and has a permanent tendency to engage in unsafe behavior in a particular job. Major characteristics associated with accident proneness include ignorance, lack of neuro-muscular coordination, and inattention.[5] It would seem that accurately identifying accident proneness could greatly improve employee selection techniques and reduce the number of accidents. However, in practice, accident proneness does not appear to explain accident causes very well. One major study of some 27,000 industrial and 8,000 nonindustrial accidents found that "those who suffer injuries year after year over a period of three years (3 to 5 percent) account for a relatively small percentage of all the accidents (0.5 percent)."[6]

Research into socio-demographic characteristics (age, sex, race, and so forth) has suggested that younger employees have more accidents than older employees and that females tend to have fewer work-related accidents than males.[7] Socio-demographic data can give general clues into what characteristics are associated with accidents. Yet, these analyses do not take into account variations within categories and differences in situations. For example, we do not know if females are more careful or if they tend to be assigned to jobs in which the chance of accidents is less. For example, studies have found that black employees have a much greater likelihood of having accidents than white employees. This finding is in part due to the fact that black employees have historically been assigned to more dangerous jobs in several industrial situations.[8]

Relationship between the Work Environment and Employees' Abilities In some cases, there may be little relationship between the work environment and employees' abilities. Consider, for example, a competent, well-trained employee who is injured in an explosion. Here is a case where the unsafe condition, not the employee's actions, caused the accident. Other examples of unsafe conditions include poor machine maintenance and illumination, lack of warning devices and machine guards, and so forth.

However, the work environment often interacts with employee deficiencies to produce an accident. Work scheduling, particularly when night shifts (12:00 a.m. to 8:00 a.m.) are involved, may adversely affect employees who are not mentally and physically alert during certain time periods. One body of safety research has even attempted to establish a relationship between accident occurrence and *biorhythms* (fixed time cycles during which physical, emotional, and intellectual capabilities are in positive, neutral, and negative phases).[9] Problems can also occur when the employee physically interacts with the work environment. Tools may be inadequate to accomplish certain jobs or equipment and machines may require excessive physical reach, strength, and endurance.[10]

Accident Measurements and Trends

Accident reporting should be based on consistent measurements. These measurements, if assessed over time, may reflect safety trends and areas for improvement. Safety statistics can provide general insights and serve as a rough means to assess the company's safety efforts. However, any safety statistic should be interpreted with attention to four possible cautions. First, accident reporting systems are narrow in scope and do not give a complete picture of safety and health. These statistics only reflect injuries or deaths occurring at the workplace. They do not reflect close calls—situations in which accidents were barely avoided and could occur in the future. Also excluded are longer-range health problems that may be caused by conditions in the workplace.

Second, problems can also be caused by the sample used in the reporting system. The most widely cited accident statistics are compiled and reported by the National Safety Council, an organization that relies largely on the voluntary reports of its own members, who are among the most safety-conscious of companies. This sample bias probably causes understatement of the accident statistics. Many of the reporting companies also view their safety records in competitive terms, particularly since safety awards are given out at the end of the year. Some suggest that this competition can result in coverup of accidents. An employee who was safety chairman of one reporting company made the following comments:

The company put a big push on for no disabling accident for the year, to receive an award. They achieved their goal. I have a picture to prove it. I was right there receiving the award. They had a big testimonial dinner. We received a nice, beautiful plaque from the National Safety Council. They come out with all kinds of figures, less than 1.2 disabling injuries, out of every one million man-hours.

Gentlemen . . . when we lose a hand this is not a disabling injury, when we break a leg this is not a disabling injury. When we have people literally torn apart, receiving hundreds of stitches, and laying in the dispensary for three days, it is not classified as a lost-time accident. . . .

We average about ninety people a day going to our dispensary over accidents, yet this year we have not had a lost-time accident. I feel sorry when I get a call at home saying we have a lost-time accident, because that means somebody is injured very seriously.[11]

Third, safety statistics may be of little value to the individual employee. As one author points out, "death does not come in increments of hundreds of thousands, but to one person at a time. . . . It is pointless to say that more people die in automobile wrecks than in industrial accidents; one premature death from either cause is one too many."[12]

Fourth, many employers have changed some of their methods of reporting accident statistics. Many employers have reported work-related accidental death statistics (absolute totals and deaths per

100,000 workers) to the National Safety Council (figures are available for the years 1933 to 1939). They have also reported accident *frequency* and *severity* rates, as well as average days lost per person from temporary disability, for the years 1926–1976. In 1976, many employers switched their accident reporting methods to those recommended by the Occupational Safety and Health Administration (OSHA). The accident frequency and severity statistics have been compiled for many years and cannot be ignored, even though the last meaningful reporting date for them was 1976. On the other hand, the OSHA statistics have not been compiled over a sufficient number of years to indicate the presence of trends.

Accident frequency and severity rates are calculated in the following manner:

$$\text{Injury Frequency Rate} = \frac{\text{Number of Disabling Injuries} \times 1,000,000}{\text{Total Number of Employee Hours Worked}}$$

$$\text{Injury Severity Rate} = \frac{\text{Number of Days Lost} \times 1,000,000}{\text{Total Number of Employee Hours Worked}}$$

These measurements are fairly straightforward and easy to calculate. The severity rate, however, does use somewhat arbitrary figures when fatalities or permanent disabilities are involved. For example, companies have been assigned 6,000 days lost for an accidental death, 2,400 days lost when an employee lost a foot as a result of an accident, and so forth.[13] Some general conclusions can be drawn from these statistics and from statistics on work-related accidental deaths reported to the National Safety Council:[14]

1. The absolute number of deaths caused by industrial accidents has not changed very much over the years. In 1933, 14,500 employees died from industrial accidents; in 1979, 13,200 employees died from this cause. (The highest number of work-related deaths, 19,000, was reported in 1937). However, many more people work today than in 1933. When adjusted for number of employees, the 1979 accidental death rate per 100,000 workers (13) is almost three times lower than the comparable figure for 1933 (37).

2. The accident frequency and severity statistics reported in 1976 (10.87 and 668, respectively) are also three times lower than comparable figures (31.87 and 2,500, respectively) reported for the first year of the study, 1926, although there have been no sharp, or even consistent, reductions in these

figures since 1950. (These findings might support the notion that companies cover up accident frequency by reporting only serious accidents.)

3. The average days lost because of permanent or total disabilities has remained the same or grown higher over the years. For example, this figure was seventeen in 1926 and twenty-four in 1976. This increase might be due to a rise in safety publicity in recent years, resulting in greater employee sensitivity to a variety of potential occupational hazards.

The incidence rates developed by OSHA are calculated as follows:

$$\text{Incidence Rate (OSHA)} = \frac{\text{Incidence of Injuries and Illness} \times 200{,}000}{\text{Total Hours Worked by All Employees during Period Covered}}$$

$$\text{Incidence Rate (OSHA)} = \frac{\text{Number of Lost Workdays} \times 200{,}000}{\text{Total Hours Worked by All Employees during Period Covered}}$$

Companies can report accidents according to one or both rates. As indicated earlier, the implications of these statistics cannot be assessed until data are reported for more survey years.

Forces Influencing Companies' Interest in Safety

Safety at the workplace can be influenced by many factors, not the least of which are the attitudes and actions of millions of employees and management officials. There are however, three general factors that exert important influences on companies, namely: social values, economic considerations, and governmental regulation.

Social Values

It is difficult to pinpoint specific social values regarding safety, much less their origins or magnitude. However, if legislation and subsequent judicial decisions approximate social values, then related shifts can be at least crudely delineated. It has already been noted in the discussion on workman's compensation that employers had little if any obligation to provide a safe working environment at the turn of the twentieth century.

This sentiment has changed, however, and commonly held values today suggest that:

Management creates and directs employment conditions and is therefore at least partially responsible for unsafe acts that occur in the course of a workday.

Exhibit 13.1   **Actual and Planned Investment in**
                          Employee Safety and Health
                          (Millions of Dollars)

Industry	Actual					Planned	
	1972	1973	1974	1975	1976	1977	1980
All Manufacturing (Durables and Nondurables)	$ 938	$1,207	$1,577	$1,481	$1,164	$1,475	$1,774
All Nonmanufacturing (Transportation, Mining, Utilities, Commercial, etc.)	1,571	1,362	1,497	1,233	1,212	1,410	1,923
All Business	2,509	2,569	3,074	2,714	2,376	2,885	3,697

Unsafe working conditions have consequences that can extend beyond the employee's workday. An employee may never have had an accident or disabling injury at the workplace but might contract a serious, even fatal, disease from exposure to a variety of working conditions such as noise and chemicals.

A related belief is that safety and working conditions are not regulated by the marketplace or subject to market forces. Publicity concerning unsafe automobiles, children's toys, and so forth will probably result in reductions in purchases of those products. The manufacturers will then be forced to make them safer. Few consumers, however, are aware of the safety conditions surrounding the products' manufacture. One union official maintains that "it is unconscionable to expect that individual workers should pay with their lungs and their health so that members of the public may enjoy lower prices for the products which they consume."[15]

These values reflect a general awareness that safety is an important issue and that something other than traditional market forces might be necessary to ensure management's obligation to provide a safe workplace. Two developments stemming from these social values are unions' efforts to include safety issues in contract negotiations and labor agreements and government legislation (discussed later in this section).

Economic Considerations

Management, however socially responsible, must at least consider the economic implications of its safety program. Exhibit 13.1 shows the considerable expenditures various industries have assigned to safety over recent years. Exhibit 13.2 furnishes a perspective on these expenditures by comparing them with total capital spending. Most tables are subject to diverse interpretations, and Exhibit 13.2 is no exception. Some might conclude that the results in the exhibit indicate a relatively insignificant and declining commitment to safety (for exam-

Exhibit 13.2   **Employee Safety and Health Investment
                                 as a Percentage of Capital Spending**

Industry	1972	1973	1974	1975	Planned 1977	Planned 1980
All Manufacturing	3.0%	3.2%	3.4%	3.1%	2.4%	2.6%
All Nonmanufacturing	2.8	2.2	2.3	1.9	1.8	2.0
All Business	2.8	2.6	2.7	2.4	2.0	2.3

Source: Modified from material that was prepared by the Economics Department of McGraw-Hill, "Annual McGraw-Hill Survey(s) of Investment in Employee Safety and Health," mimeographed (New York: McGraw-Hill, 1972–1977), and presented in Herbert R. Northrup, *The Impact of OSHA* (Philadelphia: University of Pennsylvania Press, 1978), p. 167. Used by permission of the Industrial Research Unit, Wharton School, University of Pennsylvania. © Trustees of the University of Pennsylvania.

ple, compare the years 1972 and 1980). Others might maintain that (1) safety concern could be reflected in other expense categories (such as safer equipment, improved ventilation systems in new plants, and so forth); (2) some safety expenditures have continuing results; therefore, less financial outlay might be needed in subsequent years; and (3) safety commitment and success should be assessed in results (possibly in terms of the safety measurements discussed earlier), not in dollars.

Money is spent to solve safety problems for social and economic reasons. At least some safety expenditures are incurred to minimize economic costs associated with accidents. One classic book on safety has pinpointed several accident costs (see Exhibit 13.3).

In addition to the costs enumerated in the exhibit, other less direct costs can result from long-term consequences of the accident, even when the injured employee returns full strength to the workplace. Employees may become cynical if they do not believe management is making a serious attempt to prevent similar accidents. This attitude can result in reduced productivity and even occasionally in militant actions such as work slowdowns and wildcat strikes. If the accident is labeled as serious or as being due solely to management's negligence, then the company's public image could suffer.[16]

Governmental Regulation— Occupational Safety and Health Act

Origin, Purpose, and Coverage of the Act President Johnson somewhat abruptly announced in 1968 his desire to implement federal legislation aimed at promoting and regulating on-the-job safety. He appeared to justify this legislation on two general grounds:

Many of the nation's employees were not covered by existing legislation.

"Regulation [was] necessary to correct a system underinvestment in the protection of workers against occupational hazards and to achieve optimal investment in safety and health."[17]

| Exhibit 13.3 | **Costs That May Be Incurred in an Industrial Accident** |

1. Cost of lost time of injured employee.
2. Cost of time lost by other employees who stop work:
   a. Out of curiosity.
   b. Out of sympathy.
   c. To assist injured employee.
   d. For other reasons.
3. Cost of time lost by foremen, supervisors, or other executives as follows:
   a. Assisting injured employee.
   b. Investigating the cause of the accident.
   c. Arranging for the injured employee's production to be continued by some other employee.
   d. Selecting, training, or breaking in a new employee to replace the injured employee.
   e. Preparing state accident reports, or attending hearings before state officials [possibly also preparing federal safety compliance forms].
4. Cost of time spent on the case by first-aid attendant and hospital department staff, when not paid for by the insurance carrier.
5. Cost due to damage to the machine, tools, or other property or to the spoilage of material.
6. Incidental cost due to interference with production, failure to fill orders on time, loss of bonuses, payment of forfeits, and other similar causes.
7. Cost to employer under employee welfare and benefit systems.
8. Cost to employer in continuing the wages of the injured employee in full, after his return—even though the services of the employee [who has not yet fully recovered] may for a time be worth only about half of their normal value.
9. Cost due to the loss of profit on the injured employee's productivity, and on idle machines.
10. Cost that occurs in consequence of the excitement or weakened morale due to the accident.
11. Overhead cost per injured employee—the expense of light, heat, rent, and other such items, which continues while the injured employee is a nonproducer.

Source: From *Industrial Accident Prevention*, 4th ed., by Herbert William Heinrich, pp. 51–52. Copyright © 1979 by McGraw-Hill Book Company. Used with permission of McGraw-Hill Book Company.

The Johnson administration's safety bill, when sent to Congress, caught most people, even Labor Secretary W. Willard Wirtz, by surprise.[18] This situation probably resulted in inadequate testimony and consideration of the proposed legislation. One observer noted:

Congress fiddled with and finally passed a comprehensive occupational safety and health bill late in 1970. The debate was both dismal and desultory. Even the proponents seemed to know little or care less about what they were voting on. Only a handful quibbled over the final language of the bill. Mostly they exchanged frightening statistics on deaths, accidents, injuries, and disease. No price tag was even suggested for implementation of the new law.[19]

Nobody disagreed that attention should be devoted to employees' safety, although a few were concerned about the implementation and enforcement of the act. Ronald Reagan, then Governor of California, expressed concern that federal safety legislation would supersede "effective" safety programs conducted by several states, including California.[20]

Other concerns were expressed as well. One prominent business magazine, for example, speculated that an unsuccessful job applicant could show up at the company's offices as an OSHA inspector and "threaten to padlock your gates and have you fined $1,000 a day if you don't do as he says."[21]

Though lobbying efforts by business groups delayed and altered President Johnson's initial intentions,[22] final passage of the Occupational Safety and Health Act (OSHAct) eventually took place in December 1970. The act covered some 55 million industrial, farm, and construction workers employed by nearly 5 million firms engaged in interstate commerce. Firms covered by other forms of federal safety legislation may be exempted from OSHAct coverage, although related provisions can become quite complicated.[23] The act does not specifically cover state, local, and federal government employees.[24]

The purpose of the OSHAct is broad and far reaching: its goal is to assure safe and healthful working conditions by authorizing enforcement of safety standards, helping states in related efforts, and providing for research, information, education, and training in the field of occupational safety and health. Three federal agencies have been established to achieve these purposes:

OSHA (Occupational Safety and Health Administration). OSHA, the agency responsible for the administration of the act, is located within the Department of Labor. It is mainly responsible for setting occupational safety and health standards and conducting inspections of workplaces to ensure that employers are providing the safe working conditions obligated under the act.[25] OSHA can issue citations against employers and assess penalties for violations.[26]

OSHRC (Occupational Safety and Health Review Commission). OSHRC is an independent quasi-judicial review board consisting of three members appointed by the president. OSHRC rules on all challenges to OSHA's citations and penalties.

NIOSH (National Institute for Safety and Health). NIOSH is a governmental research body responsible for developing and recommending occupational safety and health standards.

The act gave many responsibilities to these agencies and to the Secretary of Labor. Two major efforts in terms of time, money, and controversy are: 1) inspecting and correcting safety problems at company facilities; and 2) providing safety standards for company compliance.

OSHA and Company Safety Inspections There are approximately 1,500 OSHA inspectors and 5 million workplaces to be investigated. Thus, many businesses have little chance of being inspected.[27] OSHA therefore established the following safety inspection priorities:

First Priority. Inspect when a catastrophe or fatality has occurred.

Second Priority. Inspect when an employee complaint has been received. Employees who file complaints can be assured their names will be kept confidential.

Third Priority. Inspect target industries that are more prone to safety hazards. There are five target industries: (1) meat and meat products; (2) longshoring; (3) roofing and sheetmetal; (4) lumber and wood products; and (5) mobile homes.

Fourth Priority. Inspect randomly selected sites from all types and sizes of workplaces in all sections of the country.

Recently, OSHA has considered modifying its priorities. The current head of OSHA has noted that "We don't have unlimited resources. We have to do the most good we can for the most people involved."[28] Three modifications are being considered or implemented in various degrees: (1) not following up on every employee complaint with a safety inspection;[29] (2) considering the unique aspects of small business;[30] and (3) focusing on job sites posing the greatest risks instead of on the broad industrial classifications indicated in the third safety inspection priority.[31]

A safety inspector must arrive at the inspection site unannounced; there can be no advance notice given to the company. Until 1978, OSHA inspectors could enter the company's property without a search warrant. In the 1978 Barlow decision, the Supreme Court declared this procedure unconstitutional.[32] Thus, an employer may legally require that an OSHA inspector provide a search warrant. Some hailed the Barlow decision as a "victory for the little man," while others predicted it would seriously harm OSHA's inspection efforts. In retrospect, it appears the decision was a "symbolic victory," offering relatively few problems for OSHA.[33] For example, in the 98,000 inspections initiated after the Barlow decision, inspectors have been refused entry only 1,200 times.[34]

Another controversial inspection issue involves *walkaround pay,* compensation given by employers to employees who accompany safety inspectors on their tours of the facilities. OSHA officials have changed their position on walkaround pay several times, largely as a result of court decisions declaring this requirement invalid.[35] Currently OSHA has dropped the walkaround pay rule—employers do not have to compensate employees for their inspection tour efforts.[36]

After touring the facility, an OSHA inspector can issue a citation or a penalty for a safety violation. If the employer does not lodge a challenge within fifteen days, the decision becomes final and is no longer subject to review by either OSHRC or the courts. A challenge during the fifteen-day period institutes appeals procedures within OSHRC as well as clearing the way for possible judicial review.

Controversy has surrounded the cost of complying with OSHA's citations and penalties. Some contend that the penalty structure does not effectively deter some businesses from continuing their unsafe practices. If an employer repeatedly or willfully violates the regulations, a maximum of $10,000 per penalty can be assessed.[37] Yet, most penalties are well below the maximum. For example, in 1977, the average penalty for serious safety violations was $303; and the average penalty for minor violations was $9.31[38]

On the other hand, a very expensive OSHA assessment to correct an unsafe condition might also be counterproductive. One union official contends that stiff assessments will almost certainly result in lengthy judicial appeals by employers: "It simply pays to . . . fight the agency when it costs $50,000 to litigate and $1 million to abate."[39]

OSHA and the Development of Safety Standards The OSHAct indicated that OSHA's primary responsibility is to formulate and enforce safety standards. The act mandated three types of standards: "(1) *interim* (initial) standards consisting of federal standards from other Acts and national consensus standards existing at the time of the implementation of the OSHAct; (2) permanent standards to replace or augment the interim standards; and (3) temporary emergency standards which may be issued immediately upon the finding of serious danger to employees."[40]

Some controversy has occurred when OSHA has attempted to implement interim and permanent standards. The agency, particularly in its early years, was accused of doing too many of the wrong things and too few of the right things. As an illustration, consider a professor who gives students several pages of detailed technical requirements for term papers—number of centimeters for margin width, number of lines per page, and so forth. Students might contend that these requirements are irrelevant to the purpose of term papers—namely, developing abilities to define, research, and communicate particular subjects.

This situation is not unlike that faced by employers in the early days of OSHA. Interim standards needed to be established quickly, and the agency responded by publishing some 5,000 safety standards. Most criticisms of these standards, which came equally swiftly, fell into two general categories. First, the sheer number and content of the standards made it difficult for managers to interpret and implement them. (Sometimes even OSHA administrators and the courts cannot agree on their interpretation. For example, some OSHA officials believe that the words *shall* and *should,* which are often found in the standards, are synonymous. Other OSHA officials and the courts disagree. They believe *shall* represents a command, while *should* represents a recommendation.[41])

A second criticism of OSHA's interim standards was that they had limited applicability to the industrial setting. Some standards were regarded as outdated, since they were originated in the early 1940s.[42] Other standards—such as those that dealt with the design of toilet seats and the placement of coat hooks on bathroom stalls, the possibility of slipping on cow manure, and the color of the safety lanes painted on shop floors—were regarded as trivial. OSHA has recently responded to these criticisms by eliminating some 1,000 allegedly trivial standards.[43]

Criticism has also followed OSHA when it has attempted to design and implement permanent safety and health standards.[44] Establishing safety standards is, after all, a difficult task. Consider, for example, a common piece of safety equipment—the hard hat, or safety helmet, used to protect the employee from falling objects. Nobody doubts the value of hard hats; the question is, how do you test a hard hat's effectiveness?' The most realistic standard would result from tests on human subjects—clearly, an option that cannot be used.

One safety standard is based on tests that place hard hats on aluminum head forms. An eight-pound steel ball is dropped on the top of the hat from a height of five feet, and the resulting impact is measured at the bottom of the head form. When a sample of three hard hats of a particular brand transmit an average force level less than 850 pounds, with no single hard hat registering more than 1,000 pounds of measured force, that brand has passed the test.[45] While employees may feel more secure knowing their hard hats have passed some systematic safety test, they cannot be sure the laboratory-determined standard will help them in real work situations.

There have also been problems with the National Instutute for Occupational Safety and Health (NIOSH), the agency charged with helping OSHA formulate standards. According to one government official, NIOSH had problems when it was created: "The agency was underfunded, and we tried to pretend it wasn't there."[46] The agency has subsequently been shifted from one bureaucratic structure in HEW to another; as a result, employee morale is low and communication with other agencies is poor.

Finally, formulating a standard does not mean it will be implemented. A recent OSHA standard lowering the permissible amount of employee exposure to the chemical benzene was overturned by the Supreme Court, largely on the basis that OSHA did not establish its claim that employees' health would be jeopardized by such exposure.[47]

Assessing OSHAct's Impact Thus far, we have indicated that OSHA has encountered some problems with its inspection and standard formulation procedures. Another problem can occur when unions use the act's provisions for purposes other than those intended. One management official explains this potential for abuse:

> Hardly a day goes by, even in my own company, without some disturbance in our labor-management relations because of OSHA. Its abuse has produced bitter confrontations and consequences over such matters as rate retention, walk-arounds, alleged discrimination, [and] refusal to work protected by the "smoke screen" claim of unsafe conditions, "calling in the Feds" (or state agencies) in retaliation against employers' direction of the workforce, and generally obtaining through OSHA and the Act what normally should be subject to collective bargaining.[48]

However, the extent of this abuse is limited by the fact that when safety citations are issued, the burden of proof is placed on OSHA, not management.[49]

These and other problem areas raise the issue of the act's effectiveness. Useful starting points in assessing it are furnished by the statements of a former head of OSHA and of a former Secretary of Labor:

> There are some fundamentals in this administration's approach to the Occupational Safety and Health Act. We believe that a worker should not have to lay his or her life on the line just to have a job. American workers should never have to choose between their health and their paycheck. And we believe that workers have the right to know the nature of the substances in their workplace environments, and to know just how effectively their employers and their government are acting to protect them.[50]

> OSHA's ultimate impact . . . is the signals it sends to key institutions.[51]

These quotations suggest a first dimension of OSHA's impact—namely, *increased awareness of and attention to safety by employers and employees.* Some evidence suggests that employers have received OSHA's message. For example, "a Lou Harris poll has estimated that 6 out of 10 companies who now have a safety and health program, did not have a comparable one prior to OSHA."[52] Further, employees may become aware of a publicized safety and health hazard even if a standard proposed to control it is not eventually implemented. The president of the AFL-CIO recently commented:

Before 1970, on-the-job health and safety protections were a benefit provided by a few benevolent employers. Provisions in collective bargaining contracts relating to health and safety were effective in direct proportion to the strength of the union and the obvious seriousness of the health and safety issue. A peaceful alternative to a work stoppage or strike was rarely available. And the non-union worker could only grumble and hope to be lucky enough to escape the menace. For years workers were brainwashed by management to believe that workplace hazards were all part of the job. Now workers are learning that hazardous conditions are a violation of the law and they are taking steps to get them corrected.[53]

Evidence related to employees' awareness of safety issues is subject to differing interpretations. For example, OSHA's safety inspection data for 1979 revealed that the percentage of inspections initiated by employees' complaints dropped for the first time in four years.[54] These results suggest at least three interpretations: (1) employers have received OSHA's message and corrected safety problems, thereby reducing employee complaints; (2) employees believe OSHA is incapable of handling their safety complaints; or (3) OSHA is giving less attention to employee complaints, focusing instead on major safety and health problems.

A second dimension along which OSHA's impact can be assessed is *whether a reduction in accidents has occurred.* Here, conflicting evidence exists. One study concluded that "there is little evidence that regulation has yet served to reduce significantly the risk of work-related health impairment among workers in any of the industries studied."[55] Other studies have shown that the presence of OSHA has resulted in a statistically significant drop in accidents.[56]

OSHA's impact can also be assessed along a third dimension—*cost versus benefit.* The OSHAct requires that funds be spent not only to operate the agencies involved but also to ensure business compliance with OSHA directives. Total cost figures vary; however, in 1979, OSHA required a budget of $171.2 million to administer the act.[57] Critics say OSHA's cost far exceeds its benefits. However, others say that the benefits are worth the cost—that no employees should have to risk safety and health so that the general public can consume certain goods or services.[58]

Consider the situation in companies that use a particular ingredient (*acrylonitrile*) in the manufacture of many plastics and synthetic fibers. This ingredient, in large doses, produces malignant tumors in laboratory rats. OSHA ordered that the presence of this substance in the air of factories be reduced. The government states this directive will prevent about seven cancer deaths a year and cost industry $24.3 million, or $3.5 million for each life saved. The value of this directive can be heatedly argued along financial versus moral dimensions.[59] Additional arguments can be made over how OSHA allocates its funds. Some contend that OSHA should spend more of its monies on education and research and less on safety inspections.[60]

Any discussion of OSHAct's effectiveness must be qualified by two considerations. First, OSHA, in enforcing the act's provisions, will inevitably provoke negative publicity. One OSHA official states that, because approximately 50,000 OSHA safety inspections are conducted each year, "even if we did everything completely correct 98% of the time that's still 1,200 inspections that OSHA critics can find fault with. We're under close scrutiny, and . . . 'horror' stories are going to come to light."[61]

Second, the OSHAct was designed to apply across companies and industries. This type of regulation often overlooks the uniqueness of individual situations. "[OSHA] regulations cannot be written with enough specificity to accommodate all of the unique conditions encountered in the nation's five million workplaces."[62]

Organizational Efforts to Improve Safety and Health

Company Safety Policies

Most organizations have some type of safety policy, which, at a minimum, symbolizes management's commitment to safe working conditions. A good safety policy must also apply to a broad range of existing and potential hazards and provide incentives for managers and employees to develop specific ways to remove these hazards.[63]

Another characteristic of a good safety policy is that it raises questions and answers them. The value of a questioning approach is described by a writer who asked a safety expert in the Department of Labor whether anything can be done about the noise of a piledriver.

My question was answered with such surprising ease that I realized how much we are victims of accumulated folklore, mainly because we don't ask simple questions and keep asking them until we get satisfactory answers. So many questions in worker safety and health just never get asked, either by workers, by unions, by government, or by the academic community.[64]

Any safety policy must ask two general questions:

1. What causes accidents?
2. What activities should be included in the safety program?

The first question has already been discussed in this chapter; the second question is discussed next.

Activities and Techniques for Improving Safety

Safety policies usually cover three general areas of activity:[65]

Investigating various areas (content of chemicals used in the operation, exposure levels, use of safety equipment, conditions of mechanical equipment and shop floor, employees' complaints, and so forth) to determine and evaluate risks.

Reducing risks at the workplace.

Reporting and following up to determine that the present safety program is implemented in an effective manner, to ensure that no new, intolerable risks are introduced, and to comply with governmental (OSHA) forms and procedures.

Several specific techniques can be applied to these safety activities. They include the use of careful selection of employees, safety research, accident analysis, safety engineers, safety committees, protective equipment, safety incentives and contests, and communication and training.

Careful Selection of Employees Principles of employee selection have already been discussed in Chapters 6 and 7 and will not be repeated here. It is important to note, however, that careful selection offers at least the potential for accident reduction. The limitations of the theory of accident proneness and the like have been mentioned earlier in this chapter; employee selection along these lines, then, might not be effective. However, selection based on job analyses in relation to applicants' skills (eye-hand coordination, depth perception, and so forth) will likely be effective. An analysis of the applicant's previous experience in performing tasks similar to those in the current job vacancy will also be helpful.

Safety Research Research can suggest effective approaches to preventing accidents and increasing safety awareness. Safety surveys and reports from other companies or industries can be reviewed for their implications and applicability. Even more important is in-house safety research. Accident and injury forms (see Exhibit 13.4 for an example) are used by most companies and provide a useful starting point for safety research. Analysis of these records can furnish valuable safety insights for a particular facility; for example:

Certain departments—for example, subassembly or shipping—may have more accidents than others.

Older employees may have higher accident rates than others, possibly because they believe they know all the short cuts.

While experience with the company may have no statistical relationship to accident frequency, employees new to a particular job (whatever their seniority with the company) may be more likely to have accidents than other employees.

More accidents may occur on the night shift, perhaps because fewer supervisors are present during those hours.

Exhibit 13.4 **Accident and Injury Report Form**

AGENCIES (Circle Only One)
THE OBJECT, SUBSTANCE OR EXPOSURE MOST CLOSELY ASSOCIATED WITH THE INJURY

MACHINES

0000 Agitator, Mixer	0015 Mill	0026 Planer, Shaper,	0044 Hacksaw (Power)
0400 Conveyor	0053 Mower	Jointer	0042 Saw (Table)
0017 Drill	0021 Packaging Mach	0029 Presses	0048 Shears & Dicer
0009 Extruder	0083 Picture Proj.	0038 Rolls	0007 Valve Grinder
0005 Floor Polisher	0086 Pile Driver	0090 Sandblast Mach.	Machine
0018 Lathe	0094 Pipe Threader	0004 Sander, Grinder	0012 Welding Machine

STEAM, BOILERS and PRESSURE VESSELS

1510 Boilers	1931 Filters	0525 Piping	0522 Reactor
0523 Columns	0074 Furnace	0528 Tanks	
0521 Exchangers	0530 Hose	0529 Trap	

ELECTRICAL APPARATUS

0940 Batteries	0902 Generators	0901 Motors	0910 Transformers
0920 Conductors	0960 Heating Appl.	0930 Switch Gear	

PUMPS AND PRIME MOVERS

0134 Compressors	0110 Eng. & Prime Movers	0124 Fans & Blowers	0120 Pumps

FLAMMABLE and HOT SUBSTANCES

1225 Fire	1255 Steam	1956 Water	1953 Welding Rod
1954 Metal Plate			or Slag

HAND TOOLS

1010 Axe	1017 Glasscutter	1023 Pipecutter	1066 Saw (Power)
1011 Blowtorch	1051 Grinder	1051 Plane	1069 Screwdriver
1012 Broom, Brush	1018 Hammer, Hatchet	1027 Pliers	1032 Shovel, Spade
1013 Chisel, Punch	1059 Hydroblaster	1056 Pneumatic	1031 Sickle
1014 Dies & Taps	1020 Jack	Hammer	1029 Tapeline
1015 Drill (Hand)	1021 Knife	1062 Pump	1070 Torch
1053 Drill (Power)	1025 Oilcan	1065 Sandblaster	1035 Wrench
1016 File	1026 Pick, Fork,	1032 Sandpaper	
	Pickaxe	1030 Saw (Hand)	
	1019 Pry Bar, Cheater		

CHEMICALS, DUST and RADIATION

1121 Acid	1133 Caustic	1129 Hexane	1400 Radiation
1157 Additives	1123 Chlorine	1131 Lime	1127 Refrigerants
1132 Ammonia	1159 DM	1125 Methanol	1156 Solvents
1128 AN	1300 Dust	1126 Mercury	1151 Styrene
1134 Benzene	1152 EB	1155 Nitrogen	1140 Sulphur
1122 Carbon Monox.	1153 EDC	1137 Oils	1153 VAM
1135 CCl 4	1110 Explosive Gases	1138 Polymer	1154 VCM
1158 Catalyst	1124 HCN	1235 Paint, Varnish	1160 Unknown

MECHANICAL POWER TRANSMISSION

0814 Belts	0804 Couplings	0807 Gears	0811 Ropes, Cables
0812 Chain	0810 Drums	0809 Pulleys	

ELEVATORS and HOISTING APPARATUS

0310 Crane	0200 Elevators	0330 Hoists	0320 Shovel

WORKING SURFACES

1530 Floors	1576 Roofs	1583 Sidewalks	1582 Stairs, Ramps
1578 Roads			

VEHICLES

0650 Aircraft	0660 Bicycles	0691 Hand trucks,	0610 Motor Vehicle
0640 Barges, Ships	0611 Fork-lift	Tool Box &	0630 Railway
		Wheelbarrows	

MISCELLANEOUS

1916 Bags, Boxes	1934 Glassware	1954 Manholes	1978 Scaffold
1914 Barrels, Drums	1979 Handrails	1958 Nails	1980 Splinter, Sliver
1915 Bottles (ICC)	0720 Insects & Snakes	1957 Nuts, Bolts	1581 Structure or
1918 Cans	1947 Kitchen Equip.	1963 Office Equip.	Brace
1923 Ditches, Trenches	1952 Lab Equip. Misc.	& Machines	1991 Wire-Non-Elect.
1922 Doors, Windows	1950 Ladders	1966 Person	1992 Workbench,
1930 Floor Openings	1951 Load. Platforms	1967 Pipefittings	Desk
1932 Food		& Valves	

1999 Misc. Matl. or Obj.   Please Specify_____

ACCIDENT TYPE
(Circle One)

CC 65-66
00 Striking Against
01 Struck By
02 Caught in or Between
03 Fall - Same level
04 Fall - Different level
05 Slip
06 Temperature Extreme
07 Inhalation, Ingestion
08 Electrical Contact
09 Chemical Contact
10 Lifting, Pushing, Pulling
20 N.E.C.

UNSAFE MECHANICAL OR PHYSICAL CONDITION

CC 67   (Circle One)
0 Improperly Guarded
1 Defect of Agency
2 Housekeeping
3 Improper Illumination
4 Improper Ventilation
5 Defective Apparel
6 Improper Design

9 _____
(Please Specify)

UNSAFE ACT

CC 68-69   (Circle One)
00 Operating Without Authority
01 Using Unsafe Speed
02 Making Safety Devices Inoperative
03 Using Unsafe Equipment or Using Unsafely
04 Unsafe Loading, Piling, Mixing
05 Unsafe Posture or Position
06 Working on Moving Equip.
07 Horseplay, etc
08 Failure to Use Protective Equipment or Clothing
09 _____
(Please Specify)
10 Improper Method
11 Failure to be Warned

UNSAFE PERSONAL FACTOR

CC 70   (Circle One)
0 Improper Attitude
1 Lack of Knowledge or Skill
2 Bodily Defects
3 Lack of Instructions
4 Inattention - Injured
5 Wilful Disregard of Safety Rule or Instruction
6 Inexperience
7 Inattention - Fellow Worker
9 None
(Please Specify)

Is this a late report?
If "Yes", please comment below.   CC 71
3 Yes   4 No

Correction Action Taken To Prevent Recurrence

Employee was cautioned to use extreme care when working in close quarters. Work order has been written to insulate the pipe.
Frank Smith
(Supervisor's Signature)

Accident Analysis Accident analysis is a detailed, point-by-point reconstruction of a serious accident. This written report, which may be over 100 pages long, consists of graphs, diagrams, interviews of witnesses and supervisors, and so forth. The principal advantage of using this technique is that the findings may suggest ways to prevent similar accidents in the future.

Some believe that accident analysis is not an effective technique because it is reactive. A major accident (one that causes injuries or fatalities) has to occur before analysis is implemented; and it offers little, if any, help to people involved in this accident. Yet this criticism seems unfounded. Perhaps the only thing worse than a serious accident is not learning from it.

More serious criticisms can be leveled at the timing of the accident analysis and the quality of the information it obtains. An accident analysis must be conducted soon after the accident, or important details will likely be lost. However, interviews conducted at this time often elicit distorted information because of the emotional state of the witnesses. Distortion can also be caused by people's desire to avoid blame for the accident.

Safety Engineers *Safety engineer* (or sometimes *safety supervisor* or the like) is the title given the individual who heads up the company's safety program, usually at the plant level. Major duties typically include establishing safe practices, training employees and supervisors in various safety subjects, keeping abreast of the latest safety and health developments, conducting daily safety inspections, maintaining and reviewing safety statistics and accident records, and investigating serious accidents for cause and remedy. A safety engineer is a necessary ingredient in a company's safety program; not having such an individual to coordinate safety efforts would likely result in slipshod and unsystematic safety measures.

However, the safety engineer alone does not comprise a sufficient program. Some aspects of the safety engineer's job tend to weaken his or her effectiveness in the organization. First, safety engineers are *made accountable for conditions beyond their control.* Their performance is often judged according to accident statistics; however, they simply cannot ensure that everyone will perform in a safe manner. Consider the following example:

A woodworking machinist had operated a bandsaw for some nine years without so much as breaking the skin of his fingers. Then a disabling laceration, index finger right hand. When he presented for interview with the safety practitioner next morning he was obviously ill and his condition not to be reconciled with severity of injury. A little applied questioning produced the explanatory information. He had spent the night before the accident day in endeavouring to surprise his allegedly faithless wife in adultery.[66]

Second, the safety engineer typically *does not have sufficient authority to correspond with the responsibilities of the job.* One writer points out that "until the early seventies 'paper-hanging' safety supervisors were commonplace. Their value to the organization was illustrated most vividly by the fact that they were often the first to go out the gate in any workforce reduction."[67] Theoretically, the safety engineer has the authority to shut down the entire production operation if he or she spots an unsafe condition. Realistically speaking, however, the safety engineer uses this authority sparingly—if at all—and is expected to have an extremely good reason for a shutdown.

Third, the safety engineer *cannot have enough knowledge and staff to adequately perform necessary functions.* A thorough knowledge of safety and health issues might require extensive familiarity with all the engineering disciplines, medicine, and the behavioral sciences. It is unlikely that one individual could accumulate such a background. At the same time, few safety departments have more than one or two individuals for facilities employing several hundreds, or even thousands, of employees.

Safety Committees *Safety committees* are composed of management officials and hourly employees who attempt to uncover and resolve actual
and potential safety problems. Safety committees offer several possible advantages. Hourly employees are, of course, most familiar with
their jobs and workplace. Safety committees can draw on this expertise in approaching and resolving safety issues. Even heated differences of opinion can generate productive results: "The way to get at
the true merits of the case is not to listen to the fool who considers
himself impartial, but to hear the matter argued with reckless bias
both for and against."[68]

Procedures and practices recommended by participative safety committees might be more easily accepted by those individuals (employees and first-line supervisors) who work on the shop floor.[69] Safety
committees can also symbolize management's sincerity in conducting
ongoing efforts to resolve health and safety issues.

However, safety committees also involve disadvantages for management. Some evidence suggests that hourly employees who sit on
safety committees believe their recommendations are either ignored
or acted upon too slowly.[70] Real controversy can occur when management contends that employees' safety suggestions are too expensive.
Management can seldom win this type of argument with employees,
because it involves putting a dollar value on employees' safety or even
on their lives. Finally, if the safety committee includes union officers,
the union may use the committee to obtain concessions it has not been
able to receive in collective bargaining.

Protective Equipment *Protective equipment* refers to items placed on
machinery and tools (guards, for example) or on employees. The potential value of protective equipment is obvious. However, there are
also some obstacles to this safety technique's use. A previously mentioned obstacle (which used hard hats as an example) is the difficulty
of establishing realistic standards. For example, one test of safety
glasses involves dropping a small steel ball onto a lens. One safety
researcher believes this test is "like dropping a pea on your bare
foot."[71]

Another obstacle is that supervisors and employees often disregard
safety equipment. These individuals are often caught between production and safety pressures; and in some cases, the use of safety
equipment is sacrificed to obtain more production output. Another
reason for disregarding safety equipment is the attitude that only
"sissies" wear such equipment. An example of this sort of machismo-
oriented attitude on the part of a truck driver follows:

**The money's good so you have to accept these dangers the way other
real tough men accept the dangers of their occupations. In effect, the
man is told: What kind of a chicken-heart are you anyway? It's like**

the situation with the United Mine Workers, which also stresses the point that the money's good but to get it, you have to go down into those bloody mines for 20 years. The idea that comes out is this: Any red-blooded male confronted with the choice of being a truck driver despite all the dangers isn't going to let himself be typed as the gutless type who would back away from such an assignment.[72]

Safety Incentives and Contests Incentives and contests are based on the notion that employees will follow safety rules if adherence is reinforced in a direct, immediate, and consistent manner.[73] The incentive does not have to be costly. Indeed, one classic study found that an estimated 2,800 man-hours were saved as the result of a safety contest among employees at five construction sites. The incentive was that each employee at the winning site was given a chance in a minibike raffle.[74] Some safety contests between facilities or departments have awarded the winning employees a trophy or a steak dinner. This technique is used to bolster safety awareness on a daily basis. Employees are motivated to look out for themselves and their peers so that their group will win the contest. However, the technique involves two major problems: (1) accidents may go unreported so that safety statistics will look better, and (2) employees may return to previous attitudes and activities once the contest is over.

Safety Communication and Training Communication and training are used to inform employees of safe operating procedures and to reinforce the importance of safety-conscious attitudes and practices at the workplace. Substantial, but contradictory, literature can be found on mass communication safety techniques, such as safety posters. Two necessary ingredients appear to be attractiveness and credibility. The principle of credibility should also extend to safety training, where "the closer the worker identifies with his supervisor or with management, the more the safety message will be accepted by him."[75]

Safety training is often administered to new employees during their orientation. Unfortunately, much of the training during this period is ineffective. New employees are often told to read a safety rule book and are given such advice as to "use common sense" and "be careful how you lift things." Perhaps this vagueness has some value, since detailed, graphic instructions might overwhelm or unnecessarily scare new employees. However, there are risks in postponing safety training, particularly if adequate instruction is not offered at a later date.

The Role of the Personnel Department and Other Managers in Safety Activities

Personnel representatives' roles (particularly those of the safety engineer) have been discussed in previous sections and won't be extensively reiterated here. These individuals are mainly responsible for keeping informed on the latest legal and research developments in safety. They are also charged with the daily monitoring of safety procedures and practices and can even enforce these efforts (though possibly only on rare occasions) by shutting down production operations.

However, these personnel activities, like others, rely on the support and efforts of other management officials. Top management sets the climate for safety awareness and concern. Often, however, its involvement in safety activities is limited to signing the company safety policy or presenting the awards to the winners of a safety contest. Top management can perhaps more effectively demonstrate the company's concern by viewing safety from the shop floor instead of from corporate headquarters. For example, the president of division or company operations might dramatize his or her concern by taking an extensive safety tour of the facility with a few hourly employees whenever he or she visits.

Effective inspections have many purposes, one of the most important being that they display management's determination that unsafe conditions and practices will be observed and corrected. There are no inspections more effective than those made by senior executives. It's amazing how much scurrying about and beneficial results these produce.[76]

Top management can also support safety efforts by holding lower management officials accountable for safety. First-line supervisors are key individuals whose efforts can make or break a safety program. The first-line supervisor is often involved in safety inspections, accident investigations, and safety training. If he or she ignores safety equipment or condones unsafe working conditions, employees will likely do the same.[77] Seldom, however, are supervisors held accountable (through salary increases, performance appraisals, and so forth) for safety activities and results.[78]

Issue:

What are the Legal Rights of Employers and Employees in Safety Activities?

Chapter 2 noted that employers' personnel approaches underwent a major historical shift when they began to consider adapting some of their activities and objectives to employees' concerns instead of vice versa. This shift was due to changing employer and employee values and to the development and enforcement of numerous laws affecting personnel activities.

In the area of safety, an example of this legal influence is the OSHAct, which was discussed earlier in the chapter. Some specific implications of the OSHAct for employer-employee relationships will be discussed here, along with the actual and potential effects of a Supreme Court decision (*Whirlpool Corp. v. Marshall*).

The writers of personnel legislation cannot possibly consider all the situations that exist under its provisions; thus, many matters are typically interpreted and resolved through judicial decisions. The OSHAct realizes that safety is the obligation of both employers and employees; however, only employers are subject to penalties for noncompliance. This situation raises the following question: *Can employers be penalized for their employees' unsafe acts?*

There is no clear-cut answer to this question; however, many OSHA citations have been dismissed (either by OSHRC or the courts) when the presence of unforeseeable conduct has been established. *Unforeseeable conduct* describes a situation in which a reasonable employer could not have expected an employee's unsafe act and therefore could not have prevented the act from occurring. Examples of unforeseeable conduct include the following:[79]

A production machine operator was injured when he reached into a machine to clear a jam. He had operated this machine for many years and, until the accident, had always followed the proper procedure of stopping the machine before clearing it.

A guard was removed by employees in one industrial facility, and the machine thereafter operated without the guard.

Of course, even in this situation, an employer has some obligations under the act—namely, ensuring that the equipment complies in general with standards and that employees are competent to perform the work assigned them. The employer must also make a reasonable effort to prevent employees' hazardous conduct.[80]

Other implications of the act involve the area of employees' safety complaints, which, as previously mentioned, are often investigated by OSHA. Some employees might not file safety complaints because they fear their employers will retaliate, possibly even by firing them. A related question is: *What legal rights do employees have when they file safety complaints?* The OSHAct anticipated this question in its provision 11-c, which in effect states that an employee cannot be discharged or discriminated against in any manner for filing a safety complaint or assisting in an OSHA investigation. This provision also enables the Secretary of Labor to bring court action against any person who discriminates against an employee for those reasons. Remedies for discrimination include reinstating a discharged employee to his or her former job with back pay.

Employees have used the 11-c provision; for example, at the start of fiscal year 1977, a backlog of nearly 1,000 such cases existed. There are well-established procedures for investigating these cases;[81] however, the cases' resolution is often controversial. Approximately 20 percent of the safety discrimination cases are decided in the employees' favor.[82] Employers contend that this relatively low figure illustrates the potential for abuse of the OSHAct; poor performers may file a bogus safety complaint and then try to hold onto their jobs through provision 11-c's protections. Union leaders, on the other hand, contend that these statistics reflect employers' cleverness; they say an employer can fabricate other reasons for the discharge, the merits of the safety complaint nonwithstanding.[83]

None of the OSHAct's provisions (including 11-c) explicitly protect employees who refuse to perform work because of safety or health hazards. This situation raises the following question: *Under what circumstances, if any, are employees who refuse unsafe work assignments protected against discipline?* This situation was considered in a recent Supreme Court case, *Whirlpool Corp. v. Marshall.* The case involved a Whirlpool manufacturing facility that had overhead conveyors to transport appliance components through the plant. A horizontal wire mesh screen covered with paper was installed approximately twenty feet above the plant floor to protect employees working below from the objects and the grease that occasionally fell from the overhead conveyors. The company's maintenance employees spent several hours each week on top of the screen removing fallen objects and replacing the paper.

Approximately one week after a maintenance employee fell to his death through the guard screen, two maintenance employees refused to remove debris from the screen, claiming that it was unsafe. They were then instructed to leave the premises without working or being paid for the remaining six hours of the shift. The Secretary of Labor contended that this action represented a disciplinary suspension that constituted discriminatory treatment under 11-c of the act.

The Supreme Court, in deciding this issue, agreed with the employer that the OSHAct did not specifically address the work refusal issue. However, the Supreme Court stated that safety legislation must be "liberally construed to effectuate the congressional purpose."[84] The decision affirmed the Secretary of Labor's inclusion of work refusal under the scope of the act. It did, however, place two cautions on employees who refused work:

The employees have no power under the regulation to order their employer to correct the hazardous condition or to clear the dangerous workplace of others. Moreover, any employee who acts in reliance on the regulations runs the risk of discharge or reprimand in the event a court subsequently finds that he acted unreasonably or in bad faith.[85]

Some contend that these cautions, as well as the context of the decision, restrict its applicability to other cases.[86] In other words, employees at other facilities will not be encouraged to refuse to work simply because of the *Whirlpool* decision. Many employers, however, believe the decision has far-reaching implications. At a minimum, an employer appears to have two options when an employee refuses to perform an allegedly unsafe assignment: It can allow the employee to refuse the work or discipline the employee, thereby risking litigation. The magnitude and impact of the decision can only be assessed in the light of future experience.

Summary

Both managers and employees want a safe working environment, although controversy may arise over how this mutual goal is to be achieved. *Safety* refers to the avoidance of accidents, while *health* also includes physical conditions other than injuries, which may not be easily detected. Many potential hazards exist in the workplace—noise, dust, fires, explosions, electrocution, toxic materials, and so forth. Companies do not have identical types or amounts of safety hazards, since they are influenced by different technologies. Yet all companies have the potential for safety and health problems.

Accidents result from unsafe acts, unsafe conditions (mechanical or physical hazards), or a combination of unsafe acts and unsafe conditions. Several measurements are used to chart accident trends. Statistics show no consistent increases or reductions in accidents in over fifty years of industrial accident reporting. It should be remembered that accident statistics are narrow in scope, are affected by the sample used, may be of little value to the individual employee, and are affected by a recent change from traditional measurements of injury frequency and severity to two accident incidence measurements developed by the Occupational Safety and Health Administration (OSHA).

Company interest in safety is influenced by social values and economic considerations. A third influence is the Occupational Safety and Health Act, which was enacted by Congress in 1970. The OSHAct established the Occupational Safety and Health Administration (OSHA), which is located in the Department of Labor and is mainly responsible for setting occupational safety and health standards and conducting inspections of workplaces. It also established two other agencies—the National Institute for Safety and Health (NIOSH), which helps develop safety standards, and the Occupational Safety and Health Review Commission (OSHRC), which rules on challenges to OSHA's citations. There has been considerable controversy over OSHA's safety inspections and standards; this controversy has extended to assessments of the overall impact of the OSHAct.

Organizational efforts to improve safety usually begin with a company safety policy, which symbolizes management's commitment to safe working conditions, encourages managers and employees to resolve a broad variety of hazards, and raises and answers questions concerning safety. Three general areas of activity for safety programs are investigating, reducing risks, and monitoring the program through reporting and follow-up efforts. Related safety techniques include the use of careful selection of employees, safety research, accident analysis, safety engineers, safety committees, protective equipment, safety incentives and contests, and safety communication and training.

Both employers and employees have legal rights concerning safety issues. Employers are seldom liable for an employee's unsafe act if the presence of unforseeable conduct has been established. Employees may not be penalized for filing safety complaints and can refuse to perform assignments they consider unsafe, although the Supreme Court in its Whirlpool decision did not give a blanket endorsement of this latter practice.

Discussion Questions

1. Explain the difference between *safety* and *health,* including a discussion of accident causes in your answer.

2. Fully explain why accident statistics, while sometimes helpful, are always inconclusive.

3. Assess OSHA's safety inspections and safety standards and describe the controversy they have created. Also tell why it is difficult to assess the impact of the OSHAct.

4. Name several characteristics of a good company safety policy. Describe three specific techniques for improving safety, along with the advantages and disadvantages of each technique.

5. Explain how both employers and employees have some degree of legal protection under the OSHAct.

Notes

1. Rachel Scott, *Muscle and Blood* (New York: E. P. Dutton and Company, 1974), p. 3.
2. Gail M. Martin, "Safety and Health in the Magic Kingdom," *Job Safety and Health* 5 (July 1977), p. 7.
3. Dan Petersen, *Safety Management: A Human Approach* (Englewood, N.J.: Aloray, 1975), pp. 17–18.

4. D. Keith Denton, "Effective Safety Management: Focus on the Human Element," *Management Review* 69 (December 1980), pp. 47, 48.

5. Ronald Cole, *Industrial Safety Techniques* (Sydney, Australia: West Publishing Corp., 1975), p. 134.

6. Petersen, *Safety Management,* p. 239.

7. See, for example, James R. Chelius, "Economic and Demographic Aspects of the Occupational Injury Problem," *Quarterly Review of Economics and Business* 19 (Summer 1979), pp. 65–70; Alan E. Dillingham, "Age and Workplace Injuries," *Aging and Work* 4 (Winter 1981), pp. 1–10; Norman Root and Judy R. Daley, "Are Women Safer Workers? A New Look at the Data," *Monthly Labor Review* 103 (September 1980), pp. 3–10.

8. Morris E. Davis, "The Impact of Workplace Health and Safety on Black Workers: Assessment and Prognosis," *Labor Law Journal* 31 (December 1980), pp. 723–732.

9. For related literature and interpretations, see Davis W. Carvey and Roger G. Nibler, "Biorythmic Cycles and the Incidence of Industrial Accidents," *Personnel Psychology* 30 (Autumn 1970), pp. 447–454.

10. For a thoroughly researched look into related safety approaches (including extensive bibliography), see C. Michael Pfeifer, Jr., et al., eds., *An Evaluation of Policy Related Research on Effectiveness of Alternative Methods to Reduce Occupational Illness and Accidents* (Columbia, Md.: Behavioral/Safety Center, Westinghouse Electric Corporation, 1974).

11. Franklin Wallick, *The American Worker: An Endangered Species* (New York: Ballentine Books, 1972), pp. 50–51.

12. Ray Davidson, *Peril on the Job: A Study of Hazards in the Chemical Industries* (Washington, D.C.: Public Affairs Press, 1970), p. 1.

13. Roland P. Blake, *Industrial Safety,* 3d ed. (Englewood Cliffs, N.J.: Prentice-Hall, 1963), pp. 43–44.

14. Data for these conclusions were obtained from *Accident Facts: 1977 Edition (Chicago: National Safety Council, 1977), pp. 28–29; Accident Facts: 1980 Edition (Chicago: National Safety Council, 1980), p. 28.*

15. James D. English, "A Union Viewpoint," *Labor Law Journal* 29 (August 1978), p. 499.

16. *Ibid.,* p. 502.

17. Herbert R. Northrup, *The Impact of OSHA* (Philadelphia: University of Pennsylvania, 1978), p. 537.

18. Dan Cordtz, "Safety on the Job Becomes a Major Job for Management," *Fortune* 86 (November 1972), p. 115.

19. Wallick, *American Worker,* p. 25.

20. U.S. Congress, House, Subcommittee on Labor of the Committee on Education and Labor, *Occupational Safety and Health Act of 1969, Hearings, on H.R. 843, H.R. 3809, H.R. 4294, and H.R. 13373, Part 1,* 91st Cong. 1st sess., September 24, 25, 30 and October 9, 15, 16, and 29, 1969, p. 405.

21. "Life or Death for Your Business?" *Nation's Business* 56 (April 1968), p. 37.

22. Some of these associations were: the Chamber of Commerce of the United States, the National Association of Manufacturers, the American Iron and Steel Institute, and the American Medical Association. Perhaps the biggest outside backer of the legislation was the AFL-CIO. *Congress and the Nation, Vol. II, 1965–1968* (Washington, D.C.: Congressional Quarterly Service, 1969), p. 821.

23. See, for example, Timothy F. Cleary, "Inter-Agency Relationships under OSHA: A Brief Review of OSHRC Decisions," *Labor Law Journal* 29 (January 1978) pp. 3–8.

24. It should be noted that Section 19(a) of the act places responsibility on each federal agency to establish and maintain an occupational safety and health program that is consistent with the standards set forth by the Secretary of Labor.

25. The agency currently relies on 10 regional offices and 100 local offices to carry out federal law enforcement. "In addition, 23 states—covering 40% of the U.S. workforce—rely on state OSHA plans for their protection." Michael A. Verespej, "Has OSHA Improved?" *Industry Week,* August 4, 1980, p. 55.

26. In 1977, the Supreme Court affirmed two decisions of the lower courts that upheld OSHA's capacity to fine employers. The decision disagreed with the employers' contentions that they were entitled to a jury trial under the Seventh Amendment before a penalty could be assessed. Bureau of National Affairs, *Daily Labor Report,* March 23, 1977, p. A-11.

27. The authors are grateful to Steve Smittle, who aided in the preparation of this section. For more information about inspections, see "OSHA's Bad Image Blamed on Politics," *The National Underwriter: Property and Casualty Insurance Edition,* October 16, 1978, pp. 19–20; "Restraining OSHA: It's Just a Matter of Time," *Business Week,* May 5, 1980, p. 110; Michael A. Verespej, "OSHA Revamps Its Inspection Policies," *Industry Week,* September 17, 1979, p. 19; Eula Bingham, "The New Look at OSHA: Vital Changes," *Labor Law Journal* 29 (August 1978), p. 488.

28. Jill Wechsler, "Overhauling OSHA," *Dun's Review* 117 (June 1981), p. 93.

29. OSHA handles employees' complaints it deems to be "nonserious" by writing to the companies involved and requesting corrective action. "OSHA will also attempt to weed out and dismiss 'frivolous' complaints." Verespej, "OSHA Revamps Its Inspection Policies," p. 19.

30. See, for example, Bureau of National Affairs, *Daily Labor Report,* April 11, 1980, p. 2.

31. Wechsler, "Overhauling OSHA," p. 93. Also see Everett E. Adam, Jr., "Priority Assignment of OSHA Safety Inspectors," *Management Science* 24 (November 1978), pp. 1642–1649.

32. *Mashall v. Barlow's Inc.,* May 23, 1978. See Bureau of National Affairs, *Daily Labor Report,* May 23, 1978, pp. D-1–D-9. For a perspective on this situation, see Daniel L. Reynolds, "OSHA and the Fourth Amendment," *Human Resource Management* 17 (Fall 1978), pp. 17–24.

33. Urban C. Lehner, "Job-Safety Inspectors Seldom Required to Get Warrants Despite Justices' Ruling," *Wall Street Journal,* July 17, 1978, p. 13.

34. "Now OSHA Must Justify Its Inspection Targets," *Business Week,* April 9, 1979, p. 64. For additional information, see Mark A. Rothstein, "OSHA Inspections after *Marshall vs. Barlow's Inc.," Duke Law Journal* 1979 (February 1979), pp. 63–103.

35. See, for example, Bureau of National Affairs, *Daily Labor Report,* July 11, 1980, p. 1.

36. "The Door at OSHA Opens Up to Industry," *Business Week,* April 6, 1981, p. 32.

37. Frederick D. Braid, "OSHA and NLRA: New Wrinkles on Old Issues," *Labor Law Journal* 29 (December 1978), p. 758.

38. Sidney M. Wolfe and Robert B. Stalberg, "Oversight on Administration of OSHA, 1978," in U.S. Congress, Senate, *Hearings before the Subcommittee on Labor of the Committee on Human Resources,* 95th Cong. 2d sess., p. 422.

39. Verespej, "Has OSHA Improved?" p. 55.

40. Nicholas Askounes Ashford, *Crisis in the Workplace: Occupational Disease and Injury* (Cambridge, Mass.: MIT Press, 1976), p. 145.

41. Edwin A. Bowers, "OSHA: The Government Gang That Can't Shoot Straight," *Iron Age,* July 10, 1978, p. 31.

42. "OSHA: Hardest to Live With," *Business Week,* April 4, 1977, p. 74.

43. For related information, see Walter S. Mossberg, "Changing Emphasis: Safety Agency Will Tighten Regulations on Health Hazards," *Wall Street Journal,* May 19, 1977, p. 48, and Bureau of National Affairs, *Daily Labor Report,* October 24, 1978, pp. 1, 2.

44. Bingham, "New Look at OSHA," p. 488.

45. James C. Hyatt, "Protecting the Worker: Job Safety Equipment Comes Under Fire: Are Hard Hats a Solution or a Problem?" *Wall Street Journal,* November 18, 1977, p. 48.

46. Gail Bronson, "Ailing Agency: Set Up to Do Research on Health on the Job, NIOSH Is Sick Itself," *Wall Street Journal,* April 19, 1978, p. 1.

47. Bureau of National Affairs, "Decision of Supreme Court in AFL-CIO Industrial Union Department *v.* American Petroleum Institute," *Daily Labor Report,* July 2, 1980, p. E-1. See also Tom Alexander "OSHA's Ill-Conceived Crusade against Cancer," *Fortune,* July 3, 1978, pp. 86–89.

48. Douglas Soutar, "A Management Viewpoint," *Labor Law Journal* 29 (August 1978), p. 493.

49. Morton Corn, "An Inside View of OSHA Compliance," *Personnel Administrator* 24 (November 1979), p. 39.

50. Bingham, "New Look at OSHA," p. 487.

51. Verespej, "Has OSHA Improved?" p. 54.

52. Robert E. McClay, "Professionalizing the Safety Function," *Personnel Journal* 56 (February 1977), p. 73.

53. Lane Kirkland, "OSHA: A 10-Year Success Story," *AFL-CIO American Federationist* 87 (July 1980), p. 2. Used by permission of the *AFL-CIO American Federationist,* the official monthly magazine of the AFL-CIO.

54. *Labor Law Journal* 31 (April 1980), p. 250.

55. Northrup, *Impact of OSHA,* p. 539. See also James J. Cicchetti, "Does OSHA Help or Hinder Loss Control?" *Risk Management* 27 (December 1980), pp. 38–39.

56. Robert Stewart Smith, "The Impact of OSHA Inspections on Manufacturing Injury Rates," *Journal of Human Resources* 14 (Spring 1979), pp. 145–170; Lawrence P. Etkin and J. Brad Chapman, "Is OSHA Effective in Reducing Industrial Injuries?" *Labor Law Journal* 26 (April 1975), pp. 236–242.

57. Wolfe and Stalberg, "Oversight on Administration of OSHA, 1978," p. 417.

58. Richard E. Ginnold, "A View of the Costs and Benefits of the Job Safety and Health Law," *Monthly Labor Review* 103 (August 1980), pp. 24–26.

59. Niles Howard and Susan Antilla. "What Price Safety? The Zero Risk Debate," *Dun's Review* 114 (September 1979), pp. 49–57.

60. Leo Kiebala, "OSHA after Four Years," *Personnel Administrator* 20 (May 1975), pp. 32–33.

61. Verespej, "Has OSHA Improved?" p. 51.
62. Lawrence S. Bacow, *Bargaining for Job Safety and Health* (Cambridge, Mass.: MIT Press, 1980), pp. 49–50.
63. *Ibid.,* p. 51.
64. Wallick, *American Worker,* p. 65.
65. These areas were suggested by two sources: Leon Schenkelbach, *The Safety Management Primer* (New York: Dow Jones–Irwin, 1975), p. 11; Henry M. Taylor, "Occupational Health Management by Objectives," *Personnel* 57 (January/February 1980), p. 61.
66. Cole, *Industrial Safety Techniques,* p. 137.
67. McClay, "Professionalizing the Safety Function," p. 74.
68. This quotation is attributed to George Bernard Shaw and is cited in Cole, *Industrial Safety Techniques,* p. 47.
69. Petersen, *Safety Management,* p. 202.
70. John Zalusky, "The Worker Views the Enforcement of Safety Laws," *Labor Law Journal* 26 (April 1975), p. 226.
71. Hyatt, "Protecting the Worker," p. 48.
72. Bureau of National Affairs, *Daily Labor Report,* January 3, 1974, p. C-3, cited in Petersen, *Safety Management,* p. 358.
73. Pfeifer et al., *Evaluation of Policy,* p. 53.
74. K. Goodyear, "An Experiment in Safety Incentives," *British Journal of Industrial Safety* 7 (1966), pp. 30–31.
75. Petersen, *Safety Management,* p. 219.
76. Fred A. Manuele, "How Do You Know Your Hazard Control Is Effective?" *Risk Management* 27 (December 1980), p. 28.
77. Scott, *Muscle and Blood,* pp. 50–51.
78. Petersen, *Safety Management,* p. 61.
79. Gordon Betz, "You Make It Safe, Workers Won't Cooperate—Now What?" *Automation* 23 (March 1976), p. 60.
80. *Ibid.,* p. 62; see also Roger B. Jacobs, "Employee Resistance to OSHA Standards: Toward a More Reasonable Approach," *Labor Law Journal* 30 (April 1979), pp. 219–230.
81. For a discussion of these procedures, see Richard T. Foote, "How OSHA Handles Discrimination Complaints," *Job Safety and Health* 5 (August 1977), pp. 4–9.
82. *Ibid.,* p. 9.
83. "Labor Letter," *Wall Street Journal,* June 8, 1976, p. 1.
84. Bureau of National Affairs, *Daily Labor Report,* February 26, 1980, p. D-4.
85. *Ibid.,* p. D-6.
86. See, for example, Kenneth Kirschner, "Workers in a Whirlpool: Employees' Statutory Rights to Refuse Hazardous Work," *Labor Law Journal* 31 (May 1980), pp. 283–294. For additional dimensions of this issue, see Nancy K. Frank, "A Question of Equity: Worker's 'Right to Refuse' under OSHA Compared to the Criminal Necessity Defense," *Labor Law Journal* 31 (October 1980), pp. 617–626; Larry Drapkin, "The Right to Refuse Hazardous Work after Whirlpool," *Industrial Relations Law Journal* 4 (1980), pp. 29–60.

Chapter 14

Labor Relations in Perspective

We think the obituaries for workers and their unions have been premature, based principally on superficial reading of available materials, and distorted references drawn from short-term trends. We cannot, however, wholly discount the influence of simple anti-labor and anti-working-class bias.

Brendan and Patricia Cayo Sexton, "Labor's Decade—Maybe," in *The Seventies: Problems and Proposals,* ed. Irving Howe and Michael Harrington (New York: Harper and Row, 1972), p. 283.

We noted in Chapter 1 that labor unions can affect the personnel function. Unionized firms may have specialized personnel functions such as negotiating labor agreements and resolving employees' grievances. Even the personnel function of nonunion firms and employees may be affected by collective bargaining. For example, a union-negotiated wage increase in a particular industry may be passed on to employees in nonunion firms that want to remain nonunion.

It is therefore necessary to examine the relationship between management and unions as well as the problems and prospects associated with labor relations activities. This chapter first presents an overview of the labor relations process by describing its focal point (work rules), participants (union and management organizations, employees, and the government), and steps or phases. Historical and legal aspects of labor unions are briefly discussed to put the subject into proper perspective. Later sections discuss two topics of particular interest to personnel students—the reasons why employees join unions and the attitudes and activities of nonunion employers. Finally, the chapter approaches a most controversial issue: Have unions outlived their usefulness?

The Labor Relations Process

The labor relations process occurs when *management and the exclusive bargaining agent for the employees (the union or labor organization) jointly decide upon and enforce terms and conditions of employment (work rules)*. Management in nonunion situations unilaterally determines and administers its many personnel activities. However, where unions represent employees, firms become involved in the labor relations process, which has various elements and steps, each having implications for personnel activities and the organization.

Elements in the Labor Relations Process

Focal Point of Labor Relations—Work Rules Union and management organizations are concerned with the formulation and implementation of work rules that apply to: (1) compensation in all its forms (overtime payments, vacations, holidays, and the like) and (2) employees' and employers' rights (production standards, layoff procedures, ground rules for disciplining employees, and so on). Some work rules can apply to almost any organization—a no-smoking rule in areas where there are explosive or combustible materials, for example. Other work rules are unique to a particular company or industry. For example, the following work rule has been negotiated in the entertainment-nightclub industry:

Discharge and Suspension for Lack of Bunny Image. (1) The parties acknowledge the great importance of Bunny Image and its maintenance to PCI, to the Clubs and to Bunnies, due in part to the established recognition of Bunnies as unique and distinctive Playboy employees. . . . The parties acknowledge the difficulty of defining

"Bunny Image" and agree that determination of Bunny Image for purposes of discharge or suspension may include, but is not limited to, the physical appearance of a Bunny and the impression she conveys to customers and others.

This example illustrates another dimension of work rules—their degree of specificity. In many cases it is impossible to formulate a work rule that will specifically include every possible situation. Yet vague work rules can return to haunt management, particularly if a neutral arbitrator (discussed in Chapter 15) does not accept management's interpretation of the rule (for example, disagrees with management that an employee has lost her "Bunny Image").

Work rules also change over time, either because of changing industrial conditions or changing external influences such as public opinion. One example of such a change is the case of a Milwaukee police union's attempting to alter management's rule prohibiting unmarried couples from living together.[1]

Participants in the Labor Relations Process There are four general categories of participants: union organizations, management organizations, employees, and government. Several union and management officials negotiate and administer the work rules: however, these individuals do not always represent a consensus within their organizations.

There is seldom a single union or a single management position on a particular labor relations issue. As noted in Chapters 1 and 2, an organization has several functions; and line-staff relationships between the personnel department and other departments often involve differing interests. Thus, the production, sales, and accounting departments might view labor relations quite differently from the personnel department.

The union is similarly subject to differences of opinion. Most union organizations have at least three organizational levels—local, national (or international), and federation. The *local union* is a branch of the national union; it receives its charter from the national union and operates under the national union's constitution, bylaws, and rules. The national union's constitution establishes the number and types of local union officers and the limits of their authority.

The typical union member identifies more closely with the local union than with the other union levels. He or she knows the local officers and is involved in union matters at the local workplace. When the union member has a grievance, the local union is the first to assist. When a strike occurs, the local union officers are the ones in contact with the strikers on the picket line. However, local union meetings are not widely attended (estimates have ranged from 5 to 10 percent of the membership) unless crucial issues—strikes, contract negotiations, or election of officers—are to be discussed.

Exhibit 14.1	Approximate Membership of Selected National Employee Organizations	
	Employee Organizations	Membership
	International Brotherhood of Teamsters, Chauffeurs, Warehousemen and Helpers of America (IBT)	2,300,000
	National Education Association (NEA)	1,600,800
	International Union, United Automobile, Aerospace and Agricultural Implement Workers of America (UAW)	1,500,000
	United Steelworkers of America (USWA)	1,400,000
	United Food and Commercial Workers International Union (UFCWIU)	1,300,000
	American Federation of State, County and Municipal Employees (AFSCME)	1,200,000
	International Brotherhood of Electrical Workers (IBEW)	1,000,000
	International Association of Machinists and Aerospace Workers (IAM)	927,000
	United Brotherhood of Carpenters and Joiners (UBC)	800,000

Source: *Encyclopedia of Associations,* 16th edition, edited by Denise S. Akey (copyright © by Gale Research Company), 1981, pp. 504, 1281–1283, 1285, 1288. Used by permission.

The national or international union in the United States occupies the chief position in organized labor because of the size of its membership (see Exhibit 14.1) and its ability to exert collective bargaining influence over locals (through policies, research, and strike funds). In many cases, such as in the automobile, trucking, steel, and electricial industries, collective bargaining over major issues occurs at the national level, although representatives from various local levels may be present at the bargaining table.

The American Federation of Labor and Congress of Industrial Organizations (AFL-CIO), while it does not include all U.S. labor unions, is composed of 105 national and international unions that have more than 60,000 local unions and 13,600,000 members.[2] Examples of AFL-CIO services include the following:

Speaking before Congress and other branches of government.

Representing U.S. labor in world affairs, and keeping in direct contact with labor unions in other nations.

Coordinating activities such as community services, political education, lobbying, and voter registration.

Helping to coordinate efforts to organize nonunion workers throughout the United States.

Employees, the third participant category, can have loyalties to both union and management organizations. This situation is found in both the private and public sectors; for example, public employees such as firefighters, police, and teachers may feel torn between their job duties and the strategic advantages of a strike. Employees can also be indifferent or even cynical about both union and management organizations, as typified by the comments of a steelworker: "I fantasize about a sexy blonde in Miami who's got my union dues. . . . I think of the head of my union the way I think of the head of my company. Living it up."[3]

In many instances, employees' backgrounds may influence work rules. For example, if most employees at a facility are black, then there will probably be pressure for a holiday commemorating Martin Luther King's death or birthday. If the average age of employees at a facility is fifty, they probably will emphasize pension plan improvements, whereas a younger workforce might stress maternity benefits or higher hourly wages.

Union and management officials and employees must take into account a fourth participant—government, with it regulations, legislation, and judicial decisions. Government's influence is discussed throughout the book and won't be elaborated upon here. Suffice it to say the government can modify work rules in spite of the preferences of unions, management, or employees.

Even governmental actions that do not directly pertain to labor relations can have an impact on work rules. For example, the government has recently reformed regulation of the trucking industry in the hope that competition among trucking firms will be increased, thereby reducing inflationary pressures. These efforts could increase management pressure to obtain concessions from unions in the labor agreements so they might more effectively deal with competition from nonunion firms resulting from deregulation.

Steps in the Labor Relations Process

The labor relations process consists of three phases:

1. *Recognition of the legitimate rights and responsibilities of unions and management representatives.* Considerations involved in this phase include the legal right of employees to join unions, union organizing drives, and the reasons employees join unions. All these dimensions are at least briefly discussed in the remainder of this chapter. Another consideration is the attitude of labor and management officials toward each other. Managerial attitudes may vary from outright resistance to recognition that a union represents an important aspect of labor relations activities.

2. *Negotiation of the labor agreement, including appropriate strategies and tactics.* This phase includes the actual writing and signing of the collective bargaining agreement. The media tend to give this phase the most publicity, primarily because key union and management personnel are involved, the outcomes can have a major impact on the rest of the economy, and the tactics are dynamic and newsworthy.

3. *Administration of the negotiated labor agreement—applying and enforcing the terms of the agreement on a daily basis.* This phase includes activities that occur during the life of the agreement and account for the most time and energy spent by union and management officials. Administering the agreement usually involves a larger number of these officials than the preceding phases.

Of course, not all labor-management relationships involve all three phases. Indeed, employees and their representative unions at some facilities are still striving to accomplish the first phase of the process.

Historical and Legislative Aspects of the Labor Relations Process

History of the Labor Movement

Page limitations prohibit a detailed discussion of labor history, although citations for additional readings are given.[4] Brief descriptions are given of the following periods: 1869 to World War I, World War I to World War II, and World War II to the present.

1869 to World War I Unions as we know them today did not exist before the 1800s, but three major national unions were formed in the period from 1869 to World War I: the Knights of Labor (KOL), the American Federation of Labor (AFL), and the Industrial Workers of the World (IWW). Only the AFL survived; however, insights into contemporary labor relations can be gained by contrasting the goals and strategies of the AFL with those of KOL and IWW.

The Knights of Labor was formed in 1869. One of its most prominent leaders, Terence Powderly, stressed that its goal was social reform. Powderly claimed that members should not concern themselves unduly with material working conditions, as they were but stepping stones to "a higher cause, of nobler nature . . . the more exalted and divine nature of man, his high and noble capabilities for good."[5]

The moralistic and reform-oriented overtones of the Knights guided its membership policies, organizational structure, and strategies. Since moral betterment affected all members of society, the Knights encouraged people of all callings—even employers—to join their organization. (They did not, however, welcome professional gamblers, stockbrokers, lawyers, bankers, and those who lived in whole or in part by the sale or manufacture of intoxicating liquor.) The KOL's organization at the local level included many employee classifications; however, centralized authority rested at the top. A major strategy of the KOL was to educate its members on how to achieve a better society. Strikes were actively discouraged, since they would lessen the needed unity between employees and employers.

In retrospect, it is easy to furnish reasons why the KOL failed:

Faulty assumption that a group of employees with different backgrounds and employers would have identical interests.

Inability of the KOL's leadership to identify with members' short-range material goals.

Further, since there was no labor legislation, the rights of individuals to join labor organizations such as the Knights were not protected.

Finally, a violent event—the Haymarket Riot—illustrated how vulnerable the Knights were to negative public opinion. At a public gathering in Chicago of some 3,000 people who favored a change from a ten-hour work day to an eight-hour one, a bomb was thrown at policemen and several bullets were exchanged. Several people were killed, and some two hundred were wounded. The event destroyed the effectiveness of the KOL in two paradoxical ways. First, substantial negative public opinion associated the KOL with the Haymarket Riot, even though its leaders, particularly Powderly, strongly discouraged participation in the event. Second, Powderly was criticized by many KOL members for this very inaction.

The American Federation of Labor (AFL) was formed in 1886. One of its founders was Samuel Gompers, who had once been a member of the KOL. Gompers had come to believe that social reform was a hopeless cause and that the major, if not the only, goal of U.S. unions should be to *improve the material conditions of members through the existing capitalistic system.*

Without egotism and I hope very little of vanity, I will say I came to the conclusion many years ago that it is our duty to live our lives as workers in the society in which we live, and not to work for the downfall or destruction, or the overthrow of that society, but for its fuller development and evolution.[6]

Though Gompers realized capitalism could provide material gains for employees, he also realized that labor unions had to prod management in order to receive a fair return for their efforts. Unlike Powderly, Gompers believed that strikes were sometimes necessary; and he encouraged unions to set aside funds to support employees who were on strike. Another AFL strategy was political action, which was based on working within the existing two-party system rather than forming an independent labor party. The AFL worked hard to get "friends" of organized labor elected and "enemies" of organized labor defeated.

The AFL's organizational structure featured two related principles: *exclusive jurisdiction* and *decentralized authority.* The AFL recognized that each craft or trade had unique working conditions; therefore, it assumed that each craft should have its own union. Gompers also believed the AFL's success depended on the acceptance of its members. Thus, the real authority rested with member local and national unions, not with the AFL. The early growth of the AFL was not spectacular, but it did endure even through the Great Depression of 1893.

The AFL also fared well against the challenge of a revolutionary group, the Industrial Workers of the World (IWW). The IWW was founded in 1905 by "Big Bill" Haywood, who opened the first convention with the following words:

Fellow Workers . . . We are here to confederate the workers of this country into a working class movement that shall have for its purpose the emancipation of the working class from the slave bondage of Capitalism. . . . The aims and objects of this organization should be to put the working class in possession of the economic power, the means of life in control of the machinery of production and distribution without regard to capitalist masters.[7]

The initial goal of the IWW was to overthrow the existing capitalistic system by any means, because its followers believed employers and employees had nothing in common. It, however, had ceased to exist by 1918, largely because it ignored the short-run material goals of its members, had no real organizational structure or financial base, and alienated the public and the mass media by being associated with violence and antiwar statements during World War I.

World War I to World War II Between 1920 and 1924, AFL membership dropped from 4,078,000 to 2,866,000. This decline was largely due to aggressive counteractions by employers (discussed in Chapter 2) and the unwillingness or inability of AFL unions to organize mass production industries (the steel, automobile, electrical, rubber, maritime, and textile industries).

Many AFL leaders and members thought it would be impossible to apply AFL organizational principles to a mass production company. For example, if General Electric had fifty different products, then fifty different AFL unions (each with exclusive jurisdiction over its members' interests) would be needed for effective collective bargaining.

However, some AFL leaders thought that mass production facilities could be organized along industrial lines. For example, all employees working at a facility (electricians, carpenters, janitors, assemblers, fork lift operators, and so on) would be members of the same union. The disagreement over this issue resulted in seven national unions' pulling out of the AFL in 1936 and forming an independent, rival organization, the Congress of Industrial Organizations (CIO). By November 1937, the CIO had made tremendous gains in organizing the mass production industries.

Although the CIO's structure resembled those of the KOL and the IWW in that it included different jobs in one union, the similarity was superficial. Important differences, as well as several reasons related to events of the time, contributed to the CIO's success.

Differences in goals and leadership. The CIO's aims strongly differed from the vague long-range goals of the KOL and IWW. Indeed, the CIO was similar to the AFL in its emphasis on tangible, short-range goals. The CIO leaders also were aggressive and experienced in organizing unions.

Passage of favorable labor legislation in 1935. Labor legislation is discussed in more detail later in this chapter.

Changes in employees' attitudes. Many newly enrolled union members had experienced the Great Depression of the 1930s and realized that job security could not be solely achieved through hard work and loyalty to the employer. These employees now viewed unions as a mechanism that could promote job security as well as other material benefits.

Thus, by the onset of World War II, organized labor had reversed its membership decline of the 1920s, rising to almost 9 million members in 1940. Yet the rivalry between the CIO and the AFL remained intense and violent, as AFL and CIO organizers often physically clashed over the right to represent factory employees.[8]

World War II to the Present Perhaps the most dramatic postwar development in organized labor was the merger of the AFL and the CIO in 1955. Both organizations realized that competing for the same employees was costly and ineffective—organized labor would benefit if the energies devoted to raiding each other for members were spent on organizing nonunion employees. Both organizations also realized that combined efforts might have helped to elect to the presidency a supporter of organized labor, Adlai Stevenson, instead of Dwight D. Eisenhower.

The merger of the AFL and the CIO did reduce raiding; it also reduced the power of local unions, who could no longer threaten to leave their national union and switch to the rival organization. But while the merger reduced the divisiveness within organized labor, it cannot be concluded that it prompted significant growth and change.

Comparing organized labor as it existed at the end of World War II with its present state appears to reveal more similarities than differences. Organized labor still is a minority movement, never representing more than 28 percent of the employees in the civilian workforce. Yet organized labor's influence on society can on occasion be pronounced. Clearly, a settlement negotiated between a major corporation and a labor union can have spillover effects on the wage policies of other corporations, union and nonunion. And no political leader aspiring to the U.S. presidency proclaims himself or herself antiunion.[9]

Another similarity is organized labor's continual push for short-range material goals instead of long-range reform. The Knights of

Labor taught organized labor a permanent lesson—goals should relate to members' needs instead of being abstract attempts to change the social system.[10] The bargaining tactics used to achieve these goals (discussed in more detail in Chapter 15) have also tended to remain the same during this period.

Finally, consensus among diverse national unions and among members within the AFL-CIO federation is still rare. This problem occurs in any large organization, particularly one that grants much autonomy to its members. The AFL-CIO is always subject to national unions' withdrawing from its organization. One major union, the Teamsters, left the AFL-CIO and does not appear to have suffered financially or lost membership as a result. Within unions, leaders have had to deal with the changing values of younger members, who sometimes challenge traditional old-line union leaders with new goals and priorities.

Labor Legislation

Organized labor before 1935 did not enjoy many legal protections. Collective bargaining depended on management's voluntary acceptance of labor organizations. However, the situation changed dramatically in 1935 with the passage of the Wagner Act. This piece of legislation, also called the National Labor Relation's Act (NLRA), was amended in 1947 (Taft-Hartley provisions) and in 1959 (Landrum-Griffin provisions).

The National Labor Relations Act is a detailed piece of legislation, particularly when we consider its modifications and interpretations by thousands of judicial decisions. Briefly summarized from a current perspective, some of the main provisions are grouped below in two general and related categories: rights of employees and unfair labor practices. The government agency charged with administering the act, the National Labor Relations Board (NLRB), will also be discussed.

Rights of Employees The Wagner Act, in establishing a new labor relations policy, gave an indication of the changing role of the federal government in national economics.[11] It recognized that employers' denials of employees' right to organize and employers' refusal to bargain with employees' organizations had led to strikes and industrial conflicts. It also acknowledged that inequality of bargaining power between employees and employers affected the flow of commerce and aggravated recurring economic depressions by reducing wages and purchasing power.

Section 7 of the NLRA attempted to correct this situation by assuring employees of certain rights—the right to form and organize their own labor organizations; to become members of labor unions or to refuse to join; to bargain collectively through representatives of their own choosing; and to engage in other concerted activities in a union or nonunion setting for the purpose of mutual aid or protection, such as strikes, picketing, and boycotts.

However, these rights are not unlimited; they have frequently been restricted. For instance, the right to strike can be limited by a strike's objective, its timing, and the conduct of the strikers. A strike can be declared illegal, for example, if its purpose is to achieve a contract provision limiting employment to union members. If a strike occurs when there is a no-strike provision in the contract, the timing of the strike is inappropriate; and all striking employees can be discharged. Strikers cannot threaten or engage in acts of violence, such as refusing to leave the plant or blocking persons from entering it.

In 1959, Congress, through passage of the Landrum-Griffin amendments, guaranteed employees certain rights in dealing with their labor organizations. Some of the provisions of Landrum-Griffin include the following:

Title I guarantees union members equal participation in internal union affairs; the right of free speech and assembly; reasonable and uniform dues, fees, and assessments; freedom to sue the union and its officers; and fair and equitable treatment in discipline cases.

Title II requires disclosure by union officers and employees (and employees and their agents) about financial dealings, trusteeships, and any private arrangements made with employees.

Title III regulates union trusteeships, including rules for their establishment and maintenance and the protection of the rights of members of unions under trusteeship.

Title IV regulates the conduct of union elections. These provisions are designed to ensure fairness and participation in election and to challenge the results should any illegality be found.

Title V sets forth fiduciary responsibilities of union officers and representatives, disqualifies criminals and former communists from holding union offices, and requires certain union officers to be bonded to assure the faithful discharge of their duties and responsibilities.

Unfair Labor Practices Congress also protected employees' rights by prohibiting unfair labor practices by the employer (Wagner Act) and the union (Taft-Hartley amendments). Employers, for example, cannot interfere with, restrain, or coerce employees as they engage in activities that relate to joining a union. Violations include threats to fire employees if they join a union or to close the facility if a union is organized. However, employers can explain their positions on unions to employees, as long as they offer ''no threats of reprisal or force or no promise of benefits.''[12]

Employers are also prohibited from attempting to dominate a union, interfering with the formation of a union, and financing and supporting a union. For instance, the existence of a *company union,* one that receives financial help from the company, is illegal. Nor are companies allowed to pressure employees into joining a particular union or to take an active part in organizing a union.

Employers cannot discriminate against employees in terms of hiring, length of employment, wages, or other working conditions for the purpose of encouraging or discouraging union membership. (However, if the labor agreement requires union membership as a condition of employment, a practice illegal in nineteen states, an employee can be discharged for not paying the required union initiation fees and membership dues.) Similarly, employers cannot take adverse job actions (demotion, discharge, or the like) against an employee because he or she has filed charges or given testimony at hearings (for example, before the National Labor Relations Board or the courts). A final unfair labor practice is an employer's refusal to bargain in good faith about wages, hours, or other working conditions with the representative chosen by the employees. The good faith bargaining requirement is discussed in more detail in the next chapter.

Unions also are prohibited from unfair labor practices. First, they may not restrain employees in the exercise of their rights as guaranteed under the act by doing such things as threatening employees for not supporting the union or refusing to process the grievance of an employee who has criticized union officers. Second, they may not place pressure on the employer for purposes of encouraging or discouraging union membership. For example, they cannot pressure employers to discharge employees who circulate petitions challenging a union practice or who make speeches against a contract proposal. A third provision imposes on unions the same duty as employers to bargain in good faith.

Other unfair labor practices for unions pertain to rather technical activities. Unions cannot negotiate agreements whereby union members will not be required to handle goods made by either nonunion labor or striking workers. Neither can they cause or attempt to cause an employer to pay for services that are not performed or not to be performed (a practice called *featherbedding*).

The Role of the National Labor Relations Board An independent government agency, the National Labor Relations Board, or NLRB, was established to administer the NLRA's provisions. The NLRB has two major functions: (1) supervising and conducting representation elections to determine which, if any, union will represent the employees at a particular facility and (2) adjudicating matters relating to unfair labor practices. The NLRB's procedures are set in motion only when requested by either employees, the union, or the employer. Such requests are called petitions when they involve elections and charges when they involve unfair labor practices.

The NLRB has authority to order affirmative remedies where appropriate. Examples include the following:

It can offer employees improperly discharged for union activities immediate and full reinstatement to their former positions with back pay for wages lost.

It can set aside a representation election and order a new one if the winner of the first election (either employer or union) committed an unfair labor practice.

It can order the union or the employer to cease and desist from unfair labor practices and bargain in good faith.

The NLRB's decision can be appealed to the courts by the employer or the union. The NLRB can also petition the courts for an injunction when either an employer or a union fails to comply with an NLRB order.

The NLRB is an active agency. For example, in fiscal 1980, 44,063 charges of unfair labor practices were filed and 8,198 representation elections among 458,114 employee voters were conducted.[13] Quantitative success, however, is only one effectiveness criterion. Two studies conducted in different NLRB regions (New England and Texas) found that a majority of employees ordered reinstated by the NLRB either were not put back on the job or left their jobs after reinstatement.[14] Further some critics claim that the NLRA has given the NLRB rather limited remedies for violations of labor law. For example, George Meany, former president of the AFL-CIO, believed that the cease and desist remedy doesn't discourage the employer from bargaining in bad faith.

The Act permits an employer to put off, for a year or two or three [the length of time it takes to appeal an NLRB decision], the day when he has to sit down and bargain with the representative chosen by his employees. There is no sanction other than an order to begin bargaining—bargaining that should have begun long before the order was issued.[15]

Recently, the AFL-CIO conducted extensive but unsuccessful efforts to reform existing labor legislation. These efforts will probably continue.

Organizing and Joining Unions

This section examines reasons why unions are organized and the reasons why employees join them. Attention also is given to the unique situations of white-collar and professional employees.

**Conditions That
Favor Employee
Interest in Unions**

Work and Job Conditions The remarks of an automotive spot welder illustrate two reasons that may prompt employees to join unions:

I stand in one spot, about two- or three-feet area, all night. The only time a person stops is when the line stops. We do about thirty-two jobs per car, per unit. Forty-eight units an hour, eight hours a day. Thirty-two times forty-eight times eight. Figure it out. That's how many times I push that button. . . . I know I could find better places to work. But where could I get the money I'm making?[16]

Working conditions like those described above have generated two prominent theories on why employees organize unions—namely, *alienation* and *scarcity consciousness.*

Proponents of the alienation theory believe that the extensive use of machinery in manufacturing operations results in a situation in which employees are completely dominated and depersonalized by the production process and derive neither meaning nor satisfaction from work (in terms of creativity, self-expression, pride in accomplishment, input in decision making, and the like). Employees recognize their common plight, and their resulting class consciousness results in collective action such as organizing unions.

Yet the alienation theory as the primary explanation for employees' joining unions rests on several assumptions that appear faulty. First, there is little evidence of clear-cut, extensive class consciousness in the United States; geographical, occupational, and social mobility result in loosely defined social groupings that make membership identification difficult.[17]

Alienation theorists also assume that many employees are dissatisfied with their work. However, one study (*Where Have All the Robots Gone?*) found that fewer than 25 percent of the employees surveyed expressed negative attitudes toward their work.[18] Another study found a rather low correlation between employees' dissatisfaction with their work and their vote for union representation.[19] An interesting perspective on this situation is supplied by two observers of the labor movement who contend that many employees either deny or repress their alienation, pursuing instead the more immediate gratifications generated by "the spectacles of the market place"—new cars, sports events, and so on.[20]

Finally, alienation theory assumes that employees believe unions can change job characteristics. However, as discussed further in Chapter 17, few, if any, U.S. unions actively bargain for more "meaningful" work. Perhaps the only aspect of employee alienation addressed by unions is employees' desire to speak their minds without fear of management reprisal. (One article, written over thirty years ago, stated that "intertwined with the motives for union membership is the almost universal desire to tell the boss to 'go to hell.'"[21]) Unions often inform potential members ther their rights to state their opinion of management policies will be protected by negotiated grievance procedures (Chapter 15) and just cause disciplinary policies (Chapter 17).

The theory of scarcity consciousness appears to be a more appropriate explanation of why employees join unions. Proponents of this theory contend that the average employee is interested neither in political ideology nor in class consciousness. Instead, many employees strongly believe they are living in a world of limited opportunity and that jobs are difficult to find. Though it tends to be strongest among manual workers, this feeling can apply to employees of any occupation. For example, a former college basketball coach, Al McGuire, when asked about the major job-related problem facing coaches, responded:

Security, mainly. Your life depends on a 19-year-old, freckle-faced player. Your unity and your whole season can be blown if the cheerleader gets pregnant. Look, I know the fears coaches have. I know how it is when you've lost five or six in a row and the flower of your youth is gone and you're worrying about what you can do next. I know what it's like when the student body is booing and the papers are writing bad things.[22]

Unions, then, are attractive to the many employees concerned about job security today. Unions approach job security in several ways:

Work scheduling and staffing rules can be negotiated. Such rules prescribe certain procedures for performing a job, thereby ensuring that a certain number of employees will be assigned work. One example is the requirement that no more than two floral sprays can be carried with a casket in a funeral hearse. This rule ensures in many cases that a second employee will be needed to drive a flower car.

Apprenticeship programs can be set up. These programs usually represent an attempt to ensure that qualified people are available for certain jobs. However, they can also ensure that jobs will be given only to those individuals (union members) who complete the training.

Seniority and layoff provisions can be negotiated. These provisions usually do not prevent management from reducing the number of employees at a particular facility; however, they typically offer some degree of protection to the employees with the most work years at the facility. These senior employees will be the last to be laid off and the first to be called back from a layoff. Such provisions can even appeal to the younger employee who plans to work for the same company for a period of years. Since seniority is determined by an objective measurement, it also prevents management from applying favoritism in the layoff procedure.

Lobbying for legislation protecting employees' job rights can be used. Lobbying has been important to unions throughout the years. They can use it to strengthen job security by pressing for measures against cheap labor (foreign citizens, child labor, or prison labor), in favor of quotas or restrictions on imported products, and in favor of adjustment assistance to employees displaced as a result of foreign competition.

In addition to alienation and scarcity consciousness, a third, working condition prompts employees to join unions. This condition is a contract provision called a union security clause, which requires union membership or the tendering of dues as a condition of employment. Such a provision is currently found in approximately 74 percent of labor agreements.[23] It is difficult to determine how many employees in these situations would drop their membership if union security provisions were eliminated.

Employees' Social Backgrounds and Desires Two union-related aspects of employees' social backgrounds are their own previous experiences with unions and the attitudes and experiences of significant others such as parents, spouses, and friends. For example, one union member commented, "My dad was a great union man and that's where I got it—if it wasn't union, it wasn't no good."[24] Of course, conflict among opinions can exist. Indeed, it appears that employees' social backgrounds do not explain group voting behavior,[25] probably because of the combination of complex and potentially offsetting relationships among all the variables in employees' social backgrounds.

Employees may join unions to satisfy social needs such as the need for affiliation or belonging and the need for status. An employee who sees his or her work associates expressing strong preferences for unions might likewise vote to be represented by a union (called the *bandwagon effect* or *peer pressure*).

The benefit of social affiliation the union offers depends on the degree of prestige or self-esteem it gives members. Some employees join a union for the same reason they would join any organization—to enjoy the responsibility and status associated with being a member of that organization. Employees who become union officers can often win their fellow employees' approval by "standing up to the boss." Indeed, the grievance procedure enables union members and officers to discuss problems with management officials up to six levels higher on the organization chart. This ability to challenge without fear of reprisal is seldom afforded nonunion employees or even management officials when they deal with their organizational superiors.

**Union Organizing
and the White-
Collar Employee**

White-collar employees have traditionally posed an interesting and difficult challenge to union organizers. Shifts in labor force distribution toward more service industries and white-collar occupations have attracted unions to this potential membership base. However, white-collar employees often differ from blue-collar employees in that they tend to have more education, closer identification with management, and greater interest in job design changes.[26] Labor organizers have traditionally had some difficulty in convincing white-collar employees that a union organization could effectively relate to these characteristics.

Though difficult, the situation is far from hopeless for organized labor. Union gains in organizing white-collar employees in 1979 showed a significant increase over previous years. Particularly significant is the high proportion (nearly 60 percent) of union victories in representation elections.[27] Additional grounds for union optimism are found in studies reflecting a change in the attitudes of white-collar employees, who are beginning to focus on traditional union issues such as higher wages and job security.[28] It also appears that white-collar workers are increasingly disenchanted because of problems related to personnel policies, such as limited opportunity for advancement, problems with merit-based promotion systems, lack of career progression programs, and routine and uninteresting jobs.[29] The extent to which unions are able to organize white-collar employees depends largely on management's personnel policies and actions, which are discussed in the following section.

**Characteristics
and Policies of
the Nonunion
Employer**

The fact that less than one-fourth of the nonagricultural labor force are union members is in part due to the nonunion employers' "environmental characteristics" and personnel practices.[30] Two important environmental characteristics of many nonunion firms—rapid growth and good profitability—facilitate personnel programs favorable to employees. These characteristics are often found in high-technology firms.

For example, the combination of growth and the personnel policy of promotion from within creates many promotional opportunities. Growth aids full-employment practices. It helps make layoffs less necessary. Rapid growth and good profits make profit-sharing and/or other bonus plans worthwhile from the employees' standpoint. Similarly, if the company offers an employee stock-purchase plan, and not only has the stock greatly appreciated but its dividends have continued to rise, the employees have reason to be pleased with the plan. High profits also mean that a company can afford to implement leading policies on pay and benefits, and can also afford to invest the resources necessary for good personnel staffs and programs.[31]

Other typical environmental characteristics of nonunion firms include the following:

Date of founding. They were either small or nonexistent during the surge of union growth in the 1930s and 1940s.

Geographic location. They are located in rural, nonunion settings where public opinion is not particularly prolabor.

Size of production facilities. They have facilities small enough to enable managers to have closer, more personal contacts with employees; of course, plants must be large enough to justify the expenses of good supervision.

Environmental characteristics do not completely control whether a firm will be nonunion. Many of these characteristics are subject to change. For example, antiunion sentiment appears to be weakening in some rural areas.[32] Companies are also subject to dramatic shifts in growth and profitability; recently, one renowned high-technology firm reduced many of its employees' work schedules because demand for its computer products had fallen.[33]

The extent to which employees and employers prefer (or do not prefer) to have a union conditions the effects of environmental characteristics. Employees' reasons for joining a union have been previously discussed. Some employers initially formulate their preferences to remain nonunion through written personnel policies. For example, a portion of Texas Instruments' company handbook, which is given to all employees, states:

TI believes a union would be detrimental to TI and to TIers because it would reduce the operational flexibility and efficiency that have contributed greatly to both TI's success and the growth goals of individual TIers. Most TIers apparently agree, since historically they have not felt the need for a union in their quest for job security, job satisfaction and good economic benefits. As a result, TI is one of the largest non-union companies in the U.S. TI hopes that TIers will continue to feel the same way and, in turn, expects to continue its pledge to make company and employee goals as compatible as possible.

TI has instituted many personnel programs, such as Success Sharing, including a profit sharing plan, a pension plan and an employee stock option purchase plan, that are designed to relate your personal goals for financial security to TI's own goals for growth, productivity and profitability.[34]

Nonunion policies must be implemented through related activities, including the following:

Offering wages, benefits, and so on, that are equal to or better than union firms'.

Instituting grievance procedures.

Posting job openings so that eligible employees can apply.

Improving supervision through better selection, training, and evaluation.

Ensuring downward communication by use of bulletin boards, company newspapers, and handbooks.

Ensuring upward communication by use of group meetings, complaint boxes, ombudsman programs, attitude surveys, open-door policies, and counseling.

Restructing the organization—providing a climate to keep the organization alive and vibrant by reducing the levels of supervision, forcing delegation, building work teams, enlarging and enriching jobs, and experimenting with methods of training.[35]

Some nonunion companies also actively attempt to provide job security for their employees, even when their businesses are declining. Jobs can be safeguarded by use of hiring freezes, inventory buildups, maintenance work, transfer of work normally done by subcontractors to full-time employees, and retraining and relocation of employees. However, as illustrated in Exhibit 14.2, these activities—as well as other such activities—carry costs as well as benefits.

The nonunion employer confronts legal as well as cost considerations, particularly when it is faced with a union organizing drive. All such elections are conducted according to NLRB standards, which are designed to assure that employees in the bargaining unit can indicate freely whether they want to be represented for collective bargaining purposes. Unions have an advantage in that they determine when the organizing drive will start (usually when the employees are believed to be most receptive to unionization). However, the employees realize that their jobs have been furnished by the employer and must speculate whether the union could actually improve their working conditions.

Union representation elections are conducted under a variety of strategies and tactics. An estimated 1,500 lawyers, psychologists, and personnel consultants offer advice to employers on the best way to defeat unions.[36] Some of this advice encourages employers to preserve the benefits of nonunion status by committing unfair labor practices such as discharging employees who are union sympathizers or leaders.[37] Unfortunately, some employers deliberately violate the National Labor Relations Act because the risks are relatively low. Violations are not criminal; no one is imprisoned or fined for violating the

Exhibit 14.2	Costs and Benefits of Activities That Provide Job Security	
	Costs	Benefits

	Extra payroll and payroll related expenses:
	  Training costs
	  Possible temporary red circle rates
	  Extra overtime because of reluctance to hire
	  Extra costs of any special early retirement plans
	Moving expenses
	Possible slower delivery schedule
	Productivity losses associated with people assigned to different jobs
	Extra financial charges because of larger-than-necessary inventory
	Extra employment costs associated with extreme selectivity in hiring
	Possible slower rate of methods or technological change due to need to avoid displacing any permanent employees
		Better employee morale because of lack of insecurity
		Productivity advantages associated with less employee resistance to methods or technological changes due to fear of job loss (greater acceptance of methods and technological changes)
		Lower unemployment insurance costs
		Savings of subsequent employment and training costs if there had been a layoff
		Favorable image in the community

Source: Fred K. Foulkes, *Personnel Policies in Large Nonunion Companies,* © 1980, p. 118. Adapted by permission of Prentice-Hall, Inc., Englewood Cliffs, N.J.

act. Social costs are not high, because most of the public is unaware of employers' flagrant violations of the law. Too, the potential gains for these employers include not only the possibility of forestalling immediate unionization but also the possibility that employees will completely lose interest in unions after a long period of judicial appeals.[38]

Unions have attempted to counter employers' strategies to maintain nonunion status. One tactic is the use of taped telephone speeches. An employee can call a well-publicized number and receive the union message for the day or week during an organizing campaign. These messages range from information about joining unions and anticompany messages to the personal testimony of popular, well-known plant employees.

A second union strategy is the exercise of financial clout. Unions, through their stocks, investments, and bank accounts, have placed pressure on banks and insurance firms by threatening to withdraw funds unless they stop dealing with certain antiunion firms.

One publicized unionization effort concerns an agreement between General Motors and the United Auto Workers. The agreement requires that preferential consideration be given current UAW members if they seek jobs in twelve new GM plants in the South. While only about 2 percent of GM's 475,000 employees would end up working in southern plants, those transferred could help the UAW organize workers.[39]

| Issue: | ## Have Unions Outlived Their Usefulness? |

This chapter and the next discuss unions as an influential aspect of personnel activities and organizational life. Yet, some individuals contend that unions are no longer necessary in today's industrial setting. Three general arguments are often used to support this contention:

1. Union membership has declined and public opinion has grown more negative.
2. Labor organizations are unwilling or unable to become actively involved in areas in which social reform is needed.
3. Unions' original goals have been accomplished, and nothing is left to achieve.

As noted earlier, unions in the United States represent only a small fraction of the labor force (approximately 20 percent). Furthermore, this proportion has steadily dropped since the 1950s. A similar decline has occurred in the unions' rate of success in union representation elections, which the National Labor Relations Board conducts to determine whether employees will be represented by a labor organization. In 1950, labor organizations won 83 percent of such elections; in 1977, the percentage had fallen to 46 percent.[40] Making matters worse for labor unions is the increase since 1947 in decertification elections, in which employees have the opportunity to remove an existing union from their facility.[41]

Some suggest that these trends reflect the public's dissatisfaction with unions, a contention supported by public opinion polls. For example, a 1979 nationwide Gallup opinion poll found that 55 percent of respondents approved of labor unions, the lowest approval rate in forty-three years.[42]

Caution must be taken, however, in interpreting these statistics. Lane Kirkland, president of the AFL-CIO, states that success of labor organizations cannot be measured solely in membership figures, because "unions are not economic institutions competing for market shares."[43] Mr. Kirkland also points out that aggregate labor force statistics include a wide variety of categories (unemployed persons, high school students looking for part-time jobs, supervisors, farmers, lawyers, and so on); therefore, percentages derived from these categories may understate organized labor's influence. Further, as this chapter has mentioned, the wages and working conditions of many nonunion employees are strongly influenced by union collective bargaining agreements. Finally, the decline in union victories in representation elections may be due in part to the aggressive—and in some cases illegal—anti-union tactics used by some employers.[44]

Public opinion figures are also difficult to interpret. The previously cited 1979 Gallup poll also asked people the following question: "In your opinion, which of the following will be the biggest threat to the country in the future—big business, big labor, or big government?"[45] The respondents viewed big government as the greatest future threat to the United States, followed by big business and, far behind, big labor.[46]

It must also be recognized that newspaper and television accounts of labor relations activities can strongly influence public opinion. The news media are profit-making businesses, and at least one prominent union official believes this orientation biases the reporting of labor relations activities:

The media tend to cover collective bargaining as if it were a pier six brawl. The intricate moves and tradeoffs that really make up bargaining aren't as newsy as impassioned rhetoric or a picket line confrontation.

Reporters are given little training in covering collective bargaining. They are told to look for the "news"—the first fight, the walkout, the heated exchange—and, as a result, frequently miss the "story," which is the settlement. . . . Every union proposal is a "demand," every management proposal is an "offer."[47]

Regardless of the source, a double standard is often applied to business and labor organizations:

Corporate heads who enlarge profits are hailed as masters of the bottom line; union officials who do the equivalent for their stockholders—the dues paying members—run the risk of being castigated for fueling inflation. . . .

Businessmen are accorded a leniency and understanding that unions are not. Businessmen who break the law commit white-collar crime; union officials who do the same are racketeers.[48]

Unions have also been considered obsolete because they tend to support social issues and causes. Some people claim that unions have dropped their militancy of the 1930s, preferring instead to become members of the "establishment."[49] Organized labor has not become deeply involved with such issues as civil rights, nuclear disarmament, poverty, and the energy crisis. This lack of involvement signifies to some that organized labor is not a viable social institution.

Yet, this line of reasoning can be countered:

Why should American unions turn from the well-understood and tangible goals of collective bargaining for a place in the never-never land of radical social reform? . . . Unions in America have chosen to define a role for themselves that is intimately tied to the collective bargaining system which, in turn, is concerned with the welfare of employees and the success of management at the workplace.[50]

History suggests that unions' focal point should be members' needs and goals. Some available evidence indicates that union members believe social issues should be resolved in the political arena and that unions should concentrate on job-related issues.[51] A recent survey of union members found that they perceived unions as being very effective in promoting membership interests such as improved wages, working conditions, job security, and protection against unfair practices. The survey did not find membership support for union involvement in social issues.[52]

It is harder to refute the argument that says unions' goals have all been achieved. Clearly, employees' working conditions are far different today than in the late 1800s when the American Federation of Labor was formed. Employers no longer have unlimited discretion in selecting and handling employees. A variety of laws regulate safety, pensions, minimum wage, discrimination against minorities, child labor, and other employment issues; and related governmental agencies protect employees' job rights and working conditions.

Thus, perhaps we should ask whether unions are still needed given the fact that many of their concerns have been minimized by governmental actions. It is impossible to adequately answer this question. Some might argue that improvements in working conditions, while impressive, are not complete and that organized labor must remain to press for further gains.

It is even more difficult to predict how employers would treat employees if unions vanished from the scene. Organized labor has been compared to the military in peacetime—each may be seen as a strong, countervailing power needed to preserve the existing situation.[53] Management certainly could make unions obsolete, since it is the ultimate grantor of working conditions in the labor agreement. Whether it would agree to many conditions that favor employees without the pressure of labor organizations is uncertain.

Summary

Labor organizations, or unions, can represent an internal constraint to the personnel function. Unions and management combine to carry out the labor relations process, in which management and the exclusive bargaining agent for the employees (the union) jointly decide upon and enforce terms and conditions of the labor agreement. Work rules represent the focal point of the labor relations process and involve management organizations, union organizations, employees, and government.

The earliest unions were the KOL, AFL, and IWW. The short-run, material goals of the AFL contrasted sharply with the long-range reform goals of the KOL and the destructive goals of the IWW. The AFL's organizational objectives were modified by the CIO. However, a comparison of the labor movement at the end of World War II with the labor movement today reveals more similarities than differences, the merger of the AFL and the CIO notwithstanding.

Organized labor before 1935 did not enjoy many legal protections. The National Labor Relations Act of 1935 (Wagner Act), along with the 1947 (Taft-Hartley) and 1959 (Landrum-Griffin) amendments, established the following: rights of employees in union representation elections; unfair labor practices for unions and employers; and unions' responsibilities toward their members. The National Labor Relations Act also established an administrative agency, the NLRB, to administer and monitor its various provisions. The Act's lengthy appeal procedures and limited remedial powers have been criticized.

Employees may join unions because of working conditions that alienate them or because of job security concerns. Employees' social backgrounds do not predict very well whether they will join unions. However, their desires for affiliation and status may prompt them to join.

Many nonunion employers have typical environmental characteristics, such as rapid growth, rural locations, and small production facilities. These characteristics are not completely predictive, since they are subject to change and are conditioned by employees' and employers' preferences to remain nonunion. Nonunion employers also typically rely on a variety of personnel policies, which involve both benefits and costs. Such employers may encounter union organizing drives. Unions and employers use a variety of tactics in these drives.

Unions are sometimes said to have outlived their usefulness. However, it is impossible to say whether this is the case.

Discussion Questions

1. Compare and contrast the alienation and scarcity-consciousness theories of why employees join unions. Which, if either, seems more appropriate in explaining why professional baseball players would join a union?

2. Assume you are a union organizer. Formulate and explain a list of arguments you would use to convince white-collar employees to join a union.

3. "Strive for the better day" is a quotation from Gompers (AFL); however, the remark could just as easily have been made by Powderly (KOL) or Haywood (IWW), with entirely different meanings. Explain.

4. Discuss two similarities between organized labor as it existed at the end of World War II and as it exists at present. Speculate on how these similarities might be modified in the near future.

5. "Unions win most of the representation elections, because employers have their hands tied by rigid rules on unfair labor practices and severe penalties for their infraction." Assess the validity of this statement.

6. Consider a nonunion employer with whom you are familiar. To what extent do the characteristics of this firm agree with, disagree with, or expand the characteristics of nonunion employers discussed in the chapter.

Notes

1. "Cohabitation Costs Cops Their Jobs," *New Times,* October 16, 1978, p. 16.
2. *This Is the AFL-CIO* (Washington, D.C.: American Federation of Labor and Congress of Industrial Organizations, 1977), p. 1.
3. Studs Terkel, *Working* (New York: Avon Books, 1974), p. 6. Reprinted by permission of Pantheon Books, a division of Random House, Inc.
4. There are many fine overviews of labor history, two of which are: Philip Taft, *Organized Labor in American History* (New York: Harper and Row, 1964); Joseph G. Rayback, *A History of American Labor* (New York: Macmillan, 1968).
5. T. V. Powderly, *Thirty Years of Labor: 1859–1889* (Columbus, Ohio: Excelsior Publishing House, 1889), p. 163.
6. Louis Reed, *The Labor Philosophy of Samuel Gompers* (1930; reprint ed., Port Washington, N.Y.: Kennikat Press, 1966), p. 481.
7. *Proceedings of the First Convention of the Industrial Workers of the World* (New York: Labor News Company, 1905), p. 1.
8. For additional information on the CIO, see Walter Galenson, *The CIO Challenge to the AFL* (Cambridge, Mass.: Harvard University Press, 1960).
9. B. J. Widick, *Labor Today: The Triumphs and Failures of Unionism in the United States* (Boston: Houghton Mifflin, 1964), p. 117.
10. John Schmidman, *Unions in Post Industrial Society* (University Park: Pennsylvania State University Press, 1979), p. 89.
11. Herbert L. Sherman, Jr., and William P. Murphy, *Unionization and Collective Bargaining,* 3d ed. (Washington, D.C.: Bureau of National Affairs, 1975), p. 9.
12. Cindy M. Hudson and William B. Werther, Jr., "Section 8(c) and Free Speech," *Labor Law Journal* 28 (September 1977), pp. 608–614. See also George W. Bohlander, "Employee Protected Concerted Activity: The Nonunion Setting," *Labor Law Journal* 33 (June 1982), pp. 334–351.
13. National Labor Relations Board, *45th Annual Report of the NLRB* (Washington, D.C.: Government Printing Office, 1980), pp. 3 and 9.
14. For the New England study, see Les Aspin, "Legal Remedies under the NLRA," in *Proceedings of the Annual Meeting of the Industrial Relations Research Association,* ed. G. G. Somers (Madison, Wis.: Industrial Relations Research Association, 1970), pp. 265–267. For the Texas study, see Elvis C. Stephens and Warren Chaney, "A Study of the Reinstatement Remedy under the National Labor Relations Act," *Labor Law Journal* 25 (January 1974), pp. 31–46.
15. George Meany, "Common Sense in Labor Law," *Labor Law Journal* 27 (October 1976), p. 605. For additional insights into the problems and prospects of the NLRB, see Frank W. McCulloch and Tim Bornstein, *The National Labor Relations Board* (New York: Praeger Publishers, 1974).
16. Terkel, *Working,* pp. 221–222, 224. Reprinted by permission of Pantheon Books, a division of Random House, Inc.
17. Kenneth E. Boulding, *The Organizational Revolution* (Chicago: Quadrangle Books, 1968), pp. 166–167.
18. Harold L. Sheppard and Neal Q. Herrick, *Where Have All the Robots Gone? Worker Dissatisfaction in the '70s* (New York: Free Press, 1972), p. 193.
19. Jeanne M. Brett, "Why Employees Want Unions," *Organizational Dynamics* 8 (Spring 1980), p. 51.
20. Daniel Bell, *Work and Its Discontents* (New York: League for Industrial Democracy, 1970), p. 33; Stanley Aronowitz, *False Promises: The Shaping of American Working Class Consciousness* (New York: McGraw-Hill, 1973), pp. 409–410.
21. Clinton S. Golden and Harold Ruttenberg, "Motives for Union Membership," in *Union, Man-*

agement and the Public, ed. E. Wight Bakke, Clark Kerr, and Charles W. Anrod (New York: Harcourt Brace, 1948), p. 49.

22. Larry Keith, "A Conversation with Chairman Al, *Sports Illustrated,* November 28, 1977, p. 36.

23. Bureau of National Affairs, *Basic Patterns in Union Contracts,* 9th ed. (Washington, D.C.: Bureau of National Affairs, 1979), p. 85.

24. Joel Seidman, Jack London, and Bernard Karsh, "Why Workers Join Unions," *Annals of the American Academy of Political and Social Science* 274 (March 1951), pp. 775–784.

25. A study of 1,200 employees found no significant correlation between employees' voting to join the union and members of their families' being union members. Similarly, prior union membership was not significantly associated with voting for the union. J. G. Getman, S. B. Goldberg, and J. B. Herman, *Union Representation Elections: Law and Reality* (New York: Russell Sage Foundation, 1976).

26. Claude Edwards, *Some Reflections on White-Collar Collective Bargaining* (Kingston, Ontario: Queens University, 1977), pp. 1–2; Everett M. Kassalow, "White-Collar Unions and the Work Humanization Movement," *Monthly Labor Review* 108 (May 1977), pp. 9–13.

27. Bureau of National Affairs, *Daily Labor Report,* July 22, 1980, pp. B-1–B-5.

28. Edward R. Curtin, *White-Collar Unions* (New York: National Industrial Conference Board, 1970), pp. 71–72.

29. Edwards, "Some Reflections," p. 3.

30. Fred K. Foulkes, *Personnel Policies in Large Nonunion Companies* (Englewood Cliffs, N.J.: Prentice-Hall, 1980), pp. 18–19.

31. Fred K. Foulkes, *Personnel Policies in Large Nonunion Companies,* © 1980, pp. 17–18. Reprinted by permission of Prentice-Hall, Inc., Englewood Cliffs, N.J.

32. John Filiatreau, "The White Workers in the South, *Dissent* 19 (Winter 1972), pp. 78–82.

33. "Texas Instruments to Trim Work Weeks, Cites Soft Market for Computer Products," *Wall Street Journal,* December 19, 1980, p. 3.

34. *TI and You . . . The TIer's Handbook* (Dallas: Texas Instruments Incorporated, 1978), p. iv. Copyright © Texas Instruments Incorporated 1978. Used by permission.

35. V. Clayton Sherman, "What the Nonunion Employer Can Learn from the Unionized Company," *Industrial Relations Guide* (Englewood Cliffs, N.J.: Prentice-Hall, 1970), pp. 42, 142–145, 148; Peter J. Pestillo, "Learning to Live without the Union," in Barbara D. Dennis, ed. *Proceedings of the Thirty-First Annual Meeting: Industrial Relations Research Association* (Madison, Wis.: Industrial Relations Research Association, 1979), pp. 233–239.

36. "Labor Fights Back against Union Busters," *U.S. News and World Report,* December 10, 1979, pp. 96–98. For thorough coverage of this subject, see *Pressures in Today's Workplace,* vols. 1 and 2 (Washington, D.C.: Government Printing Office, 1979).

37. Charles R. Greer and Stanley A. Martin, "Calculative Strategy Decisions during Organization Campaigns," *Sloan Management Review* 19 (Winter 1978), p. 73.

38. *Ibid;* pp. 61–74.

39. "Developments in Industrial Relations," *Monthly Labor Review* 101 (November 1978), pp. 45–46; "Why GM Abandoned Its Southern Strategy," *Business Week,* October 16, 1978, p. 50; James A. Craft, "The Employer Neutrality Pledge: Issues, Implications and Prospects," *Labor Law Journal* 31 (December 1980), pp. 753–763; and Joann S. Lublin, "Laborious Task: Union Organizer Faces Harder Job Than Ever in Recession-Hit South," *Wall Street Journal,* August 3, 1982, p. 1.

40. Al Bilik, "Corrupt, Crusty or Neither? The Poll-ish View of American Unions," *Labor Law Journal* 30 (June 1979), p. 323.

41. See, for example, Ralph D. Elliott and Benjamin M. Hawkins, "Union Decertification—Some Recent Trends," *Employer Relations Law Journal* (Spring 1980), pp. 533–548; John C. Anderson, Charles A. O'Reilly III, and Gloria Busman, "Union Decertification in the U.S.: 1947–1977," *Industrial Relations* 19 (Winter 1980), pp. 100–107. For some insights into unions' and employers' strategies and the outcomes of decertification campaigns, see William E. Fulmer, "When Employees Want to Oust Their Union," *Harvard Business Review* 56 (March/April 1978), pp. 163–170.

42. *The Gallup Opinion Index #167,* June 1979, p. 12.

43. Bureau of National Affairs, *Daily Labor Report,* February 25, 1980, p. E-1.

44. In 1978, for example, a record number of unfair labor practices (for example, disciplining employees who were union supporters, threatening to close the plant if employees voted for a union, spying on union meetings, and the like) were committed by employers during union organizing campaigns. Bilik, "Corrupt, Crusty or Neither?" p. 328.

45. *Gallup Opinion Index,* p. 18.

46. The specific 1979 response totals were: big government, 43 percent; big labor, 17 percent; big business, 28 percent; and no opinion, 12 percent. The responses to the same question the first time it was asked in 1959 were: big government, 14 percent; big labor, 41 percent;

big business, 15 percent; and no opinion, 30 percent. An assessment of these differences reflects another difficulty of assessing public opinion polls—namely, attributing meaning to responses. On the one hand, the comparison of 1959 and 1979 responses could be interpreted as a current vote of confidence for big labor. On the other hand, the comparison could support the view that organized labor is a weak, nonthreatening force in contemporary society.

47. Lane Kirkland, "Labor and the Press," *American Federationist* 82 (December 1975), p. 3. See also Albert J. Zack, "The Press Bias on Labor," *American Federationist* 84 (October 1977), pp. 1–7.

48. Nicholas von Hoffman, "The Last Days of the Labor Movement," *Harper's* 257 (December 1978), p. 24.

49. See, for example, Paul Jacobs, "Old before Its Time: Collective Bargaining at 28," in *Contemporary Labor Issues,* ed. Walter Fogel and Archie Kleingartner (Belmont, Calif.: Wadsworth, 1968), pp. 187–192; Robert Schrank, "Are Unions an Anachronism?" *Harvard Business Review* 57 (September/October 1979), pp. 107–115.

50. Tim Bornstein, "Unions, Critics, and Collective Bargaining," *Labor Law Journal* 27 (October 1976), p. 617.

51. Sar Levitan, ed., *Blue-Collar Workers* (New York: McGraw-Hill, 1971), pp. 165–171.

52. Thomas A. Kochan, "How American Workers View Labor Unions," *Monthly Labor Review* 102 (April 1979), pp. 23–31.

53. Kenneth A. Kovach, "Do We Still Need Labor Unions?" *Personnel Journal* 58 (December 1979), p. 850.

Chapter 15

Negotiating and Administering the Labor Agreement

How much of the collective bargaining process has any real meaning: How much of it is empty ritual?

Albert A. Blum, "Collective Bargaining: Ritual or Reality?" *Harvard Business Review* 39 (November/December 1961), p. 65.

Collective bargaining, commonly referred to as negotiating the labor agreement, involves agreeing on the terms and conditions under which employees will work. It is the most highly publicized phase of the labor relations process; the national media usually give daily coverage to negotiations in major industries such as steel, automobile, or trucking or in popular sports such as baseball. The public seems interested in the activities surrounding the negotiations as well as in how it will be affected by them.

Managers and employees who will be directly affected by the outcome of the negotiations and by any impasse or strike are even more interested. An excessive wage settlement could seriously weaken the company's competitive position and cause employees to be laid off, and a strike could cause losses of sales and profits and possibly even result in personal bankruptcies among individual employees.

Contract administration, or applying the terms of the labor agreement through the grievance procedure, usually occupies more of labor and management officials' time than contract negotiation. This activity gives meaning to the labor agreement and in some cases modifies the negotiated contract provisions.

This chapter first discusses the general characteristics and activities of collective bargaining. It must be remembered, though, that there are currently some 160,000 labor agreements in effect in the United States, each reflecting unique situations and concerns.[1] Also discussed are several procedures used to resolve negotiation impasses. Next, the chapter discusses contract administration—more specifically, grievance procedures and how union and management officials resolve grievances. The role of personnel representatives and other management officials in labor relations activities are described. Finally, the chapter's issue concerns the possibilities for union-management cooperation.

Negotiating the Labor Agreement

Characteristics of Negotiations

Collective bargaining between union and management officials can involve a large number of work rules (see Exhibit 15.1 for an illustration). Union and management enter collective bargaining with their own ideas of acceptable settlements, although each party knows the other will not agree entirely with its position. Therefore both parties usually enter negotiations with a variety of acceptable positions, which gives them some room for maneuvering.[2] There are, however, limits for both union and management negotiators. Management will not likely agree to a collective bargaining settlement that is incompatible with the company's objectives, such as profitability or growth,[3] while union representatives typically press for a settlement that does not result in layoffs or in membership dissatisfaction.[4] The eventual settlement is shaped by three general considerations: the style of negotiations, the activities to prepare for negotiations, and the bargaining power model.

Ability, Definition of
Absence
Reporting of
With Leave
Without Leave
Arbitration
Bargaining Unit,
Definition of
Benefits, Employee
Funeral Pay
Glove, Hat, and Shoe
  Allowance
Jury Duty
Layoff Allowance
Nonoccupational
  Disability Pay
Occupational Disability
  Pay
Pension and Insurance
Vacation
Bidding
Bulletin Boards
Call-out
Definition of
Holiday
Regular
Seventh Consecutive Day,
  in P/R
Sixth Day Worked in
  Holiday Week
Change of Rate
Permanent
Temporary
**Company Service Credit
Rules**
Contract
Duration
Purpose of
Termination
Differentials, Shift
Disability Pay Plans
Nonoccupational
Occupational
Discipline
Discharge
Unsatisfactory Attendance
Dues Deduction
Authorization Form
Duration
Withdrawal, Method
  and/or Date of
Funeral Pay
Glove Allowance
Grievances
General Committee
Procedure—General
      Other
      Discharge
      and
      Suspension
      Job Rate
      Establishment
Handicapped Employees
Hat Allowance
Health and Safety

Holidays and Holiday Pay
**Hospitalization
Agreement**
Hours of Work
Insurance Plan
Interchange of Work
**Job Classifications and
Rate Schedule**
Job Rate Establishment
Job Sequence Charts
Jury Duty Allowance
Layoff
Allowance Plan
Procedure
Recall after
Seniority Rights during
Temporary
Leave-of-Absence
General
Military
Seniority, Accumulation of
Service Credit,
  Accumulation of
Union Business
Lunch, Overtime
**Maintenance of Union
Membership**
Management Rights
**Master Overtime
Agreement**
Military Service
**Nonoccupational
Disability Pay**
**Occupational Disability
Pay**
Overtime
Daily
Distribution of
Lunch
Pyramiding of
Weekly
Pay
Call-out
For Grievance Meetings
Hiring
Holiday
Overtime
Progression
Rate Schedule
Report-in
Seventh Consecutive Day
  in Workweek
Shift Differential
Sixth Consecutive Day in
  Workweek
Sunday Premium
Pension Plan
Probationary Period
Progression
Rate Schedule
Recall
Recognition, Union
Rehire and Reinstatement
Company Service Credit

Rate of Pay
Seniority Rights
Vacation Eligibility
Safety and Health
Safety Shoes
Seniority
Application of
Bidding in
Curtailment in
Definition of
Departmental
Equality of
Handicapped Employees
Layoff during
Loss of
Plant
Recall after
Rehire after
Reinstatement after
Strike Notice during
Supervisors
Ties of
Veterans
**Seventh Day, Overtime
Pay for**
Shift Differential
Shoe Allowance
**Sixth Day, Overtime Pay
for**
Stewards
Strikes and Lockouts
General Provisions
Suspension
Temporary Change of Rate
Termination of Contract
Time and One-Half Pay
Transfers (Vacancies)
Out of Bargaining Unit
Pay Changes Because of
Temporary
Within Bargaining Unit
Transportation
Union
Bulletin Boards
Officials, Leave-of-Absence
Plant Visit of Business
  Representative
Recognition
Security
Vacancies
Permanent
Temporary
Vacation Plan
Voting Time
Wages (Pay)
Hiring Rate
Progression
Rate Schedule
Work
Conditions
Day, Basic
Hours of
Supervisors
Week, Basic

The Style of Negotiations For some issues, collective bargaining occurs when one party's goals conflict with those of the other party. Certain issues, particularly wages, heighten conflict of interest, because higher wages mean higher income for union members and at the same time create higher costs for the employer. However, there are some issues, such as safety and drug prevention programs, that management and union negotiators attempt to resolve to their mutual benefit. Collective bargaining also includes activities employed by negotiators to achieve consensus within their own organizations.[5] A bargaining team, whether union's or management's, is seldom unified. For example, older union members might want more bargaining emphasis placed on pensions, while female union members might want more flexible working hours. Within the management group, production managers might want mandatory overtime provisions, while personnel representatives might state their major bargaining priority to be promotions based on merit alone. Because none of these groups can have everything it wants, union and management negotiators often have more difficulty with members of their own negotiating teams than with each other.[6]

The style of a particular negotiation is influenced by the familiarity of the parties with each other and the extent to which the bargaining relationships have been established and are viewed by the parties as being mutually acceptable. A union negotiator for a large utility firm tells how negotiations (and negotiators) can mature over time:

There used to be a lot more fist slamming, name calling and shouting. . . . Sometimes both sides got so carried away, they forgot what they were arguing about. . . .

I think both sides grew up. . . . Instead of automatically taking opposite sides and refusing to bend, we began compromising and coming up with solutions that benefited both sides.

We still have different opinions on matters, that's to be expected. But with mutual respect and trust, we're getting a lot more accomplished.[7]

As this quotation suggests, most negotiations are conducted in an atmosphere of respect and honesty.[8] Respect is an interpersonal variable seldom researched by academicians. It is not synonymous with friendship—one can dislike and respect an individual at the same time. Management and labor negotiators seldom socialize with each other; however, they can respect each other's technical competence and experience, as well as each other's personal qualities, such as willingness to stand up for what is right, ability to admit to a mistake, and—perhaps most important—*credibility,* the result of keeping one's word.

Closely related to respect is honesty, which permits each party to rely on the statements of the other. There is, however, a thin line between dishonesty and withholding the truth—union and management officials are not going to volunteer information that could damage their bargaining positions.[9] Successful negotiators are skilled in asking the correct questions and interpreting omissions from the other party's remarks.

As suggested earlier, many union and management negotiators realize that their interactions are constrained by other members of their bargaining teams. Each chief negotiator realizes that the other has to look good before his or her team; consequently, a negotiator seldom issues unnecessary ultimatums or forces the other party to take an unyielding position. In short, negotiators often give each other a chance to save face by giving several options or alternatives in the bargaining sessions.

The style and substance of the negotiations are affected by the legal requirement to bargain in good faith. *Good faith* indicates the presence of an honest and sincere intent to consummate a labor agreement as well as the presence of reasonableness in bargaining positions, tactics, and activities. This requirement also includes the obligation to negotiate most issues within the general context of "wages, hours, and other terms and conditions of employment."

Employers' obligations in good-faith bargaining include supplying the union with requested information related to negotiations, making proposals and counterproposals, and giving the management representative sufficient authority to negotiate the labor agreement. The employer cannot drag its feet in negotiations, insist on meeting at unreasonable times, or bypass the elected employee bargaining agent (the union).

Good-faith bargaining is a vague and sometimes confusing concept. For example, it does not require that an agreement be reached; indeed, "no" can be regarded as a valid counterproposal. Also, the employer does not have to open its financial books to the union unless it pleads inability to pay.

Preparing for Negotiations Before negotiations begin, management and union must determine who will be on their negotiation teams. Members are often selected for their interpersonal skills, such as abilities to work with members of the other team and to keep emotions and opinions in check. Technical knowledge, experience, and background are also considered in the selection process. Management wants at least one line manager who supervises bargaining-unit employees on its team to help interpret related negotiation issues. Unions prefer to select team members from a variety of operating departments to ensure broad membership representation and the inclusion of the working concerns of each department.

The union is usually the initiating party in negotiations and is usually requesting better wages, benefits, and so on. Management officials must prepare for negotiations by anticipating, formulating, and costing proposals. Management relies on several sources in anticipating what the union will seek in collective bargaining. A review of recent contract settlements negotiated by the company's competitors and by other firms located in the same geographical area may suggest issues likely to be emphasized by the union. The company and the union may have negotiated settlements at other facilities; if so, these negotiations also may be used as a starting point for planning the current ones. Some management officials obtain bargaining insights by reviewing the proceedings of the national union's convention.[10]

A review of the local bargaining situation at the company's facility is essential in anticipating union bargaining issues. Much attention is given to grievances that have occurred since the last negotiations and to previous bargaining issues that the union actively sought and reluctantly dropped. Compromise settlements on previous issues also generate valuable clues, since compromise does not mean permanent resolution of the issue.

The present labor agreement can be also reviewed for possible language changes to increase managerial flexibility, conform with recent NLRB and judicial decisions,[11] and minimize difficulties of implementation on the shop floor.

Management's overriding concern in negotiation preparations is the eventual cost of the union's proposals. Costing the proposals can become a very involved process; however, most management officials do not use sophisticated costing practices in labor-management negotiations. Indeed, they often fail to take several things into account:

The precise financial impact of the labor agreement on corporate profits.

The opportunity costs of new contract provisions in terms of lost production time (for example, the effect of a proposed ten-minute cleanup time provision).

Expertise and figures available from financial managers, who usually do not sit in on formal negotiations and are not consulted by industrial relations managers during the negotiations.[12]

Management negotiators use at least some costing methods in their negotiation efforts. Two such methods are preparation of employee background data and calculation of the cost of a cent-per-hour wage increase. Management usually obtains statistical summaries of employees cross-tabulated by several variables (age, sex, marital status, seniority, job classifications). These summaries provide immediate information necessary to cost out a variety of union negotiation proposals such as those involving vacations, funeral pay, and pensions.

A significant calculation pertains to the cost of a cent-per-hour wage increase. Since wages are inevitably discussed in negotiations, a cost figure is needed to help set management's bargaining range and determine whether a union's wage proposal is excessive. An illustrative calculation of a cent-per-hour wage increase for a bargaining unit of 1,000 employees is presented below:

$20,800   Straight Time Pay (1,000 Employees × 40 Hours a Week × 52 Weeks × $0.01)

   900   Premium Pay Related to Wages (1,000 Employees × Estimated 60 Hours per Year Overtime, Holiday, and Call-out Premium × $0.015)

 5,200   Benefits Directly Affected by Wage Increase (Profit Sharing, Pensions, Life Insurance, Employer Contributions to Social Security, and so on; Estimated for Illustrative Purposes at 25 percent of Straight Time Wage Rate)

$26,900   Cost of a Cent-per-Hour Increase for 1,000 Employees

The wage total calculated above does not take into account alternative ways to spend the same amount of money or spillover effects on wages of nonunion employees of the same company, who will probably receive a comparable wage gain. Additionally, many cost categories, such as overtime and holidays worked, have to be estimated from past payroll records and future production and employee requirements.

Some union proposals, such as extending employees' paid three-day funeral leave to include deaths of first cousins, are impossible to cost. For strategic purposes, the union prefers to stress proposals that cannot be costed out, thereby weakening management's ability to raise statistical objections during negotiations. However, management should maintain accurate and separate cost records on benefits paid during the previous year to help it estimate at least some of the union's proposals.

Before the negotiations begin, both parties must determine the initial proposal they will make to the other party and the outside limits of their bargaining ranges. Management must also decide the issues over which it will be willing to risk a strike, and the union must decide the issues over which it will be willing to strike.[13]

Determining the Eventual Settlement: The Bargaining Power Model During negotiations, each party has to actively try to persuade the other to accept its bargaining position. In essence, there are three bargaining positions—yes, maybe, and no. Each party attempts to force the other to take the first or at least the second alternative by increasing its own bargaining power. One of the better-known bargaining power models was suggested by Neil Chamberlain and James Kuhn; such a model is presented in Exhibit 15.2[14] The equations in the exhibit can be applied to individual issues or to the eventual package settlement.

The bargaining power model contains at least two major assumptions.

1. Union and management negotiators are rational individuals.
2. If it costs more for a party to disagree than to agree with the other, then the party will agree to the other's position.

Therefore, each side can increase its bargaining power by reducing the cost to the other of agreement or increasing the cost to the other of disagreement.

Many variables can affect the bargaining power model. Some of these variables are discussed later in the chapter as strike decision criteria. However, two variables, unemployment and timing of negotiations, will be briefly discussed here for illustrative purposes.

Unemployment can affect both equations. High unemployment increases the union's cost of disagreeing with management, since employees on strike would find it difficult to find employment with other firms. It also reduces management's disagreement costs, since high unemployment tends to make it easier for management to find replacements for strikers.

The timing of negotiations can also have a significant impact on the bargaining power model. If a backlog of customer orders or an inventory imbalance exists at the contract expiration date, for example, management's cost of disagreeing could be increased. Employees who receive company profit-sharing checks the day before the labor agreement expires have additional money to spend, and their costs of disagreeing with management are reduced.

The bargaining power model has at least two limitations:

Exhibit 15.2   Bargaining Power Equations for Union and Management

$$\text{Union's Bargaining Power} = \frac{\text{Management's Cost of Disagreeing with the Union}}{\text{Management's Cost of Agreeing with the Union}}$$

$$\text{Management's Bargaining Power} = \frac{\text{Union's Cost of Disagreeing with Management}}{\text{Union's Cost of Agreeing with Management}}$$

Source: Equations are modified slightly from Allan M. Cartter and F. Ray Marshall, *Labor Economics*, rev. ed. (Homewood Ill.: Richard D. Irwin, 1972), p. 283. © 1972 by Richard D. Irwin, Inc. Used by permission.

1. *Cost* is a term covering many imprecise considerations. For example, it is difficult to compare political cost units such as possible defeats of incumbent union officials with economic cost units such as those associated with wage increases. Imprecision is increased when each party assigns probabilities to the other's actions—for example, management must estimate both the cost of a strike and the probability that the union will actually call a strike.
2. The model is subject to sudden, dramatic change; for example, management's receiving a sudden influx of rush orders from a major customer near the contract expiration date. Management's disagreement costs could be sharply increased by such an occurrence, particularly if the major customer threatens to take unfinished orders to a competitor.

These limitations do not eliminate the model's predictive usefulness or its applicability in a real-world setting. Union and management officials do assign costs, however crudely, and direct their strategies toward increasing the other party's disagreement costs.

Resolving Impasses in Negotiations

An impasse occurs when one party has exhausted its options and cannot accept the other party's position. Impasses can also occur when the union membership rejects a tentative negotiated settlement, as union memberships did in about 11 percent of the negotiations that took place in 1980.[15] Negotiation impasses can be resolved through a variety of procedures, the two most common being mediation and strikes.[16]

Mediation Many union-management impasses are resolved with help from third-party mediators, whose services can be obtained either from the Federal Mediation and Conciliation Service (FMCS) or from state agencies. Mediators perform a number of functions; they help to schedule meetings, keep the parties talking, carry messages back and forth, and make suggestions. The mediator has no authority to make binding decisions and must rely on persuasion and recommendations; the mediator's assistance is valuable, but the negotiators make the final decisions.[17] The mediator is an invited guest who can be asked to leave. However, acceptance of mediators is an indication of good faith. The FMCS was involved in over 21,000 cases in 1980.[18]

Mediators depend on interpersonal skills and on the cooperation of union and management officials. There are no universal guidelines for mediators;[19] however, these individuals can help resolve a negotiation impasse in at least three general ways:[20]

1. *By giving management and union officials opportunities to save face.* Assume, for example, that union officials walk out

of negotiations vowing that they will not bargain with management unless bargaining concessions are made. After some thought, the union leaders realize they made a mistake but believe that saying so to the management officials would be a sign of weakness. The alternative is to call the mediator, who could schedule a meeting between the parties.

2. *By clarifying faulty perceptions or miscalculations of either party regarding the actual costs or benefits of a particular issue.*

3. *By proposing alternative solutions to the negotiation impasse.* Sometimes the mediator can offer imaginative solutions because of his or her experience with a large number of employers and unions.

Strikes Union and management officials may attempt to resolve the negotiation impasse by using economic sanctions to increase the other party's cost of disagreement. Management can use lockouts and unions can use strikes, boycotts, and picketing. Strikes involve several considerations.

Cost Considerations Employees on strike have to consider that their wages will be lost for an indefinite period. Unions and employers also incur strike costs. Unions may pay out funds to striking employees (usually less than $50 per week) to offset wages lost during the strike.[21] Management must consider a wide variety of fixed and potential costs, such as rent, interest on loans, payments for equipment, and lost customers.[22]

Each party attempts to minimize strike costs. Employers may establish strike insurance and mutual aid pacts (MAPs). These arrangements include "an agreement by which competing employers contract that, if one of them is struck, the others will indemnify it by some predetermined amount of money to help withstand the impact of the strike."[23] Strike activities are often controversial; indeed, some question whether employees should have the right to strike.[24]

One of the most controversial aspects of a strike concerns strikers' eligibility to receive state or federal public aid, such as food stamps, aid to families with dependent children (AFDC), medical assistance, and unemployment insurance.[25] Advocates of public aid and assistance for strikers argue that strikers and their families should receive these funds, since other taxpayers receive aid when they are out of work. These people say strikers are as deserving of aid as prison inmates and people in foreign countries.[26] Others contend that giving public aid to strikers violates legislative intent, particularly since strikers refuse to go back to work. Aid is said to reduce employees' incentive to work and thereby increase the roles of public aid recipients.[27]

Other Considerations *Goodwill* considerations pertain primarily to union-management relationships; neither management nor the union wants antagonistic attitudes—for example, distrust—to develop and linger after the strike. Both groups are also concerned about their *public image*—the opinions of people not directly involved in the strike—and do not want their actions labeled irresponsible or dangerous.

Strikes can also serve *strategic functions* such as releasing union members' frustrations and tensions resulting from monotonous jobs. In some cases, the union calls a strike just to show management it can unify the membership over a collective bargaining issue. Further, over a period of time, the threat of a strike loses its effectiveness. If such threats are not carried out, management comes to view the union leader as "the boy who cried wolf." Therefore, union leaders are sometimes forced to carry out a bluff or threat in order to substantiate future threats.

Union leaders may also believe that members who are not satisfied with a settlement would be more willing to accept a slightly modified final offer if they have not received wages during a brief strike. In this sense, strikes are used to reduce employees' initially unrealistic expectations.[28]

Unions also have to consider the effects of a strike on their institutional security. During the strike, some union members might accept jobs elsewhere and decide not to return after the strike. Sometimes employers hire permanent replacements for union strikers, and the negotiations are never consummated. Possibly, rival unions are waiting on the sidelines for the legally recognized union to falter.[29] With these considerations in mind, the union must be aware that a decision to strike may be a risk to its own survival. All these considerations must be evaluated in terms of past strike experiences and legal interpretations of strike activities.

Union and management officials, then, are cautious about the strike option. Indeed, publicity tends to exaggerate the use of strikes. For example, the number of work days lost to labor-management disputes in 1979 dropped to 1.5 days per 1,000, the lowest level since 1973.[30] Relatively little publicity is given to peaceful resolution of collective bargaining issues or to important long-range collective bargaining settlements such as the one described below:

Printers represented by the International Typographical Union ratify a 10-year contract with Baltimore's three daily newspapers. Retroactive to January 1, 1980, the agreement with the *Baltimore Sun, Evening Sun,* and *Baltimore News American* will expire on December 31, 1989. The agreement gives the publisher "full flexibility" to introduce new technology in return for guarantees that the number of employees will not fall below 110 at the *Sun* and 40 at the *News American.*[31]

However, the absence of strikes does not mean the absence of tensions, as neither side often obtains all it wants from the other. Tensions and conflict can also occur after the labor agreement has been reached; more specifically, they arise as the labor agreement is administered.

Administering the Labor Agreement

The core of contract administration consists of resolving employees grievances. A *grievance* can be defined as an employee's written concern over a perceived violation of the labor agreement that is submitted to the grievance procedure for eventual resolution. Thus, a grievance is distinguished from an employee's concern or complaint expressed, independent of labor agreement provisions, during the course of a typical workday. Unresolved employee grievances can result in a nonunion firm's becoming unionized or in union members' growing dissatisfied with the existing union.[32]

Employees file grievances for a variety of reasons such, as to protest a contractual violation, to draw attention to a problem in the plant, or to make themselves or their union feel important. Grievances are processed through the grievance procedure specified in the labor agreement. The interactions between union and management representatives give meaning to the grievance procedure as well as insights into the quality of the labor-management relationship at a particular facility.

Characteristics of a Grievance Procedure

Grievance procedures vary.[33] However, a fairly typical grievance procedure is presented in Exhibit 15.3 and described more fully below.

First Step The first stage actually consists of two phases. First, the employee (with or without the union steward) discusses the alleged contract violation with his or her immediate supervisor. Usually, if the grievance is not filed within a certain period, the employee forfeits the right to grieve. If agreement is not reached, then a written grievance is filed by the grievant or the union steward acting on the grievant's behalf. The supervisor then answers the employee's grievance in writing.

The purpose of the discussion phase is to resolve the grievance as early and as informally as possible. However, in some cases, the oral discussion is simply a matter of form—the employee has initiated this step with a written grievance in hand on the assumption that no amount of discussion will change his or her mind. As is true with the next two steps of the grievance procedure, if the employee accepts management's answer to the written grievance, then the grievance is considered resolved and subsequent steps are unnecessary.

Second Step In the second step, the union grievance committeeperson and management's industrial relations representative join the first-step participants to discuss the supervisor's first-step written answer

Exhibit 15.3   **Typical Grievance Procedure**

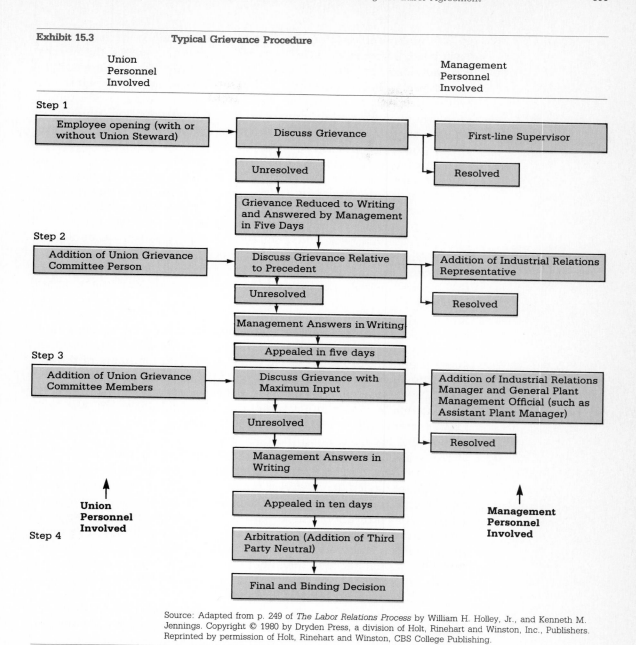

Source: Adapted from p. 249 of *The Labor Relations Process* by William H. Holley, Jr., and Kenneth M. Jennings. Copyright © 1980 by Dryden Press, a division of Holt, Rinehart and Winston, Inc., Publishers. Reprinted by permission of Holt, Rinehart and Winston, CBS College Publishing.

to the grievance. Both these individuals are aware of administrative precedent throughout the entire shop; their main role is to determine whether the grievance should be resolved at this stage on the basis of this precedent.

For example, say Employee A files a grievance protesting management's unilateral action in reducing wash-up time in her work area. The grievance committeeperson might be aware, however, that (a) the contract does not have a provision pertaining to wash-up time and (b) employees in other departments do not receive any time before the end of the shift to clean their hands. In this case, he or she would probably encourage the grievant to accept the reduction in wash-up time rather than risk losing the privilege entirely in subsequent steps of the grievance procedure.

On another issue—for example, an employees' working out of his or her normal work classification and demanding an upgrade in pay for the time worked—the industrial relations representative might be the one to concede. He or she might reverse the supervisor's first-step answer to avoid sending the grievance to the third step, where it might affect employees with similar work experiences in other departments. The second-step written grievance answer is furnished by the industrial relations representative, and any precedent resulting from this answer usually applies only to the particular work department involved.

Third Step The third-step meeting involves the industrial relations manager and another management official (such as a general foreman, superintendent, or assistant plant manager) and members of the union's grievance committee in addition to the participants in the second step. These individuals are added because the answer to the grievance at this level can affect the entire industrial operation, and both management and union representatives wish to obtain as much input as possible before making the decision.

These additional individuals serve other purposes, particularly from the union's standpoint. First, the third-step meeting can be used as an educational device for relatively new union officers. Since many labor agreements require paid time off for grievance meetings, a new union official can learn about the often complex issues and strategies involved in grievance resolution at the company's expense. The union grievance committee can also serve tactical purposes and perform political functions, because the sheer number of individuals on the committee can impress upon the grievant that the union is forcefully representing his or her interests.

Also, the committee can serve as a buck-passing device for the union steward or committeeperson, who can inform the grievant that he or she did all that was possible to win the grievance but was turned down by other members on the committee. Buck passing is not restricted to union personnel, since supervisors can claim to their peers that they were not wrong, merely "sold out" by higher-level management officials in subsequent steps of the procedure.

This step can also function as a therapeutic device for the grievant, who simply wishes to express concern to many levels of management officials. Perhaps the most important function of the third-step meeting is the inclusion of additional union and management officials who are not personally involved in the outcome of the grievance procedure and can assess the merits of the case with relative objectivity. The third-step answer is usually written by the industrial relations manager, because the decision probably will have plantwide implications.

Fourth Step—Arbitration The final step in the procedure, particularly in the private sector, involves the same individuals as step three and adds a neutral third party—the arbitrator—who hears the grievance and makes a final, binding decision.[34] Both management and union officials select the arbitrator and typically share the arbitrator's expenses. The arbitrator has the often complicated task of interpreting the provisions of the labor agreement, the intent of the parties, past practice, and the credibility of the testimony and evidence.

The arbitrator has no loyalties to either management or the union. Indeed, either may be frustrated by the arbitrator's decision:

The last case he had ended here at about 4:00. Mr. _____ expressed considerable concern since he had to make a plane for New York and was running late. I assured him that he would have no problem. I carried his bags to his car, drove in excess of all the speed limits, went through back roads, even proceeded through changing traffic lights. After a hectic ride and at considerable risk, I got him to the airport just in time to make the plane. I parked my car in a no parking zone. I even carried his bags to the gate. After all this, you know, that son-of-a-bitch ruled against me.[35]

Activities and Relationships Involved in Grievance Administration

The most frequent interaction in grievance resolution takes place between the first-line supervisor and the union steward. This relationship can be classified as *codified*, *power-oriented*, or *sympathetic*.[36]

Codified Relationships The rights and privileges of foremen and union stewards often stem from a defining code established through labor agreements and various union and management publications. Union steward handbooks and management publications emphasize mutual rights and respect.

Generally, every effort should be made to settle a grievance as close to the source of the dispute as possible. The representatives of both groups have to live with any settlement reached. If they can arrive at one, rather than having it imposed on them from above, both parties will be better off. In addition, the further the grievance travels up the procedure the more difficult it becomes to settle, because it becomes a matter of pride or prestige. Therefore, both sides tend to back up their subordinates even when they feel they may have been wrong originally.

It is absolutely essential that the steward talk to the foreman after getting the worker's story. He can probably evaluate the complaint only after hearing both sides. The foreman may provide certain facts that were not available to the worker or the steward.[37]

In labor management relations, there is no room for prejudice toward union representatives. The presence of the union organization in the plant effects a union-management marriage, and a corresponding obligation to observe the vows of recognition and good faith. In their grievance relationships, the foreman and the stewards are co-equals.[38]

Power-Oriented Relationships Codified relationships can erode when supervisors and union stewards attempt to use power to pursue different interests or goals. One dimension of the power relationship is knowledge of the labor agreement. Union stewards tend to know the labor agreement better than first-line supervisors, since supervisors must spend more time on production issues than on labor agreement analysis. One union steward tells how this knowledge can be used: "Any steward who knows his stuff can talk rings around a foreman. If he says the foreman's wrong and talks enough, whether he's entirely accurate or not, he's apt to buffalo him."[39]

A second dimension of the power relationship is intimidation. Union stewards can file many grievances, a practice that demands the time-consuming attention of several management officials. Even if the grievances are without merit, top management may wonder why the first-line supervisor can't solve employee problems. This practice is explained by a union official:

A short time ago we had a lot of trouble with a certain foreman. . . . He was making them toe the line . . . no quitting early, work from whistle to whistle, no sitting down, no horseplay, this and that. I told the committeeman there, "You do the same thing. Every time he does any work, even if he picks up a box, write a grievance. . . . " The first thing you know grievances started mounting—finally had a pile like that.

Things got so bad . . . this foreman was removed from that department. He was moved to our department and it's his last chance. If he doesn't do good in this department, out he goes. So I went to the guy and told him, "It's your last chance here and you know it. You cooperate with us and we will cooperate with you. If you don't we'll put the screws on you and out you go." Things are working out pretty good so far.[40]

Intimidation tactics are not one-sided; it is possible for a supervisor to make life very difficult for a union steward, probably without incurring an unfair labor practice charge. For example, many job classifications include a wide variety of work assignments, some of them less desirable than others. A foreman can assign undesirable work to the union steward, who has little recourse as long as the work is within his or her job classification.

Sympathetic Relationships Grievance participants may also have sympathetic relationships, which evolve when each is aware of the other's situation. The following remarks by a union steward illustrate this relationship:

> You can't have industrial relations without giving and taking on both sides. You'll always win more cases by getting along with supervision than be being tough. You've got to swap and make trades. . . . Sometimes I have to talk like hell to explain some of the deals I make with them and sometimes I keep what I'm doing to myself if I see a chance to get something good later on. The thing some grievers never get through their heads is that a lot of bosses are on the spot themselves. If you go a little easy on them when they're on the pan, by God—you make friends—they'll stand by you sometimes when you're back of the eight ball. Sometimes when I have a rotten grievance, I'll take the case up to the soop [superintendent] and let him know I won't push it hard.[41]

Sympathetic relationships are aided when the supervisor and the union steward realize that both occupy marginal positions within their own organizations. For example, many first-line supervisors do not have full authority to resolve grievances at the first step, because other management officials, concerned with the precedent-setting impacts of grievance decisions, like to be continually informed of related supervisory activities. These supervisors usually also receive advice from the personnel or employee relations department on contract administration matters; and this advice often is, in effect, direction.[42]

Union stewards are also subjected to a variety of pressures in their contract administration activities. Constituents expect their union steward to actively press every grievance, reasoning that the union's sole purpose is to represent its members. Consequently, it is difficult for the union steward to accept a supervisor's first-step rejection of a grievance, even if he or she agrees with the supervisor's position. On the other hand, union officials receiving such a grievance in subsequent steps of the grievance procedure tend to view the union steward as either ignorant of the labor agreement or too timid to stand up to grievants.

These varieties of interpersonal relationships reveal how *real* grievance procedures vary from the procedure outlined in the labor agreement.[43] Individual objectives, strategies, and personalities force the procedure to be more flexible in practice than it is on paper.

Role of the Personnel Department and Other Managers in Labor Relations Activities

This chapter and the last have described a broad spectrum of labor relations activities, including maintaining a nonunion firm and dealing with union organizing drives, collective bargaining, and contract administration. Exhibit 15.4 schematically reflects the overlap between personnel managers and other managers in these activities.

Many of the personnel activities can be grouped into two general categories: front-line behavior and research. Personnel officials often serve as the firm's first point of contact with the union. Here, their role is to discover the union's position, offer resistance when appropriate, and serve as a conduit to transmit information to and from other managers. Personnel officials also undertake research efforts to help in the formulation of management's final positions on such matters as collective bargaining and grievance issues. Some of these efforts might be termed *clerical;* however, this term is not synonymous with *insignificant* or *routine.* For example, consider the time-consuming efforts required to calculate the costs of various union proposals (extra safety equipment, alterations in overtime premiums, and so forth). The results must be accurate; a slight miscalculation could result in the company's spending considerable extra funds. Exhibit 15.4 also suggests that other managers typically retain approval authority over the personnel department's collective bargaining activities.

The extensiveness of labor relations activities and the potential for conflict between personnel officials and other managers can be illustrated by use of the policy statement in Exhibit 15.5. Many personnel activities, such as those involving wage adjustments, performance appraisals, training, and college recruiting, may directly involve other management officials only a few times a year. However, the exhibit illustrates that labor relations activities tend to be continuous and pervasive. Some of these activities strain the relationships between personnel representatives and other managers. This situation has already been suggested in the discussion of the grievance procedure, which pointed out that a first-line supervisor's actions are often directed by personnel officials. The conflict produced by this relationship is illustrated by one supervisor's remarks: "How the hell do they expect us to get the job done! . . . They expect me to go along with their stupid orders when I can't even raise my voice without the permission of "high and mighty" personnel."[44]

Other tensions can result from more subtle conflicts when the personnel department attempts to implement an organizational labor relations policy. For example, the policy outlined in Exhibit 15.5 says that

Exhibit 15.4   **Role of Specialized Personnel Representatives
and Line Managers in Labor Relations
Activities**

(Percent of Companies in Which Function Is Carried out by "Specialized," as Opposed to "Line," Managers)

Percent Specialized

For Bargaining

Background Research for Bargaining

Developing the Final Language of the Agreement

Costing Out Union "Demands" and Management Proposals

Conducting Contract Negotiations with the Union

Developing the Company's Initial Benefit Proposals

Developing the Company's Initial Wage Proposals

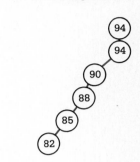

Union Organizing Situation

Directing Union Prevention Activities

Directly Dealing with a Union-Organizing Campaign

Developing Overall Policy Toward Unions and Unionization

Contract Administration

Handling Grievances and Arbitration

Monitoring Operations to Anticipate Problems and Carry Out Policy

General Administration of the Contract, Informing Foremen, and So On

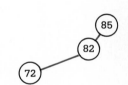

Cost Decisions

Developing Wage Position

Developing Pensions and Benefits Positions

Establishing Outside Limits

Determining Strike Issues

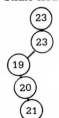

Approving Wage Items

Approving Pensions, Benefits, and So On

Approving Outside Limits

Approving Strike Issues

Approving Complete Package

Note: Data obtained from 668 companies with some unionization in 1978.
Source: Audrey Freedman, *Managing Labor Relations,* (New York: Conference Board, 1980), p. 18.
Reprinted by permission.

Exhibit 15.5	**Policy Statement of a Large Manufacturing Corporation**

The corporation will:

Recognize the place which labor organizations hold within today's social and industrial structure, and will conduct its relationships with these organizations in a responsive manner;

Establish and cultivate relationships with union officials at all levels, so that communications with labor organizations can continue to be maintained despite a breakdown at one particular level of the organization;

Recognize a labor organization as the duly elected representative of its employees;

Take a realistic posture toward collective bargaining, and attempt to use the contract negotiation process as a constructive, rather than a destructive, process. . . .

In its contracts with labor organizations at all levels, the corporation will:

Be continually conscious of the quasi-political nature of these organizations, and will give due consideration to this factor in reaching all decisions in the labor relations area;

Continue to recognize the individual needs of its employees who are represented by collective bargaining agents and, where practical, will meet these needs without undermining the role of the labor organization. . . .

Vigorously resist positions taken by a labor organization which run counter to the interests of the preponderance of employees in the bargaining unit. . . .

The maintenance of good relations between the company and its employees and their collective bargaining units is the responsibility of all management.

Source: Audrey Freedman, *Managing Labor Relations* (New York: Conference Board, 1979), p. 57. Reprinted by permission.

the organization will "establish and cultivate relationships with union officials" and recognize the "quasi-political nature" of unions. However, in some cases, a production official might become suspicious of a personnel representative who spent more time talking with union officials than with managers.

| Issue: | ## Can Union-Management Cooperation Become the Rule Rather Than the Exception? |

As previously mentioned, strikes, perhaps the most dramatic symbol of union-management conflict, are not frequently used. However, many terms encountered in the chapter—*bargaining power, impasse, grievance procedure, power relationship,* and so forth—suggest that cooperation between the two parties is not prevalent.

Many employees join a union because they believe they will obtain benefits through the union that they could not achieve otherwise. Unions, then, must continually justify their existence to members by obtaining concessions from management. Union-management relationships have commonly been labeled *adversary*—characterized by resistance and opposition. Unions cannot be perceived as partners with management; members would question paying dues to an organization that supported the status quo. This logic appears sound and generally applicable; however, another perspective on it is furnished by one company president's remarks: "I wouldn't know how to run a big company without a strong union. The unions are management's mirror. They tell you things your own people won't admit."[45]

Perhaps, then, we should ask what conditions, if any, are conducive to labor-management cooperation. Some authors suggest that union-management cooperation is enhanced by the existence of *superordinate goals*— goals that are desired by both union and management but that cannot be accomplished with the resources and efforts of either group alone.[46] One such goal is safe working environment. An effective safety program often requires large expenditures from the employer. It also requires a daily commitment from the employees and from the union, which might sometimes have to enforce safety rules over the objections of some union members. Some industries, such as the automobile, rubber, and steel industries, have recently experienced the superordinate goal of economic survival. Union and management officials in these industries have cooperated, with unions accepting wage cuts and both parties' joining to form productivity committees.

Communication and *mutual trust* are also necessary to cooperative relationships. The following comments of a union official illustrate these elements, as well as another, risk taking:

[There must be] a willingness on the part of management "to leave its authoritative hat at the door and talk eyeball to eyeball and gut to gut across the table and hear what those people really feel. Let them lay it out to you without feeling hostile, without having elements of reprisal.

"On the union side, are you willing to go in there and make suggestions to improve the quality of work and reduce the inefficiency of that plant that you and your people walking around in that plant see every day? Are you willing to take the initiative in this crisis situation that this American economy finds itself in?"[47]

Finally, the level of cooperation is influenced by the length and quality of the relationship between union and management officials.

It is important to note that *cooperation is likely when management believes unions offer at least some advantages.* These perceived advantages do not necessarily have to outweigh perceived disadvantages for cooperation to occur, on at least some issues. For example, management might cooperate with the union on such issues as safety, introduction of technological change, or United Way campaigns even though they believe that, overall, the union's presence involves more disadvantages than advantages. In any case, though, unions must be seen to offer at least a potential advantage before management will think of initiating cooperative efforts.

One area in which unions can offer management advantages is contract negotiation. Unions frequently receive membership input before formulating and presenting their bargaining proposals to management. Therefore, the negotiated labor agreement that takes these proposals into account is at least somewhat relevant to the concerns of a cross-section of employees. Another advantage exists when the union, not management, convinces members to accept the recommended labor agreement—not always an easy task, as union officials at Chrysler Corporation can testify. Contract negotiation and administration can also be useful as means to institutionalize conflict—provide mechanisms for resolving conflict in an orderly fashion instead of through the sporadic outbursts and inconsistent methods of several employee factions.

The labor agreement also provides management with a consistent framework for decision making. Supervisors are guided by contract provisions instead of individual, possibly haphazard, decision-making methods. Some decisions are made easier by the labor agreement. Assume, for example, that a supervisor must lay off one of two employees of equal ability in his or her department because of a reduction in production operations. This decision is difficult to make, particularly if the supervisor likes and respects both employees. The labor agreement's seniority provisions may well offer the supervisor a way out, since many agreements specify that the junior employee (the one having less work experience) must be laid off first. Thus, the supervisor can blame the choice on the labor agreement or on the union and management officials who negotiated it.

Summary

Union and management enter collective bargaining with their own bargaining priorities. Their positions have upper and lower limits but also include a variety of acceptable alternatives. The eventual settlement is affected by the style of negotiations, the preparations for negotiations, and the bargaining power model.

The style of negotiations involves the efforts to reach consensus among each negotiation team's members, the presence of mutual respect and honesty, and the use of face-saving techniques. Management and union negotiators prepare for negotiations by formulating and costing proposals. The eventual settlement is determined by the bargaining power model, which describes the attempts of each side to increase the other's disagreement costs or reduce the other's agreement costs.

Two methods for resolving negotiation impasses are mediation and strikes. Mediation occurs when a third, neutral party helps union and management officials reach a settlement. Strikes are usually used only after assessing cost, goodwill, and strategic considerations.

Administering the labor agreement is an underpublicized but highly important union-management activity. This activity typically involves a four-step grievance procedure (including arbitration). The activities and relationships (codified, power-oriented, and sympathetic) involved in grievance administration constitute the real grievance procedure.

Discussion Questions

1. Assume that you are a management negotiator and that the union presents the following negotiation proposal: "Any overtime assignment will be guaranteed to last a minimum of two hours at time and one-half the base hourly rate for the classification." Previously, employees working overtime received time and one-half pay for the hours they worked but no two-hour guarantee. Indicate in some detail how you would cost out this proposal. Also discuss some arguments the union might use to make it easier for you to accept the proposal (that is, to reduce your agreement costs).

2. Our discussion of bargaining power touched on only two variables: timing of negotiations and unemployment. Describe, from your own experience or from research you conduct, two other variables that could affect the bargaining power equations.

3. What specific qualities should a mediator possess? Why do these qualities facilitate impasse resolution?

4. What are your views on public aid to strikers?

5. Why does a grievance procedure have so many steps, since the employee is either right or wrong and a one- or two-step procedure would save time and money? In your answer, discuss the various functions, opportunities, and problems, involved in each of the steps.

Notes

1. A. Dale Allen, "A Systems View of Labor Negotiations," *Personnel Journal* 50 (February 1981), pp. 103–114.

2. Carl M. Stevens, *Strategy and Collective Bargaining Negotiations* (New York: McGraw-Hill, 1963), p. 34; see also Robert W. Johnston," Negotiation Strategies: Different Strokes for Different Folks," *Personnel* 59 (March/April 1982), pp. 36–44.

3. Richard E. Walton and Robert B. McKersie, *A Behavioral Theory of Labor Negotiations* (New York: McGraw-Hill, 1965), pp. 19, 23.

4. Jeffrey Z. Rubin and Bert Brown, *The Social Psychology of Bargaining and Negotiation* (New York: Harcourt Brace Jovanovich, 1975), p. 50.

5. Walton and McKersie, *A Behavioral Theory,* pp. 4–6. For an empirical study of union and management negotiators that lends some support to these dimensions, see Richard B. Peterson and Lane Tracy, "Testing a Behavioral Theory Model of Labor Negotiations," *Industrial Relations* 16 (February 1977), pp. 35–50.

6. David L. Cole, *The Quest for Industrial Peace* (New York: McGraw-Hill, 1963), pp. 9–13.

7. Southern Bell, *About Bargaining,* July 23, 1980, p. 1.

8. Paul Diesing, "Bargaining Strategy and Union-Management Relationships," *Journal of Conflict Revolution* 5 (December 1961), p. 369.

9. Hjalmar Rosen and R. A. H. Rosen, "The Union Bargaining Agent Looks at Collective Bargaining," *Personnel* 33 (May 1957), p. 540.

10. Bruce Morse, *How to Negotiate the Labor Agreement* (Detroit: Trends Publishing, 1974), p. 19; see also Ronald L. Miller, "Preparations for Negotiations," *Personnel Journal* 57 (January 1978), pp. 36–39.

11. Meyer S. Ryder, Charles M. Rehmus, and Sanford Cohen, *Management Preparation for Collective Bargaining* (Homewood, Ill.: Dow Jones-Irwin, 1966), p. 64.

12. Michael H. Granof, *How to Cost Your Labor Contract* (Washington, D.C.: Bureau of National Affairs, 1973), pp. 5, 19. For another costing approach, see W. D. Heisel and Gordon S. Skinner, *Costing Union Demands* (Chicago: International Personnel Management Association, 1976).

13. Audrey Freedman, *Managing Labor Relations* (New York: Conference Board, 1980), p. 7.

14. Neil W. Chamberlain and James W. Kuhn, *Collective Bargaining,* 2d ed. (New York: McGraw-Hill, 1965), pp. 162–190. For an overview of related models, see Jonathan Monat, "Determination of Bargaining Power," *Personnel Journal* 50 (February 1981), pp. 513–520.

15. Federal Mediation and Conciliation Service, *Thirty-Third Annual Report* (Washington, D.C.: Government Printing Office, 1981), p. 6.

16. Other, less common, impasse resolution techniques involving a third-party neutral include interest arbitration, mediation-arbitration, and fact finding. Space limitations, however, preclude a discussion of these techniques here.

17. William E. Simkin, *Mediation and the Dynamics of Collective Bargaining* (Washington, D.C.: Bureau of National Affairs, 1971), pp. 25–28.

18. Federal Mediation and Conciliation Service, *Thirty-Third Annual Report,* p. 4.

19. Carl Stevens, "Mediation and the Role of the Neutral," in *Frontiers of Collective Bargaining,* ed. J. T. Dunlop and N. W. Chamberlain (New York: Harper & Row, 1967), p. 271.

20. *Ibid.,* pp. 280–284.

21. Sheldon M. Kline, "Strike Benefits of National Unions," *Monthly Labor Review* 98 (March 1975), p. 17.

22. Albert Rees, *The Economics of Trade Unions* (Chicago: University of Chicago Press, 1962), pp. 34–37.

23. John S. Hirsch, Jr., "Strike Insurance and Collective Bargaining," *Industrial and Labor Relations Review* 98 (March 1975), p. 17.

24. Henry Hazlitt, in *The Strike: For and Against,* ed. Harold Hart (New York: Hart Publishing, 1971), p. 64.

25. The Supreme Court upheld New York's law authorizing the payment of unemployment compensation after eight weeks. *New York Telephone Co. et al. v. New York State Department of Labor et al.,* Supreme Court of the United States, Slip opinion no. 77–961, March 21, 1979.

26. G. C. Pati and L. G. Hill, "Economic Strikes, Public Aid, and Industrial Relations," *Labor Law Journal* 23 (January 1972), p. 32.

27. Marc E. Thomas, "Strikers' Eligibility for Public Assistance: The Standard Based on Need," *Journal of Urban Law* 52 (August 1974), pp. 115–154; Armand J. Thiebolt and Ronald M. Cowin, *Welfare and Strikes: The Use of Public Funds to Support Strikers* (Philadelphia: Industrial Research Unit, University of Pennsylvania, 1972), pp. 217–219.

28. William Serrin, *The Company and the Union* (New York: Knopf, 1973), p. 4.

29. Walton and McKersie, *A Behavioral Theory,* pp. 31–32.

30. Bureau of National Affairs, *Daily Labor Report,* January 29, 1980, pp. 1, 2.

31. Bureau of National Affairs, *Daily Labor Report,* November 12, 1980, p. 1.

32. See, for example, George Getschow, "Aggrieved over Grievances: Revised Complaint Sys-

tem Raises Tension in Coal Mines, Will Be Issue in 1977 Talks," *Wall Street Journal,* March 4, 1977, p. 30.

33. An example of this variation is the possibility of including mediation as a step in the grievance procedure. This practice is found in an estimated 3 percent of private-sector labor agreements. For more details of this alternative, see Mollie H. Bowers, "Grievance Mediation: Another Route to Resolution," *Personnel Journal* (February 1980), pp. 132–136, 139.

34. Grievance procedures also exist in nonunion firms; however, these firms' grievance procedures seldom include arbitration by a third-party neutral. For a discussion of some of the implications of grievance procedures in nonunion firms, see Steven R. Michael, "Due Process in Nonunion Grievance Systems," *Employee Relations Law Journal* 3 (Spring 1978), pp. 516–527; R. L. Epstein, "The Grievance Procedure in the Non-Union Setting: Caveat Employer," *Employee Relations Law Journal* 1 (Summer 1975), pp. 120–127.

35. Harry J. Dworkin, "How Arbitrators Decide Cases," reproduced by permission from the April 1974 issue of the *Labor Law Journal,* published and copyrighted 1974 by Commerce Clearing House, Inc., 4025 W. Peterson Ave., Chicago, Illinois 60646. For a more detailed description of labor arbitration, see Frank Elkouri and Edna Asper Elkouri, *How Arbitration Works,* 3d ed. (Washington, D.C.: Bureau of National Affairs, 1973); C. Ray Gullett and Wayne H. Goff, "The Arbitral Decision-Making Process: A Computerized Simulation," *Personnel Journal* 59 (August 1980), p. 663.

36. Herbert Blumer, "Social Structure and Industrial Conflict," in *Industrial Conflict,* ed. Arthur Kornhauser, Robert Dubin, and Arthur Ross (New York: McGraw-Hill, 1958), p. 234.

37. *AFL-CIO Manual for Shop Stewards* (Washington, D.C.: AFL-CIO, March 1971), p. 36.

38. Walter E. Baer, *Grievance Handling: 101 Guides for Supervisors* (New York: American Management Association, 1970), p. 53.

39. James W. Kuhn, *Bargaining in Grievance Settlement* (New York: Columbia University Press, 1961), p. 29.

40. Delbert C. Miller and William Form, *Industrial Sociology,* 2d ed. (New York: Harper & Row, 1964), pp. 401–402.

41. Melville Dalton, "Unofficial Union-Management Relations," *American Sociological Review* 15 (October 1950), p. 613. Reprinted by permission of the American Sociological Association.

42. Kuhn, *Bargaining,* p. 19; Charles Myers and John Turnbull, "Line and Staff in Industrial Relations," in *Organizations: Structure and Behavior,* ed. Joseph Litterer (New York: Wiley, 1966), p. 313. For supervisors' reaction to personnel's role, see Ross Stagner and Hjalmer Rosen, *Psychology of Union Management Relations* (Belmont, Calif.: Wadsworth, 1965), p. 62.

43. Leonard R. Sayles and George Strauss, *The Local Union,* rev. ed. (New York: Harcourt, Brace & World, 1967), p. 22.

44. Stagner and Rosen, *Psychology of Union Management Relations.*

45. T. George Harris, "Egghead in the Diesel Industry," *Fortune* 56 (October 1957), p. 264, cited in Fred K. Foulkes, *Personnel Policies in Large Nonunion Companies* (Englewood Cliffs, N.J.: Prentice-Hall, 1980), p. 12.

46. Leon C. Megginson and C. Ray Gullett, "A Predictive Model of Union-Management Conflict," *Personnel Journal* 49 (June 1970), pp. 495–503. See also Edgar Weinberg, "Labor-Management Cooperation: A Report on Recent Initiatives," *Monthly Labor Review* 99 (April 1976), pp. 13–14.

47. Reprinted by permission of the Harvard Business Review. Excerpt from "Labor-Management Cooperation Today," by William L. Bott, Jr., and Edgar Weinberg, *Harvard Business Review* 56 (January–February 1978) pp. 103–104. Copyright © 1978 by the President and Fellows of Harvard College; all rights reserved; see also A. H. Raskin, "Can Management and Labor Become Partners?" *Across the Board* 19 (July–August 1982), pp. 12–16.

Wage and Salary Administration: The Point System

Assume you are a wage and salary analyst for Muscadine, Inc., and are constructing a wage structure for hourly employees in your grape plant (follow the steps explained in the discussion of the point system in the appendix to Chapter 10).

You have obtained the data below:

Benchmark Jobs	Total Points	Present Wage Rate	Average Wage Rates from the Wage Survey
Janitor	180	$4.50	$4.60
Beginning Secretary	280	5.75	5.85
Executive Secretary	385	7.50	7.70
Tool and Die Maker	470	8.80	8.85
Electrician	485	8.90	9.10

Using the data above, construct the following:

1. A wage curve for the company's present rates.
2. A wage curve from the data obtained in the wage survey.
3. An adjusted wage curve that will become the new company wage curve.
4. Wage classes (one class for every 100 points) with 20-percent ranges (10 percent above and 10 percent below the midpoint of each wage class).

Then complete the table below to show the starting wage, the midpoint wage, and the maximum wage for each class.

Class	Point Range	Starting Wage	Middle Wage	Maximum Wage
I	0–100	———	———	———
II	101–200	———	———	———
III	201–300	———	———	———
IV	301–400	———	———	———
V	401–500	———	———	———

Now that the wage structure for benchmark jobs has been completed, you begin to look at other jobs and find that welders are assigned 460 points and earn $7 per hour and that gardeners are assigned 180 points and earn $6.50 per hour.

How will you handle these two jobs' wage rates?

Omega's
Wage System

Omega Manufacturing Company makes dinette furniture for large retail and wholesale dealers. Its product is fairly standardized and is sold under various retailer and wholesaler labels. The plant produces an average of 400 dinette sets per working day. The wages average 15 percent below the labor market rates, and all employees are paid by the hour.

In one department, chair assembly, four teams of four employees each sit at tables and assemble the seat, back, and legs for each chair in the production line. Even though the plant has produced dinette sets for ten years, no production standard has been established. However, the employees are reminded by their supervisor whenever production goes below 400 sets (1,600 chairs, with 4 chairs per set).

Because most of the employees have worked in the department since the plant started, they all realize that the implicit standard is 400 sets of chairs per day. In addition, while keeping a count of the chairs is not their responsibility (the shipping department makes an official count of the chairs ready for shipment), an employee in the department unofficially keeps count every day. When the count of 1,600 chairs approaches, the work pace slows—employees go to the bathroom or simply find something else to do. Rarely does the department produce more than 1,600 chairs in a day, and rarely does it produce less.

Questions

1. Explain the employees' behavior. Why do they not produce more than 1,600 chairs in a day?
2. If you were the plant manager, would you install a wage incentive system? If so, what type? How would it work?

Romain University's New Policy

Romain University is a middle-sized public university with about 10,000 students. Recently, Romain had a change in its presidency. The former president had been a grandfatherly figure well liked by faculty and students. Everyone seemed to trust the president and to believe that he had the best interests of all concerned at heart when he made decisions. However, a cloak of secrecy surrounded most administrative decisions, especially those concerning salaries. On many occasions, the president said that the amount of people's salaries was a private, personal matter. Even though the institution was public, not even the state budget office had an itemized list of salaries for faculty members.

The new president, on the other hand, is considered a businesslike manager and an expert on university budgeting. One of his first statements underlined his intention to get the university "back on track in terms of accountability for resources and on the road to responsible accounting." To further this effort, he directed the university budgeting office to place a copy of the budget in the university library for all to see and study if they chose. He wanted to let the faculty, employees, and public know how university funds were being spent. Included in the budget was an itemized list of faculty and employees with their respective salaries and merit increases for the previous year.

Needless to say, the budget has created a tremendous stir on campus. Comments such as the following have often been heard:

"Did you see what Professor _____ makes a year?"

"Why do computer science professors in engineering make more than computer science professors in education?"

"Did you see the low starting salaries in mathematics and English?"

"The only way to get a big salary increase is to change jobs every three or four years."

"Do you know that we just hired a new Ph.D. for more than I get, and I've been here six years?"

After studying the budget, some professors went directly to their department heads and asked for a justification of their salaries. On two occasions, professors were seen slamming the book and storming out of the library. Generally, the morale of the faculty has nose-dived, at least in the short-run. Very few faculty members seem to believe they are being paid about what they deserved.

Questions

1. Evaluate the organizational climate under the former president.
2. Did the new president make a mistake by placing the budget in the library?
3. What implications can be drawn about secrecy in pay?
4. Explain the faculty's reaction to the disclosure of salary information.
5. What should the new president do to keep things from getting out of hand?

Scheduling a Golf Tournament

You are a plant personnel manager who has been informed by the production manager at your facility that the president of your division wants to get closer to her employees. Since (a) she is an avid golfer and (b) three of the largest plants in the division are within a 100-mile radius, the president suggests an annual golf tournament to be initially hosted by your facility (Plant A). The plant manager is quite enthusiastic about the idea and places you in charge, giving you $1,500 to implement the suggestion. The tournament will involve the employees on the chart below.

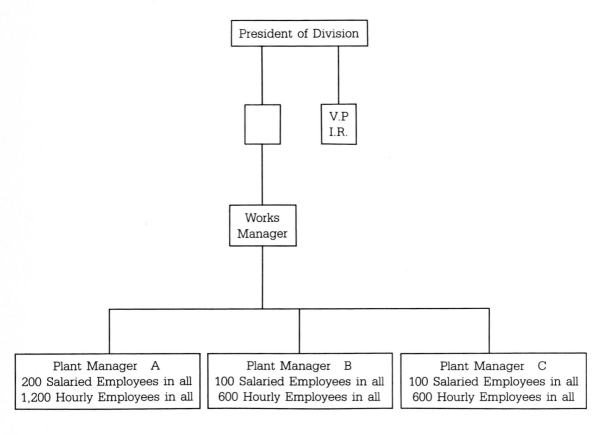

Question

1. Where do you start? What do you do?

Labor
Relations
Incidents

1. A group of workers, during their off-job time, establish a picket line at the plant gate (on a public road) and hold placards that say "This company pays slave wages." The company believes these activities adversely affect its image as a fair employer and demonstrate a lack of loyalty among the workers. The company officials debate their alternatives and decide to discharge the group leader.

   Is this action legal? Is it fair?

2. On January 5, 1980, workers vote by secret ballot for union representation. Then, after six weeks of negotiations, no agreement can be reached, and the union alleges unfair bargaining. The NLRB investigates and finds on behalf of the union. On June 3, 1980, the NLRB issues an order stating that the company is guilty of an unfair labor practice and requires the company to commence bargaining in good faith. The company offers the union a 3-percent wage increase; however, the CPI has increased 7 percent since the last wage increase.

   The company and union return to the bargaining table. The union wants a 10-percent wage increase, but the company stays with its offer of 3 percent. On October 1, 1980, the union contacts the NLRB again alleging that the company has committed an unfair labor practice by refusing to bargain in good faith.

   Are the company's actions legal? Are they fair?

3. A unionization campaign is taking place in a plant. One day, company officials tell workers to leave their work stations and go to the company cafeteria. There, the president makes a statement that includes the following comments:

   "We would rather deal directly with the workers."
   "We cannot continue this business if we do not make a profit."
   "Union membership across the United States is declining."
   "Some union bosses earn over $100,000 from members' dues."

   The union organizers believe these statements are unfair representations of the facts. They demand equal time during working hours. The company refuses.

   Is this refusal legal? Is it fair?

4. The union at XYZ Company has represented the workers there for over twenty years. The wages are excellent, benefits comparable, and personnel policies liberal. About 5 percent of the workforce remains non-

union. These employees do not pay dues but receive everything the labor agreement provides.

The union's leaders and membership believe it is time that all workers supported the union and joined the brotherhood. Union negotiators demand that all workers covered by the labor agreement be required to join the union and pay dues (equal to one hour's pay per month).

Situation A: The company refuses because the state has passed a law prohibiting such provisions. Is this position fair to the majority?

Situation B: The company refuses because it believes every worker should be free to make his or her own decision on union membership. Is this position fair to the majority?

5. A recession has caused you to cut back the workforce in your plant. You are aware that your employees are unhappy about this cutback, as well as about the lessened opportunities for advancement it has produced and the fact that wage and benefit increases have been postponed until the recession ends. You are also aware that some employees have been in contact with labor union representatives and have held meetings to determine employees' interest in joining a union.

Your first appointment this Monday morning is with Mr. I. M. Able, a union representative.

Situation A: Mr. Able opens the conversation by saying, "As the representative of your employees, I would like to discuss with you your wage problems, lay-off policies, and promotion procedures."
What is your reaction?

Situation B: Mr. Able opens the conversation by saying, "I represent a strong majority of your employees and wish to begin negotiations today and discuss additional issues at a later date."
What is your reaction?

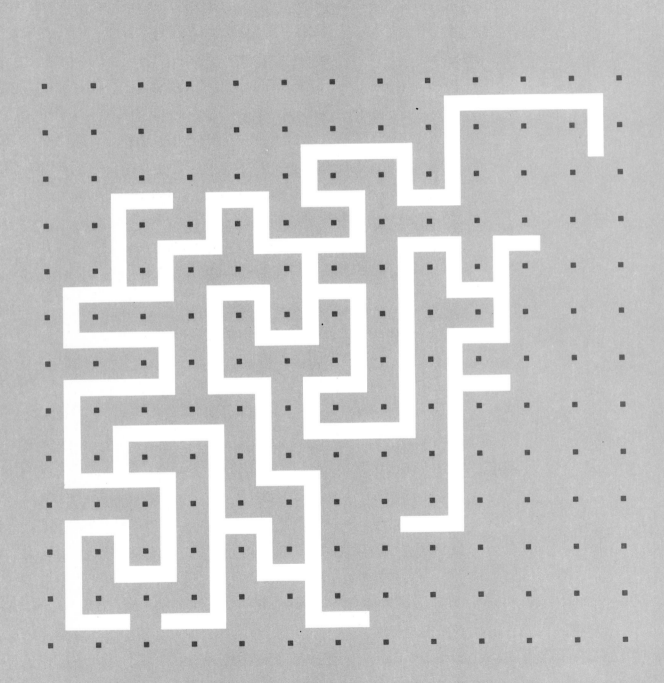

Part Five

Uncovering and Resolving Employee Problems

Even if the organizational efforts discussed in preceding chapters are successful in preserving effective employee-management relationships, employees can still have problems. Managers are not exempt from these problems, since they may personally experience them or have their departments' productivity negatively affected by subordinates who bring problems to work. Personnel representatives make significant contributions to the organization when they uncover employees' problems and implement appropriate solutions.

Chapter 16 identifies two sources of employees' problems—stress and changing employee values—and then discusses related behaviors such as absenteeism, alcoholism, white-collar crime, and turnover. Potential solutions to these problems fall into two general categories: (1) interpersonal activities relating to communication, counseling, and discipline and (2) work design alternatives, such as job enrichment, self-management, and so forth, which attempt to improve the quality of employees' working life. These solutions are discussed in Chapter 17.

Chapter 16

Sources and Types of Employee Problems

Except for layoffs or prolonged periods of illness, a work-life is laid out in front of a person: Five-day, forty-hour pieces stretch out like a seemingly endless passing train, terminating abruptly at age sixty-five at a chicken á la king banquet where a gold watch is presented and the boss picks up the tab for the drinks. Unless we dearly love our work or are blessed with a rare professional flexibility, we tend to work toward 5:00 o'clock, the weekend, vacations, and retirement itself.

Paul Dickson, *The Future of the Workplace* (New York: Weybright and Talley, 1975), p. 209.

The subject matter of this chapter should challenge organizational managers, including those located in the personnel department. Some companies prefer to ignore employees' problems, assuming that their managers effectively prevent problems from occurring. Others, however, contend that this attitude avoids reality, which is reflected by such often-used terms such as *blue-collar blues, burnout, alienation,* and *boredom.* Further, ignoring employee problems runs counter to the contemporary personnel philosophy, discussed in Chapter 2, that says organizations should at least partially adapt to employees' concerns. Personnel representatives as well as other organizational managers should be aware of sources and types of employee problems as well as able to suggest solutions. Attention to employees' problems can enhance these employees' physical and mental health and thus help the organization achieve its objectives.

The first part of this chapter discusses two sources of problems—stress and contemporary values—and the relationship between employees' problems and organizational performance. Next, a wide variety of problem-related behaviors are grouped into three general categories—relief, revenge, and removal.

Employees' problems can eventually involve managers in several ways. An employee's problem can reduce departmental productivity. In some cases, managers themselves may have experienced the problem source (stress, for example) or the problem itself (such as alcoholism). Managers also are often involved with personnel representatives in identifying a particular employee problem and determining whether the organization should become involved in dealing with it. This role of the personnel representative and other organizational managers is approached in the chapter's issue, which discusses difficulties in establishing personnel policies concerning controversial employee problems such as alcoholism.

Stress

The relationship between stress and the work environment has long been recognized. For example, one author has traced the origins of literature on executive stress to a 1920 medical journal article.[1] The flood of more recent articles (sixty-two in the August 1979/July 1980 *Business Periodicals Index,* for example) and books indicates the importance of organizational stress in the contemporary business environment.[2]

Stress occurs in a relationship between a person and his or her environment. "Where either an environmental (job) demand exceeds a person's response capability (overload), or the person's capabilities exceed the environmental demand (underload), the resulting misfit represents stress."[3]

It appears that stress occurs whenever there is a departure from optimum conditions which the individual is unable, or finds difficult, to correct. It arises as a result of too much *or* too little of situational characteristics which are important to the individual.[4]

Defining stress is easier than measuring either the extent to which it occurs at work or the degree to which it harms the individual employee. Some authors believe that the job is a main source of stress.[5] Others question whether that is often the case. For example, one survey of 2,659 top and middle managers found that "managers who normally have more work than they can handle, who never are sure what their authority is, or who always feel caught in the middle on important issues . . . are in the minority."[6]

Some stress can be helpful, as it can increase alertness, effectiveness, and performance. However, too much stress can cause a person to feel defeated, immobilized, and incapable of achieving goals. Physical consequences also are associated with stress. Some studies have suggested that psychosomatic and stress-related illnesses represent 50 to 80 percent of all health problems and are a major cause of death.[7] Physiological indicators of stress include uncontrolled eating, frequent urination, insomnia, muscular aches, rashes, diarrhea, headaches, tightness in the chest, increased blood pressure, twitching, nausea, and increased perspiration. Psychological indicators may include feelings of disorganization, anger, frustration, depression, apathy, helplessness, indecision, fear, irritability, withdrawal, and inability to concentrate.[8]

Individual reactions to stress vary according to how each person defines the potentially stressful situation; does the person view it as a threat or a challenge?[9] The idea of individual variations in reactions to stress can be refined to include the following:[10]

1. Individuals may react differently to the same *stressor,* or potentially stress-producing incident or situation.
2. An individual may react differently to the same stressor on different occasions.
3. Individuals may cope differently with the same stressor.
4. An individual may cope differently with the same stressor on different occasions.

Sources of Stress

The number of potential sources of stress is almost endless; however, many of these sources can be grouped into three general categories—external factors, job and role demands, and personal characteristics.[11]

External Factors Top executives and operating managers are faced with several external pressures that affect their organizations and themselves.

[Top executives are] increasingly unsure about the future and many managers are responding to the accelerating pace of change in business life as a personal emergency with all its attendant stress. For many managers, 1973 was a watershed year during which they learned for the first time what managing in bad times was like. Re-

covery from the 1974–1975 recession solved few problems and created many new ones including inflation, trade imbalances, energy
shortage.[12]

Economic uncertainty often can be equated with employees' fears of
being laid off. One research project (called the Termination Study)
showed that job loss caused both psychological and physiological
problems, as well as economic deprivation. Interestingly, the impact of
job loss on health was most acute from the time the workers heard
about their impending job loss through the time the job actually
ended. In other words, anxiety and uncertainty may produce as many
health problems as unemployment itself.[13]

Many external conditions, such as laws and regulations, have been
previously discussed. Other external conditions that can induce stress
are the geographic location of the organization, the weather, and the
route to and from work.

Job and Role Demands In most cases, employees receive job and work
demands from their immediate supervisors. Stress can have a multiplier effect—stressed executives are likely to cause stress in people
who work for and with them.[14]

The nature of the job can also induce stress, for a number of reasons.
For example, some jobs cause stress because they are tedious or
boring:

What bad jobs have in common is an endlessness and an imposed
rhythm, a feeling that the job never really had a beginning and will
never really end. There is also the feeling that anyone can do the
job, so the worker does not have the impression that he is making
any kind of unique contribution. Whether the worker is typing
stacks of insurance forms, or handling calls at a telephone switchboard, or going over piles of bank loan applications, it is the repeti-
tiousness that fatigues, not the actual energy required to perform
the job.[15]

Positions also have certain roles, or behaviors, attached to them. In
society, for example, individuals play several roles, such as those of
mother or father, boss or subordinate, voluntary worker or member of
the darts team. Roles can cause stress under one or more of the following conditions:

Role ambiguity. The individual does not have a clear understanding of expected job behaviors. This uncertainty often puts
pressure on employees when they have to anticipate their
duties and fear that their behaviors might not be appropriate.[16]

Role conflict. The individual receives at the same time two or
more sets of pressures, and compliance with one set would

make compliance with the other set more difficult. For example, a production foreman may be told by the personnel department to spend a great deal of time with recently hired, inexperienced minority applicants; at the same time, his or her immediate supervisor may indicate that more time should be spent overseeing production on the shop floor.

Role overload. The individual's workload is either too difficult or too great to complete in the time available.

Personal Characteristics The individual employee interprets his or her work environment in the light of various personal characteristics. Several studies, for example, have suggested that so-called Type A personalities are more susceptible to coronary diseases than other individuals.

[Type A individuals are characterized] by extremes of competitiveness, aggressiveness, impatience, restlessness and feeling of being under pressures of time and responsibility. Work activities are especially important to Type A people, and they seek out stressful jobs, work long hours and meet difficult and recurring deadlines.[17]

Two university professors, Waino Suojanen and Donald Hudson, have postulated that some employees have a predisposition to become addicted to the hormone adrenaline. These employees seek out organizational crises to increase their bodies' production of adrenaline. They refer to these employees as "ACORN," which stands for "addictive, compulsive, obsessive, really nutty worker" as opposed to an "OAK" or "an open, adaptive, knowledgeable human being."[18]

Marriage and family life represent two significant social background factors that affect reactions to stress-producing situations. One famous study, the Grant Study of Adult Life Cycles, has monitored the life patterns of 268 healthy people over a thirty-year period. This study has found that "there was probably no single longitudinal variable that predicted mental health as clearly as a man's capacity to remain happily married over time."[19] However, job demands can pose serious problems for married employees. One survey of chief executives found they "typically work 60 to 70 hours a week, travel 6 to 10 days a month and give up many of their weekends."[20] There are also a large number of employees whose working hours (such as the 4:00 p.m. to 12:00 a.m. shift) make it impossible for them to spend any time with their children during the week.[21]

Contemporary Employee Values

This section assumes that employees' values have changed over time, an assumption that is based largely on impressions rather than hard facts. Indeed, some people do not believe such an assumption can be made:

It is unproductive to compare the contemporary worker with an idealized counterpart of yesteryear, particularly since there is no clear evidence that the passage of time has created a workforce that is less motivated than its predecessors.[22]

However, in a general sense, we can say that some turbulent social changes have occurred over the past few decades. Perhaps the changes have been most evident on college campuses. Consider, for example, these comments about college students in the early 1950s from the classic book *The Organization Man:*

Liberal groups have almost disappeared from the campus, and what few remain are anemic. . . . No cause seizes them. . . . The last thing students can be accused of now is dangerous discussion, they are not interested in the kind of big questions that stimulate heresy and whatever the subject—the corporation, government, religion—students grow restive if the talk tarries on the philosophical.[23]

This situation certainly contrasts with the freedom marches, war and ecology protests, and political activism found on many campuses in the 1960s and 1970s. Many people believe that the values that so dominated campuses during this period spread at least to some extent through the rest of the U.S. culture. One prominent observer notes:

The values revolution of that shattering decade [the 1960s] was more lasting than its political protest movements. Its emphasis on sexual and personal freedom and on the ethic of self-fulfillment carried over deep into the 1970s, and to a great extent it is still with us.[24]

Although it is difficult to statistically demonstrate that values have changed, two value changes are often associated with contemporary employees. These changes—a decline in the work ethic and a decline in loyalty to the organization—will be briefly discussed.

Decline in the Work Ethic

The *work ethic* (often called the *Protestant ethic*) refers to the belief that any hard work is inherently rewarding. "In the Protestant conception, all work was endowed with virtue. 'A housemaid who does her work is no farther away from God than the priest in the pulpit,' said Luther."[25]

   Today, relatively few individuals totally embrace this ethic. One writer describes the movement away from the work ethic:

Few would deny that belief in the dignity and value of hard work represents a fundamental part of the American heritage which made the affluence of our present society possible. It was the ethic of a frontier society and it is clear that the frontier work ethic is increasingly giving way to the consumption ethic of an advanced society. Where our cultural values once stressed equality of opportunity and the value of hard work, it appears that increasingly members of our society are demanding equality of results rather than equality of opportunity. Whether one agrees or not, it is a clear pattern of our society to place less responsibility on the individual and to assume a greater responsibility on the part of society at large for providing a minimum standard of living and a constantly increasing standard of living for all members of the society.[26]

Many employees might contend that they could be dedicated to their work only if it stimulated them or served as a means of accomplishing other valued goals.

Not all employees find their work personally fulfilling. Blue-collar or hourly employees often reflect the attitude expressed by one steelworker: "It's a boring, repetitive job—nasty, hot and dirty work. I go there 'cause I have to."[27] Blue-collar employees often work in a "dungeon-like" shop floor environment that undermines the dignity and importance of their job efforts.[28] This lack of stimulation can also be found in white-collar occupations, as reflected in the following remarks from a stockbroker and from the head of an auditing department:

I can't say what I'm doing has any value. This doesn't make me too happy. . . . I'm just being manipulated (by the stock market) and moved around and I keep pretending I can understand it, that I can somehow cope with it. The truth is I can't.[29]

You check for lunch hours, making sure they take forty-five minutes and not an hour. And that they're not supposed to make personal telephone calls on the bank phone. All you're doing is checking on people. This goes on all day.

The job is boring. It's a real repetitive thing. I don't notice the time. I could care less about the time. I don't really know if it's five o'clock until I see somebody clean up their desk. . . . It's always the same. Nothing exciting ever happens.

It's just this constant supervision of people. It's more or less like you have a factory full of robots working the machinery. You're checking and making sure the machinery is constantly working. If it breaks down or something goes wrong, you're there to straighten it out.[30]

In many cases, work, particularly the uninteresting variety, takes a back seat to other activities, such as spending time with the family. One observer notes the "conspicuous loafing" of the working class,[31] while studies have shown that only about one out of five people (21 percent) say work means more to them than leisure.[32]

Decline in Loyalty to the Organization

Loyalty, or *commitment,* refers to "the strength of an individual's identification with and involvement in a particular organization."[33] Employee commitment involves three factors: "(a) a strong belief in and acceptance of the organization's goals and values; (b) a willingness to exert considerable effort on behalf of the organization; and (c) a definite desire to maintain organizational membership."[34] A loyal employee can help the organization, since this individual usually requires less supervision and performs better than an uncommitted employee and behaves more predictably in crisis situations and other situations requiring individual decision making.[35] Also significant are the legal consequences of employee loyalty to the organization. In some situations, employees can be required to sign agreements that prohibit them from taking jobs with certain employers in the future. Persuading an employee to leave his or her present organization can be an unethical, even illegal, practice.[36]

A major concern facing business leaders today is the decreasing amount of company loyalty among employees. A recent survey asked business school deans what the new generation of business executives wants. One finding suggested that a tremendous change in values has taken place over the past forty years: "Today's young executive is more of an individualist and is less apt to sacrifice for the good of his employer."[37] The comments of one ex-president of a corporation illustrate this attitude:

The most stupid phrase anybody can use in this business is loyalty. If a person is working for a corporation, he's supposed to be loyal. This corporation is paying him less than he could get somewhere else at a comparable job. It's stupid of him to hang around and say he's loyal. The only loyal people are the people who can't get a job anyplace else.[38]

Various factors have no doubt contributed to the decline in loyalty. For one thing, organizations sometimes have not been loyal to employees. Workers and managers often have been given the option of transferring to a new facility or leaving the company. Also, many mergers have forced early retirement or layoffs on managers who were performing well. Such actions have negated the idea that loyalty to the company would be rewarded by security and recognition. Finally, the bigger and more complex business and government organizations that have evolved require a larger number of employees in functional jobs. Job specialization and related formal education can make employees more loyal to their professions than to their organizations.[39]

**The
Relationship
between
Employees'
Problems and
Organizational
Performance**

Productivity, in the aggregate, can be calculated by dividing national income by total paid employee-hours in the private economy. This concept has become a major issue in the United States, largely because of publicity generated by the mass media, academic discussions and research, and related soul-searching by organizational executives and managers. Of major concern is the fact that productivity increases in the United States have been lower than those of other countries (see Figure 16.1).

Referring to productivity is easy; understanding its many facets is another matter, particularly in terms relevant to a specific organization.[40] A prominent productivity expert comments:

Figure 16.1

Average Annual Productivity
Growth for Several Countries
(Output per Employee Hour, 1950–1978)

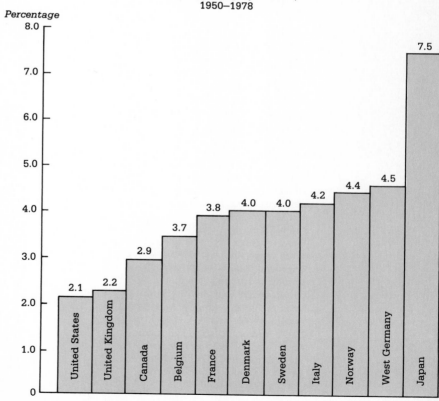

**Average Annual Productivity Growth
for Several Countries**
Output per Employee Hour,
1950–1978

Source: U.S. Bureau of Labor Statistics, cited in George W. Bohlander, "Declining Productivity: Trends and Causes," *Arizona Business* 28 (February 1981), p. 5.

What is productivity? It's like the Loch Ness monster. A few people claim to have seen it, but nobody has yet run it to earth. It is not definable in any precise terms. It's going to be up to you in your own individual firms to define productivity for wherever you sit. The most general and the only definition I ever use is output over input. That's productivity. It's a ratio. Ask me what's output and I'll tell you that you have to define it for whatever it is you do. What's input? You have to define that. We don't have neat definitions to fit it.[41]

Many factors affect productivity, causing even more confusion. Exhibit 16.1 lists some twenty-five considerations that may be associated with

Exhibit 16.1	Percent of Respondents Considering Each Factor Very Important or Unimportant in Terms of Influencing the Organization's Productivity		
		Very Important[a]	Unimportant[a]
	Better Planning	66	2
	More Effective Management	65	4
	Improved Job Procedures	49	7
	Improved Communications	48	9
	More Recognition for Achievement	45	10
	Better Training of Employees	45	8
	More Management Attention to Productivity	39	11
	Better Human Relations	36	13
	Improved Technology	35	23
	New Ways to Motivate Workers	34	17
	Increased Market Demand	31	32
	Changes in Government Regulations	30	38
	Greater Capital Investment	27	23
	Harder Work by Employees	25	20
	More Employee Loyalty	23	24
	Greater Union Cooperation	22	42
	More Opportunities for Advancement	18	25
	Improved Quality of Working Life	16	27
	Improved Working Conditions	16	34
	Job Redesign and Enlargement	12	44
	Greater Participation by Workers in Decision Making	10	49
	More Worker Incentive Programs	10	52
	More Democracy in the Organization	6	64
	More Competition among Companies	6	67
	Better Transportation to Work	4	83

[a]Percentages are based on questionnaires received from 563 executives.
Source: Reprinted, by permission of the publisher, from *Productivity: The Measure and the Myth, AMA Survey Report,* by Mildred E. Katzell, © 1975 by AMACOM, a division of American Management Associations, p. 12. All rights reserved.

productivity. Interestingly, the responses in the exhibit suggest that executives do not assign much importance to harder work by employees as a means of improving their organizations' productivity. Respondents rank this item fourteenth in importance; the more important items are largely, if not solely, management's responsibility.

This does not mean that employees cannot affect productivity; they can affect it, in either a positive or a negative way.[42] Employees, particularly those under stress or those who do not have an attachment to their work or their organization, sometimes engage in behaviors that have negative consequences for the organization. We will group these behaviors into three general categories: relief, revenge, and removal.

Relief

Relief from job demands can take many forms, such as horseplay, daydreaming, extended work breaks and lunch periods, and tardiness. Two significant relief mechanisms are intoxicants (alcohol and drugs) and absenteeism.

Intoxicants

Alcohol Many Americans have drunk alcohol in a variety of locations and on a variety of occasions. Individuals have used alcohol to be sociable, to celebrate, to reduce anxieties, and to avoid depression.[43] Problems can occur when individuals consume alcohol in large enough quantities to become dysfunctional. Alcoholism is a most complicated concept, not easily defined. The American Medical Association states:

[Alcoholism represents] an illness, characterized by preoccupation with alcohol and loss of control over its consumption such as to lead usually to intoxication if drinking is begun; by chronicity, by progression, and by tendency toward relapse. It is typically associated with physical disability and impaired emotional, occupational and/or social adjustments as a direct consequence of persistent and excessive use.[44]

This definition is helpful but vague. Other insights are equally profound and vague: "Alcoholics Anonymous . . . has a definition that goes: One drink too much, 1,000 not enough. The Japanese have a proverb which says: First man takes a drink, then the drink takes the man."[45]

One step in defining alcoholism involves classifying drinking behaviors. This can be done in several ways. One useful starting point is offered by Harrison Trice, who suggests three general categories: normal drinking, deviant drinking, and alcohol addiction.[46] *Normal drinking* is confined to periods of relaxation and sociability. This practice does not undesirably alter behavior, nor does it impair efficient performance of role assignments and obligations. *Deviant drinking* both exceeds the bounds of community definitions and impairs role expectations. An individual in this category normally drinks to excess, and his or her performance is negatively affected by being under the influence of alcohol or recovering from a hangover. *Alcohol addiction* involves physiological loss of control over drinking behavior and inability to function without alcohol.

These distinctions are not clear-cut. They sometimes can overlap, and it is difficult to determine in many cases whether a person's drinking habits extend beyond the normal category. Exhibit 16.2 offers some suggestions to help determine whether an individual has or will likely have a drinking problem. However, few general conclusions can be drawn concerning the type of individuals who will become alcoholics. Some organizations have defined alcoholism as an equal opportunity disease:

Exhibit 16.2   **Factors That Help Identify
                               Excessive Drinking**

**Warning Signals
How to Determine if You Are
Drinking Too Much**

As part of its educational program, The National Council on Alcoholism has prepared a poster listing a number of early warning signals of alcoholism. They are:

Difficult to get along with when drinking.
Drinks because he is depressed.
Drinks to calm his nerves.
Drinks until he is dead drunk at times.
Can't remember parts of some drinking episodes.
Hides liquor.
Lies about his drinking.
Neglects to eat when he is drinking.
Neglects his family when he is drinking.

A Test

Mrs. Marty Mann, founder of the National Council on Alcoholism and long its executive director, suggests that anyone seriously concerned to determine if he is an alcoholic should submit himself to this test proposed in her book, *New Primer on Alcoholism,* (Holt, Rinehart & Winston, 1958, p. 83).

"For the next six months at least, decide that you will stick to a certain number of drinks a day, that number to be not less than one and not more than three. If you are not a daily drinker, then the test should be the stated number of drinks, from one to three, on those days when you do drink. (Some heavy drinkers confine their drinking to weekends but still worry about the amount they consume then.) Whatever number you choose must not be exceeded under any circumstances whatever. . . . Absolutely no exceptions or the test has failed. . . . Even an extremely heavy drinker should have no trouble passing it. . . . The chances are a hundred to one, however, against a true alcoholic's being either willing or able to undertake the test."

Source: Stephen Habbe, *Company Controls for Drinking Problems.* (New York: National Industrial Conference Board, 1970), p. 6. Reprinted by permission.

[Alcoholism] erases barriers of male versus female, rich versus poor, educated versus disadvantaged, talented versus pedestrian. It strikes one out of every nine or ten persons who drink and there is no way to determine—at the onset of drinking—who will be the target.[47]

The image of an alcoholic as an "unkempt, unemployed boozer on skid row" is false; some estimates place only 3 to 5 percent of alcoholics in this situation.[48] However, many people still associate this image with alcoholics, and it actually hinders organizational efforts to curb alcoholism. Managers are reluctant to confront employees who they believe may be alcoholic, since these employees are not similar to the stereotype.

There are an estimated 9 million alcoholics in the United States—approximately ten percent who drink has a problem. The estimated proportion of alcoholics in the total workforce ranges from 5 to 10 percent,[49] although many organizations are either unable or unwilling to furnish related information.[50] Organizational silence or ignorance concerning alcoholism may be costly, since recent estimates indicate alcoholic employees cost corporations $12.5 billion a year in lost productivity.[51]

Some costs are direct and obvious. Estimates suggest that the alcoholic employee is absent two to four times more than the nonalcoholic employee and has two to four times as many accidents on the job.[52] The morale and possibly the productivity of other employees can also suffer when they are forced to pick up the slack of the alcoholic employee.[53] Other, less easily calculated organizational costs associated with alcoholism involve tardiness, poor managerial decisions, waste of supplies and materials, and training of replacements.[54]

Drugs Some have suggested that alcohol and drugs present similar problems, since both are labeled intoxicants. However, two major differences can be identified.[55] First, alcohol can be legally obtained and consumed, although employers usually frown on employees' drinking on company premises. The use of many drugs, however, involves illegal activities—both sale and use. Thus, law enforcement agencies can become involved. This situation can result in negative publicity for the organization.

Second, many organizational members have experienced the effects of having had too much to drink and can understand, to some extent, an employee's drinking problem. Widespread drug use, on the other hand, represents a relatively new phenomenon, one that has not been experienced and is not fully understood by many industrial representatives. For example, one industrial medical director explains that: "most of us have only a rudimentary knowledge of the effects and implications of drug abuse and we are spending a lot of time now brushing up and otherwise trying to educate ourselves."[56]

Managerial uncertainty over drug use extends to estimates concerning the number of employers with drug-related problems, as shown by Exhibit 16.3. The responses shown in the exhibit suggest two general conclusions: (1) very few organizations perceive marijuana or hard drug abuse to affects more than 5 percent of their employees, and (2) organizations perceive blue-collar employees to be more likely to have these problems than professional and managerial employees. Organizations probably underestimate the prevalence of drug use among their employees. Exhibit 16.4 suggests that a higher proportion of individuals have used various types of drugs than the responses in Exhibit 16.3 might lead us to believe. Of course, the estimates of drug *abuse* in Exhibit 16.3 might naturally be lower than the figures for drug *use* in Exhibit 16.4. Further, managers might contend that careful employment screening activities could reduce the drug use problem in a particular organization. However, it is possible that managers are out of touch with real-world considerations regarding drug use.

Managers continue to receive dramatic, if sometimes isolated, accounts of drug abuse in their organizations; for example:

A supervisor must be rushed to a hospital in critical condition because an employee laced his brownie with LSD.[57]

An assembly-line employee informs a reporter that it easier to obtain drugs in the shop than it is on the streets.[58]

| Exhibit 16.3 | **Survey of Sixty-Five Companies Concerning Estimated Druge Use among Various Employee Groups** |

	No Response or Unknown	0%	Percent of Employees		
			1–2%	3–5%	10 + %
			Percent of Companies		
Marijuana Abuse					
Production/Service	62	6	8	15	9
Office/Clerical	62	17	9	5	8
Technical/Professional	68	12	8	8	5
Managerial	68	15	11	3	3
Hard Drug Addiction					
Production/Service	66	17	11	5	2
Office/Clerical	62	23	11	5	0
Technical/Professional	69	22	6	3	0
Managerial	66	23	9	2	0

Note: A number of respondents returned the survey unanswered, indicating that they had too little experience with this problem to provide adequate information.
Source: Reprinted by permission from *Bulletin to Management*, no. 1495, March 23, 1978, p. 2, copyright 1978 by The Bureau of National Affairs, Inc. Washington, D.C.

A prominent security agency, Pinkerton's, reports that 25 percent of its current corporate undercover assignments involve employee drug use.[59]

A *Wall Street Journal* article claims that marijuana use occurs throughout companies, from the factory floor to washrooms to executive suites.[60]

No widespread and systematic organizational response to drug use exists today. Whether this situation will change in the near future depends in part on the initiative and capability of personnel representatives and the cooperation of other managers.

Absenteeism

Widespread organizational concern over employee absenteeism began during World War II, when many companies operated on tight, critical production schedules with relatively few available employee replacements.[61] Such concern increased during the early 1970s, particularly when publicized productivity reports for the years 1960–1972 indicated that the average annual productivity increase in the United States fell behind productivity increases for other countries. Productivity was discussed earlier in the chapter, but it should be emphasized that employee absences negatively affect most, if not all, productivity measurements. Many organizations also became aware that absences

Exhibit 16.4

Drug Use by Type of Drug and by Age Group, 1979

Type of Drug	Percent of Youths (12–17 Years)		Percent of Young Adults (18–25 Years)		Percent of Adults (26 Years and Older)	
	Ever Used	Current User	Ever Used	Current User	Ever Used	Current User
Marihuana	30.9	16.7	68.2	35.4	19.6	6.0
Inhalants	9.8	2.0	16.5	1.2	3.9	0.5
Hallucinogens	7.1	2.2	25.1	4.4	4.5	(Z)[a]
Cocaine	5.4	1.4	27.5	9.3	4.3	0.9
Heroin	0.5	(Z)	3.5	(Z)	1.0	(Z)
Analgesics	3.2	0.6	11.8	1.0	2.7	(Z)
Stimulants[b]	3.4	1.2	18.2	3.5	5.8	0.5
Sedatives[b]	3.2	1.1	17.0	2.8	3.5	(Z)
Tranquilizers[b]	4.1	0.6	15.8	2.1	3.1	(Z)
Alcohol	70.3	37.2	95.3	75.9	91.5	61.3
Cigarettes	54.1	12.1	62.8	42.6	83.0	36.9

Note: Current users are those who used drugs at least once within the month prior to this study. The survey is based on national samples of 2,165 youths, 2,044 young adults, and 3,015 older adults. It is subject to sampling variability.
[a]Z = less than 0.5 percent.
[b]Prescription drugs.
Source: U.S. Department of Commerce, Bureau of the Census, *Statistical Abstract of the United States, 1980* (Washington, D.C.: Government Printing Office, 1980), p. 129.

for illness (real or falsely claimed) and those from the "all other" category (a catch-all including absences to attend a funeral, serve on a jury, take a day off to go fishing, and so forth) increased at an average annual rate of 2.8 percent for the years 1957 through 1973.[62]

At first glance, absenteeism seems easily defined. In fact, the Department of Labor uses two straightforward measurements in compiling absenteeism statistics:

Total Incidence Rate of Absenteeism = Number of Workers Absent ÷ Total Employed × 100.

Total Inactivity Rate of Absenteeism = Number of Hours Absent ÷ Number of Hours Usually Worked × 100.

According to these measurements, employee absenteeism has remained fairly stable throughout the 1970s. For example, the incidence rate for the years 1973–1978 remained around 6.4 workers, and the total inactivity rate for this same period was about 3.4 hours.[63]

Yet absenteeism has many dimensions that no one measurement can accurately gauge. One study found forty-one measurements of absenteeism that covered such aspects as paid versus unpaid absences and incidental (short-term) versus long-term absences.[64] Some companies distinguish between excused and unexcused absences. Others believe that an employee can exhibit *on-the-job absenteeism*— the employee is present at work but his or her mental or physical capabilities are not fully involved with organizational concerns. On-the-job absenteeism includes daydreaming. One punch press operator explains how he relieves job monotony:

You try to fill up your time with trying to think about other things; what you're going to do on the weekend or about your family. You have to use your imagination. If you don't have a very good one and bore easily, you're in trouble.[65]

Organizations view absenteeism as an expense, particularly if they must pay employees wages for not working and must also pay premium (overtime) wages for replacements. Further, an association may exist between absenteeism and turnover (permanent separation from an organization), discussed later in this chapter.[66]

It might benefit organizations to determine the extent to which absenteeism affects their workforces. One analysis of an organization's absenteeism statistics found that an average of 17 percent of the organization's employees accounted for 90 percent of the paid absences during three-month periods. However, a second analysis over a longer period (twenty-one months) found that 50 percent of the employees accounted for 90 percent of the paid absences. The authors concluded that a relatively small core of employees are responsible for absences occurring within a quarter (three-month period) but that the core changes from quarter to quarter.[67]

Managers assessing the extent of absenteeism in their organizations should try to determine what organizational factors contribute to absenteeism. One author contends:

> We live in an absenteeism culture. Taking a day off and calling in sick is supported and encouraged by our society. Many people's attitude is: "The time is coming to us."

> Employers are also guilty of supporting absenteeism as a cultural phenomenon. They *expect* people to take sick days when they aren't sick, and accept it as one of the costs of doing business. Absenteeism is so routine that employers budget around it, making overtime allowances for it, and hire more workers than they need to take up the slack it causes.[68]

Organizational leaders who neither express a commitment to good attendance nor set an appropriate example will likely encounter absenteeism problems among their employees. Exhibit 16.5 presents several employees' comments that reflect both negative and positive organizational attitudes toward attendance.

Revenge

Miscellaneous Forms of Revenge against the Organization

Employees attempt to get even for real or imagined injustices at the workplace in several ways. Two common tactics are attempting to organize unions and "blowing the whistle," or publicizing organizational problems such as product defects or financial irregularities. A third tactic is filing legal suits to protest termination or organizational conditions that cause such complaints as "mental anguish."[69]

A fourth tactic involves sabotage, which often includes the deliberate destruction of company property. This activity has often been publicized in accounts of early employer-employee differences. More modern examples of sabotage are typically reported to occur on automobile assembly lines. One first-line supervisor encountered a variety of such incidents:

> They would do things like turn the air pressure off in the chute for the tires to come down and call me and say the chute broke. So I'd call the repairman to look at it, and they'd say the air's not turned on. . . . But in the engine room the line would have to be stopped and I would have to let five or six jobs go on without tires.

> Another thing they used to do was a job called the W-500. It's a large fourwheel drive vehicle. They would take a two-by-four and join it

Exhibit 16.5

Comments Reflecting Differing Organizational Commitments and Cultures Pertaining to Employee Attendance

Comments Indicative of Negative Norms

"You can get around it. Just don't take Monday or Friday off, and it won't show up in their records."

"There's no reward for coming in, no punishment if we're out. So what the hell?"

"We've got personal time coming to us. If they don't want us to take the day, they shouldn't have offered it to us."

"It's a fringe benefit. Everybody does it."

"I'm going to get paid anyway."

"There's no time clock. It means the company isn't all that concerned."

"They're doing all right. They can afford my days off."

"I get in more hot water for being 15 minutes late than I do for taking a sick day."

"Don't worry about the dispensary if you're out more than two days. They just sign you back in."

"There's always somebody to cover for you around here. Nobody's going to miss me."

Comments Indicative of Positive Norms

"Look, if I'm not in, it screws up the whole schedule."

"I get hassled when somebody doesn't show up. I don't want to do that to somebody else."

"The last time I was out, the supervisor called every day and dropped my check off at the house on payday. He calls everybody who's out, even for a day."

"We've got targets to meet, and that takes teamwork."

"I was out for a day last week, and this morning a VP tells me he's glad I'm back on the job."

"The less you're out, the more money you make."

"They've got a lot of benefits around here, including a free checkup whenever you're out sick."

Source: Adapted from Robert F. Allen and Michael Higgins, "The Absenteeism Culture: Becoming Attendance Oriented," *Personnel,* January–February 1979 (New York: AMACOM, a division of American Management Associations, 1979), pp. 36, 37.

down in the line so I couldn't see it, and when the cradle came by, it would hit the 2-by-4 and throw it out of kilt. The line would be shut down. It would cost us $2,000 a minute.[70]

The extent of sabotage is difficult to measure. Yet its effects, however sporadic, can result in high organizational costs.

Theft and White-Collar Crime

The problems of theft and white-collar crime are widespread and costly in organizations. For example, the U.S. Chamber of Commerce estimates that over 50 percent of employees who work in plants and offices steal; and approximately 5 to 8 percent steal in volume.[71] The organizational costs of such theft are estimated at $50 billion a year.[72]

Theft can take a wide variety of forms. Consider, for example, a small supermarket that was losing money and a large gold mine whose operators suspected its ore was being stolen despite elaborate security provisions. Both situations were eventually traced to dishonest employees. The supermarket manager had installed his own private cash register at one of the check-out counters and pocketed the take, while at the gold mine, employees packaged gold dust in plastic capsules, flushed them down the toilet, and recovered them from a trap a half-mile away.[73]

One of the most recently publicized forms of theft can be categorized as *white-collar crime*[74] which is currently defined as an illegal act or series of illegal acts committed by nonphysical means and by concealment or guile, to obtain money or property, to avoid the payment or loss of money or property, or to obtain business or personal advantage."[75] The tremendous variety of white-collar crimes this definition includes is illustrated in Exhibit 16.6.[76] A description of such activities cannot even be approached in the space available here; further, many white-collar crimes do not involve employee revenge. It is, however, appropriate to briefly discuss three factors that may be associated with those that do.

First, we should consider *employees' motives,* which can range from greed to anger. There is evidence to suggest that many employees commit white-collar crimes to get even with the organization for unsatisfactory working conditions, including lack of recognition for good performance.[77] An example of this situation is presented by the computer programmer who embezzled approximately $250,000 a year for several years. "His disgruntlement with his employer was obviously very strong. He seemed to differentiate between doing harm to people generally and doing harm to get even with his employers, who presumably cheated and treated him so badly."[78]

Many actual or potential white-collar criminals are encouraged by a second factor—relatively light penalties.[79] One study found that the jail sentences for people convicted of embezzlement were much lower than those for people convicted of auto theft or transporting stolen property.[80] A third factor that affects white-collar crime is *work group norms,* which may provide group members with general guidelines concerning acceptable methods and tolerable limits for such crimes and so forth.[81]

Removal

Turnover, or employee separation from the organization, is of two general types: *voluntary* (quits) and *involuntary* (discharges and layoffs). Turnover is measured in a variety of ways, but the most common one appears to be the following:[82]

Exhibit 16.6

A. Crimes by persons operating on an individual, ad hoc basis

1. Purchases on credit with no intention to pay, or purchases by mail in the name of another.
2. Individual income tax violations.
3. Credit card frauds.
4. Bankruptcy frauds.
5. Title II home improvement loan frauds.
6. Frauds with respect to social security, unemployment insurance, or welfare.
7. Unorganized or occasional frauds on insurance companies (theft, casualty, health, etc.).
8. Violations of Federal Reserve regulations by pledging stock for further purchases, floating margin requirements.
9. Unorganized "lonely hearts" appeal by mail.

B. Crimes in the course of their occupations by those operating inside business, Government, or other establishments, in violation of their duty of loyalty and fidelity to employer or client

1. Commercial bribery and kickbacks, i.e., by and to buyers, insurance adjusters, contracting officers, quality inspectors, government inspectors and auditors, etc.
2. Bank violations by bank officers, employees, and directors.
3. Embezzlement or self-dealing by business or union officers and employees.
4. Securities fraud by insiders trading to their advantage by the use of special knowledge, or causing their firms to take positions in the market to benefit themselves.
5. Employee petty larceny and expense account frauds.
6. Frauds by computer, causing unauthorized payouts.
7. "Sweetheart contracts" entered into by union officers.
8. Embezzlement or self-dealing by attorneys, trustees, and fiduciaries.
9. Fraud against the Government:
   (a) Padding of payrolls.
   (b) Conflicts of interest.
   (c) False travel, expense, or per diem claims.

C. Crimes incidental to and in furtherance of business operations, but not the central purpose of the business

1. Tax violations.
2. Antitrust violations.
3. Commercial bribery of another's employee, officer or fiduciary (including union officers).
4. Food and drug violations.
5. False weights and measures by retailers.
6. Violations of Truth-in-Lending Act by misrepresentation of credit terms and prices.
7. Submission or publication of false financial statements to obtain credit.
8. Use of fictitious or over-valued collateral.
9. Check-kiting to obtain operating capital on short term financing.
10. Securities Act violations, i.e. sale of non-registered securities, to obtain operating capital, false proxy statements, manipulation of market to support corporate credit or access to capital markets, etc.
11. Collusion between physicians and pharmacists to cause the writing of unnecessary prescriptions.
12. Dispensing by pharmacists in violation of law, excluding narcotics traffic.
13. Immigration fraud in support of employment agency operations to provide domestics.
14. Housing code violations by landlords.
15. Deceptive advertising.
16. Fraud against the Government:
    (a) False claims.

Exhibit 16.6   **Continued**

(b) False statements:
    (1) To induce contracts.
    (2) AID frauds.
    (3) Housing frauds.
    (4) SBA frauds, such as SBIC bootstrapping, selfdealing, cross-dealing, etc., or obtaining direct loans by use of false financial statements.
(c) Moving contracts in urban renewal.

17. Labor violations (Davis-Bacon Act).
18. Commercial espionage.

D. White-collar crime as a business, or as the central activity

1. Medical or health frauds.
2. Advance fee swindles.
3. Phony contests.
4. Bankruptcy fraud, including schemes devised as salvage operation after insolvency of otherwise legitimate businesses.
5. Securities fraud and commodities fraud.
6. Chain referral schemes.
7. Home improvement schemes.
8. Debt consolidation schemes.
9. Mortgage milking.
10. Merchandise swindles:
    (a) Gun and coin swindles.
    (b) General merchandise.
    (c) Buying or pyramid clubs.
11. Land frauds.
12. Directory advertising schemes.
13. Charity and religious frauds.
14. Personal improvement schemes:
    (a) Diploma Mills.
    (b) Correspondence Schools.
    (c) Modeling Schools.
15. Fraudulent application for, use and/or sale of credit cards, airline tickets, etc.
16. Insurance frauds
    (a) Phony accident rings.
    (b) Looting of companies by purchase of over-valued assets, phony management contracts, self-dealing with agents, inter-company transfers, etc.
    (c) Frauds by agents writing false policies to obtain advance commissions.
    (d) Issuance of annuities or paidup life insurance, with no consideration, so that they can be used as collateral for loans.
    (e) Sales by misrepresentations to military personnel or those otherwise uninsurable.
17. Vanity and song publishing schemes.
18. Ponzi schemes.
19. False security frauds, i.e. Billy Sol Estes or De Angelis type schemes.
20. Purchase of banks, or control thereof, with deliberate intention to loot them.
21. Fraudulent establishing and operation of banks or savings and loan associations.
22. Fraud against the Government:
    (a) Organized income tax refund swindles, sometimes operated by income tax "counselors."
    (b) AID frauds, i.e. where totally worthless goods shipped.
    (c) F.H.A. frauds.
        (1) Obtaining guarantees of mortgages on multiple family housing far in excess of value of property with foreseeable inevitable foreclosure.
        (2) Home improvement frauds.
23. Executive placement and employment agency frauds.
24. Coupon redemption frauds.
25. Money order swindles.

Source: Herbert Edelhertz, *The Nature, Impact and Prosecution of White-Collar Crime* (Washington, D.C.: Government Printing Office, 1970), pp. 73–75.

$$\text{Separation Rate} = \frac{\text{Number of Employees in a Month}}{\text{Total Number of Employees at Mid-month}} \times 100$$

The Department of Labor has compiled annual turnover rates based on averages of monthly observations. An assessment of total turnover statistics for the twenty-year period 1960–1980 shows little change over time. The 1980 separation rate equalled 4 percent of total employees, a figure similar to other separation rates during this period.[83] This measurement is, of course, crude. A great deal of variation can exist among and within organizations; and identical separation rates for two organizations do not always reflect similar situations, particularly if one organization's percentage includes many key personnel.

Turnover can offer both advantages and disadvantages to the organization. The movement of employees in and out of a company gives it vitality by introducing fresh ideas, different frames of reference, and unique experiences. Turnover can also rid the organization of potential troublemakers. The longer an employee dislikes an organization or a job, the more likely this individual is to become inattentive or even hostile in work situations. Turnover can also offer financial benefits to the organization when higher-priced employees leave and are replaced by lower-priced employees with equal capabilities.[84]

However, many organizational costs are also associated with employees' leaving the organization. Some can be directly calculated—for example, severance pay and added social security costs incurred when employer-paid contributions must be made for new employees. Other direct costs result from the recruitment, selection, and training of new employees. Intangible costs associated with turnover include losses in employee morale, customer relations, and the reputation of the organization in the community.[85]

Research concerning employee turnover has been both extensive and contradictory.[86] Studies conducted at different organizations often reach different conclusions concerning the ability of a particular variable (satisfactory peer group interactions, for example) to predict turnover. Although no variable seems a certain predictor of turnover, some variables appear to be stronger predictors than others. These variables are included in the following tentative conclusions:

1. Employees with low lengths of service usually have higher rates of turnover than employees with high lengths of service.
2. Younger employees usually have higher rates of turnover than older employees.
3. Periods of high employment usually involve higher rates of turnover than periods of low employment.[87]
4. Employees with a high degree of job satisfaction have lower rates of turnover than employees with little job satisfaction.[88]

Issue:

What are the Difficulties in Establishing Personnel Policies Concerning Controversial Employee Problems Such as Alcoholism?

This chapter's issue summarizes much of the material presented in the chapter and at the same time introduces considerations explored in the next chapter, which outlines possible solutions to employee problems. The common denominator between the chapters is a personnel policy that reflects both recognition and solution of problems; it is easier to recognize the need for a policy than to develop and implement one. This situation can be more fully appreciated with reference to personnel policies associated with a controversial employee problem such as alcoholism (see Exhibit 16.7).

Personnel policies in such areas must extend beyond written words; they must demand organizational commitment. For example:

Success will elude any company that tries to treat the problem of alcoholism glibly, casually, or superficially. The design of a control program merits careful attention.

If a company announces a flu-shot program, for example, or a cancer-check program, employees step forward with little or no persuasion, because they understand how they might benefit. This is not so with alcoholism-control programs. Alcoholism is a disease of denial and concealment—people are as unwilling to confess themselves alcoholics as they would be to cry "Leper!" In consequence, the control program must be energetic. The alcoholic will not identify himself; he must be identified. And, once identified, he must be given more than an X-ray or a shot in the arm. This point, strange as it may seem, escapes management in all echelons; and hence most management efforts to deal with the problem are too weak-kneed to succeed.[89]

Action-oriented policies of this magnitude must be carefully formulated. At least three general considerations affect personnel policies related to employees who abuse alcohol (as well as drugs). Each consideration must be resolved in order for an effective program to be established.

1. Does Management Have an Obligation to Attempt to Correct Employees' Behavior?

For many reasons, management may prefer not to become involved with a personnel policy dealing with a controversial subject such as alcoholism. Some might contend that such a program is undesirable for the following reasons:

It is not needed, since only a few serious drinkers are employed at a particular company and they can be helped by various community agencies.

Exhibit 16.7

**Example of a Personnel Policy
Concerned with Problem Drinking**

Attendance, job performance or conduct unsatisfactory due to excessive drinking; consult
company physician and staff advisor

Frank and firm talk by supervisor

Condition not corrected within short time

Evaluation of employee and
medical prognosis
(jointly with medical and
staff advisor)

Service less than several years,
value to company questionable,
employment may be terminated

Evaluation indicates rehabilitation
advisable—employee promises
cooperation

Evaluation reveals drinking is
within employee's control, or
employee is not cooperative—
disciplinary action

Rehabilitation measures:
Plan program with aid of staff advisor and
medical.
Medical consultant arranges for treatment.
Use of A.A. or other agency.
Help of church and family.
Transfer to new job if desirable.
Adjust work schedule if necessary.
Defer disciplinary action.

Evidence of satisfactory progress

Rehabilitation unsuccessful

Tolerant attitude toward
occasional relapse

Disciplinary action

Substantial experience and service;
up to 3 suspensions, with follow-up
of progress during suspensions, pension,
or termination

Less than several years' service:
disposition discretionary with local
organization

Source: Reprinted from "Employee Alcoholism: Response of the Largest Industrials" by August Ralston, p. 53 of the August 1977 issue of *Personnel Administrator*, copyright 1977, the American Society of Personnel Administration, 30 Park Drive, Berea, OH 44017, $26 per year.

It would harm stockholders in at least two respects: (1) added costs and (2) negative publicity that might result if consumers believed a company had a sizable number of alcoholics on its payroll.

It would intrude on the private lives of employees. An organization should not be concerned with how employees behave off the job.

Others believe that an organization has an obligation to become involved in alcoholism prevention and rehabilitation programs for at least three reasons. First, legal considerations may encourage involvement in this area. Sections 503 and 504 of the Vocational Rehabilitation Act of 1973 indicate that affirmative action principles apply to handicapped applicants, which can include alcoholics and drug addicts. Further, civil suits may be filed by employees or their relatives who claim that organizational pressures for drinking (at company parties, sales meetings, and so forth) have jeopardized, altered, or claimed employees' lives.[90]

A second reason for undertaking alcoholism programs is that resulting savings may offset costs. It is difficult to calculate this particular cost-benefit relationship;[91] however, it is clear that alcoholic employees can cause the organization to incur costs in terms of increased absences and accidents and reduced productivity. Moreover, as many as 95 percent of alcoholic employees are helpless to correct their problems without some strong outside aid.[92] In many cases, company-sponsored alternatives, including the threat of job loss, represent the strongest incentives for employees to change their drinking behaviors.

Finally, organizational involvement in this area might be prompted by the recognition that organizational conditions can contribute to employees' drinking problems. Two contributing factors, particularly for managerial and professional employees, are absence of supervision and low visibility.[93] Many employees at these levels do not have to account for every minute in the workday; they are often free to leave their offices for several hours at a time to visit their favorite bars.

For the more affluent [business executives and professionals] the liquid lunch can extend into an afternoon of serious drinking. It is not rare for bartenders to receive calls from frantic secretaries trying to track down their delinquent charges. "One stockbroker calls a guy here every day. The broker thinks this is his office."[94]

Expense accounts can also make it easier for employees at this level to purchase alcohol.

2. If Management Officials Determine They Have an Obligation to Correct Employees' Drinking Problems, When Should They Become Involved?

Many organizational policies concerning alcoholism are vague with regard to intervention points; they may call for intervention "when an employee's drinking affects his or her job performance." There are some advantages to such definitions. It is impossible to define a drinking problem in terms of quantity of alcohol consumed in a manner acceptable to all organizational members. Tying the problem to reduced work performance minimizes some of this confusion, and management officials are more comfortable focusing on work-related consequences of drinking. Yet this approach may involve some drawbacks. In many cases, employees whose work performance is affected by drinking are in advanced stages of alcoholism and thus are difficult to rehabilitate.

3. Who Has Major Responsibility for Implementing Alcoholism Programs?

Usually, personnel policies that deal with alcoholism involve many people. Alcoholism appears to cut across organizational levels. One study found that the proportion of alcoholics in an organization is fairly equally distributed across skilled, unskilled, and managerial and professional employees.[95] Related programs and policies should therefore cut across all levels, and difficulties can arise if individuals responsible for the program (say, at top-management levels) are also in need of its services.

In many cases, overall responsibility for the program's design and implementation is given to either the medical or the personnel department. Both of these departments cut across organizational levels; therefore, representatives of these departments can help ensure that alcoholism programs are applied in a uniform, consistent manner. Medical doctors offer the additional advantage of technical expertise in identifying drinking problems. Unfortunately, the organizational members usually responsible for identifying the problem—employees' supervisors—are not highly qualified in this area, a situation further discussed in the next chapter.

Responsibility in many cases includes provisions for confidentiality. Many employees do not want others to know about their drinking problems. However, it is difficult to guarantee an employee that his or her drinking problem will not become known to others, particularly if that employee is frequently away from work receiving assistance.

Summary

Recognizing employees' problems should concern personnel representatives and other organizational managers, since such efforts can benefit employees and organizations alike. Two major sources of problems are stress and contemporary employee values. Stress occurs when an environmental demand does not match an individual's capability to respond. Stress has many causes, but three major sources of stress are external factors, job and role demands, and personal characteristics. Contemporary employee values, such as a decline in the work ethic and a decline in employees' loyalty to the organization, can also contribute to problems, such as declining productivity growth.

Some employees create individual and organizational problems when they seek relief from job demands through intoxicants such as alcohol and drugs. Many organizations, however, appear unable to unwilling to recognize alcohol and drug abuse among their employees, particularly those at the managerial level. Another form of relief is absenteeism. A company can even experience on-the-job absenteeism—here, employees are present at work, but their mental or physical capabilities are not fully involved with organizational concerns.

Some employees may attempt to resolve their problems by getting even with the organization. Revenge tactics can take many forms, such as attempting to organize a union; "blowing the whistle"; filing legal suits against the organization or its officers; and engaging in sabotage, theft, or white-collar crime. A final alternative is removal, or turnover, which includes voluntary removal (quits) and involuntary removal (discharges and layoffs). Turnover has been relatively constant over a recent twenty-year period. It can offer both advantages and disadvantages to the organization.

In many cases, personnel policies must be designed to recognize, define, and eventually resolve employee problems. Such policies can be controversial, since some maintain that organizations should not get involved in employees' problems. Additional controversy can occur in policy formulation and implementation.

Discussion Questions

1. Explain how a secretary, a university professor, and a policeman can all experience a high degree of stress even though their jobs are completely different.

2. Explain how productivity is both a commonly used and a complicated concept, particularly when sources of productivity problems are considered (see Exhibit 16.1).

3. Discuss the following statement: "Alcohol and drugs present similar problems, since both are intoxicants, problems with both are easily defined, and both evoke the same reactions from organizational participants."

4. Approach the concept of absenteeism by discussing related measurements and trends. Also, indicate factors that can distort or influence these measurements.

5. Discuss the many forms of revenge against the organization.

6. Discuss three general considerations involved in establishing a personnel policy concerning alcoholism. Your discussion should explore one consideration that was not discussed in the chapter.

Notes

1. Warren Boroson, "The Myth of the Unhealthy Executive," *Across the Board* 14 (February 1978), p. 10.
2. Books include Jere E. Yates, *Managing Stress* (New York: American Management Association, 1979); Cary L. Cooper and Judi Marshall, eds., *White Collar and Professional Stress* (New York: Wiley, 1980); Alan A. McLean, *Work Stress* (Reading, Mass.: Addison-Wesley, 1979); James S. House, *Work Stress and Social Support* (Reading, Mass.: Addison-Wesley, 1981); Arthur B. Shostak, *Blue-Collar Stress* (Reading, Mass.: Addison-Wesley, 1980). For an earlier classic book on this subject, see Harry Levinson, *Emotional Health: In The World of Work* (New York: Harper & Row, 1964).
3. Gary Blau, "An Empirical Investigation of Job Stress, Social Support, Service Length, and Job Strain," *Organizational Behavior and Human Performance* 27 (April 1981), p. 280.
4. Peter Warr and Toby Wall, *Work and Well-Being* (Baltimore: Penguin, 1975), p. 141.
5. See, for example, M. Zippo, "The Executive under Stress: A Profile," *Personnel* 57 (September/October 1980), p. 41; J. C. Quick and J. D. Quick, "Reducing Stress through Preventive Management," *Human Resource Management* 18 (Fall 1979), p. 17.
6. "Management Stress: Sifting Fact from Myth," *Management Review* 68 (May 1979), p. 35.
7. K. R. Pelletier, *Mind as Healer, Mind as Slayer* (New York: Dell, 1977), p. 156.
8. The authors are grateful to Robert W. Beyer for arranging these symptoms.
9. Daniel Coleman (interview of Richard S. Lazarus), "Positive Denial: The Case for Not Facing Reality," *Psychology Today* 13(November 1979), p. 52.
10. J. E. Newman and T. A. Beehr, "Personal and Organizational Strategies for Handling Job Stress: A Review of Research and Opinion," *Personnel Psychology* 32 (Spring 1979), p. 38.
11. For a useful categorization of stress, including many of the categories discussed in this section, see Terry A. Beehr and John E. Newman, "Job Stress, Employee Health, and Organizational Effectiveness: A Facet Analysis, Model, and Literature Review," *Personnel Psychology* 31 (Winter 1978), pp. 670–674. See also Benjamin B. Wolman, *Victims of Success: Emotional Problems of Executives* (New York: Quadrangle New York Times Book Co., 1973); Lawrence Ingrassia, "Executive's Crisis: Aftermath of Failure," *Wall Street Journal,* March 12, 1982, pp. 1, 4.
12. Kurt R. Student, "Personnel's Newest Challenge: Helping to Cope with Greater Stress," *Personnel Administrator* 23 (November 1978), p. 120.
13. "Faltering Economy Takes Its Toll on Americans' Mental Health, ISR Social Psychologists Say," *ISR Newsletter of the Institute for Social Research, University of Michigan* 8 (Autumn 1980), p. 3.
14. D. D. Warrick, "Managing the Stress of Organizational Developments," *Training and Development Journal* 35 (April 1980), p. 39.
15. Judson Gooding, *The Job Revolution* (New York: Walker and Company, 1972); see also Amos Drory, "Individual Differences in Boredom Proneness and Taste Effectiveness at Work," Personnel Psychology 35 (Spring 1982), pp. 141–152.
16. Donald W. Cole, *Professional Suicide* (New York: McGraw-Hill, 1981), p. 28. See also Warr and Wall, *Work and Well-Being,* pp. 146–150.
17. Warr and Wall, *Work and Well-Being,* p. 161.
18. Swan Harrigan, "For Managers, Stress Must Be an Addiction," *Wall Street Journal,* March 26, 1981, p. 29.
19. George E. Vaillant, "Adapting to Marriage," *Across the Board* 15 (October 1978), p. 44.
20. Mortimer R. Feinberg and Aaron Levenstein, "How Busy Executives Can Manage on the Home Front," *Wall Street Journal,* June 15, 1981, p. 20.
21. See, for example, Peter J. Frost and Muhammad Jamal, "Shift Work, Attitude and Reported Behavior: Some Associations between Individual Characteristics and Hours of Work and Leisure," *Journal of Applied Psychology* 64 (February 1979), pp. 77–81; David Margolick, "The Lonely World of Night Work," *Fortune,* December 15, 1980, pp. 108–114; "A Tale of Two Cities Has an Unhappy End for Some Executives," *Wall Street Journal,* February 1, 1980, pp. 1, 27.
22. Paul Bernstein, "Work Ethic That Never Was," *Wharton Magazine* 4 (Spring 1980), p. 25.
23. William H. White, Jr., *The Organization Man* (Garden City, N.Y.: Doubleday, 1956), p. 70.
24. Max Lerner, "The 'Me' Generation Fading Out," *Florida Times Union,* April 25, 1981, p. A-3.
25. Daniel Bell, *Work and Its Discontents* (New York: League for Industrial Democracy, 1970), p. 54.
26. Reprinted from "Human Resource Management: Key to the Future" by Fred E. Shuster, pp. 34–35 of the December 1978 issue of *Personnel Administrator,* copyright 1978, the American Society for Personnel Administration, 30 Park Drive, Berea, OH 44017, $26 per year. See also D. Yankelovich, "The Meaning of Work," in *The Worker and the Job: Coping with Change,* ed. J. Rosow (Englewood Cliffs, N.J.: Prentice-Hall, 1974), p. 20.
27. "The Job Blahs: Who Wants to Work?," *Newsweek,* March 26, 1973, pp. 79–82.
28. Alexander L. Taylor III, "A Shortage of Vital Skills," *Time,* June 6, 1981, pp. 46–48.

29. Studs Terkel, *Working* (New York: Avon Books, 1974), pp. 446–447. Reprinted by permission of Pantheon Books, a division of Random House, Inc.

30. *Ibid.,* p. 524.

31. Bell, *Work and Its Discontents,* p. 15.

32. D. Yankelovich, "New Psychological Contracts at Work," *Psychology Today* 12 (May 1978), p. 47.

33. Lyman W. Porter, Richard M. Steers, Richard T. Mowday, and Paul V. Boulain, "Organizational Commitment, Job Satisfaction, and Turnover among Psychiatric Technicians," *Journal of Applied Psychology* 59 (October 1974), p. 604.

34. *Ibid.*

35. Wilbert E. Moore and Arnold Feldman, eds., *Labor Commitment and Social Change in Developing Areas* (New York: Social Science Research Council, 1960), p. 2.

36. For more details of the legal and practical aspects of this situation, see Jeffrey L. Liddle and William F. Gray, Jr., "Review of the Law of Restrictive Covenants, Noncompetition Agreements, and Employee Loyalty," *Employee Relations Law Journal* 6 (Spring 1981), pp. 601–619; Lawrence Stessin and Ira Wit, *The Disloyal Employee* (New York: Man and Manager, Inc., 1967), pp. 21–36.

37. "Understanding Today's Young Executive—a Summary," *Nation's Business* 65 (September 1977), pp. 90–94. See also Abraham K. Korman, Ursula Wittig-Berman, and Dorothy Lang, "Career Success and Personal Failure: Alienation in Professionals and Managers," *Academy of Management Journal* 24 (June 1981), p. 342.

38. Terkel, *Working,* p. 535. See also Morris Massey, *The People Puzzle* (Reston, Va.: Reston Publishing Company, 1979), p. 210; Edward Peters, "What Constitutes Employee Loyalty," *Personnel Journal* 40 (February 1961), pp. 370–371.

39. Arch Patton, "The Boom in Executive Self-Interest," *Business Week,* May 24, 1976, pp. 16, 20; Simeon J. Touretzky, "Changing Attitudes: A Question of Loyalty," *Personnel Administrator* 24 (April 1979), p. 35.

40. Ralph E. Winter, "Multiple Choice: Many Culprits Named in National Slowdown of Productivity Gains," *Wall Street Journal,* October 21, 1980, p. 1.

41. Reprinted from "Productivity's Impact on Our Economic Future," by C. Jackson Grayson, p. 23 of the June 1975 issue of *Personnel Administrator,* copyright 1975, the American Society for Personnel Administration, 30 Park Drive, Berea, OH 44017, $26 per year.

42. For insights into this situation, see L. L. Cummings, "Strategies for Improving Human Productivity," *Personnel Administrator* 20 (June 1975), pp. 40–43.

43. Harrison M. Trice and Paul M. Roman, *Spirits and Demons at Work: Alcohol and Other Drugs on the Job* (Ithaca: New York State School of Industrial and Labor Relations, Cornell University, 1972), p. 1.

44. Elmer L. Whyte, "Coping with Alcoholism in Industry," *Occupational Health Nursing* 25 (July 1977), p. 9.

45. Luther A. Cloud, "Industrial Alcoholism Program: Rationale and Results" (keynote address for a series of seminars introducing the New York State Employees Alcoholism Program, Spring 1968), p. 3., cited in August Ralston, "Employee Alcoholism: Response of the Largest Industrials," *Personnel Administrator* 22 (August 1977), p. 50.

46. Trice and Roman, *Spirits and Demons,* pp. 16–17.

47. Muriel M. Zink, "Alcoholism: The Disease That Drains Hospital Resources Away," *Hospital Financial Management* 32 (August 1978), p. 32.

48. Dorothy Schaeffer, "Alcoholism; Challenge for Today's Supervisor," *Supervision* 41 (September 1979), p. 11.

49. Catherine D. Bower, "Alcoholism: Industry's $9 Billion Headache," *Personnel Administrator* 20 (January 1975), p. 32.

50. Ralston, "Employee Alcoholism," p. 51.

51. T. Pike, "Alcoholism in the Executive Suite: Robbing Their Employers Blind," *Vital Speeches* 46 (January 1, 1980), p. 1.

52. F. Kuzmits and H. Hammons, "Rehabilitating the Troubled Employee," *Personnel Journal* 58 (April 1979), p. 239; J. Walker, "Supervising the Alcoholic," *Supervisory Management* 23 (November 1978), p. 29.

53. Trice and Roman, *Spirits and Demons,* p. 3.

54. Charles Elliot Blackford III, "What Does Employee Alcoholism Really Cost?" *Labor-Management Law Journal* 7 (May/June 1978), pp. 23–24.

55. Ken Jennings, "The Problem of Employee Drug Use and Remedial Alternatives," *Personnel Journal* 56 (November 1977), pp. 554–555.

56. Harold Rush, "Combating Employee Drug Abuse," *Conference Board Record* 8 (November 1971), p. 58.

57. Carol Kurtis, *Drug Abuse as Business Problem—the Problem Defined with Guidelines for Policy* (New York: U.S. Chamber of Commerce, 1970), p. 8.

58. Hayes Johnson and Nick Kotz, *The Unions* (New York: Pocket Books, 1972), pp. 43–44.

59. Stanley Penn, "Losses Grow from Drug Use at the Office," *Wall Street Journal,* July 29, 1981, pp. 25, 35.

60. "Prevalence of Pot, Marijuana Use Grows among Younger Aides in Business, Industry," *Wall Street Journal,* August 25, 1978, pp. 1, 31.

61. See, for example, Elton Mayo, *The Social Problems of an Industrial Civilization* (Cambridge, Mass.: Harvard University Press, 1945), p. 88.

62. "Rising Absenteeism," *Morgan Guaranty Survey,* January 1974, p. 9.

63. U.S. Department of Labor, *Handbook of Labor Statistics,* December 1980, p. 124.

64. Kathleen R. Garrison and Paul M. Muchinsky, "Evaluating the Concept of Absentee-Proneness with Two Measures of Absence," *Personnel Psychology* 30 (Autumn 1977), p. 390.

65. Terkel, *Working,* p. 58.

66. For further consideration of the complex relationship between absenteeism and eventual turnover, see Thomas F. Lyons, "Turnover and Absenteeism: A Review of Relationships and Shared Correlates," *Personnel Psychology* 25 (Summer 1972), pp. 271–282; Lyman W. Porter and Richard Steers, "Organizational, Work, and Personal Factors in Employee Turnover and Absenteeism," *Psychological Bulletin* 80 (August 1973), pp. 151–176.

67. Garrison and Muchinsky," Evaluating the Concept of Absentee-Proneness," p. 392.

68. Robert F. Allen and Michael Iggins, "The Absenteeism Culture: Becoming Attendance Oriented," *Personnel* 56 (January/February 1979), p. 30.

69. See, for example, Ralph E. Winter, "Rough Going: More Office Workers Battle Being Fired by Suing Their Boss," *Wall Street Journal,* June 18, 1975, pp. 1, 22; "Cashier May Sue for Mental Anguish," *Daily Labor Report,* April 10, 1980, p. 2.

70. Johnson and Kotz, *The Unions,* p. 36.

71. William L. Taylor and Joseph P. Cangemi, "Employee Theft and Organizational Climate," *Personnel Journal* 58 (October 1979), p. 686.

72. Paul A. Gigot, "Companies Try Harder to Recover Money Stolen by Their Employees," *Wall Street Journal,* January 5, 1981, p. 13.

73. Stressin and Wit, *The Disloyal Employee,* p. 77.

74. For one of the earliest treatments of this subject, see Edwin H. Sutherland, *White Collar Crime* (Chicago: Holt, Rinehart and Winston, 1949).

75. Herbert Edelhertz, *The Nature, Impact and Prosecution of White Collar Crime* (Washington, D.C.: Government Printing Office, 1970), p. 3.

76. For a more thorough discussion of this topic, see Gilbert Geis, ed., *White Collar Criminal* (New York: Atherton Press, 1968); August Bequai, *White-Collar Crime: A 20th-Century Crisis* (Lexington, Mass.: D. C. Heath, 1978).

77. See, for example, *A Handbook on White Collar Crime* (Washington, D.C.: U.S. Chamber of Commerce, 1974), p. 55; "Labor Letter," *Wall Street Journal,* January 6, 1981, p. 1.

78. D. B. Parker, *Crime by Computer* (New York: Charles Scribner's Sons, 1976), p. 77.

79. For example, see Blake Fleetwood and Arthur Lubow, "America's Most Coddled Criminals," *New Times,* September 19, 1975, p. 29.

80. *Ibid*.

81. Taylor and Cangemi, "Employee Theft," p. 687.

82. Rudolph L. Kagerer, "The Warm Body Syndrome: An Approach to Employee Turnover," *Personnel Administrator* 24 (November 1979), p. 58.

83. U.S. Department of Labor, *Handbook of Labor Statistics,* December 1980, p. 170; *Monthly Labor Review* 104 (September 1981), p. 68.

84. Dan R. Dalton and William D. Todor, "Turnover Turned Over: An Expanded and Positive Perspective," *Academy of Management Review* 4 (April 1979), p. 231; Saul W. Gellerman, "In Praise of Those Who Leave," *Conference Board Record* 11 (March 1974), pp. 35–40; and Edward Roseman, *Managing Employee Turnover: A Positive Approach* (New York: AMACOM, 1981), pp. 7–8.

85. Roseman, *Managing Employee Turnover,* pp. 69–70.

86. For extensive reviews of literature and conceptualizations relating to turnover, see Porter and Steers, "Organizational, Work, and Personal Factors"; L. K. Waters and Darrel Roach, "Job Satisfaction, Behavioral Intention, and Absenteeism as Predictors of Turnover," *Personnel Psychology* 32 (Summer 1979), pp. 393–397; Dalton and Todor, "Turnover Turned Over"; James L. Price, *The Study of Turnover* (Ames: Iowa State University Press, 1977).

87. Price, *The Study of Turnover,* pp. 24–43.

88. Porter and Steers, p. 175.

89. Reprinted by permission of the Harvard Business Review. Excerpt from "Company/Union Programs for Alcoholics" by Marion Sadler and James F. Horst, *Harvard Business Review,* September–October 1972, pp. 23–24. Copyright © 1972 by the President and Fellows of Harvard College, all rights reserved.

90. See, for example, "Former Executive Sues Ford for Losses Due to Alcohol," *Industry Week,* August 4, 1975, pp. 11–12; Brent E. Zepke, "Employer Liability for Intoxicated Employees," *Supervisory Management* 22 (July 1977), pp. 32–40.

91. See, for example, J. Michael Swint, Michael Decker and David R. Lairson," The Economic Returns to Employment-Based Alcoholism Programs: A Methodology," *Journal of Studies on Alcohol* 39 (September 1978), pp. 1633–1639.

92. Whyte, "Coping with Alcoholism," p. 9.

93. Trice and Roman, *Spirits and Demons,* pp. 101–120.

94. "The Noonday Tripple," *Newsweek,* October 7, 1968, p. 104.

95. Steven F. Buckley, *The Impact of Alcoholism* (Center City, Minn.: Hazeldon, 1978), p. 71.

Chapter 17

Resolving Employee Problems

Ideally, the personnel office should provide a stable, intelligent workforce that is seldom absent and makes few mistakes. Unfortunately, the perfect worker is hard to find and keep. And there is no guarantee a good worker will not be affected by personal problems that damage work performance. . . .

In the past, management has favored a hands-off approach to employee personal problems. They didn't want to get involved, or they couldn't measure what good their involvement accomplished. But this attitude is changing.

Robert Witte and Marsha Cannon, "Employee Assistance Programs: Getting Top Management's Support," *Personnel Administrator* 24 (June 1979), p. 23. Reprinted by permission of the authors.

There are many potential solutions to employee problems. Some organizations use screening devices, such as lie detectors to uncover dishonesty and urinalysis to detect drug use.[1] Other organizations use various incentives to reduce absenteeism. Space limitations prevent our discussing all potential solutions for each employee problem; instead, we will explain some general approaches that cut across a variety of problems.

The first section deals with three interpersonal activities—communication, counseling, and discipline. These activities are interrelated, since counseling and discipline involve communication and discipline can both prompt counseling and serve as a last resort if counseling efforts fail.

The second section first discusses quality of worklife, which represents a contemporary personnel philosophy. As noted in Chapter 2, early personnel philosophies stressed that employees did not have input into organizational decisions; employees who did not like this situation were free to leave the organization. The current approach recognizes that in some cases organizations must adapt to employees' interests and concerns. The remainder of the section discusses related work restructuring programs (job enlargement and enrichment, quality circles, and self-management) and possible challenges to these programs. The chapter's issue discusses flexible working hours, which may reduce some employee problems.

Interpersonal Activities Used to Resolve Employee Problems

Communication

Sending and receiving messages through various intentional or unintentional networks is both a common and a challenging aspect of organizational life. Some 2,000 verbal messages are directed toward most employees during every normal working day. However, these individuals receive and assimilate only about 25 percent of these messages.

This situation has been illustrated in a university setting. One professor had fifty other faculty members present a group of several hundred students with their "best" ten-minute lectures. Each faculty member submitted in advance a transcript of his or her lecture to the professor, who built an objective test on its content. After each lecture, the group was tested. The professor found that on the average his students could answer only half the items on the quizzes; when they were retested some time later, they could answer only 25 percent.[2]

Communication related to organizational objectives can be classified according to three functions:[3]

Production. Messages help ensure that employees will carry out tasks necessary for generating the organization's output.

Innovation. Messages are used to obtain new ideas or to implement these ideas.

Maintenance. Messages bolster employees' feelings of personal worth and significance and of satisfaction from interaction with coworkers, supervisors, and subordinates.

Accomplishing these functions often depends on communication subjects, styles, and techniques.

Communication Subjects Most, if not all, top managers believe employees should receive communication so that they feel they are a part of the organization and can effectively contribute to organizational objectives. Most employees want to send and receive communication for the same reason. However, problems can occur when intermediaries (middle-level managers who relay messages downward and upward in an organization) are unsure about appropriate subjects for communication;[4] more specifically, they are uncertain about:

1. The areas about which they can communicate.
2. How much they can reveal.
3. Whether they should become involved in discussions of controversial or sensitive issues.

Communication Styles Communication style refers to a range of things, such as whether communicators are assertive or timid, whether their tones of voice are loud or soft, whether they use gestures, and so forth.[5] Effectiveness in communication often depends on style. For example, students have, on occasion, accused some university professors of clouding the meaning of communication by using *gobbledygook*—wordy, unnecessarily difficult language. This situation can occur in any large organization. Consider, for example, two written communications, the first an office manager's memo to his boss, the second an announcement from a government department:

Verbal contact with Mr. Blank regarding the attached notification of promotion has elicited the attached representation intimating that he prefers to decline the assignment.
Translation: Mr. Blank doesn't want the job. . . .

Voucherable expenditures necessary to provide adequate dental treatment required as adjunct to medical treatment being rendered a pay patient or in-patient status may be incurred as required at the expense of the Public Health Service.

Translation: You can charge your dentist bill to the Public Health Service. Or can you?[6]

Communication must be clear and concise to avoid causing confusion and bringing about results contrary to intended objectives.

Communication Techniques There are several techniques for transmitting communication downward and upward in an organization. The frequency of use and effectiveness of some of these techniques are illustrated in Exhibit 17.1. A review of the exhibit suggests the following general observations:

1. Employee meetings in small groups are perceived to be the most effective downward communication technique; employee inquiries, the most effective upward communication technique. However, no communication technique is overwhelmingly regarded as being most effective. This lack of consensus is probably due to the availability of many communication devices and the inability of some respondents to verify the effectiveness of the techniques.

2. No clear relationship can be seen between the extent to which a communication technique is used and its perceived effectiveness. For example, bulletin boards are used in nearly all organizations, although relatively few respondents consider them effective.

Exhibit 17.1	**Frequency of Use and Perceived Effectiveness of Downward and Upward Communication Techniques in Organizations**

	Percentage of Surveyed Companies Indicating Use of Technique	Percentage of Surveyed Companies Indicating Technique Effective
Downward Communication Techniques		
Bulletin Boards	98	6
Supervisor's Meetings	86	14
Company Publications on a Regular Basis	80	23
Employee Meetings in Small Groups	77	39
Pay Inserts	68	7
Letters to Employee's Homes	64	8
Employee Mass Meetings	41	11
Upward Communication Techniques		
Informal Inquiries of Discussion with Employees	86	31
Exit Interviews	81	6
First Level Supervisors	78	22
Grievance of Complaint Procedure	66	7
Union Representatives (Percentages Are of Companies with Some Union Represented Employees)	56	6
Counseling	49	6
Formal Meetings	40	5
Formal Attitude Surveys	30	9

Note: Percentages based on responses from 219 personnel executives.

Source: Reprinted by permission from Mary Green Miner, *Personnel Policies Forum No. 110: Employee Communications,* pp. 2, 5, 7, copyright 1975 by The Bureau of National Affairs, Inc., Washington, D.C.

Many organizations modify the general techniques presented in Exhibit 17.1:

Pitney Bowes spends $850,000 a year on "job holder meetings" at which employees "fire sharp questions at executives."[7]

Cobe Laboratories, Inc., holds buffet lunches each week for various groups of 50 of its 1,600 employees to uncover employees' concerns and give updates on profits.[8]

Ford Motor Company and General Motors have established joint union-management programs at several of their facilities to increase employees' participation in workplace issues.[9]

General Motors awards employees financial bonuses for suggestions. One hourly employee earned $30,000 in one year and has earned over $100,000 since the suggestion system was implemented.[10]

The success of any communication technique depends on the *degree of organizational commitment to its use* and *the willingness of organizational members to listen to and consider communications, and implement the ideas they obtain.*

Counseling and Employee Assistance Programs

Scope and Definition of Employee Counseling Employee counseling is a personnel activity that has not received widespread attention from organizations over the years. One of the earlier and more publicized counseling efforts occurred at Western Electric's Hawthorne facility. This effort was no doubt suggested by interviews with some 20,000 employees conducted from 1927 to 1932. Two significant findings based on these interviews are applicable today:

1. The [employee's] complaint, as stated, was frequently not the real source of the individual's difficulty. Consequently, action based on the *manifest* content of the complaint did not assure that the underlying difficulty would be eliminated.

2. With the opportunity to express themselves freely, the employees were able to more clearly formulate their complaints, and in many cases the complaints disappeared entirely. In addition, many employees developed a new enthusiasm for their work as they talked out their problems and lost some of their tensions.[11]

The scope of employee counseling is extremely wide in terms of subject matter. Consider, for example, the following description of some employees seeking counseling at one industrial facility:

A mother of three children [who] wanted to get from a night to a day shift because she feared that her alcoholic husband was not tak-

ing proper care of the children while she was at work; a . . .
woman of 42, in her seventh pregnancy, whose alcoholic and sadistic
husband abused her and her children; a middle aged . . . woman
who was caught in the net of an illicit love affair from which she
could not extricate herself; a middle aged father, greatly concerned
about the conduct of a daughter over whom he felt that he lost all
control; a rehabilitated alcoholic, who is making good but who came
by for a little encouragement.[12]

Other behaviors that would probably call for counseling include the
following:

A secretary starts to use abusive language, exhorts her fellow workers to adopt her religious beliefs, and accuses the office staff of sin-
ful behavior.

A messenger positions himself on his mail cart, wraps toilet paper
around his head, and refuses to communicate with anyone.

An experienced, high-level attorney ceases productive activity and
merely sits at his desk all day, staring at the wall.[13]

Equally broad are definitions of counseling. One author who asked
managers and employees for a definition of counseling found that the
practitioners conceived of this process as "giving advice and controlling performance in a friendly and helpful way."[14] This definition,
while easily understood, could lead to haphazard, inconsistent, and
superficial counseling activities in an organization. In a more professional sense, counseling might be defined as *a problem-focused interaction process in which learning, growth, and changes in behavior are
facilitated by the counselor's attitudes and capabilities.*[15] Implications
of this definition are reflected in the following discussion.

Counseling Goals and Considerations The goals of counseling include the
following:[16]

1. Reducing anxieties and tensions.
2. Increasing self-respect, self-confidence, and morale.
3. Lowering defensiveness, thereby opening channels of communication.
4. Enhancing the organization's effectiveness and productivity.

The variety of counseling approaches are too numerous to cite, much
less describe.[17] However, most, if not all, these approaches rely on the
attitudes and skills of counselors.

Professional counselors and other organizational members concerned with counseling must first consider their relationships with
their clients. A classic treatment of this subject posed the following
questions:

Do we tend to treat individuals as persons of worth, or do we subtly devaluate them by our attitudes and behavior? Is our philosophy one in which respect for the individual is uppermost? Do we respect his capacity and his right to self-direction, or do we basically believe that his life would be best guided by us? To what extent do we have a need and a desire to dominate others? Are we willing for the individual to select and choose his own values, or are our actions guided by the conviction (usually unspoken) that he would be happiest if he permitted us to select for him his values and standards and goals?[18]

Counselors, then, must respect the individuals who seek their assistance and regard them as partners in the problem-solving relationship. Manipulation, as well as the affixing of blame, should be avoided. Instead, emphasis should be placed on what can be done to correct the problem.

Counseling skills include listening, understanding, initiating effective communication, and evaluating solutions. Each of these skills can include many dimensions. For example, evaluating solutions includes:[19]

Defining the problem, its dimensions, and its significance for the individual and the organization.

Determining alternative solutions to the problem, their probable outcomes, and their relative advantages and disadvantages.

Monitoring and evaluating the proposed solution and determining what can be done in the event of failure.

Employee Assistance Programs Counseling activities can be formalized and included in an employee assistance program (EAP), a program that attempts to systematically identify problem employees and refer them to agencies inside and outside the workplace for treatment or rehabilitation.[20] These programs began slowly in the 1940s, when they focused primarily on alcoholism. By 1959, only about 50 U.S. companies had such programs; but in 1975, 700 EAPs existed in public and private work environments.[21] A recent survey of some 500 firms found that 21 percent of the respondents reported that their organizations had an EAP. This survey also found that the more educated or the larger the workforce, the more likely was the organization to have an EAP.[22]

Exhibit 17.2 shows the many functions that can be included in an EAP. These functions involve previously discussed counseling considerations as well as three general activities: identifying employees who might be eligible for the program, determining appropriate assistance alternatives, and relating employee assistance to work performance.[23]

Identifying Employees Who Might be Eligible for the Program Employees need to be aware of an EAP in order to use its services. Most organiza-

Exhibit 17.2	**Percent of EAP Organizations Offering Various EAP Services**

Program	Percent Offering Program
Alcohol Rehabilitation	100%
Drug Abuse Programs	99%
Emotional Counseling	94%
Family and Marital Counseling	91%
Financial Counseling	87%
Legal Counseling	79%
Career Counseling	70%

Note: Based on responses of 106 organizations having EAPs.

Source: Reprinted from ''Employee Assistance Programs: A Descriptive Survey of ASPA Members'' by Robert C. Ford and Frank S. McLaughlin, p. 29 of the September 1981 issue of *Personnel Administrator*, copyright 1981, the American Society for Personnel Administration, 30 Park Drive, Berea, OH 44017, $26 per year.

tions publicize their EAPs through meetings and printed materials. An introduction to one company's EAP states:

Few people escape having some type of serious personal problem during their lifetimes.

When emotional or psychological problems, marriage and family problems, alcoholism, financial and other personal problems get out of hand, they begin to interfere with our lives, making life miserable. When this happens, a person usually needs some type of professional help in order to resolve the problem.[24]

Referrals to the program can come from many sources. Perhaps the best source is the employee who needs assistance. Chances are that employees who voluntarily seek EAP services recognize the need for help and are willing to receive advice. In other cases, the employee may be referred to the EAP by his or her immediate supervisor or union steward.

Determining Appropriate Assistance Alternatives Employees can receive help from many possible sources. In some cases, the employee's own organization may provide assistance, while in other cases, established services in the community, such as Alcoholics Anonymous, are used. Some private-sector services also offer a variety of employee counseling services for a fee.[25] For example, Control Data's employee assistance program features a round-the-clock hotline that has been so successful the company now sells the service to other employers.[26] Any successful EAP relies on careful consideration of available alternatives to avoid costly duplication of efforts. The administrator of the EAP must also be aware of existing and potential employee benefit plans that might apply to outside services.

Relating Employee Assistance to Work Performance Work performance can be related to EAPs in several ways. Many supervisors use an employee's declining work performance as a justification for referring the employee to an EAP. Supervisors are often ill-equipped to diagnose employees' mental or physical problems; however, they can monitor declining work performance and suggest that affected employees visit an EAP for guidance. In some cases, employees realize that declining work performance may eventually result in their being discharged from the organization, a realization that may prompt the troubled employee to seek help. This situation often occurs with alcoholics. "Get alcoholics into treatment while they still have something to lose, something at stake, becomes the motto."[27] Many employer-sponsored alcoholism programs have recovery rates of 60 percent to 80 percent, far higher than most programs that are not job related.[28]

An EAP's procedures often are tied directly to job performance—an employee who fails to complete the steps specified by an EAP or whose job performance does not improve might be terminated from the organization, for example. On the other hand, provisions must be made to assure an employee that his or her reputation will not be negatively affected by attending the EAP. Also, the employee successfully completing the program should be guaranteed a clean slate— that is, future career opportunities should not be jeopardized by participation in the EAP.

Benefits and Limitations of Counseling and EAPs The success of EAPs can be measured along several dimensions. Personnel representatives generally believe that their EAPs have been effective in accomplishing the various functions stated in Exhibit 17.2.[29] A survey found that personnel representatives believe counseling offers the following organizational benefits: improved morale, improved efficiency, reduced absenteeism, reduced turnover, and fewer grievances.[30] A study of Kennecott Copper's EAP supported the existence of some of these benefits and also found that hospital, medical, and surgical costs decreased by 55.4 percent.[31]

Benefits of EAPs can also be seen when alternatives are considered. Some of these alternatives, such as pretending the employee's problem does not exist or discharging the employee, do not improve the employee's situation. Other alternatives, such as placing the employee on a disability pension or early retirement, may finance the employee's drinking or drug habit. Another indication of success appears to be the large number of employees who participate in EAPs, a figure that typically increases each year the EAP is in operation.

However, many organizations have neither employee counseling nor EAPs.[32] This situation may be due to perceived or actual limitations in such programs. Two possible limitations are cost and illegitimate use of the information obtained from counseling sessions.

Cost *Cost* is a precise-sounding term for an imprecise relationship. It is difficult to compare the cost-effectiveness of different EAPs, because different definitions and measurements are used. Also, some costs may be incidental to the value received. As one executive has stated, "Where the disease of alcoholism is concerned, the 'bottom line' is life for the individual employee. There is no need to quantify such a saving."[33]

However, many costs are associated with counseling and EAPs, including the costs of publicizing the program, training supervisors as to the program's objectives and their roles in the program, and staffing the program with qualified personnel. One estimate has suggested that at least one full-time counselor should be hired for each 300 employees.[34] Another consideration is the ongoing nature of this type of program. Counseling is seldom completed with just one session. One employee, and perhaps his or her family, may require several sessions. An increase in employee entrants into counseling can have a multiplier effect, since many follow-up sessions may be required.

Illegitimate Use of Information Information obtained in employee counseling sessions can be sensitive, even damaging, in the hands of other organizational members. Many programs stress confidentiality; indeed, when outside services are used, some EAPs ask only two questions of the outside counselors: Is the employee attending the outside service? Is the employee making sufficient progress? Both questions can be answered with a simple yes or no, and no other information need be exchanged.

Yet the possibility for release of information does exist. In some cases, this situation is due to conflicting pressures placed on the counselor. For example, the American Personnel and Guidance Association has published extensive ethical standards for counselors to help establish and maintain professional counseling behavior; however, these standards represent broad and sometimes contradictory principles.[35]

A counselor has an ethical responsibility both to the individual who is served and to the institution within which the service is performed. Other obligations may also arise. Consider, for example, a situation that occurred at a California university. A patient informed a university counselor that he intended to kill a particular person. The counselor informed the university police, who detained the patient for a short time. However, the intended victim was not warned of the patient's intentions. After he was released, the patient carried out his threat. The parents of the slain individual sued university personnel, an action upheld by the California Supreme Court, which found the defendants negligent in their "duty to warn."[36]

Some counselors may feel their primary obligation is to their employer. At least one executive whose organization engages in in-house counseling maintains that counselors can trick employees into revealing confidential information, which can then be passed on to top management.[37] However, there is little evidence that this situation occurs on a widespread basis. For example, one official of the American Civil Liberties Union is unaware of any cases in which companies have used information obtained in counseling sessions against employees.[38] Nevertheless, the possibility of this occurrence, whether real or imagined, can hinder the effectiveness of counseling activities and programs.

Discipline

In some cases, management must take disciplinary action against employees who—because of problems discussed in Chapter 16 or for other reasons—violate organizational rules and practices. The nature of disciplinary actions taken against employees has varied over time. During the eighteenth and nineteenth centuries, the employer exercised uncontrolled discretion in directing the work crew. Often, managers administered harsh physical punishment to problem employees. For example, employees who were verbally insolent to their superiors could expect to have their tongues burned with a hot iron. Public humiliation was another popular form of discipline, the guilty person was either whipped in the town square or forced to wear a sign indicating that he or she was an unsatisfactory employee.[39]

This situation had changed by the 1920s because of several factors previously discussed in Chapter 2 (psychological reform, scientific management, growth of labor unions, and so forth). The new point of view stressed that arbitrary and unsystematic employee discipline could reduce organizational efficiency.

Legislation pertaining to collective bargaining and various forms of employee discrimination has also encouraged management to temper its disciplinary actions. Consider, for example, the following negative consequences of improper disciplinary actions:

An arbitrator or the National Labor Relations Board reinstates a unionized employee with back pay. One study of 400 arbitration decisions concerning discharged employees found management's actions completely upheld only 42 percent of the time.[40]

Employees claim their discharges represent racial, sexual, or age discrimination and win related legal suits.

A white male employee under forty years of age in a nonunion firm receives a disciplinary action that he believes is unfair. While this employee does not have recourse through the courts, he or she might eventually leave the organization over this incident. If other employees believe that the action was unfair and that the same thing could happen to them, they might vote to have a union represent their interests.

More recently, nonunion employers have found that their authority to discharge employees has been further restricted by court decisions. For centuries, employers and employees have entered into an unwritten arrangement called *employment at will*. According to this arrangement, as long as the employer and the employee are satisfied with the employment situation, employment continues. However, when either the employer or the employee wants to sever the relationship, either may do so at its will.

With courts in California, Washington, and Michigan leading the way, employment at will has been restricted. For example, judges have ruled that dismissals must be for just cause in nonunion settings, that an employee's length of service must be taken into account in dismissals, and that employees are entitled to fair hearings. Further, employee handbooks promising fair treatment, personnel policies providing equity, and promises of fairness by management during preselection interviews have been used in court cases to overturn discharge decisions by employers.[41]

Thus, employee discipline can have significant consequences for organizations, nonunion and union alike. The following discussion of general elements of employee discipline draws heavily from the experiences of unionized firms but is applicable to any organization.

Elements of Employee Discipline The most significant elements of employee discipline are its purpose, the nature of work rules, and mitigating circumstances.

Purpose The purpose of employee discipline is to correct the employee's behavior. This purpose involves two assumptions: (1) the vast majority of employees are well intentioned and are willing to change if they are shown the correct course of action, and (2) corrective discipline benefits both the employer and employee. The first assumption might be difficult for some to accept, particularly since every organization has its share of employees who seem to take pride in avoiding work. However, if the first assumption is accepted, then the second assumption logically follows. Correcting an employee through proper discipline can save the employer the cost of recruiting and training a replacement. Also, some believe an employee's discharge represents "economic capital punishment," since the employee no longer receives income from that employer and may find it difficult to find another job with the discharge on his or her record.

Many employers have adopted a *progressive discipline* policy, which imposes increasingly severe penalties for repeated, identical offenses. Management typically must give an oral warning, a written warning, and at least one suspension before it can discharge an employee for repeatedly committing similar offenses, such as failing to wear safety equipment. Oral and written warnings inform the employees of inappropriate actions, indicate how their behavior can be improved, and warn them that repetition of the offense may lead to more serious consequences. A suspension—time off the job without pay—typically ranges in length from one day to two weeks. It serves as an example of the economic consequences of discharge and at the same time indicates that management is willing to retain the employee who will comply with directives and change errant ways. Discharge is not a corrective measure, since it means the employee is permanently released from the company. Under corrective discipline principles, this penalty is only appropriate under two conditions: (1) when all previous attempts at correction have failed, or (2) when the nature of the offense is so awful (fighting, stealing, and so forth) that other forms of correction seem inadequate.

Work Rules Most disciplinary actions taken against hourly employees involve violations of written work rules. An effective work rule relates to corrective discipline in several ways. Work rules must first be reasonable—that is, they must be job related and intended to promote safe and efficient work efforts. A no-smoking rule instituted because of concern over employees' health would not be reasonable unless management established that smoking created a safety hazard, perhaps because of flammable materials or processes in the work area. In some cases, the reasonableness of a work rule depends on the industry or company. A unilateral ban on moonlighting (working a second shift for another employer) is regarded as reasonable in the utilities industries, which often need emergency work performed during off-shifts. Industries that do not experience these concerns might have a difficult time establishing the appropriateness of such a rule. The reasonableness of the rule can also vary within a company according to job classifications. It would be reasonable for a utility company to prohibit linespersons from moonlighting; however, extending the same rule to the secretarial staff would probably be unreasonable.

Work rules should also be clear and state the consequences for violations. These characteristics are important in corrective discipline, since employees cannot adequately evaluate or correct behavior if they do not know what is expected of them and how serious the organization considers a rule infraction to be.

Consider, for example, the following work rule: "Horseplay can inflict serious physical harm on other employees and therefore will not be tolerated in any form by the company." The term *horseplay* covers a wide variety of activities. Does the company really intend to ban them all, whether they actually cause harm or not? Also, employees cannot tell from the company's language whether breaking the rule would result in a stern oral reprimand (which they might consider a small price to pay for successfully completing a practical joke) or a suspension or discharge (which they would no doubt take more seriously).

Mitigating Circumstances Corrective discipline also considers mitigating circumstances that might have influenced the offense. One major mitigating circumstance occurs when management has contributed to the problem and must therefore assume part of the responsibility; for example:

1. Management provides employees with faulty tools, then disciplines them for low production output.
2. A supervisor provokes an employee by making vulgar comments about his wife.

Some mitigating circumstances are so unusual that they will not likely occur again. For example, an employee with a long, unblemished work record with the company might get into a fight with another employee the morning after her husband left her.

An employee receiving discipline, particularly discharge, should be given full opportunity to present his or her side of the story to determine whether mitigating circumstances are present. The existence of such circumstances should reduce the proposed discipline.

Resolving Employees' Problems through Work Design

Quality of Working Life Considerations

Many work design programs are undertaken to enhance the quality of work life (QWL). Improved quality, in turn, can reduce the employee problems discussed in the previous chapter. QWL is a very broad concept that refers to the job's impact on the worker and on others whose welfare the worker affects (coworkers, employers, family, community, and so forth).[42] QWL commonly represents "the quality of the relationship between the worker and his working environment as a whole [with emphasis on] the human dimensions so often forgotten among the technical and economic factors in job design."[43] QWL covers such elements as the following:

Availability and security of employment, adequate income, safe and pleasant physical working conditions, reasonable hours of work, equitable treatment and democracy in the workplace, less red tape and bureaucracy, the possibility of self-development, control over one's work, a sense of pride in craftsmanship or product, wider career choices, and flexibility in matters such as the time of starting work, the number of working days in the week, job-sharing and so on.[44]

The concept of quality of working life therefore fully embraces the contemporary personnel philosophy discussed in Chapter 2. More specifically, it recognizes that employees are unique, adult individuals and that their decision-making inputs might benefit the organization and should therefore be encouraged.[45] QWL stresses sincere cooperation in which organizations and employees respond and adapt to each other on a continuing basis.[46] This situation differs from the traditional view of cooperation, which involved employees' obeying managerial directives without question.

It is important also to understand what QWL is not:

> [It] is not a happiness program, although happy employees may certainly be a by-product. It is not a Personnel Department program, although quality of work life has important implications for personnel management. It is not a subtle employee incentive program, although employees motivated to achieving the goals of the organization certainly ought to be one of the outcomes. And it is not another productivity program, although better productivity is certainly one of the important results.[47]

Interest in QWL did not appear overnight but slowly and methodically emerged as a result of several factors. First, as discussed in the previous chapter, the values of U.S. workers changed significantly. Many employees demanded more challenge on the job and more participation in decision making. Second, the 1980s introduced U.S. industry to new economic phenomena—slower growth, declining rates of productivity growth, and heightened international competition. Finally, management and labor realized increasingly that solving people problems could be as important as generating capital and introducing technology. This enlightened view includes the perception that most employees want to be productive and that, with the proper incentives and a climate of trust, they will eagerly involve themselves in their jobs. Their involvement may call for a process in which workers gain a voice in decision making on the shop floor. It may include self-managed work teams, labor-management steering committees, problem-solving groups, quality circles, or work redesign committees that help to wed social and technical ideas in workplace and job design.[48] QWL, then, may serve various purposes and take various forms.

Work Restructuring Techniques

Job Enlargement and Enrichment Both job enlargement and job enrichment add tasks and responsibilities to existing jobs; however, the additions are of different types. Generally, job enlargement refers to a horizontal change in the job—that is, additional work assignments from jobs at the same organizational level are added to the existing job. An example of job enlargement might occur on an assembly line. Suppose one employee assembles part of a product in five minutes and then passes that part to another employee, who completes the product in another five minutes. A job enlargement program might assign both assembly tasks to each employee. The time needed to complete a product—ten minutes—would probably remain the same; however, the employees might feel a greater sense of job accomplishment, since each would be responsible for a completed product rather than an isolated task.

Job enrichment, on the other hand, makes horizontal and vertical changes in the existing work. Increasing the horizontal dimension increases task complexity by adding work stages as described above. Increasing the vertical dimension enriches the job by giving the jobholder more responsibility for making decisions that affect how the job is to be done. For example, the jobholder may take over some supervisory tasks such as assigning work to other employees. Employees may also form teams and make other changes, such as job rotation and group decision making, that positively influence personal behavior, growth, and motivation.[49]

Job enrichment received its stimulus from Herzberg's motivation-hygiene theory (see Chapter 3) and other works that focused on the intrinsic or motivational aspects of jobs. It involves assessing the degree to which individuals perceive certain characteristics (variety, autonomy, task significance and identity, and feedback) to be present in their current jobs and restructuring work or redesigning the job so that these characteristics will be more prevalent.[50]

An enriched job is one in which the employee completes an entire piece of work. The person performing the job can tell where his or her work starts and where it ends, what responsibilities are his or hers, and what responsibilities are others'. In addition, the enriched job permits high degrees of discretion, decision making, and control. The jobholder decides what the procedures and priorities will be and what to do in situations that are not routine. Finally, the jobholder receives frequent, direct, nonsupervisory feedback. While supervisory feedback is important, the jobholder on an enriched job can tell how well he or she is doing from the job itself.[51]

Most of what is written about job enrichment is written by advocates who dramatize its virtues; but, as one researcher has concluded:

Everyone talks about the benefits of job enrichment, but no one ever mentions the cost involved. If the issue of cost is referred to at all, it is in an offhanded manner, yet the issue of cost is one of the paramount concerns a firm must face. A manager does not simply make a few adjustments in the way employees perform their work and then stand back while the organization is showered with benefits. The changes come hard. They are usually time consuming—and they are often costly to make.[52]

Five types of costs must be considered with regard to job redesign programs such as job enlargement and enrichment: wage and salary increases, costs of changes to the facility, inventory costs, charges for implementing the new work design, and training expenses. These costs will be discussed with reference to a study of fifty-eight organizations with job enrichment programs.[53]

Wage and salary increases. In some wage determination systems, adding authority and responsibility is considered to increase the value of a job. Therefore, a higher wage for an enriched job may be justified. Twelve of the fifty-eight organizations studied increased the employees' pay by an average of 14 percent. The study concluded that the thirty-six other organizations did not increase pay because of "unwillingness by management to horse-trade with workers in order to implement a project, and the lack of flexibility that exists in many pay systems."[54]

Facility costs. Because job redesign usually combines related tasks to form new and more complex jobs, it can lead to increased requirements for floor space, tools, and equipment. While some organizations showed increased costs, others reported savings. Thus, the costs or savings are a function of the changes made and must be tied to specific projects.

Inventory costs. Job redesign often combines tasks formerly performed in interdependent work stations to form a semi-autonomous work unit. As a result, in-process inventories and supplies for production may accumulate. However, carefully managed job redesign can synchronize the processes to minimize this problem; and in-process inventories can even be lowered.

Implementation costs. The time and money invested in designing and executing job redesign projects depends in part on whether the organization uses company personnel or hired consultants. In the fifty-eight organizations studied, the average investment in time and money was 2.5 employee-years and $33,141; the average investment per employee was 0.08 employee-years and $1,075.

Training costs. Because the complexity of the redesigned jobs increases, time and money must be invested to prepare the employees to do the work satisfactorily. In the organizations studied, the average number of days in training was 12.52, and the instructor costs per employee were $283.

While the costs may seem discouraging, economic benefits were also reported by the organizations; increased production output (69 percent), increased job satisfaction (64 percent), improved quality (48 percent), lower turnover (48 percent), lower absenteeism (45 percent), and reduction of number of workers needed (43 percent).[55]

An additional consideration concerning job enrichment programs involves individual differences among employees. Organizations are finding that enriched jobs do not appeal to all workers. Some employees who would like opportunities for growth and satisfaction at work find more complex, challenging, and responsible jobs appealing. However, employees who are not interested in such opportunities may be intimidated by more complex jobs.[56] Others may fear they will be laid off when their job duties are combined with those of another job. Further, some supervisors might be reluctant to allow any of their former responsibilities to be given to their subordinates. It may be advisable to retain present job designs for employees who do not perceive that an enriched job will be satisfying to them.[57] An appropriate approach may be to seek volunteers for job enrichment programs, because employees who volunteer for enriched jobs should be those who want to satisfy the personal needs job enrichment is designed to fill.

Quality Circles (QCs) The United States is importing more than cars, televisions, calculators, and watches from Japan; it has recently been importing a Japanese management technique called the *quality circle*

Employee involvement in organizational decisions can be enhanced through quality circles or "self-management."

(called the control circle in Japan). A quality circle (QC) is "a small group of employees from the same working group who voluntarily meet . . . each week to discuss their quality problems, investigate causes, recommend solutions, and take corrective action when authority is under their control."[58]

The QC members are trained in problem-solving techniques such as brainstorming, cause and effect diagramming, and so on. Then the members select a problem to which they can apply these techniques. At the conclusion of an investigation, members present their solutions to management, who will make the final decision as to their implementation. While management has final authority, it is understood that rejection of a solution will be accompanied by a reasonable explanation. Further, management commits itself to responding to the circle within a predetermined period of time. According to one report, 80 percent of the solutions presented by QC groups have been implemented.[59]

The quality circle has a solid foundation in theories of motivation (Maslow, Herzberg, and expectancy, discussed in Chapter 3) and leadership (McGregor and path-goal, also discussed in Chapter 3).

A QC program provides personal as well as group gratification. The presentation to management offers individual employees the opportunity to satisfy their highest goals of self-actualization. The face-to-face communication of their efforts and results with supervisors and, perhaps, even the chief executive officer provides a very high level of satisfaction. Through this interaction, the message to the worker is clear—"management recognizes you as a productive worker capable of managing your work.". . .

Members assume responsibility to identify and analyze problems in their work areas. The opportunity to do interesting and meaningful problem-solving provides the Herzberg work challenge.

The design of QCs provides a vehicle for implementing McGregor's theory. He says that the employee will exercise self-direction and become more involved in working toward organizational objectives only to the degree that he or she is committed to those objectives. Through QCs, employees gain the opportunity to be part of a team seeking common goals. Matching the workers' needs to company goals can be accomplished in a Quality Circle effort.

Organizational goals can be reached while personal needs keep the process moving. During Circle meetings, an employee can discover the relationship between a 10 percent increase in productivity and his/her own acquisition of a new car. This congruency of goals maximizes employee self-direction and thus minimizes the need for external controls.

A Circle goal set by members often benefits the company more than it does the employee but becomes vital to the group because it is they who perceived the need and set the goal. The determining variable is the employee's perception of the situation, regardless of the objective reality.[60]

Ideally, then, the QC is considered a people-developing process, not a people-using process. Because the Japanese see people as their "most valuable, if not their only natural resource,"[61] QCs in Japan are consistent with other company practices.

However, one Japanese executive has indicated that the employee-oriented philosophy behind QCs may have difficulty taking hold in many U.S. companies, which have traditionally emphasized short-term financial goals.[62] Indeed, U.S. companies have sometimes used workers "as scapegoats for corporate productivity and quality problems."[63] The comments of an auto worker laid off in the 1980 recession illustrate this situation:

I am—or was—an American auto worker. I built General Motors cars for 16 years. Then, in March, I was laid off indefinitely. Although I don't think the major cause of the layoff was consumer's perception of my work ability, I believe that it was a factor.

When we lament the lack of quality in television programming, we don't fault the writers or cameramen; we blame the producers and network executives who put the shows on the air. By the same token, it is not the worker who determines the quality of a car but the executives in Detroit and the plant supervisors. . . .

The worker who performs a certain task 320 times a day, 5 days a week knows more about the specifics of his particular job than anyone else. Yet, in 16 years, I have never been consulted or seen any other assembly line worker consulted on how to improve a job qualitatively or quantitatively. There are "suggestion programs," but their main concern is always how to save the company's money.

I don't believe it is inherent in human nature to do a lousy job. Man innately wants to do good work, but he needs to be involved. He needs to know how his job relates to the work as a whole. Nothing is as frustrating as to not be able to do your job properly because a job earlier down the line was omitted. To instruct a worker in such a case to go ahead and do his job anyway is absurd. Yet, this happens, because the basic operating philosophy is to get the job done at any cost. . . .

The auto worker can only build as good a car as he is instructed or permitted to build. Quality is not something to be concerned with only when there is a slack in production. We on the line take our cue

from those in the head office. If they don't really care about quality, they can't expect us to either.[64]

This comment suggests that workers might benefit from introduction of QCs. For organizations, the benefits of QCs are measurable and have included increased productivity, lower turnover, better attitudes, cost containment, higher attendance, and improved product quality. Whether quality circles will be integrated into U.S. firms in the long term remains to be seen.

Self-Management One step beyond job enrichment and quality circles is the self-managed work team. This organizational arrangement is being tried with preliminary success in several U.S. locations. At a new Shaklee Corporation plant in Norman, Oklahoma, thirteen self-managed work teams set their own production schedules based on management volume goals, decide their hours, select team members from an applicant pool provided by the personnel department, and initiate discharges, if necessary. Employees' salary increases are based in part on their demonstrating proficiencies in a new skill every six months. The results, thus far, include production equal to that of older plants at 40 percent the labor cost. It is believed that two-thirds of this efficiency is due to management style; one-third, to better equipment.[65]

The concept of self-management can also be applied on an individual basis through several approaches.

Self-observation. The employee systematically gathers data about his or her performance to serve as a basis for self-evaluation and self-reinforcement.

Goal specification. Setting specific goals tends to improve performance, contribute toward organizational objectives, and provide strong, self-regulatory reinforcement of behavior.

Incentive modification. Self-reinforcement and self-punishment based on self-evaluation are used. Each person determines the sets of reinforcers that will result from various types of behaviors.[66]

Challenges to Work Design Programs

Organized labor has generally remained cautious and skeptical about various quality of working life projects such as work design programs. In fact, most cooperative union-management efforts in these areas have been initiated by management. Union leaders believe that such concerns go beyond the scope of the union's role as the representatives of employees. These leaders have received little demand from the rank and file to become involved in work design programs and have not been prepared to trade off concrete economic gains, such as wage increases, to enhance the quality of working life.[67] William

Winpisinger, President of the International Association of Machinists, has claimed that he never has carried a membership mandate to seek such provisions into labor-management negotiations. He remarked:

In view of the increased rate of inflation that's projected for the years ahead, I expect wages to remain the focal point of our negotiations despite a lot of sociological malarkey about today's workers being less interested in money than in job satisfaction, shared responsibility, rotating work assignments and other esoteric benefits.

As one who's had plenty of grease under my fingernails, I say you can jazz up the work place all you want. You can paint it pretty colors, pipe in Muzak, rotate jobs, put in a suggestion box and share all the responsibility you want.

But, in the final analysis the reason people work is to make money.

The overwhelming majority want to make as much money as they can. And that's true whether we're talking about fabricating airplane parts or collecting garbage.[68]

Another view expressed by unions is that management wants to cooperate with them only in hard times but that, when hard times are over, management will return to its former methods. (This position caused a General Motors executive to respond: "When you ask a bear to dance, you can't quit just when you get tired."[69])

It appears, however, that unions are becoming more receptive to labor-management cooperation such as that found in many QWL programs.[70] A strong advocate for union involvement in QWL programs is Tom Donahue, secretary-treasurer of the AFL-CIO, who has spoken in its favor:

The best, and the most productive employer-employee relationships are formed where there is open communication, a sense of worth and mutual respect flowing back and forth between the participants. The least productive relationships are those based on paternalism, where the workers are treated like unruly children, or on the "license plate shop" theory where the workers are treated as prisoners, or on the plantation theory where they are treated as a combination of both.

The problem of a statistical decline in American productivity—a state of affairs of which nobody approves—and the issue of improving the quality of working life are not going to be resolved until we engage in constructive, truly cooperative examination of all of the factors involved.[71]

As mentioned earlier, union members on the whole seem to prefer that union leaders devote most of their time to dealing with economic issues such as wages and benefits and spend a much smaller amount of time and effort on issues related to quality of working life.[72] Of course, these collective views may not accurately reflect the opinions of employees who belong to the union but do not actively participate in it. Also, individual differences based on attitudinal and demographic factors probably exist. Thus, unions may need to more carefully assess members' preferences.[73]

Unions do not pose the only challenges to work design programs. As one of the pioneers in job redesign has stated: "One of the most important challenges for management in the 1980s is to find creative ways to unlock the potential that exists in the overwhelming majority of our work force."[74] The tasks that lie ahead include the following:

The readiness of the organization for changes in job structure must be assessed, and the commitment of top management and union leadership tested. Decisions must be made about the level of involvement of job incumbents in the change process, and (if they are to participate significantly) they must be coached in the theory and practice of work redesign. Structural, social, and political problems and opportunities that are idiosyncratic to the work must be identified, and plans laid for dealing with them. The criteria to be used in judging the success or failure of the project must be determined, and appropriate evaluative measures found and devised. The list is long, and the tasks are difficult.[75]

Issue: **How Much Can Employers and Employees Adapt to One Another's Concerns? The Case of Flexible Working Hours**

Most of the activities discussed in this chapter assume that organizations can reduce employees' problems by focusing on employees' interests and concerns. This assumption relates to a general personnel issue discussed in Chapter 1—the extent to which organizations and employees can adapt to each other's concerns. Adapting in a mutually satisfactory manner is not always easy. The process typically involves three interrelated steps:

1. Recognizing that employees could benefit from a new organizational policy or action. This recognition can be expressed by either employees or managers, particularly personnel representatives.
2. Assessing the proposed change in terms of the extent to which employees would receive advantages from its implementation as well as the costs and benefits to the organization.
3. Determining whether the proposed change should be implemented even if its cost effectiveness cannot be directly established. In some cases, controls such as a pilot project and related follow-up might be appropriate.

This procedure can be applied to evaluating the introduction into an organization of flexible working hours (often called *flexitime*).[76] After briefly describing flexitime, this section will discuss the potential applicability of such a program (Step 1); assess the potential advantages and disadvantages of flexitime for employees and organizations (Step 2); and suggest situations in which flexitime might be appropriate, at least on a trial basis (Step 3).

Industrial use of flexitime appears to have first occurred in the Federal Republic of Germany in 1967, where a company believed this approach could better accommodate the preferences of its female employees and fluctuations in its work requirements. By 1975, flexitime was found in approximately one-third of all German firms.[77] Organizations in the United States began implementing such programs in 1973; in 1981, about 15 percent of U.S. firms offered flexitime to at least some of their employees.[78]

Although many variations exist, flexitime programs typically are based on an eight-hour workday and a forty-hour week. Each workday contains a *core time,* a period during which all employees are required to be present, and *flexible bands,* periods in which employees can select their work hours to make up the balance of their eight-hour workday. The following example includes core time, flexible bands, and lunch breaks.[79]

8a.m.–10a.m.	Flexible Band
10a.m.–4p.m.	Core Time with Lunch Included
4p.m.–6p.m.	Flexible Band

Employees working under this schedule can to some degree select the hours of their workdays; for example, one employee might choose to work from 8:00 a.m. to 4:00 p.m., while another employee might choose to work from 9:30 a.m. to 5:30 p.m. Organizations can vary schedules by varying the number and length of flexible bands and core times.[80]

Significant employee interest in flexitime appears to exist. For example, one survey of 1,503 adults found that more than 40 percent of the respondents said they would prefer this type of work arrangement. Reasons for this preference are varied, although many working parents indicated that they would like to be able to spend more time with their children.[81]

Flexitime could therefore reduce one source of employee stress discussed in this chapter—conflict between work demands and family demands.[82] In some cases, such an arrangement can also enable employees to pursue personal interests such as playing golf, attending college courses, spending less time commuting (if traffic congestion is less at certain hours), and so forth.[83] Employees' sense of being in control of their work setting may also be increased, along with their belief that management is sincerely interested in their well-being.[84]

It would seem that these advantages could be translated into organizational benefits. For example, employees who scheduled their workday to begin later than the normal 8:00 a.m. starting time might be tardy fewer times.[85] The number of unpaid absences might also be reduced, particularly for employees who were unable to run errands before the former starting time and took an entire day off rather than report late to work.[86] Flexitime can also serve as an effective recruiting technique; and service organizations (banks, government offices, insurance companies, and so forth) can increase hours of operation, thereby providing better service to customers or clients.

At first glance, flexitime appears ideally suited to both employer and employee concerns. However, this may not be the case. Some research has shown that flexitime has neither reduced the number of paid absences (sick leave) taken by employees nor improved organizational productivity.[87] This situation may be due to disadvantages to organizations, employees, or both. Some organizations might need to increase record keeping for pay purposes; in fact, some might need to install the dreaded time clock for employees working varied schedules. Supervisory and communication problems might also occur when employees are not all working during the same time period. Management may find it more difficult to schedule meetings requiring everyone's attendance.[88] Extended hours necessary for flexitime increase the organization's energy costs and possibly result in adding employees in certain job categories, such as receptionists and switchboard operators.[89] In some cases, organizational benefits received from flexitime—for example, fewer overtime hours and thus less overtime pay—might work to the detriment of employees.

Thus, organizations and employees must assess the real potential of a personnel change such as introduction of flexitime before implementing in on a widespread basis.[90] Both participants should also consider the situations in which flexitime might be most appropriate. Such situations include one or more of the following characteristics.[91]

Younger employees, particularly females with young children.

A large number of employees who could cover the many time combinations possible under flexitime.

Technology that does not require a high degree of interaction among employees or close supervision.

Location in an area in which varied schedules could help alleviate traffic congestion.

A nonunion setting or a union whose leaders recognize some potential advantages in the flexitime approach.[92]

Summary

Many employee problems and their negative impact on organizational productivity can be reduced through interpersonal activities (communication, counseling, and discipline) and work-restructuring techniques (job enlargement and enrichment programs, quality circles, and self-management). Communication messages typically serve three organizational functions—production, innovation, and maintenance. The effectiveness of organizational communications depends on the particular styles and techniques used.

Employee counseling first received publicity with the Hawthorne studies, which were concluded in 1932. Not much attention was given employee counseling until the recent development of employee assistance programs (EAPs), which typically allows for counseling employees on a wide variety of problems ranging from alcoholism to careers. According to one survey, EAPs are found in approximately one out of five organizations today.

In some cases managers may have to consider disciplining employees who have violated work rules. The major purpose of such discipline is to correct employees' behavior. Effective discipline is usually progressive in nature—that is, it calls for increasingly severe penalties (oral warning, written warning, at least one suspension, and discharge) for repeated, identical offenses. Also necessary are reasonable and clear work rules and consideration of any mitigating circumstances that may have been present in the rule infraction.

Any discussion of work restructuring techniques must initially consider the quality of working life (QWL), which emphasizes human dimensions of employees' jobs. QWL covers a wide variety of factors (security of employment, safety and pleasantness of working conditions, control over work, and so forth) that can affect employees' work behavior. This concept also embodies a contemporary personnel approach—an approach that says the organization must in some cases adapt to employees' interests and concerns.

Both job enlargement and job enrichment programs add tasks and responsibilities to existing jobs, although the additions usually are of different kinds. Generally, job enlargement refers to a horizontal change in the job, while job enrichment also involves a vertical change. These programs should receive careful attention before implementation, since they involve many potential costs.

Quality circles are small groups of employees from the same working unit who voluntarily meet each week to discuss quality problems, investigate causes, recommend solutions, and take appropriate corrective action. Self-managed work teams extend the principles of job enlargement and enrichment and quality circles; employees in such teams set their own production schedules, decide their hours, select team members from an applicant pool provided by the personnel department, and initiate discharges if necessary. Self-management can also be applied on an individual basis.

Work design programs must meet several challenges, such as union skepticism. Many such programs and other activities designed to reduce employees' problems call for employers and employees to adapt to each other's needs, a sometimes complicated situation, as indicated in the "flexitime" concept.

Discussion Questions

1. Indicate how organizational communications can be inefficient by discussing potential problems (1) with communication styles and (2) with three communication techniques.

2. Discuss the many dimensions of employee counseling by indicating its goals, the skills it requires, and some considerations and limitations involved in employee assistance programs.

3. Explain how improperly administered discipline can have negative consequences for both union and nonunion firms. Also, fully discuss, with some original examples, the significance of correction and work rules in a typical disciplinary procedure.

4. Put into practical terms the concept of quality of working life, indicating both what the concept represents and what it does not represent.

5. Define the following terms: *job enlargement, job enrichment, quality circles,* and *self-management.* Give some unique features of each, and cite two ways in which all are similar. Finally, indicate the problems and prospects offered by unions to work design programs.

6. Discuss the following statement, qualifying it when appropriate: "Flexitime is found in most organizations today, since it is easily implemented and offers many benefits to employers and employees."

Notes

1. See, for example, David Thoresen Lykken, *A Tremor in the Blood: Uses and Abuses of the Lie Detector* (New York: McGraw-Hill, 1981).
2. Ernest G. Bormann, William S. Howell, Ralph G. Nichols, and George L. Shapiro, *Interpersonal Communication in the Modern Organization* (Englewood Cliffs, N.J.: Prentice-Hall, 1969), pp. 183–185.
3. Richard V. Farace and Donald MacDonald, "New Directions in the Study of Organizational Communication," *Personnel Psychology* 27 (Spring 1974), pp. 12, 13. See also, Otis W. Baskin and Craig E. Aronoff, *Interpersonal Communications in Organizations* (Santa Monica: Goodyear, 1980), pp. 149–160.
4. Norman B. Sigband, "What's Happened to Employee Commitment?" *Personnel Journal* 53 (February 1974), p. 133.
5. Edgar H. Schein, *Process Consultation: Its Role in Organization Development* (Reading, Mass.: Addison-Wesley, 1969), pp. 19–20.
6. Stuart Chase, "Executive Communications: Breaking the Semantic Barrier," in *Management, Organizations and Human Resources: Selected Readings,* ed. Herbert G. Hicks (New York: McGraw-Hill, 1972), p. 216.
7. "Labor Letter," *Wall Street Journal,* April 18, 1978, p. 1.
8. "Labor Letter," *Wall Street Journal,* December 2, 1980, p. 1.
9. Bureau of National Affairs, *Daily Labor Report,* June 11, 1980, p. 2.
10. "Labor Letter," *Wall Street Journal,* July 20, 1976, p. 1. See also Steve R. Massey, "Bosses Enlist Workers in Cost-Cutting Battles," *Wall Street Journal,* May 28, 1981, p. 27.
11. W. J. Dickson, "The Hawthorne Plan of Personnel Counseling," *American Journal of Orthopsychiatry* 15 (1945), pp. 343–347. Reprinted with permission from the American Journal of Orthopsychiatry, copyright 1945 by the American Orthopsychiatric Association, Inc. Also see Harry Levinson, "Employee Counseling in Industry: Observations on Three Programs," in *Industrial Mental Health and Employee Counseling,* ed. Robert L. Noland (New York: Behavioral Publications, 1973), p. 139. For an early account of counseling in industry, see V. V. Anderson, *Psychiatry in Industry* (New York: Harper & Brothers, 1929).
12. Clifford H. Peace, "Pastoral Counseling with the Problem Employee," in *Industrial Mental Health and Employee Counseling,* ed. Robert L. Noland (New York: Behavioral Publications, 1973), pp. 263–264. Reprinted by permission of Human Sciences Press.
13. Hana Rostain, Peter Allan, and Stephen Rosenberg, "New York City's Approach to Problem-Employee Counseling," *Personnel Journal* 59 (April 1980), p. 305.
14. Raymond G. Hunt, *Interpersonal Strategies for System Management: Applications of Counseling and Participative Principles* (Monterey, Calif.: Brooks/Cole Publishing Company, 1974), p. 88.
15. *Ibid.,* p. 89.
16. *Ibid.,* pp. 107–108.
17. For useful starting points in studying counseling approaches, see Raymond J. Corsini, ed., *Current Psychotherapies,* 2d ed. (Itasca, Ill.: F. E. Peacock, 1979); Richard E. Walton, *Interpersonal Peacemaking: Confrontations and Third-Party Consultation* (Reading, Mass.: Addison-Wesley, 1969).
18. Carl R. Rogers, *Client-Centered Therapy* (Boston: Houghton Mifflin, 1951), p. 20. See also Robert Stensrud and Kay Stensrud, "Counseling May Be Hazardous to Your Health: How We Teach People to Feel Powerless," *Personnel and Guidance Journal* 59 (January 1981), pp. 300–304.
19. Hunt, *Interpersonal Strategies,* p. 121.
20. Martin Shain and Judith Groeneveld, *Employee Assistance Programs: Philosophy, Theory and Practice* (Lexington, Mass.: Lexington Books, 1980), p. 142.
21. Julian L. Carr and Richard T. Hellan, "Improving Corporate Performance through Employee-Assistance Programs," *Business Horizons* 23 (April 1980), pp. 57–58.
22. Robert C. Ford and Frank S. McLaughlin, "Employee Assistance Programs: A Descriptive Survey of ASPA Members," *Personnel Administrator* 26 (September 1981), pp. 30–31.
23. These activities were suggested by two sources: Shain and Groeneveld, *Employee Assistance Programs,* pp. 7–10; James T. Wrich, *The Employee Assistance Program* (Center City, Minn.: Hazelden, 1974), pp. 24–25.
24. Anheuser-Busch, Inc., "Employee Assistance Program," p. 2.
25. "More Help for Emotionally Troubled Employees," *Business Week,* March 12, 1979, pp. 97–99, 102.

26. "Labor Letter," *Wall Street Journal,* February 21, 1978, p. 1.

27. Shain and Groeneveld, *Employee Assistance Programs, p. 2.*

28. Roger Ricklefs, "In-House Counsel: Firms Offer Employees a New Benefit; Help in Personal Problems, "*Wall Street Journal,* August 13, 1979, p. 27.

29. Ford and McLaughlin, "Employee Assistance Programs," p. 33.

30. Bureau of National Affairs, *Personnel Management: BNA Policy and Practice Series,* no. 333, p. 245:106.

31. Carr and Hellan, "Improving Corporate Performance," p. 59.

32. See, for example, Bureau of National Affairs, "ASPA-BNA Survey No. 34: Counseling Policies and Programs for Employees with Problems," *Bulletin to Management,* March 23, 1978, pp. 1–10.

33. *Labor-Management Alcoholism Journal* 7 (May/June 1978), p. 1.

34. "Guidelines for Setting Up Your Counseling Program," *Prentice-Hall* pp. 23, 402.

35. See, for example, Marvin E. McMillan, "Conflicting Loyalties: A Literature Review," *Personnel and Guidance Journal* 58 (October 1979), pp. 97–100.

36. Lou Culler Talbutt, "Ethical Standards: Assets and Limitations," *Personnel and Guidance Journal* 60 (October 1981), p. 111.

37. Patricia O'Toole, "The Menace of the Corporate Shrink," *Savvy*[1] (October 1980), pp. 50–51.

38. Ricklefs, "In-House Counsel."

39. Lawrence Stessin, *Employee Discipline* (Washington, D.C.: Bureau of National Affairs, 1960), pp. 2–3.

40. Ken Jennings and Roger Wolters, "Discharge Cases Reconsidered," *Arbitration Journal* 31 (September 1976), pp. 164–184.

41. "The Growing Costs of Firing Nonunion Workers," *Business Week,* April 6, 1981, p. 95; Stuart Youngblood and Gary L. Tidwell, "Termination at Will: Some Changes in the Wind," *Personnel* 58 (May/June 1981), pp. 22–33.

42. Raymond A. Katzell, "Work Attitudes, Motivation, and Performance," *Professional Psychology* 11 (June 1980), p. 411.

43. Louis E. Davis, "Enhancing the Quality of Working Life: Development in the United States," *International Labour Review* 116, no. 1 (July–August 1977), p. 53. Reprinted by permission of the International Labour Office, Washington, D.C. 20006.

44. *Ibid.,* pp. 53–54. See also, Richard Walton, "Quality of Work Life Activities: A Research Agenda," *Professional Psychology* 11 (June 1980), p. 484.

45. Irving Bluestone, "Implementing Quality-of-Worklife Programs," *Management Review* 66 (July 1977), p. 43.

46. Stephen H. Fuller, "Quality of Work Life in America: Today's Potentials and Tomorrow's Constraints" (remarks at Industrial Relations Research Association meeting, Atlanta, Georgia, December 29, 1979), p. 2.

47. *Ibid.*

48. "The New Industrial Relations," *Business Week,* May 11, 1981, pp. 84–86.

49. Antone F. Alber, "The Real Cost of Job Enrichment," *Business Horizons* 22 (February 1979), pp. 60–61.

50. William F. Giles, "Volunteering for Job Enrichment: Reaction to Job Characteristics or to Change?" *Journal of Vocational Behavior* 11 (October 1977), pp. 232–238; J. R. Hackman and E. E. Lawler, "Employee Reaction to Job Characteristics," *Journal of Applied Psychology* 55 (June 1971), pp. 259–286.

51. David A. Whitsett, "Where Are Your Unenriched Jobs?" *Harvard Business Review* 53 (January/February 1975), p. 75.

52. Alber, "The Real Cost," p. 60.

53. *Ibid.,* pp. 61–66.

54. *Ibid.,* p. 61.

55. *Ibid.,* pp. 61–66.

56. Greg Oldham, J. Richard Hackman, and Joni L. Pearce, "Conditions under Which Employees Respond Positively to Enriched Work," *Journal of Applied Psychology* 61 (August 1976), pp. 395–403.

57. Giles, "Volunteering for Job Enrichment," p. 237.

58. Union Carbide, *Q News* 1 (3d quarter 1980), p. 1.

59. Elaine Rendall, "Quality Circles—a 'Third Wave' Intervention," *Training and Development Journal* 35 (March 1981), p. 29.

60. *Ibid.* Copyright 1981, Training and Development Journal, American Society for Training and Development. Reprinted with permission. All rights reserved.

61. Robert R. Rehder, "What American and Japanese Managers are Learning from Each Other," *Business Horizons* 24 (March/April 1981), p. 68.

62. *Ibid.*

63. *Ibid.,* p. 69.

64. Martin Douglas, "Car Quality—Blame the Executives, Not the Workers," *Los Angeles Times,* July 15, 1980, part 2, p. 5. Used by permission of the author.

65. "The New Industrial Relations," p. 96.

66. Charles C. Manz and Henry P. Sims, Jr., "Self-Management as a Substitute for Leadership: A Social Learning Perspective," *Academy of Management Review* 5 (July 1980), pp. 361–367.

67. William H. Holley, Hubert S. Feild, and James C. Crowley, "Negotiating Quality of Worklife, Productivity, and Traditional Issues: Union Members' Preferred Roles of Their Union," *Personnel Psychology* 34 (Summer 1981), pp. 310–311.

68. William W. Winpisinger, "Bargaining Focus Remains on Wages," *AFL-CIO News,* November 3, 1979, p. 4. Reprinted by permission of the AFL-CIO News, the official weekly newspaper of the AFL-CIO.

69. "Quality of Work Life: Catching On," *Business Week,* September 21, 1981, p. 80.

70. For example, see the comments of Lloyd McBride, president of the United Steelworkers of America, in "Steel Seeks Higher Output via Workplace Reform," *Business Week,* August 18, 1980, p. 98. A successful QWL program based on union-management cooperation is described in Julius N. Draznin, "Labor Relations: QWL," *Personnel Journal* 60 (September 1981), p. 684.

71. Thomas R. Donahue, speech to Conference on Joint Labor-Management Approaches to Productivity and the Quality of Working Life in the Federal Sector, Washington, D.C., at the Hyatt Regency, November 13, 1980. Reprinted by permission of the AFL-CIO.

72. William F. Giles and William H. Holley, Jr., "Job Enrichment versus Traditional Issues at the Bargaining Table: What Union Members Want," *Academy of Management Journal* 3 (December 1978), pp. 725–730. Union members also seem to consider collective bargaining the appropriate way to deal with traditional issues, and union-management committees more appropriate for dealing with QWL issues. Holley, Feild, and Crowley, "Negotiating Quality of Worklife," pp. 317–323.

73. Holley, Feild, and Crowley, "Negotiating Quality of Worklife," pp. 324–325.

74. Robert H. Guest, "Review of Work Redesign," *Harvard Business Review* 59 (January/February 1981), p. 46.

75. J. R. Hackman and Greg Oldham, *Work Design* (Reading, Mass.: Addison-Wesley, 1980), p. 242.

76. The authors are grateful to Lynne Ashmead for researching much of the material on flexitime.

77. D. Maric, *Adapting Hours to Modern Needs* (Geneva, Switzerland: International Labour Office, 1977), pp. 27–28.

78. Bureau of National Affairs, *Daily Labor Report,* July 28, 1981, p. A-4.

79. For additional variations see Heinz Allenspache, *Flexible Working Hours* (Geneva, Switzerland: International Labour Office, 1975), p. 10; and Maric, *Adapting Hours,* p. 26.

80. J. Caroll Swart, *A Flexible Approach to Working Hours* (New York: AMACOM, 1978), p. 55.

81. Bureau of National Affairs, *Daily Labor Report,* May 6, 1981, p. A-7.

82. William D. Hicks and Richard J. Klimoski, "The Impact of Flexitime on Employee Attitudes," *Academy of Management Journal* 24 (June 1981), p. 339.

83. William F. Glueck, "Changing Hours of Work: A Review and Analysis of the Research," *Personnel Administrator* 24 (March 1979), p. 47.

84. Allan R. Cohen and Herman Gadon, *Alternative Work Schedules: Integrating Individual and Organizational Needs* (Reading, Mass.: Addison-Wesley, 1978), p. 39.

85. See, for example, Simcha Ronen, "Arrival and Departure Patterns of Public Sector Employees before and after Implementation of Flexitime," *Personnel Psychology* 34 (Winter 1981), p. 821; Talmer E. Curry, Jr., and Deane N. Haerer, "The Positive Impact of Flexitime on Employee Relations," *Personnel Administrator* 26 (February 1981), p. 63.

86. Jay S. Kim and Anthony F. Campagna, "Effects of Flexitime on Employee Attendance and Performance: A Field Experiment," *Academy of Management Journal* 24 (December 1981), p. 739; Joe L. Welch and David Gordon, "Assessing the Impact of Flexitime on Productivity," *Business Horizons* 23 (December 1980), p. 63.

87. Kim and Campagna, "Effects of Flexitime," p. 739.

88. Cohen and Gadon, *Alternative Work Schedules,* p. 739.

89. Allenspache, *Flexible Working Hours,* p. 41.

90. For a thorough discussion of various considerations involved in the implementation of flexitime, see Swart, *A Flexible Approach,* pp. 221–248.

91. The first four characteristics are from Sally A. Coltrin and Barbara D. Barendse, "Is Your Organization a Good Candidate for Flexitime?" *Personnel Journal* 60 (September 1981), pp. 714–715.

92. The last characteristic was suggested by John D. Owen, "Flexitime: Some Problems and Solutions," *Industrial and Labor Relations Review* 30 (January 1977), p. 156.

The Alcohol Problem

Bill Smith, a fifty-year-old sales representative for a private electric utility company, is an alcoholic. He has been employed by the company for twenty-five years, and his performance has been adequate during these years. His office is located in a small town of 45,000 about fifty miles from the major city where the company headquarters is located. About forty employees are assigned to his office—linepersons, meter readers, clerks, salespersons, and so on. Bill's job is to call on clients and make sure that their needs are being met by the company, to help builders in developing subdivisions with all-electric houses, and to help industrial developers in recruiting new industry.

Bill has been a social drinker since he was in college and has never tried to hide it. However, his drinking has become very frequent. He often takes two-hour lunch breaks, and his breath smells of whiskey when he returns. The personnel staff has examined his attendance record and has found that he has missed twenty Mondays in the last two years. However, his performance is adequate. In fact, some believe that his coworkers are helping to protect Bill by picking up part of his workload. His supervisor requested that he take a physical exam, and his personal physician diagnosed his problem as gastritis brought about by an acid stomach.

The company is worried about Bill Smith's situation, because it seems to be affecting other employees. The company has no policy for dealing with employees with alcohol problems but knows that it must do something.

Questions

1. Explain the coworkers' behavior.
2. How should the company handle Bill Smith's situation?
3. What policy do you recommend for the company?
4. What responsibility does the company have for Bill Smith's welfare?

**Red Dot
Drug Stores:
The Polygraph
Test**

Ben Danford, owner and president of Red Dot Drug Stores, a small retail chain specializing in discount sales of toiletries, cosmetics, and medicine, was preparing his end of the year report. In an attempt to stop inventory shrinkage caused by employee theft, Mr. Danford had contracted the services of a polygraph testing agency for a one-year trial period. During this time, each Red Dot employee was required to submit to a polygraph test every six months. The contract for polygraph services was up for renewal next week, and Mr. Danford was evaluating the results of the trial program.

Mr. Danford felt strongly that the polygraph testing had been effective in reducing employee theft, but the program produced a marked increase in personnel problems. To provide some insight into these problems, four employee case histories are presented:

Case I Tom Walker served as manager of one of the Red Dot stores for three years. He was very active in community and church activities and was doing graduate work at a local college. At one time he borrowed a tape recorder from the store to catch up on company work. The polygraph indicated that he had stolen the recorder, and he was almost fired before the facts were known.

Case II Paul Johnson, an assistant store manager, argued that the administering of polygraph tests was clearly immoral. He said that ''man shouldn't be humiliated by allowing a machine to determine who is telling the truth.'' Johnson had worked for Red Dot Drugs for two years and seemed to be highly satisfied until the polygraph tests were begun. His test results showed that he had stolen from the company on several occasions. At first, he denied that he had stolen, but after several questions he finally confessed. He was immediately fired.

Case III Donna Waters worked as a cashier at a Red Dot store for seven years without missing a day of work except for a two-month leave of absence due to pregnancy. Ms. Waters was happy with her job until the polygraph policy was implemented. She considered the polygraph test an insult to her integrity and chose to resign rather than to take the test. Everyone assumed that she probably had stolen from the company and had quit for fear of being caught. After several months, Ms. Waters returned and consented to the test; she passed and resumed her employment.

Case IV Bob Dennis, a twenty-year-old college student, worked part-time as a stockboy at a Red Dot store. Several months before he was administered the polygraph test, Bob had witnessed another employee steal a cigarette lighter. Although the incident bothered him for several weeks, he decided against reporting the theft to his supervisor. From the polygraph test results it was concluded that he was dishonest, and this resulted in Bob's suspension.

Many other employees were displeased with the testing policy, and their dissatisfaction was reflected by an increase in turnover. Mr. Danford was well aware of the deteriorating employee morale, and this weighed heavily on his mind. A decision whether or not to continue the polygraph testing program or to find other methods for controlling employee theft had to be made.

Negotiating Quality of Working Life

Sharon Atkinson, the personnel director of Wingfield Products, a steel fabricating plant, was directed by the company's president to initiate a management-union cooperative program on productivity and quality of working life. After reading the professional literature on the topic, she called Frank Brooks, a union official, to discuss the matter.

Sharon was enthusiastic about the prospects, because much of the literature was very positive. Frank, however, had serious reservations, because the union literature advised caution, for the following reasons:

1. Quality of working life programs are used by labor relations consultants (union busters) to keep unions out of plants.
2. Quality of working life programs are introduced so that employees will see no need for union representation.
3. Management increases employees' autonomy and responsibility, but does not increase their wages.
4. Management seeks employee input into decision making, but without offering monetary incentives and without involving the union.

After hours of discussion on several occasions, Sharon and Frank finally decided to find out how the employees felt about these programs. Both agreed in advance that they would follow the employees' wishes. Together they constructed a questionnaire to determine workers' preferred method of union involvement in several union-management issues. The types of involvement included the following:

1. Union would be involved in a joint program as an equal partner with management.
2. Union would be involved through collective bargaining.
3. Union would not be involved.

The questionnaire was distributed to the employees as a joint union-management study, and the response rate was 98 percent. The results are listed on page 559.

Assignment

1. Analyze the data and develop a strategy for Sharon Atkinson.
2. Analyze the data and develop a strategy for Frank Brooks.
3. As a neutral party, what would you recommend to Sharon and Frank?

Types of Issues	Joint Program	Collective Bargaining	No Union Involvement
Fringe Benefits	11%	88%	1%
Pay	5	95	0
Job Security	19	77	4
Hours	19	77	4
Grievances	21	77	2
Productivity	49	29	22
Workload	40	44	16
Safety	54	44	2
Promotions	33	30	37
Job Duties	50	40	10
Interesting Work	70	16	14
Flexibility in Choosing Work Methods	61	30	9
Adequacy of Tools and Equipment	57	38	5
Relationships with Supervisors	56	25	19

Part Six

Anticipating and Coping with Organizational Change

Personnel representatives are continually faced with changing situations which can affect personnel activities discussed in preceding chapters. Three major sources of change are: governmental legislation and related judicial decisions; organizational settings such as those found in the public sector or in multinational companies; and organizational concerns as identified through personnel research.

Chapter 18 is entirely devoted to accommodating fair employment legislation and legally protected employee groups. Laws, legal rules and procedures, and problems relating to minorities are discussed; and special attention is devoted to black employees, females, older workers, and handicapped employees.

Chapter 19 covers the personnel function in two special sectors with which students will likely be associated at some time during their careers. The chapter first highlights multinational corporations, focusing on differences among countries and resulting differences in personnel activities. The personnel function in the public sector is then described and its unique qualities explained.

In a dynamic, rapidly changing world, organizations and individuals must not only cope with change but anticipate it. The role of personnel research in helping organizations anticipate and cope with change is described in Chapter 20. The chapter also discusses measuring the effectiveness of personnel activities and concludes with a number of expert opinions on the future of the personnel function.

Chapter 18

Accommodating Fair Employment Legislation and Legally Protected Employee Groups

From numerous and uncoordinated laws, from volumes of Federal regulations and guidelines, from countless pages of comments by enforcement officials, employers, and other individuals there emerges, somewhat surprisingly, a rather consistent and coherent theme. That theme indicates that the problem of employment discrimination is still with us; it is widely recognized and thought to deserve continuing attention and relentless opposition; and the desire for its eventual eradication is strong.

U.S. Commission on Civil Rights, *Promises and Perceptions* (Washington, D.C.: U.S. Government Printing Office, October 1981), p. 3.

Organizations must respond to various legislative mandates that can change work relationships and personnel practices. Much of this legislation pertains to fair employment practices concerning minorities and female employees, a situation first discussed in connection with the affirmative action concept in Chapter 5. The first section of this chapter presents a brief overview of fair employment legislation and the Equal Employment Opportunity Commission (EEOC).

The next section discusses both black and female employees, since these groups share several similarities in terms of fair employment legislation and practices. A third section outlines some personnel considerations that relate to older employees and handicapped employees. Particular attention is given to these considerations, since they have not been discussed in previous chapters. The chapter's issue describes problems that can arise in dealing with vague legal concepts—more specifically, religious discrimination and sexual harassment.

Fair Employment Legislation in Perspective

A Brief History of Fair Employment Legislation

Fair employment legislation tries to ensure that employment decisions are made solely on the basis of job-related criteria instead of on the basis of such characteristics as age, sex, or race. A wide variety of laws and executive orders at the local, state, and national levels, as well as decisions and guidelines of agencies and the courts, have contributed to this concept. Fair employment legislation may specify various procedures organizations must take with regard to certain employees, prohibit discriminatory employment practices, and prescribe remedies for affected employees or applicants. This legislation represents an extremely broad, complicated field; for example, an estimated 15,000 pages of judicial decisions have pertained to this subject.[1] However, some general considerations concerning fair employment legislation should be stressed because of their implications for personnel and management practices.

In 1941, President Franklin D. Roosevelt introduced Executive Order 8802, which stated the federal government's intention to provide fair employment practices. Related executive orders were issued by Presidents Truman, Eisenhower, and Kennedy. However, enforcement strength and results were weak.[2] Consider, for example, the following testimony of a personnel representative, given in 1962 before the U.S. Civil Rights Commission:

Chairman Hannah: I would like to ask Mr. Ladd if I understood him correctly to say that Southern Bell has not as yet opened up its employment to Negroes in either the operators or mechanical or clerical?

Mr. Ladd: That is correct, sir, here in Memphis.

Chairman Hannah: That is based on the assumption that the Negroes are not able to perform these services?

Mr. Ladd: No, sir. That's based on the assumption that local traditions and customs have not changed to the point that we feel it is the thing to do in our company at this time.[3]

Fair employment legislation before 1963 stressed voluntary compliance; little attention was given to specific unlawful employment practices.[4] Federal legislation during this period often deferred to fair employment laws enacted in states, which were often ineffective. Further, no agency was charged with requiring employers to comply with fair employment practices or with imposing penalties if necessary.[5]

This situation was dramatically changed with the passage of the 1964 Civil Rights Act. Title VII of the act pertained to fair employment practices, which were to be monitored by a newly created agency, the Equal Employment Opportunity Commission (EEOC). For the first time, many employers were held accountable for discriminatory practices; and employees or applicants affected by discrimination had recourse through the EEOC, the Justice Department, and the courts. Title VII has since been amended by the Equal Employment Opportunity Act of 1972; and the EEOC has also been altered, most notably through President Carter's Executive Orders 12067 and 12144 in 1978[6]

Current Scope of Fair Employment Legislation

Many legislative provisions attempt to ensure fair employment practices. The most inclusive set of provisions results from combining Section 702(a) of Title VII with Section 4(a) of the Age Discrimination in Employment Act (discussed in more detail later in this chapter). Combined, these sections make it unlawful for an employer to do the following:

1. Fail or refuse to hire any individual, discharge any individual, or otherwise discriminate against any individual with respect to compensation, terms, conditions, or privileges of employment because of such individual's race, color, religion, sex, national origin, or age (forty to seventy).
2. Limit, segregate, or classify employees or applicants for employment in any way that would deprive or tend to deprive any individual of employment opportunities or otherwise adversely affect his or her status as an employee because of such individual's race, color, religion, sex, national origin, or age (forty to seventy).

Title VII applies to most employers in the private sector, as well as to state and local governmental employers and educational institutions. There are some exceptions; for example, Title VII does not apply to employers who regularly employ fewer than fifteen persons, to tax-exempt private membership clubs, or to corporations owned by the government of the United States.

An employer can discriminate against employees in three general ways: through evil intent, differential treatment, and disparate effect.[7]

Evil Intent Evil intent was primarily considered in discrimination cases after World War II and before 1965, when Title VII took effect. There were relatively few cases during this period; therefore, there was little specific guidance on how to place antidiscrimination concepts into operation. Employees seeking recourse through the courts typically had to establish the evil nature or intent of employers—a difficult, if not impossible, task. Today, more reliance is placed on the other two means of discrimination. However, proof of evil intent in a case can be very detrimental to the employer's position. For example, a comment by a management representative to the effect that "black employees cannot be trusted" will likely discredit any subsequent defense raised by the employer.

Differential Treatment Differential treatment is one of the most common discrimination complaints. It occurs when employees protected by Title VII are treated differently from other employees. Examples include the following:

A black employee and a white employee fight on company property. The white employee receives an oral warning and the black employee is discharged.

Male employees in a certain job classification receive overtime assignments; female employees in the same job classification do not.

Only white male employees in a particular department are asked to participate in an experimental job enrichment program.

Disparate Effect Disparate effect occurs when barriers that are on the surface neutral have an adverse impact on minority employees. Such employment criteria as a college degree, the absence of an arrest record, a passing score on an intelligence test, or a minimum weight requirement may result in fewer minority or female employees' being hired. The employer may not intend to discriminate against these groups with such criteria. However, job requirements that have a disparate effect on groups protected by Title VII (that result in fewer minority or female employees' being employed in a job category than could be reasonably or statistically expected, for example) are a *prima facie* proof of discrimination. The employer must then establish that the employment criterion was job related, was justified by business necessity, and complied with EEOC guidelines, if applicable.

These general sources of employment discrimination can involve numerous personnel activities and policies pertaining to:[8]

Discharge, including the manner of discharge (whether it is consistent or inconsistent with company policy) and *constructive discharge,* whereby a person quits because of unbearable circumstances either encouraged or tolerated by the employer.

Failure to hire, when selection methods—tests, word-of-mouth recruiting, and so forth—have not been validated as described in Chapter 6 or are inconsistent with the principles of affirmative action discussed in Chapter 5.

Terms and conditions of employment, which refer to nearly every aspect of the work arrangement, such as wages, promotions, training, discipline, benefits, social and recreational activities, bias-free working atmosphere, leaves of absence, and so forth.

Current Procedures under Fair Employment Legislation[9]

The EEOC is an independent government agency currently responsible for administering most fair employment legislation (Title VII, Equal Pay Act, Age Discrimination Act, and Rehabilitation Act) as well as coordinating all federal equal employment programs. (See Figure 18.1 for the EEOC's organization chart.[10]) Five presidentally appointed commissioners make up the EEOC; one commissioner serves as chairman, and three members constitute a quorum. The president also appoints a general counsel who provides legal advice and manages any litigation involving the EEOC.

Two major responsibilities of the EEOC are formulating procedural rules, regulations, and guidelines and resolving complaints concerning alleged discriminatory practices. EEOC guidelines concerning substantive issues of Title VII (sexual harassment guidelines discussed at the end of this chapter, for example) do not have the force of law, although they are often given considerable weight by the courts.

Individuals or their representatives may file charges against persons or employers engaging in discrimination. Any commissioner of the EEOC may also file charges alleging either a single act of discrimination or a pattern and practice of discrimination. Numerous procedural variations can complicate these charges; however, the following general steps must be considered:

Charges filed with the EEOC usually must be delivered or made within 180 days after the alleged discriminatory act.

State or local fair employment agencies are given the opportunity to act first on discrimination charges.

The EEOC, if it eventually assured jurisdiction, must determine reasonable cause.

Efforts at conciliation and persuasion must be initiated by the EEOC to resolve discriminatory practices if reasonable cause is

Figure 18.1   Organization of the Equal Employment
                      Opportunity Commission

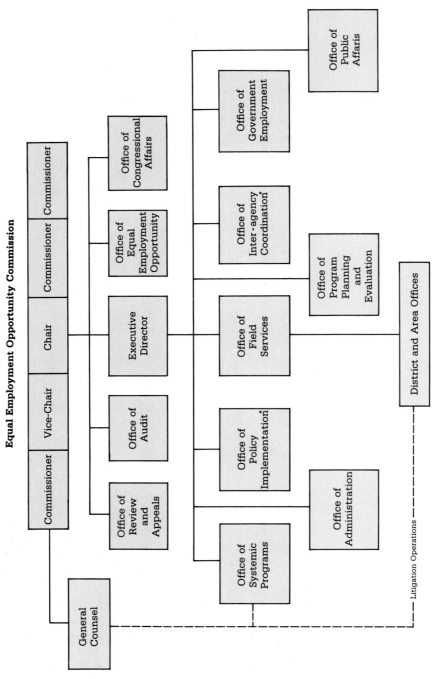

*Reports to the Commission on Policy Matters

found. The parties must be informed by the EEOC if a legal suit is likely to be filed.

Controversy Concerning the EEOC

Like most government agencies, the EEOC has its controversial aspects; charges against it have ranged from incompetence to corruption.[11] Many criticisms focus on two general areas—*leadership* and *administrative capability of the agency.* Turnover of top officials in the agency has been sharp. In the EEOC's first thirteen years, it had nine chairpersons or acting chairpersons and ten general counsels.[12] The ability to establish a clear, consistent policy is hampered by this turnover. Conflict among some staff members' priorities for investigation and action may also cause problems. For example, one EEOC official was quoted by "CBS Evening News" as having said that the EEOC existed primarily for the protection of blacks.

From a practical point of view, white women don't need any protection—they can protect themselves. . . . But we couldn't. We needed some people to protect us. Because nobody ever told white women or other minorities that they couldn't sit in the front of a bus.[13]

Other problems focus on procedural delays, which have in the past resulted in a yearly backlog of some 130,000 cases.[14] Such delays often are due to administrative details and to the large number of cases that reflect individual employees' concerns instead of broad patterns of job bias.[15] Sometimes the EEOC has to follow up on trivial or nuisance complaints; for example, one man filed 150 charges, alleging he was a victim of job discrimination because he was a Transylvanian and a vampire.[16] Delays can discourage individuals who have legitimate employment concerns from filing complaints, creating a situation that perpetuates job discrimination.

The EEOC has recognized some of these problems; its current scope and procedures reflect the willingness of Congress, the courts, and the agency to modify original activities so that fair employment legislation can be implemented in a more effective manner.[17] (It should be noted that some believe the Reagan administration has not encouraged this agency in its activities, however.[18]) The ultimate success of the EEOC's efforts remains to be seen, although some clues can be found in the following discussion of black and female employees.

Black and Female Employees

Making generalizations concerning members of even one employee category is difficult. The problem is compounded when comparisons made between two categories, such as black employees and female employees.

Differences and Similarities

Some concerns of female employees are unique. The legal rights of pregnant female employees and related employer obligations have

Employment discrimination can be measured by results and/or intent.

FRANK AND ERNEST by Bob Thaves

HOW CAN A WOMAN BE SUING US FOR SEX DISCRIMINATION?... WE'VE NEVER EVEN HAD ONE WORK HERE!

© 1981 by NEA, Inc., TM Reg. U.S. Pat. & TM Off.   THAVES 1-5-82

been extensively considered in court cases.[19] The Pregnancy Discrimination Act of 1978 requires that employers who provide benefits to employees for other disabilities arising outside the job situation also provide them for pregnancy. This situation has several implications for benefit plans and related insurance costs.[20]

The issue of sex discrimination can also be raised through the EEOC and the courts when females are denied employment because of potential exposure to materials that allegedly threaten their fertility.[21] Another complicated fair employment issue, sexual harassment, is discussed at the end of this chapter.

A final legal difference related to sex concerns employee pension plan contributions. Previously, some employers required female employees to contribute more to their pension funds than males, on the rationale that their longer life expectancy would enable them to receive more pension benefits. However, the Supreme Court prohibited this practice in its *Manhart* decision in 1978.[22]

Black and female employees also have many similar concerns. These groups represent the focal point of fair employment legislation and related EEOC activities. Members of each group often lack the preparation necessary to understand and participate in organizations. Much of this situation has been due to previous employment discrimination, which has either excluded them from organizations or permanently restricted their opportunities to enter certain job categories. In some cases, such discrimination is reinforced by cultural factors (family, school, and societal values), which traditionally did not explain organizational realities, particularly at the executive level, to blacks and females and which often instructed them to "know their place."[23]

Managers and executives who are black or female are usually more visible than their white male counterparts. One black manager comments, "As you move up, everything you do and say is being watched."[24] One study of upper-level women managers found that:

All the women were the subject of conversation, questioning, gossip, and careful scrutiny. Their positions were known and observed throughout the divisions, while those of most men typically were not. Their names came up at meetings where they would easily be used as examples. . . .

One woman swore in an elevator, in an Atlanta hotel, while going to have drinks with colleagues, and a few days later it was known all over Chicago that she was a "radical."[25]

Increased visibility coupled with inadequate preparation (whether perceived or actual) can endanger the employee's self-image.[26]

Black and female employees have also tended to share relatively poor economic and occupational positions in U.S. society. Exhibit 18.1 compares the occupational distribution of black and female employees

Exhibit 18.1   **Distribution of Employed Persons by Major Occupation Group, Sex, and Race for Selected Years from 1960 to 1980**

Total Employed (in Thousands)

	1960			1970			1975			1980		
	Total	Black and Other	Female	Total	Black and Other	Female	Total	Black and Other	Female	Total	Black and Other	Female
Occupational Categories	65,778 (100%)	6,927 (100%)	21,874 (100%)	78,627 (100%)	8,445 (100%)	29,667 (100%)	84,783 (100%)	9,070 (100%)	33,553 (100%)	97,220 (100%)	10,890 (100%)	41,283 (100%)
White-Collar Workers	43.4%	16.1%	55.3%	48.3%	27.9%	60.5%	49.8%	34.7%	62.9%	52.2%	39.2%	65.6%
Professional and Technical	11.4	4.8	12.4	14.2	9.1	14.5	15.0	11.4	15.7	16.1	12.7	16.8
Managers and Administrators	10.7	2.6	5.0	10.5	3.5	4.5	10.5	4.4	5.1	11.2	5.2	6.9
Sales Workers	6.4	1.5	7.7	6.2	2.1	7.0	6.4	2.7	6.9	6.3	2.9	6.8
Clerical Workers	14.8	7.3	30.3	17.4	13.2	34.5	17.8	15.7	35.1	18.6	18.4	35.1
Blue-Collar Workers	36.6	40.1	16.6	35.3	42.2	16.1	33.0	37.4	14.1	31.7	35.9	13.8
Craft and Kindred	13.0	6.0	1.0	12.9	8.2	1.1	12.9	8.8	1.5	12.9	9.6	1.8
Operators, Including Transportation Equipment Operators	18.2	20.4	15.2	17.7	23.7	14.5	15.2	20.0	11.6	14.2	19.4	10.7
Nonfarm Laborers	5.4	13.7	0.4	4.7	10.3	0.5	4.9	8.7	1.1	4.6	6.9	1.2
Service Workers	12.2	31.7	23.7	12.4	26.0	21.7	13.7	25.8	21.6	13.3	23.1	19.5
Farm Workers	7.9	12.1	4.4	4.0	3.9	1.8	3.5	2.6	1.4	2.8	1.8	1.2

Note: Some columns do not total to 100 because of rounding.

Source: Compiled from information in U.S. Department of Commerce, Bureau of the Census, *Statistical Abstract of the United States* (Washington, D.C.: Government Printing Office 1980), tables 696 and 698, pp. 418 and 421; and "Employment and Unemployment: A Report on 1980" (Washington, D.C.: U.S. Department of Labor, Bureau of Labor Statistics, April 1981), p. A-21.

with the occupational distribution of all employees. This exhibit illustrates that black and female employees are traditionally underrepresented in craft and managerial positions and overrepresented in the service worker category. Also, black employees have been underrepresented in professional, technical, and sales positions, while the clerical worker category has a disproportionate number of females. Exhibits 18.2 and 18.3 illustrate additional dimensions of the economic difficulties of blacks and females. Exhibit 18.2 shows the higher unemployment rate of blacks, while Exhibit 18.3 shows the comparatively lower salaries of female employees. Some factors that might explain these situations are explained in the following discussion.

Problems and Prospects

Many of the organizational difficulties faced by black and female employees are due to factors beyond their immediate control. Three such organizational barriers are: managerial philosophies, inefficient communication of EEO objectives and policies, and faulty employment practices.

Managerial Philosophies Two negative management philosophies are indifference and exclusion. On the surface, indifference may appear to be a neutral or even an objective attitude. However, this attitude does not reflect the spirit and intent of affirmative action. Indifferent managers do not actively seek ways in which blacks and females can obtain equal employment opportunity; instead, they place the entire burden on blacks and females to adjust to and rise above negative

---

Exhibit 18.2   **Unemployment Rates for Persons Sixteen Years Old and Over by Race for Selected Years**

	Annual Average Unemployment Rate		Ratio of Black and Other Races to White
Year	Black and Other Races	White	
1948	5.9%	3.5%	1.7%
1950	9.0	4.9	1.8
1955	8.7	3.9	2.2
1960	10.2	4.9	2.1
1965	8.1	4.1	2.0
1970	8.2	4.5	1.8
1975	13.9	7.8	1.8
1980	14.1	6.3	2.2

Source: Compiled from information in Bureau of the Census, *The Social and Economic Status of the Black Population in the United States: An Historical View, 1790–1978* (Washington, D.C.: Government Printing Office, 1979), p. 69; "Current Population Reports," special studies, series P-23, no. 80, and, "Employment and Unemployment: A Report on 1980" (Washington, D.C.: U.S. Department of Labor, Bureau of Labor Statistics, April 1981), p. A-44.

Exhibit 18.3 **Median Annual Earnings of Year-round Full-Time Workers Fourteen Years Old and Over by Sex, 1955–1978**

	Annual Earnings		
Year	Women	Men	Women's Earnings as Percent of Men's
1955	$2,719	$4,252	63.9%
1956	2,827	4,466	63.3
1957	3,008	4,713	63.8
1958	3,102	4,927	63.0
1959	3,193	5,209	61.3
1960	3,293	5,417	60.8
1961	3,351	5,644	59.4
1962	3,446	5,794	59.5
1963	3,561	5,978	59.6
1964	3,690	6,195	59.6
1965	3,823	6,375	60.0
1966	3,973	6,848	58.0
1967	4,150	7,182	57.8
1968	4,457	7,664	58.2
1969	4,977	8,227	60.5
1970	5,323	8,966	59.4
1971	5,593	9,399	59.5
1972	5,903	10,202	57.9
1973	6,335	11,186	56.6
1974	6,970	11,889	58.6
1975	7,504	12,758	58.8
1976	8,099	13,455	60.2
1977	8,618	14,626	58.9
1978	9,350	15,730	59.4

Note: Data for 1955–1966 are for wage and salary workers only and exclude self-employed persons.

Source: U.S. Department of Labor, Bureau of Labor Statistics, *Perspectives on Working Women: A Databook* (Washington, D.C.: Government Printing Office, 1980), p. 52.

employment conditions. Exclusion (racism or sexism) denies black employees and female employees respect, self-determination, and the right to fully participate.[27]

Managerial attitudes can often be influenced by stereotypes. One example of a stereotype was expressed in an 1873 Supreme Court decision, which upheld Illinois's refusal to license women attorneys. The court based its decision in part on the following reasoning:

The civil law, as well as nature herself, has always recognized a wide difference in the respective spheres and destinies of men and women. . . .

The natural and proper timidity and delicacy which belongs to the female sex evidently unfits it for many of the occupations of civil life. The constitution of the family organization, which is founded in the divine ordinance, as well as in the nature of things, indicates the domestic sphere as that which properly belongs to the domain and functions of womanhood. The harmony, not to say identity, of interests and views which belong, or should belong to the family institution is repugnant to the idea of a woman adopting a distinct and independent career from that of her husband. . . . The paramount destiny and mission of woman are to fulfill the noble and benign offices of wife and mother. This is the law of the Creator.[28]

Stereotypes have the following characteristics:[29]

1. They are usually negative or restrictive in nature. The previously cited comments make it clear that the Supreme Court believed women should be restricted to the home.
2. They apply to members of one group and do not transfer to people outside that group. For example, the stereotype that women are more emotional than men is reinforced if a woman cries at work. If a man cried at work, holders of the stereotype would not believe that men had become more emotional than women but would assume the individual was under unusual pressure.
3. People who hold stereotyped ideas do not respond to rational evidence to the contrary. Studies have disproven a variety of employment stereotypes, such as that women only work for extra money and that women have higher absenteeism and turnover rates than men.[30] However, many managers stubbornly retain such stereotypes in spite of contrary statistical evidence.

Major organizational efforts are necessary to uncover and dispel negative managerial attitudes and stereotypes so that black and female employees' job prospects will be enhanced.

Inefficient Communication of EEO Objectives and Policies Ineffective communication often occurs after general statements of EEO objectives and policies have been made at executive levels. Managers and supervisors responsible for directing black and female employees are often either uninformed or subjected to contradictory information.

One study, for example, examined the integration of previously underemployed or unemployed inner-city poor into a corporate workforce. This study found the following communication difficulties and problems:[31]

Intrasender conflict. Supervisors received different priorities from people within an organizational level. For example, employees under a supervisor's direction may not agree with each other or even be consistent within themselves about what they expect the supervisor to do.

Intersender conflict. People at different organizational levels placed conflicting demands on the supervisor. For example, higher management officials wanted the newly hired employees treated with more leeway, while the other employees wanted all workers treated alike.

Faulty Employment Practices Employment practices such as relying on word of mouth recruiting, using invalid employment tests, failing to recruit at black or female universities, and so forth have been discussed in previous chapters and will not be repeated here. However, many organizations appear to use another faulty employment practice—placing black and female employees in jobs in which they will receive the least resistance from other employees. For example white males who have worked for an organization for a long time may resent a black or female employee's with less experience becoming their boss.[32] Such resistance can result in two alternative practices. The first is to keep black and female employees in traditional positions at lower levels in the organization.[33] For example, as recently as 1972, one utility company had at least eight black janitors with college degrees.[34] This alternative, of course, runs against the legal mandates of fair employment and affirmative action.

A second alternative is to select for managerial positions highly qualified black or female candidates whose expertise is clearly superior to that of the individuals they will supervise.[35] This practice may overcome employees' resistance; yet it may also be unfair in certain respects. Many black or female employees may be overlooked in this search for a "superstar," while white male employees, perhaps with fewer qualifications, are promoted. Some have suggested that establishing black or female "buddy" systems or "networks" might aid in job development for black or female employees.[36] However, it might be difficult to establish such systems if these employees are placed in isolated positions that deprive them of the opportunity to share problems and experiences with other blacks or females in similar positions.

Some evidence suggests that blacks and females have made some progress under fair employment legislation. Some believe that organizations and employees now realize that EEO is not just a concept, but an obligation.[37] However, Exhibits 18.1, 18.2, and 18.3 suggest that continued efforts are needed to achieve equal employment opportunity. Organizations must take active steps to minimize problems such as those discussed here and must implement additional, sometimes imaginative, strategies.[38] Perhaps most important—particularly from the personnel department's point of view—are two related attitudes. First, there are two groups of acceptable employees: *qualified* and *qualifiable.*[39] Employees in the qualifiable category cannot be ignored; indeed, every organizational effort should be made to ensure that they become qualified. Second, organizations must achieve a sincere commitment to EEO policies, including establishing rewards and sanctions for managers charged with implementing EEO policies.[40]

Older Employees

Supreme Court Justice Thurgood Marshall has eloquently described the employment situation faced by many older workers:

It cannot be disputed that they constitute a class subject to repeated and arbitrary discrimination in employment. While depriving any employee of his job is a significant deprivation, it is particularly burdensome when the person deprived is an older citizen. Once terminated, the elderly cannot readily find alternative employment. The lack of work is not only economically damaging but emotionally and physically draining. Deprived of his status in the community and of the opportunity for meaningful activity, fearful of becoming dependent on others' . . . support and lonely in . . . new found isolation, the involuntarily retired person is susceptible to physical and emotional ailments, as a direct consequence of his enforced idleness.[41]

Statistical evidence illustrated this employment situation in the early 1960s. One study of employees who were permanently laid off because a production facility ceased operations found that employees forty-five years of age and older were less likely to find new jobs than others. Employees forty-five and older who found new jobs experienced an average reduction in earnings over a five-year period.[42] Another study found that only 8.6 percent of 89,000 new hires in 1964 were forty-five years of age and over.[43]

Today, two trends may have negative consequences for older employees and organizations alike. The first trend relates to *the aging of the U.S. population.* The percent of the population aged sixty-five and older was 11 percent in 1980; it is estimated that this proportion will increase to 13 percent in the year 2000 and 39 percent in the year 2050. The second trend relates to *older employees' declining participation in the labor force.* The labor force participation rate of men aged fifty-five and over fell from 65 percent in 1955 to 46 percent in 1980.[44] Simply put, if these trends continue, more older persons will be unemployed in the future. This situation affects not only older people's adjustment problems but also employers' benefit costs, such as those for pension payments. The problems of older employees have been addressed by legislation and by various personnel policies voluntarily adopted by organizations.

Age Discrimination Legislation

Scope, Purpose, and Procedures The Age Discrimination in Employment Act (ADEA) was enacted in 1967 and amended in 1978. The EEOC oversees the ADEA, which protects employees aged forty to seventy (with the exception of certain executives and persons in high, policy-making positions). In essence, ADEA protections parallel those of Title VII, which were discussed earlier in this chapter. Employers cannot discriminate against protected employees in terms of hiring, firing, and other terms of employment such as wages. However, unlawful actions can be difficult to establish in a court of law. Establishing a *prima facie* case of age discrimination is not a matter of statutory law; instead, the federal courts are left to determine the issue, with varying results. One of the more common ways to establish age discrimination is to show that the employee is in the protected age group, has the ability to perform the job, and has been replaced by an employee younger than forty years of age.[45] Once the employee has established these conditions, the defendant (employer, employment agency, or labor organization) has the burden of producing evidence to show that factors other than age were the basis for the allegedly discriminatory employment practices.

An employee, regardless of age, can legitimately be discharged for *good cause* according to the disciplinary principles discussed in Chapter 17. Unsatisfactory job performance, such as failure to meet sales quotas, does not have to be tolerated by an organization simply because the employee is between the ages of forty and seventy.

Several courts have also found that employees can sometimes be discharged regardless of their job performance. These courts have determined that there can be *reasonable factors other than age* for discharge; one of the more common involves business conditions that necessitate a reduction in number of employees. When such conditions exist, an organization can eliminate some of its operations or functions, such as branch sales offices; and the employees at these operations can be permanently removed from the organization regardless of their age.[46]

The ADEA acknowledges that age can be a *bona fide occupational qualification (BFOQ)*—a qualification reasonably necessary to perform the normal operation. An employer is not discriminatory when it rejects persons forty years old and older who apply for jobs modeling or advertising teen-age clothes or acting in youthful roles in a play or movie.

Employers can also refuse to hire older persons on the basis of BFOQ by indicating these individuals can represent a threat to public safety. Here, however, the courts have not been clear regarding the necessary burden of proof. In two cases, bus companies said "compelling concerns for safety" prompted their decisions not to hire inexperienced bus drivers between the ages of forty and sixty-five. Their actions were eventually upheld in courts of appeals, even though the evidence supporting their contentions was at best limited.[47] However, another judicial decision indicated that a company was discriminatory when it discharged a fifty-two-year-old test pilot, since the company could use available medical technology that can predict a disabling physical condition in a test pilot with virtually foolproof accuracy."[48]

Impact of the ADEA One way to gauge the ADEA's impact is by looking at the number of legal suits filed under its provisions. Initial response to these provisions was slow, receiving less attention than employment discrimination cases involving charges of racial or sexual bias.[49] However, concern has increased dramatically over the years.[50] Now, it is acceptable—even fashionable—for disgruntled employees to claim age discrimination.[51]

One potentially significant influence of the 1978 ADEA amendments was their raising the upper employee protection limit from sixty-five to seventy years of age. The history of the previous mandatory retirement age—sixty-five—shows that it was arbitrary; few attempts were made to relate this figure to social and economic realities.[52] Extending, if not eliminating, the mandatory retirement age is based on the following rationale:

Mandatory retirement wastes valuable talent, squanders important human resources, denies funding sources for pension plans, places a further burden on public and private pension systems, and affronts the dignity of older persons. The forced retirement of older persons to make room for younger workers is morally bankrupt because productive people are severed from their livelihood and sense of self-worth.[53]

Yet extending the mandatory retirement age could create problems. It is true that postponing retirement age may help alleviate the social security problem (discussed in Chapter 12) by reducing the ratio of people at work to retired people who receive social security payments. Yet, extending mandatory retirement could create other economic and social costs. For example, retaining large numbers of older employees might stifle efforts to reduce unemployment levels. Further, many of the retained employees will be white males, because of past hiring practices. Thus, the affirmative action plans of organizations with stable employment might be hampered, since fewer new employees, including women and minorities, will be hired.[54]

The organizational implications of extending the mandatory retirement age are also speculative. For example, will organizations have smaller pension fund payouts, larger medical insurance costs, and fewer promotional opportunities for younger employees?[55] The answers to these questions may depend on the number of employees who work beyond age sixty-five. Some believe that older employees make their retirement decisions independent of any legislated retirement age. In 1974, mandatory retirement provisions existed in less than half of private employers' pension plans. "To assume that now workers will not electively retire is to ignore this ingrained social behavior.[56] Exhibit 18.4 illustrates the previously mentioned fact that, for one reason or another, older employees have become less involved in the labor force over the years. Three factors that may contribute to this trend are a decline in the work ethic (discussed in Chapter 16), older employees' health status, and availability of retirement income. Employees who are in declining health may take advantage of retirement income sources, such as social security, disability payments, and private pensions, which allow them to leave the labor force voluntarily.[57]

The social trends on which predictions are based are subject to dramatic shifts, particularly if social and economic conditions change. We have been living in inflationary times. Many employees who retire before the mandatory retirement age will likely suffer reduced purchasing power, since very few pension plan payments fully cover current rates of inflation.[58] Older employees might therefore increasingly choose to remain on the job because of inflationary pressures.

One major corporation, Sears, has calculated the personnel impact of some employees' continuing their employment beyond age sixty-five. An employee at the executive level who stays with the organization past this age can block another employee's promotion to that position, which in turn blocks lower-level promotions needed to fill appropriate vacancies. Sears calculated the cumulative effect of employees' remaining on the payroll from age sixty-five to seventy and found that the retention of twenty-five senior executives would result in the loss of 5,900 promotions or hirings during the five-year period.[59]

The ADEA has also affected the organization and the personnel function in other ways.[60] Personnel representatives will have to ensure that employees' performance appraisals[61] and benefits[62] are in line with ADEA legislation and with judicial decisions in related legal suits. Perhaps age discrimination legislation has also enhanced voluntary organizational efforts to help the older employee.

Exhibit 18.4 **Labor Force Participation Rates for Men**

Year	Age Category 60–64	65 and Over
1957	82.5%	37.5%
1962	80.2	30.3
1967	77.6	27.1
1972	72.5	24.4
1977	62.9	20.1

Source: Philip L. Rones, "Older Men—the Choice between Work and Retirement," *Monthly Labor Review* 101 (November 1978), p. 4.

Personnel Policies and the Older Worker

Most employees eventually need to consider how to spend their time once they leave their organizations. However, many employees at all levels of the organization postpone making retirement plans until that event occurs.[63]

Retirement can subject the individual with no plans to sudden aimlessness, since established feelings of worth and social acceptance, goals, influence, routine patterns of time consumption, and social relationships associated with employment are lost.[64] These difficulties can be made even more serious by two other factors: inflation and marital adjustments. As mentioned earlier, inflation weakens most retirement assets and creates in retirees fears that they will not be able to continue their former standards of living. Marriages can be subject to strains when husbands and wives must adjust to being with each other twenty-four hours a day.

By providing preretirement planning, organizations can help employees minimize these difficulties by counseling and informing them in such areas as estimated retirement income from company benefits and social security, financial planning and investment possibilities, housing options, leisure time interests such as volunteer work, psychological adjustments to retirement, health and safety considerations, and legal affairs such as consumer protection.[65] Some companies limit participation in such programs to employees who will be retiring in the near future, while other companies permit any employee to attend. This latter option may help the organization, since people fearing retirement difficulties might perform their jobs better if relieved from those concerns.[66] Research into the history of retirement patterns at the facility may help identify likely age groups to participate in retirement planning programs and may also help organizations in their human resource forecasting efforts.[67]

Many organizations are also considering alternative work patterns for older employees, for two reasons. First, a reduction in the number of people between the ages of eighteen and twenty-four will occur between the years 1977 and 2000.[68] Estimated reductions range from 1.5 million to 7.2 million. Employees in the older age categories may have to assume a greater proportion of the workload. Second, older workers may offer many benefits to the organization. One study found that properly placed older workers have fewer accidents, a lower rate of absenteeism, and greater stability on the job than younger employees.[69] However, older employees can pose some problems, such as those caused by physiological changes and a more cautious approach to solving work-related problems.[70]

Jobs can in some cases be altered to meet unique demands of older employees. The pace of work, equipment used, and physical tasks performed can sometimes be changed with little inconvenience to the employer. Some organizations have used older employees on a part-time basis. Department stores, for example, have relied on part-time employees, since these stores are open for longer hours than could be covered by a full-time work schedule and must handle an uneven flow of customers. Some department stores, such as Macy's, rely on older part-time employees.[71] Other companies take advantage of retirees' "institutional memory" when they return to work on special projects. One executive of an architectural firm says: "Talking to them for five minutes on a given project can sometimes save us hours of searching back through files."[72]

Handicapped Employees

Difficulties Confronting Handicapped Employees

Handicapped people have historically experienced a great deal of employment discrimination. Consider, for example, the following statistics:

Eighty-seven percent of paralyzed veterans are unemployed, compared with a 10-percent unemployment rate prior to their disability.

Twenty-five percent of the 1.4 million epileptics between the ages of sixteen and sixty-four are unemployed.

The employment rate of the handicapped adult population has recently been estimated at 42 percent, contrasted with a 59-percent employment rate for the total adult population.[73]

The extent of discrimination depends in part on the particular disability, the place of employment, and the type of position. Some believe that certain diseases, such as epilepsy and cancer (even in people free of the disease for five or more years), frighten employers, who refuse to hire affected employees.[74] Employees who work in sheltered workshops typically designed for rehabilitation purposes often receive wages lower than the minimum wage. Recent articles describe a blind employee who, after twenty years on the job, receives $1.85 an hour,[75] and other disabled employees who receive as little as 10 cents an hour.[76] There is also some evidence to suggest that physically handicapped employees are unlikely to advance to top management positions, particularly when visibility and company image are considerations.[77] Worse yet, this situation will probably not improve sharply in the near future. One survey of approximately 3,000 executives found that 47 percent of the respondents felt that handicapped people would make the least significant employment gains in the next five years.[78]

Defining *handicapped* and identifying the employees who should be classified in this category is difficult. This difficulty is reflected in related legislation—Sections 504 and 7(6) of the Rehabilitation Act of 1973:

Section 504. No otherwise qualified handicapped individual in the United States, as defined in Section 7(6), shall, solely by reason of his handicap, be excluded from the participation in, be denied the benefits of, or be subjected to discrimination under any program or activity receiving Federal financial assistance.

Section 7(6). The term "handicapped individual" means any individual who (a) has a physical or mental disability which for such individual constitutes or results in a substantial handicap to employment and (b) can reasonably be expected to benefit in terms of employability from vocational rehabilitation service provided pursuant to Titles I and III of this Act.[79]

Considerable controversy has surrounded the inclusion of alcoholics and drug addicts in the handicapped category. Employers were concerned that they would have to actively seek such individuals as part of some affirmative action program. However, these concerns should be minimal, for two reasons. First, Section 504 specifies that the person must be *otherwise qualified*. The employer is not obligated to keep an employee on the payroll if drinking or drug problems continue to affect his or her job performance.[80] Second, legislation concerning handicapped employees has stressed voluntary affirmative action by the employer. Attention has shifted away from the emphasis on numbers of many affirmative action programs (see Chapter 5) toward a concern with systematic discrimination.[81]

Some situations are exempt from legislation regarding handicapped employees. For example, people who are overweight do not appear to be specifically covered by Section 504, although some individuals and the National Association to Aid Fat Americans have lobbied for federal legislation concerning size discrimination.[82] The Supreme Court has also suggested that an organization does not have to hire a person whose physical handicap might cause a safety hazard (for example, a nurse with a serious hearing impairment could present substantial dangers to patients).[83]

These exclusions notwithstanding, the legal definition of *handicapped* is extremely broad. Employers cannot equate disability with inability to perform the job.[84]

Every individual carries color, age and sex as undeniable personal characteristics from the cradle to the grave, but this is not the case with disability. . . . One paralyzed man in a wheel chair is on relief, whereas another serves more than three terms in the White House.[85]

Varied definitions, adjustments, and reactions concerning physical handicaps must be considered in personnel policies and activities.

Organizational Considerations Involving Handicapped Employees

Two general reasons for employers' failure to hire more physically handicapped people are prejudice and lack of knowledge about the employment of handicapped workers.[86] In some cases, these reasons are not entirely the fault of the employer. For example, employees with handicaps that observers cannot easily detect may not inform the employer of their problems, either because of personal embarrassment or fear of adverse job actions such as discharge or denial of promotion.[87] Yet, organizations must bear a major responsibility for eliminating such problems, as emphasized in the following discussion.

Identifying and Modifying Attitudes Concerning Handicapped Employees Talking about handicapped employees in the abstract is sometimes easier than first encountering them on an interpersonal basis. For example, a minister born without arms recently astounded a group of businessmen:

He eats with his feet, dresses with his feet, turns the pages of a book he is reading with his feet. He writes with his feet. He sometimes startles commuters on the subway when he deposits the change in the turnstyle with his feet . . . shocks passersby when he dials a pay phone with his feet . . . or floors an unsuspected hitchhiker he picks up when the hiker sees the driver has the steering wheel by his feet.[88]

Lack of knowledge about handicapped persons combined with various attitudes described in Exhibit 18.5 can create barriers. One observor notes; "Any affliction within reason can be gotten used to. Being treated funny cannot. Cripples do not, as you might suppose, sit around thinking, 'I'm a cripple' all day. It takes other people to remind them."[89] Organizations must modify negative attitudes in order to comply with the implementation of Section 504. They should also realize that in many cases, handicapped individuals are highly productive employees. Studies, for example, have indicated that handicapped employees compare equally or favorably with other employees in terms of total work performance; they also tend to be absent fewer times and have lower turnover rates.[90]

Implementing Activities That Ensure Reasonable Accommodation of the Handicapped *Reasonable accommodation* is a relatively vague legal concept that suggests that employers must make some effort to adjust workplace conditions to handicapped employees, though they need not incur substantial costs in doing so. Many related activities can be grouped into four general areas—job descriptions, adjustments of the workplace or working conditions, outreach, and counseling and follow-up programs.[91]

Job descriptions should be reexamined to ensure that any specified physical activities such as lifting are indeed essential to the job. For example, one job description might say the jobs involves "heavy work"; reexamination might show that a person with strong arms in a wheelchair could perform the necessary tasks.[92] Other physical com-

Exhibit 18.5   **Possible Organizational Attitudes Concerning**
                   Handicapped Employees

All that matters is your label. Employers label a handicapped employee according to his or her deficiencies rather than his or her assets. For example, deaf people are good for one particular job assignment, while blind employees are suited for another. This attitude, of course, has little regard for individual differences, interests, and abilities.

I feel sorry for you. The handicapped employee is pitied and regarded as fragile and as a victim of tragic misfortune. Work-related problems such as poor productivity and deteriorating peer relationships are not handled in a constructive manner. Instead, the supervisor explains the situation entirely according to perceived problems attributed to the employee's physical difficulty.

You present too many problems for us to handle. The attitude that the handicapped employee presents too many problems in a sense is opposite from the second attitude. Here, the handicapped employee is viewed as adding too many responsibilities and requiring too much time and energy from an already stretched supervisory staff.

If I'm lucky, we won't see each other today. The employee's physical disability is an unpleasant, sometimes painful stimulus that makes interactions with other employees difficult. The handicapped employee, whose adjustment to the workplace could be aided by support of fellow employees, is instead avoided or treated with contempt.

Source: Robert B. Nathanson and Jeffrey Lambert, "Integrating Disabled Employees into the Workplace," *Personnel Journal* 60 (February 1981), pp. 110–112. Adapted with the permission of Personnel Journal, Costa Mesa, California; all rights reserved.

ponents of the job suggested by the job description might be inexpensively redesigned; for example, an assemblers' table might be raised or lowered to accommodate a wheelchair.

Other adjustments of the work environment or working conditions might also be necessary. Examples include the following:[93]

Allowing a person with epilepsy to avoid rotating shifts, because people with this condition often physically respond poorly to frequent shift changes.

Providing an air-conditioned workspace for a worker with a respiratory condition, even though this action contradicts the organization's energy conservation program.

Moving a mobility-impaired assembly-line worker to a work station near the door so she will not be jostled during the rush to lunch or to work breaks.

Handicapped employees also need access to other parts of the building, such as parking lots, elevators, and rest-room facilities. These areas can be made accessible with a variety of adjustments, including ramps, rails, braille floor numbers on elevators, wider doors, and nonslip surfaces on all floors and ramps.[94]

Outreach involves active efforts to attract and employ handicapped persons. Some handicapped people may not seek jobs because their job experience is limited. Others may be reluctant to seek employment because of financial disincentives. (For example, many jobs do not pay enough to provide for necessary medical services, which a person may receive at low cost by remaining unemployed.[95]) *Outreach programs* often have to modify existing employment practices. For example, many organizations traditionally have several interviews with an applicant; the final employment decision may require a consensus of several organizational representatives, including the personnel representative and the direct supervisor for the position. It may be difficult to reach consensus when the interviewers have had little experience with handicapped employees. Also, this interview process may require the applicant to return to the organization several times before being hired, a situation that might encourage the applicant to seek a job elsewhere.[96] Organizations also need to consider using various employment sources that can refer handicapped employees, such as hospitals, state and local agencies concerned with vocational rehabilitation, and organizations for handicapped people. Referrals from handicapped employees who are presently working for the firm also represent a valuable recruiting source.

Counseling and follow-up programs help ensure that handicapped employees and their work associates (supervisors, for example) can resolve any employment problems that arise. These sessions can also obtain valuable suggestions to enhance previously cited accommodation factors, such as work environment adjustments.[97]

Issue:

How Are Fair Employment Laws Interpreted? The Cases of Religious Discrimination and Sexual Harassment

Legislation concerning fair employment is seldom clear cut. Governmental agencies and the courts often have to interpret and define vague provisions and concepts, causing confusion and controversy. This situation can be illustrated with reference to two topics: religious discrimination and sexual harassment.

Religious Discrimination

Many employment decisions in the past have been made on the basis of the applicants' religious affiliations.[98] Title VII of the 1964 Civil Rights Act attempted to eliminate this problem by prohibiting religious discrimination in employment practices. However, no immediate attempt was made to define or enforce these prohibitions.[99] The EEOC's efforts to clarify this situation through related guidelines (in 1966 and 1967) were not successful, and Congress in 1972 amended Title VII by enacting Section 701(j):

(j) The Term 'religion' includes all aspects of religious observance and practice, as well as belief, unless an employer demonstrates that he is unable to reasonably accommodate to an employee's or prospective employee's religious observance or practice without undue hardship on the conduct of the employer's business.

This provision was far from conclusive, since it defined neither *religion* nor *undue hardship.*

The Supreme Court has suggested that religious beliefs need not be related to an established church or religion. However, these beliefs must be "sincere and meaningful" and not based on pragmatism and expediency. Employers faced with a religious discrimination suit seldom challenge the employee's sincerity, since this criterion is extremely difficult to establish. In one exception, the court did find the plaintiff's beliefs were insincere:

The plaintiff allegedly had a life-long conviction against Sunday work. He claimed a renewed conviction after a "miraculous improvement" in the health of his son, but occasionally worked Sundays even after this "rebirth." The court used these factors in order to conclude that a showing of sincere convictions had not been made.[100]

Religious beliefs and related Title VII protection do not pertain to political ideology. However, the definition of religious beliefs is so broad as to permit a tremendous variety of interpretations.

As noted, the employer does not have to incur undue hardship in adjusting to an employee's religious preferences; a firm facing this situation can discharge the employee. A problem remains in determining what constitutes undue hardship. For example, one employer discharged a registered nurse who refused to wear the requisite nurse's cap on the job because her "Old Catholic" faith required her to wear a close-fitting scarf on her head. The EEOC determined that the employer had violated Title VII unless it could show that wearing the nurse's cap was essential to its business or was necessary for sanitation.[101]

The Supreme Court approached the notion of undue hardship in a 1977 decision, *Trans World Airlines Inc. v. Larry G. Hardison et al.* The employee in this case, Larry Hardison, was a member of the Worldwide Church of God, which requires that members observe the Sabbath by not performing any work from sunset on Friday until sunset on Saturday. His seniority enabled him to avoid Saturday work; however, when he asked to be transferred to another department, his low seniority in that department required him to perform Saturday work. The company permitted the union to seek a work scheduling change for Hardison, but the union was not willing to change related seniority provisions in the labor agreement. The Supreme Court upheld the employer's discharge of Hardison, in effect stating that replacing him on Saturday assignments could require that the employer incur overtime costs for a replacement, which apparently represents an undue hardship.[102] What constitutes reasonable accommodation to an employee's religious preferences depends on the facts of each case, an uncertain situation.[103] The EEOC has recently attempted to provide guidance through additional guidelines.[104] The ability of these guidelines to provide employers and the courts with a clear and acceptable direction remains to be seen.[105]

Sexual Harassment

According to one source, the practice of obtaining sexual favors for employment considerations probably first occurred on a large-scale basis in an industrial setting around 1820, when large groups of female employees were used to operate textile mills.[106] As noted in Chapter 2, the foreman or first-line supervisor often acted as an independent contractor, free to hire and fire members of his work crew, a situation that at least increased the possibility of his making sexual requests. Although these supervisory responsibilities were changed around 1920, the possibility of sexual harassment still exists throughout contemporary organizations.

Cornell University appears to have conducted the first sexual harassment survey in 1975. Seventy percent of the working women responding to this survey had experienced some form of sexual harassment at the workplace. In other surveys, conducted in a variety of settings (employees at the United Nations, employees in state government offices, readers of *Redbook* magazine, and so forth), the proportion of respondents who reported experiencing sexual harassment at the workplace ranged from 59 to 90 percent.[107] The widespread extent of reported sexual harassment represents significant costs to the organization and affected employees.

Unwanted sexual attention communicated to female employees can be demeaning to both the male and the female involved. This situation can also create a variety of unpleasant feelings for the female employee, such as confusion, fear, anger, and helplessness.[108] Sexual harassment can also have the devastating consequence of damaging females' images of themselves as legitimate and qualified competitors for organizational responsibilities and rewards.

The notion that women are fundamentally out of place in the wage-labor-force is perpetually maintained and reinforced by their treatment as passive sexual beings. That women are forced to accept the image of themselves as fair game in any public space—even if for the least serious of attacks, say, whistling from across the street—maintains and reinforces women's sense of belonging at home in the family, and hence of the most basic sexual division of labor, one of the biggest sources of sexual inequality.[109]

Females concerned about being sexually harassed at work could take their complaints to higher management officials. However, this technique has historically been unsuccessful, particularly when the employee's immediate supervisor initiated the sexual harassment. Female employees whose complaints are not resolved and who remain at their jobs often experience increased physical and mental symptoms of stress. Some might avoid this situation, either through increased absenteeism or voluntary quits. In some cases, employees who raise such a complaint may be fired or forced to resign.[110] Absenteeism, turnover, and reduced productivity cost the organization as well as the individual.[111] One recent two-year study of sexual harassment in federal government estimated related costs at $188.7 million.[112]

The extent and costs (personal and organizational) of sexual harassment have been recently recognized by the courts in their attempts to determine whether this practice is covered by fair employment legislation (Title VII). Judicial dimensions of sexual harassment are complicated and controversial, largely because of the difficulty of defining the term.[113] Sexual harassment includes many verbal and physical dimensions:

Verbal abuse.

Sexist remarks regarding a woman's clothing or body.

Patting, pinching, or brushing against a woman's body.

Leering or ogling.

Demand for sexual favors in return for hiring, promotion, or tenure.

Physical assault.

Rape.[114]

Additional confusion occurs when people have different interpretations of the same act. Consider, for example, the following remarks made by a male supervisor to his female subordinate: "Nobody who looks as good as you should be alone on a Friday night. How about going with me to a fine restaurant and having a good time afterward." The male employee might regard his remarks as being an innocent compliment or, at worst, an attempt to determine whether the female might be interested in him. The female employee, on the other hand, might regard these remarks as the ultimate sexual harassment, a thinly disguised demand for sexual favors. Both might sincerely believe their opposing versions, a situation that would cause many problems if this incident turned into a legal suit.[115]

The EEOC has recognized many different forms of sexual harassment, since it defines this concept to include "unwelcome advances, requests for sexual favors, or other verbal or physical conduct of a sexual nature."[116] This behavior is unlawful under the following conditions:

1. Submission to the conduct is either an explicit term or condition of employment.
2. Submission to or rejection of the conduct is used as a basis for employment decisions affecting the person who did the submitting or rejecting.
3. The conduct has the purpose or effect of unreasonably interfering with an individual's work performance or creating an intimidating, hostile or offensive work environment.[117]

In essence, these EEOC guidelines have increased management's involvement in the sexual harassment issue in two respects.

First, the scope of sexual harassment has been widened. Employers may be held responsible for the acts of other employees, supervisors, and nonemployees (customers, for example). Indeed, an employee who never experienced sexual harassment might file a suit under the EEOC guidelines. Consider, for example, the following situation:

A male supervisor has a staff of 20 subordinates, 10 of them female. He makes passes at four of the women, more or less promising them promotions if they come across. Two of the four tell him to get lost; they are not promoted. The other two submit, and one of them is promoted.

Who are the victims of sexual harassment and sex discrimination?

The woman who gave in but nevertheless was left to languish in her same old job?

The pair who, but for their steadfast virtue, might have been promoted, even if their professional skills did not warrant it?

The six women who were never approached in the first place?

The 10 men who, by reason of their sex, were never in the running?

And after you've sorted out the victims, please tell me how you'd make them whole.[118]

The EEOC guidelines on sexual harassment could conceivably apply to all twenty subordinates in this situation.

Second, employers are required to take affirmative steps to educate employees regarding sexual harassment and to express organizational disapproval of such activities by developing appropriate sanctions against them and providing a mechanism to encourage harassed employees to express their concerns without fear of retaliation.[119] Sexual harassment will not likely be eliminated; but it can be reduced in frequency, duration, and intensity. Companies that expose sexual harassment and remove social support from its practitioners through affirmative steps will at least minimize this source of organizational strain.[120] Efforts in this area will no doubt be improved if the definition of *sexual harassment* becomes legally sharpened and made operational.

Summary

Fair employment legislation refers to a wide variety of laws and executive orders at the local, state, and national levels. These laws and executive orders specify various employment procedures and prohibit certain discriminatory employment practices. Voluntary compliance was emphasized before 1963, but the situation was dramatically changed with the passage of the 1964 Civil Rights Act. Title VII of this act, now incorporated into the 1972 Equal Employment Opportunity Act, created the Equal Employment Opportunity Commission (EEOC). The EEOC has specified various unlawful employment practices that restrict applicants' opportunities on the basis of their race, color, religion, sex, national origin, or age. Organizations can discriminate against employees through evil intent, differential treatment, or disparate effect.

Two major responsibilities of the EEOC are formulating procedural rules, regulations, and guidelines and resolving complaints concerning allegedly discriminatory practices. Current criticisms of this agency focus on leadership and administrative capability.

Black and female employees often share employment concerns. Their problems include increased visibility in the organization and relatively poor economic and occupational situations in many organizations. They also are often harmed by counterproductive managerial philosophies (sometimes influenced by stereotypes), poor communication of EEO objectives and policies, and faulty employment practices.

Older employees also present challenges to the organization. These challenges may be increased by two general population trends: aging of the population and declining participation of older employees in the labor force. The legal impetus for organizational attention to the older worker is the Age Discrimination in Employment Act (ADEA), which was enacted in 1967 and amended in 1978. The ADEA has no doubt resulted in the filing of more employment discrimination suits; its impact on mandatory retirement, however, has been less certain. Organizations sometimes institute personnel programs that pertain to the older worker, such as preretirement counseling and alternative work patterns.

Handicapped employees are also subjected to employment discrimination, a situation prohibited under the Vocational Rehabilitation Act of 1973. Recently, corrective actions have been taken by many organizations; such actions include identifying and modifying attitudes concerning handicapped employees and implementing activities that ensure reasonable accommodation of the handicapped.

Fair employment legislation is not always clear cut; organizations often have some difficulty placing the vague principles and concepts contained in such legislation into operation. In some cases, such as with religious discrimination and sexual harassment, interpretation is left to the courts; and the results are sometimes contradictory.

Discussion Questions

1. Indicate specifically the purpose of the EEOC and the current problems or controversies surrounding this organization.

2. Specify two unlawful employment practices. Define *evil intent, differential treatment,* and *disparate effect.*

3. Describe in some detail one legal difference between black and female employees. Also discuss two similarities of these groups. (One similarity should draw some specific conclusions from Exhibit 18.1.)

4. Indicate how stereotypes can limit employment opportunities for blacks and females.

5. Discuss the rationales in favor of and against mandatory retirement. When can an organization discharge an older worker and not be guilty of age discrimination?

6. Discuss two general approaches organizations might use to ensure that handicapped persons receive fair employment treatment.

7. Indicate various problems organizations might encounter in attempts to remove religious discrimination and sexual harassment.

Notes

1. Richard Perez, *Dealing with Employment Discrimination* (New York: McGraw-Hill, 1978), p. 17.
2. Nijole V. Benokraitis and Joe R. Feagin, *Affirmative Action and Equal Opportunity: Action, Inaction, Reaction* (Boulder, Colo.: Westview Press, 1978), p. 7.
3. Hearings before the United States Commission on Civil Rights, Memphis, Tennessee, June 26, 1962, cited in Perez, *Dealing,* p. 31.

4. Paul Bernstein and Margo W. MacLeod, "Prohibiting Employment Discrimination: Ideas and Politics in the Congressional Debate over Equal Employment Opportunity Legislation," *American Journal of Sociology* 86 (November 1980), p. 520.

5. Herbert Hill, "Is the Past Prologue? The Law and Employment Discrimination," *Crisis* 82 (February 1975), p. 57.

6. For a text of President Carter's reorganization Plan of EEOC, refer to Bureau of National Affairs, *Daily Labor Report,* February 23, 1978, pp. F-1–F-6. See also U.S. Equal Employment Opportunity Commission, *Coordination of Federal Equal Employment Opportunity Programs: The First Year, 1978–1979* (Washington, D.C.: Government Printing Office, 1979).

7. Perez, *Dealing,* pp. 47–57.

8. *Ibid.,* pp. 18–27. For additional illustrations, see Gene E. Burton and Dev S. Pathak, "101 Ways to Discriminate against Equal Employment Opportunity," *Personnel Administrator* 22 (August 1977), pp. 42–49.

9. This section was derived from a more detailed, yet easily understood, treatment of fair employment legislation and its organizational implications. See Commerce Clearing House, *1981 Guidebook to Fair Employment Practice,* report 116, September 16, 1980, pp. 121–135. For a case study of the impact of these procedures on an organization, see Carol J. Loomis, "AT&T in the Throes of 'Equal Employment,'" *Fortune,* January 15, 1979, pp. 44–57.

10. For a collection of these laws, refer to U.S. Equal Employment Opportunity Commission, *Laws Administered by EEOC* (Washington, D.C.: Government Printing Office, 1981).

11. Comptroller General of the United States, *Report to Congress: The Equal Employment Opportunity Commission Has Made Limited Progress in Eliminating Employment Discrimination* (n.p., September 25, 1976); Walter Mossberg, "Reports on EEOC Charge Incompetence and Corruption, Prompt Criminal Study," *Wall Street Journal,* April 22, 1976, p. 5.

12. William J. Eaton, "Job Agency from Hope to Despair," *Miami Herald,* May 25, 1977, p. A-21.

13. Dorothy Rabinowitz, "The Bias in the Government's Anti-Bias Agency," *Fortune,* December 1976, pp. 141–142. See also, Marilyn Chase, "Mired Minority: Latins Rise in Numbers in U.S. but Don't Win Influence or Affluence," *Wall Street Journal,* June 9, 1982, pp. 1 and 26.

14. Walter S. Mossberg, "Wary Watchdogs: Besieged by Criticism, Job-Bias Agencies Seek to Bolster Programs," *Wall Street Journal,* August 25, 1977, p. 1.

15. See, for example, Mary T. Matthies, "Equal Employment Opportunity and the Business Community," *Journal of Contemporary Business* 2 (Summer 1973), p. 3; Marvin J. Levine and Anthony J. Montcalmo, "The Equal Opportunity Commission: Progress, Problems, Prospects," *Labor Law Journal* 22 (December 1971), pp. 771–779; and Elizabeth Bartholet, "Application of Title VII To Jobs in High Places," *Harvard Law Review* 95 (March 1982), pp. 945–1027.

16. Eaton, "Job Agency."

17. See, for example, Eleanor Holmes Norton, "Reform at the EEOC," *Personnel Administrator* 23 (June 1978), pp. 21–25; "The Troubled Drive for Efficiency at the EEOC," *Business Week,* December 19, 1977, pp. 90–91, 94.

18. See, for example, James Borders, "Negating Affirmative Action: The Reagan Initiative," *Black Collegian* 12 (February/March 1982), pp. 62–77.

19. See, for example, Patricia M. Lines, "Update: New Rights for Pregnant Employees," *Personnel Journal* 58 (January 1979), pp. 33–37.

20. Paul S. Greenlaw and Diana L. Foderaro, "Some Further Implications of the Pregnancy Discrimination Act," *Personnel Journal* 59 (January 1980), pp. 36–43; L. Bruce Fryburger, "Maternity Leave Policies under Title VII," *Labor Law Journal* 26 (March 1975), pp. 163–173.

21. Hugh M. Finneran, "Title VII and Restrictions on Employment of Fertile Women," *Labor Law Journal* 31 (April 1980), pp. 223–231.

22. Roger B. Jacobs, "The *Manhart* Case: Sex-Based Differentials and the Application of Title VII to Pensions," *Labor Law Journal* 31 (April 1980), pp. 232–246.

23. See, for example, Eli Ginzberg, *The Negro Potential* (New York: Columbia University Press, 1956), pp. 48–49; Louis A. Ferman, Joyce L. Kornbluh, and J. A. Miller, eds., *Negroes and Jobs* (Ann Arbor: University of Michigan Press, 1968); Ibithaj Arafat and Betty Yorburg, *The New Women: Attitudes, Behavior and Self-Image* (Columbus, Ohio: Charles E. Merrill, 1976), p. 21; Jonathan Kaufman, "Rights Frontier: Black Executives Say Prejudice Still Impedes Their Path to the Top" *Wall Street Journal,* July 9, 1980, p. 1; Robert S. Greenberger, "Up the Ladder: Many Black Managers Hope to Enter the Ranks of Top Management," *Wall Street Journal,* June 15, 1981, p. 1.

24. Richard F. America and Bernard E. Anderson, "Must Black Executives Be Superstars?" *Wharton Magazine* 3 (Spring 1979), p. 46.

25. Rosabeth Moss Kanter, "Tokenism: Opportunity or Trap?" *MBA* 12 (January 1978), p. 16.

26. J. Stephen Heinen, Dorothy McGlauchlin, Constance Legeros, and Jean Freeman, "Developing the Woman Manager," *Personnel Journal* 54 (May 1975), p. 283.

27. Robert W. Terry, *For Whites Only* (Grand Rapids, Mich.: Detroit Industrial Mission, 1970), pp. 40–67.

28. *Bradwell v. Illinois,* quoted in Donald R. Stacy, "The Intrepid Executive's Guide to Avoiding Sex Discrimination," *Atlanta Economic Review* 26 (March/April 1976), p. 9.

29. Characteristics of stereotypes suggested by Roslind Loring and Theodora Wells, *Breakthrough: Women into Management* (New York: Van Nostrand Reinhold, 1972). For additional information, see "Sex-Role Stereotypes: A Current Appraisal," *Journal of Social Issues,* vol. 28, no. 2, 1972; Virginia E. Schein, "Think Manager—Think Male," *Atlanta Economic Review* 26 (March/April 1976), pp. 21–24.

30. For related studies, see Benokraitis and Feagin, *Affirmative Action,* p. 72; Paula Greenfield, "Why Women Work," in *Women in Management,* ed. Meg Gerrard, June Oliver, and Martha Williams (Austin: Center for Social Work Research, University of Texas, 1976), pp. 27–36; Joan Crowley, Teresa E. Levitin, and Robert P. Quinn, "Seven Deadly Half-Truths about Women, *Psychology Today* 6 (March 1973), pp. 94–96.

31. R. A. Hudson Rosen, "Foreman Role Conflict: An Expression of Contradictions in Organizational Goals," *Industrial and Labor Relations Review* 23 (July 1970), pp. 541–551.

32. "How Men Adjust to a Female Boss," *Business Week,* September 5, 1977, p. 90. For a fine discussion of related implications, see Eleanor Brantley Schwartz and James J. Rago, Jr., "Beyond Tokenism: Women as True Corporate Peers," *Business Horizons* 16 (December 1973), pp. 69–76.

33. Louis A. Ferman, *The Negro and Equal Employment Opportunities* (New York: Praeger, 1968), p. 13.

34. Benokraitis and Feagin, *Affirmative Action,* p. 78.

35. Marshall H. Brenner, "Management Development for Women," *Personnel Journal* 51 (March 1972), pp. 166–167.

36. Bette Ann Stead, "Real Equal Opportunity for Women Executives," *Business Horizons* 17 (August 1974), pp. 87–92; M. Jane Kay, "A Positive Approach to Women in Management," *Personnel Journal* 51 (January 1972), pp. 38–41; "Labor Letter," *Wall Street Journal,* August 4, 1981, p. 1.

37. Alma S. Baron and Elton T. Reeves, "How Effective Has Affirmative Action Been?" *Personnel Administrator* 22 (January 1977), pp. 47–49; Fred L. Frey, "The End of Affirmative Action," *Business Horizons* 23 (February 1980), pp. 34–40.

38. For related examples, see Allen R. Janger and Ruth G. Shaeffer, *Managing Programs to Employ the Disadvantaged* (New York: National Industrial Conference Board, 1970); *Training and Jobs for the Urban Poor* (New York: Committee for Economic Development, 1970); James M. Burns, "Corporate Programs for the Hard-Core Unemployed: The Elements of Success," *SAM Advanced Management Journal* 39 (April 1974), pp. 45–50; Jerolyn R. Lyle, *Affirmative Action Programs for Women: A Survey of Innovative Programs* (Washington, D.C.: Equal Employment Opportunity Commission, n.d.).

39. John S. Morgan and Richard L. VanDyke, *White Collar Blacks: A Breakthrough?* (New York: American Management Association, 1970), p. 23.

40. Madeline Nelson, "The Precarious Life of the EEO Manager," *MBA* 9 (February 1975), p. 42; Gerald D. Klein, "Beyond EEO and Affirmative Action," *California Management Review* 22 (Summer 1980), pp. 76–77; Theodore V. Purcell, "How GE Measures Managers in Fair Employment," *Harvard Business Review* 52 (November/December 1964), pp. 99–104.

41. U.S. Congress, House, Select Commission on Aging, *Abolishing Mandatory Retirement,* 97th Cong., 1st sess., August 1981, p. 44.

42. Donald Shire, "Age Discrimination in Employment," *Personnel Administrator* 20 (June 1975), p. 28.

43. Sara Leiter, "Hiring Policies, Prejudices, and the Older Worker," *Monthly Labor Review* 88 (August 1965), p. 968.

44. Select Committee on Aging, *Age Discrimination in Employment,* p. 52.

45. It should be noted that age discrimination can also apply if an individual is replaced by another employee in the forty to seventy age group. Patricia Linenberger and Timothy J. Keaveny, "Age Discrimination in Employment: A Guide for Employers," *Personnel Administrator* 24 (July 1979), p. 88.

46. Comments and Case Notes: Recent Developments in Age Discrimination," *American Business Law Journal* 17 (Fall 1979), p. 367.

47. Ronald J. James and Michael A. Alaimo, "BFOQ: An Exception Becoming the Rule?" *Industrial Gerontology* 4 (Fall 1977), pp. 238–241.

48. Stuart H. Bompey, "Cases and Issues in Age Discrimination," *Employee Relations Law Journal* 3 (Winter 1978), p. 392. For example, stress tests, such as the widely recognized Bruce Protocol, enable physicians to determine with 98- to 100-percent accuracy that an individual in the low-risk category will not suffer a sudden cardiac death within the next year. S. Mohler, "Age Is a State, as Are Sex and Race," *Aging and Work* 2 (Summer 1979), pp. 193–194.

49. Shire, "Age Discrimination in Employment," p. 30.

50. For example, in 1973, approximately 1,000 employees received $2 million in age discrimination settlements, compared with 2,400 employees and $7 million in 1975. Bernard E. DeLury, "The Age Discrimination in Employment Act: Background and Highlights of Recent Cases," *Industrial Gerontology* 3 (Winter 1976) pp. 37–40. In 1980, the EEOC received 8,779 age discrimina-

tion complaints, a dramatic increase over similar complaints filed in 1979 (3,097). Robert S. Greenberger, "Fired Employees in 40's Filing More Bias Suits," *Wall Street Journal,* October 8, 1981, p. 31.

51. Greenberger, "Fired Employees," p. 31; Also see "Wounded Executives Fight Back on Age Bias," *Business Week,* July 21, 1980, pp. 109–114.

52. Gopal C. Pati and Randall C. Jacobs, "Mandatory Retirement at 70: Separating Substance from Politics," *Personnel Administrator* 24 (February 1979), p. 20.

53. "Work, Aging, and Retirement," *Personnel Journal* 58 (May 1980), p. 360.

54. Richard M. Cyert, "Extending the Retirement Age," Beta Gamma Sigma invited essay, p. 2.

55. Bernard Wysocki and James C. Hyatt, "Battle of the Ages: Mandatory Retirement at 65 Is Likely to End," *Wall Street Journal,* September 13, 1977, p. 1.

56. Robert S. Cuddy, "Age Discrimination Amendments and Their Impact on Personnel," *Employee Relations Law Journal* 4 (Winter 1978–1979), pp. 342–343.

57. Philip L. Rones, "Older Men—The Choice between Work and Retirement," *Monthly Labor Review* 101 (November 1978), pp. 4–5. Also see Select Committee on Aging, *Abolishing Mandatory Retirement.*

58. See, for example, Rian M. Yaffe, "Changing Retirement Patterns: Their Effect on Employee Benefits," *Personnel Administrator* 24 (February 1979), p. 29; Joann S. Lublin and Michael L. King, "Invited Out: More Companies Offer an Early Retirement; Some Workers Decline," *Wall Street Journal,* November 12, 1980, pp. 1, 24; Charles W. Stevens, "Aging Americans: Many Delay Retiring or Resume Jobs to Beat Inflation and the Blues," *Wall Street Journal,* November 5, 1979, pp. 1, 22.

59. Tom Fiedler, "What Will It Mean if Few Quit at 65?" *Miami Herald,* April 2, 1978, p. 27-A.

60. Ernest J. Griffes, "Changes Created by the End of Mandatory Retirement," *Personnel Administrator* 23 (August 1978), pp. 13–16.

61. See, for example, Michael H. Schuster and Christopher Miller, "Performance Evaluations as Evidence in ADEA Cases," *Employee Relations Law Journal* 6 (Spring 1981), pp. 561–583; James W. Walker and Daniel E. Lupton, "Performance Appraisal Programs and Age Discrimination Law," *Aging and Work* 2 (Spring 1978), pp. 73–83.

62. See, for example, Jeffrey D. Mamorsky, "Impact of the 1978 ADEA Amendments on Employee Benefit Plans," *Employee Relations Law Journal* 4 (Autumn 1978), pp. 173–184; Ronald L. Haneberg, "Is ADEA Another ERISA?" *Risk Management* (August 1980), pp. 25–34.

63. Alfred P. Diotte and Douglas M. Soat, "Employees' Attitudes toward Retirement," *Personnel Administrator* 24 (February 1979), p. 27.

64. Leland P. Bradford, "Can You Survive Your Retirement?" *Harvard Business Review* 57 (November/December 1978), p. 103.

65. Lawrence J. Holt, "Retirement: A Time to Enjoy or Endure?" *Personnel Administrator* 24 (November 1979), pp. 72–73; John C. Perham, "The Newest Employee Benefit," *Dun's Review* 115 (May 1980), p. 76.

66. "How to Help Employees Prepare for Retirement," *Business Week,* April 24, 1978, p. 137.

67. For a fine example of this type of research, see Neal Schmitt, Bryan W. Coyle, John Rauschenberger, and J. Kenneth White, "Comparison of Early Retirees and Non-Retirees," *Personnel Psychology* 32 (Summer 1979), pp. 327–341.

68. Estimated reductions range from 1.5 million to 7.2 million. Daniel D. Cook, "Older Workers: A Resource We'll Need," *Industry Week,* July 7, 1980, pp. 43–44.

69. E. Meier and E. Kerr, "Capabilities of Middle-Aged and Older Workers," *Industrial Gerontology* 3 (Summer 1976), p. 148.

70. Jeffrey Sonnenfeld, "Dealing with the Aging Work Force," *Harvard Business Review* 56 (November/December 1978), pp. 85–90.

71. Some volunteer to work between 10 a.m. and 3 p.m. to avoid rush-hour traffic and travelling in darkness. Beverly Jacobson, *Young Programs for Older Workers* (New York: Van Nostrand Reinhold, 1980), p. 5.

72. "Labor Letter," *Wall Street Journal,* May 30, 1978, p. 1.

73. The first two statistics are from Richard J. Lehr, "Employer Duties to Accommodate Handicapped Employees," *Labor Law Journal* 31 (March 1980), p. 175; the third statistic is from Ray B. Bressler and A. Wayne Lacy, "An Analysis of the Relative Job Progression of the Perceptibly Physically Handicapped," *Academy of Management Journal* 23 (March 1980), p. 132.

74. "How Bias Strikes 'Hidden Handicapped,'" *U.S. News & World Report,* June 29, 1981, p. 73.

75. Jonathan Kwitney and Jerry Landauer, "Sheltered Shops: How a Blind Worker Gets $1.85 an Hour after 20 Years on the Job," *Wall Street Journal,* January 25, 1979, pp. 1, 31.

76. Jonathan Kwitney and Jerry Landauer, "Minimal Wage: Some Workshops Pay Handicapped as Little as 10 Cents an Hour," *Wall Street Journal,* October 17, 1979, pp. 1, 24.

77. April Koral, "The Handicapped Fight to be Boss," *Parade,* September 2, 1979, p. 17.

78. Handicapped Seen 'Least Likely to Succeed,'" *Risk Management* 25 (May 1979), p. 56.

Chapter 19

The Personnel Function in Special Sectors: Multinational Corporations and Public Organizations

The current [personnel] technology [is] applicable to multinational companies. . . . [However,] current technology may rapidly become obsolete. . . . Its durability will depend on its adaptability, the extension of our transport and communication systems, and our skill in global finance and geopolitics. As the world shrinks and regional markets become one, [personnel] technology will require updating.*

The most notable fact about the field of personnel and industrial relations as it is practiced in the public sector today is that theory and practice are rapidly coalescing. And the likelihood that this development will continue into the 1980s is practically a certainty. By the mid-1970s professional practice in both the public and the private sector was practically identical, but there were still some substantial differences between the two sectors.†

*Reprinted by permission from Edwin B. Gilroy, David M. Noer, and James E. Spoor, "Personnel Administration in the Multinational/Transnational Corporation," in *PAIR Policy and Program Management,* edited by Dale Yoder and H. G. Heneman, Jr., p. 1-123, copyright 1978 by The Bureau of National Affairs, Inc., Washington, D.C.

†Reprinted by permission from Laurence C. Caffin and Terrell G. Manyak, "PAIR Management in the Public Service," in *PAIR Policy and Program Management,* edited by Dale Yoder and H. G. Heneman, Jr., p. 1-98, copyright 1978 by the Bureau of National Affairs, Inc., Washington, D.C.

The personnel function as practiced in multinational corporations (MNCs) and in the public sector are topics usually not covered in traditional personnel management textbooks. We have included them here in recognition of (1) the interdependencies and interrelationships among countries, the effects of international competition, the improvement in international communication and transportation, the growing importance of the role of the multinational corporation in world events, and the increased international orientation of curricula under the guidance of the American Assembly of Collegiate Schools of Business (AACSB) and (2) the critical roles played by local, county, state, and federal governmental units and their effects on all U.S. citizens. Another reason for the inclusion of these topics is that many students will sometime in their careers be employed by a multinational corporation or a governmental unit.

While the preceding chapters have presented the personnel function as it applies to the typical organization, Chapter 19 focuses on the unique features of these two special sectors. Although many previously discussed principles, techniques, and problems involved in major personnel activities apply to MNCs and public-sector organizations, the distinguishing characteristics of these sectors result in their having unique features as well.

The Personnel Function in Multinational Corporations

Economic expansion into international investments has stemmed from two major technological developments: the rapid, convenient, and reliable transportation provided by jet aircraft and the vast improvement in global communications provided by computers and telecommunications systems. Another contributing influence was the favorable political and economic climate after World War II, which allowed the expansion of private investments throughout the world.[1]

U.S. companies alone have foreign affiliates numbering 3,540 and have direct investments of $200 billion abroad. In 1981, it was estimated that $41 billion was earned from these investments—one-third from petroleum products, one-third from manufactured goods, and the rest from a variety of businesses.[2]

MNCs have had a great impact on much of the world:

[The multinational corporation] is domestic entrepreneurship extended to foreign opportunity . . . has developed through the creation, production, and distribution of goods and services which satisfy the needs and wants of customers in diverse locations . . . has developed without the benefit of a common currency, common language, a common government, or a common value system . . . has carried technology and capital across broad reaches of water and distance and has made possible advances in the standards of living of many people . . . has made visible the emerging global economy—the interdependence of nations on raw materials and sources of energy

> . . . has made possible the worldwide production and consumption of
> a wide array of products and services. [MNCs] could be the forerun-
> ner of business enterprises of the future.[3]

Because nations of the world have become so interdependent, MNCs
cannot simply pursue their own economic goals of expanding markets,
lowering production costs, and increasing profitability as they did in
the past. Unless these firms accept their social responsibilities and
discharge them effectively, their rights may be altered by the governments of countries in which they operate. One of the first responsibility of the MNC is to work to bridge gaps in understanding and communication between itself and its host countries.[4]

**Differences in
Countries**

The MNC must operate its business and achieve its production, marketing, and financial objectives through affiliates in numerous countries. In these countries, adjustments to cultural, educational, technological, political, climatic, and managerial differences must be made in
order for success to be achieved.

Cultural Differences Since MNCs must operate within the framework of
numerous cultures and social systems, it is surprising how many expatriate employees (employees working outside their home country but
planning to return to it) make no effort to learn the language, religious
beliefs, and customs of the host country. Without a common language,
there can be no effective communication with employees, especially
those at lower levels—the levels at which most difficulty arises. Without an understanding of religious beliefs and customs, there can be
little understanding of employees' behavior.

Criticism or ignorance of a local way of life can result in rejection,
lack of cooperation, and poor performance from host-country nationals.
Expatriate managers must know the customs of the host country and
learn to deal with cultural differences. For example, in some countries,
especially those of Latin America and the Far East, family connections
must be recognized. Key organizational positions are filled by family
members, and authority is vested not in the position but in the person.
Regardless of their organizational positions, these individuals expect
the same respect within the organization as they receive in their community. Religious beliefs can also enter the workplace. In Islamic
countries, for example, people must pray at certain times of the day,
even at work.

Consideration must be given to the local society's attitudes toward
status, prestige, position, and wealth. For example, in some countries,
there is no middle class. Authoritarian behavior is the rule, and participation by employees in decision-making is thought to reflect weak-

ness in management. In many parts of the world, particularly in underdeveloped countries, a paternalistic attitude toward employees is fully accepted.

The role of women in the various cultures must be understood and respected, even if it is not the role approved in the United States. For instance, in most countries, women do not expect to receive equal pay for equal work. Further restrictions on employment, such as allowing women to work only before they are married, are also encountered and must be respected by expatriate managers.

Educational Differences Communicating with and training employees who cannot read or write are extremely difficult. In turn, technological advancement is handicapped by the lack of technically trained employees. Because education is so intertwined with social and economic development, the lack of education makes other development improbable. Thus, education is a primary concern for the MNC.

Recognition of educational traditions is also important, however. For example, once a student in Asia or Africa becomes an engineer, he or she will refuse to do manual work, because such work is regarded as undignified. In Western Europe, strong social stratification causes educational inequality and reduces social mobility and opportunity for advancement.

For companies locating facilities in underdeveloped countries, the lack of educated workers prevents the use of modern production technology; so significant investments in training must be made at all levels. In many European countries, the status of the first-line and middle manager is low, partly because of an educational system that perpetuates the social class structure. For companies entering these European nations, supervisor training is imperative; and enhancing the supervisor's status through pay and responsibility may also be necessary.

Technological Differences The introduction of new technology is usually favored, particularly in developing countries. While this new technology promises jobs, economic development, and higher living standards, it may conflict with traditions and behavioral patterns. Consider a small village whose inhabitants have always been employed locally. When a factory locates in a neighboring town and some villagers take jobs there, they must commute; and their lifestyle is significantly altered.

Further, the new technology requires that workers become more accurate, concentrate more intensely for longer periods, and adhere to more highly regimented work schedules. Consequently, employees must be taught new practices and procedures that are essential if the foreign facility is to achieve an optimum return on its investment.

Training employees will be intensive, because local employees will have to adjust to practices of modern industrial management. Neglecting proper preparation and training will result in lack of industrial discipline, low operating efficiency, criticism of management, and possibly governmental interference. Training must be extended beyond job training; employees must be taught why the introduction of technology is necessary for their own long-term economic interests.

Differences in Political and Governmental Attitudes Businesses operating in foreign locations must fully understand the government's structure and policies and the current political issues. Frequently, political leaders are elected because they have promised broad social reforms, maybe even nationalization of foreign firms. Failure to recognize this possibility leads to problems. Other countries openly encourage foreign investments as a way to advance their technologies by introducing computers, nuclear energy, and electronics.

Climatic Differences Climatic factors in developing countries contribute to the failure rate of as many as 70 percent of expatriates. Such factors as dryness and heat in the Arabian deserts, monsoons in Asia, and extreme heat and humidity in many parts of Asia can be extremely severe. Hours worked, number of weeks worked, and productivity are affected by temperature and humidity. Such extremes sap workers' energy; they think and move more slowly, and they appear to have less initiative and ambition. Any expatriate manager who does not consider the climatic influences on employees' behavior will not survive.

Differences in Managerial Practices Vast differences in management philosophy, style, and sophistication can be observed among countries. These differences stem from all the differences explained above; however, cultural and social systems have the strongest impact. The following list gives some examples of unsophisticated management practices:

Lack of planning.

Poor definition of line-staff relationships.

No inventory controls.

Lack of employee participation in company decisions.

Personnel managers functioning as record keepers or social benefit administrators.

Absence of employee planning, training, and development.

Excessive levels of management.

No job descriptions or performance standards.

Lack of measurement skills.

Poor communication throughout.

No management by objectives.

Other differences, such as differences in social and educational structures and the presence of paternalistic and autocratic styles of management, preclude the use of many modern management tools. In addition, where management development is accepted, bureaucratic systems and reluctance to delegate authority prevent qualified local managers from being continually fed into the organizational hierarchy. All these problems make it difficult for an MNC to operate its foreign branches as it does its domestic ones.

One of multinationals' greatest challenges is to successfully transfer management expertise. This transfer can take a long time where the dominant cultural, social, and educational patterns have historically precluded the rise of a professional management group. Thus, teaching managerial skills and encouraging their subsequent implementation is difficult. In many countries where management education at universities is not adequate, disciplines such as industrial engineering are unknown. Such inadequacies have caused some MNCs to develop their own management training programs; but setting up these programs takes time, and their effects are not immediate. The problems are magnified by host country officials who ask, "When will our people move into top management positions?"

Local people who are eager for and receptive to management education are frequently not prepared to accept the consequences, such as changes in lifestyle. In some cases, local trainees become overly optimistic and view management education as a panacea for all problems. Training should allow these employees to develop slowly, solve their own problems through team effort, and apply what they have learned.[5]

Personnel Activities of MNCs

The personnel practices of MNCs must be adjusted to accommodate the wide variations among countries. The personnel activities most affected are staffing, orientation and training, compensation, and labor relations. While much of the discussion below can be applied to the personnel function of MNCs of any country, the major focus will be directed toward U.S. MNCs.

Staffing Staffing is one of the most important activities of an MNC. Not only must selection of expatriate managers be made under a unique set of circumstances, but the considerations involved in the employment of local nationals are also unique. After the expatriate's assignment is completed, another important staffing activity involves the social and organizational reentry of the executive, who may have felt out of touch during the overseas assignment.

The trend in multinational staffing is toward greater use of local nationals to staff overseas operations. In fact, some MNCs, such as IBM, employ local nationals in 99 percent of the positions in overseas facilities. The reasons for this trend include the following:

Local nationals understand the people and the country.

Local nationals can easily communicate with employees, customers, suppliers, government officials, other business leaders, and the general public.

Local nationals have no adjustment problems.

Local nationals are less expensive to employ. (For example, people transferred from the United States to Japan can pay as much as $4,000 per month for housing comparable to their U.S. housing. The MNC will have to reimburse most of this expense.)

Hiring local nationals appeases host country demands to hire more local employees and eases the shortage of qualified managers willing to take overseas assignments.[6]

As an example of local nationals' advantage over expatriates, one Japanese executive employed by a U.S. firm in Japan explains that "the foreigner has to write a letter to get an appointment. I can just call them up. It makes a hell of a difference."[7]

Of course, selecting local nationals can be difficult.

There are no specific guidelines for the hiring of foreign nationals. Much depends on the individual company; its business philosophy; its degree of internationalization; the nature of its production; product line and markets; and its management resources. Much also depends on the particular countries in which the company carries on its business.[8]

Even though the trend is toward employing local nationals, the need to employ expatriates in overseas operations still exists. The principal reason was suggested earlier: qualified local nationals are scarce in certain countries. For example, the developing countries in Asia, Africa, and Latin America can supply few engineers and managers; in industrialized countries, sales and marketing managers are scarce. In cases where the foreign operations are new, it is imperative that expatriate managers be used. Once the operations are functioning smoothly, many MNCs want to retain a few expatriate managers to maintain effective control and to retain a continuing presence at the location. Some U.S. MNCs are trying to build a core of U.S. executives who will have a multinational orientation.[9]

Because 30 to 50 percent of U.S. managers assigned to foreign operations return before the scheduled completion of their assignments,

MNCs are investing more time and effort in selection.[10] However, the selection process remains largely judgmental, intuitive, and personal, even though it is recognized to be more complicated than the difficult task of selection for domestic positions. As a general rule, the basis for selection is accomplishments in previous positions. Use of this selection criterion cannot be relied on completely, because overseas assignments are more difficult and the person selected is usually unaware of the complexities of the assignment.[11]

Several characteristics of successful expatriate managers have been identified and should be kept in mind during the selection process:

They are sensitive to foreign environments, willing to learn the local language, and empathetic toward the overall culture.

They are profit-oriented.

They are open-minded and unprejudiced.

They are motivated to work abroad for such reasons as personal interest, career development, money, and so on.

They have strong family support, especially from the spouse.

Family difficulties have been judged a major limiting consideration in the selection of expatriate managers. Assignments to underdeveloped countries can cause major difficulties because of inadequate medical facilities, inadequate schools, and various cross-cultural barriers.[12] Some companies require that a prospective manager's entire family undergo "adaptability screening" before the manager can be assigned to a foreign affiliate. The screening measures the family's suitability for life abroad in terms of its success in handling transfers within the United States and its reaction to discussions of the stresses that life in a particular country would entail. Such stresses include separation anxiety, tensions from unstable family relations, frustrations of adjusting to a strange culture, and difficulties of learning to communicate in a new language.[13]

MNCs must also consider restrictions imposed by the government of the host country, particularly those of less-developed countries. Interested in providing jobs for their citizens and motivated by nationalistic interests in economic development, many host governments persuade MNCs to replace expatriate managers with local nationals. The hosting government can constrain the employment of expatriates or at least frustrate the process through such acts as delaying the granting of work permits, imposing worker quotas, and limiting the duration of work permits. For example, the government of Pakistan requires that MNCs hire certain proportions of local nationals at various salary levels, such as 100 percent below a certain salary level and 50 percent above a certain salary level. Brazil requires that two-thirds of the MNC's local payroll be Brazilians unless the company shows that no qualified local nationals are available. However, government interference is usually not present when high-level positions are held by local nationals and when most expatriates stay for only short periods.[14]

Orientation and Training As a general rule, the cost of maintaining an expatriate manager in an overseas assignment is two and one-half to three times the domestic base salary. If the manager returns before the assignment is complete, the costs of replacement soar. Frequently, the reason overseas assignments do not work as planned is that the U.S. manager was not prepared for the assignment.

Those who are going on overseas assignments in responsible positions must be able to perceive, understand, and respond quickly in their new environments. They must possess innate receptivity to begin with; they must also be given enough knowledge of their new country to use that skill to its utmost. They need to understand how people are likely to read them, respond to them, react to them. The better a manager can do that, the better that manager can predict their actions and reactions and the better he or she can perform in this new world.[15]

Surprisingly, most MNCs do not properly prepare their executives for overseas assignments. One sample of MNCs reports that 25 percent offer no training or orientation for employees moving to foreign locations; about half include some orientation, which focuses on company matters; and less than 50 percent include training for the spouse.[16]

Proper orientation and training before foreign assignments usually make the difference between a successful and an unsuccessful experience. Such preparation should be required and not be left up to the individual. Topics in an orientation and training program should be:

Review of terms and conditions of the assignment. Terms and conditions include the MNC's policies and procedures, compensation system (including taxes and allowances such as those for housing, moving, and cost of living), living conditions, moving arrangements (passports, visas, inoculations, shipping of household goods, and temporary housing).

Cultural training. Cultural training provides an understanding of the predominant values in the host country and the way of life of its people. Training may involve studying books; hearing lectures; viewing films; discussing history, culture, and socioeconomic patterns; and participating in simulated exercises to develop interpersonal skills.

Language training. Language training, considered vital to success, requires dedication, discipline, and time in advance of the foreign assignment. Such training may use individual and formal classroom work, self-teaching exercises, and experiential exercises.[17]

Training of local nationals relies heavily on on-the-job training. For managerial positions, the trainee usually visits the home headquarters long enough to understand company policies and practices. As part of the development effort, periodic meetihgs are held so that face-to-face communications between local managers and headquarters staff can take place. When training occurs outside the company, it usually takes place at universities or international institutes.[18]

Compensation Compensation for expatriates must be sensitive and responsive to changing overseas conditions, such as cost of living and housing. Compensation should be designed to provide a net income comparable to that of an individual performing similar work in the United States (commonly referred to as the domestic equivalent) and to provide a cash incentive or premium as a reasonable financial inducement to work and live outside the home country. Where appropriate, this premium includes allowances for housing, travel, a "cultural shock," tax liability to the host country, education for children, hardships due to climate or conflict conditions, and so on. In some cases, the total cost of the premium may rise as high as 50 percent of the prevailing base salary at home. The Economic Recovery Tax Act of 1981 helped expatriates in the area of tax liability by exempting from U.S. taxes as much as $75,000 of their earned income (adjusted to $95,000 by 1986). In addition, rent on furniture and house and utilities payments are tax deductions. When the foreign country's cost of living is higher than that in the United States, a cost of living allowance is usually paid. Compensation specialists continually monitor exchange rates and fluctuations in price levels to maintain equity.

While the expatriate's pay is typically based on the domestic equivalent, variations in the exchange rate and the changing value of the dollar in relation to the foreign currency continually change the real earning of the expatriate. For example, if the dollar loses in value, the expatriate's real earnings are reduced. Further, if the inflation rate in the foreign country is 3 percent, the expatriate gains in real earnings when his or her pay is adjusted in accordance with the U.S. inflation rate, which may be 8 percent in the same year.[19]

Compensation for local nationals is usually commensurate with that in the prevailing local labor market. When taxes are extremely high, executive "perks" such as club memberships, automobiles, and deferred compensation plans are provided to executives who are local nationals.[20]

Because the expatriate's salary may exceed the local national's salary for comparable work, issues of equity may surface. For example, what problems will emerge when local nationals find out that expatriates' salaries exceed theirs by a sizable margin? Should expatriates' pay equal that of their domestic counterparts or of local nationals? How much difference in pay does it take to induce executives to work in foreign countries? Because countries differ so much, should an MNC have separate compensation policies for different countries? These issues must be resolved by organizations with operations in foreign countries if they are to reach the objectives of wage and salary programs specified in Chapter 10.

Labor Relations   Labor relations vary from country to country, and no country has a labor relations system identical to that of the United States. Organizations learn quickly that they must deal with unions in most countries as unique organizations. The fundamental principles of U.S. labor unions are majority rule, exclusive representation, and political independence. In Western Europe, there are government-mandated worker participation arrangements; and workers are represented on corporations' supervisory boards (bodies similar to boards of directors in the United States). In Japan, workers are organized into company unions. In Latin America, unions are split along ideological lines.

A detailed analysis of unions' organizational structures, and collective bargaining issues and strategies found in foreign countries is not necessary here.[21] However, MNCs need to be well versed in these subjects and related differences from labor relations activities in the United States. Some MNCs might also need to review their domestic labor agreements where negotiated work rules could prohibit certain products or parts being manufactured in foreign countries.

The Personnel Function in the Public Sector

Since 1950, employment in government has grown substantially. Federal payrolls (not including the military) have grown from 2.0 to 2.8 million, while state and local government payrolls have grown from 4.1 to 13.6 million.[22] It is estimated that 5 million of these state and local government employees are paid with federal funds to administer federal programs.[23] Overall, public employment makes up 18 percent of the overall labor force in the United States.[24]

The technical processes of staffing, training, appraisal, wage administration, and labor relations in the public sector are similar to those in the private sector. As one authority has stated:

> . . . there is no standard (personnel) practice in either the public or the private sector. . . . the professional practitioner must select from among a variety of approaches and programs, those best for each organization and situation.[25]

In spite of the similarities between the public and private sectors, differences also exist. This discussion will focus on these differences and their effects on personnel activities.

Nature of the Operations

A primary cause for the differences between the public sector and the private sector stems from internal operations and the economic environment in which each sector operates. In the private sector, the market economy serves as a constraint on the wages paid, the benefits offered, the number of employees, and the terms and conditions of employment. Any benefits that accrue to employees in the private sector must be offset by higher productivity, lower profits, or higher consumer prices.

Most firms in the private sector must compete with other firms, and most products and services can be purchased from various sources. Thus, a price increase in the products or services of one firm without a corresponding increase in the prices of competitive or substitutable products or services of other firms causes customers to shift away from the higher-priced products or services. This reduction in sales reduces the employer's ability to provide better wages, benefits, and other terms and conditions of employment. Further, employees must remember that high wages can lead quickly to automation, plant shut-downs, plant relocations, and shifts of production from one plant to another.

In the public sector, on the other hand, services provided by the public employer—for example, police and fire protection, water, garbage collection, and street maintenance—usually have no close substitute. Even where there are close substitutes, such as private schools, consumers do not usually choose between alternatives on the basis of cost alone. In other words, the consumers of public services usually do not have a real choice in the purchase of these services; and further, they may be required by law to pay for the services through taxes, regardless of the degree to which they use the services.

Any improvements in public-sector wages, benefits, and other terms and conditions of employment must be offset through increased productivity and efficiency, reduced services, higher taxes, or shifts of funds from one department to another. Unlike the private employer, the public employer usually has a monopoly; however, reduction of services, increase in taxes, or shift of funds is frequently met with resistance from citizens and various interest groups. Thus, in the final analysis, the public employer is constrained not by the discipline of market forces but by its customers, the taxpayers and voters who elect public officials.[26]

The Merit Principle and Politics

Merit system is the name that has been given to an elaborate system of civil service laws, rules, and regulations which are based on the merit principle.[27] Merit systems stem from the passage of the Pendleton Act of 1883, which established the civil service in the federal government. Executive Order 7916, signed by President Franklin D. Roosevelt in 1938, required major governmental agencies to have a bona fide personnel office. Some states already had merit systems at that time, and the approach has since spread to most other government units.[28] Today, merit systems cover 95 percent of permanent federal civilian employees, all state and county employees paid with federal funds, most state employees, almost all police and firefighters, and three-fourths of city employees.

The merit system was designed to replace the *spoils system,* which subjected all employees to the control of the political party in power. When incumbents failed in their bids for reelection, the newly elected officials would select new employees with whom they shared political allegiance; thus, others would have to seek employment elsewhere.[29]

While merit systems were founded on the principle that merit would be the primary factor in employment, promotion, wage determination, and other personnel matters, they have often been unsuccessful in achieving this goal. It has been impossible to keep politics out of public personnel management. One example of the dilution of the merit principle by politics comes from the *Malek Manual* (see Exhibit 19.1), a personnel manual used by the White House staff during the Nixon administration. Personnel rules and regulations, codes of conduct, and so on have been designed to limit administrative discretion and thus to reduce political influence. However, such limitations have also reduced employers' ability to react to changing conditions.

One critique of contemporary merit systems notes the following additional concerns:

Entry-level positions are filled on the basis of written examinations scored to two or three decimal places.

Once a ranked list of examination scores is established, management must choose one of the top three names on the list regardless of the special qualifications, knowledge, experience, aptitude, or training of other applicants on the list.

After an employee has spent six months on the job, he or she is virtually guaranteed the job for life, unless the supervisor files a special report urging that the employee be discharged or at least that the granting of tenure be deferred; it is very unusual for a supervisor to take such action.

An employee, after acquiring such tenure, can be fired only on grounds of dishonesty or incompetence of a truly gross nature and cannot be shifted to a less demanding assignment.

Promotions are generally limited to employees who occupy the next lower position within the same division; qualified employ-

Exhibit 19.1	**Excerpt from the *Malek Manual***

There is no substitute in the beginning of any Administration for a very active political personnel operation. Whatever investment is made in positions, salaries, systems, training and intelligent work in this area, will yield a return tenfold. Conversely, the failure to invest what is necessary to a political personnel program, will cost the Administration and the department or agency fiftyfold what they might otherwise have invested. These estimates are borne out by experience. Where departments and agencies, and Administrations, have failed to invest the manpower and other necessary aforementioned items into an effective political personnel program—blindly paying lip service to such a function and proceeding immediately to invest heavily in the management and program functions—they have only been plagued by such folly. The time consumed of high level Administration appointees, and the manpower and expenses involved in the creation of firefighting forces, caused by acts in attempt to frustrate the Administration's policies, program objectives and management objectives, as well as to embarrass the Administration, engaged in by unloyal employees of the executive branch, has far exceeded the investment a political personnel operation would have required. In those few organizations where an effective political personnel office was the forerunner of "new directions" in policy, program objectives, and management objectives, the ease and low visibility with which they were accomplished was markedly contrasted to the rest of the Administration. There is no question that the effective activities of a political personnel office will invoke a one-shot furor in the hostile press and Congress. But there is no question that these costs are far less than the costs of the frequent crescendos of bad publicity that are sure to occur frequently and indefinitely if you do not. In short, it is far better and healthier to swallow a larger bitter pill in the beginning, and then run rigorously toward your objectives, than to run toward your objectives stopping so frequently for small bitter pills that you become drained of the endurance, the will and the ability to ever reach your objectives. As one of the ranking members of this Administration once put it: "You cannot hope to achieve policy, program or management control until you have achieved political control. That is the difference between ruling and reigning."

Source: White House Personnel Office, "The Malek Manual," in *Classics in Public Personnel Policy,* ed. Frank J. Thompson (Oak Park, Ill.: Moore Publishing Co., 1979), p. 187. Excerpts from U.S. Congress, Senate, Select Committee on Presidential Campaign Activities, *Watergate and Related Activities,* book 19 (Washington, D.C.: Government Printing Office, 1974).

ees in other divisions of the organization are discriminated against, as are applicants from outside the organization.

Salary increases are virtually automatic and, with rare exceptions, are completely unrelated to the employee's work performance.

Supervisors belong to unions, sometimes to the same unions as the employees they supervise.

Personnel practices are regulated by commissions, frequently chaired by the director of personnel. Managers and supervisors must defer to his or her judgment on all personnel matters except those involving top-level executives.

The employees' unions have enough political power to influence the decision concerning whether the chief executive is permitted to stay on; furthermore, they also influence the appointment of top-level managers.[30]

Staffing Decisions and Employment

Since public employers have adopted merit principles in staffing, employees have at least theoretically been recruited and selected through competitive examinations; appointed to job classifications in which pay is predetermined according to duties and responsibilities; promoted on the basis of capacity and performance; and dismissed for cause, such as inefficiency and improper conduct on the job.

In regard to staffing, "examinations are the real mainstay of the public service employment process."[31] In fact, 50 to 60 percent of the 1.7 million applicants to federal government positions each year are required to take written examinations. While 60 percent of those taking the examinations pass, many of them will not obtain jobs.[32]

By use of examinations, personnel representatives determine which applicants will be certified as qualified for jobs when they become available. The employing unit can then choose from among the certified applicants. In the federal government and in thirteen states, the *rule of three* is used—selection is made from the top three eligible applicants. Including three names allows the immediate supervisor some flexibility in making the final selection decision. Complicating the rule of three and other competitive selection is the veteran's preference, which gives a bonus of five points to all veterans and ten points to all disabled veterans who pass the general competitive exam.[33]

One feature that distinguished public employment for many years was its exemption from laws that applied to the private sector. In the last ten years, this situation has changed. Since the Equal Employment Opportunity Act of 1972 expanded coverage of the Civil Rights Act to government employees, personnel departments in public organizations now must comply with the EEOC guidelines, which specify requirements for employment. State laws and local ordinances have expanded collective bargaining rights, wage and hours regulations, pension requirements, unemployment compensation, and the like to cover public employees.[34]

Numerous laws and executive orders pertain only to public employees. The Hatch Act at the federal level and numerous state statutes restrict the political activities of these employees. Personal appearance, residence, and off-the-job behavior have been regulated more closely in the public sector. Because citizens pay the taxes that pay public employees' salaries, personnel administrators have to be careful of the image public employees project. Such factors are likely to be less important in the private sector.[35] It is a challenge for public personnel administrators to balance these concerns with the protection of individual employees' rights.[36]

The rights of public employees have been abridged in the past; however, this situation has changed over time. Today, for example, public employees are entitled to *procedural due process,* which means that a dismissed public employee has a constitutional right to receive a statement of reasons for the dismissal and to rebut these reasons when the dismissal stemmed from retaliation for the exercise of freedom of speech, when the employee's reputation has been damaged, or when future employability has been impaired. These rights have been expanded to include the right to a hearing, the right to confront accusers, the right to cross-examine, and the right of counsel.[37]

While freedom of speech and association are constitutional rights, there are limits to their exercise by public employees. The Supreme Court has identified several reasons for which these rights may be limited, including the need to maintain discipline and harmony in the workforce, the need for confidentiality, and the need to ensure that the proper performance of duties is not impeded.[38]

Other cases in public employment involve equal protection under the Fourteenth Amendment. Assigning police to neighborhoods according to race, banning the hiring of aliens, and requiring that pregnant school teachers leave their jobs four to five months before the expected date of birth were determined to be in conflict with the equal protection clause of the Constitution.[39]

Performance Appraisal

In public employment, as in other service-oriented industries, performances and productivity are difficult to measure. But, since there seems to be a drive toward making government more accountable and productive, organizations are devoting more time and effort to performance appraisal.

There [is] a new obsession with measuring results—developing public equivalents of business' bottom line. The question is not how many sanitation men and how much equipment work how faithfully for how long—but whether the street gets clean.[40]

In evaluating performance, organizations must identify cause and effect relationships. Jobs can be defined, and some performance measurements can be developed. For example, the state police patrol a certain length of highway, make traffic arrests, and investigate criminal cases. Records of performance may include arrests made, tickets issued, miles covered, and so on. The problem with these measurements is that they may not be directly related to the basic objectives of police patrol work—to improve the flow of traffic, reduce accidents, and reduce crime. Further, the measurements are not totally under the control of police. Accidents may be caused by poor drivers, traffic violations, and poor roads. Crimes may result from numerous social, psychological, legal, and economic factors. Connecting cause and effect in such situations may be difficult.[41]

Public officials must also seek to define good performance. Good performance is viewed by constituents in terms of the quality of the services provided. Legislators and executive officials have tended to associate poor quality only with complaints from the public consumer. It has been assumed that performance is good unless such complaints are made.[42] In other words, some officials tend to let sleeping dogs lie.

Wage and Salary Administration

Wage and salary administration in the public sector does not differ fundamentally from that in the private sector. However, one might assume that in the public sector, this task has more importance, because wages constitute about 80 percent of the sector's total costs.

Before recent federal budget cuts, government employment remained attractive in terms of wages and job security. Most governmental units adopted the *prevailing wage principle*—public-sector jobs provided wage levels comparable to the prevailing wage for the same job in the private sector. The justification for this principle has been that public employers, although not constrained by marketplace factors, must compete for employees with private employers.

Politics also enter the wage-setting process. Most elected officials, who wish to win elections and remain in office by maximizing votes, tend to view the electorate in terms of numerous interest groups. These officials must be sensitive to the government employee groups who are directly affected by wage decisions. The larger the group, the more influence it has in the political process.

Public employers have usually provided more favorable nonwage aspects of jobs and less uncertainty. Data show that in the public sector, layoffs have been less frequent, fringe benefits generally better, and turnover lower.[43] These conditions may change as a result of the Reagan administration's budget policies.

One difficulty in public-sector wage and salary administration is the lack of ability to reward high performers. Money has become increasingly scarce, and it is frequently difficult to locate funds to institute merit pay plans. Further, raises have traditionally been awarded for time in service rather than merit. Moreover, the classification system for positions sets constraints on the amount that can be paid for specific types of jobs.[44]

Mechanisms do exist in many jurisdictions to reward outstanding employees; but these procedures are so cumbersome and difficult to employ and offer such insignificant money that for all practical purposes they do not exist.[45]

Unlike the private sector, where pay plans are still usually secret, the public sector makes pay plans open. In recent years, legislation involving freedom of information and openness has made public employees' salaries matters of public information so that citizens will know how their tax dollars are being spent. Not only are government budgets that list salaries made available, but some state and local governments also publish all salaries in newspapers.[46]

A problem not unique to the public sector is the upward pressure on wage and grade classifications. Some government agency heads contend that they cannot hire qualified persons at the salary level designated by the merit system. Some may subcontract with a university or a consulting firm, which can then hire personnel outside the merit system. Others may apply political pressure to upgrade the wage classification to justify a higher pay level. Such pressures place the personnel representative, who must administer the merit system, in a position of conflicting interests. In response to these pressures, the personnel representative seems to have three choices: (a) apply merit system standards rigidly and recognize that he or she may be forced out by the agency head because of failure to cooperate, (b) resign or seek a transfer because his or her professional integrity is being compromised, or (c) cooperate with the agency head and other administrative officials by applying the merit system standard to the extent feasible from the agency's view. Should the last alternative be chosen, the personnel representative will become an advocate for his or her agency and will quite likely have proposals for wage classification changes refused by the administrators of the merit system. Consequently, conflicts will be raised to higher levels.[47]

Labor Relations[48]

Labor relations in the public sector differ from those in the private sector in several major ways. First, the budgeting process plays a more conspicuous role in the public sector. Most budgets are posted in advance and subject to public hearings. Salaries are listed as line items, and citizens can pressure officials to keep salaries in line.

Further, the budgeting process seems to be highly flexible; budgets are padded, transfers of funds among items are made, and budgets are amended after the final approval date. Because of such flexibility, government labor relations specialists have been accused of showing little concern for financial activities. Likewise, union officials seldom let the budget influence their collective bargaining strategies and settlements. The union's major concern is to secure benefits for their members; it is up to management to find sufficient funds.

Negotiations differ in the public sector in that the chief negotiator often lacks authority to reach a final and binding agreement with the union. Many elected officials refuse to give up their authority to make final decisions on matters that they believe are important to effective governmental operations. They feel responsible directly to the electorate and do not want appointed negotiators to bind them to wage settlements and other provisions of collective bargaining agreements that they consider unworkable.

Negotiable issues differ in the public sector, because statutes exempt many traditional collective bargaining subjects from negotiation. In the federal government, under the Civil Service Reform Act of 1978, wages and position classifications of federal employees cannot be negotiated. In many states operating under merit system rules and regulations, subjects such as promotion, pension plans, and layoff procedures cannot be negotiated.

Bargaining tactics in the public sector differ as well. Certain bargaining practices allowed in the public sector would be considered unfair labor practices in the private sector. Negotiations in the private sector involve two parties—union and management. Public-sector bargaining, particularly at the state and local levels, also involves other groups, such as citizens and government officials. Thus, bargaining often becomes an exercise in politics—whom one knows and what one can do to help or hurt a government official's political career can play a decisive role. Public-sector unions often have opportunities, with the aid of the news media, to direct their appeal to the legislative body that will make final decisions on the agreement in the hope that they will gain a more favorable settlement.

Public-sector bargaining is complicated further by negotiations' being open to the public under the so-called *sunshine laws*. This approach to public-sector bargaining affects the flexibility and honesty that are necessary prerequisites of successful labor-management relationships; these qualities are often lost if union and management negotiators have to posture before a public audience.

The right to strike, considered by many a vital instrument for successful collective bargaining, is usually prohibited by statute in the public sector. Because services provided by public organizations are essential to the general welfare of the citizens, strikes are considered to create disorder in the community. The term *essential services,* however, is subject to diverse interpretations. Although services (police and fire protection, for example) are clearly essential, others are no more essential than their counterparts in private industry.

Even though strikes are prohibited in most states and the federal government statutory penalties for strikes exist, significant strikes have occurred in the public sector. They have involved teachers, firefighters, police, and sanitation workers in large cities and air traffic controllers and postal employees in the federal sector. Moreover, strikes are often continued until all strikers or discharged employees have been granted amnesty or reinstatement to former positions. While laws can cause employee dismissal and union decertification, as in the air traffic controllers' strike, laws have not prevented strikes, and discipline has not been invoked against all employees who have participated in them. Some believe that laws prohibiting strikes may have deterred some strikers, but prohibiting strikes by passing a law has not realized a great degree of success.

Summary

One of the most important influences on the personnel function in the multinational corporation involves the differences between countries. Differences exist among countries' cultures, educational and technological development, politics and governments, climates, and managerial practices. Recognition and adjustment to these differences play a large role in the personnel activities of the MNC.

Staffing activities for overseas assignments are unique. MNCs seek special qualifications in expatriate employees, such as sensitivity to foreign environments, open-mindedness, and strong family support. Preparation in terms of orientation and training is critical for overseas assignments, and training on company policies and the culture and language of the host country is an essential prerequisite. A compensation plan that includes allowances and incentives must be designed; its designers must consider tax laws and real earnings as well as equity with local nationals. Labor relations provide a real challenge, because each country has a unique system with its own labor laws.

The public sector has been characterized by significant increases in employment, especially at the state and local levels. Although the principles of personnel administration are the same in the private and public sectors, there are differences. The nature of operations differs, because public organizations do not operate in a market economy. Merit systems were developed to enable public organizations to hire on the basis of qualifications and to pay and promote on the basis of performance. However, the operation of these systems has been compromised by political intervention. Examinations play an important role in applying merit principles. Laws relating to public-sector employees have been changing; for example, EEO laws now extend their requirements to public staffing decisions. Performance appraisal has received increased attention because of the emphasis on accountability. One concern in wage and salary administration is to maintain comparability with similar private-sector jobs. Labor relations activities are affected by laws requiring openness, restrictions on the right to strike, and complexities of bargaining structures.

Discussion Questions

1. Design in outline form a training program for an executive who is being transferred to an underdeveloped country. What obstacles must be overcome? What adjustments must be made by the executive and by the family?

2. Design a compensation package that would make a foreign assignment attractive to a fast-track executive.

3. Explain the unique aspects of the public sector and how this uniqueness affects the personnel function.

4. Why are the principles of personnel management generally the same in the public sector as the private sector?

5. What principles studied in Chapters 14 and 15 can be used in public-sector labor relations?

6. Under what conditions, if any, do you think public employees should be allowed to strike?

Notes

1. Edwin B. Gilroy, David M. Noer, and James E. Spoor, "Personnel Administration in the Multinational/Transnational Corporation," in *PAIR Policy and Program Management,* ed. Dale Yoder and H. G. Heneman, Jr. Washington D.C.: Bureau of National Affairs, 1978), pp. 1-121–1-147.

2. Richard F. Janssen, "U.S. Companies Profit from Investments They Made Years Ago in Plants Overseas," *Wall Street Journal,* March 11, 1981, p. 56.

3. Gilroy, "Personnel Administration," p. 1-147.

4. R. L. Desatnick and M. L. Bennett, *Human Resource Management in the Multinational Company* (New York: Nichols, 1978), p. 4.

5. *Ibid.,* pp. 5-28.

6. Franklin R. Root and David A. Heenan, "Staffing the Overseas Unit," in *Handbook of Modern Personnel Administration,* ed. Joseph J. Famularo (New York: McGraw-Hill, 1972), pp. 56-3–56-15.

7. "A U.S. Turn to Native in Japan," *Business Week,* December 8, 1980, p. 56.

8. Root and Heenan, "Staffing the Overseas Unit," p. 56-14.

9. *Ibid.,* pp. 56-12–56-13.

10. Desatnick and Bennett, *Human Resource Management,* p. 5.

11. Frederick A. Teague, "International Management Selection and Development," *California Management Review* 12 (Spring 1970), pp. 1–2.

12. Root and Heenan, "Staffing the Overseas Unit," pp. 56-4–56-8.

13. "Gauging a Family's Suitability for a Stint Overseas," *Business Week,* April 16, 1979, p. 127.

14. Root and Heenan, "Staffing the Overseas Unit," pp. 56-14–56-15.

15. Alison R. Lanier, "Selecting and Preparing Personnel for Overseas Transfers," *Personnel Journal* 58 (March 1979), pp. 161–162.

16. *Ibid.,* p. 160.

17. Edwin B. Gilroy, pp. 1-132–1-133.

18. Root and Heenan, "Staffing the Overseas Unit," p. 56-14.

19. Kenneth Lefkovwitz, "Getting More Mileage from Overseas Pay," *Compensation Review* 8, (1st quarter, 1976), pp. 27–29.

20. Alfred J. Figliola, "Compensation of Overseas Personnel," in *Handbook of Modern Personnel Administration,* ed. Joseph J. Famularo (New York: McGraw-Hill, 1972), pp. 57-1–57-7.

21. For more coverage, see pp. 494–518 of *The Labor Relations Process* by William H. Holley, Jr., and Kenneth M. Jennings. Copyright © 1980 by Dryden Press, a division of Holt, Rinehart and Winston, Inc., Publishers. Reprinted by permission of Holt, Rinehart and Winston, CBS College Publishing.

22. John T. Tucker, "Government Employment: An Era of Slow Growth," *Monthly Labor Review* 104 (October 1981), p. 19.

23. Richard A. Snelling, "How Competent Are the State Governments?" *Wall Street Journal,* October 30, 1981, p. 30.

24. Tucker, "Government Employment," p. 19.

25. Laurence C. Caffin and Terrell G. Manyak, "PAIR Management in the Public Service," in *PAIR Policy and Program Management,* ed. Dale Yoder and H. G. Heneman, Jr. (Washington, D.C.: Bureau of National Affairs, 1978), pp. 1-99.

26. William H. Holley, Jr., "Unique Complexities of Public Sector Labor Relations," *Personnel Journal* (February 1976), pp. 72–73.

27. E. S. Savas and Sigmund G. Ginsburg, "The Civil Service: A Meritless System?" *Public Interest,* Summer 1973, pp. 70–71.

28. Caffin and Manyak, "PAIR Management in the Public Service," p. 1-100.

29. Savas and Ginsburg, "The Civil Service." pp. 71–73.

30. *Ibid.* pp. 70–85. Adapted by permission. © 1973 by National Affairs, Inc.

31. Jay M. Shafritz, Albert C. Hyde, and David H. Rosenbloom, *Personnel Management in Government* (New York: Marcel Dekker, 1981), pp. 164–165.

32. *Ibid.*

33. N. Joseph Cayer, *Managing Human Resources: An Introduction to Public Personnel Administration* (New York: St. Martins Press, 1980), pp. 110–111.

34. Robert D. Krause, "Public Personnel in a Changing World," *Public Personnel Management* 8 (September/October 1979), p. 341.

35. Cayer, *Managing Human Resources,* pp. 4–5.

36. *Ibid.,* p. 151.

37. David H. Rosenbloom, "Public Personnel Administration and the Constitution: An Emergent Approach," *Public Administration Review* 35 (February 1975), pp. 52–59.

38. *Ibid.*

39. *Ibid.*

40. Russel E. Palmer, "Making Government Accountable," *Business Week,* February 11, 1980, p. 21.

41. Shafritz, Hyde, and Rosenbloom, *Personnel Management,* pp. 336–338.

42. *Ibid.,* p. 327.

43. Walter Fogel and David Lewin, "Wage Determination in the Public Sector," *Industrial and Labor Relations Review* 27 (April 1974), pp. 410–431.

44. *Ibid.*

45. Shafritz, Hyde, and Rosenbloom, *Personnel Management,* p. 335.

46. Cayer, *Managing Human Resources,* p. 88.

47. Bernard H. Baum, *Decentralization of Authority in a Bureaucracy* (Englewood Cliffs, N.J.: Prentice-Hall, 1961), pp. 89–104.

48. For more coverage, see Holley and Jennings, *Labor Relations Process,* pp. 430–492.

Chapter 20

The Personnel Function: Research, Assessment, and Prospects for the Future

One of the perennial problems with research in any field has been
the translation of research findings into practical applications. This
problem seems to be especially critical in connection with
behavioral science developments. In many companies there is more
than just a time lag in adopting innovative approaches that have
been proven effective; often there is failure to adopt any
innovative approaches at all.

Reprinted by permission from Herbert H. Meyer, "PAIR Research," in
Planning and Auditing PAIR, edited by Dale Yoder and H. G. Heneman,
Jr., p. 2-127, copyright 1976 by The Bureau of National Affairs, Inc.,
Washington, D.C.

This chapter surveys three interrelated subjects that contribute to the advancement of the personnel function. First, personnel research will be considered broadly. We include in this category not only the critical assessment of innovative and creative personnel activities but also investigative analyses concerning organizational problem solving for improving the personnel function. Much of this book has assumed that the personnel function could be improved. The second section, on assessment of the personnel function, will reveal the current status of the major personnel activities based on expert opinion. This assessment will focus on the degree to which the objectives of personnel activities are being achieved in organizations today. Finally, based on past and present assessments and on contributions of innovative personnel activities, projections and directions for the personnel function will be discussed.

Personnel Research

Personnel research is becoming more relevant and more prevalent, essentially because of externally imposed demands related to equal employment opportunity and internally imposed demands related to accountability for personnel activities and to increasing the productivity of human resources. Personnel researchers are involved in these challenging areas, which have given impetus for renewed interest in research by both personnel professionals and academicians.[1] However, personnel research also faces problems. One researcher describes the situation as follows:

Personnel research pervades all of the functional areas of personnel administration. In many respects, the future of the personnel administration field rests upon our ability to refine and develop techniques, practices, and strategic approaches to the ongoing problems in personnel. Research has traditionally produced innovations in areas such as job analysis, staffing, and performance measurements, job satisfaction and employment morale and personnel forecasting and planning. More recently, research has provided answers to organizational problems in the areas of equal employment opportunity and equal pay administration.

Why then does there remain the doubt and skepticism about the practicality of [personnel] research among practitioners and administrators? For years we have observed that there is a large gap between the subject matter and findings of personnel research efforts and the practical problems in the field. Concern over the sometimes 'esoteric'' nature of personnel research creates frustration on the parts of those who are involved in producing research as well as those who are involved in solving personnel problems. More importantly, however, much potential understanding and useful information is lost because of misunderstanding over the means and ends of personnel research.[2]

**Types of Personnel
Research**

Personnel research can be categorized according to six major types—experimental research, case studies, surveys, analysis of employee data, legal and quasi-legal research, and secondary research.

Experimental Research The most creative type and the one most likely to advance the personnel function is experimental research.[3] Experimental research usually involves a new program or a new direction for an existing program, such as a wage incentive program to increase productivity. The research design calls for an experimental group (a group to work under the new wage incentive program, for example) and a control, or comparison, group (a group that will *not* work under the new program); also skilled researchers must be employed if any sophisticated analysis is required.

Before the new program is introduced on a broad scale, it should be carefully analyzed and assessed. Because many organizations are reluctant to experiment when the risks of failure are high, researchers—especially academicians—often rely on laboratory studies, which can be carefully controlled. Many such experimental studies are conducted on campuses; a typical example might involve a comparison of negative and positive feedback concerning a performance appraisal interview. While the natural concern about the results of laboratory studies involves their transferability to the real world, each experiment advances our knowledge about personnel activities. Ideally, the results should be published so that others can share in the researchers' findings.

Case Studies The intensive case study revolves around an organization or a specific personnel activity. Personnel researchers may rely on sources of information, such as company policies and records, or interviews with organizational personnel. One of the most noted examples of the case study method is the Hawthorne Studies, discussed earlier in this text. Many other case studies have been written by personnel professionals about their experiences in specific programs, such as job enrichment programs, drug-abuse programs, union-management quality of working life programs, and the like. All help others become more knowledgeable and thus help advance the personnel function.

Surveys Surveys may be conducted within or outside the organization. Surveys within the organization usually include attitude or organizational climate surveys, which assess employees' opinions, attitudes, and beliefs about their jobs, organization, pay, supervision, and other job-related considerations. Some organizations conduct these surveys routinely so they can continually monitor personnel-related concerns. Analysis of the survey data enables the organization to identify such things as early signals of employee dissatisfaction, possible problems with particular supervisors, and employees' reactions to new programs.

External surveys are frequently conducted by organizations to determine what other organizations are doing with regard to a particular personnel activity. As mentioned in an earlier chapter, a commonly conducted external survey is the wage survey, which is used to determine the labor market wage rate. On a broader scale, national surveys are conducted by government agencies, trade associations, groups such as the Conference Board, and reporting services such as the Bureau of National Affairs, Commerce Clearing House, and Prentice-Hall. Although these national surveys cannot be readily applied to an individual organization, the survey results give an indication of what other organizations are doing, provide the current status of particular personnel activities on a national scale, and give trends and projections for these activities.

Analysis of Employee Data Analysis of employee records and data takes advantage of records and data that are currently available within the organization or that can be secured. Exhibit 20.1 shows various types of employee data that can be obtained. If the personnel data are kept in a computerized form called a *personnel information system*—skilled researchers can analyze enormous volumes of data highly useful to the organization. Typical studies include the relationships between turnover and personnel characteristics such as age, sex, race, education, and so on. Further, measurements of performance can be correlated with test scores, interviewers' assessments and biographical data. Performance, absenteeism, turnover, and other employee data can be translated into employment costs per unit output. Examples of more uses of personnel data appear in Exhibit 20.2. Such analyses can contribute significantly to the effectiveness of personnel activities by enabling personnel managers to assess the costs of human resources and by making the personnel department more accountable for many of its activities.[4]

The ready availability of personnel records and banks of data stored in computerized personnel information systems has led to a rise in employees' concern about the privacy of their records. Employees are raising the question of possible misuse of these data by unauthorized personnel. Casual handling of private records by personnel departments has heightened the possibility of governmental intervention in personnel activities. In fact, twenty-four states already have legislation to protect employees' privacy; six more states have had legislation introduced; and the federal government has enacted a law guaranteeing privacy of personnel data.[5]

Legal and Quasi-Legal Research Legal and quasi-legal research may not be considered personnel research in its purest form, even though it is extremely important to the personnel function. This type of research involves analysis of employment discrimination and labor arbitration cases, which may take a sizable amount of time in some large organizations. In analyzing employment discrimination cases, personnel researchers may seek legal cases in which they can identify principles useful to the company's positions in an EEO suit. For example, suppose that a minority employee denied promotion files a discrimination charge and that performance appraisal was used as the basis for the promotion decision. A review and analysis of similar cases would assist the company in formulating the position it would take before the EEOC or, later, the court. While this work may be assigned to corporate attorneys, familiarity with the legal research process will add significantly to the value of the personnel researcher.

Similarly, in preparing for an arbitration hearing (called a quasi-legal procedure), researchers will find it valuable to conduct case analysis to identify principles and apply these principles to the company's positions in the forthcoming arbitration hearing. Such cases are available in their original form from the Bureau of National Affairs, Commerce Clearing House, Prentice-Hall, and the American Arbitration Association. Personnel researchers frequently take advantage of these sources.

Secondary Research In using the last type of personnel research, secondary research, the researcher synthesizes information from publications on a particular topic for a specific purpose. Although this research is not classified as creative or innovative, it often requires creative and innovative analysis and interpretation. For example, an organization may be considering the introduction of a management-by-objectives

---

Exhibit 20.1   **Components of a Personnel Information System**

Personal Data
Name
Pay number or social security number
Sex
Date of birth
Physical description of employee
  (height, weight, color of eyes, etc.)
Names, sex, and birth dates of
  dependents
Marital status
Employee association participation
United Fund/Community Chest
  participation
Minority group classification

Recruiting Data
Date of recruiting contact

Responsible recruiter or interviewer
Source of candidate referral (newspaper
  ad, employment agency, etc.)

Benefit Plan Data
Medical and/or life insurance plan
  participation
Pension plan participation
Savings plan participation (U.S. bonds,
  etc.)
Pay for time not worked (vacation,
  illness, lost-time accidents, personal
  time off, death in family, jury duty,
  military reserve duty, etc.)
Tuition refund plan participation
Etc.

Exhibit 20.1   **Continued**

Separation from Payroll Data

Date of removal from payroll
Reason for leaving
Forwarding address
Name and address of new employer
Amount of pay increase obtained with
    new employer
Eligibility for rehire

Safety/Accident Data

Noise level (in decibels) in work area
Exposure to noxious fumes or chemicals
    on job
Record of injury (date of accident, date
    reported, nature of injury, cause of
    injury, record of medical attention
    given, name of attending physician)
Classification of injury (disabling or
    nondisabling, days of work lost, lost
    time charged)
Physical limitations resulting from injury
Workmen's compensation claim data

Open Jobs or Positions Data

Job request control number
Job title
Position or job code
Educational requirements
Experience requirements
Permissible salary range
Date by which the position must be
    filled

Work Environment Data

Average educational level of co-workers
Average salary of co-workers
Number of job openings in component
Date of referral of candidate or
    application to interested management
Names of supervisors or managers
    referred to
Date of interview(s)
Date of offer of employment
Date added to payroll
Reasons for selection/rejection of
    candidate
Test scores and interviewer ratings
Number of jobs open for which
    candidate was potentially qualified
Number of other applicants for same
    open job or jobs.

Work Experience Data

Names and locations of previous
    employers

Prior employment chronology
Military service
Job skills possessed
Percent employees terminating
    employment (for some standard
    period)
Accident frequency and severity rates
    for position or component
Relative frequency of job changes in
    component
Manager's or supervisor's age
Manager's or supervisor's years
    supervisory experience
Selection or inheritance of employee by
    present manager
Relative frequency of manager's or
    supervisor's disciplinary actions
Manager's or supervisor's tendency
    toward strict or lenient rating of
    employees
Amount of overtime worked in
    component
Percent of employees dissatisfied with
    work, pay, supervisor, etc. in
    component

Position/Job History Data

Job or position ID number
Job or position code
Date job or position was established
Permanent/temporary classification
    of job
Identity of past incumbents in the job
Dates of change in job incumbents
Dates of vacancies in positions
Type of change involved for each
    person leaving the position (newly
    hired, lateral transfer, promotion from
    another position)
If a promotion, identity of position
    promoted from
Location of job in organization structure
Manager or supervisor to whom
    position reports

Labor Market Data

Analysis of local manpower availability
Unemployment levels by skill,
    occupation, age, sex, etc.
Predicted future manpower needs
Identification of scarce and surplus
    manpower pools
Wage and salary, shift differentials, etc.
Product line experience
Managerial or supervisory experience

Exhibit 20.1	Continued

Foreign languages spoken, written, read
Publications authored
Special skills or hobbies of potential value to the business
Patents held
Elective governmental positions
Security clearances held

Educational Data

College degree, high school diploma, level of educational attainment
Field of degree
Date of degree
Schools attended
Special employer sponsored courses completed
Professional licenses held

Compensation/Work Assignment Data

Exempt/nonexempt or hourly/salaried classification
Current salary or pay rate
Date of current salary level
Date and amount of next forecast salary/pay increase
Previous pay rates and dates effective
Previous dollar and percent increase and dates of increase
Organizational reporting level
Position title
Supervisor/individual contributor status
Job code
Hours worked
Premium time hours worked

Performance Evaluation Promotability Data

Personal interests
Work preferences
Geographical preferences (for multiplant operations)
Level of aspiration
Rank value of contribution in current work group
Special nominations and awards
Appraisal reports
Date of last appraisal
Growth potential as rated by manager
Previous promotions considered for, and dates of consideration
Dates of demotion
Reason for demotion

Date of last internal transfer
Dates considered for apprenticeship or other special training
Reasons for elimination from consideration for apprenticeship or other special training
Dates of, type, and reason for disciplinary action

Length of Service/Layoff Data

Date hired by employer (actual or adjusted for lost service)
Seniority date (if different from date of hire)
Date of layoff
Last pay rate
Recall status

Employee Attitude/Morale Data

Productivity/quality measures
Absenteeism record
Tardiness record
Suggestions submitted (usually to a formal suggestion plan)
Grievances
Anonymous inquiries/complaints
Perceived fairness of management practices regarding employees
Perceived fairness and soundness of management philosophy
Attitudes about credibility/honesty of management
Attitudes toward work, pay, supervisor, etc.

Union Membership Data

Union membership/representation status
Controlling union contract
Union officer status
Dues checkoff status

Location/Contact Data

Home address
City and state
Zip code
Home phone
Present component and work assignment
Geographic location of work assignment
Office phone
Emergency notification

Source: Reprinted by permission from Glenn A. Bassett, ''PAIR Records and Information Systems,'' in *Planning and Auditing PAIR*, edited by Dale Yoder and H. G. Heneman, Jr., pp. 2-66–2-68, copyright 1976 by The Bureau of National Affairs, Inc., Washington, D.C.

Exhibit 20.2   **Uses of Personnel Data**

Employee age distributions and retirement analyses
Equal employment opportunity reports and analyses
Budgeting for recruiting
Prediction of success in finding specific work skills at desired salaries
Identification of good and poor selection practices
Description of the candidate pool attracted by the employer
Description of the time span required to fill an open position
Identification of effective and ineffective recruitment sources
Identification of employees for promotion, reassignment, or special assignment
Justification of salaried or job titles
Analyses of the availability of existing job skills for changes in product mix or work
Planning for availability of critical manpower types
Planning college recruitment
Comparison of individual salary growth rates
Creation of salary curves
Control of salary budgets
Tracking and control of pay increases
Tracking of pay increase policies and practices
Analyses of employee losses by component, educational level, quality of
    performance, etc.
Systematic control of bumping and recall situations
Monitoring appraisal practices
Analysis of absenteeism and tardiness patterns
Tracking of changes in attitudes for comparison with observed changes in the
    business
Monitoring relations with the union
Sending out special notices and letters
Drawing samples for representative surveys of employees
Identifying geographic distribution of employees for purposes of distributing United
    Fund gifts, encouraging car-pools, etc.
Analyzing the return on investment from benefits expenditures
Analysis of the competitiveness of pay rates from losses to other employers
Identification of patterns of safety hazards
Provision of OSHA reports and analyses
Control of hiring requests to assure consonance with manning authorizations
Identification of environmental factors which most affect attitudes, turnover,
    productivity, etc.
Analysis of career movement patterns, including identification of fast-track or dead-
    end jobs, etc.
Prediction of potential skill shortages and training needs.

program, a flexitime program, or a retirement preparation plan. Top
management may want an analysis of the program's effect on the personnel function, its advantages and disadvantages, the experiences of
other organizations, and so on. The personnel professional can research the professional literature, such as the journals in Exhibit 20.3,
to make the analysis and prepare recommendations.

As to the future of personnel research, one view is offered by Herbert
H. Meyer, who was General Electric's personnel research manager for
two decades.

| Exhibit 20.3 | Journals Covering Topics Relating to the Personnel Function |

Employee Relations Law Journal
Industrial Relations
Industrial and Labor Relations Review
Journal of Applied Psychology
Labor Law Journal
Personnel

Personnel Administrator
Personnel Journal
Personnel Psychology
Public Personnel Management
Training and Development Journal

The success of American industry has been attributed to the fact that technical and organizational problems have been approached in a very *systematic* manner. Innovative practices emanating from the scientific management movement were adopted and developed to their fullest potential by American business leaders in the first half of this century. There is no reason to expect that in the second half of the century American business leaders will not also apply this systematic approach to the complex area of human relations.[7]

Because the role of personnel research is so important and has so much potential for contributing to organizational effectiveness, it seems inevitable that this role will expand. With rapid technological advances affecting attitudes and behavior of employees, creative approaches to work-related concerns must be sought and examined. Younger employees are less receptive to authoritarian leadership, and researchers must therefore continue to study supervisory behavior and leadership styles. Shifts from a blue-collar workforce to a predominantly white-collar workforce with more education and a stronger need for self-actualization will require imaginative approaches to management of personnel. The value of personnel research and personnel researchers is yet unrealized. However, large companies are organizing specific research units, and small companies are participating in joint research efforts. The latter part of this century will show significant progress in this personnel activity.[6]

Assessment of the Personnel Function

U.S. employers spend 2.5 percent of their payroll costs and a median of $437,448 on personnel activities and employ one personnel department employee for every hundred employees in the workforce. Thus, organizations are becoming increasingly interested in assessing the personnel function.[8] In fact, some firms now systematically assess their present personnel activities and programs in terms of ease of implementation, net economic benefits, and economic risks of not acting. Systematic assessment has instilled discipline in the personnel staff and encouraged them to move away from intuitive techniques to more rigorous assessment of the likely benefits to be achieved.[9] "Personnel must establish credibility with management by justifying its programs and clearly demonstrating how it contributes to the attainment of organizational goals. Personnel must be evaluated in terms of its contribution to the effectiveness with which an organization attains its particular goals."[10] Organizations are developing criteria and indices (or yardsticks) to measure the effectiveness of the personnel function. Several instruments, called *audits*, have been designed to assist in the assessment.

Before determining whether the personnel department is effective in administering its responsibilities, we must consider some of the indicators of effectiveness. One indicator of effectiveness is the degree to which top management supports personnel representatives and relies on their inputs and recommendations in its decision making and planning. Because top management sets the tone for the personnel function in the organization, managers' and employees' perceptions of top management's view of the personnel function influence their own views and thus influence the extent to which the personnel department can serve the organization.

Another indicator of effectiveness is the contribution of the personnel function to overall profitability. Assessment should be made of the various personnel activities' relative benefits and costs and the savings they make possible by preventing personnel problems. An assessment of how well the personnel department's goals mesh with those of the company and how effectively they contribute toward the achievement of these goals is desirable. The degree to which the personnel staff is effective in dealing with special problems and changes in the operating departments should be considered. Data on other, more quantifiable, indicators of effectiveness—such as job satisfaction, absenteeism, turnover, productivity, and accidents—can be collected, maintained, analyzed, and assessed.

While it is important to recognize the indicators of effectiveness, it is also important to identify factors that indicate ineffectiveness. They include the following:

Top management deemphasizes the role of operating department managers in carrying out personnel functions.

Management underestimates the capacity of the personnel staff to contribute to organizational effectiveness.

The personnel staff provides too many services within its limited budget allotment.

Personnel goals are integrated with company goals in the planning stages but not in the results stages.

The personnel staff is used by top management as its "eyes and ears" in dealing with lower management, thereby raising suspicions of the personnel representatives' role.[11]

Measurements of Performance

Determining the return on the corporation's personnel dollar involves taking a profit-oriented approach to assessing the effectiveness of personnel activities. One advocate of this approach has stated:

> Management must constantly demonstrate that its efforts make sense quantitatively—in objective, cold, hard-cash terms. Of course, such matters as the quality of worklife, employee morale, social responsibility, and business ethics are also concerns of every company today, and they are attended to—right after the profit plan. Profits aren't measured in terms of goodness, righteousness, or other esthetic indexes. They are expressed in hard dollars. Therefore, if the human resources department wants to join the profit team along with marketing, manufacturing, and the rest of the high-status departments, it will have to start looking for and pointing out its contribution to profits.[12]

Personnel professionals must seek accurate and acceptable tools of persuasion. Nothing is more convincing to top management than contributions to profit and productivity shown in objective indices. Personnel departments, with so much data available—salary and benefits costs, employment information required by federal agencies, absentee and turnover data, and so on—have an objective measurement system at their fingertips. Reports on staffing, training, wages and benefits, performance, and other personnel activities can provide top management with a clear picture of contribution of the personnel function. Moreover, these reports provide information in language top management understands.[13]

Because of top management's performance orientation, data on the personnel activities have been converted into quantifiable terms. Exhibit 20.4 displays typical data that can be quantified for use in profit-oriented assessment.

Personnel Audits

The personnel audit is an assessment technique that provides a comprehensive analysis of all aspects of the personnel function. The audit is conducted to upgrade personnel activities, help achieve overall organizational objectives, and raise the consciousness of the organization concerning the personnel function and a data base from which constructive change can take place. Because the audit usually uncovers needs for change, it serves as a useful instrument for change.[14]

The personnel auditing process includes five steps:

1. Preparing a diagnostic instrument, such as a questionnaire or interview guide. This instrument includes items to assess

Exhibit 20.4

Typical Data Used in Assessing the Personnel Function

Personnel Activity	Examples of Data for Assessment
Hiring	Costs per applicant source; offers made compared with offers accepted; time spent interviewing, testing, etc.; relocation costs; selection ratios by job type
Recruiting	Cost of hiring, by source; hiring rate; types of interview, rejection rates and reasons, retention rates and reasons for applicants' declinations
Training	Knowledge and skill improvement on prehiring and post-hiring tests for each training module; retention of trainees; cost per training activity; comparison of in-house and outside programs.
Salary Administration	Salary comparison by race, sex, age, etc.; comparison of merit increases with performance ratings; comparison of salary levels with external labor market levels
Benefits Administration	Average costs per employee; percent of payroll; participation in various plans; cost of record keeping and claim processing; turnaround time per claim; employee knowledge of benefits
Performance Appraisal	Errors (halo, inflation, central tendency); reliability and validity; time spent on performance feedback
Labor Relations Activities	Number of grievances per 100 employees; grievances settled at each step; disciplinary action taken, by offense and penalty; cost of negotiation and preparation; costs of strikes; costs of union avoidance programs; effect of cooperative programs
Safety Administration	Severity and frequency rates; lost time; accidents, by type and time of day; overall costs
Provision of Services (Publications, Cafeteria, Recreation, Credit Union, Stress Reduction and Health Programs, etc.)	Participation; time spent; costs; effect on attitudes
Employee Behavior	
Lost Time	Absences, turnover, accidents, and sick leave by job, department, and employee characteristics; results of counseling and exit interviews
Job Satisfaction	Attitude surveys (comparison over time and with comparable organizations); absences; turnover; grievances; tenure of service; performance

Sources: Information from Jac Fitz-Enz, "Quantifying the Human Resources Function," *Personnel* 57 (March/April 1980), pp. 41–52; Frank E. Kuzmits, "How Much Is Absenteeism Costing Your Organization," *Personnel Administrator* 24 (June 1979), pp. 29–33; W. F. Rabe, "Yardsticks for Measuring Personnel Department Effectiveness," *Personnel* 44 (January/February 1967), pp. 56–62.

managers' and employees' contacts with the personnel department, to evaluate the department's performance, acceptance of suggestions, follow-up on requests, assistance in promotions and transfers, compliance with government regulations, communication of personnel policies, and so on.

2. Selecting respondents. Respondents may include a random sampling of employees for broad representation and may include all supervisors for political reasons, if it is discovered that supervisors do not want to be left out.
3. Gathering data by questionnaires or interviews. Respondents are guaranteed confidentiality and anonymity.
4. Analyzing data. Analysis includes tabulation of data by hand or computer to provide a general assessment of various personnel activities and also includes appropriate content analysis of handwritten comments and suggestions.
5. Taking corrective action based on employees' and managers' evaluations and recommendations. Examples of positive steps include reorganizing the personnel department so that each personnel representative will specialize in one personnel activity in order to provide better service to line management, devoting more time to staffing activities that will facilitate promotion and hiring decisions, and making more effort to help line management determine training need.[15]

The audit, if it is conducted by people within the organization, should be conducted by experienced line managers and personnel professionals from another division of the organization.[16] A few organizations hire teams of outside professionals to conduct personnel audits. While insiders know more about the organization, and the costs of using them are lower, outside auditors are more objective, have less ego-involvement in company activities, and tend to uncover problems that in-house auditors may overlook. When sensitive issues such as compliance with government regulations, compatibility between the organization's goals and those of the personnel department, and performance of the personnel department are considered, an external team may be more appropriate.[17]

Prospects for the Personnel Function

As noted in Chapter 1, personnel representatives attempt to work with and through employees to achieve organizational objectives. The personnel department also helps other managers realize that employees are a most important resource, particularly under today's changing conditions.[18]

Signs of the times include unprecedented problems of inflation, widespread youth unemployment, energy supply, environmental improvement, consumerism, minority rights, gay power, and political activism. The tide of working women continues unabated, with altered family and workplace values in its wake. Government no longer concentrates merely on legislating new benefits or protecting traditional ones, but instead increasingly regulates to assure compliance with administrative law and to cater to the sentiments of special interest groups. Users of human resources in our nation are learning to manage enterprises successfully in a low-growth economy where productivity gains are harder to find and where relatively expensive capital and credit continue to be funneled to clean up the environment and develop domestic supplies of energy. The times have changed and many segments of our society are marching to the beat of a different drummer.[19]

The efforts of the personnel department to help the organization cope with these changing conditions are influenced by three general issues also cited in Chapter 1:

To what extent can the organization adapt to employees' concerns, and vice versa?

What is the relationship of the personnel department to other organizational departments?

To what degree is the personnel department presently effective in its various activities?

The final issue has been discussed in the preceding section; of the other two issues, the first can be said to involve the personnel department's relations with employees, while the second involves the personnel department's role in the organization. These issues are addressed in the remainder of this section.

The Personnel Department and Employees

Changing employee characteristics and values have been discussed elsewhere in this book, particularly in Chapters 1 and 16, and won't be discussed here in great detail. Suffice it to say that employees want organizations to recognize their unique qualities[20] and fulfill their increased expectations,[21] even though many of these employees are more loyal to their occupations or professions than to their employers.[22] Adding to these problems is a potential decline in the absolute numbers of the workforce,[23] and many organizations are having difficulties in replacing employees in certain skilled job classifications.[24]

Some organizations appear to have dramatically adapted to employees' concerns. One example is provided by Eaton Corporation. The chairman explains:

When we looked at our traditional practices, it was obvious that they weren't designed for rushing into the 21st century. These practices were born of mistrust, agitation, and negotiation. This was apparent in the paraphernalia and terminology that went along with them. We had the tyrannical time clocks and mindless bells and buzzers. We had probationary periods, posted work rules, disciplinary proceedings, and restrictive holiday-eligibility rules for production workers that stamped them as second-class members of the total team.

The building of so many new plants gave us a unique opportunity to start from scratch, and our employee relations people were challenged to break away from tradition and develop a program built on mutual trust.[25]

Today, about twenty of Eaton's plants operate without time clocks or whistles. All employees—managerial, office, and production—are salaried and participate in major operational decisions. Attendance policies have been liberalized as well. As a result of this new approach, employees' attitudes have changed dramatically; and they exhibit a feeling of involvement and a sense of belonging. Production increases have ranged as high as 40 percent, absenteeism averages 2 percent and turnover is almost nonexistent.[26]

Other organizations, through various personnel activities such as human resource planning, internal staffing activities, performance appraisals, and so on, have also recognized and met employees' unique needs.

In the future, significant employee-oriented changes in personnel activities probably will involve compensation and reward systems. Compensation plans will become more and more individualized to accommodate employees' preferences and reinforce individual behavior. In addition, the use of cash bonus plans (lump-sum merit increases) identified with predetermined work standards and productivity goals will likely increase.[27] Use of peer input in bonus determination as well as goal-oriented performance appraisals may become common for managerial positions. While the debate will continue on whether performance appraisals can serve two purposes (appraisal for development versus appraisal for merit increases),[28] pay-for-performance policies probably will be continued regardless of whether they will be operationalized.

In the area of training and development, changes may be more apparent than real. In spite of new directions such as assertiveness training and value clarification sessions, one personnel expert concludes that:

The bread-and-butter of training will remain: apprenticeship programs; trainee foreman and new first-level staff supervisory programs; college graduate orientation and induction efforts; on-site and off-site middle management seminars; specialized training for sales and marketing personnel; and refresher training for engineers, technicians, and skilled trades employees.

Such programs will continue for the next two decades, although formal programs for highly educated employees in management positions (defined as those who supervise the work of others) may actually be less numerous than today. There will instead be greater use made of on-the-job training and senior executive coaching, well-arranged job rotation, fast track programs especially for minority group members, and sophisticated career planning.[29]

The personnel function will continue to identify more ways to use computers to effectively serve employees and the organization. The speed of processing information and the capacity for storing personnel data will progress rapidly. Many more personnel professionals will have desk-top computer terminals that tie into the central computer, enhancing their ability to retrieve information and solve problems. The computer facilitates human resource planning activities by quickly providing personnel data from skills inventory systems; maintaining records of transactions such as promotions, retirements, and changes in employee status; retrieving employee records rapidly; and modeling human resource needs under conditions of growth, stability, or decline. Computers can help plan career paths for younger managers and professionals and help coordinate executive succession planning.[30] Labor relations specialists will rely more on computers to develop the company's positions and estimate the costs of union proposals. Computers will reduce the normal drudgery of paperwork required to comply with government regulations, especially those involving EEO matters. Further, the rapid processing of personnel data allows up-to-date analysis of workforce composition and allows the company to monitor its status on a continuing basis.[31]

Organizations have come a long way from the commodity approach to employees discussed in Chapter 2. The personnel department in most cases has played a significant role in changing this organizational attitude, and its various activities have enabled the organization to adapt to employees' interests. Employees, too, must be willing to adapt to organizational objectives. Determining and effecting the proper balance will be a major challenge and opportunity for the personnel function in the years ahead.

The Personnel Department in the Organization

As discussed in Chapter 1, personnel activities involve various organization members. Some activities, such as wage surveys, are undertaken solely by personnel representatives, while other activities, such as personnel forecasting, involve personnel representatives and other organizational managers. The relationship between personnel and other managers has been discussed throughout the book and will not be reiterated here. Instead, this discussion will focus on the changing role of the personnel department in the organization.

The remaining years of this century will see changes in the personnel job itself as well as in the expectations of and the requirements for it. These changes are very much intertwined, because changes in the job will occur only if the personnel function performs in accordance with changed expectations and demands.[32]

One change already occurring in many organizations involves the role of the personnel department as an anticipator of problems concerning employees and personnel activities. The personnel professional must identify problems and must view himself or herself as a preventor of problems, rather than a reactor to them.

This means that personnel departments will have to develop more extensive sensing devices to discover what the problems of the future will be rather than awaiting their arrival when it may be too late. The occupational safety and health law of the late 60s and early 70s caught many unaware; yet, such a law had been thrown into the legislative hopper many times before. In its enactment it contained a three-year early warning period for emergency convenience, but many personnel and safety departments were caught napping. In their preoccupation with immediate problems, personnel departments often ignore the many services which provide early warning for impending major changes. Keeping up with legislation and watching for changing cultural and social values which could alter personnel strategy will become a major requirement.[33]

Top management will depend more on the personnel function in organization-wide planning and controlling activities. Human resource planning, staffing, compensation, government compliance, and training are activities that affect total organizational performance and thus profitability.

Increasingly, top management looks to personnel for some very practical means to get better people, train them better, organize their work more effectively, evaluate them, and compensate their performance on a more equitable and effective basis.

The key word for personnel executives has become "motivate"; the key objective, creating a "climate of motivation." And this climate of motivation, as explained by one executive, calls for managing people so that their imagination and initiative, as well as their hands, are directed to the task of company survival and growth.[34]

Accompanying the emphasis on developing a motivational climate is the greater involvement of the personnel function in setting objectives, establishing standards, and measuring performance. The personnel staff has input into the planning process and provides information on such measures as turnover, absenteeism, accidents, incentive payments, performance appraisals, and training participation, which are important in the evaluation phases of the controlling process.

Personnel departments will continue their important role as internal consultants to line management. This role introduces and applies behavioral science insights in a manner contributing to the effective management of human resources. However, "consultants" must also understand the operational end of the organization; their knowledge must extend beyond personnel techniques to several management areas such as sales, production, and accounting.[35]

Additional Challenges

There will be other challenges to personnel professionals that will call for the highest degree of creativity. These challenges include:

Charges of sex and race discrimination resulting from women and minority employees' experiencing career stagnation while white males continue to dominate the upper circles of the corporate structure.

Demands for flexible policies to handle the responsibilities of two-career families.

Shortages of entry-level workers to operate machines. Loosening of immigration regulations to allow admittance of unprecedented numbers of new workers, predominantly from third-world countries. Litigation on national origin discrimination may increase as these workers seek to move upward.

Reassignments and lateral transfers of older employees who have contributed a lifetime to their employer but whose technical skills have become obsolete and who are too young (or are unwilling) to retire.

A workforce with an average age of forty in 1990, one-fourth of whom will be college graduates. Accommodating these mature, educated employees while positions at the upper levels of the corporate structure are not growing at the pace of the supply of potential managers will be difficult.[36] (One projection says that only 25 percent of jobs in 1985 will require college education.[37])

Inflation and its effect on salary compression and merit pay plans.

Displacement that results from foreign competition, technological advances, and plant relocation.

Summary

Personnel research is playing an increasingly important role in organizations because of internal demands for accountability and productivity and external demands regarding equal employment opportunity. Personnel research can be considered creative (designing innovative personnel activities) or evaluative (measuring the effectiveness of the activities). Types of personnel research include experimental research, case studies, surveys, analysis of employee data, legal and quasi-legal research, and secondary research.

Assessment of the personnel function involves use of measurements (indices) that determine relative effectiveness. Because top management is very much performance-oriented, such measurements as job satisfaction, absenteeism, turnover, productivity, and accident reduction are useful to demonstrate accountability and contribution to profitability. The personnel audit is a technique designed to comprehensively analyze all aspects of the personnel function in order to upgrade the personnel function, contribute to organizational objectives, and raise the consciousness of the organization concerning the personnel function.

Prospects for the personnel function can be addressed in terms of the three general issues cited in the beginning of the text. In addition to effectiveness, these issues relate to the personnel department's relations with employees and its role in the organization. Not only this chapter, but the entire text, has attempted to deal with these issues. The effectiveness with which management and personnel representatives deal with them in their own organizations will determine the contribution of the personnel function.

Discussion Questions

1. If experimental research is so important to the advancement of the personnel function, why are so few organizations involved in such activities?

2. For each type of personnel research, describe a project that would be appropriate for a recent college graduate who has joined a corporation (do not use examples from the text).

3. How can a manager make use of the personnel-related journals named in Exhibit 20.3.

4. How can the data in the personnel information system be used to assess the effectiveness of the personnel function?

5. How can the personnel department show that its activities are contributing to profitability and organizational objectives?

6. To what extent do you believe organizations will be able to adapt to employees' concerns?

7. To what extent do you believe employees will be able to adapt to organizational needs?

8. What do you believe is the appropriate relationship between the personnel department and other departments?

Notes

1. Richard W. Beatty, "Research Needs of PAIR Professions in the Near Future," *Personnel Administrator* 23 (September 1978), pp. 15–16.
2. Reprinted from "Personnel Research for Problem-Solving," by Fred Crandall, pp. 15–16 of the September 1978 issue of *Personnel Administrator,* copyright 1978, the American Society of Personnel Administration, 30 Park Drive, Berea, OH 44017, $26 per year.
3. Herbert H. Meyer, "PAIR Research," in *Planning and Auditing PAIR,* ed. Dale Yoder and H. G. Heneman, Jr. (Washington, D.C.: Bureau of National Affairs, 1976), p. 2-120.
4. *Ibid.,* pp. 2-118–2-120.
5. "Privacy Rights Protections under State Statutes," in *Fair Employment Practices Digest* (Washington, D.C.: Bureau of National Affairs, February 12, 1981), p. 4.
6. Meyer, "PAIR Research," pp. 2-127–2-128.
7. Reprinted by permission from Herbert H. Meyer, "PAIR Research," in *Planning and Auditing PAIR,* edited by Dale Yoder and H. G. Heneman, Jr., p. 2-128, copyright 1976 by The Bureau of National Affairs, Inc., Washington, D.C.
8. "ASPA-BNA Survey No. 41, Personnel Activities, Budgets, and Staffs: 1980–1981," in *Bulletin to Management* (Washington, D.C.: Bureau of National Affairs, 1981), p. 1-4. Based on survey of 507 employers with employment of 1,051,532. One-half were manufacturers; 28 percent were nonmanufacturing businesses; and 21 percent were nonbusiness organizations. Fifteen percent had fewer than 250 employees; 19 percent, between 250 and 499; 23 percent, between 500 and 999; 24 percent, between 1,000 to 2,499; and 19 percent, 2,500 or more.
9. Logan Cheek, "Cost Effectiveness Comes to the Personnel Function," *Harvard Business Review* 51 (May/June 1973), pp. 96–103.
10. Vytenis P. Kuraitis, "The Personnel Audit," *Personnel Administrator* 26 (November 1981), p. 29.
11. Robert L. Malone and Donald J. Peterson, "Personnel Effectiveness: Its Dimensions and Developments," *Personnel Journal* 56 (October 1977), pp. 498–501.
12. Jac Fitz-Enz, "Quantifying the Human Resources Function," *Personnel* 57 (March/April 1980), pp. 41–42.
13. *Ibid.,* p. 52.
14. Walter R. Mahler, "Auditing PAIR," in *Planning and Auditing PAIR,* ed. Dale Yoder and H. G. Heneman, Jr. (Washington, D.C.: Bureau of National Affairs, 1976), pp. 2-91–2-95.
15. R. Bruce McAfee, "Evaluating the Personnel Department's Internal Functioning," *Personnel* 57 (May/June 1980), pp. 56–62.
16. Paul Sheibar, "Personnel Practices Review: A Personnel Audit Activity," *Personnel Journal* 53 (March 1974), p. 213.
17. Kuraitis, "The Personnel Audit," pp. 30–33.
18. Fred E. Schuster, "Human Resource Management: Key to the Future," *Personnel Administrator* 23 (December 1978), pp. 33–35, 66–68.
19. George A. Rieder, "The Personnel Function—Marching to the Beat of a Different Drummer," in *Management of Human Resources,* ed. E. L. Miller, E. H. Burack, and M. H. Albrecht (Englewood Cliffs, N.J.: Prentice-Hall, 1980), p. 69.
20. Jack English, "The Road Ahead for Human Resources Function," *Personnel* 57 (March/April 1980), p. 36.
21. Elizabeth Hartzell, "Rising Expectations . . . or Who Pays for the Pie," *Personnel Journal* 60 (June 1981), p. 446.
22. Schuster, "Human Resource Management," pp. 34–35.
23. Warren T. Brooks, "Coming: A Severe Labor Shortage in 1980s," *Human Events* 34 (February 10, 1979), p. 12.
24. Alexander L. Taylor III, "A Shortage of Vital Skills," *Time,* July 6, 1981, pp. 46–48.
25. E. M. DeWindt, quoted in James C. Toldtman, "A Decade of Rapid Changes: The Outlook for Human Resources Management in the 80's," *Personnel Journal* 59 (January 1980), pp. 30–31. Reprinted with permission of Personnel Journal, Costa Mesa, California; all rights reserved.
26. *Ibid.*
27. Jerry L. Selletin, "Commitment to the Future," *Personnel Administrator* 26 (January 1981), p. 20.
28. Thomas H. Patten, Jr., "Personnel Management in the 1990's" in *Management of Human Resources,* ed. E. L. Miller, E. H. Burack, and M. H. Albrecht (Englewood Cliffs, N.J.: Prentice-Hall, 1980), p. 80.
29. *Ibid.,* p. 83 Reprinted by permission of the author.
30. *Ibid.,* p. 76.
31. Allen Janger, *The Personnel Function: Changing Objectives and Organizations* (New York: Conference Board, 1977), p. 42.
32. Patten, "Personnel Management in the 1990's," pp. 88–89.

33. Reprinted by permission from George S. Odiorne, "Personnel Management for the 1980's," in *PAIR Policy and Program Management,* edited by Dale Yoder and H. G. Heneman, Jr, p. 1-151, copyright 1978 by The Bureau of National Affairs, Washington, D.C.

34. Janger, *The Personnel Function,* p. 35. Used by permission.

35. Edwin L. Miller and Elmer Burack, "The Emerging Personnel Function," *MSU Business Topics* 25 (Autumn 1977), p. 31; John B. Miner, "Managerial Talent in Personnel," *Business Horizons* 22 (December 1979), p. 10-17.

36. Elizabeth Hartzell and Roger Lewis, "Soothsayers and Parables: The Workforce Now and Tomorrow," *Personnel Journal* 60 (June 1981), pp. 444–448.

37. Ben Burdetsky, personal communication, December 20, 1981.

Case/6.1

Personnel Research at Quality Manufacturing Company

One conclusion that could be drawn from the discussion of the problems faced by Quality Manufacturing Company, the calculator manufacturing firm that was the subject of Case 1.3 is that more in-depth investigation and analysis of the problems should be conducted. Possible areas for investigation and analysis include the following:

Low productivity and performance.
High absenteeism.
Low employee morale.
Inability to recruit and retain qualified employees.

Questions

1. What data should be available within the company to you as a personnel representative to help you analyze these areas? How would you go about analyzing these data? If data are not available or are not readily accessible, what do you recommend doing?
2. If you conduct a survey, what will be the content of the questionnaire? How will you conduct the survey?
3. What additional personnel activities can be studied? What approach would you take for each of these activities?

Name Index

Subject Index